DISCOVERIES IN THE JUDAEAN DESERT · XXVII

THE SEIYÂL COLLECTION

II

DISCOVERIES IN THE JUDAEAN DESERT

EMANUEL TOV, EDITOR-IN-CHIEF

CLAIRE PFANN, PRODUCTION

DISCOVERIES IN THE JUDAEAN DESERT · XXVII

ARAMAIC, HEBREW AND GREEK DOCUMENTARY TEXTS FROM NAḤAL ḤEVER AND OTHER SITES

WITH AN APPENDIX CONTAINING ALLEGED QUMRAN TEXTS

(THE SEIYÂL COLLECTION II)

BY

HANNAH M. COTTON

AND

ADA YARDENI

CLARENDON PRESS · OXFORD

1997

Oxford University Press, Great Clarendon Street, Oxford OX2 6DP
Oxford New York
Athens Auckland Bangkok Bogota Bombay
Buenos Aires Calcutta Cape Town Dar es Salaam
Delhi Florence Hong Kong Istanbul Karachi
Kuala Lumpur Madras Madrid Melbourne
Mexico City Nairobi Paris Singapore
Taipei Tokyo Toronto Warsaw
and associated companies in
Berlin Ibadan

Oxford is a trade mark of Oxford University Press

Published in the United States
by Oxford University Press Inc., New York

British Library Cataloguing in Publication Data
Data available

Library of Congress Cataloging in Publication Date
Data available

ISBN 0–19–826395–3

1 3 5 7 9 10 8 6 4 2

Printed in Great Britain on acid-free paper by
St Edmundsbury Press, Bury St Edmunds

To our mothers

CONTENTS

TABLE OF FIGURES

TABLE OF PLATES

XXI.	**31**. XḤev/Se papDeed E ar
	32. XḤev/Se papDeed F (+ 4Q347) ar
XXII.	**33**. XḤev/Se papUnclassified Fragment I ar
	34. XḤev/Se papDeed G ar
	35. XḤev/Se papUnclassified Fragment J ar
	36. XḤev/Se papUnclassified Fragment K
XXIII–XXIV.	**37**. XḤev/Se papDeed H ar?
XXV.	**38**. XḤev/Se papUnclassified Fragment L
	39. XḤev/Se papUnclassified Fragment M
	40. XḤev/Se papUnclassified Fragment N
	41. XḤev/Se papUnclassified Fragment O
	42. XḤev/Se papUnclassified Fragment P
	43. XḤev/Se papUnclassified Fragment Q
	44. XḤev/Se papUnclassified Fragment R
	45. XḤev/Se papUnclassified Fragment S
	46. XḤev/Se papUnclassified Fragment T
XXVI.	**47a**. XḤev/Se papUnclassified Fragment U
	47b. XḤev/Se papUnclassified Fragment V
	47c. XḤev/Se papUnclassified Fragment W
	47d. XḤev/Se papUnclassified Fragment X
	47e. XḤev/Se papUnclassified Fragment Y
	47f. XḤev/Se papUnclassified Fragment Z
	47g. XḤev/Se papUnclassified Fragment AA
	47h. XḤev/Se papUnclassified Fragment BB
XXVII.	**49**. XḤev/Se Promissory Note (133 CE)
XXVIII–XXX.	**50**. XḤev/Se papDeed of Sale H (+ Mur 26) ar
XXXI.	**60**. XḤev/Se papTax (or Rent) Receipt from Maḥoza gr
	61. XḤev/Se papConclusion to a Land Declaration gr
	63. XḤev/Se papDeed of Renunciation of Claims gr
	67. XḤev/Se papText Mentioning Timber gr
	68. XḤev/Se papText Mentioning a Guardian gr
	70. XḤev/Se papUnidentified Fragment A gr
	71. XḤev/Se papUnidentified Fragment B gr
	72. XḤev/Se papUnidentified Fragment C gr
XXXII.	**60**. XḤev/Se papTax (or Rent) Receipt from Maḥoza gr
XXXIII.	**61**. XḤev/Se papConclusion to a Land Declaration gr

FOREWORD

THE present volume is the second and last of the so-called 'Seiyâl Collection', that amorphous group of documents attributed to Wadi Seiyâl on the witness of the clandestine excavators, but which actually, in most cases, came from Naḥal Ḥever, a fact which soon became evident as a result of controlled archaeological excavations. The undersigned presented the first volume of this collection in *The Greek Minor Prophets Scroll from Naḥal Ḥever (8ḤevXIIgr), The Seiyâl Collection I* (Discoveries in the Judaean Desert VIII; Oxford: Clarendon, 1990). In his preface to that volume, J. Strugnell, then editor-in-chief of the series, pointed out the difficulty of attributing that text to Wadi Seiyâl. The true provenance of that text is apparent in the title of the volume, namely *The Greek Minor Prophets Scroll from Naḥal Ḥever*, while the connection with the collection as a whole was preserved in the subtitle, *The Seiyâl Collection I*. A similar method has been adopted in this volume: the title expresses the conviction that most of the texts in this volume originated in Naḥal Ḥever, while the connection with the collection as a whole is preserved in the subtitle, *The Seiyâl Collection II*. The same duality is also reflected in the designation of the individual documents in this volume as XḤev/Se. The texts from Naḥal Ḥever found in the course of controlled excavations, and designated P.Yadin, are published elsewhere by N. Lewis in *The Documents from the Bar Kokhba Period in the Cave of Letters*. Vol. I: *Greek Papyri* (Judean Desert Series 2; Jerusalem 1989) and Y. Yadin, J. C. Greenfield, A. Yardeni, and B. Levine, *The Documents from the Bar Kokhba Period in the Cave of Letters*. Vol. II: *Hebrew, Aramaic and Nabatean Documents* (forthcoming).

A very special case is presented by the inclusion in an appendix to this volume of some documentary texts from Qumran cave 4 (4Q**342–346a**, **348**, **351–354**, **356–360b**), entrusted to A. Yardeni and ascribed by her to localities other than Qumran, in one case perhaps, Naḥal Ḥever. These documents will not be republished in the Qumran volumes in the DJD series. The issue of the provenance of these texts, which are allegedly from Qumran, has repercussions for our understanding of the Qumran community and site, if they did indeed derive from Qumran, but cannot be considered relevant to this issue if they derived from another site, as claimed by A. Yardeni with convincing arguments (see pp. 283–4).

Several additional XḤev/Se texts are to be published in DJD XXXVI (phylacteries [XḤev/Se **5**], prayer [XḤev/Se **6**], four biblical texts, and five or six Nabataean texts).

Within the DJD series, the reader will find additional documentary texts in DJD II (Murabbaʿat), III (Qumran cave 6, 6Q**26–29**), XXXVI (Naḥal Mishmar, Naḥal Ṣeʾelim, and additional sites), and XXXII and XXXVIII (Wadi Daliyeh I and II; in press). The documents from Masada and Ḥirbet Mird are published elsewhere.

The two authors of this volume, H. M. Cotton and A. Yardeni, are to be congratulated on their achievement of deciphering and editing these texts, making many new joins between fragments previously found in different locations, and obtaining so much information from often rather unreadable and almost always very fragmentary texts. The hand-drawn figures presented by A. Yardeni are a welcome innovation in the

Discoveries in the Judaean Desert series. The authors applied much background information from areas and disciplines beyond the Judaean Desert texts to the description of the texts in this volume.

Professor David Wasserstein kindly agreed to read the whole volume and to offer his very helpful comments to the authors on matters of content and style.

The volume underwent a long production procedure skilfully executed by the Jerusalem team. A large part of the section by A. Yardeni was initially translated by Matthew Morgenstern from the author's Hebrew monograph and subsequently type-set by him; the base files of the section by H. M. Cotton were provided by the author herself. In both cases, Matthew Morgenstern performed the initial editing of these texts. Subsequently, the whole volume was copy-edited by Valerie Carr Zakovitch, while additional type-setting was performed by Eva Ben-David, Miriam Berg, and Janice Karnis. The indices to the Greek texts were compiled by H. M. Cotton and those to the Aramaic and Hebrew texts by Claire and Stephen Pfann in consultation with A. Yardeni. The plates were prepared by Claire Pfann, who was also very much involved in every stage of the production. Her knowledge of the content of the texts and their presentation in the plates and figures allowed her to guide this volume graciously and skilfully through the production process.

We are grateful to the Oxford University Press for its professional production of the manuscript and the plates. It is a pleasure to present plates in this and other volumes which give, in fact, better contrast than the photographs presented by us to the plate makers.

As always, we are very much indebted to Gen. (ret.) Amir Drori, director of the Israel Antiquities Authority (IAA), and the staff of the IAA for their substantial efforts on behalf of the publication of the Discoveries in the Judaean Desert series. The excellent photographic services provided by Tsila Sagiv had often to be invoked for this volume.

The Qumran Project of the Oxford Centre for Hebrew and Jewish Studies is to be thanked for its support for the typesetting of this volume and for the work of the international Dead Sea Scrolls Publication Project as a whole.

Jerusalem
April 1997

EMANUEL TOV
EDITOR-IN-CHIEF

PREFACE

IN autumn 1992 I was entrusted by the Advisory Committee for the Dead Sea Scrolls of the Israel Antiquities Authority with the publication of the Greek papyri in this volume. The core of the present collection had been assigned to the papyrologist J. Schwartz of Strasbourg some time after their arrival in the Rockefeller Museum in the early 1950s. Schwartz died in the summer of 1992, without, it seems, having made any attempt to publish them.

I have incurred very many debts along the way, but my greatest debt is to the papyrologist John Rea without whose promise of help at the very beginning I would not have undertaken the publication of such difficult texts: for the last three years, until his retirement in summer 1996, he corrected and improved my readings of the texts. Coming from another discipline, a Roman historian by training, I was fortunate and privileged to enjoy and to benefit time and again from the *papyrologorum amicitia*: Dieter Hagedorn (Heidelberg) helped me in person and via electronic mail. David Thomas (Durham) agreed to write on the palaeography of these texts for the present publication. I benefited greatly from Naphtali Lewis' publication of the Greek part of the Babatha Archive in 1989, and from his personal help in the initial stages of my work in Greek papyrology. I am also grateful to Klaus Maresch and Robert Daniel (Cologne), Roger Bagnall (Columbia University), Ravel Cole (Ashmolean Museum, Oxford), Isaac Fikhman (Jerusalem), Jean Gascou (Strasbourg), Alan Bowman (Oxford), Walter Cockle (London), and last but not least my fellow travellers in the papyrology room of the Ashmolean Museum, Nicholas Gonis (Oxford), Juan Chapa (Pamplona), and Michael Sharp (Oxford).

My co-author, Ada Yardeni, and the late Jonas Greenfield were generous in showing me transcriptions of the unpublished Aramaic, Nabataean and Hebrew texts, which are to appear in Judaean Desert Studies, and for discussing them with me. My debt to them is evident in the multiple references to those texts in the commentaries to the individual documents in the present publication. To Ada Yardeni I am also indebted for reading the Aramaic and Nabataean subscriptions and signatures to the Greek documents and for close collaboration over the last four years. I remember with affection and gratitude my friend and colleague, the late Jonas Greenfield.

I owe much to my friend and colleague, Lisa Ullmann (Jerusalem), whose careful reading of the text saved me, not for the first time, from mistakes of judgement and form. Ra'anana Meridor (Jerusalem) read and corrected some of the preliminary publications. Deborah Gera (Jerusalem) and Yuliya Krivoruchko (Jerusalem) helped me with the proofreading of the last versions.

During his last illness, my teacher and friend, the late Abraham Wasserstein, discussed with me the larger picture of a Jewish society as part of an Aramaic Near East subject to the impact of Hellenization under Roman rule—a subject which preoccupied him for years. My debt to him can be detected everywhere in the interpretation of the documents.

The historical commentary has benefited from the advice of Roman historians, who read extensive parts of the text in their preliminary and final versions: Werner Eck (Cologne), Benjamin Isaac (Tel Aviv), and Fergus Millar (Oxford). For the rabbinic sources I consulted my cousin, the talmudist Shlomo Naeh (Jerusalem). Christopher Howgego (Oxford) and Wolfram Weiser (Cologne) helped me with numismatics.

During the past three years I was the guest of universities and institutions in Israel and in Europe, and benefited from advice and criticism on these occasions. Above all I am grateful to Werner Eck and Henner von Hesberg, who in summer 1993 invited me to give a graduate seminar at the University of Cologne, where I presented some of the new texts for the first time, and began to shape my ideas. I am also grateful to Ranon Katzoff of Bar Ilan University, to Dieter Hagedorn and Géza Alföldy of the University of Heidelberg, to Johannes Meier of the Martin Buber Institut für Judaistik in Cologne, to Peter Schäfer of the Institut für Judaistik in the Freie Universität of Berlin, to Leonhard Schumacher of the University of Mainz, to Jan Krysztof Winicki of the Institute of Papyrology in Warsaw, to Willy Clarysse and Leon Mooren of the University of Leuven, to Menahem Mor and Uriel Rappaport of Haifa University, to Jonathan Price of Tel Aviv University, to Miriam Pucci ben Zeev of Ben Gurion University, to Elio Lo Cascio of the University of Naples, and to Peter Arzt of the University of Salzburg. I learnt much from the participants' comments on all these occasions.

Werner Eck and Dieter Hagedorn, editors of *ZPE*, and Andrew Wallace-Hadrill, then editor of *JRS*, agreed to publish without delay preliminary versions of some of the texts, thus enabling me to receive reactions, which I hope have improved the final product.

Lena Libman, conservator of the Dead Sea Scrolls Laboratory in the Rockefeller Museum, gave me access to the papyri, cleaned them and prepared them for photography by Tsila Sagiv of the Israel Antiquities Authority, to whom I am much indebted for the quality of the reproductions. I am also grateful to Magen Broshi, formerly curator of the Shrine of the Book, and to Adolfo Roitman, its present curator. Yuval Goren (Tel Aviv) and Charles Crowther of the Centre for the Study of Ancient Documents in Oxford scanned some of the more difficult papyri on the computer, thereby helping to improve some of the readings.

Emanuel Tov, the editor-in-chief of the series, gave me the wonderful opportunity of being the first to uncover the past from documents never before read by anyone—a rare privilege for an ancient historian. Claire Pfann, production manager of the series, read every single word of my text (more than once), and helped me with the compilation of the index. To Emanuel Tov, Claire Pfann, Valerie Carr Zakovitch (my copy editor), Miriam Berg, Eva Ben–David, Janice Karnis, and Matthew Morgenstern I owe a great debt for the conscientious editing of the text.

Much of the groundwork was done in the Haverfield Room and the Griffith Institute in the Ashmolean Museum in Oxford, to whose librarians' help, courtesy and consideration I owe a great debt. Using this resourceful library was made easier by the hospitality extended to me by my college (Somerville College, Oxford), where I spent much time during these last three years. I also benefited from working in the library of the Institut für Altertumskunde-Alte Geschichte in Cologne in summer 1993. I am grateful to the members of the Kommission für Alte Geschichte und Epigraphik in

Munich, for making me welcome in the summer of 1996, as well as to Dieter Nörr for use of the library at the Leopold Wenger-Institut für Rechtsgeschichte in Munich.

My research was supported by grants: from the Israel Science Foundation founded by the Israel Academy of Sciences and Humanities (1993); the Gerda Henkel Stiftung, Düsseldorf (1994-96); the Dead Sea Scrolls Foundation (1995); and the Paula and David Ben-Gurion Prize for Research in Jewish Studies (1993-95). These generous grants enabled me to travel abroad, work in the institutions and libraries mentioned above, consult my colleagues there, and employ Olga Bondarchuk, my assistant for many years, as well as Anat Kluger, Nurith Shoval and Aviah Gubbuy.

My friend David Wasserstein (Tel Aviv) read the entire manuscript from beginning to end, as he has read all my work for the last twenty years, shaping it and improving it with insight, precision and tact.

Finally I thank my children, Tor and Yotham, for putting up with my frequent absences, and my husband, Ari, for help and encouragement, so unstintingly given for so many years.

Jerusalem
February 1997

HANNAH M. COTTON

PREFACE

MY contact with the Seiyâl Collection came in 1986 as part of my dissertation on the palaeography and epigraphy of the Wadi Murabbaʿat and Naḥal Ḥever documents. At the start of my work with the Wadi Seiyâl documents it became clear to me that, due to their poor state of preservation and due to the shifting of the fragments and the labels bearing their numbers over the course of the years, it would be necessary to reposition and renumber many of them. The large number of fragments and their dispersal demanded considerable papyrological work in order to reunite fragments from individual documents. The first stage of my preparatory work was carried out with the aid of black and white photographs of the museum plates. These I hand-copied while making a first attempt to decipher and read the texts and to categorize the fragments according to their contents. In the second stage, I examined the fragments themselves while attempting to combine them by matching the script, the fibres, and the colour of the papyrus. When this assemblage was complete, I copied once again virtually all the fragments from the originals and took colour photographs.

During the composition of the commentary to the texts, further identifications were made and the positioning of several fragments was corrected in the figures. However, I was not able to alter their position on the museum plates, as preservation work had begun on the fragments at the museum and they were no longer accessible. Therefore, the majority of the early PAM photographs, especially those of the very fragmentary documents, do not reflect the final stage of restoration, which is found in the figures, transcriptions, and plates in this volume. Only in 1994 were the fragments rearranged on the museum plates on the basis of the drawings. Most of the documents were ultimately renumbered, with only a few retaining their original numbers and two retaining their provisional numbers. Furthermore, because the fragments of the original No. **20** were apparently reassigned to other documents, this number is unused.

I am indebted to several persons and organizations for their assistance at various stages in the preparation of this book. First and foremost, gratitude is extended to the Israel Antiquities Authority for placing this material at my disposal and to Mr. Magen Broshi, former curator of the Shrine of the Book, for enabling me to examine the documents and produce hand-copies thereof in his office. Furthermore I wish to thank Dr. Penina Shor for responding to our request to arrange for the restoration and photographing of the documents, and conservator Lena Libman and photographer Tsila Sagiv for performing their tasks with careful attention to my instructions. Translation of the greater part of the book into English was done by Matthew Morgenstern who also corrected errors and laboured assiduously in locating the English versions of the bibliographical items. I thank my friend Prof. Hannah Cotton who carefully read the manuscript, made many helpful suggestions, and saved me from egregious errors, and Prof. David Wasserstein for his many corrections. Finally, I am indebted to the Dead Sea Scrolls Publication Project under the direction of Prof. Emanuel Tov. Special thanks are due to Claire Pfann for her untiring labour in preparing the book for printing, to Miriam Berg and Eva Ben-David for typing repeated drafts of the Aramaic and Hebrew texts, to Valerie Carr Zakovitch for copy-editing, and to the staff of the Dead Sea Scrolls Foundation for providing financial support.

Jerusalem
February 1997

ADA YARDENI

SIGLA

The documents presented in this volume should be cited hereafter as XḤev/Se. Boldface numerals refer to texts listed in *The Companion Volume*.[1]

SIGLA USED IN THE ARAMAIC AND HEBREW TEXTS

א̇	probable letter
א̊	possible letter
~~אב~~	word crossed out
א̇ב̇	scribal deletion
א̣	scribal deletion
{א}	erasure
(א)	modern editor's deletion
<א>	modern editor's addition
[א]	reconstructed letter

SIGLA USED IN THE GREEK TEXTS

[ ]	lacuna in the text
< >	letters added by the editor
{ }	letters excised by the editor
α̣ β̣ γ̣	uncertain letters
....	traces of letters

Papyri are cited according to the *Checklist of Editions of Greek Papyri, Ostraca and Tablets*, ed. J. F. Oates, R. S. Bagnall, W. H. Willis and K. A. Worp (4th ed., *BASP* Sup. 7, 1992).

---

[1] E. Tov with the collaboration of S. J. Pfann, *The Dead Sea Scrolls on Microfiche, Companion Volume* (2nd rev. ed., Leiden, 1995).

General Introduction

THE title of the present volume, *Aramaic, Hebrew, and Greek Documentary Texts from Naḥal Ḥever and Other Sites*, reflects the common belief, based on sound evidence, that most of the documents in it come from the caves of Naḥal Ḥever.[1] The subtitle, *The Seiyâl Collection* II, serves as a reminder that, as in the case of *The Seiyâl Collection* I, the papyri which constitute the core of the present collection were once attributed to Wadi Seiyâl. Both these facts stand behind the decision taken by the compilers of the *Companion Volume* to designate these documents XḤev/Se. The X stands for the fact that the cave number is unknown. Depending on the language in which they were written, the documents are designated XḤev/Se for the Hebrew, XḤev/Se ar for the Aramaic, XḤev/Se nab for the Nabataean documents (not included in the present volume), and XḤev/Se gr for the Greek documents.

Provenance of the Original Seiyâl Collection

The original Seiyâl Collection was composed of documents which were not discovered in the course of controlled excavations, but rather were found by Bedouin and brought, in August 1952 and July 1953, to the Palestine Archaeological Museum (PAM),[2] where they have been kept to this day. The plates were labelled 'Se', i.e. Wadi Seiyâl (Naḥal Ṣeʾelim).[3] Although the labelling suggests that the papyri came from Naḥal Ṣeʾelim, those directly in charge of the documents at the time of their discovery never made this claim in print.

For the historical record, it would be amiss not to cite in full the first announcement by Father Roland de Vaux of the École Biblique in Jerusalem, on 30 September 1952, of the arrival in Jerusalem of papyri from 'a region not yet properly identified':

> Un autre lot important est sorti de plusieurs grottes qui paraissent voisiner dans une region qui n'a pas été sûrement identifiée. Le genre des documents, les dates qui y sont inscrites et les monnaies qui les accompagnaient assurent qu'ils proviennent comme ceux de Murabbaʿat, d'un groupe de révoltés de la seconde guerre juive. Ici encore les textes bibliques en hébreu sont peu nombreux; ils appartiennent à la *Genèse*, aux *Nombres* et aux *Psaumes* et, ici encore, il y a un phylactère complet. Le plus nouveau, dans le domaine biblique, est la version grecque des Petits Prophètes sur laquelle le P. Barthélemy, dans ce même fascicule de la *Revue*, donne une première information. Une lettre en hébreu et adressée à Shimeʿon ben Kosebah, le chef de la Révolte, Bar Kokeba. Deux contrats en araméen sont datés de la '3e année de la libération d'Israël au nom de Shimeʿon ben Kosebah'. Deux documents grecs donnent l'ère de la Province

---

[1] S. J. Pfann, 'Sites in the Judaean Desert Where Texts have been Found', in Tov with Pfann, *Companion Volume*, 117.

[2] Subsequently known as the Rockefeller Museum. See Barthélemy, *Devanciers*, 163.

[3] See also Appendix 1: 'The Photographer's Logbook of the Photographic Sessions taken at the PAM between 20.12.1947 and March 1961', *Companion Volume*, 155-62, for the designation 'Seiyâl'.

> d'Arabie et deux documents araméens suivent la même chronologie. Le plus étonnant a été de trouver dans ce lot une série de papyrus nabatéens, certains assez longs et fournissant plus de texte continu en cette langue que n'en avaient donné toutes les inscriptions. Mais leur écriture cursive demandera un gros effort de déchiffrement.[4]

D. Barthélemy gives no more details about provenance in his report on the scroll of the Twelve Prophets mentioned by de Vaux above.[5] The same vagueness is retained in a subsequent volume of *Revue Biblique*. J. Starcky speaks of 'un . . . groupe [de grottes], sur lequel on manque encore des précisions nécessaires', as the source of some Nabataean documents—one of which he publishes—'ainsi qu'un certain nombre d'autres documents (araméens, grecs ou hébreux)'.[6] In the same volume, in the introduction to what has become known as 'the Kefar Bebayu Conveyance', J. T. Milik says: 'Le document araméen qui fait l'objet de cet article provient du même lot qui contient le texte nabatéen publié ci-dessus, les fragments d'une version grecque de l'Ancien Testament ainsi que des fragments bibliques et d'autres documents juridiques en araméen et en grec'.[7]

In 1957, another document from the same lot was published by Milik[8] with the information that: 'Il fait partie de la cachette de la Deuxième Révolte dont l'emplacement n'est pas jusqu'ici repéré avec certitude'.[9] Finally, at a congress in Strasbourg, Milik presented a report on the documents from the Judaean Desert in which he gave an incomplete inventory of 'un autre lot de la Seconde Révolte, dont le lieu de provenance exact n'est pas certain'.[10] This was the most detailed inventory of the so-called Seiyâl Collection until J. C. Greenfield's lecture in Madrid in 1991.[11]

Suspicions and rumours that the documents offered by the Bedouin to the Palestine Archaeological Museum actually came from the Israeli side of the Judaean Desert[12] led to a series of surveys of the caves of Naḥal Ḥever by Israeli missions in 1953 and 1955,[13] and again in 1960 and 1961.[14] On each occasion, the teams discovered evidence that the Bedouin had previously searched the caves. During the survey of 1960 and 1961, however, they found tangible proof that some of the documents said to have come from an 'unknown place', in fact came from the caves of Naḥal Ḥever.

---

4 De Vaux, 'Fouille', 85–6.

5 'Redécouverte', 19; or in the full publication, *Devanciers*, 163.

6 Starcky, 'Contrat Nabatéen', 161. This document is XḤev/Se nab **1** = P.Yadin **36**, see Tov with Pfann, *Companion Volume*, 66.

7 'Un contrat', 182; republished with corrections in 'Deux documents', 264–8. This document is No. **8a**.

8 'Acte de vente d'un terrain', in 'Deux documents', 255–64. This is No. **50**.

9 Ibid., 245.

10 Milik, 'Travail', 20–21.

11 Greenfield, 'Naḥal Ṣeʾelim'. This lecture was based on a preliminary sorting and identification of the Aramaic and Hebrew texts by A. Yardeni.

12 E.g. Aharoni, 'Expedition B', 11: 'Rumour had it that part of the material from the period of Bar Kokhba from "unknown caves" which were being sold by Beduin in Jordan, had been found in Wadi Seyal, that is Naḥal Ṣeʾelim'.

13 Yadin, *Bar Kokhba*, 1971.

14 The 1960–61 surveys were part of a large-scale Judaean Desert Survey, which included Naḥals Ḥever, Ṣeʾelim, David (Wadi Sdeir), Mishmar, and Hardof (Wadi Mardif); see Pfann, 'Sites in the Judaean Desert', 116–19.

The following is a survey of all the texts which originally belonged to the so-called Seiyâl Collection and which certainly come from Naḥal Ḥever:

1. 8ḤevXIIgr (*DJD* VIII): Additional fragments from the scroll of the Greek translation of the Minor Prophets, which Barthélemy had published preliminarily, were found in the Cave of Horror in Naḥal Ḥever, thus proving that Naḥal Ḥever was the source of Barthélemy's text.[15]

2. Two biblical fragments from Psalms (15:1-5 and 16:1) and from Numbers (20:7-8) discovered at Naḥal Ḥever, turned out to belong to two larger scrolls (XḤev/Se **1** and **4**) which had been labelled in the Rockefeller Museum as coming from Wadi Seiyâl, thereby establishing the real provenance of the larger scrolls as Naḥal Ḥever.[16]

3. Fragments of the Nabataean document published by Starcky in 1954[17] were discovered by Yadin in the Cave of Letters in 1961.[18] These are XḤev/Se nab **1** (= P.Yadin **36**). The other five Nabataean papyri, XḤev/Se nab **2–6**, were surely found there, too. XḤev/Se nab **1** may belong to the Babatha Archive if the Γαννaθ Νικαρκος in the possession of Babatha's second husband, Judah son of Eleazar Khthousion,[19] is named after Nikarchos (ניקרכס), who was the father of the author of the Nabataean contract.[20]

4. Nos. **12**, **60**, **61** frg. b, **63**, and **64**, which belong to the Archive of Salome Komaïse daughter of Levi, were found in the Rockefeller Museum labelled as coming from Wadi Seiyâl. However, No. **65** (= P.Yadin **37**),[21] the marriage contract of Salome Komaïse daughter of Levi, was found by Yadin's expedition in a passage between two chambers in the Cave of Letters.[22] The unity of the archive is the best proof that Naḥal Ḥever is the source of Nos. **12**, **60**, **61** frg. b, **63**, and **64**.

The identification of some of the people who feature in this archive with those in the Babatha Archive also points to Naḥal Ḥever as the source of the entire archive of Salome Komaïse daughter of Levi. The heirs of Yosef son of Baba, whose property abuts that given to Salome Komaïse daughter of Levi in a deed of gift (no. **64** lines 11 and 32–3), are also the abutters to two pieces of land owned by Babatha's father in P.Yadin **7** lines 6, 11 (= lines 38, 45). Two of the witnesses in this deed of gift, Yeshuʿa son of Yoḥanan and Yohesaf son of Ḥananiah (No. **64** lines 46 and 49), appear as witnesses in papyri from the Babatha Archive (the first in P.Yadin **20** line 47, and the second in P.Yadin **14** lines 39, 48; **15** line 43; **17** line 49; **18** line 79; **21** line 33; **22** line 40).

---

15 For details, see Tov, *Prophets Scroll*, 1.

16 Yadin, 'Expedition D', 40; 'Expedition D—Cave of Letters', 229; see Greenfield, 'Naḥal Ṣeelim', 662 and n. 6.

17 Above, n. 6.

18 Yadin, 'Expedition D—Cave of Letters', 228–9.

19 P.Yadin **21** line 10 and **22** line 11.

20 See Yadin, 'Expedition D—Cave of Letters', 242, n. 21; Bowersock, 'Babatha Papyri', 340, suggests that Babatha's husband and the author of XḤev/Se nab **1** are related.

21 Published by Lewis together with the Babatha Archive: *Documents*, 130–33.

22 See Yadin, 'Expedition D—Cave of Letters', 231: 'In the connecting passage between [the second] chamber and the next chamber (C) we came upon . . . a Greek papyrus which formed the *interior* of a "tied" deed'; Lewis, *Documents*, 3.

5. Since Nos. **60**, **61** frg. b, and **63**, which belong to the Archive of Salome Komaïse daughter of Levi, were all found on the plate designated XḤev/Se gr **5** in the Rockefeller Museum, it may be safely assumed that the other items on that plate also came from Naḥal Ḥever, namely Nos. **67**, **68**, **70**, **71**, and **72**.

6. No. **13** contains the signature of Masabalah son of Shimᶜon who appears in P.Yadin **50** line 3 and **45** line 32—both found in the Cave of Letters. Masabalah without a patronym appears in many of the other papyri found in this cave: P.Yadin **49**, **52**, **54–56**, **58**, **63**. It is reasonable to suppose that No. **13**, too, came from Naḥal Ḥever.

7. No. **7** is written by the same hand as No. **13** and P.Yadin **47b**—both from the Cave of Letters in Naḥal Ḥever.

Provenance of Other Papyri in this Volume

Among the papyri designated XḤev/Se in the *Companion Volume* and included in this volume are several which were not part of the original Seiyâl Collection but which shared the similar fate of not being discovered in a controlled excavation. These are divided into five groups.

I. The first group includes papyri which can be shown to have come from the Cave of Letters in Naḥal Ḥever. These papyri were not found in the course of the two seasons of excavations in 1961 and 1962, but were discovered among Yadin's papers after his death. They may have reached his hands at about the same time that they were sold by the Bedouin to the PAM. It seems likely that Yadin had access to the same 'mysterious' sources which supplied the PAM.

1. No. **61** frgs. a, c, and d were found among Yadin's papers.[23] No. **61** frg. a fits precisely with No. **61** frg. b (see above, no. 4).[24] The fragments contain the conclusion to a land declaration from the Archive of Salome Komaïse daughter of Levi, which, as we have seen, comes from the Cave of Letters in Naḥal Ḥever. Thus, there is no doubt in this case that both Yadin and the PAM were in possession of fragments from the Cave of Letters in Naḥal Ḥever.

2. No. **62** (*olim* XḤev/Se gr **7**) is another document found among Yadin's papers. This is a land declaration from Maḥoza submitted in Rabbath Moab on the occasion of the census held in the province by the governor of the province of Arabia. The declarant, Sammouos son of Shimᶜon (line 12) is likely to be Salome Komaïse's first husband, mentioned in No. **63** line 2. Admittedly, only the last letter of the first name has survived there, a fact which does not make the identification compelling.[25] If the identification is nevertheless accepted, then No. **62** also belongs to the Archive of Salome Komaïse daughter of Levi, whose source has been proven to be the Cave of Letters in Naḥal Ḥever (see above).

---

[23] Cotton, 'Fragments'.

[24] Cotton, 'Another Fragment'.

[25] [cυμπαρόντοc αὐτῇ ἐπιτρόπου + 7]ụ Cιμωνοc ἀνδρὸc α[ὐτῆ]c (no. **63** lines 1–2), but see the INTRODUCTION TO THE ARCHIVE OF SALOME KOMAÏSE DAUGHTER OF LEVI and COMMENTS ad No. **63** line 2.

However, even if the identification of Sammouos son of Shimᶜon as Salome Komaïse's husband of No. **63** line 2 is rejected, his presence in two documents from the archive, namely as the middle man between the addressee of No. **60**, Menaḥem son of Iohannes, and the tax (or rent) collectors (line 8), and one of the abutters to the half courtyard in No. **64** (line 14 = line 35), points to Naḥal Ḥever as the source of his land declaration. Furthermore, two other land declarations, P.Yadin **16** and No. **61**, both made by people from Maḥoza, and both found in the Cave of Letters in Naḥal Ḥever, make it extremely likely that No. **62** was also found in the Cave of Letters.

II. The second group consists of two papyri likely to have come from a cave in the upper part of Naḥal Ḥever (some 12 km west of the Cave of Horror and the Cave of Letters), excavated in December 1991: the Aramaic No. **9** from Yakim (or Yakum) and the Greek No. **69** from Aristoboulias. Both Yakim (present day Kh. Yuqin, or Kh. Bani Dār) and Aristoboulias (present day Kh. Istabûl) are located close to the cave (Kh. Istabûl lies only three km west of the cave). The excavations revealed evidence of occupation during the Bar Kokhba Revolt; among this the most important was a tetradrachm of Bar Kokhba from 134/5. This cave bore evidence of prior excavation, in all probability by Bedouin.[26]

III. The documents in the third group were also found among Yadin's papers. The provenance of this group, however, is uncertain.

1. No. **8**, a house sale deed from Kefar Baru.[27] At the Rockefeller Museum, fragments of the deed were identified on plates containing papyri said to have come from Wadi Seiyâl. It may also be recalled that another deed written in Kefar Baru and published by Milik in 1954—No. **8a**—is said to come from an 'unknown place'.[28] Furthermore, both these documents, as well as No. **26**, were written by the same hand.[29] Admittedly, all this does not reveal the provenance of these papyri. However, the fact that Naḥal Ḥever can be shown to have been the source for at least part of the original Seiyâl Collection said to come from 'an unknown place' or 'caves', lends credibility to the assumption that others described in this way also originated there.
2. A photograph of No. **49**, an acknowledgement of debt on parchment, was found among Yadin's papers and published in 1989.[30] Again, the provenance of the document is unknown, but it may well have come from the same sources which supplied the PAM.
3. A large group of Greek fragments (Ḥev/Se? **1–58**, reproduced on Pls. L–LIII), were also found among Yadin's papers. They are not transcribed here due to their fragmentary state.

---

[26] 'All over the cave there was evidence of extensive illicit digging' (Amit and Eshel), 'Tetradrachm', 33; cf. *AJA* 97 (1993), 152–3.

[27] Broshi and Qimron, 'House Sale Deed', 203.

[28] Above, n. 7.

[29] But there are some reservations; see the INTRODUCTION to No. **8a**.

[30] Broshi and Qimron, 'I.O.U.'. The parchment itself has not been found. The editors suggest that it may have been returned to the antiquities dealer who showed it to Yadin.

IV. The fourth group consists of 4Q**342–348**, 4Q**351–354**, and 4Q**356–360b**. Despite their designation, it is unlikely that they came from Qumran cave 4.[31] 4Q**347** is a fragment of No. **32**.[32] The name מתת בר חזק (Mattat son of Ḥazaq) occurs in 4Q**359**, whereas חזק בר מתת (Ḥazaq son of Mattat) occurs in No. **7**. Both sets of facts may suggest that at least part of this group shares its provenance with the Seiyâl material. For additional arguments, see the INTRODUCTION to the Appendix.

V. The fifth group consists of a single papyrus. No. **50**, first published by Milik in 1957,[33] joins with Mur **26**.[34] In this case, therefore, the provenance of the papyrus is Wadi Murabbaʿat.

The provenance of some of the papyri included in this volume must remain moot, though a provenance in the caves of Naḥal Ḥever (Cave of Letters or Cave of Horror) can be proven for most of the papyri, and for others can reasonably be assumed. Some may well have come from other places, too, perhaps even from where their labels in the Rockefeller Museum suggest, namely Naḥal Ṣeʾelim: 'On the basis of the amount of work which Bedouin put into the search of Cave 32 [in Naḥal Ṣeʾelim], it can be assumed that at least part of the material from "unknown caves" comes from here'.[35]

Contents

This volume contains only non-literary documents. Most of these documents were written on papyrus, and a very few on skin. There is one bilingual archive, that of Salome Komaïse daughter of Levi, which resembles the much larger Babatha Archive.[36] Most of the documents which could be restored are legal deeds. The one letter in Hebrew (No. **30**) is addressed to Bar Kokhba. The collection also includes many small fragments which could not be placed or transcribed.[37]

---

[31] J. C. VanderKam, *The Dead Sea Scrolls Today* (Michigan, 1994) 69, does not seem to be aware of the false attribution.

[32] A daughter of Levi, ברת לוי, is mentioned in No. **32**. Could No. **32**, and, therefore, also 4Q**347**, be part of the archive of Salome Komaïse daughter of Levi? See the INTRODUCTION TO THE ARCHIVE OF SALOME KOMAÏSE DAUGHTER OF LEVI.

[33] Above, n. 8. The papyrus is in Paris, labelled BTS 7163.

[34] The identity of the hand was noticed by Milik, see *DJD* II, 137.

[35] Aharoni, 'Expedition B', 24; cf. 18–19.

[36] The Greek papyri of the archive were published by N. Lewis in *Documents* as P.Yadin **5** and **11–35**. The Aramaic and Nabataean papyri have so far been only partially published. They are to be published in final form by Y. Yadin, J. C. Greenfield, A. Yardeni, and B. Levine in *Judean Desert Studies*.

[37] Cf. Pls. XLVIII–LIII.

ARAMAIC AND HEBREW DOCUMENTARY TEXTS

Introduction to the Aramaic and Hebrew Documentary Texts

THE non-literary material in Aramaic and Hebrew in the XḤev/Se group consists of small and large fragments, the majority written on papyrus and two on hide (Nos. **7** and **49**). They comprise some thirteen documents (Nos. **7**, **8**, **8a**, **9**, **10**, **12**, **13**, **21**, **23**, **26**, **30**, **49**, and **50** + Mur **26**) for which it is possible to restore a modicum of running text and thus to identify their nature. Among them are four documents already published (Nos. **8**, **8a**, **49**, and **50** + Mur **26**) and newly collated. In addition to these, there are tiny remnants of fifty-five documents, represented by one or more fragments, the texts of which are mostly too fragmentary or obscured to reveal the document type. A further thirty-six small fragments belong to No. **8**; eight of these have been directly joined to the large fragment already published, while the twenty-eight remaining fragments have been tentatively placed. The majority of the documents are in Aramaic with only two documents (Nos. **30** and **49**) and the lower part of No. **8** being written in Hebrew. Fragments of approximately twenty documents which were assigned to Qumran cave 4 but seem to have been found in other sites in the Judaean Desert are also included in this volume (see APPENDIX). One of those fragments—4Q**347**—has been joined with No. **32**.

General Description

About half of the documents identified are deeds of sale. The others are a waiver of claims given by a woman to her divorced husband, a receipt for dates, a tiny fragment—perhaps of a ketubbah, a fragment of a deed dealing with deposits, one promissory note (in Hebrew), a few fragments of accounts, and one letter (in Hebrew) addressed to Shimᶜon son of Kosibah. Most of the deeds of sale, as well as the tiny ketubbah(?) fragment, are double documents which are witnessed on the verso. Of these, two are written on hide, whereas the remainder are on papyrus, written across the fibres.[1] The waiver of claims is written along the fibres, and witnessed on the recto. The receipt for dates is also written along the fibres, and there are no remains of signatures. The letter is written along the fibres. The promissory note is written on hide. The documents were written by many different people, and the large variety of individual handwritings indicates that at least some of the documents were not written by professional scribes. The script in most of the fragments is the Jewish cursive script

---

[1] Ancient papyrus documents are usually made up of two layers of papyrus laid one over the other, with the direction of the fibres of the one layer perpendicular to the direction of the fibres of the other. The documents were generally rolled so that the fibres on the outside were parallel to the direction of the rolling, in order to avoid their stretching and breaking. In Egypt in the Persian period it was customary to distinguish between documents which were written in columns along the fibres and rolled sideways (literature, lists), and documents in which only one column was written across the fibres, which were rolled from bottom to top or from top to bottom (deeds and letters). The majority of the double documents from the Judaean Desert were written across the fibres and rolled from top to bottom. In the 'simple' documents (see below), it is difficult to point to any clear intent.

style used in the Herodian and post-Herodian periods. The Hebrew letter, as well as another tiny fragment, are written in a non-calligraphic bookhand. Eleven or twelve of the remaining unidentified fragments are written on papyrus along the fibres. Among them is a fragment which is possibly the receipt for the payment of a fine, four or five groups of fragments from accounts, and a fragment containing only two words from the root פקד. The rest of the papyrus fragments are all written across the fibres.

The deeds of sale are similar in form and linguistic usage to other Aramaic deeds of sale from the Judaean Desert. The waiver of claims, the receipt for the dates, and several unidentified fragments have no parallels within the contemporary Aramaic and Hebrew documents already published.

Dating the Manuscripts

Only six of the documents in the group published here bear full dates. Of those one (No. **49**) is dated to the second year and four (Nos. **7**, **8**, **8a**, **13**) to the third year of the freedom or redemption of Israel. One document (No. **12**) is dated to the 'twenty-fifth year of the Eparchy' (Provincia Arabia). A further two fragments (Nos. **11**, **32**) bear the number of the year, but the era is missing; since the year is 'year eight', it is clear that they predate the Bar Kokhba Revolt.

The correspondence of the date by the year of the Bar Kokhba Revolt to the Gregorian calendar is not always entirely clear. The question is, when does the calendar indicated by לחרות ישראל ('freedom of Israel') or לגאולת ישראל ('redemption of Israel') begin? Is it from the start of the revolt, i.e. the summer of 132, or from the New Year, i.e. Nisan or Tishrei of the year 132? (Perhaps following a victory by the rebels; it is difficult to believe that they began the calendar from Tishrei 131.)

Three possible ways of calculating the years of the revolt are laid out in the following table:

TABLE 1: *Years of the Revolt*

Year	New Year in Nisan	New Year in Tishrei	Calendar from Start of Revolt
1	Nisan 132—Adar 133	Tishrei 132—Elul 133	summer 132—summer 133
2	Nisan 133—Adar 134	Tishrei 133—Elul 134	summer 133—summer 134
3	Nisan 134—Adar 135	Tishrei 134—Elul 135	summer 134—summer 135
4	Nisan 135—autumn 135	Tishrei 135—autumn 135	summer 135—autumn 135

P.Yadin **27** from Naḥal Ḥever, which is apparently the latest of the deeds in the Babatha Archive, bears the date parallel to 19 August 132. Since the deed was drawn up in the Roman recorder's office, it seems that the rebellion had not yet begun, or was still in its initial stages. Since there is no decisive proof regarding any one of the three possible calculations, the documents dated to Iyyar and Sivan of the third year, for example, are either from 134 (calendar starting in Nisan) or from 135 (calendar starting in the summer or Tishrei).

The Eparchy dating system began with the foundation of the Provincia Arabia by the Romans in place of the Nabataean Kingdom on 22 March 106 CE. Thus the receipt for dates that is dated to the 15th of Shevat, year twenty-five of the Eparchy, was written in January 131 CE. The calendar of the Eparchy is further attested in other deeds from the Judaean Desert (e.g. in two Nabataean deeds from Naḥal Ḥever: P.Yadin **6** line 2 ועל] מ[ני]ן הפר[כיה]דא and P.Yadin **9** line 2 ועל מ[נין הפר]כיה דא). Jews lived within the borders of the Nabataean kingdom and the Eparchy up until close to the days of the Bar Kokhba rebellion.

Document Types and Signatures

One of the ways of categorizing the different deeds is into 'simple deeds' and 'double deeds'. The simple deed (גט פשוט in rabbinic literature) is a deed written only once, as distinguished from the double deed (שטר כפול) or 'tied document' (גט מקושר) which was written twice, with the upper version tied. In a simple deed, the witnesses' signatures are found on the recto, whilst in a tied document they appear on the verso; *m. B. Bat.* 10.1 גט פשוט עדיו מתוכו גט מקושר עדיו מאחוריו.

The first of the signatures on the back of a double deed was that of the person in whose name the deed was written. According to the finds from the Judaean Desert, the writer of the deed would start the signature on the back of the deed close to the tie, opposite the start of the lines of the lower version on the recto. In Aramaic, Nabataean and Hebrew deeds, the first signature was opposite the right margin of the text on the recto, and in Greek deeds, opposite the left margin. The direction of the signatures is also determined by the language of the deed: in the Aramaic, Nabataean, and Hebrew deeds, the signatures were written in these scripts downwards from the stitching, while signatures in the Greek script were written upwards towards the stitching. In the Greek deeds, the signatures in the Greek script were written downwards from the stitching, while signatures in the Aramaic or Nabataean scripts were written upwards towards the stitching.

Language and Orthography of the Aramaic Documents

Two linguistic phenomena stand out in the documents, in spite of the relative paucity of material: (a) variant forms of individual words and particles and (b) lack of uniformity in orthography. Both of these are characteristic of a change-over period in the development of the language. The following examples may be noted:

1. מן/מ. The apocopated, proclitic form of מן appears occasionally in the Aramaic texts alongside the independent form regular in earlier Aramaic (see for example No. **9** line 2 מרעותי. The short form is not common in Aramaic. Occasional occurrences of it are found in the Masoretic text of the Bible, for example 𝔐 Jer 10:11 מארעא; Dan 2:25 מטורא; Ezra 5:11 מקדמת דנה. Compare also in the Aramaic letters from Naḥal Ḥever, P.Yadin **57** line 3 מלותך; P.Yadin **55** line 3 מתר (= מאתר).

2. Relative pronoun די/ד. In texts from the Judaean Desert the relative pronoun appears as an independent particle (די) or prefixed to the following word (ד: דיתה, דיתב, דלי). Alongside the independent form, the relative pronoun is already found in an

earlier period prefixed to the possessive pronoun; compare זלי in the Asshur Ostracon[2] and -זיל (with possessive pronouns) in the Elephantine documents; compare also in Hebrew, Song 3:7 מטתו שלשלמה.

3. Final *nun* added to words ending with a long vowel. The forms דנן and תמן reflect the tendency to add a *nun* after a long vowel at the end of the word, one of the characteristics of the language at the end of the Second Temple Period. The form דנן appears in deed formularies in the Babylonian Talmud, and is attested in *Tg. Onqelos* and *Tg. Jonathan* along with the shortened form דין/דן (see דן also in P.Yadin **42** line 7). It appears as standard in the deed formulae from the Middle Ages (below, n. 9). In different documents we find the forms דנה and דנן alongside one another (see for example No. **9**; compare דנא with דנן in *b. Giṭ* 85b, pointing to the antiquity of the formula cited in the Talmud). Compare also the word תמן (for example No. **9** line 2 מן ת[מן and line 13 מ[ן]תמן, and No. **8** line 1 יהונתן בר עלי מן כפר ברו אמר לשאול בר חרשה מן תמן).[3]

4. Infinitive with *mem*. One of the most notable linguistic phenomena in the Aramaic deeds from the Judaean Desert is the appearance of the infinitive form with a prefixed *mem* in all the conjugations (as in the Western Aramaic dialects) alongside forms without the *mem*—for example, No. **9** line 8 למשפיה ולמקימה in contrast to No. **50** line 12 לקימא and many others. See the detailed discussion of this phenomenon in the article by J. C. Greenfield.[4]

5. Gerund forms with a *he* or *ʾalep* ending alongside forms without the ending, e.g. No. **9** lines 5, 16 מעל ומפק in contrast to No. **21** lines 4–5 מעלה ו[מפ]ק[ה] and No. **8** line 5 מ[עלה ומפקה. Compare also Mur **25** line 3 מעלא ומפק]א and No. **50** line 6 מעלא ומפקא.

6. Interchange of *ʾalep* and *he* at the end of words. One of the linguistic characteristics of this period is the interchange between *ʾalep* and *he* at the end of the word (see for example No. **9** line 4 ארחה, against line 15 ארחא; and see also above מ[עלה ומפקה, in contrast to מעלא ומפקא; etc.). It is interesting to note that the scribes were not meticulous regarding the use of *ʾalep* for the definite article, even though its power to determine was preserved. As a result of interchanges between *ʾalep* and *he* at the end of words, it is difficult to understand the role of the ending in certain cases. So it is, for example, in the words indicating the compass directions in the boundaries clause, e.g. למדנחה etc. (also written sometimes with an *ʾalep* ending and sometimes without the *lamed*).

7. Interchange of *śin* and *samek*. In the XḤev/Se documents, the name כ(ו)ש/סבא/ה is only attested with a *samek* (see, however, the orthography with a *śin* in P.Yadin **50** and **55**). The name משבלה (attested with a *śin* and a *samek* in the letters from Naḥal Ḥever)

---

[2] Lidzbarski, 'Aramäischer Brief', 195, line 13.

[3] The supposed occurrence of the form תמן in an ostracon from Elephantine (Sachau, *Papyrus und Ostraka*, 239) is a mistaken reading, which should be read ומן; compare the photograph in the volume of plates (pl 65/3, obverse, line 2). Compare also the names בעין, יודן, חזקין and עזרין (see too the explanation of Yadin in *IEJ* 15 [1965] 112 n. 97. See Kutscher, *Studies*, 55 [Hebrew Section]). The names חזקין and עזרין appear, for example, in a synagogue inscription from Ein Gedi; see Naveh, *Stone and Mosaic*, 107, and the correction of the reading according to Yadin's suggestion; Naveh, 'Synagogue Inscriptions', 20. See too the name חנינין in a papyrus fragment from Wadi Murabbaʿat: Mur **38** line 4; Milik explained the ending as morphology on the basis of Greek; see Milik in Benoit et al., *DJD* II, 153.

[4] Greenfield, 'Infinitive'. It is worth noting that in addition to the form למעמקה mentioned (p. 79) there is also the form ולהעמקה (No. **21** line 7).

appears with a *śin* in a signature in No. **13** and in P.Yadin **45**. The word סלעין is usually written with a *samek*, but in No. **10** line 3 it appears with *śin* שלעין. This scribe also used a *śin* for the word שמוקא (= סמוקא). The words עשרין/עשר are generally written with a *śin*, but occasionally with a *samek* (see, for example, חשע עסרה in No. **50** line 8; בעסר[ה/ין in No. **8a** line 1), and so too the word נשי/נשיא (the word is written with a *samek*, for example, in the Hebrew letter, No. **30**).

8. Plene vs. defective orthography in use of *waw* or *yod*. E.g. in the words חרות/חרת; כושבא/כוסבא/כשבה/כסבה; אוחרן/אחרנין/אחרנן.

9. The dropping of the *ʾalep* in the word וחרנין (No. **9** lines 4, 15–16) as opposed to ואחרנן (No. **7** line 3) apparently attests to its suppression in pronunciation. The *ʾalep* in the word אחרן was dropped in several dialects of Late Western Aramaic, such as Jewish Palestinian Aramaic, Samaritan Aramaic (עורן/חורן) and Palestinian Syriac.

10. *He* to indicate the vowel *e*? Unusual orthography in two words (in two documents written by the same scribe), may imply that *he* at the end of the word might have been used to represent the *ṣere* vowel (perhaps through analogy with the 3rd masc. sing. possessive pronoun?); thus the words ירתה (= 'inheritors of'? No. **7** line 3) and עינגדה (= עין גדי, No. **13** line 5; and perhaps also בעלה in line 6, מנה in line 7, and עלה in line 9).

11. Another interesting phenomenon is the method of building compound numbers, i.e. numbers composed of tens and units. These appear in two forms—sometimes in the compound form, and sometimes with the tens preceding the units (perhaps influenced by the order of writing numerals, in which the tens precede the units). See, for example, No. **12** lines 4–5 עשר ותשע; lines 9–10 עשרה וחמשה; No. **7** line 4 בכסף דנרין עשרה ותרין, as opposed to line 1 בארבעה עשר לאיר; compare, e.g., P.Yadin **7** line 2 שנת עשר וחמש; P.Yadin **8** lines 2–3 שנת] עשר] ושבע; No. **21** line 6 סלעין חמש עשרה; No. **50** line 8 סלעין תשע עסרה; P.Yadin **47a** line 3 בארבעת עשיר לטיבת; and in Hebrew, Mur **29** line 9 בארבעה עשר לאלול; P.Yadin **44** lines 20, 23 דנרין ששה עשר; P.Yadin **45** line 23 זוזין שנים עשר.

Structure and Formulation of the Deeds

Prominent in the legal documents from the Judaean Desert is the phenomenon of common phrases and frozen expressions characteristic of conservative legal language. Nevertheless, there is a wide variety in the orthography and morphology of the words themselves, and so too in the use of synonymous expressions (e.g. למרקא ולקימא/ למשפיה ולמקימה; ועד לעלם/לעלם/עד עלם—and see further examples in the discussions on the documents). In addition to these, there are differences in formulation, such as change in person (subjective or objective formulation), expansion or contraction of the clauses, changes in the order of the boundaries of the property, etc. The differences in formula and linguistic variety reflected in the deeds from the Judaean Desert witness to the fact that their writers formulated the deeds independently according to the differing circumstances, and to the freedom allowed at that time in writing legal documents. Nevertheless, a picture emerges of a unified and well-established structure as to the order of the clauses in the most common deeds (deeds of sale for immovable property, and promissory notes)—evidence of an accepted tradition. The other types of deeds (such as bills of marriage and divorce, receipts, etc.) are fragmentary or are not represented in a number sufficiently large to permit one to draw any conclusions regarding their formula and structure, though it should be assumed that the situation was the same in their case.

The order of the clauses, with the differences in formulation, as reflected in the deeds of sale of property, may be reconstructed as follows:

1. *The Date*. The date appears in the opening formula of the deed of sale, and it includes, in the following order, the day of the month, the year, and the calendrical system in use. In the corpus of Aramaic and Hebrew deeds from the Judaean Desert, the dating clause appears in different formulations, such as: ב. . . ל. . . שנת . . . לחר(ו)ת ישראל (Nos. **7**, **8** [Kefar *Brw*], **8a** [Kefar *Bryw*], **13**), or לחרות ירושלים (Mur **25**); ב. . . ל. . . שנת . . . לגא(ו)לת ישראל (No. **49**[5]; Mur **22**, **24**, **29**, **30**; P.Yadin **42**). In a few of the deeds this is followed by the words על ידי (No. **49** line 2) or על ימי (No. **8** and perhaps P.Yadin **42** [reconstructed]) or לשם (Nos. **7**, **13**[6]) preceding the name and title שמעון בר/בן כ(ו)סבא/ה נשיא ישראל (P.Yadin **44–46**, **47b**), and once only לשמעון בר כסבא (P.Yadin **43**). The attempt to explain the difference as a linguistic distinction between the Hebrew and Aramaic deeds, as if the word לחרות is unique to the Aramaic deeds, and לגא(ו)לת to the Hebrew deeds, is unsuccessful, as there are deeds written in Aramaic in which the (Hebrew) word לגאולת appears in the date (such as P.Yadin **42**). The words על ידי that appear in the dating formula after גאלת ישראל are not suitable after the word חר(ו)ת, which is an abstract noun (see No. **8** שנת תלת לחרות ישראל על ימי שמעון בן כוסבה נשי ישראל; the original editors[7] viewed the words על ימי as a mistake for על ידי, but that phrase is actually more suitable after the word לחרות, and it is possible that the words על ימי were written intentionally).

2. *The Place*. After the date, the place in which the deed was written is sometimes indicated (for example, No. **9** line 1 ביקים; No. **8a** line 1 בכפר בריו; No. **8** line 1 בכפר ברו).

3. *The Parties and the Sale*. In the few deeds of sale in which this clause has survived two formulae are attested. The first version opens with indirect speech—'*x* said to *y*'[8]—and goes into direct speech in the name of the seller—'I of my own free will, this day have sold to you . . .' etc. (thus Nos. **9**, **8a**[9]). The second version uses only direct speech in the name of the seller: 'I *x* sold to you, you *y*' (thus No. **7**). The parties

---

[5] M. Broshi and E. Qimron, 'I.O.U.'.

[6] H. Misgav has brought the formula כתב לשם מלכות in *m. Giṭ* 8:5 to the author's attention; see Mur **18** line 1 שנת תרתין לנרון קסר.

[7] Broshi and Qimron, 'House Sale Deed'.

[8] A similar formula is attested in Hebrew deeds from the Judaean Desert (such as P.Yadin **45**, P.Yadin **46**, and Mur **24**) and it is the regular formula in the Aramaic deeds from Egypt (Porten and Yardeni, *TAD* II). In the mediaeval deed formularies the formulation in the name of the witnesses is common, and the writer of the deed 'declares' before the witnesses and not necessarily to the other party. See Assaf, *Shetaroth*.

[9] אנה מ/מן רעותי יומה דנה זבנת לך. In No. **8** the text is shortened to [אנה] זבנת לך יומה דנה. The writer of the deed declares that the transaction was carried out by his own will and not under duress. The formula is common in deeds. See also in a divorce document, Mur **19** line 2 שבק ומתרך מן רעת[י]יומא דנה, and line 13 שבק ומתרך [אנ]ה מן רעתי יומא דנה; and in lease deeds in Hebrew: P.Yadin **44** lines 2–3 רצו וחלקו בינותים מן רצונם היום הזה; Mur **24** col. B lines 6–7 אני מרצונ[י חכרתי ה]מך; col. C lines 5–6 אנ[י מ]רצוני חכרת[י]המך היום; col. E line 5 אני מרצוני [ח]כרת[י] המך היום. Compare in this matter the marriage document from Antinoupolis in Egypt from the year 417 CE (lines 6–8) אנה שמ[ואל בר]סמפטי [מן אפ]סוס ושרי באנטינו אמרת ובעית מן דעתי מן ציב[יו]ני [נפש]י למסב לי יאת מיטרא ברת לעזר . . .; Sirat et al., *Ketouba*.

appear in their names and the names of their fathers, and sometimes their grandfathers' or family names. In addition to the name, or in its place, an appellative may appear. The parties are further identified by their place of origin, מן . . . , or their place of residence, יתב ב . . . , or by both of these.

4. *The Property*. The property is either indicated explicitly, or with the word אתרה/א or אתריא. Occasionally, the property is identified by an appellative, די מתקרה . . . (thus No. 9[10]). A tract of land or a field is indicated by its ground area, בית זרע . . . סאין , and in this case it is indicated that if the area is smaller or larger than the measure given, the gain or loss will be that of the purchaser: הן חסיר או יתר לזבנה (e.g. Nos. **9** and **50**).

5. *The Boundaries*. The boundaries clause is found in all deeds dealing with the transfer of immovable property, including Aramaic deeds from Elephantine[11], and mediaeval deed formularies.[12] The boundaries are indicated according to the points of the compass. The order is generally: east, west, south, north (regarding the orthography, see above), though sometimes this changes (see for example No. **8a** lines 8–9: south, east, north, west; in a Hebrew sale document, Mur **30** lines 16–17: east, west, north, south; and so too in a deed of gift from Naḥal Ḥever [P.Yadin **7** lines 5–6]; in the Aramaic deeds from Elephantine there is no consistency in the order of the directions of the compass).

6. *Description of the Property*. In most of the deeds there is a detailed description of the property. The clause opens with a *casus pendens* such as אתרה דך בתחומה (in No. **50** the formula reads אתרא דך בתחומה ובמצרה) followed by a list of features found within the boundaries of the property, and its entry and exit—מעלה ומפקה (on the orthography and morphology of these, see above), as is fitting (according to the law)—כדי חזה.

7. *The Sum*. The clause opens with the words דך/לקבלדך זבנת לך 'that/corresponding to that I have sold to you for silver . . .', followed by the sum, generally formulated in two units of coinage—*zwzyn* or *dinarin* and *slʿyn* (one *selaʿ* is equal to four *zwzyn* or *dinarin*; in No. **50** the חקל also appears, which is half a *selaʿ* and equal to two *zuzin*). The duplication is apparently used to prevent error in the indication of the sum. The formula is בכספ זוזין/ד(י)נרין . . . די המון/אנון כספ סלעין . . . .[13] In two deeds (No. **9** and No. **50**) the word לחוד ('only') is added at the end (cf. לבד in P.Yadin 44 line 21).

8. *Receipt*. The full text of the receipt clause is וכספה אנה מקבל דמין גמרין (thus for example in No. **9**). Syntactically, the sentence is constructed of direct object, subject and predicate. The word מקבל appears in the participle form in most of the deeds of sale from the Judaean Desert.[14] The expression דמין גמרין reflects an expression that appears in Babylonian and Neo-Assyrian deeds. It also appears in Nabataean deeds

---

[10] See parallels from Greek deeds in the discussion of No. **9**.

[11] See Porten and Yardeni, *TAD*.

[12] See Assaf, *Shetaroth*.

[13] See for example No. **9** lines 5–6 זבנת לכ בכספ זוזין עשר[ין] ותמניה ד[י המון סלעי]ן ש[ב]ע לחוד; No. **50** lines 7–8 כספ זוזין שבעין ותמניה די המון סלעין תשע עסרה ותקל חד לחוד; P.Yadin **8** line 5 זוזין צו[רין עש]רין די המון כספ סלעין צורין חמש; No. **21** lines 5–6 זוזין שתין די המון סלעין חמש עשרה; P.Yadin **47b** line 6 דנרין מאה די אנון סלעין צרין עשרין וחמש; No. **8** line 5 זוזי[ן תלתי]ן ושתה[די המו]ן סל[ע]ין תשע; P.Yadin **10** lines 8–9 זו[זי]ן [א]רבע מאה די הימון סלעין מאה; and in Hebrew deeds: Mur **30** line 21 ש[מו]נים ושמונה זוז סלעים עשרים ושתים and P.Yadin **44** lines 20-21 דנרין ששה עשר שהם סלעים ארבע לב[ד].

[14] The intention is apparently that the seller has already received the sum. See the discussion of this word by Broshi and Qimron, 'House Sale Deed', 210, who believe that this is a passive participle form.

from Naḥal Ḥever,[15] and is found in a deed from Wadi ed-Daliyeh.[16] Compare also Gen 23:9 כסף מלא.[17] The precise meaning of the expression in this context is not certain. Is it possible that the seller receives the payment in full at once (i.e. rather than in instalments)? Is it in order to distinguish this document from a lease document? (For payment in instalments, see P.Yadin **42**.[18])

9. *Ownership*. For different formulations of the ownership clause, see for example No. **9** lines 6–7 לעלם רשי ושלט יהו[דה] זבנה ויר[תוהי בזב]נה דך למקנה ולמז[ב]נה ול[מ]עבד בה כל די תצבה (see the discussion and notes *ad loc*); No. **21** lines 6–8 לעלם רשי יהוסף זבנה וירת[ו]הי באת[ריא]אלך למחפר ולהעמקה למב[נה] ולהרמא למקנה ולמזבנה[ולמעבד בהון כל די יצבון . . .]; No. **50** lines 9–10: לעלם רשאין זבניא די מן עלא באתרא דך וירתהן למקנה ולמזבנה ולמעבד בה כל די יצבון וירתהן . . . . Compare also in Hebrew, Mur **30** lines 22–23 ו[ר]שי הלוקח וירשו להמכר הזה לעשות בו כל שתחפץ. See also the legal formulae for the sale of houses and land in the collection of deeds of Rav Hai Gaon[19]. The clause ends with the words: מן יומה דנה/דנן ולעלם/ועד (ל)עלם.

10. *Responsibility and 'Cleansing'*. The full text of this clause is ואנה . . . מזבנה וכל די איתי לי ודי אקנה אחראין וערבין למרקא ולקימא/למשפיה ולמקימה זבנה/אתרה דך קדמך וקדם ירתיך מן יומה דנה/דנן ולעלם/ועד (ל)עלם מן כל חרר ותגר נזקן ובטלה/ן די יתנ(ו)ך על אתרה דנה. The clause appears with changes and omissions in different deeds (see the discussion of the clause in No. **9**).

11. *Guarantee*. In this clause the seller pledges to recompense the purchaser for losses incurred as a result of claims on the property. The text of this clause is פרען תשלמתה מן נכסי ודי אקנה לקבלדך (this is attested in No. **9** line 9, but in the majority of the deeds of sale this clause has not survived).

12. *Exchange of the Deed*. In this clause, the seller pledges to exchange the deed whenever the purchaser so requests. The full text runs וכל זמן די תמר לי אחלף לך שטרא דנה כדי חזה. The question remains as to what the meaning of exchange is in this context—is it exchanging an old deed for a new one (compare שטר חדת ועתיק in deeds from Elephantine[20]) or an exchange of the deed for its value as explicated in the deed itself? A basic reason for exchanging an old document for a new one can be damage to the old deed, and not necessarily changes in the content of the deed. However, one may also conclude that exchange of the deed for its value is intended, that is to say, payment of claims that might arise following the deal may be carried out only if the claimant returns the deed in exchange for the payment, i.e. the deed serves as an exclusive receipt.[21] The clause also appears in other deeds.[22] כדי חזה—'as is fitting'.

---

[15] See שי חרץ דמין זבנין/דרבין(?) גמרין בשלין חלטין in P.Yadin **2** lines 9, 30 and P.Yadin **3** lines 32–33 (to be published).

[16] Cross, 'Samaria Papyrus 1', 11*.

[17] See Greenfield, 'Legal Terminology', 70–71.

[18] P.Yadin **42** lines 6–7 כספא דן תהוא תקל לנה בכל שנה [. . .]רין תלת חדא באחד בטבת וחדא ב[אח]ד בסיון וחדא באחד באלול. The expression דמי כסף (value in silver) appears in deeds from Elephantine. See for example *TAD* B2.7 (Cowley 13) lines 5–6: אנה יהבת לכי לביתא זנה חלף נכסיך אלך דמי כסף כרשן; etc.

[19] Assaf, *Shetaroth*, 26, lines 12–16; 27, lines 13–18; and see above, n. 9.

[20] *TAD* B2.3 (Cowley 8) line 16.

[21] See the discussion of this question by R. Katzoff in Lewis, et al., 'Papyrus Yadin 18', 242–3. In the opinion of H. Cotton (private conversation), exchange of the deed is indeed exchange for its value. Proof may be found in the deeds 'crossed out' with lines, which are apparently deeds returned after being paid. Thus, for example, in a Greek divorce document from Oxyrhynchus (no. 266) the wife declares to the husband that she is returning the marriage document crossed out. But compare also *b. Ketub.* 56a מי שפרע מקצת חובו רבי יהודה אומר יחליף

13. *The Signatures of the Parties and Witnesses.* The majority of the deeds of land sale that have survived from the Judaean Desert are double documents, with their signatures on the verso. From the documents in which all or most of the lines of signatures have survived, it emerges that the first two signatures are those of the seller and the purchaser, and the remainder are those of the witnesses. The documents can be divided into at least two distinct groups as far as the number of witnesses is concerned. In the first group (Nos. **9**, **22**, and **50**) the number of witnesses is apparently five. In the second group it is three (No. **8a**;[23] and the Hebrew documents Mur **29** and Mur **30**). In all the remaining Hebrew and Aramaic deeds of sale from the Judaean Desert known to me the signatures are damaged.

Proper Names

A total of about seventy people, among them six women, appear by name (whether intact or damaged) in all the fragments of documents in the Jewish script presented in this volume, including the signatures in the Jewish script on two of the Greek documents. Four of them (in addition to Shimᶜon bar Kosibah) appear also in documents from Naḥal Ḥever (see above in the general introduction on the provenance of the documents). Most of the people are indicated by their names and the names of their fathers, as has been noted. As in the documents from Wadi Murabbaᶜat and Naḥal Ḥever, the common names are those of the Hasmoneans: Elᶜazar, Yehudah, Yehonathan, Yehosef and Shimᶜon (this name is the most common). The names Ḥananyah, Yehoḥanan, Yeshuᶜa, Levi (only as the father's name), Mattat and perhaps Menaḥem and Ḥoni appear more than once. The remainder of the names (some of them by-names) appear only once. The women's names which are legible are Shlamṣion, Shalam and Sarah.

Apparently only six place names have survived in the fragments of the Aramaic and Hebrew documents presented in this book: כפר ברו, כפר בריו (Kefar *Brw*, *Bryw*, Nos. **8** and **8a**), החרמ/סת (*hḥrm/st*, No. **49**), ירושלם, חברֹן (Jerusalem, Hebron[?], No. **50**), עינגדה (Ein Gedi, No. **13**) and יקו/ים (*yqym*[?], No. **9**).[24]

רבי יוסי אומר יכתוב לו שובר (here the meaning of the word יחליף is that he will write for him a new deed for the remainder of the debt).

[22] Mur **26** line 7; No. **8** line 7; Mur **27** lines 5–[6]; Mur **20** lines [13–]14; Mur **21** line 19; P.Yadin **10** lines 16–[17]; Mur **19** lines 10–11, 24; Wadi Sdeir (unpublished) lines 5–6. See also Koffmahn, *Doppelurkunden,* 70–76; she bases herself on the mistaken reading כדי חיא.

[23] No. **8a** differs from the majority of the deeds of sale both in its structure and in its being a simple deed, with its signatures thus on the recto.

[24] The place name בית אפק (Beit Aphek) appears in the Nabataean fragments 4Q**343a+b** in line 2.

7. XḤev/Se Deed of Sale A ar (134 or 135 CE)

(FIG. 1 AND PL. I)

THIS is a fragment of a double deed of sale.[1] The right half of six lines of the upper version and the remains of three lines of the lower version have survived. The upper version is written in a smaller script, as is usual in tied documents. There are remains of pen strokes in ink on the verso which are perpendicular to the text on the recto; these may be the remains of signatures. However, it is difficult to identify the letters with any certainty, and there are no tying holes before them. The remains of two folds are clearly visible along the width of the deed (the lower is three times wider than the upper), and it is possible that an additional, no longer detectable, fold was made between them. The maximal measurements of the fragment are 11.5 x 7.5 cm.

The deed is written on hide, unlike the majority of the deeds surviving from the period, which are written on papyrus. (There are fragments of deeds on hide among the material from Qumran cave 4,[2] but their provenance is uncertain; two of them apparently date to the Herodian period. Similarly, there is a promissory note (IOU) on hide from 133 CE of unknown provenance.[3]) The fragment appears to have been cut with a knife on the right side of the deed (it is difficult to imagine a natural tearing occurring in an arch, with smooth edges and not along the fold). It is possible that it was cut in modern times.[4]

No. **7** is written in the name of the seller. The property involved is a courtyard and houses, including the gates (the entrances and exits).[5] The formulation of the deed is similar to that of other deeds of sale that have survived from Wadi Murabbaʿat and Naḥal Ḥever.[6]

---

[1] For a discussion of double deeds, see Koffmahn, *Doppelurkunden*.

[2] 4Q**344**, 4Q**345**, 4Q**346**, 4Q**348**, see below.

[3] No. **49**.

[4] No. **60**, a Greek land declaration from 127 CE, was also possibly cut with a knife, and two fragments from it were purchased separately. See COMMENTS, ad loc. However, since the height of the fragment is equal to the height of the fold, the possibility that the deed was not cut, but rather tore at the fold, cannot be ruled out.

[5] See No. **21** 4–5 ותרעא ומפתחא מעלה ו[מפ]ק]ה. See also No. **8** 5 [מ]עלה ומפקה; No. **50** 6 מעלא ומפקא; Mur **25** 3 מעלא ומפק[א.

[6] The full text of a deed of sale contains formulaic clauses in an almost fixed order; see the discussion of the structure of a deed of sale in the INTRODUCTION TO THE ARAMAIC AND HEBREW DOCUMENTARY TEXTS. See also the deeds of sale from Wadi Murabbaʿat and Naḥal Ḥever (including deeds whose provenance is uncertain, though they possibly also originate from the caves of Wadi Murabbaʿat [No. **50**] and Naḥal Ḥever [Nos. **8** and **8a**]).

Palaeography

Two other deeds are in the hand of the same scribe, No. **13** and P.Yadin **47b**. The name of the scribe, מתת בר שמעון, appears in No. **13** 12.[7] The *šin*, which rests on its left side, is striking for its unique form. The script lacks fluency. In spite of an intended division between the individual letters (in both sections of the deed), there are a few ligatures, including the conventional ligature for the word מן. The script in the lower version is larger than that in the upper version, but there is no difference between the two parts in the degree of cursiveness. In spite of variations in the forming of some of the letters, the basic stylistic features of this scribe's handwriting fit well into the sequence of the development of the Jewish script.

Orthography and Language

The scribe uses defective orthography in חרת (= חרות, 'freedom'; the word appears in this orthography also in No. **13** 1 [same scribe (for his identity see No. **13** 11–12)] and in No. **8a** 1); the definite article is indicated with a *he* instead of an *ʾalep*, in keeping with the common practice in later Palestinian Aramaic.[8] In the plural construct a *he* appears instead of a *yod* in the form ירתה.[9] In דיתב and דיתה, the short, proclitic, form of the relative pronoun די appears. *Samek* possibly replaces *śin* in the name סרה. For the question of לשם in the dating formula, see below.[10] The formulaic phrase [מן יומא] דנן ועד עלם is used.[11]

Mus. Inv. 889
PAM 42.192
IAA 440114, 440115*, 449726*

---

[7] Two deeds in a somewhat similar script (P.Yadin **42** and **43**) were written by a different scribe, חורון בר ישמעאל. It is possible that the similarity results from a common scribal school.

[8] The indication of the definite article with a *he* rather than an *ʾalep* occurs occasionally in the Elephantine documents (e.g. ביתה in *TAD* B3.4 [Kraeling 3] 4; B3.5 [Kraeling 4] 11; etc.) and is the normal practice in the Hermopolis papyri (see *TAD* A2.1–7). See also in Biblical Aramaic (e.g. ביתה Ezra 6:15).

[9] See 1QapGen XXII 1–2 אתה חד מן רעה ענה, 'one of the shepherds came'; Kutscher, *Studies*, 27 (English section) and n. 123; but cf. the interpretation of Muraoka, 'Notes', 37, who wishes to read אתה חד מַן רעה ענה, 'There came one, he who tended the flock'. ירתה here, however, perhaps supports Kutscher's interpretation. (I am grateful to Cordelia Hoestermann who brought this article to my attention.)

[10] See the discussion of the dating formula in the INTRODUCTION TO THE ARAMAIC AND HEBREW DOCUMENTARY TEXTS.

[11] See P.Yadin **47a** 10 מן יומה דנ[ה וע]ד לעל[ם]; P.Yadin **47b** (the same scribe as No. **7** and No. **13**) 7 מן יומה ד[נה ע]ד עלם; No. **50** 10 מן יומא דנה ולעלם; No. **8a** 11 מן ימה דנה ולעלם; No. **9** 7–8, 20–21 מן יומה דנן ולעלם.

Recto

Upper Version

בארבעה עשר לאיר שנת תלת לחרת ישראל לשם[שמ]ע֯ון בר [כסבה נשיא ישראל 1
ב   אנה חזק בר מתת זבנת]

לך אנת אלעזר בר לוי השפ֯י מן ב֯נ֯י֯ י֯ר֯שאל ד֯יתב ב֯כ֯פ֯ר֯[תחומי אתרה דך] 2

למדנחה ירתה מתת בר אבי ואחר֯נ֯ן ולמערבה ד◦◦[לצפונה 3
ולדרומה   דך זבנת לך]

בכסף דנר֯ין עשרה ותרין דרתה ובתיה ותר֯ע֯יה [מן יומה] 4

דנן ועד עלם ואנה חזק בר מתת וס֯רה ברת י֯מ֯[מזבניא אחרא֯ין וערבין למרקה 5
ולק֯ימה זבנה דך מן]

קדמך אנת אלעזר דיתה ר֯ש֯ו מן כל אנש ו[   ]◦[6

Lower Version

בארבעה לאיר שנת תל֯ת֯[לחרת ישראל לשם שמעון בר כסבה נשיא ישראל] 7

ב[   ]◦ אנה חזק בר מת[ת 8

אנה לך ית [9

TRANSLATION

Recto

Upper Version

1. On the fourteenth of Iyyar, year three of the freedom of Israel, in the name of[Shim]ʿon son of [Kosibah the prince of Israel, at . . ., I, Ḥazaq son of Mattat have sold]
2. to you, you ʾElʿazar son of Levi, the wine seller, of the sons of Israel, who is dwelling in the village[. . . . The boundaries of that place:]
3. To the east—the inheritors of Mattat son of Abi and others; and to the west— . . .; [to the north— . . .; and to the south— . . . . That I have sold to you]
4. for twelve silver *dinarin*. The courtyard and the houses and the gates[. . . from today]
5. and forever. And I, Ḥazaq son of Mattat, and Sarah daughter of *ym*[. . ., the sellers, are responsible and guarantors for cleansing and establishing that purchase
6. before you, ʾElʿazar, who has permission from everyone and [. . . .]

Lower Version

7. On the four<teenth> of Iyyar, year three[of the freedom of Israel, in the name of Shimᶜon son of Kosibah the prince of Israel,]
8. [at . . .,] I, Ḥazak son of Matta[t . . .
9. I (. . .) to you the [

NOTES ON READINGS AND COMMENTS

L. 1 בארבעה עשר לאיר שנת תלת לחרת ישראל. Iyyar of the third year of the rebellion fell in 134 or 135 CE.[12]

L. 1 לשם [שמ]ע֯ון בר [כסבה נשיא ישראל]. לשם is used only by this scribe (see also No. **13**).[13]

L. 1 [אנה חזק בר מתת זבנת]. The reconstruction is according to the formula appearing in other deeds (e.g. No. **8**; No. **8a**; No. **13**). The reconstruction of the name of the seller, חזק בר מתת (possibly hypocorisms for חזקיה and מתתיה), is on the basis of line 5 (though there is no room here to add the name of the wife, who is apparently a partner to the transaction; see COMMENTS on line 5; see also No. **8a** 12–13, where the wife is mentioned as a party to the transaction), and also on line 8, in the corresponding position of the lower version.

The formulation begins in the first person, i.e. is written in the name of the seller, and not in the third person, with '*x* said to *y*' as a precursor of direct speech.[14] (See e.g. the change of persons in the formulation of No. **13**.)[15]

L. 2 לך אנת. The independent pronoun אנת is in apposition here in order to emphasize the suffixed pronoun לך, and separates it from the name. This is a common means of expression in Aramaic deed formulae.[16]

L. 2 אלעזר בר לוי השפי. לוי is written with a ligature; השפי follows extremely close to it. Nevertheless, reading both words together as one name is impossible (no other division of the letters provides a reasonable meaning). Another difficulty is the *he* at the beginning of השפי, apparently the Hebrew definite article. Accordingly, one must assume that the man was known by his Hebrew appellative. The Hebrew definite article rather than an Aramaic one sometimes appears in the context of personal names or appellatives even in Aramaic texts (see e.g. הקבש in P.Yadin **43** 3). Furthermore, one cannot tell if the appellative refers to the father or the son, though it seems likely that it is a by-name for the father.[17]

The last two letters of השפי are written with a ligature, and it is difficult to know whether the last letter is a *yod* or a *reš*. It seems that we have here a *šin* (not a *śin*), thereby excluding the possibility of the word השפר = הסופר. The word השפי ('the wine seller') is derived from the root שפי, of which one of the meanings is 'to incline', and hence also to pour, and especially to sell wine (see e.g. *b. B. Meṣ.* 60a השופה יין לחבירו). In Aramaic, שפאי, שפיי, is attested meaning 'wine dealer'.[18]

L. 2 מן ב֯נ֯י֯ ירשאל. Had the scribe not meticulously distinguished between the letters *kap* and *bet*, it would have been possible to read the word כפר instead of the word בני. Indeed, we would have expected to find here the name of ᵓElᶜazar bar Levi's place of origin, since, afterwards, the words דיתב בכפר] appear, which attest to the fact that at the time of writing the deed he was living in a place different

---

[12] See the discussion of the dates in the INTRODUCTION TO THE ARAMAIC AND HEBREW DOCUMENTARY TEXTS.

[13] See above, n. 10.

[14] See, e.g. No. **9** 1–2 יעקוב בר שמען בר דקנה אמר ליהודה; No. **8a** 2 חדד בר יהודה מן כפר בריו אמר לאלעזר בר אלעזר שטר/יא; No. **8** 1 יהונתן בר עלי מן כפר ברו אמר לשאול בר חרשה מן תמן. A similar formulation is also found in the Hebrew deeds from Naḥal Ḥever (P.Yadin **45–46**).

[15] In lines 6–9 the formulation is in the scribe's words.

[16] See, e.g. the phrase עמי אנה in 4Q**344** (see Appendix I) and its Hebrew equivalent עמי אני in No. **49** 5. See also עמך אנת in No. **13** 5, 8.

[17] See, e.g. the inscriptions on an ossuary from Jerusalem חנניה בר יהונתן הנזר and שלום אנתת חנניה בר הנזיר (Avigad, 'Burial Vault', 47–8). The *nazir* is the father, Yehonathan. But cf. ישעיהו הנביא בן אמוץ in 2 Kgs 19:2 with ישעיהו בן אמוץ הנביא in 2 Kgs 20:1.

[18] See, e.g. *Lev. Rab.* 12.2 עברין שפיין בתרע בית עלם, 'wine dealers pass the gate of the cemetery'.

from his place of origin. If the place of writing the deed is not indicated, one cannot know whether the deed was written in his place of residence, or, alternatively, in a third location; similarly, one cannot know where the property was situated. A different problem is raised by מן בׄנׄי ירׄשאל (assuming that metathesis has taken place here) that comes after לוי: Is the son, ʾElʿazar, an Israelite and his father a Levite? Or, are both father and son Israelites in spite of the father's name, Levi?

L. 2 דיתב בׄכׄפׄרׄ[. 'Who sits (who resides) in the village of[' (the name of the village is missing; for the full formula, see e.g. Mur **18** 2–4). The relative pronoun is already appearing here in its short, proclitic form, similar to later usage. (See also דיתה in line 6; and cf. the usage of ד alongside די in No. **8** 3 תרעה דביתה די זבנת.)[19]

In the continuation of the line it is perhaps possible to reconstruct [דרתה ובתיה ותרעיה] on the basis of line 4. The remainder of the reconstruction—the opening of the boundaries clause—is also based on other deeds (see e.g. No. **50** 3; No. **8** 4; No. **8a** 8).

L. 3 למדנחה ירתה מתת בר אבי ואחרׄנׄ ולמערבה ד°°[. The *he* at the end of למדנחה and ולמערבה is apparently the definite article (see the same words with a final *ʾalep*, e.g. in No. **8a**; No. **21** [fragment]; No. **50**) and not a retrospective pronoun ('to its east'). Interchanges of *ʾalep* and *he* are common in documents from this period. In spite of the *he* found at the end of ירתה, its meaning is apparently ירתי ('inheritors of') in a plural construct, and not 'his inheritor' in the singular (the form of the sing. construct would be ירת). This conclusion is supported both by the absence of a following די/ד, which would indicate a genitive relationship, and also by the formulae found elsewhere (e.g. No. **21** 7 וירת[ו]הי; but it is also possible that this is the sing. emphatic form 'the inheritor'; see also No. **50** 9, 10 וירתהן). If the plural is intended here, the *he* perhaps indicates an *e* vowel (perhaps under the influence of the 3rd masc. sing. possessive pronoun?). It is difficult, however, to determine.[20]

מתת and אבי are apparently hypocorisms for מתתיה and אביה (see also חזק בר מתת, line 1; מתת בר חזק, 4Q**359a**). The name מתת is attested amongst the signatures in No. **13** and in P.Yadin **26** (מתת בר שמעון is found in both; in P.Yadin **26** אלעזר בר מתת also appears). The name אביה is rare, and does not appear in other documents from this period known to me.

L. 3 ואחרׄנׄ 'and others'. In No. **9** lines 4, 15, 16, the word appears in the form וחרנין, indicating the assimilation of *ʾalep*. This addition indicates that there are further landmarks in the territory bordering the property in the direction mentioned, but it is sufficient to define the boundary by the mention of a single, recognizable landmark. אחרן in the singular and plural, meaning 'another', appears as both an adjective and a noun in the deeds from Elephantine.[21]

At the end of the line begins the sale and sum clause (the reconstruction is based on a similar formula in No. **9** 5–6; No. **8** 5; No. **8a** 5; No. **50** 7).

L. 4 בכסף דנרׄין עשרה ותרין דרתה ובתיה ותרׄעׄיה]. The property is sold for twelve *dinar*s (here the orthography lacks a *yod*, similar to P.Yadin **17**; P.Yadin **18**; P.Yadin **43**). The *dinar* is a Roman coin of equal value to the *zuz*, to half a shekel, and to a quarter of a *selaʿ* (in the deeds from Naḥal Ḥever and Wadi Murabbaʿat the two units of currency appear interchangeably).[22] In other documents, the sum sometimes appears in a small unit of currency, with its equivalent in a large unit of currency after the words די המון.[23] Here there is no indication of the equivalent value. The receipt formula, which should

---

[19] See the discussion of the relative pronoun in the INTRODUCTION TO THE ARAMAIC AND HEBREW DOCUMENTARY TEXTS.

[20] See above, n. 8.

[21] Cf., e.g. *TAD* B2.3 18–19 מחר או יום אחרן לא אהנצל מנכי למנתן לאחרנן. The word אחרן appears for the first time as an introduction to a new subject at the beginning of a sentence, with the meaning '(something) else' or 'further', on ostraca from approximately the beginning of the first century CE (see Yardeni, 'Jewish Aramaic', esp. 133–4).

[22] See, e.g. P.Yadin **44–46** (Hebrew). In P.Yadin **44** *dinar*s are mentioned, while in P.Yadin **45** and P.Yadin **46** *zuzin* appear in connection with the same transaction.

[23] See, e.g. P.Yadin **8** 5 זוזין צו[רין עש]רין די המון כסף סלעין צורין חמש; No. **21** 5–6 זוזין שתין די המון סלעין חמש; No. **50** 7–8 דנרין מאה די אנון סלעין צרין; P.Yadin **47b** 6 זוזין שבעין ותמניה די המון סלעין תשע עסרה ותקל חד לחוד עשרה; P.Yadin **10** 8–9 זו[זי]ן [א]רבע מאה די הימון סלעין מאה; No. **8** 5 זוזין] תלתי[ן ושתה] די המו[ן סל[ע]ין תשע עשרין וחמש; and in

follow the indication of the sum, is missing here, i.e. the declaration of the seller that he has received the money (see e.g. No. **9** 6; No. **8** 5); it is possible that a separate receipt was written for the payment, even though the receipt of the money is, in practice, embodied in the formula זבנת לך. The order of the words in the number עשרה ותרין reflects the picture in numeric symbols, in which the tens precede the units (see also No. **12** 4–5, 9–10).

Immediately following the sum, the nature of the property is indicated דרתה ובתיה ותרֿעֿיה, 'the courtyard, the houses and the gates' (it is perhaps possible to restore here מעלה ומפקה כדי חזה; see n. 5). Here, too, a *he* rather than an *ʾalep* appears at the end of the word to represent the definite article. The remainder of the line is missing. In this place we would expect the ownership clause, but there is not enough room for the formula in its entirety, and it is thus hard to know whether the sentence continues or if a new, short clause begins here.

Ll. 4–5 מן יומה] דנן ועד עלם. It is possible that this formula closes a short clause which begins in the broken area of line 4 (possibly a shortened ownership clause, such as לעלם רשי אלעזר זבנה באתרה דך למעבד בה כל די תצבה; or something like No. **8a** ורשה לא איתי לך עמי בגו דרתה, but see line 6).

The form דנן appears in four other deeds, two by the same scribe (No. **13**; P.Yadin **47b**) and two by others (No. **9**, which is earlier and has both דנן and דנה; and P.Yadin **43**, in which only דנן appears). In the remainder of the documents the demonstrative pronoun is always דנה/דנא.[24]

L. 5 ואנה חזק בר מתת וסֿרה ברת ימֿ[מזבניא. From what is written here it is clear that another partner to the transaction is סרה ברת ימ[(perhaps the wife of Ḥazak bar Mattat?[25] In line 1 there is no space to restore her name.) Accordingly, מזבניא 'the sellers' is reconstructed.[26] The name סרה is the biblical שרה written with a *samek*. In that form it is attested on an ossuary from Jerusalem in Palmyrene script: וסרה וברתה ('and Sarah and her daughter).[27]

Ll. 5–6 אחראין וערבין למרקה ולקימה זבנה דך מן] קדמך אנת אלעזר. The reconstruction of the end of line 5 is according to the text that appears in Mur **26** 4, No. **50** 12, and No. **9** 8 (למשפיה ולמקימה);[28] it is required by קדמך at the beginning of line 6. This is the 'cleansing' clause, which appears in a variety of formulations in the different deeds.[29] The independent personal pronoun אנת appears once again, as above,[30] in apposition to and as a strengthening of the suffixed pronoun on the word קדמך. So, too, the name of the purchaser, אלעזר, appears once again explicitly, this time without the name of his father.

Hebrew deeds, Mur **30** 21 ש[מו]נים ושמונה זוז סלעים עשרים ושתים; P.Yadin **44** 20–21 דנרין ששה עשר שהם סלעים ארבע לב[ד]; etc. Cf. R. Yaron, 'Note on a Judaean Deed of Sale of a Field', *BASOR* 150 (1958) 26, (a).

[24] See the discussion of דנן in the INTRODUCTION TO THE ARAMAIC AND HEBREW DOCUMENTARY TEXTS.

[25] The wife as a partner to a transaction is also mentioned in other deeds; see, e.g. No. **8a** 12 and Mur **30** 25–28, and the discussion of this matter in *m. B. Bat.* 10.2.

[26] The form מזבניא (a pl. noun in the form of a *Paʿel* participle) is according to the model of the sing. מזבנה in Mur **25** 6; No. **50** 11; No. **8a** 9; No. **8** 6. The buyer is indicated by זבנה (e.g. No. **9** 7; No. **21** 7). Two roots serve in the Aramaic documents from the Judaean Desert for the meaning 'purchase', קנה and זבן in *Qal*. For selling, only זבן is used in the *Paʿel*. In the mediaeval legal formularies (Assaf, *Shetaroth*), different forms of קנה and זבן are used for purchase and sale. See, e.g. למקנא ולאקנויי ולזבונא ('to buy and to cause to be bought and to sell'; p. 27, line 14); לזבונא ולמיזבן ('to sell and to buy'; p. 30, line 13).

[27] See P. J.-B. Frey, *Corpus Inscriptionum Iudaicarum*, vol. II (Roma, 1952) 250, no. 1222, line 3. סרה as a male name perhaps appears in a burial inscription from Edfu (Kornfeld, *Grabinschriften*, 132, no. 5). Kornfeld read חרה, but the first letter may be a *samek* in its late form from the fourth century BCE. The suggestion remains only hypothetical, and in any case it is apparently the name of a man and not a woman (cf. the name שרה/שרא on labels on sarcophagi from Egypt: Cairo 55247 שרא בר פסי; Cairo 55227 פטאסי בר שרה; see Aimé-Giron, *Textes*, no. 96. It may be that this name was pronounced with a *šin* and has a different etymology).

[28] See No. **9**, nn. 54 and 56.

[29] See No. **9** 8, 20 למשפיה ולמקימה; No. **50** 12 למרקא ולקימא; No. **8** 6–7 (?) למקימה [ולמרק]א; and in Hebrew, Mur **30** 24 למרק.

[30] See above, n. 16.

L. 6]ו דיתה רשׁו מן כל אנש. ‘Who has[31] the right from every person and . . .’. This seems to be the opening of the ownership clause; however it connects as a relative clause to the previous sentence. In place of the word רשי, which opens the ownership clause in other deeds (see e.g. No. **21** 6; No. **50** 9) or רשי ושלט (e.g. No. **9**), the phrase דיתה רשׁו מן כל אנש, ‘who has the right from every person’, appears here with the same meaning. The scribe moves here from 2nd to 3rd person sing. The relative pronoun ד (without a *yod*)[32] is prefixed to the following word. The word רשו appears here in the independent, indefinite form.[33]

אנש (אנוש in Hebrew and Nabataean; see also in the Aramaic deeds P.Yadin **7** 21, 23, 27, 60, and P.Yadin **8** 7) serves in Aramaic as an indefinite pronoun, for both masculine and feminine.[34]

The reconstruction of the ownership clause is required here, stating that the purchaser has the right to do with the property all that he may desire. This clause also appears in deeds in different formulations.[35] It may perhaps be possible to restore at the end of the line a short version of the formula, such as למעבד בזבנה דך כל די יצבה מן יומא דנן ועד עלם.

Ll. 7–9 These lines belong to the the lower version of the double document, and are written in larger letters. The date is lacking עשר (see line 1).] אנה לך ית in line 9 perhaps attests to a formula different from that of the first lines of the upper version. At the end of line 8 the verb זבנת is required, but the group of words in line 9 makes an accurate reconstruction of the text difficult. The continuation of the text is missing.

---

[31] Cf. No. **8a** 5, 9 לא איתי לך (= רשו?) ורשה. The form ית appears in several Western Aramaic dialects as an object pronoun before suffixed personal pronouns and is the etymological parallel to the Hebrew את meaning ‘with’ (see the detailed discussion in Kutscher, *Studies*, 48–52 [Hebrew section]). Here, too, it would be possible to translate ‘with whom there is the right from every person’, but there is evidence that ית may also represent אית/איתי (= Hebrew יש) with the omission of the *ʾalep* and the final *yod*. This form is apparently already attested with a 1st person pronominal suffix in a deed from Elephantine from the beginning of the fifth century BCE (*TAD* B2.1 [Cowley 49] 2 יתלי עליך). In No. **7** it acts as a noun to which has been attached a 3rd masc. sing. possessive pronoun (e.g. ביתה). Compare, however, No. **50** 5 בתחומה (= בתחומוהי?). Compare the form without an *ʾalep* in the negative לית ליה רשו (= לא איתי), ‘he has no right’ (e.g. *Tg*. Exod 27:8). The word דית (= Hebrew שיש) appears in an amulet of unknown provenance (to be published by J. Naveh) ועין בישה וסטן וטלני דית על גופה דחבובי בר לילין.

In Official Aramaic the form is generally איתי or אתי (see, e.g. Dan 2:10). It is on the basis of this form, which ends in the diphthong *-ai*, that איתוהי is built (e.g. Dan 2:11), with a possessive pronominal suffix (on the pattern of עלוהי from עלי). In Middle Aramaic, אית without a final *yod* predominates; such a form already appears in an early document from Egypt from 515 BCE (*TAD* B1.1 [Bauer–Meissner] 15 ואית לך) and also in later documents (e.g. *TAD* B6.3 [Cowley 46] 3 אית לה).

[32] See above, n. 19.

[33] The *-u* vowel ending appears in feminine abstract nouns.

[34] Cf. P.Yadin **47b** 10, and, among the Bar Kokhba letters, P.Yadin **50** 13 (די לא יקרב בה אנש) and P.Yadin **55** 3. Compare the Hebrew parallel אדם in P.Yadin **45** 28. אנש serves in Official Aramaic as an indefinite pronoun alongside איש. איש is not attested in the Aramaic sections of the Bible, but it appears frequently in the Aramaic documents from Elephantine (e.g. *TAD* B4.1 [Cowley 49] 3, and many others). גבר usually indicates a male. אנשא, איש, and גבר appear in the Proverbs of Aḥiqar, with the latter indicating only men. In Middle and Late Aramaic, אנש and גבר serve as indefinite pronouns, and they have replaced איש.

[35] See the INTRODUCTION TO THE ARAMAIC AND HEBREW DOCUMENTARY TEXTS, for the different formulations of the ownership clause.

8. XḤev/Se papDeed of Sale B ar and heb (135 CE)

(FIGS. 2–3 AND PL. II)

Previous discussions: M. Broshi and E. Qimron, 'A House Sale Deed from Kefar Baru from the Time of Bar Kokhba', *IEJ* 36 (1986) 201–14; Y. Yadin, M. Broshi, and E. Qimron, 'שטר של מכירת בית בכפר ברו מימי בר כוכבא', *Cathedra* 40 (1986) 201–13.

THIS document is a deed of sale dated to the month of Adar in the third year of the freedom of Israel by Shimᶜon bar Kosibah, i.e. 135 CE. The maximal measurements of the large fragment (which is composed of several small fragments) are approximately 12 x 25 cm. This is a 'double' document, the upper version being written in Aramaic and the lower in Hebrew. The writing runs across the fibres. The average height of the letters in the upper version is approximately 3 mm, and in the lower version 4–5 mm. The average space between the lines in the upper version is approximately 3 mm, and in the lower version 5–7 mm (the size of the letters as well as the spacing becomes larger as the text proceeds downwards).

The document was first published by M. Broshi and E. Qimron in 1986. While working on the group of documents assigned to Naḥal Ṣeʾelim, the present editor found additional fragments belonging to the document scattered among fragments from other documents in four different museum inventory plates (nos. 542, 734, 735, 736) and attached some of the additional fragments directly to the fragments already published, while others were tentatively placed in the same inventory plate (no. 533).

The fact that the additional fragments, as well as No. **26** (see below), written by the same scribe, belong to the group assigned to Naḥal Ṣeʾelim confirms that the fragments already published also belong to that group (see the discussion of the provenance of that material in the GENERAL INTRODUCTION).

From the upper, Aramaic version, large portions of all seven lines have survived. From the lower, Hebrew version, remains of the first four lines have survived on the fragments which were attached directly to the already published fragments, and remains of about ten lines have survived on the remaining fragments.

Three of the newly found fragments belong to the upper version. One of them contains the beginnings of lines 1–4, with part of the date formulation including the name of the month. Another fragment was placed to the right of lines 6–7. It has not been possible so far to place the third fragment. On the verso of one of the newly attached fragments, illegible traces of a signature (perhaps the first or second one) have survived. The remaining fragments have been grouped together by this editor according to their contents. On the verso of one of those (frg. e), part of the first signature has survived with the notation על נפשה ('for himself'). Its script is the same as that on the recto, indicating that the seller himself wrote the document. If that is so, that person, Yehonathan son of ᶜEli, perhaps also wrote No. **8a** (but see the discussion concerning the handwriting in both documents in No. **8a**, PALAEOGRAPHY).

In addition to the textual corrections, based on the newly placed fragments (see the text and the translation below), this editor would suggest that an additional correction be made in the reconstruction of the already published text. In line 3, the authors reconstructed ולד[לת before תרעה דביתה ('the gate of the house'). Instead of the Hebrew דלת (door), an Aramaic word, מע[לת (entrance), is to be preferred. For the interpretation of the document, see Broshi and Qimron's commentary in their article.

Mus. Inv. 533
PAM 42.198-201
SHR 6205
Photo: A. Yardeni*

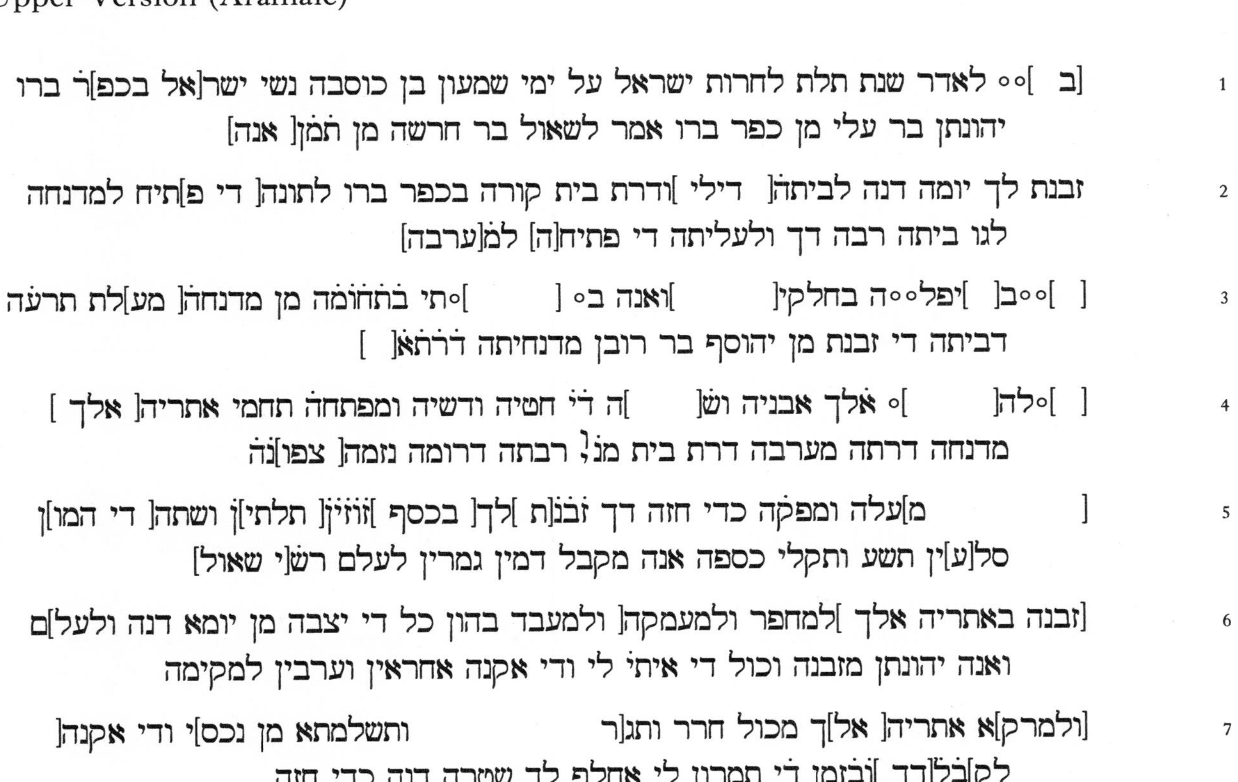

Recto
Upper Version (Aramaic)

1 [ב]○○ לאדר שנת תלת לחרות ישראל על ימי שמעון בן כוסבה נשי ישר[אל בכפ]רׄ ברו
יהונתן בר עלי מן כפר ברו אמר לשאול בר חרשה מן תׄמׄ[ן אנה]

2 זבנת לך יומה דנה לביתהׄ[דילי]ודרת בית קורה בכפר ברו לתונהׄ[די פ]תיח למדנחה
לגו ביתה רבה דך ולעליתה די פתיח[ה] למׄ[ערבה]

3 [ ]○○ב[ ]יפל○○ה בחלקיׄ[ ]ואנה ב○ [ ]○תי בׄתׄחׄומׄה מן מדנחהׄ[מע]לת תרעׄה
דביתה די זבנת מן יהוסף בר רובן מדנחיתה דׄרׄתׄאׄ[ ]

4 [ ]○להׄ[ ]○ אׄלך אבניה ושׄ[ ]ה דׄי חטיה ודשיה ומפתחהׄ תחמי אתריה[אלך]
מדנחה דרתה מערבה דרת בית מנׄ? רבתה דרומה נזמהׄ[צפו]נׄהׄ

5 [מ]עלה ומפקׄה כדי חזה דך זׄבׄנׄ[ת]לך[בכסף]זׄוׄזׄיׄ[ן תלתי]ן ושתהׄ[די המו]ן
סל[ע]ין תשע ותקלי כספה אנה מקבל דמין גמרין לעלם רשׄ[י שאול]

6 [זבנה באתריה אלך]למחפר ולמעמקהׄ[ולמעבד בהון כל די יצבה מן יומא דנה ולעל]ם
ואנה יהונתן מזבנה וכול די איתׄי לי ודי אקנה אחראין וערבין למקימה

7 [ולמרק]א אתריה[אל]ך מכול חרר ותג[ר ותשלמתא מן נכס]י ודי אקנהׄ[
לק[בׄלׄ]דך]ובׄזמן דׄי תמרון לי אחלף לך שטרה דנה כדי חזה

Lower Version (Hebrew)

8 [ב לא]דר שנת [תל]ת לחרות ישראל] על ימי שמעון בן כוסבה נשי ישרא]ל בכפר ב[רו
יהונתן בר ע]לי מן כפר ברו

9 [אמר לשאול בן חרשה משם מכרתי לך היום הזה תמקומות שלי בכפר ברו את החדר]
ש[פ]תוח למזרח ∘∘∘[   ]∘∘∘ [   ]ת חדר שפתוח

10 [למערב   ]∘∘ה בחלקי בחצר ו[   ]
ל[   ]ל ב[   ]

11 [במ]ערב

TRANSLATION

Recto

Upper Version

1. [On the . . .] . . . of Adar, year three of the freedom of Israel in the days of Shimᶜon son of Kosibah, the prince of Israel, at Kefar *Brw*, Yehonathan son of ᶜEli from Kefar *Brw* said to Shaʾul son of Ḥarrashah from there: [I]
2. sold to you today the house[that I own]and the courtyard of the beam(?)-house in Kefar *Brw*, the/its room [that o]pens to the east inside that large house and the/its upper storey that open[s] to the w[est.]
3. [. . .] . . . [. . .] . . . in my share[. . .] and I, in . . . [. . .] . . .. Within its boundaries, to the east, [the ent]rance-gate of the house which I bought from Yehoseph son of Ruben, to the east of which is the coutyard[. . .];
4. [. . .] . . . [. . .]those[. . .] . . ., the stones and the p[its?]for the wheat, and the doors and the key. The boundaries of[those]places (are): (to) the east—the courtyard; (to) the west—the large courtyard of the house of *Mny/w*; (to) the south—*Nzmh*; [(to) the nor]th—
5. [. . . the en]trance and the exit as is fitting. That [I have]sold to you[for thirt]y-six[silver] *zuzin*[which ar]e (equal to) nine *sil*ᶜ[*i*]*n*. And the silver coins I received, the full price. Forever entit[led (is) Shaʾul]
6. [the seller, regarding those places,]to dig and to deepen[and to do with them whatever he desires from this day and forev]er. And I, Yehonathan, the seller, and whatever I own and whatever I shall acquire, are responsible and a security to establish
7. [and to cleans]e [tho]se places from any dispute and challen[ge which will come upon you . . .. And the payment (will be) from] my[property] and (from) whatever I shall acquir[e acco]rding (to) [that.]And at (any) time that you say to me, I shall exchange for you this document as is fitting.

Lower Version

8. [On the . . . of A]dar, year [thr]ee of the freedom of Israel[in the days of Shimᶜon son of Kosibah, the Prince of Israe]l, at Kefar *B*[*rw*, Yehonathan son of ᶜE]li from Kefar *Brw*
9. [said to Shaʾul son of Ḥarrashah from there: I sold to you today my places in Kefar *Brw*, the room] that[o]pens to the east . . . [. . .] . . . [. . .]the room that opens
10. [to the west . . .] . . . in my share in the courtyard and[. . .] . . . [. . .]
11. [. . . in the we]st

Fragments from Recto

Upper Version
Frg. a

ו֯מ֯ובצ֯ר◦[
]ל ◦◦◦◦◦[

Lower Version
Frg. b

מז]רח מן ב֯יתי [
]◦ת עמ֯[

TRANSLATION
1. . . . ea]st of my house [. . .
2. . . .] . . . [. . .

Frgs. c–d

]ח וכ֯[
ה]דלת[ות והמפ]תח [
בדרום]נזמ[ה

TRANSLATION
1. . . .] . . . [. . .
2. . . . the] door[s and the k]ey [. . .;
3. to the south]*Nzm*[*h*

Frgs. e–k

]◦◦◦◦◦[1

]◦ה בחלקי במע[רב 2

שקניתי מיהוס]ף בן[רובן ב]מזרח הח[צר 3

]◦תרח◦[ ]ין[4

]מה ◦◦[5

]ן̇ בכסף[זו]זין ש[לושין וששה שה]ן סלעין תשע [6

]חת[ ]מעלן וירשה[7

]ב ו ◦◦ ◦[שא/כ]ול ◦◦[ואני י]הונת[ן 8

תמכר הזה מ]כול חרר[ותגר] שי[בואוך 9

]ךה◦ ד◦[אח]לף לך ת[שטר הזה 10

TRANSLATION

1. . . .] . . . [. . .
2. . . .] . . . in my share, to the we[st . . .
3. which I bought from Yehose]ph son of[Ruben; to]the east the cou[rtyard . . .
4. . . .] . . . [. . .
5. . . .] . . . [. . .
6. . . .] . . . for th[irty six silver[*zuzin* which ar]e (equal to) nine *silʿin*.[. . .
7. . . .] . . . [. . .]above(?) and [. . .] will permit/entitle[. . .
8. . . .] . . . [. . . Sha]ʾul/that a]ll . . . [and I, Ye]honatha[n the seller, and whatever I own and whatever I shall acquire are responsible and a security for establishing
9. and cleansing that sale from a]ny dispute[and challenge] that will c[ome upon you . . . .
10. . . .] . . . [. . . and whenever you will say to me I shall exch]ange for you t[his document as is fitting(?)]

Frg. l

מע]רב 1

TRANSLATION

1. we]st

Frg. m

]◦ו֯ת◦◦ מ֯[1

Frg. n

] ◦[1

]א֯ז֯[2

Frg. o

יהונ]תן ב[ר 1

TRANSLATION

1. Yehona]than s[on of

Frg. p

]פ֯[1

Frg. q

]◦ז֯למ֯[1

Frg. r

]ב֯[1

Frg. s

]וא [1

Frg. t

]◦[1

]◦[2

Frg. u

]◦ ◦[1

]ב הש[2

Frg. v

]◦◦[1

]◦◦[2

Frg. w

]◦◦ז[1

Frg. x

]ש[1

]תו/ן◦[2

Frg. y

1 ח
]ג[
ה

2]מ[
ת

Frg. z

1] ∘∘[

Frg. aa

1]ן וי[

2]מא [

Frg. bb

1]מ[

2]ל∘[

Fragment from Verso

Frg. e

2]על נפש]ה כתבה

TRANSLATION

1.]for [him]self[wrote it

8a. XḤev/Se papDeed of Sale C ar (134 or 135 CE)

(FIGS. 4–5 AND PL. III)

Previous discussions: S. Abramson and H. L. Ginsberg, 'On the Aramaic Deed of Sale of the Third Year of the Second Jewish Revolt', *BASOR* 136 (1954) 17–19; K. Beyer, *Die aramäischen Texte vom Toten Meer* (Göttingen, 1984) 320–1; S. A. Birnbaum, 'The Kephar Babhayu Conveyance', *PEQ* 89 (1957) 108–32; J. T. Milik, 'Un contrat juif de l'an 134 après Jésus-Christ', *RB* 61 (1954) 182–90; 'Note additionnelle sur le contrat juif de l'an 134 après J.-C.', *RB* 62 (1955) 253–4; 'Acte de vente d'une maison, daté de 134 après J.C.', *Biblica* 38 (1957) 264–8; J. Naveh, 'Marginalia on the Deeds from Kefar Baro', *Studies in Hebrew and other Semitic Languages Presented to Chaim Rabin*, eds. M. Goshen-Gottstein, S. Morag, and S. Kogut (Jerusalem, 1990) 231–4; J. J. Rabinowitz, 'Some Notes on an Aramaic Contract from the Dead Sea Region', *BASOR* 136 (1954) 15–16.

THIS document was first published by Milik in 1954. Following the initial publication, two articles appeared in the same year, one by J. J. Rabinowitz and the other by S. Abramson and H. L. Ginsberg. In both, a few corrections to Milik's readings and interpretation of the document were suggested. Milik himself added a few corrections in 1955. The document was further discussed by S. A. Birnbaum. In 1957 Milik published a revised version of his readings and interpretation of the document in which he stated: 'nous considérons la transcription et la traduction . . . comme pratiquement definitives . . .'. In 1984, K. Beyer published his reading and translation of the text, adding more corrections. In an article by J. Naveh the author discussed in detail the reading of the place-name appearing in the document (כפר בריו), proving that Milik's reading of the name (כפר בביו), which had also been accepted by Birnbaum, Beyer and other scholars, should be rejected, as already suggested by Abramson and Ginsberg as well as by Broshi and Qimron. Although the present editor in general accepts most of Beyer's corrections, Naveh's reading of the place-name is to be preferred.

One additional major correction remains, concerning the reading and reconstruction of the clauses dealing with the borders of the property (lines 8–9).

Milik's reading and reconstruction of those clauses are as follows (pp. 264–5):

תחמא בתה דך [די לך ל]אלעזר זבנה מדנחא ^{9}יהונתן [בר י]שוע לצפנה דרתה מערבא ודרמא בנה

He translates: 'Les limites de cette maison [qui appartient à toi, E]léazar, acheteur, sont: à l'Est (9)Yehonathan fils de Yešuaᶜ, au Nord la cour, à l'Ouest et au Sud le (terrain) bâti.' ('The borders of this house [which belongs to you, ʾE]lᶜazar, the buyer, are: In the east $^{(9)}$Yehonathan son of Yeshuaᶜ, in the north the courtyard, in the west and in the south the built up [land]').

Beyer's reading and reconstruction are as follows (pp. 320–1):

תחמא בתה דך [די לך ל]אל[ע]זר זבנה מדנחא ^{9}יהונתן <בר> [י]שוע לצפנה דרתה מערבא [ו]דרמ<א> זבנה

He translates: 'Die Grenzen jenes Hauses, [dass dir gehört], dem Käufer Eleasar, sind: Im Osten (9)Jonatan <der Sohn des> Jesus, im Norden der Hof, im Westen und im Süden der Käufer.' ('The borders of that house, [which belongs to you], the buyer ʾElᶜazar, are: In the east $^{(9)}$Yehonathan <son of> Yeshuaᶜ, in the north the courtyard, in the west and in the south the seller'.)

The present editor suggests the following corrected reading and reconstruction:

תחמא בתה דך[דרומא אלע]זר זבנה מדנחא [9]יהונת]ן <בר> י]שוע לצפנה דרתה מערבא [ח]דד מזבנה

'The borders of that house (are): [(to) the south—ʾElᶜa]zar the buyer; (to) the east—[9]Yehonatha[n <son of> Ye]shuaᶜ; (to) the north—the courtyard; (to) the west—[Ḥa]dad the seller.'

Following this correction I have changed the scheme of the property as presented by Milik (268). The altered scheme would appear thus:

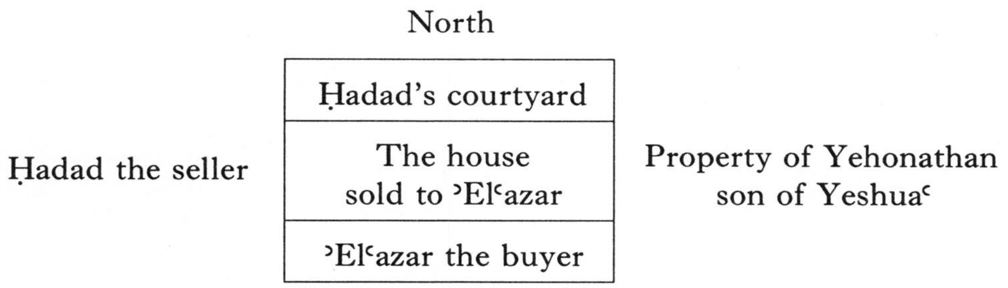

	North	
	Ḥadad's courtyard	
Ḥadad the seller	The house sold to ʾElᶜazar	Property of Yehonathan son of Yeshuaᶜ
	ʾElᶜazar the buyer	

Palaeography

The handwriting, which is a Jewish cursive, very much resembles the handwriting of the כפר ברו deed, as already recognized by Broshi and Qimron, as well as Naveh, who claimed that both deeds were written by the same hand. Because of the differences between the deeds in the average size of the script and in the form of several letters, as well as in the spelling of certain words, the present editor at first doubted that conclusion. However, a comparative and statistical examination of the characteristics of the script in those documents, as against other handwritings in the Jewish cursive dating to the same period,[1] shows that the letter-forms in both deeds, as well as in another fragment (No. **26**), have many common features which distinguish them from the other deeds.

Mus. Inv. 651
SHR 72–560*
PAM 40.996

---

[1] See A. Yardeni, 'Cursive Script', 333, 342–3.

Recto

בעסר[ין] לאדר שנת תלת לחרת ישראל בכפר בריו 1

חדד בר יהודה מן כפר בריו אמר לאלעזר בר אלעזר שטרא 2

מן תמן אנה מן רעותי >יומא דנה< זבנת לך ימה דנה לבתה דילי 3

די פתיח צפן לגה דרתי די תפתחנה לגה בתך 4

ורשה לא איתי לך >לך< עמי בגו דרתה דך זבנת לך בכסף 5

זוזין די המון תמניא וסלעין תרתן דמין גמרין לעלם רשי 6

אלעזר בזבן בתה דך אבניה ושרית[א]ודגריא כול די בה 7

∘כו ∘∘∘ וקרקעא תחמא בתה דך[דרומא אלע]זר זבנה מדנחא 8

יהונת[ן י]שוע לצפנה דרתה מערבא [ח]דד מזבנה ורשה לא 9

איתי לך עמי בגו דרתה די לי ולא מעל ול[א] מפק עלי אנ>ת<ה חדד 10

[מ]ן ימה דנה ולעלם ואנה אחרי וערב ל[ך בז]בן בתה דך מן ימה דנה 11

ולעלם ואנה שלם ברת שמעון אנ[תת]חדד דנה מלין לאיתי 12

לי ולעלם בזבן בתה דך ולעלם ותש[למ]תה ודי נקנה לוקבלך 13

כ[תב]א דנה פשיט וחתים בגוה   שלום[בר]ת שמעון על נפשה כתב 14

חדד בר יה[ו]דה על <נ>פשה   אלעזר בר מתתא ממרה 15

שמעון בר יהוסף עד 16

אלעזר בר שמעון שהד 17

יהודה בר יהודה שהד 18

Translation

Recto

1. On the ten[th]/twen[tieth] of Adar/Iyyar, year three of the freedom of Israel, at Kefar *Bryw*,
2. Ḥadad son of Yehudah from Kefar *Bryw* said to ʾElʿazar son of ʾElʿazar the . . .
3. from there: I, of my own will, >today< sold you today the house of mine
4. that opens (to the) north into my courtyard, that you might open it into your house.
5. And you >you<, have no right with me in that courtyard. That (house) I sold to you for silver,
6. eight *zuzin* which are (equal to) two *silʿin*, full price. Forever entitled is
7. ʾElʿazar regarding the sale/purchase of that house, the stones and [the] beams and the steps, anything that is in it—

8. . . . and the ground. The boundaries of that house (are):[(To) the south—ʾElʿaz]ar the buyer; (to) the east—

9. Yehonatha[n and/son of Ye]shuaʿ; to the north—the courtyard; (to) the west—[Ḥa]dad the seller. And no ṛight

10. (will) you have with me within my courtyard, and neither entrance nor exit upon me, you Ḥadad,

11. from this day and forever. And I am responsible and a guarantor for y[ou regarding the sa]le/pur]chase of that house, from this day

12. and forever. And I, Shal(o)m, daughter of Shimʿon, the wi[fe of] this Ḥadad, have no claims

13. (now) and forever, regarding the sale/purchase of that house, and forever. And the pa[yment] <is from my property> and whatever we shall acquire, according to that.

14. This d[e]ed is simple and signed inside. Shalom [daughte]r of Shimʿon, for herself. Wrote

15. Ḥadad son of Yeh[u]dah, for hi<m>self; ʾElʿazar son of *Mttʾ*, at her word.

16. Shimʿon son of Yehoseph, witness;

17. ʾElʿazar son of Shimʿon, witness;

18. Yehudah son of Yehudah, witness.

9. XḤev/Se papDeed of Sale D ar

(FIGS. 6–8 AND PLS. IV–V)

THIS is a double deed of sale on papyrus broken into many fragments. The text on the recto is written across the fibres. The date has been lost, but according to the script it is likely to be from the end of the Herodian period.[1] According to the reconstruction suggested by the present editor, the original width was approximately 26.5 cm. Because the bottom lines are missing, it is difficult to estimate the original height. Parts of all eleven lines of the upper version and of thirteen lines of the lower version have survived. The original position of an additional six small fragments has not been determined so far with certainty. On the back of the document seven lines of signatures have partially survived; the first two lines seem to be those of the seller, Yaʿaqob bar Shimʿon bar Diqna, who also acted as the scribe of the deed. The handwriting in these lines is similar to that on the recto. After the first two lines another signature, apparently that of the buyer (Yehudah), is possibly missing. The three following lines are apparently the signatures of the witnesses, but in spite of their being in a large, formal script, only a few letters can be read with certainty and these do not yield recognizable names. Accordingly, the placing of these fragments remains uncertain and what is presented here is only a suggestion, albeit supported by the agreement between the verso and the recto. The lower two signatures, of the witnesses, have been partially deciphered.

The deed is written in the name of (and by) the seller. The property referred to as אתרה ('the place') is not described, but apparently comprises a field (line 3), referred to as פרדסה ('garden' or 'orchard').

Palaeography

The size and fluency of the letters are similar in the upper and lower versions. Virtually no ligatures are used. There is notable regularity in the forms of the letters, so that there are only a few variations in the form of each letter of the alphabet. There is sporadic use of non-final forms of letters at the ends of words (לכ lines 2, 5, הנ line 3; the regular differentiation between non-final and final forms consolidated during the Herodian period). Several letters are unique in their form (*he*, *ḥet*, *mem*, medial and final *nun*, *ʿayin*, *ṣade*, *qop*, *reš*, and *šin*), producing a distinguishable, personal handwriting. In spite of its unique forms, a large number of characteristics enable the placing of this script in the sequence of the development of the Jewish cursive towards the end of the Herodian period.

[1] See Yardeni, 'Cursive Script'.

Orthography and Language

The definite article is generally indicated by *he* (e.g. דקנה, אתרה), in keeping with the orthography characteristic to Palestine, though sometimes with *ʾalep* (ארחא); יעקוב appears in *plene* orthography, as opposed to שמען, which is written defectively. The text also reflects the penetration of spoken forms into the more conservative written language. Thus, for example, we find a *nun* closing an open syllable at the end of a word: דנן (דנה also occurs), תמן;[2] the apocopated, proclitic form of the relative pronoun ד (דילי = דלי) alongside the older, independent form די;[3] assimilation of an opening *ʾalep* in the word וחרנין; the apocopated, proclitic form of the preposition מן (מרעותי) alongside the independent form regular to earlier Aramaic; infinitive forms of the *Paʿel* conjugation with a *mem* prefix: למשפיה ולמקימה;[4] and the use of the root שפי in place of the root מרק which appears in other documents (see lines 8–9).

With regard to syntax, אתרה דך בתחומה is a *casus pendens* with a retrospective pronoun. וכספה אנה מקבל represents the characteristic word order in Eastern Imperial Aramaic in which the predicate follows the subject. ארח ירתי צפן represents a double construct.

Formulaic expressions include דמין, לקבלדך, כדי חזה, בית זרע חנטין, הן חסיר או יתר, יומה דנה, נזקן, חרר ותגר, למשפיה ולמקימה, אחראין וערבין, מן יומה דנה ולעלם, למעבד בה כל די תצבה, רשי ושלט, גמרין, ובטלה, תשלמתה מן נכסי ודי אקנה לקבלדך.

Mus. Inv. 543
PAM 42.202, 42.203
IAA 445123*, 445125*

Recto
Upper Version

1 בעׄשׄ[ר]ין ל שנת ל]ביקים יעקׄובׄ[בר]שׄמען בר דקנה אמר

2 ליהודה כ∘∘[מן ת]מן אנה מרעותי יומה דנה זבנׄ[ת] לכ לׄאתרה דלי די מתקרה

3 ח[ק]לׄ פרדסהׄ[בית זרע חנטי]ן סאין תלת הנ חסיר או יתר לזבנה[ת]חׄומי אתרה דך מד[נח]ה

4 ארחה וחׄ[רנין מערבה יהוד]הׄ זבנה ו[ח]רנין[דרומה] ארח∘ יׄ[ר]תי צפן וחרנין צפונה ירת[י]צפׄן וחׄ[רנין]

5 אתׄרׄה דך בתחׄו[מה תרעה די]מעל ומפק לכ לאת∘תׄרׄ כדי חזה לקבלד[ך]זׄבׄנׄת לכׄ

---

[2] See the discussion of דנן in the INTRODUCTION TO THE ARAMAIC AND HEBREW DOCUMENTARY TEXTS.

[3] See the discussion of די in the INTRODUCTION TO THE ARAMAIC AND HEBREW DOCUMENTARY TEXTS.

[4] See Greenfield, 'Infinitive'.

בכסף זוזין עשר[ין]

6 ותמניה ד[י המון סלעי]ן שׄ[ב]ע לחׄוׄד וכסׄ[פ]ה אנה מקבל דמין גמרין לעלם רׄשׄי ושלטׄ
יהו[דה]

7 זבנה ויר[תוהי בזב]נה דך למקנה ולמז[ב]נה ול[מ]עׄבד בׄהׄ כל די תצבה מן יומה דנן

8 [ולעלם ואנה יעקוב ודי אי]תי לי א[חר]איׄן וערׄבׄ[י]ן למשפיה ולמקימה אתרה קדמךׄ
וׄ[קד]םׄ

9 ירתׄ[י]ך מׄ[ן יומה דנן ולעלם מן]כל חרר ותגר נזׄקׄן ובׄטׄלׄהׄ ד[י יתנך]על אתרה[דנן]

10 פטר◦◦[פר]ען תשלמתה מן נכ[סי ודי אק]נה לקבלדך וכל זמן די ת[מר לי אחלף]

11 לׄךׄ ש[טרא דנה]◦נבׄא רבׄה כדי חזה

Lower Version

12 בעש[ר]הׄ ל שנת]ל[ ]◦◦[יעקוב בר שמען בר
דקנה]

13 מן יקׄים[אמר ליהודה כ◦◦ בר שמ]ען בׄרׄ ◦[◦◦]אׄל מׄ[ן]תׄמן אנה מרעותי יומׄהׄ דׄ[נה זבנת
לכ]

14 לאתׄ[רה דלי די ביקי]ם די בת[חומה חקל פרדסה]בׄיׄתׄ [זר]עׄ חׄנׄטׄ[י]ן [ס]אין תלת הן

15 [חסיר או יתר לזבנה תחומי אתרה דך מ]דׄ[נ]חה ארחא וחרנין מערבה יהודה

16 [זב]נה[וחרנין דרומה ארח יר]תי צפן וחרנין אתרה דך בׄתׄחׄוׄ[מה תרעה]דׄיׄ מעל
ומ[פק]

17 לך לאת[כדי חזה לקבל דך זבנת]לׄ[כ בכסף זוזין עשרין ותמניה די המון]סׄלׄ[עין
שבע]

18 [לחוד וכספה אנה מקבל]דמין גמרׄיׄן לעלם רשי ושלט יהודה זבנה וירתוהי]

19 [בזבנה דך למקנה ו]לׄ[מ]זׄ[בנה ו]לׄ[מ]עבד בה [כל די תצבה מ]ן[יומה דנן ולעלם
ואנה]

20 [יעקוב ודי איתי לי אחראין וערבין למשפיה ו]לׄ[מקימ]הׄ[א]תׄ[ר]הׄ קדמך וקדם ירתיך
מן יומה דנ[ן]

21 ולעל[ם מן כל חרר ותגר נזקן וב]טלה די יתנך על אתרה דנה ◦[פׄ]רׄעׄ[ן]תשלם די ל[

22 דין]תׄ[ ]◦ר לׄךׄ ול◦◦ל[ ]◦◦◦ת◦[ ]◦אׄתׄרה דנן

23]   ]עוֹדהו°ם[[

24]   ]°°°[   ]לֹ[[

25]   ?   [

Frg. a

1]בֹרֹ בֹ[

Frg. b

1]עלֹםֹ רשֹׁתֹ[

2]לֹ[

Frg. c

1]אנֹה כדי °[

Verso

26 [יע]קֹוב בר שמעוֹן[בר דקנה ע]ל נפשֹׁ[ה כתבה]

27]   ]ביקֹ֯ם ש[[

[?]

28]°°   ]בֹרֹ בֹ[[

29]°°בֹ   ]דהֹ בֹ[   ]ה֯ח֯ זֹ֯ל אֹ֯יֹשֹׁ[   ]זפֹ[ ]

30]°   [°   ]מֹן יֹ°קֹ֯ים[°[

31 יהֹ[   ]בֹר יהוסף ש[הד]

32 שמע[ון בר   ]° שהד

Frg. d

]נב[1

Translation

Recto

Upper Version

1. On the ten[th/twe[ntieth of . . ., year . . . of . . .,] at *Ykym,* Yaʿaqob[son of]Shimʿon son of *dqnh* (= 'the beard'?) said to
2. Yehudah *k* . . . [. . . of the same plac]e: I, of my own will, on this day have sol[d] to you the place of mine that is called
3. the F[iel]d of the Orchard (or: Garden),[the area of sowing of]three *seʾah*'s of[whea]t. If it is less or more—that is the buyer's. [The bou]ndaries of that place: ea[st]—
4. the road and oth[ers; west—Yehud]ah the buyer and[o]thers;[south—]the road/s of the in[her]itors of *Ṣpn* and others; north—the inherit[ors of]*Ṣpn* and o[thers.]
5. That place—within its bounda[ries: a gate that is] an entrance and exit for you to/for . . . as is fitting. According to th[at]I have sold (it) to you for silver *zuzin,* twen[ty-]
6. eight whi[ch are (equal to)] seven [*silʿi*]*n* only, and the mo[n]ey I received, (the) full price. Forever entitled and empowered are Yehu[dah]
7. the buyer and his inherit[ors regarding that sa]le, to buy and to se[l]l, and to [d]o with it whatever you desire, from this day
8. [and forever. And I, Yaʿaqob, and (all) that] I [ow]n, are re[spon]sible and a securi[t]y for cleansing and establishing the place, before you and be[fo]re
9. your inherit[o]rs, f[rom this day and forever,] from all dispute and challenge, damage and annulment th[at may come upon you]regarding [this]place[. . .]
10. . . . [. . . the fulfill]ment of the payment (will be) from my prop[erty and (from) whatever I will acq]uire, according to that. And any time that you s[ay to me, I will exchange]
11. for you [this]d[ocument . . .] . . . as is fitting.

Lower Version

12. On the ten[th/twentieth of . . ., year . . .]of[. . . at *Yqym,* Yaʿaqob son of Shimʿon son of *dqnh*
13. from *Yqym* [said to Yehudah *k* . . . son of Shim]ʿon son of .[. . .] . . ., of the same place: I, of my own will, on th[is] day [have sold to you]
14. the pla[ce of mine, that . . . in *Yqy*]*m,* in whose bo[rders there is a field of the Orchard/Garden,] the area of [so]wing of three [*s*]*eʾah*s of whe[a]t. If
15. it is [less or more—it is the buyer's. The boundaries of that place: e]a[s]t—the road and others; west—Yehudah
16. the [bu]yer[and others; south—the road(s) of the inhe]ritors of *Ṣpn* and others. That place—within its boun[daries: a gate] that is an entrance and ex[it]

17. for you to/for . . . [. . . as is fitting. According to that I have sold (it) to]yo[u for twenty-eight silver *zuzin* which are (equal to) seven] *silᶜi*[*n*]
18. [only, and the money I received,] the ful[l] price. [Forever entitled and empowered are] Yehu[dah the buyer and his inheritors]
19. [regarding that sale . . . to buy and to se]l[l, and] to[do with it whatever you desire, fr]om[this day and forever. And I,]
20. [Yaᶜaqob, and (all) that I own, are responsible and a security for cleansing and]for[establish]ing the[p]la[ce], before you and before your inheritors from th[is] day
21. and forev[er, from any dispute and challenge, damage and an]nulment that may come upon you regarding this place. . . . [. . . the ful]fill[ment]of the payment of/that . . . [. . .]
22. . . . and . . . [. . .] . . . to/for you and to/for . . . [. . .] . . . [. . .] . . . this place
23. [. . .] . . . [. . .]
24. [. . .] . . . [. . .]
25. [?]

Verso

26. [Yaᶜa]qob son of Shimᶜon[son of *dqnh*, for [him]self[wrote it].
27. [. . .] in *Yqym* [. . .];
(line missing?)
28. . . . [. . .]son of *B*[. . .];
29. . . . *b*[. . .]*dh* s[on of . . .] . . . [. . .]*Zp* (=*Zif?*)[. . .];
30. . . . [. . .]from *Yqy*[*m* . . .] . . .;
31. *Yh*[. . .] son of Yehosef, wi[tness];
32. Shimᶜ[on son of . . .] . . . , witness.

Notes on Readings and Comments

L. 1 [בעׂשׂ]ר[ין]. The date of the month is broken (see also in the lower version). Similarly, the name of the month, the year, and the calendrical system are missing. (It is possible to fit six or seven words into the gap: the name of the month, the word שנת [year of], the number of the year, and another two to four words indicating the calendrical system in operation).

L. 1 ביקים. This is apparently the name of the place in which the document was written. This assumption is supported by the *bet* before the name, but see below, line 13 (in the lower version), where מן יקים indicates the origin of the seller. Though there is no direct evidence of a place with this name, a Greek document from the XḤev/Se group from 130 CE,[5] which was written in Aristoboulias (in the vicinity of biblical זיף, in the region of Hebron) mentions Ακαβας Μηείρω τῶν ἀπ̣ὸ κ̣ώμης Ἰακείμων τ̣[ῆς Ζειφηνῆς ('to ᶜAqabas son of Meir from the village of Iaqim [of the Zephene . . .'). H. Cotton suggests identifying this settlement with Khirbet Yaqin (= Khirbet Bani Dar), identified by M. Kochavi[6] with the הקין that appears in the list of cities in the Judaean district in Josh 15:57, together with זיף, מעון, and כרמל.

L. 1 יעקוׂב[בר]שמען בר דקנה. This is the seller's name. The name יעקוב was not common in the Herodian period.[7] The father's name, שמען (one of the most widespread names in this period), is written

[5] Mus. Inv. 870. See No. **69** below.

[6] Kochavi, *Judaea*, 21.

[7] יעקוב/יעקב appears as the name of two people (בן יהודה and בן יהוסף) in a letter from Wadi Murabbaᶜat (Mur **42** 3 [missing], 10, 13), and in a broken signature from Mur **40** בן יעקב עד]; see Benoit et al., *DJD* II, 154, 156. The name יעקוב appears also on an ossuary from Jerusalem (see Avigad, 'Inscribed Ossuaries'). It seems that the custom of naming children after the Patriarchs was not widespread at the end of the Second Temple period (אברם appears on

without a *waw*, though in the signature on the verso the remains of a *waw* can be seen between the *ʿayin* and the head of the *nun*. After the father's name appears the name of the grandfather, who was known by his by-name דקנה (the beard?).[8] The orthography with *he* in place of *ʾalep* (for the definite article) at the end of the word is widespread in documents from the Judaean Desert, and is the normal orthography in Jewish Palestinian Aramaic.[9] (See also ארחה in line 4, as opposed to ארחא in line 15.)

Ll. 1–2 אמר ליהודה כ°°[. The formula '*x* said to *y*' as a precursor of direct speech appears in other deeds from the Judaean Desert,[10] and is the standard formula in Aramaic deeds from Egypt.[11] (In legal formularies of the Middle Ages,[12] such formulation in the name of witnesses is common, with the writer 'declaring'—אמר—in front of the witnesses, and not necessarily to the other side.) After the name Yehudah, we would expect בר; however, the letters appear to be *kap* and possibly *yod* or *waw*, or another damaged letter. It is thus possible that we have here a by-name or family name of Yehudah.[13]

L. 2 מן ת[מן. The restoration is based on line 13, and also No. **8a** 3; No. **8** 1; cf. a Hebrew deed (P.Yadin **46** 2–3) שניהם משם. This indicates that Yehudah, the purchaser, is from the same place previously mentioned, i.e. יקים. For the form תמן, see the discussion of דנן.[14]

L. 2 אנה מרעותי יומה דנה. The writer of the deed declares that he carried out the transaction of his own free will. The formula is common in deeds.[15] The short, proclitic form of the particle מן (with the assimilation of the *nun*) is not common in Aramaic, but occasional examples of it are already found in Biblical Aramaic.[16] It is found in the Aramaic Targums of the Bible, generally corresponding to Hebrew -מ, and also in Aramaic deeds and letters from the Judaean Desert.[17]

L. 2 זבנ[ת] לכ לֿאתרה דלי. The *lamed* of לֿאתרה is short and joined to the final *nun* that descends from the line above.

אתרה, 'the place', indicates the property, which is not described here.[18] The definite article is represented by *he* (see also above, line 1 דקנה). It is difficult to know whether the writer omitted the *yod*

---

an ostracon from Egypt of the fourth century BCE; see Sachau, *Papyrus und Ostraka*, plate 62/1 line 23), while יצחק is extremely rare in the non-literary epigraphic material; see Hachlili, 'Names'.

[8] One should reject the translation 'the elder', in spite of the fact that several people were known by that name (הזקן מביתאל, הלל זקן, etc.), as the Aramaic word for 'elder' is סבא/סב. For the issue of appellatives, see Naveh, 'Nameless People?'. See e.g. the nickname בר קרזלא on a sherd from Masada (Yadin and Naveh, *Masada* I, 114 no. 421).

[9] In most cases, the definite article preserved its emphatic meaning; this is one of the characteristics of Western Aramaic as opposed to Eastern Aramaic, in which it lost this function.

[10] See e.g. No. **8a** 2–3 חדד בר יהודה מן כפר בריו אמר לאלעזר בר אלעזר . . . מן תמן; No. **8** 1 יהונתן בר עלי מן כפר ברו אמר לשאול בר חרשה מן תמן; and in Hebrew lease documents such as P.Yadin **45** 3–6 אלעזר בן אלעזר בן חיטא מן עין גדי אמר לאליעזר בן שמואל משם; P.Yadin **46** 1–3 ישוע קבי[ש] בן שמעון מן עין גדי אמר לאלעזר בן אלעזר בן חיטא ולאליעזר בן שמואל שניהם משם; see also Mur **24** ii 5, iii 5, v 4.

[11] Cf. e.g. *TAD* B1.1 lines 1–2; B2.2 lines 2–3.

[12] Assaf, *Shetaroth*.

[13] Yehudah is one of the most common names in this period. According to T. Ilan, this name was especially widespread amongst converts; see Ilan, 'Ossuary Inscriptions'.

It is possible that a by-name or family name follows the name Yehudah; cf. כתושיון (e.g. P.Yadin **15**; P.Yadin **17–20**); קביש (P.Yadin **42**; = Hebrew הקבש, P.Yadin **43**); קבשן (No. **13**); קיבשא (No. **10**; the reading is uncertain); קנבר (P.Yadin **18**, according to Puech's suggestion, and not קמבר), that appear after Jewish personal names.

[14] See INTRODUCTION TO THE ARAMAIC AND HEBREW DOCUMENTARY TEXTS.

[15] Cf. No. **8a** 3; and see in the INTRODUCTION TO THE ARAMAIC AND HEBREW DOCUMENTARY TEXTS, n. 10.

[16] Thus in 𝔐 Jer 10:11 מארעא (but 4QJer^{b} reads here מן); Dan 2:45 מטורא.

[17] See e.g. P.Yadin **57** 3 מלותך; P.Yadin **55** 3 ומתר (= ומאתר [J. Naveh]); cf. also No. **8** 7 מכול.

[18] Cf. No. **50** 3, 5 אתרא; No. **8** 4 אתריה, as the equivalent of 'house and courtyard' of line 2; No. **21** 3, 7 את[ריא], detailed in lines 3–5.

in דלי by mistake, or if the form already heralds the use of the short form of the relative pronoun (thus also No. **7**[19]). Everywhere else the writer of the deed uses the independent די.

L. 2 די מתקרה. The property is sometimes identified by its appellative. So, e.g. in an Aramaic deed of gift (P.Yadin **7** 7) אתרא די מתקרא כרבא; and in a Hebrew deed of lease, P.Yadin **44** 11–12 המקום שנקרה החפיר והמקום שנקרה הסלם. Evidence of this custom is found also in Greek deeds from Naḥal Ḥever; see e.g. P.Yadin **16** 22 'a date orchard called Algifiamma' (λεγόμενον Αλγιφιαμμα), and 25, where there is another orchard 'called Bagalgala' (λεγόμενον Βαγαλγαλα).[20]

L. 3 ח]ק[ל̊ פרדסה̊] בית זרע חנטי]ן סאין תלת. The expression ח]ק[ל̊ פרדסה̊, 'the field of the garden/orchard', is difficult, since both words are general terms and such an expression is otherwise unattested. It is thus possible that פרדסה indicates the nature of the field—that it is a garden, and not, e.g. a grain field, in spite of its being measured by בית זרע חנטין; cf. *m. B. Bat.* 3.1, where שדה האילן, a tree-planted field, is distinguished from שדה הלבן, a shadeless vegetable or grain field.[21] If we read a *waw* in place of a short *lamed*, the name of the property will be only two letters long and the פרדסה will be additional to the property itself. The first possibility seems more likely.[22]

The ground area of the site is indicated by the amount of wheat that it is possible to sow in it (here three *seʾah*'s). This unit already appears in an Aramaic document from the fifth century BCE.[23] See also No. **50** 2 בית זרע חנטין סאין תלת וקבין תלתה (and see Milik's discussion of the size of the area).[24]

L. 3 הנ חסיר או יתר לזבנה. According to this clause, if the area of the land is smaller or larger than that specified, the loss or gain is that of the purchaser. In No. **50** the same expression appears.[25] חסיר with a *yod* seems to be an adjective in the *Qaṭṭil* pattern. (The form can also be interpreted as a passive participle, חֲסִיר, or as an active participle in plene orthography, חָסֵיר.) If so, יתר is written defectively. זבנה is apparently a substantive in the form of the active participle with the definite article זָבְנָה (cf. Hebrew הקונה). The seller is indicated in the documents by מזבנה.[26]

---

[19] No. **7** 2 דיתב; 6 דיתה.

[20] Lewis, *Documents*, 66.

[21] Cf. ארעא חורתא, 'the white ground', P.Yadin **7** 10, 44.

[22] In order to save space, it was customary to sow between the trees in plantations; for example, grain was sown between vines or olive trees; see Feliks, *Agriculture*, esp. 118–22. The phrase חקל פרדסה may refer to a field within a garden/orchard, but, because of the lack of data, this remains only an hypothesis.

[23] See בית זרע א ר̇ך (א is an abbreviation for the Persian word ארדב, the dry measure for wheat and barley), a phrase indicating the area of a domain (בגא) in an Aramaic letter from the fifth century BCE found in Egypt (*TAD* A6.11 [Driver 8] lines 2, 4).

[24] Milik ('Deux documents') claims that, according to Talmudic data, a *bet seʾah* is equal to 782 square metres. According to the Talmud, the size of the *bet seʾah* is 50 x 50 cubits, but there is a dispute as to the length of a cubit (44.65 cm is a small cubit; 56 cm a large cubit), and therefore Broshi ('Seven Notes', 234) adopts the average measurement for a *bet seʾah,* 625 square metres; see also Feliks, *Agriculture*, 144–5; Kaufman, 'Median Cubit'.

[25] Milik, 'Deux documents', 258. Milik's reading of the second line is incorrect. At the end of the line, he reads ומח]ס[ר. I have suggested the reading אם י]תיר א]ו]ח[ס̊יר (Yardeni, 'Cursive Script', 81), but on further examination it seems to me that the correct reading is אם ח]סיר]א[ו י]תיר, in keeping with the word order here (in this case the orthography of the word יתיר is *plene*). However, compare the Hebrew deed of sale, Mur **30** 3, 14–15 אם יתיר או חסר ללוקח. See also the discussion in *m. B. Bat.* 7.1–4.

[26] See מזבנה ('the seller') in Mur **25** 6; No. **8a** 9, etc. For זבנה ('the buyer'), see e.g. No. **21** 7, No. **8a** 8. The word זבונא ('the buyer') in the form of the nomen agentis (*pāʿōl*) appears in a Syriac slave transmission document of 243 CE; see Welles, *Dura-Europos*, 54–7.

L. 3 ת]חומי אתרה דך. Here begins the definition of the site according to its boundaries. This clause is found in all deeds of real estate transfer. See e.g. the boundaries clause in the Aramaic deeds from Elephantine[27] and in the mediaeval legal formularies.[28]

Ll. 3–4 מד[נח]ה ארחה וח[רנין מערבה יהוד]ה זבנה ו[ח]רנין[דרומה] ארח° י[ר]תי צפן וחרנין צפונה ירת[י]צפן וח[רנין]. The boundaries are indicated according to the directions of the compass point. The order is generally east, west, south, north, though it occasionally differs; see e.g. No. **8a** 8–9 (south, east, north, west); a Hebrew deed of sale, Mur **30** 16–17 (east, west, north, south); the deed of gift, P.Yadin **7** 5–6 (east, west, north, south). In the deeds from Elephantine, there is no unity in the order of the directions.

The name of the direction appears here with a *he* at the end (apparently the definite article, and not a retrospective pronoun), with no directional *lamed* prefix. (Some deeds use *ʾalep* and not *he* at the end of מדנחא, למדנחא, etc.,[29] while some have both a directional *lamed* and *he* למדנחה, etc.)[30]

The repeated word וחרנין (here without *ʾalep*)[31] indicates that there are other abutters in the direction in question, but explicitly naming a single neighbour or landmark in each direction suffices to define the boundaries of the area. A similar formula appears in No. **7** 3 ואחרנן; No. **50** 4 ואחרנין. From the text it is clear that the buyer, Yehudah, was the neighbour to the west of the property. Apparently this was one of the reasons for the purchase (see also No. **8a**[32]). The nominal use of the adjective אחרן, אחרנן is already attested in the documents from Elephantine.[33]

The land to the north of the property, and the road(s?) to it from the south, belonged to the members of a single family who are referred to as ירתי צפן, 'inheritors of *Ṣpn*'. The ink after the *ḥet* in ארח° suggests that there might have been a *yod* there of the plural construct form (ארחי 'roads'). The first letter of the name צפן is similar to both *qop* and *ṣade*, though the top stroke of the right arm, which is arched, is short compared with other examples of *qop* (cf. יקים and דקנה in line 1), and the downstroke is short compared with the other example of *ṣade* (cf. צפונה later in line 4). The name קפן is not known from any source. The name צפן is rare but attested;[34] it is possible that it is an apocopated form of the theophoric name צפניה (cf. מתת and חזק, which are possibly hypocoristics of מתתיה and חזקיה).[35]

L. 5 אתרה דך בתח[ו]מה . . .]מעל ומפק לכ לאת°תר. A new clause begins here. The restoration is based on parallel formulae found in other deeds, in which תחום appears in the singular form (תחומה rather than תחומוהי); thus, e.g. in No. **50** 5; No. **8** 3; and, in Hebrew, Mur **30** 13 (בתחומו).[36] Not everything that is

---

[27] E.g. *TAD* B2.2 (Cowley 6) lines 8–11; B2.3 (Cowley 13) lines 13–15. See discussion on the boundaries in the Aramaic legal papyri in Levine, 'Formulary', 48–53, and 'Topography' in *TAD* B, 177. The boundaries clause is already attested in Old Babylonian deeds.

[28] See Assaf, *Shetaroth*; e.g. in a שטר זביני דבאתי (a deed for the sale of a house, p. 25): ואילין מצרונה . . . מצד אחד דפל׳ ומצד שני דפל׳ ומצד שלישי דפל׳ ומצד רביעי דפל׳.

[29] See e.g. No. **50** 3–5: (1) מדנחא, (2) מערבא, (3) דרומא, (4) צפונא. See also P.Yadin **7** למדנחא, etc.

[30] See e.g. No. **7** 3 למדנחה, ולמערבה.

[31] The word is spelled with an *ʾalep*, in e.g. No. **7** 3; No. **50** 4; P.Yadin **21** 5. The *ʾalep* of אחרן was dropped in several dialects of Late Aramaic, such as Jewish Palestinian Aramaic, Samaritan Aramaic (חורן, עורן), and Christian Palestinian Aramaic.

[32] In this document, ʾElʿazar acquired the neighbouring house to the north of his place of residence.

[33] E.g. *TAD* B2.3 (Cowley 8) 19: למנתן לאחרנן, as opposed to line 10 בר וברה אחרנן. See also the inscription from Sheikh Fāḍel (*TAD* IV [in preparation]) plate 4 line 7 לאחרנן.

[34] The name צפן appears on a seal from the 8th century BCE from Tel Baṭash. Cf. also צפיון among the sons of Gad (Gen 46:16) and ציפן on a sherd from Masada (Yadin and Naveh, *Masada* I, 28, no. 436).

[35] The name צפניה is rare in documents from the end of the Second Temple period. It appears in Aramaic documents from Egypt, such as a name list from the year 400 BCE (*TAD* C3.15 [Cowley 15] 7). The names מתת and חזק appear, e.g. in No. **7** 3, 5; cf. also מתתה in Ezra 10:33. The reading of an Aramaic graffito in the Temple of Abydos is apparently erroneous; see Kornfeld, 'Neues', Sonderband 11, 202.

[36] According to Beyer, the form is plural; see Beyer, *Die Aramäischen Texte*, esp. 35, 53, 118 (n. 1), and 322: 'Südostjudäische Pluralsuffix "seine" ה -ōh'. Cf. in the equivalent place in the Hebrew sale document, Mur **30** 18 בתחומו—is it a sing. form, or a pl. in orthography lacking the *yod*?

found within the borders of the property is specified here. The only elements explicitly laid out are those likely to be contested for any reason, such as routes of access to and from the property, as the words following מעל ומפק ('entry and exit') show. It may therefore be possible to restore here תרעה ('the gate').[37] There remains minimal room in the gap for more letters; it may be possible to fit in די. It is difficult to know if there was a *lamed* before מעל. מעל (root עלל) and מפק (root נפק) are either *Qal* infinitives, or substantives with a prefixed *mem*; cf. also Mur **25** 3 מעלא ומפק[א]; No. **8a** 10 לא מעל ולא מפק; No. **8** 5 מ[עלה ומפקה; and possibly, in Hebrew, Mur **30** 19–20 מובא [ומוצא] (as suggested by E. Qimron).

The words following ומפק are unclear. לכ is confirmed by לך in the parallel text of the lower version (line 17). The next word is broken after לא in the lower version. In the upper version, the letters cannot be combined to form a word which suits the context. (This may perhaps be a scribal error; the scribe intending to write לאתרה דך, or something similar.)

L. 5 כדי חזה. 'As is fitting'. These words seem to close the ownership clause (but see לקבלדך in the continuation of the line).[38] In *Tg. Onq.* Lev 5:10, כדחזי translates כמשפט.

L. 5 לקבלד[ך]. In the Hebrew documents from Naḥal Ḥever, the equivalent of this expression is לעומת ככה (e.g. P.Yadin **44** 22, 30). The expression generally comes at the end of the clause, but here it is unclear if it is pertinent to the previous clause or opens a new clause, the payment that the seller collects in return for the property (according to its nature).

Ll. 5–6 זבנת לכ בכסף זוזין עשר[ין] ותמניה ד[י המון סלעין] ש[ב]ע לחוד. This clause outlines the sum received in return for the property. The sum is indicated in two units of currency, זוזין and סלעין (one *selaᶜ* equals four *zuzin*). It seems that the purpose of the repetition is to avoid mistakes regarding the sum.[39] לחוד (cf. No. **50** 7–8 זבנת לכן בכסף זוזין שבעין ותמניה די המון סלעין תשע עסרה ותקל חד לחוד; and, in a Hebrew deed, P.Yadin **44** 20–21 דנרין ששה עשר שהם סלעים ארבע לב[ד]) appears in texts from Qumran and in Nabataean texts.[40] It apparently originates from the word חד 'one'[41] and in the Targum translates לבד (Exod 26:9) and רק (Gen 6:5). It also appears in several Aramaic dialects. Its use here is similar to the modern use of 'only' written after the sum specified in official documents such as cheques or accounts (cf. בלחוד, 'alone', in P.Yadin **7** 4, 24, 65).

L. 6 וכס[פ]ה אנה מקבל דמין גמרין. This is the receipt clause. The remnants of the *samek* in וכס[פ]ה resemble the lower part of a *ṣade*, but note the left stroke of the *samek* in פרדסה in line 3. מקבל represents the root קבל in the participle;[42] this is the form found in most Aramaic deeds of sale from the Judaean Desert. Apparently, the intention is to state that the seller has already received the sum (but see the form קבלן 'we have received' in No. **12**, a receipt).

The expression דמין גמרין mirrors an expression that appears in Babylonian and Neo-Babylonian deeds.[43] The precise meaning of the expression in this context remains uncertain. It is possible that the

---

[37] So, too, for example in No. **21** 4–5 ותרעא ומפתחא מעלה ו[מפ]קה.

[38] See Mur **19** 11, 25; Mur **21** 3; No. **50** 6–7. Milik read here כדי חיא; Y. Yadin corrected the reading to כדי חזא. A corrected reading of this phrase appears in *Inscriptions Reveal* (Jerusalem: Israel Museum, 1972) 200. Cf. also כראוי in a Hebrew deed, P.Yadin **44** 13, 16.

[39] See above in the INTRODUCTION TO THE ARAMAIC AND HEBREW DOCUMENTARY TEXTS, n. 14, for examples from other deeds.

[40] In Nabataean, e.g. CIS II 212 line 6; 209 line 7 (בלחוד); in texts from Qumran, e.g. 1QapGen XIX 15; 11QtgJob XXXIV 32.

[41] Greenfield ('Azatiwada', 76) believes that the word was pronounced with the vowel *o*, and that only thus is it possible to explain the *waw* in Aramaic. (The explanation is based on the assumption that the vowel in the word חד was long, and that the *waw* reflects the Canaanite vowel shift of long *a* to long *o*.)

[42] See the INTRODUCTION TO THE ARAMAIC AND HEBREW DOCUMENTARY TEXTS, n. 15, and the discussion of מקבל in Broshi and Qimron, 'House Sale Deed', 210. The authors hold that this is the participle passive form.

[43] See the discussion of the sum clause in the INTRODUCTION TO THE ARAMAIC AND HEBREW DOCUMENTARY TEXTS.

seller receives the full payment at once (as opposed to payment by installments, or perhaps to distinguish it from a lease document? An example of payment in installments appears in P.Yadin **42**).[44]

L. 6 לעלם. This word appears in most deeds of sale at the opening of the ownership clause in the phrase לעלם רשי, and at its close in the phrase מן יומה דנה ולעלם (or עד עלם, or עד לעלם; see line 8 at the end of the clause and line 9 in the middle of the sentence; see also No. **21** 8–9; No. **50** 9–10; P.Yadin **47a** 9–10; No. **8** 5–6).[45]

Ll. 6–7 ד̊ש̊ר̊ ושלט יהו[דה] זבנה ויר[תוהי בזב]נה דך. In the context, the first word must be read רשי, even though the first letter resembles a *dalet* (the scribe meticulously distinguishes *reš* from *dalet*), and the remnants of the final letter resemble a *reš*, so that what one sees is דשר. However, the expression דשר ושלט is not attested, so that it seems that this is a scribal error. רשי and שלט in this context are to be taken as synonyms.[46] The root שלט, requiring the preposition *be*-, appears with a similar meaning in deeds from Elephantine (see e.g. *TAD* B2.3 [Cowley 8] 9, but cf. also the formula of a deed of sale from the Middle Ages [Assaf, *Shetaroth*, 26] ושליט יהיה פל׳ דנן על זביני אלין, possibly under the influence of the vernacular). The phrase רשי ושלט appears also in P.Yadin **47b** 6 (cf. P.Yadin **7** 15, 53 רשיה ושליטה). In most of the other deeds from the Judaean Desert the root רשי alone appears in this context.

Ownership of the property is transferred also to the heirs of the buyer. (The reconstruction ויר[תוהי, probably in the plural, is according to No. **21** 7 יהוסף זבנה וירת[ו]הי.[47])

The restoration בזבנ]ה דך is hypothetical. It is also possible to restore באתר]ה דך, as in No. **50** 9 and No. **21** 13; cf. the use of מכר ('sale') in the equivalent position in a Hebrew deed of sale (Mur **30** 16, 17, 22, 28). The expression, which is the indirect object of the clause, appears before the predicate, i.e. before the verbs immediately following.

L. 7 למקנה ולמז[ב]נה ול[מ]עבד בה כל די תצבה. 'To buy and to sell and to do with it all that you desire'. After the array of verbs comes the preposition *be*- with a pronominal suffix referring back to the object, זבנ]ה דך or אתר]ה דך.

With the word תצבה there is a change in the formulation of the deed from 3rd sing. to 2nd sing. (see also a Hebrew deed of sale, Mur **30** 23 תחפץ; No. **50** 10 יצבון in 3rd masc. pl.; and see the detailed discussion by Greenfield of the *kyrieia* clause).[48] The formula expanded in the course of time. A variety of verbs describing what the buyer is 'permitted' (רשי) to do with אתריא אלך appears, for example, in the

---

[44] See Greenfield, 'Legal Terminology', 70–71.

[45] See the discussion of the parallels to the biblical formula מעתה ועד עולם (e.g. Ps 113:2) in documents from Alalakh and Ugarit in Loewenstamm, 'Alalakh', 221–2; see also Yaron, *Law*, 110.

[46] The root רשי appears in Aramaic with two basic meanings (for a detailed discussion of the root רשי and its different uses, see Greenfield, 'Legal Terminology', 79–82):

1. A 'positive' meaning of 'right', similar to the meaning in Hebrew of רשאי, רשות. In this meaning it is the parallel of שלט ב-, which occurs in the deeds from Elephantine and is generally attested before an indirect object (רשי ב-). The root רשי appears in this meaning parallel to the root משל in the Ancient Aramaic inscription from Sefire (III 9) ולתרשה לי עלי]ה, paralleling לתמשל בי בזא (but see the discussion of the root רשה at Elephantine in Kutscher, *Studies*, 43 [Hebrew]). It is also attested with this meaning in deeds of sale from the Judaean Desert, such as No. **21** 6; No. **50** 9; No. **7** 6; P.Yadin **47a** 9; No. **8a** 9; No. **8** 5; and also in Hebrew, Mur **30** 22. It also appears in a deed of lease, P.Yadin **42** 8; cf. in a Hebrew deed of lease, P.Yadin **44** 24.

2. A 'negative' meaning covering the issue of debt and the issue of legal claim. In this meaning the verb is generally attested before a direct object. See the occurrences of the verb רשי meaning 'legal charge' in the deeds from Elephantine (e.g. *TAD* B2.3 [Cowley 8] 24). As a noun, see e.g. מרשא, whose meaning is apparently 'debt' in an account list from the middle of the third century BCE (*TAD* C3.29 [Levi della Vida papyrus] 2). See also Assaf, *Shetaroth*, 20 (a deed of loan, line 9) בזכו (read בזפו) וברשו ('in loan and in debt').

[47] Cf. also in the Elephantine deeds, e.g. *TAD* B3.4 (Kraeling 3) 11–12 אנת ענניה בר עזריה שליט בביתא זך ובניך מן אחריך.

[48] Greenfield, 'Legal Terminology', 67–70. See also A. Hurvitz, 'The History of a Legal Formula', *VT* 32 (1982) 257–67.

ownership clause of No. **21**; an accumulation of verbs also appears in a deed of gift from Naḥal Ḥever (P.Yadin **7**),[49] all the more so in the mediaeval legal formularies.[50]

Ll. 7–8 מן יומה דנן [ולעלם. The buyer and his heirs have ownership rights over the property forever (cf. also the deeds from Elephantine[51] and from the Middle Ages[52]). Regarding דנן, see INTRODUCTION TO THE ARAMAIC AND HEBREW DOCUMENTARY TEXTS, n. 2.

L. 8 ואנה יעקוב ודי אי[תי לי א[חר]אין וערב[י]ן. Here begins the clause dealing with responsibility and 'cleansing' (מירוק). The formula is short (see e.g. the longer formula in No. **50** 11 ואנה . . . מזבנה וכל [די איתי לי ודי אקנה אחראין ו]ערבין). The long version will not fit here, and the reconstruction is based on No. **21** 9 (see also below, lines 19–20).

Although most of the letters in א[חר]אין וערב[י]ן are damaged, the reading is almost certain given the standard formula (see e.g. No. **8** 6).[53]

Ll. 8–9 למשפיה ולמקימה אתרה קדמך ו[קד]ם ירת[י]ך מ[ן יומה דנן ולעלם. 'To cleanse and establish the place before you and before your inheritors'. The seller pledges before the purchaser and his heirs to 'cleanse' the property from all claims likely to be made regarding it by another party.[54]

The formula of the defension clause appears in different forms. In a parallel text the root מרק[55] appears in place of שפי,[56] used here (see e.g. No. **50** 12 למרקא ולקימא). The verbal forms למשפיה and למקימה appear here in the infinitive with a prefixed *mem*[57] (cf. ולקימא in No. **50**, as opposed to למקימה in

---

[49] No. **21** 7–8 למחפר ולהעמקה למב[נה] ולהרמא למקנה ולמזבנה]. P.Yadin **7** 17–18, 56–57 למקנא ולמזבנו ולמנחל ולמורתו ולמרהן ולמנתן ולמזרע ולמנצב ולמבנא ולמפרוע פרענהון ('to buy and sell and bestow and bequeath and mortgage and give and sow and plant and build and pay their debts').

[50] See Assaf, *Shetaroth*, 26 (שטר זביני דבאתי): ושליט יהא פל׳ דנן על זביני אילין דזבינית ליה למקנא ולאקנויי ולאורותי ולאחסנא ולזבונא ולחלופא ולמידר ולאוגורי ולמש[כונא] ולשנאה ולגמרה ולמיסתר ולמבנא ולמעבד מחיצות ולמיהב במתנה לכל מאן דיצבי ('and *X* will be permitted regarding these sales/purchases that I sold to him to buy and give away and to bequeath and bestow and sell and exchange and dwell and rent out and mortgage and change and complete and destroy and build and make fences and to give as a gift to whomsoever he wishes').

[51] In the deeds from Elephantine the root ירת appears only as a verb (see e.g. *TAD* B2.6 21; B3.8 35), indicating the rights of the husband after the death of his wife (see Yaron, *Law*, 86, 90), while inheritors are specified according to their familial proximity and status (see e.g. n. 47).

[52] See e.g. Assaf, *Shetaroth*, 26 line 16; 27 line 18, ואינש לא ימחא בידיה ולא ביד ירתיה בתריה מן יומא דנן ולעלם.

[53] אחראי is a loan translation from Neo-Babylonian. See Greenfield, 'Babylonian/Aramaic', 478. In the mediaeval deed formularies the formula ואחריות זביני אילין עליאי ('and the responsibility for these sales is mine'; Assaf, *Shetaroth*, 27 line 18, etc.) appears. In No. **8a** 11 this formula apparently appears in the singular אחר̇י̇ וערב. The reading of the first word is doubtful since the form of *reš* and *yod* has been damaged. In my doctoral dissertation I suggested reading here אהוי ערב, but after further examination I accept Milik's reading אחרי וערב ('Deux Documents', 264), as the phrase אחראין וערבין is indeed common in the deeds, while אהוי ערב does not appear at all. From the palaeographic aspect, too, the second letter is closer to a *ḥet* than a *he*. (See Milik's note for the question of the *ʾalep* in the word אחראין, etc.; 'Deux documents', 263).

[54] On the root קום in this context, see Kutscher, *Studies*, 508–9 (Hebrew section); Yaron, *Law*, 166–7.

[55] The root מרק appears in a similar context in Neo-Babylonian deeds; it is usually accepted that it originates in Akkadian (see Kutscher, *Studies*, 425 [Hebrew section] and notes 1, 2; on the 'cleansing' clause see Kutscher, *Studies*, 428–30 [Hebrew section]). See also Greenfield, 'Defension Clause', 467–71. See the detailed discussion of the 'cleansing' terms in the Elephantine documents and their legal significance in Yaron, *Law*, 129–31; 166–8 (it is he who dubs this clause the 'defension clause'). See also ואמרק ואדכא in line 14 of the Syriac deed from Dura Europos (Welles, *Dura-Europos*). Compare the 'cleansing' terms used in the deed of sale formulary from Assaf, *Shetaroth*, 26 lines 19–20.

[56] The root שפי is common in Hebrew (לשפות, שפוי; but see the Hebrew deed of sale, Mur **30** 24 למרק). For a discussion of this root see Kutscher, *Studies*, 426 (Hebrew section); see also Greenfield, 'Defension Clause', 469–70.

[57] Infinitive forms of the verb in the derived conjugations with a prefixed *mem* such as are found in the *Qal* appear in Western Aramaic (but also Syriac). Kutscher, *History of Aramaic*, 86; see also Greenfield, 'Infinitive', 469–70.

No. **8** 6). Following אתרה, דך usually appears (see e.g. No. **50** 12; No. **8** 7 אתריה[אל]ך and in Hebrew, Mur **30** 24 את המכר הזה). The formula is shortened here, and the word appears without a demonstrative pronoun (thus also in the lower version, line 20).

L. 9 מן [כל חרר ותגר. The phrase חרר ותגר appears also in other deeds from the Judaean Desert; it refers to opponents of the transaction.[58] The precise meaning and etymology of חרר have not been established with any degree of certainty (cf. Prov 26:21 לחרחר ריב); it apparently is related to the root *ḥrr* with the meaning of heat, burning. תגר is apparently derived from the root גרי (or גור, or גרר) and means 'dispute' (like Hebrew תיגרה).

L. 9 נזקן ובטלה. 'damages and "annulling"'; cf. Mur **25** 7 ונזק ובטלן (Milik read וריק); Mur **26** 5 ובטלן. The form בטלה represents the gerund of the *Paᶜel*, equivalent to Hebrew ביטול.

L. 9 ד[י יתנך]על אתרה[דנן]. The reconstruction is according to line 21 (cf. Mur **25** 7; Mur **26** 5). The root of יתנך is apparently אתי; the form results from the dropping of the 1st and 3rd root letters and the addition of a *nun* before the suffixed pronoun in the future form of the verb. If this is the case, the literal translation is 'will come (upon) you'.[59] The use of על is in keeping with the context. The end of the line apparently lacks the word connecting it to the next line.

L. 10 פטר∘∘[. The root פטר is not attested in other deeds of sale. Possibly the word is used to declare that the buyer is exempt from paying any claims, but the context is too broken to allow us to draw any far-reaching conclusions.

L. 10 פר[ען תשלמתה מן נכ]סי ודי אק[נה לקבלדך. A similar clause usually appears in loan bills (IOUs) written in the name of the borrower (Mur **18** 7; Wadi Sdeir [unpublished] 6–7; in Hebrew, No. **49** 10–11). Remnants of the clause appear in a deed of sale from Wadi Murabbaᶜat (Mur **26** 6), and possibly also in No. **8** 7 and P.Yadin **42** 9. פרען appears in a deed of gift (P.Yadin **7** 18, 57). In deeds of sale, this clause expresses the obligation of the seller to compensate the buyer for losses resulting from claims on the property.

Ll. 10–11 וכל זמן די ת[מר לי אחלף] לך ש[טרא דנה   ]∘נבא רבה כדי חזה. With this clause the seller undertakes to 'exchange' (אחלף) the deed any time that the buyer requests. It remains uncertain what 'exchange' means in this context;[60] we are dependent on the words preceding כדי חזה, which are difficult to decipher.

Ll. 12–25 The lower version begins in line 12, and consists of an almost identical repetition of the upper version. Between the two versions there is a mark in the form of a sharp angle, whose function is to indicate a division, and possibly to prevent additions in the empty space.[61] The lower version is more fragmentary than the upper, and most of the reconstructions have been made on the basis of the latter. Only in a few places did the lower version aid in the reconstruction of the upper: בית [זר]ע חנט[י]ן (line 14 [line 3]); מערבה יהודה (line 15 [line 4]); יתנך and דנה (line 21 [line 9]). At the end of line 21 and the start of line 22, the words תשלם די ל[ ]דין ו/ית[do not fit well with what is written in line 10 תשלמתה מן נכ[סי ודי אק]נה. It is possible that the formulation has been corrected here. In any case, the text in the lower version is longer than that of the upper, and the restoration remains no more than a suggestion. The remainder of the text is missing, so that we do not know the length of the addition.

Ll. 26–33 On the verso of the deed are the remains of seven lines of signatures. The first is certainly that of the seller, [יע]קוב בר שמעו[ן] בר דקנה, who signed for himself (ע[ל נפש]ה כתבה]). The handwriting is

---

[58] See חרר ותגר in Mur **26** 5; No. **8** 7; and in a Hebrew deed, Mur **30** 25. See also Greenfield and Sokoloff, 'Qumran Aramaic', 92.

[59] Attempts to derive this word from the root תני (with the meaning 'condition') are not supported by the formulae found in other deeds.

[60] See the discussion and notes on this clause in the INTRODUCTION TO THE ARAMAIC AND HEBREW DOCUMENTARY TEXTS.

[61] One must distinguish between the sign used between sections, such as appears here, and the signs used to fill up lines, such as crosses at the end of short lines, that are attested in several deeds from the Judaean Desert (e.g. P.Yadin **44–46**, to be published). Division marks between sections, similar to the sign in this document, appear e.g. in 1QIsa^a.

identical to that on the recto, so that it is clear that Yaᶜaqob himself was the writer of the deed. The second line is also written in the same hand, but only a few letters of it survive, amongst them the word יקים (line 27), which is apparently the name of Yaᶜaqob's place of origin and possibly the place where the deed was written (see above, lines 1, 13). One may suppose that the signature of the purchaser was here, as the following five lines apparently contained the five signatures of the witnesses (only in two of them [lines 31–2] is it possible to identify parts of the names יהוסף and שמעון). Seven signatures appear on several other double documents from Naḥal Ḥever. See e.g. P.Yadin **7**; P.Yadin **15–21**; No. **22**; the Nabataean documents from Naḥal Ḥever (P.Yadin **1–4**); and the Hebrew deed of lease, P.Yadin **44**.[62] In line 29, the place name זפ (= Zif) has perhaps survived. The nature of this line is not clear. In line 30 it is perhaps possible to read מן יק]ים[('from *Yqym*'; cf. ספריא מן ירושלם alongside the signature on the verso of No. **50** 18–19).

[62] See Koffmahn, *Doppelurkunden*, 12, 63–4. See the detailed discussion of the number of witnesses on the deeds from Elephantine by Yaron, *Law*, 36–7.

9a. XḤev/Se papUnclassified Fragment A ar

(FIG. 9 AND PL. VI)

THIS fragment of papyrus was placed together with No. **9** on a single plate. Although they appear in IAA photograph 445123 as parts of a single deed, they apparently do not belong together. The maximal measurements of the fragment are 10 x 3.3 cm. On one side have survived the remains of seven lines from the left edge of the document, perhaps a deed, written along the fibres. It is not clear if this is a continuous text, as the spacing between the words is not uniform and the lines are uneven. Neither is the script uniform; it appears to be the work of several hands, one of which (second part of line 4) is apparently the same as that of No. **9**. While the letters seem to be clear, actual readings are questionable, and the nature of the text is uncertain. If the reading of שלמת לכ/הון in line 6 is correct, it is possible that this is the remains of a deed of purchase in Aramaic. On the other side are the remains of two lines written across the fibres. In the first line, שהד (witness) has survived, which indicates that it may have been a 'double' deed.

Mus. Inv. 543
PAM 42.202, 42.203
IAA 445123*, 445125*

Recto

1 כת]בה
2]ן לי   אל◦[ ]ך ◦[
3] אנחנה ה\כל/נן שתין [
4]◦◦◦ין   עשרה ◦◦◦[
5]◦ן ◦◦[
6]◦ם שלמת ל\כ/הון [
7]◦◦ל[

Verso

]שהד 8

]∘∘∘∘ 9

Translation

Recto

1. wr]ote it
2.] . . . to me . . . [. . .
3.]we are(?) sixty(?) [
4.] . . . ten(?) . . . [
5.] . . .
6.] . . . I paid you/them [
7.] . . . [

Verso

8. PN son of PN]witness
9.] . . .

10. XḤev/Se papReceipt for Payment of a Fine? ar

(FIG. 9 AND PL. VII)

THIS is a fragment of a document on papyrus. The maximal measurements are 4.4 x 4.6 cm. Remains of five lines have survived, written in Aramaic along the fibres. Part of a date—the indication of the year (עשרין ותרתין, line 4)—has survived, though the era is missing. The right and lower margins have survived, and apparently also the upper margin, so that it seems that there were no further lines. The deed is torn along the length of its left side. The division of the words in line 2 is not clear, and in fact the nature of the document is uncertain. The mention of an amount of silver (five *silʿin*) in line 3 suggests the possibility that it is a receipt of some kind, though there is no explicit evidence for this being the case. A Greek loanword—אפופס or אפופסא (see line 3)—meaning, i.a., verdict, could perhaps indicate the juridical nature of the document, perhaps being a receipt for a fine. The names of two people are mentioned at the opening of the document.

Palaeography

The form of the letters belongs to the Herodian period cursive style, as found, e.g. in No. **9** and several sherds from Masada.[1] The writing is upright and the letters clear. There are no remains of ornamental additions to the letter forms, and no ligatures.

Orthography

שׂמוׂקא (line 1) and שׂלעין (line 3) are written with *śin* and not with *samek*.[2]

Mus. Inv. 736
PAM 42.194
IAA 449734*, 449737*

---

[1] See Yadin and Naveh, *Masada,* I, pl 24, nos. 421, 422, 425, 426.

[2] Interchanges of *śin* and *samek* are a common phenomenon in this period. See e.g. the names כסבא/כשבא, מסבלה/משבלה; cf. also ימא שמוקא in 1QapGen XXII 17–18.

Recto

שמׄוׄקׄא בר בׄרׄוׄכׄא[ל]יׄהׄוׄנתן ◦[
קׄיבשאוחבראגב אש[כסׄף]
שׄלעין חמש אפופסאב◦[
שנת עשרין ותרתין לתׄ◦[
בר שׄוׄלׄיׄ כתבה

TRANSLATION

Recto

1. *smwqʾ* son of *brwkʾ* [and/to Ye]h/Yonathan . . . [. . .]
2. *Qybšʾ*(?) and [his(?)] associate(?) at(?) . . . [. . . silver(?)]
3. five *silʿin*, (according to?) the verdict . . . [. . .]
4. year twenty-two of . . . [. . . PN]
5. son of Shulai wrote it.

NOTES ON READINGS AND COMMENTS

L. 1 שמׄוׄקׄא. This is apparently a by-name (= סמוקא, 'the ruddy', 'the red'). It is attested several times, in different forms, in Jewish sources.[3] It is possible that people given this name had red hair. The name of the father is possibly בריכא or ברוכא ('the blessed').[4] The final letter is unclear, but it may be possible to restore the remains of the lower stroke of an *ʾalep* descending in a slant from left to right (cf. the other examples of *ʾalep* in this fragment).

L. 1]יׄהׄוׄנתן ◦[or]יׄוׄנתן ◦[. If this is the name of the person to whom the deed is addressed, it may be possible to restore a *lamed* before it. However, it is also possible that the second person is the writer of the deed (compare No. **12**). From the first few letters of the name, only two lower ends have survived, with the second of them apparently belonging to a *waw*, and the first possibly to a *he* or *yod*. Accordingly, it is difficult to know whether the name was written with or without a *he*. Following the name there are unidentifiable ink marks, perhaps *bet* of the word בר, after which the deed is torn.

L. 2 The division of the words in this line is not clear. The first letter may be a *qop* or the ligature מן. If the letter is a *qop*, we may have before us a personal name—קיבשא—which is possibly a by-name or a family name; cf. קביש in P.Yadin **42** 2 (= הקבש in P.Yadin **43** 3); קבשן in No. **13** 4. No meaning for these names has been suggested so far. If this is the case, the reading may be קיבשא וחברא גב אש[('Qibshaʾ and the (his?) associate at . . . ['). If the first sign is מן, the reading may be מן יבש או חבר אגב אש[or מן יבשא וחברא גב אש[. In any case, the meaning is obscure. For גב (or אגב), cf. גבי ('*chez*'). The remainder of the line is missing.

L. 3 שׄלעין חמש אפופסאב◦[. The name of the coin *selaʿ* is feminine (and therefore the form חמש), as is usual for the period (this is true in all the deeds; cf. also in a Hebrew deed[5] סלע אחת). The order of the words, name followed by number, is usual for Aramaic.

---

[3] See e.g. חילפי בר סמקאי (*Gen. Rab.* 51.2); טייפה/טיופה סמוקה/י (*y. Dem.* 3.4; *y. Yeb.* 8.1); רבי אבא סמקה (*y. Ber.* 9.1).

[4] A man by the name of רמי בר ברוכי is mentioned in *b. Sanh.* 17b. Cf. also the name Βρωκ (= ברוך; *CPJ*, vol. 3, inscr. 1438), and so, too, ברוכי in the Munich manuscript of the Talmud. Note עבדברוך in *CIJ* II, 846.

[5] No. **49** 6–7.

L. 3 אפופס or אפופסא. If the reading is correct, this may be a shortened form of ἀπόφασις or ἀπόφανσις, 'verdict, dispensation'. If so, perhaps this deals with the payment of a fine following some kind of judgement. The letters]○אב or]○ב that follow are the start of the following word. The remainder of the line is missing.

L. 4]○שנת עשרין ותרתין לה̇. This line contains part of a date, namely, the year. The reading of the letter after *lamed* is uncertain, but it is not similar to a *he* (were it a *he*, it would be possible to restore להיפרכיה). It is possible that the name of the Roman ruler appeared here.

L. 5 בר שולי כתבה. Only the scribe's father's name survives, and the reading is not certain. Instead of *waw* and *lamed* after the *šin* it might be possible to read *taw*, though the name שולי seems preferable. It may be an Arabic name; cf. the name שלי in the signature on a Nabataean deed from Naḥal Ḥever (P.Yadin **3** 53) והבדשרא בר שלי; and on a Greek deed from Naḥal Ḥever (No. **63**, verso, 6th signature) יהוסף בר שולי; cf. also the Arabic שולי (in Greek, Συλλαεος) mentioned by Josephus as one of the associates of Obdat II, King of the Nabataeans, who plotted against Herod.[6]

[6] Josephus *J.W.* 1.24.6; 1.28.6; 1.29.6; 1.32.3.

11. XḤev/Se papMarriage Contract? ar

(FIG. 9 AND PL. VII)

THIS is a small fragment of a double deed written on papyrus. It is written in Aramaic, across the fibres. The maximal measurements of the fragment are 4.7 x 3.4 cm. The upper margin and the remains of three lines of the upper version have survived, and further remains from the first line of the lower version. The deed is torn apparently close to the right margin, as the date lacks only the day of the month. On the verso are the remains of possibly the first or second letters of a signature. The words that have survived from the second line—די תהוין לי—may suggest that the fragment is the remains of a marriage document. If so, it is impossible that the three lines of the upper version comprised the complete text. The fragment is too small, however, to enable any clear assessment. The name of the month has survived along with the number of the year (line 1), but the name of the era is missing.

Palaeography

The forms of the letters fit well into the extreme Jewish cursive style attested in documents from the close of the Second Temple period up to the end of the Bar Kokhba revolt. The writing is skilled. Ligatures of a *nun* connected to the letter following it appear three times (in שנת, תמנה, ואנה).

Mus. Inv. 736
PAM 42.356
IAA 449734*, 449737*

Recto
Upper Version

1 [ב]∘∘∘ לאלול שנת תמנ̇ה [

2 [ ]∘∘ס∘כ̇י̇ (נ̇ב̇ז / י̇ן) די תהוין לי ל̇[אנתה כדין משה ויהודא

3 [ל]מ̇פ̇ר̇ע̇ה ואנה מקב̇[ל

Lower Version

[ב]עשׂ֯ר֯ ◦ ל֯◦◦[4

(continuation missing)

Verso

[◦וא֯] 5

Translation

Recto

Upper Version

1. [On the . . .] . . . of Elul, year eight [. . .]
2. [. . .] . . . that you shall be my [wife according to the law of Moses and the Jews/Judaea . . .]
3. [. . . to]pay it, and I recei[ve . . .]

Lower Version

4. [On the . . . -]teenth/twentieth of . . . [. . .]

Verso

5. . . . [. . .]

Notes on Readings and Comments

L. 1 [ב]◦◦◦ לאלול שנת תמנה [. שנת תמנה also appears in No. **32** 1, as well as in the date of a deed fragment in cursive script of unknown provenance.[1] After תמנה the document is torn, so the year may be either the eighth or the eighteenth. Since the era is missing, it is impossible to date the document; perhaps the era is that of a Roman emperor (cf. Mur **18**)[2] or possibly that of the Eparchy (cf No. **12**).[3]

L. 2]◦◦ס֯נ֯ב֯ז֯ די תהוין לי ל[אנתה. The reading of the first word is difficult. The first two letters are fragmentary. Following them is possibly a *samek*, and another letter that may be a short *nun* or a *yod*. After that there is a *bet* or a *kap* and finally perhaps a *zayin* (from the inclination of the head to the right) or a *waw* or a *yod*. In this position we would expect the name of the bride's father. Since the full version of this clause has not survived in the Jewish Aramaic marriage documents from the Judaean Desert,[4] it is difficult to restore the text. Possibly, the formulation was similar to the following:

---

[1]]באב שנת תמנה. The fragment is in the Hecht Museum in Haifa, no. H 1804. I am grateful to Mr. H. Misgav who showed me a photograph of this fragment prior to its publication.

[2] Mur **18** 1 שנת תרתי[ן] לנרון קסר.

[3] No. **12** 11–12 שנת עשרין וח[מ]ש להפרכ[יה].

[4] Apart from this document, an additional three Jewish Aramaic marriage documents have survived, all damaged to a smaller or larger extent (Mur **20**; Mur **21**; P.Yadin **10**). In Mur **20** 3 [ד]י תהוא לי לאנתה כדין מ[שה ויהודא; it is possible that the prospective husband does not address the wife directly but rather, perhaps, her father (cf. the marriage document in Greek from Naḥal Ḥever [P.Yadin **18**] formulated in the name of the bride's father). Mur **21** is torn and it is not possible to reconstruct the text of this clause. Babatha's marriage document (P.Yadin **10**) is torn

בר . . . אמר ל . . . ברת . . . די תהוין לי לאנתה כדין משה ויהודא . . . . A slightly different formula appears in the Jerusalem Talmud:[5] לכשתיכנסי לביתי תהויין לי לאנתו כדת משה ויהודאי. (Cf. also the mediaeval formula for a marriage document[6] הואי לי לאינתו כדת משה [וישראל.)

L. 3 ל]מִפְרַעֵה ואנה מקבּ[ל. This is the last line in the upper version of the deed. The text is too torn to be restored. ואנה shows it to be a declaration by the writer of the deed (the groom, if this is indeed a marriage document). The words before and after it are fragmentary. From the context it seems that ל]מִפְרַעֵה is a *Qal* infinitive of the root פרע (perhaps a lengthened infinitive form or perhaps with a retrospective pronoun, 'to pay it'). Perhaps the author of the deed is indicating here that there are obligations on his part or on the part of another person to pay the ketubbah (cf. the mediaeval formula of a marriage document[7] in which the groom obligates himself to pay the ketubbah) or to fulfill some kind of repayment. ואנה opens a new sentence. If the reading מקבּ[ל is correct (*bet* with an extended tail) it is possible that we have here a confirmation by the writer of the deed that he received some kind of payment (cf. the formula אנה מקבל in deeds of sale[8] in which the seller confirms that he received the money in exchange for the property) or that he takes upon himself some kind of obligation, perhaps responsibility for payment of the ketubbah[9] (in both cases we would have expected a syntactical construction in which the object was at the beginning of the sentence, the common formulation in Aramaic).

L. 4 [עשר̊◦ ל◦◦]. The lower version of the double deed begins here, after a gap of two lines. The letters are larger and less cursive. It seems that there are remains here of a date, possibly עשר or maybe עשרן (remains of an unidentified letter follow the *reš*). From the position, at least one word is lacking before this. Accordingly, it seems that this is part of a compound number indicating the date in the month. The name of the month must be Elul (as in line 1), but the remains of the letters after the *lamed* do not look like an *ʾalep* followed by a *lamed*, and it is difficult to identify the letters, especially as the word is broken.

L. 5 On the verso remains of a signature can be seen perpendicular to the text on the recto. From its position, it was the signature of one of the parties.[10]

---

before the words לאנת]ה כדי[ן משה ויה[ו]דא. The word ויהודא ('and Judaea') needs some explanation, as ויהודאי ('and the Jews') is the traditional version, appearing in the formula כדת משה ויהודאי (see n. 5). Thus I have read ויהודאי in both P.Yadin **10** and Mur. **19**, where the formula appears. However, after further examination of those documents, I noticed that the *ʾalep* at the end has the form of a final *ʾalep* and is rather big. The following letter, which could be either *yod* or *waw*, may belong to the following word (in both documents). I, therefore, prefer the reading ויהודא, although not attested elsewhere. There also remains the question of the spelling of the name יהודא with *ʾalep* rather than *he*, which is more common.

[5] See *y. Yeb.* 15.2 and *y. Ketub.* 4.8.

[6] Assaf, *Shetaroth*, 13 line 6.

[7] Assaf, *Shetaroth*, 15b lines 4–6 כולהון יהון [אחר]אין וערבאין לכתובתא דא ולנדוניא ולתוספת לאתפרעא מנהון בחיי [ו]בתר מותי.

[8] E.g. No. **8** 5 ותקלי כספה אנה מקבל; No. 9 6 וכס[פ]ה אנה מקבל; No. 50 8 וכספא אנה מקבל.

[9] See in a mediaeval ketubbah formulary (Assaf, *Shetaroth*) 15b 2 [ואחריות] כתובתא דא קבלית עלי ועל ירתאי בתראי, etc.

[10] See the discussion of signatures on the deeds in the INTRODUCTION TO THE ARAMAIC AND HEBREW DOCUMENTARY TEXTS.

12. XḤev/Se papReceipt for Dates ar (131 CE)

(FIG. 10 AND PLS. VIII–IX)

THIS deed has survived almost in its entirety. Thirteen short lines are written along the fibres of a rectangular piece of papyrus. The maximal measurements of the fragment are 9 x 4.8 cm. It is a receipt for dates bearing the date of the 15th of Shevat in the 25th year of the Eparchy (Provincia Arabia), i.e. 131 CE.[1]

The deed appears to be complete. However, there are no remains of signatures of the parties or of the witnesses. If the reading is correct, the writers of the deed are two men whose names have partially survived יחס° ° בר תשה and חברי שמ[עון/ואל]; the second appears without the name of his father. They declare that they received from שלם ברת לוי (line 1) a quantity of dates measuring nineteen *se*ʾ*ah*s and one and a half *qab*s, i.e. nineteen and one quarter *se*ʾ*ah*s (the precise measure of the *se*ʾ*ah* in this period is unknown).[2] In the absence of a reference to any monetary value, it seems that the dates themselves are the subject of the receipt. Since the date on the document is Shevat, while the season for picking dates was at the start of the autumn,[3] it is possible that the dates were dried. The date appears at the end of the document, unlike most of the Aramaic deeds from the Judaean Desert in which it appears at the beginning.[4] This document may represent the payment of a tax on a lease, in which case the writers are perhaps tax collectors. Since there are no signatures of witnesses, it seems that the signature of the scribe served as proof of the legal validity of the receipt. The text in lines 6–8 is fragmentary, and various attempts at reading have not produced convincing results. It is possible that information is contained within these lines which could clarify the meaning of the date שנת עשר[י]ן ('the year twenty', lines 7–8), and perhaps the circumstances in which this receipt was written.

Palaeography

The letters are relatively large; their average height is *c.*4 mm. Their forward inclination, however, and their connection to one another make the identification of several letters uncertain. Comparison of the forms of individual letters to those in other documents from the Judaean Desert shows that they are similar in basic structure to the cursive forms current in the Jewish script in this period. Noteworthy are the two forms of the ʾ*alep*: a reclining medial as opposed to an upright final (if the reading is correct), against the majority of the documents in which it is particularly the medial

---

[1] See the discussion of the dating in the INTRODUCTION TO THE ARAMAIC AND HEBREW DOCUMENTARY TEXTS.

[2] See the discussion of date crops, measures, weights, and export quantities, in Broshi, 'Seven Notes'.

[3] Broshi, 'Seven Notes', 233.

[4] But see the very similar receipt in Greek (No. **60**).

form that is upright, while the final form reclines.[5] The scribe uses two forms of medial *kap*: one more cursive and similar to a *bet* with the form of the digit 2 (להפרכ[יה], line 12) and the second less cursive and unlike a *bet* (כתבה, line 13). The forward inclination of the writing distorts the form of several letters, especially of *ʿayin*, *šin* and *gimel*. An unintended extension of the letters *waw* and *yod* into the letter following them (לוי, line 1; סאין, line 4; עשרין, line 11) may appear in an extreme cursive script, but does not constitute a stage in the development of those letters (see a similar phenomenon, e.g. in No. **13**). A further characteristic of the script in this document is the relatively short *lamed*. The scribe used a relatively wide pen with a cut end. The difference in the width between the heavier vertical and lighter horizontal strokes shows that the nib of the pen was held virtually parallel to the line.

Orthography and Language

A noteworthy feature of this short text is its means of expressing the numbers nineteen (עשר ותשׄעׄ, lines 4–5) and fifteen (עׄשׄרׄה וחׄמׄשׄהׄ, lines 9–10) with עשר preceding the number of units. This method of expressing numbers, perhaps influenced by the order of writing numerals in which the tens precede the units, is also attested in other legal documents from the Judaean Desert (both in the context of dates and for sums of money) alongside the compound form, in which single units precede the tens.[6]

Mus. Inv. 736
PAM 42.194
IAA 449734*, 449737*

1 שלם ברׄת לוׄיׄ אׄחׄוׄך
2 יׄחׄ°° ברׄ תשׄה וחׄברׄיׄ
3 שמׄ[ ]קבלן מנך צדׄמׄיׄ
4 תמרׄיׄן סאין עשר
5 ותשׄעׄ וקב ופלׄגׄ
6 עדׄ°ׄ עׄמׄך מׄן בב לׄוׄיׄ
7 אבוׄךׄ בשנת

[5] A few scribes do not distinguish between medial and final forms of *ʾalep*, and a few interchange them. Cf., e.g. ארחא in No. **9** 15: an upright final *ʾalep* against a reclining opening *ʾalep*.

[6] See the discussion of the language of the documents in the INTRODUCTION TO THE ARAMAIC AND HEBREW DOCUMENTARY TEXTS.

///
עשׄר[י]ן וׄכׄזׄאׄ 8
ביום עׄשׄרׄה וח 9
מׄשׄה בשבט 10
שנת עשרין 11
וח[מ]ש להפרכ[יה] 12
תד/ח°° כתבה 13

TRANSLATION

1. *Šlm,* daughter of Levi; your brother
2. *Yḥ* . . . son of *Tšh,* and my friend
3. *Šm*[. . . ,]we received from you the price/tax of
4. dates—*seʾah*s ten
5. and nine and a *qab* and a half,
6. which is with you(?), from . . . Levi
7. your father, in the year
8. twenty and 3/. And as such,
9. in the day ten and fi-
10. ve of Shevat,
11. year twenty-
12. fi[v]e of the Eparch[y.]
13. *Td/ḥ*[. . .] wrote it.

NOTES ON READINGS AND COMMENTS

L. 1 שלם ברׄת לוׄיׄ. The name שלם may be a hypocoristic of שלמציון or perhaps it is the Aramaic form of the Hebrew name שלום[7] (cf., e.g. Mur **30** 25 שלום). The name שלם appears also in No. **8a** 12, and elsewhere, such as an ossuary from Jerusalem שלם ומתיה ברה.[8] The name שלמציין also appears in this orthography in other documents from the Judaean Desert (e.g. No. **13** 4, 11), and so, too, in finds from Egypt from the third century BCE.[9] The two names are attested on ossuaries from the end of the Second Temple period.[10] The name Levi appears also in No. **7** as the name of the father of ʾElʿazar.

Ll. 1–2 אׄחׄוך יׄחׄ°° ברׄ תשׄה. It is possible that אׄחׄוך (if the reading is correct) does not indicate a blood relationship, but rather an equal social status (thus, for example, in documents from Egypt in the Persian period[11]), unless we take תשׄה as the name of the mother (תשא appears as a woman's name on an ostracon from Egypt from the fourth or third century BCE[12]); however, referring to a man by his mother's name is not a common phenomenon in Judaea in this period. The first letters of the name are apparently *yod* and *ḥet* or *he*. The meagre remains of the last two letters of the name make its

---

[7] For the difference between the two names see Ilan, 'Ossuary Inscriptions', 156–7.

[8] Sukenik, 'Hypogeum'.

[9] See e.g. *TAD* C3.28 80 (Cowley 81 line 2). See also Kornfeld, *Grabinschriften,* nr. 1, line 2.

[10] Ilan, 'Ossuary Inscriptions'.

[11] See *TAD* A3.6 (Cowley 40) 15 אל אחי פל[טי בר יא]וש אחוך הושע בר נתן, and many other examples.

[12] Degen, 'Die aramäischen Ostraka', ostracon Aram O 1 line 7 . . . לתשא ברת חור.

identification impossible; in any case, the name is not amongst the most common in the documents from the Judaean Desert (in a document from Egypt from the 3rd century BCE the name יחיי appears[13]).

L. 2 וחבריׄ. חבר is especially common in Hebrew but appears also in Aramaic;[14] חברי also appears in P.Yadin **15** 25.[15]

L. 3 [ ]שמׄ. Perhaps שמׄ[עון] or שמׄ[ואל]. The break is small, however, with room for just one or two letters; the name may be a hypocoristic such as שמעה, or one written in defective orthography, such as שמען[16] (though there is no trace of a final *nun*). These two people may be responsible for collecting the tax.

L. 3 קבלן מנך[. 'We have received from you'. The verb appears in the past, and not in the participle form found in several deeds of sale.[17]

Ll. 3–4 דׄמׄיׄ תמׄרׄיׄן. The reading of the first word is doubtful; the letters are too closely connected. The first letter may also be *ṣade*, as the small stroke on the final *kap* in the previous word may be a part of it (there is no other *ṣade* in this document). If this is so, perhaps the word is an Aramaic transliteration of the Greek τιμή, meaning 'value, price'. It is also possible that the letters have been erased and are not part of the text. If, in spite of this, דמי appears here, it may be interpreted as 'price' or 'payment', even though no sum of money is specified in connection to it.[18]

In תמׄרׄיׄן the letters *taw* and the final *nun* are clear. From its form, the *mem* may also be read as a *samek*, on account of its wide roof. The letters *reš* and *yod* are damaged, but it is possible to reconstruct them. The reading of the word is almost certain. It seems that the dates are the subject of the receipt.

Ll. 4–5 סאין עשר ותשׄע וקב ופלגׄ. 'ten and nine *se'ah*s and a *qab* and a half'. This is equivalent to 19 1/4 *se'ahs*. The volume of dates is measured in the units of measure for dry goods: the *se'ah* and *qab*.[19] The *ʿayin* in ותשע is apparently written on the top of a *he* (an error caused by similarity to the name תשה?). The *lamed* of ופלגׄ touches the *reš* of עשר above it. On the order of the numbers עשר ותשׄע, see ORTHOGRAPHY AND LANGUAGE.

L. 6 All of line 6 is difficult to read and the context is not clear; accordingly, it is difficult to suggest a likely restoration. The first letter may be *ʿayin* or *dalet* (there is no other *dalet* in the text with which to compare). The remains of the letter following it are too small to allow its identification and there are many possible readings. It may be the word די. After the break, which has room for one letter, there are remains of an unidentified letter which may be a *šin*, or possibly the remains of two letters followed by a *yod*. With difficulty it might be possible to read all the remains as a *mem*, followed by a final *kap*, and to restore עמך, which would fit nicely into the context. It is perhaps followed by a ligature for מן.[20] The בב in the continuation of the line is entirely clear, but its meaning is obscure. In an Aramaic list from 3rd century BCE Egypt,[21] בב appears with every occurrence of a previously mentioned name. In that context, too, the precise meaning of the word is unclear.[22] At the end of line 6 there is a *lamed* and the remains of letters which are possibly *waw* and *yod*, in which case one could read here the name לוי.

---

[13] See *TAD* C3.28 (above, n. 9) 104 יחיי בר שבניה.

[14] See also וחברוהי in a document from Egypt from the middle of the 3rd century BCE (*TAD* C3.29 [Levi Della Vida papyrus] 11). כנת is used for this meaning in Official Aramaic.

[15] Lewis, *Documents,* 139.

[16] שמעה appears in Mur **29** 12. שמען is found in No. **9** 1.

[17] E.g. No. **8** 5 ותקלי כספה אנה מקבל.

[18] Cf. also the use of דמין in deeds from Elephantine, e.g. *TAD* B2.7 (Cowley 13) 5–6 אחר אנה יהבת לכי לביתא זנה חלף נכסיך אלך דמי כסף כרשן 5. See the discussion of דמין גמירין in No. **9** 5.

[19] See also e.g. on sherds of unknown provenance, A. Yardeni, 'Cursive Script', 132, sherd 7 concave, col. 2 3 תמרין קב 1].

[20] If the reading is correct, the form of the *mem* has degraded from a circle or a small concave curve to a short horizontal line connecting to the final *nun.*

[21] *TAD* C3.28 (Cowley 81).

[22] However, M. Morgenstern (oral communication) suggests an interpretation of the word here on the basis of באב appearing in an early mediaeval prayer by the Palestinian poet Yannai, and interpreted by M. Zulay as the

Ll. 6–7 אבוך̇. This may be אבוך̇, in which case it might be possible to read די [ע]מך מן בב לוי אבוך and translate 'which is with you from papa Levi, your father'.

Ll. 7–8 בשנת עשר̇[י]ן̇. This date is apparently connected to the preceding subject. Since the year 20 is five years earlier than the year in which the deed was written (but see below, lines 9–12), it is possible that something connected with the father is mentioned here.

L. 8 ו̇כ̇ז̇א̇. The reading is uncertain. The series of letters, graphically connected to one another, may be read in differing ways. We would perhaps expect a number complementing עשר̇[י]ן̇ ('twenty-'), but the letters will not combine to form any number. One might with some difficulty read three units here written as downward strokes and connected to each other, but there is no evidence of a similar method for writing numbers in the documents from the Judaean Desert (but see figure 2 in a document from Egypt from the middle of the 3rd century BCE).[23] It seems to me that the reading ו̇כ̇ז̇א̇ is better (see כזא in a Hebrew promissory note from the year 133).[24] If that is the case, the *ʾalep* at the end of the line has a different form from the other examples of *ʾalep* in this document (all of them medial).[25] If the reading is correct, the word opens the dating clause.

Ll. 9–12 ביום ע̇שׂר̇ה וחמ̇שׁ̇ה בשבט שנת עשרין וח[מ]ש להפרכ[יה]. This is apparently the date of the receipt. For the order of the first number, see COMMENTS to lines 4–5. It is reasonable to assume that the deed was written on receipt of the dates. The date is according to the number of the Eparchy,[26] and Shevat of the 25th year fell in 131 CE.

L. 13 תד̇°° כתבה. The name of the scribe is broken. It is possible that it was a Greek name, such as תדרס (= Theudros, Theodoros), or תדיי/תדאי, or the name תחנה (the left downstroke of the *ḥet* to be restored).[27] Alternatively, it may be some other short name. The handwriting of this scribe does not appear on any other document.

---

transcription of the shortened form of the appellative בבא, 'father' (Greek and Latin 'papa') (*Eretz Israel and its Poetry*, ed. E. Hazan [Jerusalem, 1995] 458 [Hebrew]). This may be confirmed by the name בבא appearing in e.g. P.Yadin **7** 6, 12, 38 יוסף בר בבא, and P.Yadin **7** 40 יו[חנן בר בבא.

[23] *TAD* C3.29 4 (two downward strokes connected by a horizontal line).

[24] No. **49** 13 אחתם בידי/בהו כזא . . . .

[25] See above, n. 5.

[26] See above, n. 1.

[27] See e.g. Eshel and Misgav, 'Ketef Yeriḥo', lines 2, 11, 12, 23.

13. XḤev/Se papWaiver of Claims? ar (134 or 135 CE)

(FIG. 11 AND PLS. VIII–IX)

Preliminary publication: A. Yardeni and J. C. Greenfield, 'A Receipt for a Ketubba', *The Jews in the Hellenistic-Roman World, Studies in Memory of Menachem Stern*, eds. Y. Gafni, A. Oppenheimer and D. Schwartz (Jerusalem, 1996) 197–208 (Hebrew).

THIS manuscript, a waiver of claims from a wife to her husband (or a divorce document written by the wife?)[1] written on papyrus, has survived almost in its entirety. The maximal measurements of the fragment are 15.3 x 9.5 cm. The writing is along the fibres. This document was written by the scribe who wrote No. **7**, and apparently also P.Yadin **47b**. The name of the scribe was מתת בר שמעון (see COMMENTS to lines 11–12). The deed is written in the name of the wife, שלמצין ברת יהוסף קבשן, who comes from Ein Gedi. She declares that she has no claims against the man who was her husband, אלעזר בר חננ[י]ה, from whom she has received (or who received/receives from her?) a bill of divorce. The deed is a simple deed[2] and the signatures are on the recto. The scribe also signed in the name of the wife. The witnesses are both sons of Shimᶜon (the same Shimᶜon?), and are identified with the Hebrew word עד.

Shelamṣion makes three declarations in this deed: (a) that she received (or gave/gives?) a *geṭ*; (b) that she has no monetary claims against the man who was her husband, i.e. that she has received the value of her ketubbah; (c) that there is no *modaᶜa* on this deed.

Palaeography

The script is distinguished by the personal style of the scribe. The script fits well into the cursive script style that appears in the corpus of documents from the Bar Kokhba period, in spite of the variety of letter forms: *šin* is unique in its positioning, resting on its left stroke; *ʾalep* and *bet* tend to be similar to one another, as the top of *bet* is

---

[1] Determination of the nature of the deed derives from the restoration of the word די in line 6. It is not certain that this is a divorce document, as Milik believed (*DJD* II, 108); it could be a receipt for a ketubbah. The rejection of Milik's opinion may be supported by two facts: (1) The line mentioning the divorce is not at the beginning of the deed. (2) It is a 'simple' deed with the witnesses' signatures on the front, unlike the deed of divorce from Wadi Murabbaᶜat (Mur **19**) which is a 'double' deed with the signatures on the back. The matter of the receipt is mentioned several times in the Mishna and Talmud; see e.g. *m. B. Bat.* 10.3 כותבין גט לאיש אף על פי שאין אשתו עמו והשובר לאשה אף על פי שאין בעלה עמה; *m. B. Ketub.* 9.9 היא אומרת אבד גטי והוא אומר אבד שוברי; *m. Giṭ.* 8.8 כתב הסופר גט לאיש ושובר לאשה וטעה ונתן גט לאשה ושובר לאיש . . . See also *b. Giṭ.* 27a and *b. B. Meṣ* 13a מצא גיטי נשים ושחרורי עבדים דיתיקי מתנות ושוברין הרי זה לא יחזיר שמא כתובים היו ונמלך עליהם שלא ליתנם. Thanks are due to M. A. Freedman and P. Segal for their useful remarks.

[2] See the INTRODUCTION TO THE ARAMAIC AND HEBREW DOCUMENTARY TEXTS for a discussion of simple and double documents and of witnesses' signatures.

shortened while the head of *ʾalep* curves to the left.[3] The scribe rarely connected letters to one another (see *yod* and *waw* in לסיון [line 1; this does not characterize the development of these letter forms]; *samek* and *pe* in כסף [line 4] and יהוסף [line 11]).

Orthography and Language

The scribe used defective orthography in this document as in No. **7**, omitting *waw* for the *u* vowel, in לחרת (= לחרות; also, in No. **8a** 1);[4] in שבקין ותרכ[ין] (= שבוקין ותרוכין; line 7);[5] and perhaps also in לשם (= לשום; line 2); if the reading צבת (line 9) is correct, it, too, may be included in this category. The name שלמצין (lines 4, 10, 11), written without *waw,* is also found elsewhere.[6] The spelling עינגדה (line 5), in one word and with a *he*, possibly reflects the Aramaic pronunciation of the place name.[7] The *he* in בעלה and עלה (lines 6, 9, respectively) may be explained as the 3rd fem. sing. pronominal suffix, following a change in formulation, unless it is an irregular spelling of the first person, written with *he* instead of *yod* (perhaps also מנה [line 7]; cf. עינגדה [line 5]) (see below). The pronominal suffix for 2nd fem. is לך (line 7). הוא ('was') is written with *ʾalep* and not *he* (line 7). מדעם ('anything'; line 9) is written without *nun*. In this document (and also in No. **7**) the date is indicated by לשם שמעון בר כסבה נ[שי]א ישראל.[8] Regarding מדעה, which does not occur elsewhere in the documents from the Judaean Desert, see COMMENTS to line 8.

Mus. Inv. 736
PAM 42.193
IAA 449734*, 449737*

---

[3] Similarity in form between *ʾalep* and *bet* is extremely rare.

[4] Milik, 'Un contrat' and 'Deux documents'.

[5] In later deeds it was customary to lengthen the *waw* in these words. See *b. Giṭ.* 85b ולורכיה לוי״ו דתירוכין ולוי״ו דשבוקין ד[אי לא] משמע תריכין ושביקין. See also the instructions for writing a bill of divorce in Assaf, *Shetaroth,* 18(a) line 20–18(b) line 1 (with the addition of the word פטורין): ויש בו ווין שצריך לכתבם ארוכים כדי שלא יהיו דומין ליוד . . . וכדו וו ארוך פטורין תירוכין ושבוקין . . .

[6] See e.g. Lewis, *Documents,* 91 (= P.Yadin **20** 41); and, on an ossuary, see Sukenik, 'Hypogeum', שלמצין אמנה. The name also appears in defective orthography in a document from Edfu, Egypt, from the 3rd century BCE (*TAD* C3.28 line 80 [Cowley 81 line 2]); and also in a burial inscription from Edfu from about the same period; see Kornfeld, *Grabinschriften,* Nr. 1.2 שלמצין ברת עזגד.

[7] It is difficult to know how the name was pronounced. The *he* possibly indicates an *e* vowel at the end of the name. In other documents from Naḥal Ḥever the name is written עין גדי (e.g. P.Yadin **44** 2, 5–6, 7; P.Yadin **45** 3, 4–5, 20; P.Yadin **46** 2, 7) or עינגדי (P.Yadin **49** [a letter]); cf. also P.Yadin **51** (a letter) העינגדין ('the people of Ein Gedi').

[8] See No. **7** 1; and see the INTRODUCTION TO THE ARAMAIC AND HEBREW DOCUMENTARY TEXTS for a discussion of the dating formula.

Recto

1 בעשרין לסיון שנת תלת לחרת ישראל

2 לׄשם שמע[ו]ן בר כסבׄה נ[שי]א ישראל

3 [ ]∘∘[ ]∘ ו̊∘∘∘[ ]ן̊[ ]∘לאׄ אׄיתי[לי]

4 אנה שלמצין ברת יהוסף קבשׄן

5 מן עינגׄדׄה עמך אנת אלעזר בר חנׄנׄיׄ[ה]

6 די הוית בעלה מן קדמת דנן דׄ[י]

7 הוא לך מנה גט שבקין ותרכ[ין]

8 [מ]לת מדעה ל[א] אׄיתׄיׄ לי עמךׄ אׄ[נת]

9 אלעזר על צׄבׄת כל מדעם וקים עלה

10 אנה שלמצין כׄול די על כׄ[ת]בׄ

11 שלמצין ברת יהוסף על נפשה שאלה כתב

12 מׄתׄת ב[ר] שמעון מׄמרא

13 ∘∘∘∘ בר שמעון עד

14 משבלה בן שמעון עד

Translation

Recto

1. On the twentieth of Sivan, year three of the freedom of Israel
2. in the name of Shimᶜ[o]n son of Kosibah, the pr[in]ce of Israel,
3. [. . .] . . . [I admit that . . . I] do not have,
4. I, Shelamṣion daughter of Yehosef *Qbšn*
5. from Ein Gedi, with you (= you don't owe me), you, ʾElᶜazar son of Ḥanania[h]
6. who had been her/my husband from before, th[at (one)]
7. from whom you had (received)/who had (received/receives) from me a document of divorce and expuls[ion . . .,]
8. [a wo]rd of notice (that cancels in advance) I do not have with you (= you do not owe me), y[ou,]
9. ʾElᶜazar, concerning a matter of anything. It is confirmed by her/by me
10. I, Shelamṣion, all that is wri[tt]en above.
11. Shelamṣion daughter of Yehosef, for herself, borrows the writing.
12. Mattat so[n] of Shimᶜon, at her word.
13. . . . son of Shimᶜon, witness;
14. Masabalah son of Shimᶜon, witness.

NOTES ON READINGS AND COMMENTS

Ll. 1–2 בעשרין לסיון שנת תלת לחרת ישראל לשם שמע[ו]ן בר כסבה נ[שי]א ישראל. This is the full dating formula. The year is the third of the revolt, and the month of Sivan fell either in 134 or 135.[9] On the subject of לשם, see n. 8.

L. 3 The damaged beginning of the line contained the name of the place in which the document was written.

L. 3 לא א̇יתי[לי]. The reading is based on the context. It is possible that before this something like מודה אנה די must be restored (cf. מודיאנה in P.Yadin **17**;[10] מדי אנה in P.Yadin **18**;[11] מודא אני לכם, מודא אני לך in Hebrew lease documents from Naḥal Ḥever;[12] similar usage is found also in Syriac deeds from the 3rd century CE such as a deed from Dura Europos from the year 243,[13] line 7 מודינא). The subject is missing before לא א̇יתי: the thing that 'is not' (perhaps מדעם 'anything'). The *ʾalep* in both words is similar to *bet* on account of the curving of the upper stroke to the left (see n. 3). However, this stroke joins the lower stroke at its end, and not at its middle, as in the *bet*.

L. 4 אנה שלמצין ברת יהוסף קבשן. The name Shelamṣion (in both *plene* and defective orthography) is attested in several other places, and is one of the most common female names in the finds from the Second Temple period, including the documents from the Judaean Desert.[14] קבשן is a family name or an appellative.[15]

L. 5 מן עינגדה. Shelamṣion originates from Ein Gedi, whence many fled to the caves at the time of the revolt. In other deeds from the Judaean Desert the name Ein Gedi sometimes appears as two words, sometimes as one, usually with a *yod* at the end.[16]

L. 5 עמך אנת אלעזר בר חננ[י]ה. The phrase לא איתי לי עמך means 'there is nothing for me with you' (= 'you owe me nothing'). The expression עמי אנה (followed by a name and a sum of money) appears in promissory notes (cf., e.g. Mur **18** 3; and in a Hebrew promissory note from 133 CE עמי אני יהוסף בן חנניה כסף זוזין ארבעה סלע אחת).[17]

L. 6 די הוית בעלה מן קדמת דנן. 'You, who were her/my husband previously'.[18] This is a relative clause, perhaps formulated by the scribe in his own name (even though he began by writing in the name of the wife), in which he addresses the husband. One may possibly explain the change in formulation by claiming that the husband and wife sat before him at the time of writing, and the scribe turned from one to the other; otherwise an alternative explanation will be needed for the spelling with *he* instead of *yod*; cf. lines 9–10 וקים עלה אנה שלמצין.

---

[9] See the discussion of the numbering system for the years of the revolt in the INTRODUCTION TO THE ARAMAIC AND HEBREW DOCUMENTARY TEXTS.

[10] Lewis, *Documents*, P.Yadin **17** 40; cf. the Greek ὁμολογῶ (this form is found in P.Yadin **20** 42, etc.).

[11] Lewis, *Documents*, P.Yadin **18** 68–70.

[12] See P.Yadin **45** 6; P.Yadin **46** 3.

[13] See Welles, *Dura-Europos,* 142–9; Drijvers, *Inscriptions*, 54–7.

[14] See above, n. 6. See the discussion of the names Shelamṣion and Shalom in Ilan, 'Ossuary Inscriptions', 156–7.

[15] Cf. ישוע קביש בן שמעון in P.Yadin **46** 1–2; קביש בר [שמו]אל in P.Yadin **42** 2–3; אליעזר בר שמואל הקבש in P.Yadin **43** (the same man as in P.Yadin **42**, where the appellative קביש appears instead of אליעזר). See also No. **10** 2 קיבשא, which is perhaps another form of the name (the reading is not certain). Similarly, see the names (family name or appellative) יהודה בר אלעזר כתושיון in P.Yadin **18**, etc.; יהודה קנבר בר חנניה בר שמלה in P.Yadin **18** (קנבר [and not קמבר] according to Puech's reading).

[16] See above, n. 7.

[17] No. **49** 5–7.

[18] The expression קדמת זנה appears in a letter from Egypt from the year 407 BCE *TAD* A4.7 (Cowley 30) line 17; cf. also Dan 6:11 מן קדמת דנה and Ezra 5:11 מקדמת דנה. In the documents from the Judaean Desert this expression appears in No. **50** 4 (מן קדמת דנה); Mur **19** 17 (מן קדמת דנה); P.Yadin **42** 4 (מן קודמת דנה), and alternatively with קדם instead of קדמת in P.Yadin **7** 28, 29 (מן קדם דנה); Mur **19** (מן קדם דה).

L. 6 דנן. This is according to the pattern of תמן, להלן, למטן, למעלן, etc.[19]

Ll. 6–7 [דֹ[י] הוא לך מנה גט שבקין ותרכ[ין. A literal translation is 'from whom you had (or: have) a deed of abandoning and expulsion'. Assuming that the scribe continued formulating the deed in his name, it may be suggested that he now turned to the wife (לך; an alternative form of לכי, apparently pronounced לָךְ),[20] and referred to the husband in the third person (מנה). This is a parenthetical subordinate clause, continuing the previous sentence (see n. 1) and explaining the status of ʾElʿazar son of Ḥanan[iah] with respect to Shelamṣion daughter of Yehosef at the time of the writing of the deed. However, if we accept the possibility of an irregular spelling of the 1st person, written with *he* instead of *yod* (מנה for מני), another interpretation, which better fits the syntax is that the wife divorced her husband (this was suggested by T. Ilan and H. Cotton; but see above, n. 1). The verb הוא may be in the past tense or in the present. If in the present tense, the deed itself must be considered the divorce document.

L. 7 [שבקין ותרכ[ין.[21] This expression (with the addition of פטורין, according to the formula found in *b. Giṭ.* 85b) appears in Jewish divorce documents up to the present day. שבקין reflects the use of *ezēbu* in Akkadian as a term for divorce (CAD 'E' p. 422).

L. 8 [מ]לת מדעה. If the reconstruction is correct, it is possible that what is intended here is that which appears in the Talmud and in mediaeval legal formularies as שטר מודעא:[22] a declaration in writing before witnesses that any future deed to be written or promise of gifts will not be valid. The שטר מודעא anticipatorily cancels the deed or gift. In the version of the deed that appears in the Book of Shetaroth of R. Hai Gaon,[23] מלתאי ('my words') is used meaning 'contents of the deed'. Accordingly, it is possible that the expression מלת מדעה refers to the contents of a שטר מודעא; if so, this is the earliest reference to such a legal document.

Ll. 8–9 ל[א] אִיתַי לי עמך אֹ[נת] אלעזר על צִבֹת כל מדעם. '([a w]ord of notice) I don't have with you, you, ʾElʿazar, concerning a matter of anything' (see Deut 15:3 ואשר יהיה לך את אחיך, the equivalent expression to Aramaic איתי ל . . . עם). The second half of the sentence is not entirely clear because of the difficulty in reading צבת. It seems that the object of the sentence is [מ]לת מדעה, which stands at its head, with the

---

[19] See the discussion of the word דנן in the INTRODUCTION TO THE ARAMAIC AND HEBREW DOCUMENTARY TEXTS.

[20] See Kutscher, *Studies*, 89–90 (Hebrew section).

[21] See above, n. 5. The word גט means 'deed'; in documents from Elephantine from the 5th century BCE the word ספר served the same meaning. Thus, a 'deed of withdrawal' is referred to as ספר מרחק (see e.g. *TAD* B2.8 [Cowley 14] line 14). Cf. also in Hebrew, e.g. Deut 24:1 ספר כריתת. שטר in both sing. and pl. appears already in a list from the 3rd century BCE (*TAD* C3.28 90–102 [Cowley 81 14–26]).

[22] See *b. ʿArak.* 21b וכן בגיטי נשים כופין וכו׳. אמר רב ששת האי מאן דמסר מודעא אגיטא מודעיה מודעא פשיטא לא צריכה דעשאוה ואירצי מהו דתימא בטוליה בטליה קא משמע לן דאם כן ליתני עד שיתן מאי עד שיאמר עד דמבטל ליה למודעיה, 'And in like manner, concerning bills of divorce of wives: you have to force agreement (out of him,) etc. Rav Sheshet said: The one who gave a declaration regarding a divorce document, his declaration is a declaration (i.e. stands). Isn't that self-evident? No, it is necessary (to teach this), as they forced him and he complied. What if you should say that he cancelled it? It shows us (that the ruling stands), because otherwise the Mishna should teach "until he gives". What is the meaning of "until he says"—until he cancels his declaration'. See also *b. B. Bat.* 40a–b לא כתבינן מודעא . . . כל מודעא דלא כתיב בה אנן ידעינן ביה באונסא דפלניא לאו מודעא היא מודעא דמאי אי דגיטא ודמתנתא גלויי מלתא בעלמא הי וכו׳, 'One does not write a *modaʿa*; any *modaʿa* that does not contain the words "we know that *x* is acting under duress" is not a *modaʿa*. A *modaʿa* of what? If it is regarding a *geṭ* or a gift, the matter in any case is common knowledge', etc.; cf. the formula for a *modaʿa* from *The Book of Deeds of Rav Saadiah Gaon* (M. Ben Sasson, 'Fragments', 226 [for *geṭ*], 242–3 [for *modaʿa*]; our appreciation goes to R. Brody for giving us the corrected text of the *modaʿa* [to be published shortly]). Cf. also Assaf, *Shetaroth,* 45, *modaʿa* document אנחנה שהדי די לתחתא חתימיננא וכו׳ אתא לקדמנא ביום פל׳ במקום פל׳ פל׳ בר פל׳ אמר לנא דאיצטריכית לאטעייה לפלונית אנתתי בת פל׳ ולמיכתב לה גיטה ולמיהב לה בתורת גירושין ולית בדעתאי לגרשה כל עיקר וגיטא די יהבנא לה גט בטל הוא ולית למיסמך עליה ומסרית הדין מודעא קדמיכון לגלויי מלתאי קדמיכון דגיטא בטילא הוא דתיכתבון לי ראיה ואנחנא שהדי כתבנא ליה מודעא דנן דליהוי בידיה לראיה. Further, on page 47, in the context of a *modaʿa* for a sale, the witnesses write . . . וקדמאנא הות מלתא דא וכתבנא ליה לפל׳ דנן מודעא דנן. See further, A. Gulak, *Otsar Ha-Shtarot* 64–5, no. 63, a receipt for a ketubbah.

[23] Assaf, *Shetaroth*.

complement at the end (cf. *TAD* A4.3:6 מה צבו ומלה זי צחא חור יבעה מנכם ['whatever wish and thing that Ṣeha (and) Ḥor shall seek of you']); the wife declares that she does not have 'any *modaʿa* about anything' with the husband. From this, one may be able to conclude that there was not an earlier *modaʿa* deed cancelling anticipatorily any later deed; in the absence of parallels, however, the interpretation remains uncertain.

Ll. 9–10 וקים עלה אנה שלמצין כֹול די על כֹ[ת]בֹ. A new clause begins here. The word עלה perhaps has a 3rd person fem. suffix (= עליה) and is written in defective orthography. The scribe once again switches to speaking in the name of the wife אנה שלמצין (unless we assume that the intention is to indicate the 1st person sing.; see above, line 5). In this clause the wife accepts as binding everything that is written in the deed. The letters in this line are damaged and the reading is based on formulaic expressions (cf., e.g. כל די על כתב in P.Yadin **20** 42).[24] Only the lower half of the *bet* at the end of the line can be seen, drawn out in a long stroke under the line, graphically indicating the end of the body of the deed.

Ll. 11–14 In these lines appear the signatures. The scribe, מחת ב[ר] שמעון, signed in the name of the wife. The handwriting in the signatures is the same as that of the document. The words על נפשה attest to the fact that the woman was present at the time of the writing of the deed and agreed to its contents. For שאלה כתב, 'she borrows the writing', compare אשאלת כתב ידי, 'I have lent my hand', in a Palmyrene tomb inscription.[25] The name מחת—apparently a hypocoristic for מחתיה—appears also in No. **7** 3, מחת בר אבי, and 5, חזק בר מחת, as well as in other places. In the last two lines appear the signatures of two witnesses, both sons of Shimʿon, perhaps the same Shimʿon who appears in line 12. The first of these signed for himself (the handwriting is different from that of the scribe); his personal name is illegible. The handwriting of the second is somewhat similar to that of the scribe, but it seems that he, too, signed for himself. His personal name is משבלה[26] (before the first letter unidentified remains of ink appear). The Hebrew word עד, not the Aramaic שהד, appears after the signatures of both the witnesses. The Hebrew word בן appears in the signature of the second witness, unlike that of the first in which the Aramaic בר appears.

---

[24] Lewis, *Documents*, 145.

[25] See Greenfield, 'Letters', 41. Thanks are due to H. Cotton for bringing the phrase to our attention.

[26] משבלה בר שמעון (from Ein Gedi) appears in the Bar Kokhba letters (see P.Yadin **50** 3; he appears without his father's name in other letters, and משבלא or מסבלה is also written). It is very possible that it is the same person who signed here. The signature of a witness by the name of משבלה בן שמעון also appears in a Hebrew document from Naḥal Ḥever that was written in Ein Gedi (P.Yadin **45** 32); from the similarity in the letter forms in the two signatures one may conclude that they are both of the same person. For the pronunciation of the name, see Kutscher, *Studies*, 39 (Hebrew section).

14. XḤev/Se papFragment of a Deed ar?

(FIG. 12 AND PL. X)

THIS document comprises a tiny fragment of a deed. Its maximal measurements are 3 x 2.5 cm. The script resembles that of No. **13**. However, the present editor was not able to find a connection between the two fragments. Remains of five lines appear on the fragment, two of which (lines 4–5) are in a different script and seem to be remains of signatures (the word כתב appears in line 4). וקימ] appearing in line 3 may be part of the final confirmation clause in a deed. If the language is Aramaic, the phrase would resemble וקימ] על[ה [כל די על כתב]. The word עלה would then be written with the unusual spelling used by the scribe of No. **13** (instead of the usual עלי). In any case, the fragment is too damaged to enable a safe reconstruction or a determination of its nature.

Mus. Inv. 542
PAM 42.193
IAA 445132*, 445134*

Recto

]∘ ∘[1
] ∘[2
]וקימ[ ]ה[3
]כתב 4
]ע∘∘[ ]∘∘ת[5

15. XḤev/Se papUnclassified Fragments B

(FIG. 12 AND PL. X)

THIS collection is composed of five tiny, unclassified fragments from various documents, on which remains of text appear in Jewish cursive hands. Frg. a bears the remnants of three letters, the first being *taw* and the second, *lamed*. Frg. b contains remains of two unidentified letters. Frg. c, written parallel to the fibres, bears the end of the word מ]דנחה ('the East'). Its script resembles that of No. **8** and **26**. Frg. d is illegible. The remains of three or four lines on frg. e are too damaged to enable decipherment.

Mus. Inv. 542
PAM 42.198-201
IAA 445132*, 445134*

Recto
Frg. a

]תל◦[1

Frg. b

]◦◦[1

Frg. c

מ]דנחה [1

16–17. XḤev/Se papUnclassified Fragments C–D

(FIG. 12 AND PL. X)

NO. **16** contains remains of the ends of two lines, the final letter in line 2 perhaps being *he*. No. **17** contains traces of four letters, the final one being a cursive *ʾalep*. The two fragments may belong to a single document written in a Jewish cursive script.

Mus. Inv. 542
PAM 42.198, 42.199
IAA 445132*, 445134*

No. 16

∘[1

ה̇∘[2

No. 17

א∘∘∘[1

18. XḤev/Se papUnclassified Fragment E

(FIG. 12 AND PL. X)

NO. **18** has traces of letters from two words which cannot be identified with any certainty.

Mus. Inv. 542
PAM 42.200, 42.201
IAA 445132*, 445134*

]◦◦ ◦◦[

19. XḤev/Se papUnclassified Fragment F

(FIG. 12 AND PL. X)

NO. **19** bears the remains of the beginnings of two lines separated by a horizontal stroke, extending into the right margin. Line 2 contains the remains of a personal name starting with the letters יהו, written with a ligature.

Mus. Inv. 542
IAA 445132*, 445134*

○ע○[1

———

יהו[ ]○ ○[2

21. XḤev/Se papDeed of Sale E ar

(FIGS. 12–13 AND PLS. XI–XII)

ONLY the middle section of this deed on papyrus has been preserved, and that only fragmentarily: four fragments from the upper version of the deed, which fit together, and seven small fragments from the lower version of the deed, including six which have not been placed. According to the reconstruction, the original width of the deed was *c.*18.5 cm (the margins have been preserved on both sides). The text lacks its beginning and end. The deed is written across the fibres. Remains of large folds are clearly discernible and there are also signs of other, smaller folds.[1] The six tears along the length of the deed apparently occurred where the holes were placed through which passed the chord that was wrapped around the upper version (the seventh is not clearly seen). It seems that the signatures of the two parties, and possibly of five witnesses,[2] were on the verso of the lower version. Remnants of the signatures have survived on the verso of four of the fragments from the lower version, but only in three of them is it possible to identify the letters. Remains of ink can also be seen on the verso of two fragments from the upper version; *lamed* and *mem* or *samek* may possibly appear on one, and after them perhaps the remains of two strokes, possibly remnants of the dating clause (which would have been on the first line) of another deed that was previously written on the same sheet of papyrus.[3] The remains of ink on the other fragment of the upper version are illegible.

Nine continuous lines from the clauses in the middle of the upper version of the deed have survived. The formulation is in the name of the sellers, whose names have not survived. The name of the buyer is Yehosef. The property is referred to as אתריא ('the places'), and it comprises land and parts of a building or buildings. Frg. a recto, apparently belonging to the lower version, contains remains of the sale clause and the opening of the boundaries clause; its placement would therefore be towards the beginning of the lower version. The end of שהד appears on its verso after a signature which has not survived. On frg. b the beginning of סלעין appears belonging to the sum clause (the parallel clause in the upper version appears in line 6).

[1] The double deeds from the Judaean Desert were rolled from top to bottom; accordingly, the width of the folds grows larger towards the bottom.

[2] Regarding the number of witnesses, see Koffmahn, *Doppelurkunden*. See also the detailed discussion of the number of witnesses in the Elephantine deeds in Yaron, *Law*, 26-37.

[3] It may be possible to restore [ב   ]לס[ון], '[On . . .] of Si[van].

Palaeography

The letters are clear and elegant, in the cursive script style in use at the end of the Herodian period and in the post-Herodian period.[4] *ʾAlep* appears in two forms—medial and final—and so, too, *mem*. The letters are upright or lean forward. The scribe distinguishes between the forms of *dalet* and *reš*, and *bet* and *kap*. From the upright mast of the *lamed* a prong descends sloping down to the left. The *taw* has a loop. Remains of ornamental additions are on the right side of *ʾalep* and *ḥet*. There are ligatures for the letter combinations סף, מי, and ני. In frg. a 12 a diagonal cross (X-sign) appears at the end of the line as a filler. Such signs appear also in other deeds,[5] and are common in Greek deeds.

Orthography and Language

In spite of the professional dexterity displayed in the writing and formulation of this deed, the scribe was not strict in the regular distinction between *ʾalep*, to indicate the definite article, and *he*, to indicate a final *a* vowel (e.g. אבניה along with כותליא; להרמא along with להעמקה; see below, line 7). The plural morpheme is indicated with *yod* (דמין גמירין, [ב]תחומיהון). Formulaic expressions include עומקא ורומ[א], ו[מפ]ק[ה מעלה, דמין גמירין, [מן יומא] דנה ועד לעלם, למחפר ולהעמקה למב[נה] ולהרמא למקנה ולמזבנה.

Mus. Inv. 527
PAM 42.194, 42.195
IAA 449728, 449729, 541677*, 541678*

Recto
Upper Version

[ ]◦נ̇א̇ ◦[ ] 1
[י]הוסף [ ]◦ה̇ ור̊ר̊[יד]] 2
ד̇די ואחר[נ]ין את̇[ר]יא אלך[ב]תחומיהון אבניה כותליא שריתא̇ 3
קרקעא עומקא ורומ[א]◦א ותרעא ומפתחא מעלה 4
ו[מפ]ק[ה]כ[די]חזה ל[קבלדך זבן] לך בכסף זוזין שתין די המון 5

---

[4] See the discussion of the cursive script and the comparative tables of the script in Yardeni, 'Cursive Script', 264–321.

[5] Crosses of this kind appear e.g. in deeds from Naḥal Ḥever (P.Yadin **42**, **44**, **45** and **46**).

6 סלעין חמש עשרה ואנחנׄהׄ [מ]קב[לין] דמין גמירין לעלם רשי

7 יהוסף זבנה וירת[ו]הי באׄתׄ[ריא]אלך למחפר ולהעמקה למב[נה]

8 ולהרמא למקנה ולמזבנה[ולמעבד בהון כל די ת֯צבון מן יומא]

9 דנה ועד לעלם וׄכל ד[י איתי לן ודי נקנה אחראין וערבין]

10 [למרקא ולקימא]

Lower Version
Frg. a

11] [ןׄ

12]] אנחנה מן X

13 [רעותנה תחומי אתרא דך]למדנחא

Unplaced Fragments from Recto
Frgs. b + f

1 עׄרׄבׄ[

2 סל[עין חמש עשרה

Frg. c

1 לח[

Frg. d

1 אׄתׄ/שׄטׄ]רה ◦◦[

2]ב/ד לכל [

Frg. e

1]◦ די מן עלה ◦[
2]◦ שטרה דנׄהׄ[

Frg. g

1]בׄ יׄח◦[

Unplaced Fragments from Verso
Frg. a

1 ש]הד

Frgs. b + f

These fragments bear traces of ink which cannot be deciphered.

Frg. c

1]◦חׄנן[

Frg. e

1 יהוח]נׄן שה[ד

Translation

Recto

Upper Version

(beginning missing)

1. [. . . to]the[so]uth— . . . [. . .]

2. [. . . Ye]hosef [. . .] . . . [. . .]
3. *dw/ydy* and others. Those pla[c]es—[within] their boundaries: the stones, the walls, the beams,
4. the ground, the depth and [the] height, the[. . .] and the gate and the key, the entrance
5. and [the ex]i[t], a[s] is fitting. In [accordance with that I have sold (it)] to you for sixty silver *zuzin*, which are (equal to)
6. fifteen *silʿin* and we received the full price. Forever empowered (are)
7. Yehosef the buyer, and his inheritors, regarding those pla[ces]to dig and to deepen, to bu[ild]
8. and to erect, to buy and to sell[and to do with them whatever they/you desire, from]
9. today and forever. And all th[at we have and shall acquire is responsible and a security
10. for cleansing and establishing . . . this purchase before you and before your inheritors from all dispute and challenge . . .].

(continuation missing)

Lower Version

Frg. a

11. [. . .]
12. [. . .] We, of
13. [our own free will sold to you . . .. The boundaries of those places:]to the East—

Frg. b + f

1. (a) guarantor[. . .]
2. *sil*[*ʿin* fifteen . . .]

Frg. d

1. . . . the pla]ce/de]ed . . . [. . .
2. . . .] . . . for/to all [. . .

Frg. e

1. . . .] . . . which is (written) above . . . [. . .
2. . . .] . . . this deed[. . .

Verso

Frg. a

1. [. . ., wit]ness

Frg. e

1. [. . . son of Yehoḥa]nan(?), witne[ss.]

NOTES ON READINGS AND COMMENTS

L. 1]◦ מׄאׄ◦[. If the reading is correct, perhaps this is the end of the word דרומא from the boundaries clause, since line 2 and the beginning of line 3 apparently also belong to that clause. It would also be possible to restore here יומא from the expression זבנת לך מן רעותי יומא דנה, but then there would remain insufficient room for the restoration of the boundaries clause. If that is indeed the case, perhaps the order of the directions of the compass point begins here with south (see for example the order in No. **8a** 8–9: south, east, north, west).

L. 2]יד̊ו̊ר̊ך̊ ה̊ו̊[ ] י]הוסף. Yehosef is possibly one of the neighbours who border the property; he is not necessarily the buyer. The name Yehosef is one of the most commonly attested names in this period.[6]

L. 3 ואחר[נ]י̇ן ד̊ידי This is the last neighbour in the boundaries clause. The name דידי is rare. It appears in an Aramaic document from Egypt from *c*.400 BCE.[7] It may be a hypocoristic for a longer name, such as ידידיה,[8] or perhaps one should read דודי. The end of *yod* can be seen before the final *nun* of ואחר[נ]י̇ן, in keeping with the scribe's habit of writing the plural morpheme in *plene* orthography (see the discussion of this word in No. **7** 3).

L. 3 את̇[ר]יא אלך] ב]תחומיהון Thus begins the description of the property, which apparently consists of more than one site. The clause is built as a *casus pendens* with a retrospective pronoun.[9]

Ll. 3–5 אבניה כותליא שריתא קרקעא עומקא ורומ]א]◦א ותרעא ומפתחא מעלה ו[מפ]ק[ה]. 'The stones, the walls, the beams, the ground, the depth and [the] height, the[. . .] and the gate, and the key, the entrance and the [ex]i[t]'. Houses are not mentioned here, rather parts of buildings and also a gate and key[10]. The word שריתא is apparently a pl. fem. noun.[11]

L. 4 קרקעא. (See also No. **8a** 8 וקרקעא.)[12] The land includes that which is above and below ground (עומקא ורומ]א; cf. also a Hebrew deed of land-lease, Mur **24** vi 11 . . . עמוק ורם; P.Yadin **7** 3, ושפלין ועליין, and 49, ועליהון ושפליהון [relating to houses, perhaps referring to the upper and lower stories]). The simple interpretation is based on line 7, but it is possible to imagine more complex legal situations, such as treasure being discovered in the ground, and whether it belongs to the seller or buyer, etc.[13] See also the legal formulary of R. Hai Gaon,[14] p. 25: עומקא ורומה; p. 26: כל שמיתוסף עלה מתהום ארעא ועד רום רקעא; p. 27: מן תהום ארעא ועד רום רקיעא.

L. 4 After ורומ]א a word is missing that ended in an *ʾalep* indicating another item included in the boundaries of the property.

---

[6] See the discussion of Yehosef, a member of the Hasmonaean family, in Ilan, 'Ossuary Inscriptions'.

[7] *TAD* C4.6 (Cowley 23) 14.

[8] The name ידידיה (cf. 2 Sam 12:25) is unattested in the documents from the Judaean Desert. It is apparently derived from the same root as the name ודדאל or ודאל which appears on Aramaic ostraca from the middle of the fourth century BCE (private collection) and also in Sabaean inscriptions; see Harding, *Index,* 637.

[9] Cf. No. **9** 5, 14; No. **50** 5; see also in Hebrew, Mur **30** 17–18 ... המכר הזה בתחומו בית.

[10] From the form it might be possible to translate 'the gateway', but it seems that a key is intended; see Broshi and Qimron, 'House Sale Deed', 209.

[11] The singular form is שרי; the emphatic is שריתא/שריתה; the plural is שריין—also שרוון; and in the emphatic שריתא or שרוותא. The word appears in Middle Aramaic in Targumim and Midrashim (see e.g. *Tg. Jonathan* to 2 Kings 6:5 ויהי האחד מפיל הקורה: והוה חד מחי בשריתא); so, too, in Syriac, Palmyrene, Mandaic, Nabataean, and Christian Palestinian Aramaic. An early occurrence of the word (in construct) is perhaps found in a letter from Egypt from the end of the 5th century BCE (*TAD* A4.7 [Cowley 30] 11 שירית). Alongside שריתא appears the word כשורא (Akkadian *gušuru;* cf. in the Hermopolis Letters, *TAD* A2.2 line 14 גשרן and line 15 גשר), e.g. in the *Tg.* to Song 1:17 קורות בתינו ארזים רהיטנו ברותים: דכשרוהי יהוין מן ארזין דגנתא דעדן ושרתוהי יהוין מן ברתי ושני ושורבניה. The Arabic word *sāriah,* 'pillar, mast', is apparently borrowed from Aramaic (see Fraenkel, *Fremdwörter,* 11). The present editor is grateful to U. Melammed who placed at my disposal material that he had gathered on שריתא.

[12] According to Kutscher, *Studies,* 332–3 (Hebrew section), the origin of קרקע is in קרקר (Assyrian *qaqqaru*). Kutscher does not explain the *ʿayin* at the end of the word. Compare קרקרה, קורקורתה (the bottom of a vessel; *m. Ohol.* 9.16), and the Arabic words *qarār* ('bottom of a vessel') and *qarārah* ('bottom, low ground, depression'). At Elephantine, the word ארעא/ארקא serves this meaning (the etymological equivalent of Hebrew ארץ). See e.g. *TAD* B2.2 (Cowley 6) 15, 16; cf. also P.Yadin **7** 4 וארע.

[13] See *m. B. Bat.* 4.2 לא את הבור ולא את הדות אף על פי שכתב לו עמקא ורומא; cf. *TAD* B3.7 (Kraeling 6) 11 תחתיתא וז[י ע]לא, and the discussion of that expression in Szubin and Porten, 'Life Estate', 39–40.

[14] Assaf, *Shetaroth.*

Ll. 4–5 מעלה ו[מפ]ק[ה]. ‘Entrance and[ex]i[t]’. These are the emphatic infinitives of the roots עלל and נפק in the *Qal*, or nouns (cf. מעל ומפק in No. **9** 5). The expression appears also in other deeds.[15] A Hebrew parallel possibly appears in a deed from Wadi Murabbaʿat (Mur **30** 19–20) מובא [ומוצא].

L. 5 כ[די]חזה. As is fitting, according to the law.[16]

Ll. 5–6 ל[קבלדך זבן] לך בכסף זוזין שתין די המון סלעין חמש עשרה. The restoration is based on the corresponding clause in No. **9**. The verb זבן was probably in the plural (זַבֵּן; or זַבֶּנָּה?), as there is in fact more than one seller.[17] The properties were sold for 60 *zuzin* which equal 15 *silʿin*.[18] The word זוזין is written with a ligature.

L. 6 ואנחנה [מ]קב[לין] דמין גמירין. This is the receipt clause. The sellers received the full payment.[19]

Ll. 6–7 לעלם רשי יהוסף זבנה וירת[ו]הי באת̊[ריא]אלך. This is the ownership clause. Compare the corresponding formula, e.g. in No. **50** 9; see also No. **9** 6 רשי ושלט.

Ll. 7–9 למחפר ולהעמקה למב[נה] ולהרמא למקנה ולמזבנה[ולמעבד בהון כל די ת̊צבון מן יומא] דנה ועד לעלם. This is the specification of the rights of the buyer and his inheritors over the purchase. The deed explains עומקא ורומ[א (line 4) by indicating the activities that the buyer is permitted to perform on the property that he has purchased: to dig and deepen, to build, and to erect (the root רום ‘to build high’ seems to appear in Ezra 9:9 לרומם את בית אלהינו ולהעמיד את חרבתיו[20]). The buyer purchased not merely the land, but also the space above it, and he is permitted to build there and to go up as high as he wants; likewise, his ownership extends under the ground, and he is permitted to dig as deep as he wants (but see n. 13). ולהעמקה and ולהרמא have a *he* prefix, in keeping with the form of the *Hapʿel* in Official Aramaic (but see the Hermopolis papyri where it is with a *mem*). Most of the infinitive forms in the deeds from the Judaean Desert appear with a *mem* prefix in all the conjugations (see e.g. למעמקה in No. **8** 6[21]).

The restoration after למקנה ולמזבנה is based on the attested formula (see e.g. No. **50** 10). יצבון has been restored in the 3rd person, but תצבון in the 2nd person is also possible; note the change in person in No. **9** 7. The word ולמזבנה is the infinitive form of the *Paʿel* with a *mem* prefix.[22]

דנה/דנא is the common form in the deeds from the Judaean Desert alongside the rarer דנן (דנן appears in No. **7**; No. **9**; No. **13**;[23] P.Yadin **43** 7; cf. also the form דן in P.Yadin **42** 7).

L. 9 ועד לעלם. Sometimes the scribe writes the form ולעלם without עד (see e.g. No. **8a** 11, 12);[24] cf. also the formula מן יומא זנה ועד עלם in deeds from Elephantine.[25]

L. 9 וכל ד[י איתי לן ודי נקנה אחראין וערבין]. Only the opening of the cleansing clause remains. The restoration is based on the formula that appears in No. **8** 6 (cf. also No. **9** 8; No. **50** 11).

---

[15] Cf., e.g. Mur **25** 3 מעלא ומפק]א; No. **8** 5 מ]עלה ומפקה; No. **50** 6 מעלא ומפקא; cf. also No. **8a** 10 ולא מעל ולא מפק. See, too, in a mediaeval deed formulary (Assaf, *Shetaroth,* 26) מעלנה ומפקנה ומסקאנה ומהתאנה (‘its entrances and exits and its ascents and its descents’); in deeds from Elephantine the indication of right of passage through the gate in *TAD* B2.1 (Cowley 5) 14 ואנת שליט למפתח תרעא ולמנפק בשוקא; *TAD* B3.10 (Kraeling 9) 14–15 אף שליט אנת למנפק בתרע זי תחית; *TAD* B3.12 (Kraeling 12) 21–22 ותרעא זילה פתיח לשוק מלכא מן תמה תנפק ותנעל.

[16] See No. **9** 5.

[17] Cf. *TAD* B3.4 (Kraeling 3) 13 זי אנחן זבן ויהבן לך.

[18] For the question of coinage and the formulation of the sum clause in other deeds, see COMMENTS to No. **7** 4.

[19] The expression דמין גמירין appears also in other deeds from the Judaean Desert (No. **9** 6 [see the discussion there]; No. **8** 5). In No. **50** 8, only דמין appears. See the discussion of מקבל in Broshi and Qimron, ‘House Sale Deed’, 210.

[20] See Loewenstamm, ‘Parallels’; S. Lieberman, ‘Editor’s Notes’, 556–7.

[21] On infinitive forms with a prefixed *mem,* see Greenfield, ‘Infinitive’; see also Broshi and Qimron, ‘House Deed Sale’, 213.

[22] See above, n. 21.

[23] See the discussion of דנן in the INTRODUCTION TO THE ARAMAIC AND HEBREW DOCUMENTARY TEXTS.

[24] See the section on No. **9**, n. 45.

[25] See e.g. *TAD* B2.3 (Cowley 8) 9 אנתי שליטה בה מן יומא זנה ועד עלם.

Here the deed is cut off. It is possible to restore the text on the basis of the formulae attested in other deeds of sale, such as No. **9**; No. **50**.[26]

Frg. a recto, bearing the words אנחנה מן X and למדנחא is apparently from the opening of the lower version, from the sale clause, close to the left margin (the X after מן is a space-filler). The formula is apparently short, as there is not enough room to restore the complete formula. (The complete formula would be אנחנה מן [רעותנה זבן לך יומא דנה אתריא די לן די ב . . . תחומי אתריא אלך] למדנחא[, etc.) See, also, in the COMMENTS to line 1, the note regarding the order of the directions of the compass, a matter which further complicates the restoration. Frg. b, from the right margin, bears the beginning of סל[עין and may accordingly be ascribed to the sum clause. Frgs. a–c, e–f bear remains of signatures on the verso; consequently they too belong to the lower version. Frg. d, though it has no remains of ink on the verso, also belongs to the lower version because of its similarity in colour to frgs. c and e.

[26] Taking into account the length of the lines, we could possibly restore the continuation as למרקא ולקימא אתריא אלך/זבנה דך קדמכן וקדם ירתכן , in keeping with No. **50** 12, or as למשפיה ולמקימה אתריא אלך מן קדמך וקדם ירתיך מן יומה דנן ולעלם, in keeping with No. **9** 8–9, 20.

22. XḤev/Se papDeed of Sale F? ar

(FIG. 14 AND PL. XIII)

FIVE fragments have survived of this double deed on papyrus. Remains of the signatures on the verso help to place three of the fragments, while the placement of the other two fragments remains doubtful. The maximal height of frgs. a, b, and c (after being joined) is 8.4 cm; width: frg. a: 10.7 cm; frg. b: 5.8 cm; frg. c: 12.3 cm. Frg. d measures 1.7 x 8.8 cm; frg. e: 3.5 x 9 cm. The text on the recto is written across the fibres. On frg. a remains of the last line of the upper version of the double deed have survived, followed by a space of a line before the first line of the lower version. On frgs. b and c the remains of a total of five lines have survived. On frg. d the remains of one or two lines have survived, and on frg. e the remains of four lines. From the differences in the width of the folds one may perhaps conclude that frgs. d and e belong to the lower version. Part of the upper layer of the papyrus on the recto has peeled off, making the identification of letters difficult. From the few legible words it emerges that the language of the deed is Aramaic. It is possible that this was a deed of sale. The word בתחומי, which appears twice, may perhaps suggest that the deed deals with immovable property, but the text is too fragmentary to identify with certainty.

On the verso have survived the remains of seven signatures. Since this is the largest number to be expected, it seems that one can restore the width of the deed to *c*.15 cm. Among the seven signatures are four names whose reading is certain. All are common names in deeds from the Judaean Desert: Shimᶜon, ᵓElᶜazar, Yehosef, and Yehudah.

Palaeography

The script is in the scribal cursive style which developed at the close of the Herodian period and is attested up to the end of the Bar Kokhba revolt. In the absence of a date it is difficult to establish the date of writing with any greater accuracy.

Mus. Inv. 735
PAM 42.198, 42.199
IAA 449732*, 449733*

Recto

Upper Version
Frgs. a, b

1 מ[ן קׄדמי]   [°°°°°°°°°°°°להן לקבלדך

Lower Version

2]°°° °[   ]°[   ]°°

3]

4]°°°°[

5]°°°°[ ]°מ[   ]°°[   ]°°°°[   ]°[[ד{וב}{אנ}יה ° די בה[

6]°°° צפונא °°°°°° די בתׄ°°[   ]°°°°א[

7]°מא[[ואׄנה °°°° לשמעון בחול[קה   ]ע°[[מנאׄ[

8]°°א בתחומי °°°° °°°נה דׄ°[

Frgs. c, d

9–11 (illegible)

12]?[°°°°°הש{ב}כר בתחומי°°°°°°°[

Verso

Frgs. a, b

13]°°

14 [אלע]זר

15]°°°°[

16 יהו[בר א]לעזר שׂהׄ[ד]

17 יהוׄח[נן בר יה]וסף שׂהד בׄ°[

יה̇[בר]יהודה שה[ד]

שמ̇[בר י]הוסף̇ שהד

TRANSLATION

Recto

Frgs. a, b

Upper Version

(beginning missing)

1. . . . [. . .] . . . according to that.

Lower Version

2.] . . . [. . .] . . .
3.]
4.] . . . [
5.] . . . [. . .] . . . [. . .] . . . which is in it[
6.] . . . to the north . . . which is in the . . . [. . .] . . . [
7.] . . . [. . .] and I . . . to Shimᶜon in [his] sha[re . . .] . . . [
8.] . . . in the boundaries of . . . [

Frgs. c, d

9–11. (illegible)

12.] . . . in the boundaries of . . . [

Verso

Frgs. a, b

13. [. . .] . . .
14. [. . .] ʾElᶜa[zar . . .]
15. [. . .] . . . [. . .]
16. Yeho/u[. . . son of ʾE]lᶜazar, witne[ss]
17. Yehoḥa[nan son of Yeh]osef, witness, in . . . [. . .]
18. Yeh[o/u . . . son of]Yehudah, witne[ss]
19. *Šm*[. . . son of Ye]hosef, witness.

23. XḤev/Se papDeed of Sale G ar

(FIG. 15 AND PL. XIV)

THIS is a fragment of a deed on papyrus. The maximal measurements of the fragment are 7.2 x 6 cm. The text on the recto is written across the fibres. Parts of eight lines of the left side of the deed have survived, including the left margin, but only in four of them is it possible to read a sequence of words. The language is Aramaic. The text seems to be from a deed of sale, which is generally a double document. If the restoration in line 4 is correct (cf., e.g. No. **9** 7–8), the width of the missing part of the line is similar to that of the part that has survived. If this is the case, then what is missing is the right half of the deed, i.e. the deed was torn down the middle; its original width would have been 12–13 cm (cf. Mur **30** whose width is 12.5 cm). It is difficult to determine if the remains are from the upper or the lower version. The absence of remains of signatures on the verso does not necessarily prove that this is the upper version, since the lines that have survived are from the end of the ownership clause and the start of the responsibilities clause, clauses which are generally close to the end of the deed, so that the signatures would not have reached this part. The formulae in these two clauses appear to be shorter than the full versions; so, too, further on, the formulation is not the same as that found in other deeds of sale, thereby making restoration difficult. The short formulation, the extreme cursiveness of the script, and the scribal error in ארחאין in place of אחראין, perhaps suggest that this is the upper version, which was often written briefly and with relative negligence.

Palaeography

The script is in the post-Herodian extreme cursive style. The letters are small; the average height being 2.5 mm. The lines are widely spaced, with *c.*6–7 mm between each pair of lines. Final *mem* is conspicuous for its size, written with a large curve and a long diagonal stroke. Also unique in its form is the *lamed* in לעלם, which consists of two strokes, with the mast connecting to the middle of a horizontal bar that represents the main part of the letter (an intermediate form between a three-stroked *lamed* of bookhand and the single-stroked cursive *lamed*). In spite of the cursiveness of the script, there are only single ligatures (כו in כול; נה in אקנה and אנה).

Formulaic expressions include למעבד בה כול די תצבא/ה;]ודי אקנה ארחאין וערבין[.

Mus. Inv. 536
PAM 42.196, 42.197
IAA 445119*, 445122*

Recto

[ן̇ ◦]

[ש̇]   [ן̇]

[ל̇מ̇ע̇בד בה כ̇ול די תצ̇בה וא̇נ̇ה

מזבנה וכל די איתי לי]ודי אקנה אר̇חא̇ין וערבין

[למרקה ולקימה זבנה דך קדמך וקדם י]ר̇ת̇ך ◦◦◦◦◦ אנה ל̇ך̇ יום

[◦◦◦◦ ולעלם ואם

[א◦◦ה די א◦◦◦ חי̇ב̇

[ל]

TRANSLATION

Recto

(beginning missing?)

1. [. . .] . . . [. . .]
2. [. . .] . . . [. . .]
3. [. . .]to do with it whatever you desire. And I,
4. [. . . the seller, and anything I have]and shall acquire are responsible and a security
5. [to cleanse and to establish that sale before you and before your in]heritors, I . . . you, [to]day(?)
6. [. . .] . . . and forever. And if
7. [. . .] . . .
8. [. . .] . . . [. . .]

(continuation missing)

24. XḤev/Se papDeed A ar

(FIG. 15 AND PL. XV)

THREE fragments that join together survive from the lower version of a double deed on papyrus. The maximal measurements of the joined fragment are 7.7 x 6.8 cm. On the recto have survived remains of six lines in a large cursive script across the fibres; the average height of the letters is 6 mm. On the verso are the remains of two lines of signatures across the fibres and perpendicular to the writing on the recto. The last word that can be seen in line 2 (on the recto) begins with an *ʾalep*, *nun*, and *taw*, after which are signs of another letter. Perhaps one may read here אנתי ('you', fem. sing.) or אנתתה ('wife'), in which case it may be a part of a marriage or divorce document. The language is Aramaic. The two names on the verso are Shimʿon and Yehosef (the names of the fathers could not be deciphered). From the size of the letters on the recto and the distance between the signatures on the verso, it seems that the dimensions of the deed were relatively large.

Mus. Inv. 536
PAM 42.196, 42.197
IAA 445119*, 445122*

Recto

]◦◦◦ ◦◦◦◦◦◦ ◦◦[1
]◦◦צׄ(ר)יב מנהׄ אנתׄ◦[2
]הׄ ותבע(ג)ן תׄ[3
]ה בׄנׄשׄ◦◦◦[4
]◦ הׄכׄ(חב)◦[5
]פׄה ◦◦◦ ◦[6

Verso

שמעון בר ש(חט/גב)י ◦ה] 7

יהו[ס]ף[בר] יה◦◦] 8

TRANSLATION

Recto

1.] . . . [
2.] . . . from him/her, you/wife[
3.] . . . [
4.] . . . [
5.] . . . [
6.] . . . [

Verso

7. Shimʿon son of . . . [. . .]
8. Yeho[se]f[son of] *Yh* . . . [. . .]

24a. XḤev/Se papDeed B ar

(FIG. 15 AND PL. XVI)

FOURTEEN small papyrus fragments are all that remain of No. **24a**. The writing is across the fibres. Only some of the words are legible; from them it emerges that these are fragments of a deed in Aramaic. Eight fragments (frgs. a–h) have been placed by the present editor alongside one another in such a way that they preserve the remains of four lines. The arrangement of some of the fragments is uncertain due to the difficulty in reading the text at the joins. On frg. a איתי לי יו[may appear; before it לא can perhaps be restored, with the subject preceding it. The tentative reconstruction is based on the assumption that]מא דנה (frg. b) should be positioned here, so that we can join the two fragments together. On frg. c, ואנה appears; in the neighbouring word to the left (frg. g) perhaps אקנה. If we distance the fragments from one another, it may be possible to restore ואנה [ ] מזבנה (a personal name is missing after ואנה) between the two words, yielding ודי] אקנה א[חראין וערבין, the formula of the responsibilities and cleansing clause. However, the continuation is not similar to any known formula. In line 3 (frgs. d + e) it is perhaps possible to read די אסתדר ('which was arranged'[?]; the last two letters are very similar and may be either *dalet* or *reš*; the context is unclear). In the continuation of the same line (frg. f) ומקים appears and before it remains of a word which is illegible. Line 4 is illegible, apart from remains of the letters *lamed* and *taw*. A further six small fragments (frgs. i–n) bear writing, but they cannot be connected. There are no remains of writing on the verso.

Palaeography

The letters are large and broad; the average height of the letters is *c*.5 mm. The script belongs to the cursive style of the Herodian and post-Herodian periods. The *taw* is notable for its looped form, with the top of its left stroke curving backwards. The scribe distinguishes between medial and final forms in the letters *ʾalep* and *mem*. Medial *ʾalep* is upright, while the final *ʾalep* reclines. Medial *mem* connects to the letter following it by a short horizontal stroke, while the final *mem* is finished with a downward stroke sloping to the left. *Samek* is small, and almost triangular, and is stylistically close to its form in bookhand. *Qop* may be a cross-stroke connecting to the downwards stroke in a right angle (similar to a final *kap*); a medial *nun* before a *he* connects to it by a ligature close to the top of the *he*; *dalet* and *reš* are similar to one another.

Mus. Inv. 536
PAM 42.196, 42.197
IAA 455119*, 455122*

Recto

1]◦ אׄיתׄי לׄיׄ יׄומא דׄנה עׄ[מך

2]ה ואנה ◦[ ]ןׄ מזבנה ודי] אׄקׄנה אׄ[חראין וערבין

3]ה די אסתׄ˹ד˺רׄ ◦◦עׄה ומקים ◦◦◦[

4]לׄ[ ] ◦[ ]ת◦◦[ ]◦[ ]◦[

Translation

Recto

1.] . . . I have/I [do not] have this day with y[ou (= you owe me/you do not owe me)
2.] . . . and I [PN the seller and whatever] I purchase are re[sponsible and a security . . .]
3.] . . . which . . . and establish . . . [
4.] . . . [

25. XḤev/Se papDeed C ar

(FIG. 16 AND PL. XVII)

TWO papyrus fragments have been joined together on which the remains of four lines of writing appear across the fibres. The maximal measurements of the joined fragment are 3.3 x 6.8 cm. On the verso remains of four lines of signatures written across the fibres have survived, perpendicular to the writing on the recto. Before the ligature סף in line 3, just before the join between the two fragments, we would expect to find a *kap* (כסף) or the letters יהו (יהוסף); however no such letters appear. It is also difficult to reconstruct the remains of line 3 according to known formulae of deeds of sale or promissory notes. In the light of this it seems that one must consider again whether the joining of the two fragments is correct.

Only a few words may be read in line 4, amongst them the expression כסף זוזין. The reading of the two words following is difficult, though the first surely indicated the sum. מן and the beginning of a personal name following it apparently refer to the payer of the silver. The language of the deed is apparently Aramaic.

The remains of signatures on the verso prove that the fragment belongs to the first few lines of the lower version of a double deed.

Mus. Inv. 542
PAM 42.198, 42.199
IAA 445132*, 445134*

Recto

]∘∘∘∘[1

]∘∘ין ש̇[2

]ה̇ תנ∘∘[?] ול̇א̇ כ̇[ ]סף וש∘∘[3

]∘ כסף זוזין ש̇ב̇ע̇י̇ן ∘[ ]∘ מן יה̇[ו 4

Verso

]◦ בר[5

]^בר^כנ פר[6

]^כ^על ל[7

]◦◦ בר[ ]◦[8

Translation

Recto

1.] . . . [
2.] . . . [
3.] . . . and not(?) . . . and . . . [
4.] . . . seventy silver *zuzin* [. . .] from *yh*[

Verso

5.] . . . son of[
6.] . . . [
7.] . . . [
8.] . . . son of [

26. XḤev/Se papText Dealing with Deposits and Barley ar

(FIG. 16 AND PL. XVII)

THIS is a fragment from the left side of a document on papyrus. The maximal measurements of the fragment are 7 x 3.7 cm. The writing on the recto is along the fibres; on the verso are remains of ink, perhaps signatures, written along the fibres and perpendicular to the writing on the recto. The deed was written by the same scribe as that of No. **8**. Remains of nine lines have survived; the first few lines of the deed are missing, as is perhaps a line between lines 8 and 9. The language is Aramaic.

סערין טבן ('good barley'; line 3) and פקדנה אלך ('those deposits'; line 4; cf. P.Yadin **17** 42 כנמוש פקדנה) hint at the content of the deed. The transaction is between מליך (line 2), who is apparently a Nabataean (cf. the third signature on a Greek document from the XḤev/Se group[1]), and ישוע (line 6). The document is too fragmentary to identify who wrote the deed, the depositor or the person who received the deposit. If we restore אמ]ר before the name מליך, then it was he who wrote the deed, but this is only tentative. If the word in line 5 is to be read ותקבל (second person masculine singular or third person feminine singular) and not יתקבל, then perhaps the writer of the deed is the receiver of the deposit, who pledges to return the deposit or to give its equivalent. If the word in line 5 is יתקבל, perhaps the word before it—לה or אלה—is connected to it. One may perhaps interpret אלה as a combination of אם and לא = אלא ('if not') with the assimilation of the *mem* and written with a *he* rather than an *ʾalep* (on interchanges of *he* and *ʾalep* at the end of a word, see the INTRODUCTION TO THE ARAMAIC AND HEBREW DOCUMENTARY TEXTS). In that case, we may assume that the penalty clause appears here.[2] It seems that the main text of the deed ended in line 7, as the end of the line is blank.

Line 8 perhaps contained the signature of one of the parties (the receiver of the deposit?), in whose name someone signed (?), in which case one may restore something like [. . . על נפשה . . .] ממר[ה] ('[. . . for him/herself; . . .] at [his/her] word'). The remains of letters in line 9 are likely to be *he* and *dalet*, in which case it might be possible to restore [. . . בר . . . ש]הד ('[. . . son of . . ., wi]tness'). The width of the deed could then be estimated at *c*.7–8 cm (cf. No. **49** with a width of *c*.7 cm). However, the remains of the signatures on the verso cast doubt on the reading and restoration of this line. The space between lines 8 and 9 suggests the possibility that another line appeared between them; perhaps one containing another signature. Line 9 is possibly the last; part of the lower margin may have survived on the left side.

---

[1] No. **63** below.

[2] In an Aramaic promissory note from Wadi Sdeir (Mus. Inv. 985, PAM 40.217; unpublished), lines 5–6, the expression לה יתקבל לי ותשלמתה מן נכסי ודי אקנה appears. Unfortunately, the reading of the word preceding is uncertain, but, though with some difficulty, one may perhaps read the conditional particle אם.

Mus. Inv. 542
PAM 42.198, 42.199
IAA 445132*, 445134*

Recto

1 [○]
2]ר מליך בר
3] ○אׄחך/ב סערין טבן
4] פקדנה אלך נתן
5]○ אלה ׄתקבל
6]○ׄ ישוע בר
7]○ל י[שו]ע
8]ממר[ה]
8a [?
9 ש]הד

Translation

Recto

1. [. . .] . . . [. . .]
2. [. . .] . . . Malik son of
3. [. . .] . . . one/your brother, good barley
4. [. . .] those deposits Nathan/gave
5. [. . .] . . . these,/unless it will be received/and you will receive
6. [. . .] . . . Yeshuaʿ son of
7. [. . .] . . . Ye[shu]aʿ.
8. [PN for him/herself; PN] at [his/her] word

8a. [?]

9. [PN son of PN wit]ness.

27. XḤev/Se papDeed D ar

(FIG. 16 AND PL. XVIII)

THESE three papyrus fragments apparently belong to a single deed. The letters are of the post-Herodian Jewish cursive style, and the lines were written across the fibres. The text is too fragmentary to allow for the identification of the deed. Diagonal lines written over letters are apparently signs of cancellation. This seems to have been the customary way of cancelling deeds which had been paid. On this matter, see the discussion of the clause for exchanging the deed in the INTRODUCTION TO THE ARAMAIC AND HEBREW DOCUMENTARY TEXTS (and n. 21 therein).

Mus. Inv. 542
PAM 42.198, 42.199
IAA 445132*, 445134*

Recto
Frg. a

]◦[ ]◦[1

כ[תיב] [ב] [◦◦] 2

]◦ה בכל נב◦[3

]תין[4

] ◦[5

Frg. b (joined frg.)

[◦בך] 1

[שא◦ד] 2

[ן ◦◦] 3

[א ◦] 4

[◦ל ◦] 5

[כ◦] 6

Frg. c

[◦◦ 1

[◦◦ פ◦◦ 2

28. XḤev/Se papUnclassified Fragment G ar

(FIG. 17 AND PL. XIX)

THIS is a very damaged fragment of a document, on which remains of four lines of probable Jewish cursive script may be seen, written across the fibres. Its maximal measurements are approximately 5 x 5.5 cm. The average height of the letters is approximately 4 mm and the average space between the lines is approximately 6 mm. No script is evident on the verso. The script is too faint to enable its decipherment. A final *ʾalep*, perhaps following *mem* and *yod*, appearing in the second line, may indicate that the language is Aramaic. In the third line, a *lamed* appears, followed by a circle and a long downstroke, which could be a ligature of *mem* and *nun* (מן) or, alternatively, a *qop*.

Mus. Inv. 536
PAM 42.196, 42.197
IAA 445119*, 445122*

Recto

[ooooooooo]

[oooמיא ooo]

[oooל(מן/ק)ooo]

[חoooooooooooo]

29. XḤev/Se papUnclassified Fragments H

(FIG. 17 AND PL. XIX)

THIS is a group of fourteen tiny fragments from different documents, which were scattered among other fragments on two different museum plates (Mus. Inv. 732 and 733). On all of them appear remains of letters in the Jewish cursive script, written by different hands. Some of the fragments may perhaps belong to other documents appearing in this volume, but they have not thus far been successfully classified. Frg. e may belong to No. **27**. Frg. j may belong to No. **8** or No. **26**.

Mus. Inv. 732, 733
PAM 42.196-201
IAA 445132*, 445134*

Frg. a

◦◦] 1

Frg. b

[אלח̇] 1

Frg. c

◦◦] 1
ל◦] 2

Frg. d

]◦ל על̊[1
]◦◦[2

Frg. e

]◦ל̊[1
]יה̇ב ק̇[2

Frg. f

]◦[1

Frg. g

]◦◦[1
]ש̇פ ◦[2

Frg. h

]◦ ◦◦[1
]ל ◦◦◦ל̊[2

Frg. i

]◦ת◦[1

Frg. j

[◦] 1
[נ] 2

Frg. k

[◦◦◦◦] 1

Frg. l

[◦◦◦] 1
[ל◦ ו̇ח̇◦] 2

Frg. m

ק◦] 1
ח◦◦] 2
◦◦◦] 3
א] 4

Frg. n

[לפ̇◦◦] 1

30. XḤev/Se papLetter to Shimᶜon ben Kosibah

(FIG. 18 AND PL. XX)

THIS is the only letter among the XḤev/Se documents. It is written in Hebrew on papyrus along the fibres. The maximal measurements of the fragment are 12.5 x 10 cm. Parts of all eight lines have survived, written in a non-calligraphic bookhand, along with the signature of the sender written in a semi-cursive. There are further unidentified, illegible remains of a single line on the lower two fragments (one of them does not appear in the drawing). The majority of the upper and side margins have survived. On the verso remains of an address containing two words have survived. The main part of the letter has been damaged to the point where restoration, apart from occasional letters and words, is difficult, so that the contents remain unknown.

No. **30** is one of the few letters sent to Shimᶜon ben Kosibah (and not by him) which have been preserved. If the reading is correct, the sender—שמעון בן מתניה/ם (he signs שמעון בן מתנה)—apparently refers to ben Kosibah as אבה חבו/יבי (line 3).[1] The root חבב has connotations of both affection and respect, and it is therefore possibly an expression of honour. On the other hand, it is possible that the by-name refers to the father of the sender (מתניה/ם) since it immediately follows, but that interpretation seems somewhat forced. If the reading of lines 4–8 is correct, then the person is relating to Shimᶜon ben Kosiba an incident that occurred to a certain group of people (perhaps a disaster—שנטרפו (?): the reading is not certain; the dot of ink above the baseline of the third letter is possibly part of a *ṭet*), and reporting that he and some others were not among them: ולא היינו מן בין להם (line 8).

On the verso two words are written in cursive script. The second word is לשמעון. With difficulty the first word may be read as אליעזר, rendering a different name from that of the sender (Shimᶜon); in any case the reading is uncertain. Perhaps ᵓEliᶜezer was the carrier of the letter.

Mus. Inv. 542
PAM 42.193
IAA 445132*, 445134*

---

[1] חביב or חביבא is also a by-name for a paternal uncle. חביבא/ה is also the personal name of several Amoraim. A letter on papyrus discovered in Egypt (Oxford, Bodleian Library, MS Heb. e. 120) is addressed to אחי חבו/יבי רחימי, and the name אבה also appears (perhaps 'the father', or maybe a personal name). The date of the letter is not known, but from the script it appears that it is from approximately the third century. The letter reads thus: (1) חרקן ברת יוחנן כהנה לאלעזר אחי חבו/יבי (2) ורחימי סברי וסכוי ופלטתי ממביתה (3) דאבה שלם צלותי/ו דבני לחיך ודמרים (4) חתי שותפתך ודבניכון. See the picture and bibliography in Sirat, *Papyrus,* 125, pl. 88. The name חבובי בר לילין appears in an amulet from the Byzantine period (to be published by J. Naveh).

Recto

לשמעון בן כוסבא נסי
ישראל מן שמעון בן מתני[ה]ם
אבהׄ חׄבׄ[ו]בי שלם
ידוע יהיה לך שׄ◦◦◦◦◦ ◦◦
הגא[ו]ׄ◦[?] שה◦◦ [ ]ן לׄ[ ]
קצׄת֯ היך בׄישׁ[ ]בׄ ◦[ ]◦◦[ ]◦◦◦[ ]
שנׄטׄרׄפׄוׄ אׄחׄ◦ ◦[ ]ןׄ ◦[ ]
ולא הייׄנׄו מׄןׄ בין להׄםׄ שׄ[לם]
שמעון בן מתנהׄ

Verso

אׄלׄ◦◦◦◦ לשמעון

TRANSLATION

Recto

1. To Shimʿon son of Kosibah, the prince of
2. Israel, from Shimʿon son of *Mtnym/h*;
3. . . . Greetings.
4. Let it be known to you that . . .
5. . . . [. . .]
6. . . . [. . .]
7. that brothers(?) were . . . [. . .]
8. and we have not been among them(?). Greet[ings.]
9. Shimʿon son of *Mtnh*

Verso

10. *ʾEl* . . . to Shimʿon

31. XḤev/Se papDeed E ar

(FIG. 19 AND PL. XXI)

THIS is a fragment of a deed on papyrus in Aramaic. The maximal measurements of the fragment are 5.2 x 3 cm. Three lines in a small cursive script have survived, written across the fibres. The average height of the letters is *c*.2.2 cm. The spacing between the lines is relatively large: *c*.1 cm between each two lines. In line 2 it is possible to read למעבד בה, an expression common in the ownership clause, and it may therefore be possible to restore למעבד בה כ]ול די ת/יצבה/ון[('to do with it whatever you may wish'). This formula appears in deeds of conveyance such as deeds of sale. The remains of the letters in lines 1 and 3 are too scant for restoration. Following line 3 is a large space which may well be the space between the upper and lower versions of a double deed, or the lower margins of the whole document. There are no remains of ink on the verso.

Mus. Inv. 734
PAM 42.198, 42.199
IAA 445135*, 445137*

Recto

]◦סף֯[?]◦א כ֯[1

]למ֯ע֯ב֯ד בה כ֯[ל 2

]א֯מ֯ר֯ל֯ך [? 3

TRANSLATION

Recto

1.] . . . [
2.]to do with it w[hatever he/she/you desire(s)?
3.] . . . [

XḤev/Se **32** + 4Q**347**. papDeed F ar

(FIG. 19 AND PL. XXI)

FOUR small papyrus fragments from the top of a deed have been joined together. Part of the upper margin and parts of four lines in cursive script written across the fibres have survived. Another fragment (*olim* 4Q**347**), containing four lines, the upper part of which connects to the lower part of the first set of fragments, should apparently be added to them, so that a total of seven lines may be seen (the fragments join in line 4). The maximal measurements of the joined fragments are 6.2 x 6.8 cm. There are no remains of ink on the verso. The script is quite large, the average height of the letters being approximately 4 mm, and the spacing between the lines is approximately 5 mm.

In the first line part of the date has survived כס]לו שנת תמנה ב°[(the *mem* and *nun* are written with a ligature or the *nun* has been dropped). The letter following *he* is possibly *bet*, the beginning of the place-name in which the deed was written. There is no indication of the period, but since the eighth year is mentioned, it is clear that the deed precedes the Bar Kochba revolt. In line 2 it may be possible to read ברת לוי מן; before ברת there are two letters which cannot be identified with certainty (the first is possibly *dalet* or *reš*, the second *waw* or *yod*); they are apparently the end of a female name (there are no other examples of a female name ending in these letters among the documents). The name of her place of origin is also unclear. The reading of line 3 is doubtful. It is possible that מסמרא א/שכפ רב°[(']the nail. [The] great saddler/saddle-maker/cobbler[') appears here. The first word may also be read מסמיא ('blind'? 'sealing'/'sealed'?).

If the fragment 4Q**347** does indeed connect to the others it may be possible to read חד מן in line 4 (the other letters in that line do not combine to give a certain reading). In line 5 it might be possible to read פ]לגות טבא ('half of the good'?). In line 6 שותפות appears (cf. a Hebrew lease document, P.Yadin **45** 9 שותופתי עמך). The remains of the letters in line 7 are illegible. The words פ]לגות and שותפות can only give a general hint as to the nature of the transaction agreed upon in this deed between a woman, a daughter of Levi, and someone whose name has not survived. It is difficult to guess what the connection might be between the transaction, and the nail(s) and saddler(?)/saddle-maker/cobbler of line 3 (if that reading is correct). It is also difficult to know if this was a simple document (with the signatures on the recto at the end) or the upper part of a double deed (in which the signatures were on the verso of the lower version only).

Mus. Inv. 734 + 184 (4Q**347**)
PAM 42.196, 42.197, 43.406*
IAA 445135*, 445137*

Recto

XḤev/Se **32** = lines 1-4
4Q**347** = lines 4-7

[ב   לכס]לו שנת תמׄנה ב∘]

[ד/רי/ו ברׄת לוי מן נׄי/וד/ר[

]מסמרא א/שׄכׄפׄ רב∘[

]∘ חד מׄן ב/דׄיׄד/רתה/דו/יסהד/ר[

פ]לגות טׄבׄא[

]∘ב/דה שותפותי/ו∘∘[

]∘∘∘ [

Translation

Recto

1. [On the . . . of Kis]lev, year eight, at [
2.] . . ., daughter of Levi, from . . . [
3.]the nail(?), saddler/saddle/shoemaker . . . [
4.] . . . one of . . . [
5. h]alf(?) the good[
6.] . . . my/our partnership . . . [
7.] . . . [

(continuation missing)

33. XḤev/Se papUnclassified Fragment I ar

(FIG. 19 AND PL. XXII)

THIS is a fragment of a papyrus document. Its maximal measurements are 3.2 x 6 cm. On the fragment remains of three lines survive in cursive script, written across the fibres. The text of lines 1 and 2 appears to be identical, apart from the *lamed* before אוחרן (line 1), which is not seen on line 2 (though since the papyrus is torn at this point it is possible that there was a *lamed* which has not survived). Line 3 cannot be read. The torn text, the absence of any parallels from other texts, and the many possible meanings of סימניא (‘marks’, ‘signs’, ‘treasures’) prevent the identification of the nature of this document.

Mus. Inv. 734
PAM 42.196, 42.197
IAA 445135*, 445137*

Recto?

]סימניא לאוחרן נפ̇◦◦[1

]◦ סימניא [?]אודרן נפ[2

]◦◦◦◦[3

TRANSLATION

Recto

1.]the signs/symbols/treasures for another . . . [
2.]the signs/symbols/treasures [for] another . . . [
3.] . . . [

34. XḤev/Se papDeed G ar

(FIG. 19 AND PL. XXII)

THIS document consists of four fragments of a deed on papyrus. The maximal measurements of frg. a (the largest of the four fragments) are 3 x 5.2 cm. On this fragment are remains of six lines in cursive script written with a very fine pen across the fibres. Frg. b perhaps connects to the left side of frg. a. Frgs. c and d contain remnants of letters of which only a few are legible. Frgs. c and d do not seem to connect directly to frgs. a and b. Only a few words can be identified; the language of the deed is Aramaic. There are no remains of writing on the verso. In line 3, מפק seems to be visible (the infinitive form of the root נפק in *Qal* with assimilation of the *nun*), followed possibly by מן. In deeds of sale for immovable property, the expression מעל ומפק (or מעלא/ה ומפקא/ה) appears in the ownership clause. The word before מפק is illegible, but its last letter may be a *lamed* (the preceding letter cannot be identified as the *ʿayin* of מעל). In line 4 one may read contiguously: לקבלדך ברא מן. The remains of the preceding letters are illegible. The expression לקבלדך ('accordingly') is found in the responsibilities clause from the end of promissory notes, such as Mur **18**, a promissory note from Wadi Murabbaʿat (lines 7–8: תשלמתא לך מנכסי ודי אקנה לקבלדך); it is also found in a slightly different formula in deeds of sale (לוקבלך, with the *dalet* perhaps having been omitted, appears in No. **8a** 13; in No. **8** 7 the word is restored). The term further appears at the end of a deed of gift from Naḥal Ḥever in the final clause (P.Yadin **7** 28–29 in the upper version and line 72 in the lower version). It is possible that the expression is an abbreviation of a longer phrase stating the commitment of the writer of the deed to fulfill it (cf. וקים עלי לעומת ככה in Hebrew lease documents from Naḥal Ḥever, P.Yadin **45** 29–30; P.Yadin **46** 12). If the reading ברא מן ('apart from') is correct, some restriction of the commitment is apparent. The text is too fragmentary to allow for its identification.

Mus. Inv. 734
PAM 42.194, 42.195
IAA 445135*, 445137*

Recto
Frgs. a–b

1]◦◦◦◦ [ ]דׄיׄ[

2]◦◦◦◦◦ [ ]כׄעׄלׄיׄ◦[ ]?[ ]

3]◦◦לׄ מפק[ ]מׄן ◦◦◦◦◦[ ]על ח◦[

4]◦◦ ◦◦ ◦◦◦ לקבלדׄךׄ ברא מׄן דׄיׄצׄ[ ]◦◦◦[

5]◦◦◦◦םׄ [ ]◦◦םׄ ◦[ ]◦[

TRANSLATION

Frgs. a–b

Recto

1.] . . . [. . .] . . . [
2.] . . . [. . .] . . . [
3.] . . . exit[?] from . . . [. . .] . . . [
4.] . . . according to that, apart from . . . [. . .] . . . [
5.] . . . [

Frg. c

1] ◦תׄ[

2]◦א◦[

Frg. d

1] ◦◦◦◦לׄךׄ

35. XḤev/Se papUnclassified Fragment J ar

(FIG. 19 AND PL. XXII)

TWO small fragments have survived from No. **35**. The two fragments of papyrus fit together, and perhaps are from the left side of a deed. The maximal measurements of the joined fragment are 1 x 4.9 cm. The writing is along the fibres. The two words from the root פקד may hint at the content of the deed. The first word is a noun, פקדון, or a masc. pl. participle: פקדין. Before the second word there is a *lamed*, and following the letters of the root there is possibly a *taw*; פקדתא appears with the meaning of 'testament' in *b. Giṭ.* 50b: בשטר פקדתא. Two letters are written next to the word after the *taw*, the second of which is a final *ʾalep*. The first appears to be either *yod* or *waw*, but the form פקדתיא would not be correct; here accordingly one must assume a different reading. It is possible that the letter before the *ʾalep* is a large *nun*, in which case part of the lower line of the *ʾalep* belongs to the *nun* preceding it, and the word would be לפקדתנא (sing. or pl. with a suffixed pronoun of 1st person pl.). With difficulty it might also be possible to read לפקדתא דא or לפקדוניא, but these readings are even more difficult with respect to the forms of the letters. Since there is no similar text or formula, it is difficult to reach a conclusion.

Mus. Inv. 734
PAM 42.198, 42.199
IAA 445135*, 445137*

1] פקד֯ין לפקד∘∘א

TRANSLATION

1.]giving in charge/deposit this(?) will/deposit

36. XḤev/Se papUnclassified Fragment K

(FIG. 19 AND PL. XXII)

NO. **36** consists of a tiny fragment from the top of a papyrus document. Its maximal measurements are 2.2 x 1.7 cm. The upper margin has survived, along with the name כוסבה written in bookhand along the fibres. The remains of a *lamed* may be seen in line 2. Perhaps this is the remnant of a letter, but it is also possible that it is part of the dating formula of a deed; in any case, it is from the period 132–135 CE. The fragment has not been linked so far with the fragments of any other known documents. The smaller fragments associated with this fragment on the plate cannot be deciphered.

Mus Inv. 734
PAM 42.194, 42.195
IAA 445135*, 445137*

1 שמעון בר/בן]כוסבה [

2]ל[

TRANSLATION

1. Shimʿon son of]Kosibah [
2.] . . . [

37. XḤev/Se papDeed H ar?

(FIG. 20 AND PLS. XXIII–XXIV)

FIFTEEN fragments of a deed on papyrus constitute No. **37**. The present editor has not been able to join the fragments and the nature of the document remains uncertain. On some of the fragments, part of the upper layer of the papyrus containing the writing has peeled off, leaving only traces of individual words or letters. The language of the document may be Aramaic or Hebrew. The letters are written across the fibres. There are no remains of writing on the verso. In frg. h there are possible remains of the line containing the date (the end of ?יש]ראל), but if we read a *waw* instead of a *reš*, it may be possible to restore the name שמ]ואל. In the second line of that fragment *mem* and *ṣade* appear consecutively, possibly forming the beginning of מצ]דה (compare Mur **19**). If this restoration is correct, then it is possible that this is the location in which the deed was written, or the place of origin or current residence of one of the parties. In that case we would have to abandon the reading יש]ראל, and favour שמ]ואל in the previous line. In frg. i, part of the right margin has survived, but the text in that fragment is illegible. In frg. g one might possibly read כסף, and assume that this section belongs to the sum clause; two lines after that the remains of כ]ל די°[may perhaps be seen. In frg. f מן appears before a *kap*, and it is perhaps possible to restore מן כ]ל חרר תגר as part of the responsibilities and 'cleansing' clause. In that case, the fragment belongs to the bottom of the deed.

The script is in the late Herodian and post-Herodian cursive style. The letters are large (the height of the *dalet* in frg. g and of the medial *kap* in frg. l is about 5.5 mm); the nib, about 1 mm wide, was held virtually parallel to the line, and accordingly the downstrokes are generally wider than the cross-strokes. There are no connections between the letters. The lines are somewhat crammed together (with an average space of 3.3 mm between each two lines).

Mus. Inv. 734
PAM 42.200, 42.201
IAA 445135*, 445137*

Recto

Frg. a

]ב◦ ד̇[1

Frg. b

] ◦[1

]◦◦[2

]◦◦[3

Frg. c

]◦ [1

]◦◦◦◦[2

]◦   [3

Frg. d

]נ̇[1

]◦◦◦[2

Frg. e

]א[1

]◦ל[2

Frg. f

1]◦◦ ◦[ ]◦◦[

2]מן כ[

3]ה ◦[

4]◦ ◦[

5]◦◦ ע[

Frg. g

1]ב◦[

2]כ[ס]ף [

3]◦ ◦[

4]ל די ◦[

5]ע◦[

Frg. h

1]קאל [

2]מצ[

3]ך ◦◦[

Frg. i

1]ע◦ת◦ה◦[

2 ◦◦◦ ◦◦◦◦ינדנ ◦[

3 ◦ ◦◦◦◦◦◦[

Frg. j

[○○ ○○○○○○] 1

Frg. k

[○○○○] 1

Frg. l

[○ לכל ○מ○] 1

Frg. m

[○]   [○ ○○○○] 1

[○○ה○כע○] 2

Frg. n

○○ל ○] 1

Frg. o

[○○ ת○○ ○נן] 1

[○○ף וח○] 2

38–47h. XḤev/Se papUnclassified Fragments L–BB

(FIGS. 20–21 AND PLS. XXV–XXVI)

THE fragments on this plate were originally assigned the numbers 38–47. The present editor has added several fragments to them from Mus. Inv. 734, yielding groups of fragments and individual fragments from sixteen or seventeen (perhaps frgs. 47a and 47e belong together?) different documents written by different hands. Frgs. 38–46 are written across the fibres, while frgs. 47a–h are written along them. Groups of fragments from individual documents have been placed together, but their extremely fragmentary state prevents any clear reading of these texts. Frg. 38a has not been drawn.

Mus. Inv. 865
PAM 42.196-201
IAA 445127*, 445129*

Frg. 38a

]◦◦◦[1

]◦◦◦◦[2

Frg. 38b (possibly part of No. **9**)

] ◦ב◦ 1

]◦◦◦◦ 2

Frg. 39

]◦◦[1

Frg. 40

]◦◦[1
]◦◦◦◦ן ◦◦◦ ע[2
]◦ך ◦◦ ◦◦ [3

Frg. 41

[עליכי ◦◦[?] 1
]לתא [?] 2

Frg. 42

]◦די[1
]◦רבה כדי [2

Frg. 43

]◦◦◦◦[1
]◦[ ]ברתי ◦◦[2
]◦לה הו◦◦◦◦ת ת◦[3

Frg. 44

]נך די ק◦[1

Frg. 45

This fragment bears traces of ink which have not been deciphered.

Frg. 46

]◦ת◦◦תיה 1

]◦ל ◦◦◦◦◦◦◦◦◦ 2

Frg. 47a

]◦◦◦[1

?]ו לשׁ̊ה̊[2

] *vacat* [3

]◦◦◦[4

]מקבל◦[5

]◦◦[6

Frg. 47b

◦[1

ש̊י̊[2

◦◦[3

על[4

על[5

ע[6

Frg. 47c

]◦ח◦[1

Frg. 47d

This group of fragments bears traces of ink which have not been deciphered.

Frg. 47e

]חולקה[1

] שלה [2

Frg. 47f

]◦ וכתב◦◦ על[1

Frg. 47g

(illegible) 1–4

]◦◦ ◦◦ת לי[5

(illegible) 6–8

Frg. 47h

] ךסו◦[1

]◦◦אל◦[2

49. XḤev/Se Promissory Note (133 CE)

(FIGS. 22–23 AND PL. XXVII)

THIS document is written on hide. Its maximal measurements are 16 x 7.3 cm. The document is dated to the month of Kislev, the second year of the redemption of Israel by Shimᶜon bar Kosibah, i.e. the year 133 CE. The language is Hebrew and the script is a Jewish cursive hand.

This document was first published in 1989 by M. Broshi and E. Qimron (in Hebrew).[1] In 1990, P. Segal published an article dealing with some aspects of the interpretation of the document,[2] and suggested major corrections.[3] Following Segal's study and in accordance with additional corrections suggested by J. Naveh, Broshi and Qimron published a corrected, English version of their article in 1994.[4]

For the interpretation of the document see Broshi and Qimron's commentary in their English publication of this text. For minor corrections in the reading compare the following text with the text appearing in Broshi and Qimron's article (e.g. in lines 13–14, 17).

Private collection

Recto

1 [בע]סרין לכסלו שנת שתין

2 [ל]גאלת ישראל על ידי שמעון בן

3 כוסבא נשיא ישראל איתודי

4 יהודה בן יהודה ס̇רטא מן

---

[1] Broshi and Qimron, 'Shṭar'.

[2] Segal, 'Hebrew IOU'.

[3] The most important correction was the interpretation of איתודי (line 3) as referring to the moneylender who is receiving the borrower's declaration. Another correction concerns the interpretation of עמי (line 5) which stands for the phrase איתי לך עמי ('you have with me', i.e. 'I owe you'). In line 10 he reconstructed [ואל]מלא, which if correct, is the only occurrence of that word in the non-literary documents from the Judaean Desert. Therefore the reconstruction [וא]ם לא, rendering a simple conditional clause (with a dittography of לא following), seems preferable to me.

[4] Broshi and Qimron, 'I.O.U'.

5 החר̊מ̊ת עמי אני יהוסף בן

6 חנניה כסף זוזין ארבעה סלע

7 אחת תסלע הזוא אנמקבל

8 המך שאפרך בכל זמן שת

9 [ומ]ר לי ואשה את השטר הזא

10 [וא]ם לא לא יתקים לי והתשלם

11 [מן]ביתי ומן נכסי וקים עלי

12 כול שאש על̇ השטר הזא

13 שא̇[ ] °° ואחתם ב'ידי' הו כזא

14 [יהוס]ף בן חנניה על

[נפש]ה כתביה

15 מנחם בן [ ] °[ ]עד̇

16 ישוע בר יהדה שהד

17 יהודה בן יהו°[ ] עד̇

TRANSLATION

1. [On the t]wentieth of Kislev, year two
2. of the redemption of Israel by Shimᶜon son of
3. *Kosibah*, the Prince of Israel, an acknowledgement was received by
4. Yehudah son of Yehudah, the soldier from
5. the . . . : (You have) with me (= I owe you), I, Yehosef son of
6. Ḥananyah, four silver *zuzin*, (equivalent to) [7]one [6]*selaᶜ*.
7. This *selaᶜ* I receive(d)
8. from you, (on condition) that I shall pay you at any time that you
9. say to me, and take/demand this document.
10. [And i]f (it will) not >not< be fulfilled by me, then the payment (will be)
11. [from]my house and from my property. And it is confirmed by me
12. all that is on this document
13. that I [. . .] . . . and I shall sign inside/with my (own) hand, thus:
14. [Yehose]ph son of Ḥananyah, for [14a][himsel]f he wrote it.
15. Menaḥem son of [. . .], witness;
16. Yeshuaᶜ son of Yehudah, witness;
17. Yehudah son of Yeho/u[. . .], witness.

XḤev/Se 50 + Mur 26. papDeed of Sale H ar

(FIGS. 24–26 AND PLS. XXVIII–XXX)

Previous publications: Milik, 'Deux documents', 255–64; Benoit et al., *DJD* II (Mur **26**), 137–8.

FIVE fragments, apparently belonging to the lower version of a single deed of sale, comprise this document. Four of the fragments have already been published by J. T. Milik as two separate documents.[1] The maximal measurements of No. **50** (frg. d), which was published first, are 13 x 16.5 cm. The maximal measurements of Mur **26** frg. a (= Milik frg. b) are 3 x 3.4 cm, and of Mur **26** frg. b (= Milik, frg. a) are 14.8 x 9 cm. A small fragment, frg. c, published together with the latter (appearing as part of Milik's frg. a), measures *c.*7.1 x 0.8 cm. An additional fragment, which was stripped off from the verso of No. **50** (frg. e; see below), has not previously been published; it measures *c.*1.0 x 1.3 cm.

Milik noted the similarity of the script of both documents. In his comments to Mur **26**, he writes: 'Très belle écriture cursive, sans ligatures, pratiquement identique à celle du document publié en *Biblica*, xxxviii, 1957, pl. II'. However, Milik did not refer to the similarities in the size of the right margin and in the average spacing between the lines (see tracing in fig. 24). By tracing all the original fragments and reconstructing the text of Mur **26** according to the formulae attested in other deeds of sale, the present editor was able to estimate the original width of the now damaged fragment, and to conclude that it was apparently identical to the width of No. **50**, which remained intact. All these factors suggest that the fragments may have belonged to the same document. This hypothesis could not be verified, however, as the fragments are located in different places: Mur **26** is in the Rockefeller Museum in Jerusalem, whereas No. **50** is located in the Musée Bible et Terre Sainte, Institut Catholique de Paris. Remnants of letters have survived on the above-mentioned frg. e, which is located together with the fragments of Mur **26** and bears the same inventory number. These fit perfectly into the gap within the signatures on the verso of No. **50**, where a layer of papyrus has peeled off (see my tracing and reconstruction of the verso, in fig. 25). Whoever framed that fragment together with Mur **26** (Milik?) may have realized that they belong together; but this decision remains undocumented in the literature.

As indicated by the signatures on the verso, the deed was a double document.[2] The location of the signatures proves that the text which has survived in No. **50** belongs to the clauses following the beginning of the lower version.[3] Parts of clauses from the end

---

[1] See 'Previous publications' above.

[2] On double documents see the INTRODUCTION TO THE ARAMAIC AND HEBREW DOCUMENTARY TEXTS.

[3] On the practice of signing the documents see the INTRODUCTION TO THE ARAMAIC AND HEBREW DOCUMENTARY TEXTS.

of the document have survived in Mur **26** frg. b (= Milik's frg. a). On Mur **26** frg. a (= Milik's frg. b) see below.

The lines of the joined fragments have been renumbered here, their old numbers appearing in parenthesis, to facilitate comparison with the previous publication.

This is a deed of sale conveying a plot of land which includes fig trees (line 9). The seller is of Greek origin, as indicated by the first signature in Greek letters appearing in two damaged lines on the verso (24–25), as well as by the *samek* at the end of the name (apparently the Greek suffix '-os'), appearing in the guarantee and responsibility clause (line 14). The second signature (line 26), the remains of which are in Aramaic, probably belonged to the seller's wife, who did not sign for herself, as indicated by ממרה ('at her word') which has partly survived at the end of line 27. In several deeds from the Judaean Desert, certain signatures are followed by the phrase '*x* son of *y* at his/her word' written in the same hand as the signature. This indicates that the signature was not written by the person bearing that name, but rather by someone else.[4] (The clause concerning the wife appears in the body of the deed, lines 18–19).[5]

Mur **26** frg. a (= Milik's frg. b) is a small fragment which includes אנחנה ('we'). It has been placed at the beginning of the text, on the assumption that it belongs to the sale clause ('we [of our own free will sold to you', etc.). However, as its context is not clear, it may perhaps be placed further down in the text (possibly at the end of lines 15–17).

Since part of the deed is known to have come from Wadi Murabbaʿat, we may now assign No. **50** to the same location (some other fragments of unknown provenance may also have come from there).

Summation

The new collation and reconstruction of the fragments add some information to the understanding of the deed which has been published as two separate documents. Some of the corrections correspond to the standard formulae appearing in other deeds from the Judaean Desert. The seller appears to be of Greek origin, while his wife may have been a Jewess, supposing the second signature in line 26 to be hers. (If the *šin* at the beginning of line 18 is part of her name, we may perhaps reconstruct it as ש]לם ברת [ס.) The property being sold is a plot of land, containing fig trees, sold for seventy-eight denarii to more than one person, as indicated by the plural suffix in both fragments. Apparently two witnesses (rather than three, as suggested by Milik) and the scribe signed their names as well as their places of origin on the back of the document. Line 23, the end of which is missing, repeats a phrase appearing in the ownership clause (line 12), and may be an addition, as it follows the clause of exchanging the deed, which appears as the final clause in several deeds from the Judaean Desert.

The following corrections should be made to Milik's readings and reconstructions based upon the new collation of the fragments.

---

[4] See e.g. No. **8a** 14–15; Mur **29** 18; No. **13** 10–11; and others. See also Greenfield, 'Letters'.

[5] Compare the phrase by the wife of the seller, e.g. in No. **8a** 12. The wife, in that way, probably waives rights assigned to her in the marriage contract, where the husband's property is said to be a guarantee for her ketubbah money.

TABLE 1: *Corrected Readings of No. **50***[6]

Line(s) (old numbers)	Milik's reading:	Corrected to:
(2–3)	ומח[סר י]תיר	אם ח[סיר א]ו [י]תיר
(3)	אלנה	אלעזר
(4)	ל[י]ה[ו]נתן בר ר[ו]בא	°[ ]°°[ ]°°° בר °°°°°א
(6)	ודי חיא	ודי חזא
(6–7)	כדי חיא	כדי חזא
(8)	עשרה	עסרה
(8)	לחין	לחוד (Yaron, 'Note', 26)
(15)	]°על[נפשה כ]תב	]על [נפ]שה כתב
(16)	[ ]°°°[ ]ה	]°°[ ]°[ ]ן ממרה
(17)	ש]הד [מ]ן °קר°	ש]הד מן הקר°[?]
(18)	מ]נשה	] °ש°°

TABLE 2: *Corrected Readings of Mur **26***[7]

Line (old number)	Milik's reading:	Corrected to:
(2)	מ[ן יומא דנה ולעל]ם	מ[ ]°
(3)	ש[ואנה]ס	ש[ ]ס
(3)	מזב[נתה]	[ת]
(5)	[על אתרא דך]	[על אתרא דך מן יומא דנה]
(6)	ל[ק]ב[לכן	ל[ק]ב[לדך
(8)	רשין	[ר]ש[א]ין

COMMENTS TO THE CORRECTIONS:

NO. 50

Ll. (2–3) אם ח[סיר א]ו [י]תיר לזבנה. This phrase implies that in case the plot is smaller or larger than written in the preceding phrase, the loss or the gain is that of the buyer (cf. No. **9** 3).

L. (3) The name is אלעזר. In the Jewish cursive script of that time, extreme cursive *ʿayin* often resembles medial *nun* (as well as *bet* and *kap*). The two final letters are *zayin* and *reš* (there is no horizontal stroke connecting the two down-strokes representing those letters, as there would be if it were the letter *he*).

L. (3) The letters are too damaged to enable a certain reading of the second name.

6 Milik, 'Deux documents', 258–9.

7 Benoit et al., *DJD* II, 137.

L. (3) ודי חזא. This reading was proposed by Yadin, 'Expedition D—The Cave of the Letters', 249 n. 36, and corresponds to the formulae in other deeds (e.g. No. **9** 5) and to כראוי in Hebrew (see e.g. P.Yadin **44** 13 and 16).

L. (8) עסרה. *Samek* here replaces *śin*. Cf. No. **8a** 1. Regarding the interchange of *śin* and *samek* see the INTRODUCTION TO THE ARAMAIC AND HEBREW DOCUMENTARY TEXTS.

L. (8) לחוד. The final letter in this word is a large *dalet* rather than final *nun* (cf. *dalet* in the preceding word). The scribe of this document writes the final *nun* as a long downstroke. (The word appears also in No. **9** 6; see R. Yaron, 'Note on a Judaean Deed of Sale of a Field', *BASOR* 150 (1958) 26.)

L. (15) ∘על[נפ]שה כתב]. Three additional letters appear in this line on the fragment which the present editor placed (in the drawing alone!) on the verso of the document.

L. (16)]ן ממרה. Milik suggested reading ספר[ה. The new reading is based on the additional fragment (see above). This word indicates that another person signed for the person whose name appears in the preceding signature, perhaps because the latter was illiterate (see Greenfield, 'Letters').

L. (17) Part of the ligature of *mem* and *nun* appears on the additional fragment (see above). No traces are seen after the unidentified letter following *reš* . One may expect a *he* there for הקריה (Hebrew, 'the city'?).

L. (18) Milik's reading could not be verified.

According to the new readings, the first four lines of signatures belong to the seller and to another person, apparently his wife, as well as the person who signed 'at her word'. The other four lines belong to two witnesses and to the scribe, all of them apparently adding the names of their provenance.

MUR. 26

L. (2–3) The words reconstructed by Milik within parentheses were omitted because there are also other possible reconstructions for the text in those places.

L. (5) The reconstruction of the text is based on the formulae attested in other deeds from the Judaean Desert. It completes the line to its full width, which thus corresponds to the width of No. **50**.

L. (6) The correction of the reconstructed word is based on parallels in other deeds from the Judaean Desert.

L. (8) [ר]ש[א]ין. Examination of the papyrus fibres shows that a letter (*ʾalep*) may be reconstructed between *šin* and *yod* in the word (cf. רשאין in l. 12)

Mus. Inv. 725; BTS 7163
PAM 40.230, 40.345, 41.328, 41.329, 43.872
IAA 553494*

Recto
Mur **26**
Frg. a

[ ]ני∘[ ] 1

[ ]אנחנה 2

[מן רעותנה יומא דנה זבנה לכן]∘∘ל^{ב}א 3

No. **50**
Frg. d

[ ]∘∘∘[ ]∘∘ ∘∘[ ]
[ ]∘לין בית [ז]רׄע חנטין סאין תלת וקבין תלתה אׄם חׄ[סיר א]וׄ
[י]תׄיר לזבנה תחומי אתרא דך מדנחא אלעׄזׄר בר מ∘חׄי מערבא
חׄוני ואחרנין די הוא מן קדמת דנה ∘[ ]∘∘[ ] ∘∘∘ בׄרׄ ∘∘∘∘אׄ דרומא
אפתלמיס ופרׄדׄיון אחה צפונא אורחא אתרא דך בתחומה
ובמצרה תאניא וכל די בה ודי חזא עלה מעלא ומפקא כדי
חזא דך זבנת לכן בכסף זוזין שבעין ותמניה די המון
סלעין תשע עסרה ותקל חד לחוד וכספא אנה מקבל דמין
לעלם רשאין זבניא די מן עלא באתרא דך וירתהן למקנה ולמזבנה
ולמעבד בה כל די יצבון וירתהן מן יומא דנה ולעלם ואנה
או∘∘∘∘ס מזבנה וכל די איתי לי ודי אקנה אחראין ו[ערבין]
למרקא ולקימא זבנה דך קדמׄ[כן]וקדם ירתכן[

Mur **26**
Frgs. b + c

∘[ ]טׄין די יׄהׄ[ ]∘∘[ ]
מ[ ]∘ וקים ע[לי]הׄ מׄ[ ]
ש[ ]ס אנתתׄ[ ]∘ת∘[ ]
אחריא וערבה לׄמרקא ולקימׄ[א זבנ]ה [דך קדמכן וקדם]
ירׄתכן מן כל חרר [ו]תגר ובׄטׄלׄ[ן די י]תׄנכן[<על אתרא דך> מן יומא דנה]
ולעלם ותשלמתא מן נכסי[נה ודי נקנה]לׄ[ק]ב[לדך ובזמן די]
תאמר לנה נחלף לכן ש[טרא דנה כדי חזא לעלם]
[ר]ש[א]ין זבניה די מן עלא[ ]

No. **50** (Verso)
Frgs. d + e

]Ẹυ̣[....]Eυ (13) 24

]..[...].ϵ̣ (ρὶ)χϵι (14) 25

[ ]עׄל [נפ]שה כתב (15) 26

[ ]∘∘[ ]∘[ ]ן ממרה (16) 27

ש]הׄדׄ מן הׄקרׄ∘[?] (17) 28

[ ]∘ש∘∘ כתב ספריא (18) 29

מן ירושלם (19) 30

[ ]שׄהׄדׄ מׄן חׄבׄרׄן (20) 31

Translation

Recto
Mur **26**
Lower Version
Frg. a

1. [. . .] . . . [. . .]
2. [. . .]We
3. [of our own free will, on this day, sold to you . . .] . . .
(lines missing)

No. **50**
Frg. d

4. (1) [. . .] . . . [. . .]
5. (2) [. . .] . . . the area of [so]wing of three *seʾah*'s of wheat. If it is l[ess o]r
6. (3) [mo]re—it is the buyer's. The boundaries of that place: East—ʾElʿazar son of *M.ḥy*; West —
7. (4) Ḥoni and others, which has previously [belonged to . . .] . . . son of . . . ʾ; South—
8. (5) Ptolemoeus and *Prdywn* his brother; North—the road. That place—within its boundaries and
9. (6) within its borders: fig-trees, and everything which is in it and which is fitting to it, the entrance and the exit, as
10. (7) is fitting. That I have sold to you for silver *zuzin* seventy eight, which are (equal to)
11. (8) *silʿin* nineteen and one sheqel only, and the money I received, (the full) price.
12. (9) Forever entitled are the buyers, who are (mentioned) above, regarding that place, and their inheritors, to buy and to sell
13. (10) and to do with it whatever they desire, as well as their inheritors, from this day and forever. And I,

14. (11) *ʾw...s*, the seller, and all that I own and whatever I will acquire, are responsible and [guarantors]
15. (12) to cleanse and to establish that sale before[you]and before your inheritors[. . .]

Mur **26**

Frg. b

16. (1) . . . [. . .] . . . which will . . . [. . .] . . . [. . .]
17. (2) . . . [. . .] . . . and it is confirmed [by] m[e . . .]
18. (3) . . . [. . .]*s*, wife of[. . .] . . . [. . .]
19. (4) responsible and a guarantor to cleanse and to establi[sh this sal]e[before you and before
20. (5) your inheritors from any dispute [and] challenge and annulment[that will] come upon you [<regarding this place,> from that day]
21. (6) and forever. And the payment (will be) from my property[and from whatever I will acquire]acc[or]di[ng to that. And at any time that]
22. (7) you say to us, we shall exchange for you [this] d[ocument as is fitting. . . .. Forever]
23. (8) en[tit]led are the sellers who are (mentioned) above [regarding this sale, to . . .]
(the remainder is missing)

Verso

No. **50**

Frgs. d + e

24. (13) Eu[....]Eu[
25. (14) with [my own?] hand [
26. (15) [. . .] for [him/her]self; wrote
27. (16) [. . .] . . . [. . .] . . . [a]t his/her word.
28. (17) [. . ., wit]ness from the . . . [?];
29. (18) [. . .] . *š* . . wrote the deeds,
30. (19) from Jerusalem;
31. (20) [. . .], witness, from Hebron.

NOTE ON THE GREEK SIGNATURE

In his first edition of the deed, Milik wrote that lines 24 (13) and 25 (14) are occupied by one signature, that of the seller, the או○○○ס of line 14 (11).[8] He read:

Ευ[ ]Ẹụ[
..[ ]..[

In other words, the name and the patronymic start with the same syllable. I read χει in the second line. The ει is superscript in small letters, and seems to be an abbreviation since I cannot read the third letter as *rho*; if anything, it is an *epsilon*. I suggest, therefore, that we have here a case similar to that of Mur **29** which reads:

Κ[λέο]πος Εὐτραπέλ-
[ο]υ χειρὶ ἑαυτοῦ γ(έγραφε)
'Kleopos son of Eutrapelos wrote with his own hand'.

The last two words were corrected by P. J. Sijpesteijn to read: ἐ<μ>αυτοῦ γ(έγραφα) i.e, 'Kleopos son of Eutrapelos (I) wrote with my own hand'.[9]

- Hannah M. Cotton

[8] Milik, 'Deux documents', 257, 259.

[9] Sijpesteijn, 'A Note', 49–50.

GREEK DOCUMENTARY TEXTS

Introduction to the Greek Documentary Texts

CONTENTS

General Description

The Greek texts collected here are all written on papyrus. They are all documentary texts, mostly deeds. No. **67**, although phrased as a letter (see χαίρειν in line 3) is a document, as the addition in a different hand in lines 11–12 proves.[1] Some of the texts are double documents (see below, DOUBLE DOCUMENTS). The majority of the documents come from the Roman province of Arabia; some come from the province of Judaea. Although the date has not survived in all of them, those which do bear a date come from the first third of the second century CE. The Archive of Salome Komaïse daughter of Levi, with seven documents (six in Greek, Nos. **60–65**), is without a doubt the most significant part of the collection. The collection includes a variety of documents: a receipt for tax or rent (No. **60**); a land declaration (No. **62**), and a conclusion to a land declaration (No. **61**; both land declarations were submitted at the census conducted in Arabia in 127); two marriage contracts, one of them cancelled (No. **69**) and the other turning an unwritten marriage into a written one (No. **65**); a deed of renunciation of claims (No. **63**); a deed of gift (No. **64**); a deed of loan with hypothec (No. **66**); and fragments of other deeds (*olim* XḤev/Se Gr. 3 and 4), whose nature is not entirely clear. In addition, there are many fragments with only a few letters on them which cannot be placed, or even described (see pls. XLVIII–XLIX).

[1] See Mitteis, *Grundzüge*, 55, and Wolff, *Recht der griechischen Papyri*, 109ff., on the χειρόγραφον.

Context

As has been explained in the GENERAL INTRODUCTION the present volume is not a self-contained corpus, but merely a fortuitous collection of texts, the core of which comprises papyri once claimed to have come from Wadi Seiyâl, together with others which shared the same fate of not being found in the course of a controlled excavation. It is not enough, therefore, to relate the Greek texts to the Aramaic and Hebrew texts in this volume; they have to be viewed in the various, wider contexts to which they belong.

First, the Greek texts published here are part of the documentary material in different languages found in a number of sites in the Judaean Desert, not all of which has yet been published.[2] Three collections have already been published in their final form: the Hebrew, Aramaic, Greek, Latin, and Arabic texts from Wadi Murabbaᶜat were published in 1961 by Benoit *et al.* in *DJD* II; the Aramaic, Hebrew, Latin, and Greek texts from Masada were published in 1989 by Yadin and Naveh in *Masada* I and Cotton and Geiger in *Masada* II; and the Greek part of the Babatha Archive was published in the same year by Lewis in *The Documents from the Bar Kokhba Period in the Cave of Letters*: *Greek Papyri* (= Lewis, *Documents*). Another part of the material has been published, so far only preliminarily. Most relevant to the present collection are the Aramaic and Nabataean documents from the Babatha Archive,[3] and the Aramaic and Hebrew letters and leases of Bar Kokhba and his men.[4] These last two groups will be published in *Judean Desert Studies*.[5]

Secondly, the Greek texts must be seen in the context of other Greek papyri found in the Judaean Desert, all but one of which were written in Judaea or Arabia.[6] A special relationship exists between the Salome Komaïse Archive and the Greek part of the Babatha Archive (Lewis, *Documents*).[7] Yet the present collection is also related to other documentary texts in Greek from different sites in the Judaean Desert including:

1. Greek letters written by Bar Kokhba's followers, found in the Cave of Letters in Naḥal Ḥever, together with the Hebrew and Aramaic letters: P.Yadin **52** and **59** (= SB VIII 9843–9844);[8]

---

[2] See S. J. Pfann, 'Sites in the Judean Desert Where Texts have been Found', in Tov with Pfann, *Companion Volume*, 109–19.

[3] See, in general, Yadin, 'Nabataean Kingdom'. For individual documents, see Starcky, 'Contrat Nabatéen' (P.Yadin **36** = XḤev/Se nab **1**); Yadin, Greenfield, and Yardeni, 'Deed of Gift' (P.Yadin **7**); Yadin, Greenfield, and Yardeni, 'Babatha's *Ketubba*' (P.Yadin **10**). For papyri and parchments from sites other than Naḥal Ḥever, see Eshel and Eshel, 'Fragments' (Aramaic documents from sites near Jericho).

[4] See Yadin, 'Expedition D'; idem, 'Expedition D—Cave of Letters'; and Beyer, *Aramäischen Texte*; idem, *Ergänzungsband*.

[5] For other preliminary publications of the papyri from the Judaean Desert see Cotton, Cockle, and Millar, 'Papyrology', 223–33.

[6] Mur **117** is the exception; it must have been sent from Egypt.

[7] See INTRODUCTION TO THE ARCHIVE OF SALOME KOMAÏSE DAUGHTER OF LEVI.

[8] Preliminary publication in Lifshitz, 'Papyrus grecs'; for bibliography, see Cotton, Cockle, and Millar, 'Papyrology', nos. 317 and 320. There are three more Greek papyri, probably from the same site, in the Rockefeller Museum (provisional plate nos. 101, 106, and 135); these are not mentioned in Yadin, 'Expedition D', or 'Expedition D—Cave of Letters'.

2. one Greek document from 'the Cave of Horror' in Naḥal Ḥever, 8Hev **4**;[9]

3. Greek documents found in Wadi Murabba'at, published in *DJD* II as Nos. **89–107**; **114–116**, **118–155**;[10]

4. Greek papyri and ostraca found on Masada, and published in *Masada* II as nos. **741**, **743–749**, **772–793**;

5. Greek documents from Naḥal Ṣe'elim, 34Se **4** (**5**, **6**) and **7**;[11]

6. one Greek papyrus from Naḥal Mishmar;[12]

7. five Greek documents from Cave Abi'or near Jericho.[13]

The great majority of these Greek documents are legal deeds. They were written by Jews, or at least involve Jews.[14] Furthermore, it can be demonstrated that the Jews who wrote them were non-Hellenized, or only semi-Hellenized, Jews.[15] The question of why they chose to write in Greek, rather than in Aramaic (or Hebrew),[16] will be dealt with in JEWISH LAW AND SOCIETY (below).

Finally, one must view the Greek texts in this collection in the context of the rapidly growing corpus of Greek papyri from the Aramaic-speaking Roman Near East (as distinct from Greek papyri from Egypt). The area concerned is that covered by the Roman provinces of Syria (divided in the 190s into 'Syria Coele' and 'Syria Phoenice'); Mesopotamia (created in the 190s); Arabia; and Judaea, which in the 130s became 'Syria Palaestina', and to which were added the southern part of the former province of Arabia, the Negev, and Sinai in the 290s.[17] Greek is the dominant language in the papyri from the Roman Near East, alongside Latin (especially in Roman army circles), several Aramaic dialects (Palestinian Aramaic, Nabataean, Syriac, and Palmyrene), Hebrew, as well as Parthian and Middle Persian (a few scraps). The papyri published in the present volume well illustrate one of the salient features of the papyrology of the Roman Near East, namely the variety of languages employed, but, more particularly, 'the presence of two or more languages in the same archive, or even in the same document: for instance Greek and Syriac in the texts from Mesopotamia and the Middle Euphrates; Nabataean, Aramaic and Greek in the archive of Babatha; and Hebrew, Aramaic and Greek in the Bar Kochba documents'.[18] The Greek papyri from the Roman Near East share linguistic as well as diplomatic and palaeographical

---

[9] Preliminary publication Lifshitz, 'Greek Documents from the Cave of Horror', 206.

[10] No. **117** originated in Egypt, see n. 6; Nos. **108–113** are literary texts.

[11] Published by Lifshitz, 'Greek Documents', 53–8, and rearranged and corrected by Schwartz, 'Remarques', 61–3, who shows that 34Se **4**, **5**, **6** are fragments of the same papyrus. See also corrections by Benoit in *RB* 68 (1961), 466–7. They are located in the Rockefeller Museum on two plates, provisionally labelled Mus. Inv. 226 and 229. 34Se **7** is located on a plate provisionally labelled Mus. Inv. 231; 34Se **8** does not exist.

[12] Lifshitz, 'Greek Documents', 59–60, and Schwartz, 'Remarques', 61.

[13] See Cotton, Cockle, and Millar, 'Papyrology', 215 and nos. 285–6.

[14] See Sevenster, 'Greek?', 155–75; Mussies, 'Greek in Palestine'.

[15] See Wasserstein, 'Marriage Contract', 124ff.; idem, 'Non-Hellenized Jews', and in No. **69**, DATE AND PROVENANCE.

[16] Hebrew appears alongside Aramaic and Greek after the outbreak of the Bar Kokhba Revolt, see Yadin, *Bar Kokhba*, 181, who suggests that the use of Hebrew received official encouragement; cf. Rosén, 'Sprachsituation', 223ff.

[17] Millar, *Roman Near East*, 192; see below, Fig. 32, Map of the Roman Near East.

[18] Cotton, Cockle, and Millar, 'Papyrology', 215.

features. Semitisms and Latinisms, as well as other Roman influences, are the most obvious manifestations.[19] The double document, which fell into desuetude in Egypt in the first century BCE, is very typical of the texts from other parts of the Roman Near East.[20]

Language

The Greek of the documents published in this volume shares all the characteristics of the Greek of the Babatha Archive, in other words, it is 'in its essence the postclassical Greek *koinē* familiar from other sources in the eastern Mediterranean—the Old and New Testaments, inscriptions, and papyri from Hellenistic and Roman Egypt and from Dura-Europus' (Lewis, *Documents*, 13). Lewis gives an exhaustive survey of the principal Semitisms in the Greek part of the Babatha Archive (*Documents*, 14–16) which can be applied profitably to the present collection. However, at least in the case of No. **64**, we have to deal not simply with pervasive Semitisms, but probably with a literal translation of an Aramaic deed of gift by a scribe whose knowledge of Greek leaves much to be desired. The ease with which this Greek can be literally translated, with no adaptation, into the presumed Aramaic *Urtext* proves this point incontrovertibly.[21] To a certain extent, No. **64** resembles P.Yadin **19**, a deed of gift from the Babatha Archive, which Lewis contrasts with the accurate and idiomatic Greek of P.Yadin **14**: '[P.Yadin] **19**, in sharp contrast, presents in a neat, even, flowing hand a text notable for its erratic orthography, indiscriminate vowels . . . and insouciant case endings' (*Documents*, 83).

Some of the Greek papyri in this collection evince lexicographic features which they sometimes share with other Greek papyri from the Roman Near East, and which either are not attested in the Greek papyri from Egypt, or occur in them at a much later period. This may well be the result of the influence of the Aramaic world in which they were written.

1. [ἐξωμολο]γήcατο καὶ cυνεγρ[άψατο] (No. **63** line 1). The phrase is never attested in the Egyptian papyri.[22] However, it appears in four more double documents from the Roman Near East: P.Avroman I (88 BCE) A, lines 7–8 = B, line 8; P.Avroman II (22/1 BCE) A, lines 4–5 = B, lines 4–5; Mur **115** (124 CE) line 2 = line 21; P. Dura 30 (232 CE) lines 6–8.

2. μηδένα λόγον ἔχειν πρὸc αὐτήν (No. **63** lines 4, 8, 11[23]). This is the equivalent of Aramaic כל מדעם לא איתי לי עמך[24] and occurs also in P.Yadin **26** lines 15–17. In Egyptian papyri it rarely occurs before the fourth century CE.[25]

---

[19] See, in great detail, Lewis, *Documents*, 13–19.

[20] See Lewis, *Documents*, 8. The sheer quantity of double documents is palpably demonstrated in Cotton, Cockle, and Millar, 'Papyrology', which gives the specification 'double document' where it is relevant.

[21] See INTRODUCTION to No. **64**.

[22] Although, as Wolff points out (*Recht der griechischen Papyri*, 60–61, n. 21), it is a Greek formula.

[23] Cf. P.Yadin **25** lines 61–63 = 26–27.

[24] No. **13** lines 3, 8–9; P.Yadin **9** (Nabataean, unpublished) lines 6–7.

[25] See COMMENTS ad No. **63** line 4.

3. ἔχειν . . . κυρίωϲ καὶ βεβαίωϲ εἰϲ τὸν ἅπαντα χρόνον (No. **64** line 16 = line 40). This form of the guarantee is found also in P.Yadin **19** lines 20–23, P.Dura 26 (227 CE) lines 14–15; P.Euphr. 9 line 20 (without εἰϲ τὸν ἅπαντα χρόνον), but it is hardly ever attested in Egyptian papyri.[26]

For 'Latinisms and other Roman influences', the reader is referred to Lewis, *Documents*, 16–19, where linguistic and legal influences are exhaustively discussed. As in Lewis, *Documents*, here, too, the calendar is treated separately; see below.

Palaeographical Notes

THE documents published here form a small but valuable addition to the growing body of Greek papyri from sites in the Eastern Mediterranean outside Egypt. The principal collections of such papyri are now listed in *JRS* 85 (1995), along with papyri found in Egypt but written elsewhere in the Near East.[27] With regard to the palaeography of such material, there might at first sight appear to be two different views. On the one hand, C. Bradford Welles, writing of the Greek papyri and parchments from Dura, stresses the contrast between the scripts used in them and those used in contemporary papyri from Egypt,[28] a view which is shared by D. Hagedorn with reference to a slave sale from Side in Pamphylia.[29] On the other hand, P. Benoit regards the script on papyri from the Judaean desert as generally similar to that on Egyptian papyri,[30] and N. Lewis, similarly, in his edition of P.Yadin, prefers to emphasize the similarity between the hands in his documents and in papyri from Egypt.[31]

In fact there is no real conflict between these apparently different views.[32] The hand of the slave sale from Side (and those of other such documents) and many of the hands from Dura do differ appreciably from the hands in contemporary Egyptian documents; whereas the differences are much less marked between Egyptian papyri and those from the Judaean Desert. E. Crisci has recently published a detailed and thorough analysis of these hands.[33] Especially relevant for the documents being considered here are his analyses of P.Murabbaʿat and P.Yadin.[34] These analyses make it clear throughout that

---

[26] See COMMENTS ad No. **64** lines 16–17 = lines 40–41 and Lewis, *Documents*, 16, on πάντα κύρια καὶ βέβαια.

[27] Cotton, Cockle, and Millar, 'Papyrology'. For papyri from Mesopotamia, add now Feissel and Gascou, 'Documents'; 'Documents 1. Les pétitions'; 'Documents 2. Les actes de vente-achat'.

[28] See Welles et al., *Dura-Europos*, 53–5.

[29] P.Turner 22: Hagedorn comments in the introduction that the handwriting is distinctly different from that in contemporary Egyptian documents.

[30] *DJD* II, 210.

[31] *Documents*, 6.

[32] It is interesting that both sides quote W. Schubart, *Griechische Paläographie* (Munich 1925), 72–3, in support of their views.

[33] 'Scritture greche'. E. Crisci's *Scrivere Greco fuori d'Egitto*, *Papyrologia Florentina* XXVII (1996) appeared too late to be taken into account here.

[34] Crisci, 'Scritture greche', 142–7 and 148–55, respectively. The texts from the Middle Euphrates (see n. 27) were published too late to be included in Crisci's survey; while documents found in Egypt but written in Asia Minor, etc., and the Colt papyri from Nessana, fall outside his terms of reference.

the hands from the Judaean Desert have affinities with contemporary Egyptian documentary hands, but at the same time show features similar to those found in some of the hands from Dura. Some of Crisci's remarks suggest that he regards them as a halfway house between the two types of writing, but in his conclusions he lays more emphasis on their affinity to the Dura hands than to the Egyptian ones.[35] In general, Crisci's analysis seems to be sound, although I should be inclined to lay more stress on the similarities between the scripts used in the Judaean Desert papyri and contemporary scripts from Egypt, and rather less stress on the differences.

As we should expect, the hands used in the documents under consideration here resemble much more closely some of those found in P.Murabbaʿat and, especially, P.Yadin, than those from Dura. The general impression we get from them is of less cursive scripts with fewer ligatures than would be normal in papyri from Egypt of a similar type. None of the scripts makes a serious attempt at bilinearity, and indeed the variable size of the letters (e.g. *beta*, *kappa*, and *eta* are often quite tall) is a notable feature of most of the texts. As to the letter-forms employed by the different writers, however, there are few if any essential differences from those used by contemporary scribes in Egypt, though several letters do call for special comment. In some texts, *alpha* has an elongated bow which stretches well below the line. *Beta*, which never appears in the cursive form, is often made in two halves like a Latin capital B and is always large. There is no example of y-shaped *eta*, which is always h-shaped, whereas N-shaped *nu* is much rarer than the cursive form. *Iota* is often large and can descend well below the line, especially in ligatures. Many of the *sigmas* resemble a printed capital *gamma*, while the centre of *phi* is usually triangular rather than round. It is particularly noteworthy that *tau* is sometimes made as a reversed *gamma*, followed by a horizontal at top right (cf. Lewis, *Documents*, 6), a form which is often found in first-century Egyptian papyri but has more or less dropped out by the second century. These two letters (*phi* and *tau*) may therefore be considered to show archaizing features by comparison with Egyptian papyri. Note also the tendency to add a link-stroke to some letters, especially *eta*, to facilitate ligaturing, a feature which is rare in Egyptian papyri after the Ptolemaic period. On the other hand, *epsilon* is not infrequently made in two separate halves, one on top of the other, with the top half ligaturing to the right; this form is very rare in Egypt before about 200 CE.

The Individual Documents

The hands of the individual documents vary quite considerably, especially in the extent to which they are more or less rapidly written. The hand of No. **61** is the most cursive, whereas No. **60**, which is written with a thicker nib, is noticeably less cursive and has fewer ligatures. It is upright and competent, but hardly an attractive hand. Note the tall initial *iota* in the proper name Ιουδα (line 3) and at the start of line 4, where it appears to have a hook at the top. *Pi* is regularly made with a link-stroke at the right, and *beta* is narrow. Most remarkable is the form of *tau* on several occasions,

[35] See, in particular, p. 149: 'Le tipologie grafiche in essi attestate . . . se da un lato non mancano le affinità con le scritture egiziane coeve, dall'altro . . . rinviano piuttosto alle scritture di Dura Europos'; and p. 158: 'Benché numerose siano le affinità con le forme grafiche dei papiri egiziani . . ., la scrittura dei manoscritti greco-giudaici, sopratutto tra il I secolo a.C. e il II d.C., mostra innumerevoli e cospicue analogie con le scritture greche mesopotamiche, esemplificate dai materiali di Dura Europos'.

e.g. in ἔτουϲ and ὀκτω (line 6): though basically of the type described above (a reverse *gamma*, to which a horizontal stroke is added at the right), it begins with a hook above the first horizontal stroke, giving it a very eccentric appearance; it is made in a somewhat similar fashion in P.Yadin **17** and **18**.

The cursive nature of the hand of No. **61** has already been mentioned; note in particular the marked tendency to write letters such as *kappa* and *mu* in a single stroke. It is a rather untidy hand, not unlike P.Yadin **28** and **29**, which makes fairly frequent use of ligature, see e.g. γεγραπται in frg. a line 3 and μαι in frg. b line 6. Especially remarkable is the very cursive, *theta*-shaped form of the first *epsilon* in ὑποϲτειλάμενοϲ (frg. a line 3). The hook at the bottom of one arm of *chi* in frg. b line 4 is noteworthy, as is the form of *rho* in πρό (frg. b line 5), which is like *R* in some contemporary Latin hands; this feature is also found in No. **63**, and in P.Yadin **27**. There is occasional use of link-strokes, in particular after *eta*; most unusual is the one joining *omicron* to *sigma* in Πρεῖϲκοϲ (frg. b line 5).

No. **62** is written in a neat, practised cursive by a scribe who was obviously highly skilled; although written quickly it retains its legibility. There is some resemblance to P.Yadin **16** (Lewis, *Documents*, pl. 13). The script is right-sloping with a number of link-strokes, though few actual ligatures. It is more like a contemporary Egyptian hand than most of the papyri from the Judaean Desert. *Alpha* occasionally has a large loop, in which case it descends below the line, and *beta* shows clear development from the capital towards the cursive form. Note also the n-shaped *nu* (distinguishable from *pi* since the latter but not the former normally has a link-stroke) and the v-shaped *upsilon*. *Kappa* sometimes rises to the right and can have its two right-hand strokes prolonged. The bow of the *phi* is not completed at the bottom right.

In No. **63** we have a script much like that of No. **61**, but more legible and less carelessly written. It is quite cursive with several ligatures; some of these are remarkable, e.g. *sigma* and *alpha* in line 1, κατα in line 6 and ἔτι in line 8. In this hand *nu* is always in the cursive form, and *xi* is written much as one would expect *zeta* to have been made (line 5). *Omicron* is larger than in many of the other texts and *delta* is often formed cursively in a way which closely resembles *alpha*. *Upsilon* is like modern printed ν, though with its second stroke sometimes much prolonged. *Phi*, which usually has a rounded centre section, is followed by a curious link-stroke in lines 6 and 7; contrast *eta*, which in this hand is never linked to the letter following. Also noteworthy is the cursive way in which many of the letters are made, notably *theta* and *pi*, even if this does not regularly lead to ligatures. In the last line, which seems to be in a different hand, the form of *tau*, though essentially made as described above, is particularly striking; a similar form is to be found in No. **68**, line 6 ([π]ρ̣ο̣ϲ̣ηκόντων).

No. **64** has both an outer and an inner text, the latter written by the same hand but less carefully and with more ligatures. The strokes are thick and give a sprawling, rather ugly effect; it is much like Mur **115**. Letter sizes can be variable, notably *alpha* and *omicron*. One or two *alphas*, e.g. in αὐτῆϲ line 5 and βεβαίωϲ line 16, are squashed up narrowly; others have a pronounced slanting *hasta*. Some *deltas* are noteworthy, especially those which resemble a modern printed δ (e.g. in line 2, εἰδῶν), or the rounded cursively-written form found in δυϲμῶν in line 14. There are several examples of *sigmas* written like *gamma* (e.g. ἐξόδοιϲ, line 12), but other examples where they look much like a printed σ (e.g. in line 35, the two consecutive *sigmas* in Cαμμουοϲ Cιμωνοϲ).

There is some use of link-strokes, especially after *pi*, which is often the easiest way to distinguish it from *nu*. *Rho* regularly has a large loop; on at least two occasions it is written much like a Latin *R* (cf. above): κληρονόμοι in lines 10 and 11. *Nu* can be written much like a capital *eta* with a horizontal cross-stroke (e.g. αἰωνίου line 7). The centre of *phi* is triangular. In καί the *iota* can descend well below the line, especially in line 33. *Epsilon* can be a narrow letter, little more than a straight *hasta* with a mid-stroke linking to the next letter.

No. **65** (= P.Yadin **37**) is written in an ugly hand which Naphtali Lewis describes in the introduction to P.Yadin **37** (*Documents*, 130): 'unattractive writing, in small letters produced with a thick pen that . . . looks clumsy and crude'. There are numerous link-strokes, but most letters are in fact made independently with few ligatures. As a whole it has what may be called an old-fashioned look. Note the hook at the top of the cross-bar in some instances of *tau* and also at the start of *mu*; *eta* is regularly h-shaped; both *eta* and *zeta* usually also start with a hook. *Kappa* has hooks at top and bottom of the vertical and a smaller right-hand section written above the line. There is some resemblance to Mur **115** (*DJD* II, pl. 86).

In No. **66**, which is, again, competently written but rather ugly, there is a tendency to use the cursive forms of letters but with very few ligatures. *Omicron* is often a mere blob, as is the circle of *rho*, and *pi* is written as a *gamma* followed by a stroke slanting to the right; it is never linked to the letter following. *Alpha* can be surprisingly large and, in its second occurrence in ὑπατείας (line 1), descends well below the line (cf. above). In line 5, the reading τὸ δέ seems inescapable (cf. the note *ad loc.*), yet, if so, *omicron* is made very strangely—more like an *upsilon* and with an unexpected stroke linking it to the *delta*; less strange is the linking of *omicron* and *upsilon* in τοῦ in the next line. The angular *omega* is interesting: note the way the final stroke is added independently (especially in ἐξέσστω αὐτῷ in line 7 and τῷ in line 8). Also worth a comment is the *xi* in ἐξέσστω, which is virtually a straight line.

The fragmentarily preserved No. **68** is particularly interesting, since it does not resemble closely any of the other hands in this group, although the letter-forms are made in essentially the same ways. It is a right-sloping, flowing hand with few ligatures, though that uniting *tau* and the tall *rho* in line 3 is noteworthy. Note *nu* with a tall stroke at the right, which makes it look like *gamma* plus *iota*.

Finally, No. **69** is written in a clear, upright hand with few ligatures. The letters are of uneven height, e.g. the *kappa*s. The same is true of the *upsilon*s, which can be surprisingly tall (though always v-shaped or with the first stroke vertical, much like a *nu*; cf. No. **61** above). Some examples of *alpha* have a very deep bow (especially at the start of lines), and there is a remarkable form in the first *alpha* of ἀπεσκηκέναι (line 8) in which the bow has become no more than a diagonal line. Note also *chi*, in which the first stroke is horizontal rather than diagonal, and *pi* in lines 10 and 11, with the feet curving in different directions. *Beta*, in lines 3 and 4, is close to the remarkable figure-8 form found in Mur **89** (see Crisci, 'Scritture greche', fig.10 on p. 180). The neat, small hand used on the verso is very similar to that found for the names of witnesses in several texts in P.Yadin.

Diplomatics

Double Documents

Nos. **62, 64, 65** and **69** are double documents; No. **61** is a fragment of one. The topic is briefly described in the INTRODUCTION TO THE ARAMAIC AND HEBREW DOCUMENTARY TEXTS. An extensive discussion with the essential bibliography can be found in Lewis, *Documents*, 6–10.[36] Lewis emphasizes that the use of double documents fell into disuse in Egypt by the time it became a Roman province (30 BCE),[37] but survived in other parts of the Roman Near East into the Roman period.[38] Newly discovered papyri from the Middle Euphrates supply further evidence for this.[39] Nevertheless, the fact that the inner text is often abbreviated, and sometimes reduced to a mere notation (as in No. **62**), proves that even where the tradition of writing double documents continued, the inner text no longer served its original purpose of authenticating the outer text.[40] 'A common characteristic of double documents is that the inner text is produced by the same scribe in smaller, less careful writing than the outer text' (Lewis, *Documents*, 9). The writing of the outer text is likely to have preceded that of the inner text (Lewis, *Documents*, 9–10). Like other double documents from the Roman Near East, the double documents from the Judaean Desert are always written across the fibres, what Turner called *transvecta charta* (see Turner, 'Recto and Verso', *passim*, and INTRODUCTION TO THE ARAMAIC AND HEBREW DOCUMENTARY TEXTS).

The Witnesses

The technical aspects of the placing of witnesses' signatures on the verso of the documents are discussed in the INTRODUCTION TO THE HEBREW AND ARAMAIC DOCUMENTARY TEXTS. The signature consists of name and patronymic, followed by the Aramaic or Greek term for 'a witness', שהד or μάρτυϲ, respectively. The number of witnesses was briefly touched upon by Lewis,[41] but it seems necessary to review the evidence, even if, at this point, it is impossible to reach final conclusions.

The early Ptolemaic double document was called ἑξαμάρτυρον (ϲυγγραφὴ ἑξαμάρτυροϲ), since one of its standing features was the presence of signatures of six witnesses.[42] The Roman double document, however, e.g. military diplomas, required the signatures of seven witnesses.[43] It is, therefore, important to point out the presence of five witnesses in the majority of double documents from the Judaean Desert, as well

---

36 Lewis does not enter into the question of the origin of the practice (Greek or Oriental), on which see Koffmahn, *Doppelurkunden*, 10–30.

37 With the exception of documents submitted by Roman citizens, mostly stemming from military circles; see Lewis, *Documents*, 8; Turner, 'Recto and Verso', 39ff.

38 Cf. Wolff, 'Zur Geschichte der Sechszeugendoppelurkunde', 475ff.

39 See P.Euphr. 6–10 (published in Feissel and Gascou, 'Documents 2. Les actes de vente-achat') and P.Euphr. 12, 15 (described in Feissel and Gascou, 'Documents', 559–60); P.Euphr.Syr. 19–20 (= A–B; published by Teixidor, 'Deux documents syriaques'; for P.Euphr.Syr. 20 [= B] see also Teixidor, 'Un document syriaque').

40 Cf. Wolff, *Recht der griechischen Papyri*, 74f.

41 *Documents*, 12.

42 Wolff, *Recht der griechischen Papyri*, 57ff., 63f.

43 Kunkel, 'Doppelurkunde', 416ff.; Wolff, 'Römisches Provinzialrecht', 783.

as in many of the documents from elsewhere in the Roman Near East. In what follows, the papyrological evidence for the different numbers of witnesses is given. Although the main emphasis is on the Greek documents, the evidence from papyri in other languages is also provided. The investigation is restricted to double documents.

Seven Witnesses

In none of the documents in this volume is there an example of seven witnesses. There are one probable and four certain cases of documents bearing seven witnesses in the Greek part of the Babatha Archive: P.Yadin **5**, a deposit from 110 CE, which lists seven names, probably witnesses, in frg. b col. ii lines 3–10; P.Yadin **11**, a loan with hypothec from 124 CE, verso lines 31–37; P.Yadin **15**, a deposition from 125 CE, which records in the text the presence of seven witnesses (καὶ ἐπεβάλοντο μάρτυρες ἑπτά, line 35), who signed on the verso, lines 39–45; P.Yadin **19,** a deed of gift from 128 CE, which has seven signatures on the verso lines 31–37; and P.Yadin **20,** a concession of rights from 130 CE, which is signed on the verso lines 46–52 by seven witnesses.[44] P.Yadin **11** records a loan given by a centurion of a Roman unit. It is only natural that the number of witnesses followed the Roman legal practice. P.Yadin **19** and **20** concern the registration of real property with the public authorities in Ein Gedi in Judaea. Again, this may explain why the Roman practice which required the signatures of seven witnesses was followed. Finally, P.Yadin **15,** described in the document itself as μαρτυροποίημα (see line 12 = line 30), i.e. a Roman *testatio*, like others of its kind called for the signatures of seven witnesses.[45]

Six Witnesses

In the Aramaic deed of gift from 120 CE, P.Yadin **7,** six signatures of witnesses follow that of Shimʿon son of Menaḥem, the donor (lines 74–9).[46] To the best of my knowledge, this is a unique case.

Five Witnesses

There are eight certain cases of signatures by five witnesses in Greek documents. No. **62** from 127, an authorized copy of a land declaration, frg. a verso lines 1–5; No. **64**, a deed of gift from 129 CE, verso lines 45–49; No. **69**, a marriage contract from 130 CE, frg. a verso, lines 1–5; P.Yadin **12**, an authorized copy of an extract from the minutes of the *boule* of Petra from 124, verso lines 12–17; P.Yadin **14**, a summons to the governor's court from 125, verso lines 44–48; P.Yadin **16**, an authorized copy of a land declaration from 127 CE, verso lines 39–43; P.Yadin **23**, a summons to the governor's court from 130 CE, verso lines 26–30; P.Yadin **26**, a summons to the governor's court from 131 CE, lines 22–26.

P.Yadin **18** from 128 CE, a marriage contract, is a somewhat doubtful case. It has seven signatures on the verso lines 76–80: the first two are of the father and the groom,

---

[44] The first name on the verso of P.Yadin **17** is that of Judah son of Eleazar Khthousion, who cannot be a witness to this document, and, therefore, this cannot be a seven-witness document; it is also hard to determine whether there were seven witnesses in P.Yadin **21** and **22** from 130 CE, but these are not, in any case, double documents.

[45] See Wolff, *Recht der griechischen Papyri*, 78f.; idem, 'Römisches Provinzialrecht', 779ff.; Kunkel, 'Doppelurkunde', 426ff.; Gilliam, 'Sale of a Slave', 65ff.

[46] The editors make no comment; see Yadin, Greenfield, and Yardeni, 'Deed of Gift'.

who cannot be counted as proper witnesses; the third signature, in Greek, is probably that of a witness.[47]

In the Aramaic No. **9**, dated palaeographically to the late Herodian period, there seem to be five witnesses on the verso, lines 28–32. The names of the last four witnesses remained on the verso of No. **22** (i–ii CE) lines 16–19; they are preceded by three lines with traces of letters. If the arrangement here is similar to that of No. **64**, then the first two lines belonged to the subscription, and the third (line 15) carried the signature of the fifth witness.

Five witnesses are present in the Nabataean and Aramaic texts from the Babatha Archive. P.Yadin **1** from 94 CE, a Nabataean promissory note, has seven names on the recto lines 55–59 (= verso lines 62–66), but the first is that of the debtor and the last is that of the scribe; hence there are probably five witnesses. P.Yadin **2** and **3** from 99 CE, Nabataean deeds of sale, bear seven signatures on the verso (P.Yadin **2** lines 45–49;[48] P.Yadin **3** lines 51–55). The first is that of the seller and the last is that of the scribe; hence there are probably five witnesses; P.Yadin **10** from *c*.25–28 CE, an Aramaic marriage contract, has probably five witnesses on the verso.[49]

Three Witnesses

In the following Aramaic double documents from Murabbaʿat, there seem to be three witnesses: Mur **19**, a writ of divorce from 111 CE (see below), verso lines 27–29; Mur **21**, a marriage contract from the first half of the second century CE, verso lines 25–27;[50] Mur **29**, a deed of sale from 133 CE, verso lines 4–6; and Mur **30**, a deed of sale from 134 CE, verso lines 34–36.[51]

Double documents from other parts of the Roman Near East also give us a variegated picture. In the Greek papyri from Dura we find seven witnesses attested in P.Dura 18 (87 CE, deed of gift), 19 (88/9 mutual distribution), and 25 (180 CE, deed of sale). Five witnesses are attested in P.Dura 26 (= *FIRA* III^2 138, 227 CE, deed of sale); 30 (232 CE, marriage contract) and 32 (254 CE, divorce). There are also five witnesses in the third document from Avroman, Kurdistan, written in 53 CE[52] in Pahlavi.[53] Five witnesses are found in three of the Greek deeds published so far from the Middle Euphrates: P.Euphr. 6, 7, and 10 (five witnesses, four sign in Syriac and one in Greek), as well as in the Syriac P.Euphr. 19 (A).

---

[47] Though Lewis categorically excludes the possibility of reading μάρ(τυς) after the name. See Cotton, 'Subscriptions', 40, n. 48, for another suggestion.

[48] Where the first names are unreadable, but must follow the same pattern as P.Yadin **3**.

[49] The fragmentary state of the papyrus does not permit absolute certainty; see Yadin, Greenfield, and Yardeni, 'Babatha's *Ketubba*', 83.

[50] Yardeni's reading.

[51] There are only two witnesses in No. **50** + Mur **26** according to Yardeni's new reading of the signatures in lines 24 (13) – 31 (20).

[52] For the date, see *Handbuch der Orientalistik*, ed. B. Spuler, I.4: *Iranistik* (1958), 29.

[53] See Nyberg, 'Pahlavi Documents', 182–230, esp. p. 187, lines 5–6.

Subscriptions, Subscribers, and Guardians.[54]

In three of the Greek documents collected here we find subscriptions.

1. The receipt for tax (or rent), No. **60**, is subscribed in Aramaic in line 13: רישה כתבה, i.e. 'Reisha underwrote this'.[55] As his nickname, Reisha, implies, the subscriber is likely to be 'the chief' of the group of tax collectors referred to as ἑτα[ῖρ]ọị ('colleagues') in line 3.[56]

2. There are copies of two subscriptions in Greek in No. **61**, a fragment containing the conclusion to an authorized copy of a land declaration. The first subscription, that of the declarant, was written in the original declaration by the χειροχρήϲτηϲ, Onainos son of Saʿadalos (see below), who may or may not have written it in Greek. The second subscription, that of Priscus, the Roman prefect of cavalry who received the declaration, appeared in the original document in Latin. It is explicitly stated in No. **61** line 4 that the prefect's subscription in lines 4–5 is a translation (Ἑρμηνꞏ{ν}εία ὑπογραφῆ[ϲ]).

3. There were two subscriptions in Aramaic, of which only traces remain, on the verso of No. **64**, a deed of gift (lines 42–43). These were the signatures of Salome Gropte, the donor, and that of her husband and guardian, Yosef son of Shimʿon,[57] who must have signed for her. The procedure of one person signing for another and then adding his own name is well attested in the papyri from the Judaean Desert.[58]

The term χειροχρήϲτηϲ is attested for the first time in the Greek language in No. **61**. The χειροχρήϲτηϲ is the equivalent of the Egyptian ὑπογραφεύϲ. He fulfilled a distinct and specific function, which is to be distinguished from that of the scribe, on the one hand,[59] and from that of the guardian, on the other. Precisely like the ὑπογραφεύϲ, the χειροχρήϲτηϲ is the one who writes the subscription for those who are legally competent to do so, but who happen to be illiterate (or otherwise incapable of writing), when a subscription and/or a signature in their own hand is required to render a document valid. As the term implies, the χειροχρήϲτηϲ lends his hand, or rather someone else borrows his hand (χεῖρα χρηϲάμενοϲ).[60] This function is not attested for the bearer of this title before the middle (perhaps the end) of the sixth century CE. At this late date, it occurs in Latin letters in a group of papyri from Ravenna.[61] From the mid-eighth century, it occurs again in this sense in Byzantine legal rules.[62]

Proof for the distinction between the guardian and the χειροχρήϲτηϲ (although the latter term does not appear there) seems to be contained in P.Yadin **15**. This is a case of deposition against the guardians of Babatha's son. Babatha's guardian for this

---

[54] See the introduction to Y. Yadin and J. C. Greenfield, 'Aramaic and Nabatean Subscriptions' in Lewis, *Documents*, 136–7.

[55] See COMMENTS ad No. **60** line 13.

[56] On the nickname used as name see COMMENTS ad No. **60** line 13.

[57] ϲυνπαρọ́ντọϲ ạὐτ[ῇ ἐ]πιτρόπο[υ τοῦδε τοῦ πρά]γμạτọϲ χάριν Ιωϲηπου Cιμω̣ν̣οϲ [ἀ]νὴρ αὐτῆϲ (lines 4–5).

[58] See COMMENTS ad No. **64** lines 42–43 for many examples.

[59] This is argued in detail in Cotton, 'Subscriptions', 33ff.

[60] See COMMENTS ad No. **61** line 4; see Cotton, 'Subscriptions', 38ff.

[61] Tjäder, *Papyri Italiens* I: nos. 16 ('um 600?'), line 34; 20 ('um 600?'), line 72; 27 ('Mitte des 6.Jh.?), line 1.

[62] *Nov.* 27.1–2 (797–802), K. E. Zachariä von Lingenthal, *Ius Graecoromanum*, 1:48; *Ecloga legum*, 5.2 (740 CE); ibid., 2:30.

matter, Judah son of Eleazar Khthousion, did not write the subscription for her; instead, Eleazar son of Eleazar wrote it for her, since her illiteracy prevented her from doing it herself. The relevant lines are lines 31–35:

> [ἐμαρ]τυροποιήσατο ἡ Βαβαθα ὡς προγέγραπται διὰ ἐπιτρόπου αὐτῆς τοῦδε τοῦ πράγματο[ς Ἰούδου Χ]θουσίωνος ὃς παρὼν ὑπέγραψεν. (second hand) Βαβαθας Σίμωνος ἐμαρτυροποιησάμη<ν> κα̣τ̣ὰ Ἰωάνου Ἐγλα καὶ Ἀ<βδ>αοβδα Ἐλλουθα ἐπιτρώπων Ἠσοῦς υ<ἱ>ο<ῦ> μου ὀρφανοῦ δι' ἐπιτρόπου μου Ἰούδα Χαθουσ̣ίωνος ἀκο̣λ̣[ο]ύθω̣ς τε̂ς προγεγραμμένες ἑρέσασιν. Ἐλεάζαρος Ἐλεαζάρ̣ου ἔγαρψα ὑπὲρ αὐτῆς ἐρωτηθ̣εὶς διὰ τὸ αὐτ̣ῆς μὴ ε<ἰ>δένα<ι> γράμματα.[63]

It seems that διὰ τὸ αὐτ̣ῆς μὴ ε<ἰ>δένα<ι> γράμματα, in Babatha's case, does not mean that she could not write Greek,[64] but that she was illiterate in any language. A Greek subscription was not required: Judah son of Eleazar, her guardian, wrote his own subscription in Aramaic.[65] If Judah son of Eleazar did not write a subscription for Babatha, although he was her guardian and could write Aramaic, but Eleazar son of Eleazar did, then we must look for some legal reason: evidently she was legally competent to do so, but incapable of doing so because of her illiteracy. This is where a χειροχρήστης, and not a guardian, must have been used.

The term ἐπίτροπος is used in the papyri from the Judaean Desert both for the guardian of a woman and for that of a minor. The practice was common to the province of Arabia as well as to the province of Judaea.[66] That this was not due to the influence of the Aramaic environment is proved by the fact that the distinction is made in the Aramaic subscriptions: the guardian of a woman is called אדון = κύριος (P.Yadin **15** line 37; **17** line 40) while, for the guardian of the minor, the Aramaic borrowed the Greek term ἐπίτροπος: אפטרפא (P.Yadin **20** line 41; **27** line 12).[67] The use of a single term for the two types of guardians is due to the influence of Roman law,[68] but also the very requirement for a woman to be represented by a guardian seems to have been imposed by the Roman authorities.[69] In none of the Hebrew, Aramaic, or Nabataean papyri from the Judaean Desert do we find a woman represented by a guardian. Are we in the presence of two different legal systems, or is this merely a question of the language of the document? Unfortunately, the evidence is not sufficient to give an unequivocal

---

[63] 'Babatha deposed as aforestated through her guardian for this matter, Judah son of Khthousion, who was present and subscribed. [second hand] I, Babatha daughter of Simon, have deposed through my guardian Judah son of Khthousion against John son of Eglas and 'Abdoöbdas son of Ellouthas, guardians of my orphan son Jesus, according to the aforestated conditions. I, Eleazar son of Eleazar, wrote for her by request, because of her being illiterate'.

[64] As is claimed by Youtie to be the case in Egyptian papyri; see 'ΑΓΡΑΜΜΑΤΟΣ', 162–3; idem, 'Because They Do Not Know Letters', 101–8; cf. Bagnall, *Egypt* , 256–7, n. 142.

[65] יהודה בר כתושין אדון בבתה בקמי השרת בבתה ככל די על כתב יהודה כתבה: 'Judah son of Khthousion lord of Babatha: in my presence Babatha confirmed all that is written above. Judah wrote this', P.Yadin **15** line 37; cf. Yadin and Greenfield in Lewis, *Documents*, 139–40.

[66] See COMMENTS ad No. **69** line 4.

[67] Pointed out by Wolff, 'Römisches Provinzialrecht', 795f.; idem, 'Le droit', 279ff.

[68] 'In Roman law *tutor* could designate either a guardian of a minor (*tutor impuberis*) or the transactional "guardian", or attendant, of a woman (*tutor mulieris*)', Lewis, *Documents*, 17; cf. Wolff, 'Römisches Provinzialrecht', 796.

[69] Wolff, 'Römisches Provinzialrecht', 796f.

answer. The low profile kept by the guardian of a woman even in the Greek documents is conspicuous.[70] The four deeds in languages other than Greek which would have necessitated the presence of a guardian of a woman under Roman law were not written under Roman rule: the three Nabataean deeds, P.Yadin **2**, **3**, and XḤev/Se nab **2**—all three deeds of sale—were written before the annexation of the Nabataean kingdom and the creation of the province of Arabia,[71] and the Hebrew No. **13** (whether a renunciation of claims or a writ of divorce)[72] was written in Ein Gedi at the time of the Bar Kokhba Revolt. Is it mere coincidence that we do not have a document written under Roman rule in Aramaic, Nabataean, or Hebrew with a guardian representing a woman, or does this prove incontrovertibly that the Greek deeds, unlike the Semitic deeds, were meant for Roman courts—or, at least, had to conform to Roman legal formalities? (See below, JEWISH LAW AND SOCIETY.)

The Calendar

Dating Formulas

Private documents from Arabia and Judaea, like those from Syria and Mesopotamia[73] but unlike those from Egypt, use consular dates and Roman months, often in addition to regnal years of the Roman emperor and the provincial era.[74] The table below is patterned on that of Lewis, *Documents*, 28, showing the presence and order of the several dates in the documents. Three columns have been added: date of document, place, and position in the document.

In the Greek documents in this collection as well as in the Babatha Archive, the regnal year, if it appears, always occupies the first position, followed by the consular, and the provincial year. The order of the several dates differs in the Aramaic and Nabataean papyri from the Babatha Archive from the Roman period: in the two Aramaic documents, P.Yadin **7** from 120 CE and P.Yadin **8** from 122 CE, the consular year comes first; it is followed by the regnal year, with the provincial year recorded last. This is likely to have been the order in the two Nabataean documents, P.Yadin **6** from 119 and P.Yadin **9** from 122 CE, where the consular year comes first, followed, after a lacuna, by the provincial year; the regnal year may have occupied the second position. Only the very beginning of the consular date remains in P.Yadin **10**, and the

[70] See COMMENTS ad No. **65** lines 13–15 and lines 14–15.

[71] P.Yadin **2** and **3** were written in 99 CE; XḤev/Se nab **2** *c.*100? (I am grateful to A. Yardeni for letting me see the text in advance of publication).

[72] See Ilan, 'Divorce Bill'.

[73] See P.Dura 26 (Greek, deed of sale, 227 CE); 28 (Syriac, 243 CE); 29 (Greek, deposit, 251 CE); 30 (Greek, marriage contract, 232 CE); 31 (Greek, divorce, 204 CE); 32 (Greek, divorce, 254 CE); 43 (Greek, contract, 238–244 CE); P.Euphr. 1 (Greek, petition, 245 CE); 6–7 (Greek, sale of a slave, 249 CE); 8 (Greek, sale of a slave, 251 CE); 9 (Greek, sale of a slave, 252); 10 (Greek, sale of a horse, 250 CE); P.Euphr. Syr. 20 (B) (Syriac, lease of land, 242 CE).

[74] See Lewis, *Documents*, 27.

editors maintain that 'there does not . . . seem to be room for a double or triple date' there.[75]

The date is missing in most of the Aramaic (and Hebrew) documents in this volume. Apart from the five documents dated by the year of the Bar Kokhba Revolt, only one full date survives: No. **12**—which belongs to the Salome Komaïse Archive—is dated at the end of the document (lines 11–12) to 'year twenty-five of the Eparchy', i.e. 131 CE. No other dating formulas occur in the documents.[76]

TABLE 1: *Dating Formulas*

No.	Date	Place	Consular Year	Regnal Year	Provincial Year	Position of Date: Beginning/End of Document
60	125	Maḥoza, Arabia	1st	no	2nd	end
61	127	Rabbath-Moab, Arabia	(2nd)	(1st)	(3rd)	(beginning)[77] end[78]
62	127	Rabbath-Moab, Arabia	2nd	1st	3rd	beginning (end)[79]
63	127	Maḥoza, Arabia	yes	?	?	end
64	129	Maḥoza, Arabia	1st	no	2nd	beginning
65	131	Maḥoza, Arabia	1st	no	2nd	beginning
66	99 or 109	Arabia?	yes	no	no	beginning
67	before 127 or 128?	Ein Gedi? Judaea?	yes	?	?	end
68	?	Arabia?	?	?	?	
69	130	Aristoboulias, Judaea	2nd	1st	no	beginning
73	106/7 or 109	Arabia? Judaea?	2nd	1st	no	end

[75] Yadin, Greenfield, and Yardeni, 'Babatha's *Ketubba*', 85.

[76] Nos. **11** and **32** bear the year 'eight' and No. **10** bears the year 'twenty-two', but the era is missing in all three documents.

[77] The beginning is lost, but the order of the several dates must have been the same as in P.Yadin **16** and No. **62.**

[78] Only the Roman month and day were written.

[79] The subscription did not survive; it may have contained only month and day as No. **61**, or the year as well, as in P.Yadin **16**.

In the two dated Greek papyri from Murabbaʿat, written in Judaea, we find only the consular year in Mur **114** from 115 CE (at the beginning),[80] and the regnal year, followed by the consular year, in Mur **115** of 124 CE (at the beginning, cf. No. **69**). In the Aramaic Mur **18**, from 55/6 CE, only the regnal year appears at the beginning. The Aramaic Mur **19**, which bears the date 'year six in Masada', is likely to refer to the era of Arabia, i.e. 111 CE;[81] Mur **20** bears the date 'year eleven', probably referring to 'the hyparchia,' i.e. 117 CE.[82]

The Provincial Year in Arabia[83]

The era of the Roman province of Arabia began on 22 March 106.[84] The earliest document which bears the provincial year in its dating formula is the Greek P.Yadin **5** from 2 June 110: τῆϲ δὲ κατ̣[αϲτ]ά̣ϲ̣ε̣ω̣[ϲ τῆϲ] ἐπαρχείαϲ ἔτουϲ πέμπτου (frg. a, col. i, lines 3–4). The next four documents bear the formula על מנין הפרכיה דא 'according to the era of this Eparchy' (i.e. the province of Arabia), in their opening: P.Yadin **6** (119 CE, Nabataean, unpublished) line 1; P.Yadin **7** (120 CE, Aramaic) lines 1–2 = lines 31–32; P.Yadin **8** (122 CE, Aramaic, unpublished) lines 2–3; P.Yadin **9** (122 CE, Nabataean, unpublished) line 2. Next comes No. **60** from 29 January 125, where the provincial year, without τῆϲ ἐπαρχείαϲ (or τῆϲ ἐπαρχείαϲ Ἀραβίαϲ),[85] is given at the end: ἔ̣τ̣ο̣[υ]ϲ̣ ἐννεακαιδε̣[κάτ]ου (line 11). Two Greek papyri from the Babatha Archive from 11 or 12 October 125 bear an identical formula at the opening: κατὰ δὲ τὸν ἀριθμὸν τῆϲ ἐπαρχείαϲ Ἀραβίαϲ ἔτουϲ εἰκοϲτοῦ (P.Yadin **14** lines 17–18; **15** line 2 = lines 15–16).

From December 127 onwards a new element enters the formula which expresses the provincial year: the adjective νέα modifies ἡ ἐπαρχεία in the dating formula, thus no longer ἡ ἐπαρχεία Ἀραβία but ἡ νέα ἐπαρχεία Ἀραβία. It is attested for the first time in the two land declarations from that date, P.Yadin **16** and No. **62**: κατὰ δὲ τὸν τῆϲ νέαϲ ἐπαρχείαϲ Ἀραβίαϲ̣ ἀριθμὸν ἔτουϲ δευτέρου εἰκοϲτοῦ μηνὸϲ Ἀπελλαίου ἑκκαιδεκάτη (P.Yadin **16** lines 9–10; cf. No. **62** frg. a lines 8–9). The addition proves tenacious: it occurs, in one of two formulas, in all of the Greek documents which employ provincial dating in the next five years, until the documents stop altogether in 132: ἀριθμῷ δὲ τῆϲ νέαϲ ἐπαρχείαϲ Ἀραβίαϲ (cf. P.Yadin **17**, 21 February 128, line 2 = lines 18–19; P.Yadin **18**, 5 April 128, lines 30–31) or κατὰ τὸν ἀριθμὸν τῆϲ νέαϲ ἐ̣παρχείαϲ

---

80 Despite the editor's dating of 171 CE, which is too late for the papyri for the Judaean Desert. The second consul, Statilius Severus (line 2) is the suffect consul, T. Statilius Maximus Severus Hadrianus, who, together with the ordinary consul, L. Vipstanus Messala, is likely to have stayed in office till the end of June; on the restoration of the month, see in lines 2–3, and the commentary ad loc. For dating the year by *consules suffecti*, see Eck, 'Consules Ordinarii und Consules Suffecti'.

81 Although the document was written in Masada, in Judaea; cf. Freeman, 'The Era of the Province of Arabia', 43f., for the use of the era of Arabia in adjacent territories. Some take 'year six in Masada' to be Year 6 of the First Revolt, i.e. 71/2; see Yadin, *Bar-Kokhba*, 188f.; Yadin and Naveh, *Masada* I, 9–11; Yaron, 'Mesadah'.

82 See Milik ad Mur **20** line 1.

83 See, in detail, Cotton, 'Ἡ νέα ἐπαρχεία Ἀραβία'.

84 See Brünnow and von Domaszewski, *Provincia Arabia* III, 303; Bowersock, 'Annexation', 39; idem, 'Report', 231.

85 The convention of dating by the provincial era without in any way referring to the province is very common in inscriptions from this area as well as in the Nessana papyri; see Freeman, 'The Era of the Province of Arabia', 39.

'Αραβίας (cf. P.Yadin **19**, 16 April 128, lines 9–10 [without 'Αραβίας]; P.Yadin **20**, 19 June 130, lines 2–3 = lines 21–22; No. **65**, 7 August 131, lines 1–2; P.Yadin **21** and **22**, 11 September 130, line 4; P.Yadin **27**, 19 August 132, lines 2–3).[86]

In the new dating formula, the term νέα modifies ἐπαρχεία and not 'Αραβία—'the new province', not *Nova Arabia*.[87] Thus, there is no question of the creation of a new province called Νέα 'Αραβία under Hadrian.[88] This is further proved by the fact that the counting of the provincial years continues uninterrupted from 106.[89] Nor, if the interpretation offered here is accepted, does the introduction of νέα into the dating formula suggest a reorganization of the province of Arabia, 'occasioned by, or connected with, the antecedents . . . of the Bar Kokhba rebellion',[90] or 'a reform of the provincial administration'.[91]

Significantly, not only the formula expressing the provincial era is modified in 127, but also that expressing the regnal year is unlike anything we encounter before or after. Hadrian's full titulature appears in the dating formula: ἐπὶ Αὐτοκράτορος Καίσαρος θεοῦ Τραιανοῦ Παρθικοῦ ụ̣ịοῦ θεοῦ Νέρουα υἱωνοῦ Τραιανοῦ 'Αδριανοῦ Cεβαστοῦ ἀρχιερέως μεγίστου δημαρχικῆς ἐξουσίας τὸ δωδέκατον ὑπάτου τὸ τρίτον (P.Yadin **16** lines 5–7 = No. **62** frg. a lines 4–7). The appearance of the emperor's full titulature in the dating formula (i.e. following ἐπί) is quite exceptional; nowhere else in the papyri is the full titulature attested as part of the dating formula.[92]

These considerations suggest that land declarations P.Yadin **16** and No. **62** reflect, in their dating formula, the language used by the emperor Hadrian in a letter or an edict ordering a census in the new province. The letter or edict was then published by the provincial governor together with his own edict ordering the census.[93] Obviously, in Hadrian's letter or edict, the imperial titulature appeared in the nominative and not as part of the dating formula. Furthermore, since this was the first census (see below), it was only natural that Hadrian would order a census in 'the New Province'. In the land declarations, both the imperial titulature and the order to conduct a census in the 'new province' were translated into the dating formulas by the official scribes who translated the original declarations into Greek and prepared the authorized copies.[94]

---

[86] It is restored in No. **64** (9 November 129) line 2.

[87] Lewis, 'The World of P.Yadin', 35–6. Therefore, the association with the fourth century Νέα 'Αραβία in P.Oxy. L 3471 (Wasserstein, 'Marriage Contract', 96ff.) is quite irrelevant here.

[88] As pointed out by Lewis, 'The World of P.Yadin', 35–6, against Wasserstein, 'Marriage Contract', 94ff.

[89] One also notes that, although the dating formulas in the two land declarations (and elsewhere) read τῆς νέας ἐπαρχείας 'Αραβίας (P.Yadin **16** lines 9–10; cf. No. **62** frg. a lines 8–9), the text itself states 'Αραβίας with no modification: ἀποτιμήσεως 'Αραβίας ἀγομένης ὑπὸ Τίτου 'Ανεινίου Cεξστίου Φλωρεντείνου πρεσβευτοῦ Cεβαστοῦ ἀντιστρατήγου (P.Yadin **16** lines 11–13; cf. No. **62** frg. a lines 10–12).

[90] J. Geiger apud Wasserstein, 'Marriage Contract', 101, n. 27.

[91] Lewis, 'The World of P.Yadin', 36.

[92] See COMMENTS ad No. **62** lines 4–7 for the two occasions on which Hadrian's full titulature appears in the papyri.

[93] Cf. Oliver, *Greek Constitutions*, no. 19 (= P.Lond. VI 1912), where Claudius's epistle to the Alexandrians is published by the prefect of Egypt in his own edict.

[94] Cotton, 'Subscriptions', 31ff.

Provincial Divisions and Administration

The Greek documentary texts from the Judaean Desert, of which the present collection represents an important part since it contains documents from both Arabia and Judaea, broadens our knowledge of the administrative divisions of Arabia and Judaea in Roman times.

Judaea

We are now better able to confirm, revise, and reinterpret the evidence concerning the Roman province of Judaea in the literary sources, namely Josephus and Pliny the Elder.[95] The papyri confirm the survival of the administrative divisions, called toparchies, in Judaea proper, into the period following the Great Revolt of 66–70.[96] Furthermore, it is now clear that Pliny's list of toparchies (*N.H.* 5.70) is more up-to-date than that of Josephus (*B.J.* 3.55),[97] since his omission of the toparchies of Ein Gedi and Idumaea reflects conditions after the first revolt: P.Yadin **16** proves that Ein Gedi was now subsumed into the toparchy of Jericho,[98] and No. **69** proves that the new toparchy of Zif (not yet known to Pliny) replaced at least part of the toparchy of Idumaea.[99]

Josephus attaches the name of toparchy not only to a cluster of villages, of which the most important or central one gives its name to the toparchy, but also to cities with their territories.[100] Joppa and Jamnia are added as two more toparchies in Josephus's list;[101] about the latter it is said explicitly elsewhere Ἰάμνειάν τε . . . καὶ τὴν τοπαρχίαν πᾶcαν (*A.J.* 18.31). Even more revealing is the evidence of *B.J.* 2.252, where we are told that Nero annexed to Agrippa II's kingdom 'four cities with their toparchies' (πόλειc . . . cὺν ταῖc τοπαρχίαιc). The cities were Abila and Julias (that is Livias) in the Peraea, and Trachinae, and Tiberias in lower Galilee. The parallel passage in *A.J.* interprets the expression as 'a city with its toparchy': 'he (Nero) gave him also Livias (Julias) with its fourteen villages' (δίδωcι δὲ καὶ Ἰουλιάδα πόλιν τῆc Περαίαc καὶ κώμαc τὰc περὶ αὐτὴν δεκατέccαραc, 20.159). In other words, the fourteen villages constituted Livias's toparchy. The expression καὶ κώμαc τὰc περὶ αὐτήν is now echoed in No. **65** lines 3–4, in the description of the dependence of the village of Soffathe[...] on the city of Livias in the P[eraia]: Ἰηcοῦc Μαναήμου τ[ῶν ἀπὸ κώμηc ...] Cοφφαθε̣[..].... π̣ε̣ρὶ πόλιν Λιουιάδοc τῆc Π̣[εραίαc].

---

95 See the pioneer study of Isaac, 'Babatha Archive', 67–71.

96 That this was so was already known from Mur **115** (124 CE) lines 2–3 cited below; see Isaac, 'Babatha Archive', 67–71; Oppenheimer, 'Urbanization', 209ff.

97 Stern believed the opposite to be true; see 'Pliny the Elder', 227 (reprint p. 258).

98 P.Yadin 16 (127 CE) lines 15–16: Ἰουδάνου Ἐλαζάρου κώμηc Αἰνγαδδων περὶ Ἱερειχοῦντα τῆc Ἰουδαίαc; on Ein Gedi, see DATE AND PROVENANCE in No. **68**; Cotton, 'Ein Gedi Between the Two Revolts'.

99 No. **69** (130 CE) lines 3–5: ἐν Ἀριcτοβουλιάδι τῆc Ζε̣ι̣φηνῆc ἐξέδετο Cελα.ε[*c*.30 letters] δι̣ὰ Βορκ.. Ἀγλ̣α ἐπ̣ιτρόπ̣[ου] α̣ὐτῆc τοῦδε τοῦ πράγμ̣α̣[τοc *c*. 27 letters] Ακαβαc Μηείρω τῶν ἀπὸ κ̣ώμηc Ἰακείμων τ̣[ῆc Ζειφηνηc]; and see DATE AND PROVENANCE in No. **69**.

100 The same conclusions have independently been reached by Y. Shahar, 'Josephus' Geography of Eretz Israel and its Relation to Talmudic Traditions and Hellenistic and Roman Literature', Ph.D. dissertation, University of Tel Aviv, 1996, 181ff.

101 *B.J.* 3.55–7; cf. 2.567.

Like Josephus, the documents suggest the identity of the dependence of a village on the central village of the toparchy and that of a village on the city to whose territory it belongs. The dependence of Soffathe[...] on the city of Livias in No. **65** lines 3–4 is expressed in the same terms as that of Ein Gedi vis-à-vis Jericho in P.Yadin **16** lines 15–16,[102] Bethbassi vis-à-vis Herodion, Galoda vis-à-vis Akrabatta, Batharda vis-à-vis Gophna in Mur **115** lines 2–3,[103] and Aristoboulias and Yaqim (or Yaqum) *vis-à-vis* Zif in No. **69** lines 3–5[104]

Does the identity of the language imply an identity of function: would it be legitimate to maintain that the central village performed the same functions fulfilled by a city both in respect to its subordinate villages and in respect of the Roman authorities? The functions performed by central villages are unknown.[105] There is no evidence of local officials at the head of these capital villages, nor for centrally appointed officials in charge of the toparchies. And yet it is hard to believe that nothing more than a merely geographical relationship is intended by describing the dependence of a village on a central village, especially since it is described both in Josephus and in the documents in the same terms as that of the *chora* on its *polis*. Furthermore, we know that under the Severi some of these central villages received the status of a *polis*: thus Lydda became Diospolis in 199/200, and Emmaus became Nicopolis in 219 or 220. In 199/200, Beth-Govrin received the status of a *polis* (although we do not know whether it was a capital village) and was renamed Eleutheropolis.[106] The accelerating urbanization of Judaea (now called Syria-Palaestina) resulted in the eventual disappearance of the toparchies and their replacement by *poleis* with their territories. This is the picture conveyed by the fourth century *Onomasticon* of Eusebius.[107] However, if we are right to think that the capital villages achieved a degree of local autonomy and administrative responsibilities already in the first and second centuries, then this urbanization was simply a logical development.[108]

Arabia

In No. **64** Maḥoza is said to be included in the territory of Ẓoʿar: ἐ̣ν̣ Μ̣α̣ω̣ζας τῆ̣ς π̣ερ̣ὶ Ζ[ο]α̣ρ̣ω̣ν (line 3). The hierarchical relationship between Maḥoza and Ẓoʿar is already

---

[102] Ἰουδάνου Ἐλαζάρου κώμης Αἰνγαδδῶν περὶ Ἱερειχοῦντα τῆς Ἰουδαίας.

[103] ἐν Βαιτοβαι̣ϲϲαιαϲ . . . τ̣ο̣παρχείαϲ Ἡρω̣δεί̣ο̣[υ] . . . Ἐ̣λ̣ε̣α̣ῖοϲ Cίμωνοϲ τῶν ἀπὸ κ(ώμηϲ) Γαλωδῶν τῆϲ περὶ Ἀκραβα̣τ̣τῶν οἰκῶν ἐν κώμῃ Βαιτοα̣ρδοιϲ τῆϲ περὶ Γοφνοῖϲ.

[104] Cited above in n. 97.

[105] The central villages have been compared to the μητροκωμίαι ('capital villages') of the Trachonitis—a territory which like the Jewish region lacked cities, cf. Schürer, Vermes, and Millar, *History*, 195f. Again, the responsibilities of the latter towards the κῶμαι are little known; see MacAdam, *Studies*, 82–3; Jones, *Cities*, 284, pleads for the autonomy of the single village in this area; cf. Cotton, 'Administration'.

[106] See Jones, 'Urbanization', 82ff.

[107] Oppenheimer, 'Urbanization', 220ff. For example the village of Zif, which was the capital of its toparchy, to which both Aristoboulias and Yaqim belonged (No. **69** lines 3–5), is now described as 'a κωμή in the Daromas in the territory of Eleutheropolis, near Hebron, eight miles to the south', Eus. *Onomasticon*, p. 92, line 15 (Klostermann).

[108] A recent study of the Egyptian *metropolis* convincingly demonstrates that already in the Julio-Claudian period 'the *metropoleis* were to a significant degree functioning and behaving like the Greek *poleis* of other eastern provinces' (Bowman and Rathbone, 'Cities and Administration', 125). Were the central villages of the toparchies in Judaea the equivalent to these *metropoleis*?

known from the Babatha Archive, where it has the following variants: ἐν Μαω[ζοις τ]ῶν περὶ Ζ[οα]ρα;[109] ἐν Μαωζᾳ περὶ Ζοαραν;[110] ἐ[ν] Μαωζᾳ περὶ Ζοορων;[111] ἐν Μ̣α̣ω̣ζας τῆς πε[ρὶ Ζοα]ρ̣α;[112] ἐν Μαωζᾳ περιμέτρῳ Ζοορων.[113] The phrasing in all its different variations strongly resembles the locutions describing the hierarchical relationship between central villages and subordinate ones in Judaea: ἐν Βαιτο-βαι̣ςςαιας . . . τ̣ο̣παρχείας Ἡρῳδεί̣ο̣[υ] . . . ἀπὸ κ(ώμης) Γαλωδῶν τῆς περὶ Ἀκραβ̣α̣ττῶν οἰκῶν ἐν κώμ̣η̣ Βαιτοα̣ρδοις τῆς περὶ Γοφνοῖς (Mur **115** lines 2–3); κώμης Αἰνγαδδῶν περὶ Ἱερειχοῦντα (P.Yadin **16** line 16); ἐν Ἀριςτοβουλιάδι τῆς Ζε̣ι̣φηνῆς . . . τῶν ἀ̣π̣ὸ κ̣ώμης Ἰακείμων τ̣[ῆς Ζειφηνῆς] (No. **69** lines 3–5). The similarity suggests that Maḥoza was subordinate to Ẓoʿar in much the same way as a village in Judaea was subordinate to the central village which gave its name to the toparchy to which it belonged—even if the term *toparchia* never appears in the archives from the province of Arabia.[114]

Yet, as we now know, Arabia was organized differently. In the section on Judaea it was demonstrated that the province was divided into administrative units, the centre of which could be either a city (*polis*) or a village. In Arabia, on the other hand, there was double subordination, as we already knew from the Babatha Archive: both Maḥoza and Ẓoʿar were subsumed into the territory of Petra, which possessed the legal status of a *polis*:[115] Βαβθα . . . Μαωζηνὴ τῆς Ζοαρηνῆς περιμέτρου Πέτρας (P.Yadin **16** lines 13–14). This double subordination is attested in two of the papyri from the Salome Komaïse Archive: Ϲ̣α̣μ̣μ̣ο̣υ̣ος Ϲ̣ιμων[ο]ς Μαωζηνὸς τῆς Ζοαρηνῆς περιμέτρου Πέτρας (No. **62** frg. a line 12); [ἐν Μαωζᾳ τῆς Ζο]αρηνῆς .[...]...... Πέτραν μητρόπολιν τῆ[ς Ἀραβίας] (No. **65** lines 2–3). The fact that the double subordination is recorded in land declarations (No. **62** and P.Yadin **16**) confers an official status on the subordination. That this was—or came to be—the administrative structure in the whole province of Arabia is now proved by the unpublished P.Bostra 1.[116] The Bostra papyrus dates to 260 CE. It is a petition addressed to a ***beneficiarius*** by a woman called Aurelia Thopheise daughter of Azeizos, from the village Azzeira, which belongs to Aianatis in the territory of Bostra, Augusta Colonia and Metropolis: παρὰ Αὐρηλίας Θοφε̣ι̣ςης Αζειζου κώμης Αζζειρων τῆς Αἰανείτιδος ὁρίου Αὐγουςτοκολ(ωνίας) μητροπόλεως Βόςτρων (lines 2–4). The three concentric circles familiar to us from the southern part of the province are reproduced in its northern part.[117] As in the case of Petra, the vastness of Bostra's territory should be seen to account for the inclusion of villages in a subdivision of the city's territory.

---

109 P.Yadin **5** frg. a, col. i, lines 4–5.

110 P.Yadin **14** line 20; **15** line 3 = lines 16–17; **17** lines 2–3 = lines 19–20; **18** line 3 = line 32.

111 P.Yadin **25** line 28 = line 64.

112 P.Yadin **19** lines 10–11.

113 P.Yadin **20** line 4 = lines 22–23; **21** lines 5–6; **22** lines 5–6; **26** line 18; **27** lines 3–4.

114 As Lewis reminds us in 'Babatha Archive', 244; however, one notes that it is also absent in No. **69**, as well as in two out of three dependencies described in Mur **115**, all quoted above.

115 The evidence for its status as a *polis* is P.Yadin **12** lines 1–2 (= lines 4–5; 124 CE): ἐγγεγραμμένον καὶ ἀντιβεβλημένον κεφαλαίου ἑνὸς ἀπὸ ἄκτων βουλῆς Πετραίων τῆς μητροπόλεως.

116 I am much obliged to J. Gascou for allowing me to see the text and the commentary on it in advance of publication.

117 The editors regard Aianatis as a name of a district rather than as that of a village. In that case, the district of Aianatis, unlike that of Ẓoʿar, is not named after its capital village.

The Census of 127

We have now two land declarations (P.Yadin **16** and No. **62**) and the conclusion of another (No. **61**) from the census of 127 in the province of Arabia. The census was conducted by the governor of the province, L. Aninius Sextius Florentinus. It must have lasted over six months since the subscription in No. **61** is dated to 25 April[118] whereas Sammouos son of Shimʿon's declaration (No. **62**) was submitted on 4 or 11 December, and Babatha's declaration (P.Yadin **16**) was submitted on 2 December and subscribed on 4 December.[119] It could, however, have begun earlier and ended later. There are good reasons to believe that this was the first census conducted in Arabia since its annexation in 106.[120] It is worth noting the use of local units of measurements in the land declarations, the evaluation of the rate of taxation in the old Nabataean monetary unit—the *melaina*, as well as the presence in these documents of the Nabataean royal tax—the *stephnikon*.[121]

Jewish Law and Society

The contribution of the growing corpus of documentary texts from the Judaean Desert to the proper understanding of legal and social aspects of Jewish society in the Roman provinces of Judaea and Arabia in the first half of the second century CE calls for a special study. Here I shall limit myself to the conclusions we may draw from the use of the Greek language, Greek diplomatics, and non-Jewish law by non-Hellenized or semi-Hellenized Jews.

On the whole it seems that the use of Greek should be explained by the desire to make the documents valid and enforceable in a Greek-speaking court, such as that of the governor of the province, or those of the Greek *poleis* in the area. A further reason could be the need to deposit the deeds in public archives, so that they could later be produced in court as evidence.[122] Indeed, we have several references in the Greek documents to the registration in public archives (διὰ δημοσίων) of property located in Ein Gedi,[123] and of date groves located in Maḥoza (ἐν τ̣ῇ̣ ἀπ̣[ο]γ̣ραφῇ̣).[124] That Jews registered their contracts with the public authorities is neither unknown nor surprising.

[118] That the year must be 127 is argued in No. **61** DATE AND PROVENANCE.

[119] See No. **61** DATE AND PROVENANCE.

[120] See above on the provincial year in Arabia. The case for assuming that the census followed immediately upon the creation of a province is far from proven; see, in detail, Cotton, 'Ἡ νέα ἐπαρχεία Ἀραβία'.

[121] See in detail Weiser and Cotton, 'Gebt dem Kaiser, was des Kaisers ist'; Isaac, 'Tax Collection', 264, thinks this was the third census.

[122] Ạs was the case in Egypt, where public archives were used to deposit private documents; see Cockle, 'Archives', 116; Burkhalter, 'Archives'; see now P.Euphr. 6 (249 CE, Greek) lines 29–31 (= P.Euphr. 7 lines 24–26): Τούτων ἐγένετο ἀντιcύνγραφα δύο ὧν τὸ ἕτερον καταχωριcθήcεται ἐν τοῖc ἐνταῦθα δημοcί[οι]c ἀρχείοιc.

[123] ὅταν δὲ παρα̣νγείλει Cελα‹μ›ψιοῦc τῷ αὐτῷ Ἰούδατι, τευχίζ{ζ}ει αὐτὴν διὰ δημοcίων, P.Yadin **19** lines 25–27; τ̣α̣υτὴν δὲ τὴν αὐλὴν ὅπου ἂν βουληθῇc τευχίcω co[ι] δ̣ι̣ὰ δημοcίων, coῦ διδούcηc τὸ ἀνάλωμα, P.Yadin **20** lines 34–36; see Cotton, 'Courtyard(s)'.

[124] ἀπεγράψατο Ἰούδαc Ἐλεαζάρ̣ο̣[υ Χθουcίωνοc] ἀ̣π̣ο̣γ̣ενμένου cου ἀνὴρ ἐπ' ὀνόματόc cου ἐν τ̣ῇ̣ ἀπ̣[ο]γ̣ραφῇ̣ κήπουc φοινικῶνοc ἐν Μαωζα̣, P.Yadin **24** lines 4–6; on the ἀπογραφή, see Cotton, 'Deeds of Gift'.

We hear in the rabbinic sources of these 'non-Jewish archives'—ערכאות הגויים—in which the term ערכאות is simply a transliteration of the Greek word ἀρχεῖα.[125]

It is a remarkable fact that no court, Jewish or non-Jewish, other than that of the Roman governor of Arabia, is mentioned in any of the documents from the Judaean Desert, a great many of which, as already pointed out, are legal documents. We should not therefore conclude, however, that the governor's court was the only court in operation in a Roman province. Nonetheless, the absence of any reference to other courts is disturbing, especially in view of the host of references in rabbinic sources to courts of different sizes in towns and villages.[126]

The validity of contracts made in Greek, and the use of gentile witnesses, courts, and archives, are the subject of several discussions in rabbinic sources. Sometimes such activities are explicitly forbidden. The harsh language employed by the rabbis in the prohibition on using gentile courts may indicate that the Jews did in fact use them: no less is implied when the rabbis used conciliatory language and allowed practices which were in common use to have validity under Jewish law.[127]

We may assume that these non-Hellenized or semi-Hellenized Jews chose to write their contracts in Greek either because of the absence of Jewish courts and archives using Aramaic as the official language in the places mentioned in the papyri, or out of the desire to leave open their option to go to the court of their choice. That such considerations were in operation is apparent in documents which use a very faulty version of the Greek language (e.g. No. **64**, which can be shown to be almost certainly a literal translation from Aramaic).[128]

However, what we witness in the Greek texts from the Judaean Desert is not merely the use of Greek and Greek diplomatics by non-Hellenized or semi-Hellenized Jews, but the absence of anything which would mark them as Jewish apart from the identity of the parties as disclosed by their names. Thus we find deeds of sale, renunciations of claims, land registrations, receipts, mortgages, promissory notes, deeds of gift, and even marriage contracts—all of which bear a striking resemblance to their Egyptian counterparts, thereby revealing the remarkable degree of integration of Jewish society into its environment.

True, what makes a contract Jewish is not its language, nor even the laws and customs reflected in it. Some of the provisions we find in the documents existed among Jews as well as among non-Jews long before Jewish civil law—as we have it in the tannaitic sources—was codified.[129] The halakha was not created *in vacuo*, but absorbed many local, or, better, regional traditions which are reflected in its rules. Once they

---

[125] Cf. P.Dura 28 (243 CE, Syriac) lines 18–20 for the transcription of ἀρχεῖον: *'rkywn*; cf. *m. Git.* 1.5: 'Any deed is valid that is registered in the registries of the gentiles (ערכאות הגויים), although witnessed by gentiles, except a deed of divorce or a deed of emancipation. R. Shimʿon [*c*.130–160] says: "These, too, are valid; they were mentioned [as invalid] only when they were prepared by unauthorized persons (נעשׂו בהדיוט)"'.

[126] Schürer, Vermes, and Millar, *History*, 2:184–8; Alon, *Jews in Their Land*, 1:553–7; Gulak, *Towards a Study*, 54ff.; less skeptical is Safrai, *Jewish Community*, 76ff; but see Misgav, 'Jewish Courts', 17ff.

[127] See Cotton, 'Rabbis'.

[128] See INTRODUCTION to No. **64**.

[129] For an appreciation of the poly-ethnic society of Aramaic-speaking people into which these documents fit—a society whose cultural, social, and legal life absorbed many and various elements from different sources, only one of which was Hellenism, see Wasserstein, 'Marriage Contract', 121ff.; idem, 'Non-Hellenized Jews'.

received halakhic sanction, they could be described as Jewish, but not before. In the period attested in the documents from the Judaean Desert—after the destruction of the Temple in 70 and before the end of the Bar Kokhba Revolt in 135—Jewish civil law was in the process of being created in the rabbinic schools, but had yet to receive its final shape—let alone the authority it was to acquire after its formal redaction at the end of the second century CE. Thus, to say that Jews wrote 'non-Jewish' contracts is to say that the legal usage current in these contracts is not always in harmony with what eventually came to be normative Jewish law. This has been argued for various branches of personal law applied in the documents, namely marriage law,[130] the law of succession,[131] and the law of guardianship.[132] It is sometimes true of contract law as well.[133] However, even when the provisions in the documents do resemble what came to be normative Jewish law, we cannot assume without further proof that what we are witnessing is the influence of Jewish law on the documents rather than the reverse: the halakha adopted the legal usage of the documents, which, in their turn, reflect the legal usage of the environment. The diversity and fluidity manifested in the documents from the Judaean Desert, the incursion of different legal systems sometimes, but not always, overlapping with what came to be halakhic law, are the best evidence we have for the state of Jewish law and the authority exercised by the rabbis at the time.

It could be claimed that the evidence of the documents is distorted, that the Jews acting in them are not representative of Jewish society as a whole at the time, and consequently, that it would be illegitimate to rely on them in order to evaluate the state of Jewish law and the authority exercised by the rabbis at this time. These objections can be met, and refuted, by the following considerations:

1. The Jews represented in the documents from the Judaean Desert are not a fringe group, even if the corpus—whose origin is the direct result of the upheaval resulting from the outbreak of the Bar Kokhba Revolt—is limited both in place (to those parts of Judaea and the province of Arabia that were near the caves) and in time (to the period 70–135 CE). These are Jews from villages as scattered as Maḥoza and Mazraʿa in the southern part of the Dead Sea area in the province of Arabia, Soffathe[...] in the Peraea in Transjordan, which belonged to the province of Judaea, Ein Gedi near the Dead Sea, Yaqim (or Yaqum) and Aristoboulias in the area southeast of Hebron, Bethbassi near Herodium, Galoda in eastern Samaria and Batharda in southern Samaria. These Jews are indeed representative of Jewish society as a whole in the period under discussion. The documents present a faithful picture of the realities of life at the time that they were written.

2. Any notion of a distinction between Jews from the province of Arabia and those from Judaea should be dispelled: these areas were very close to each other (a day's walk, or two days at most, between the furthest destinations), and the borders had very

---

130 See INTRODUCTION to No. **65** and MARRIAGE PRACTICES in No. **69**; Wasserstein, 'Marriage Contract', 105ff.; cf. Cotton, 'Rabbis'.

131 See INTRODUCTION to No. **64**; Cotton and Greenfield, 'Babatha's Property'; Cotton, 'Deeds of Gift'.

132 Cotton, 'Guardianship'.

133 Lapin, 'Early Rabbinic Civil Law', using as a test case the Mishnaic tractate *Baba Meṣiʿa*, is able to show that Mishnaic economic and contract law is not reflected in the literature of the Second Temple Period, nor in the documents which postdate the destruction of the Second Temple.

little inhibiting effect on movement. The official names, Arabia, Judaea and Syria-Palaestina, represent artificial divisions which did not seem to matter significantly. The archives amply demonstrate that the Jews living in Arabia and the Jews living in the province of Judaea belonged to a single Jewish society whose internal ties overrode provincial boundaries: they disregarded the provincial boundaries in their residence, marriages, and property holdings.[134]

3. The Jews represented in these documents come from densely populated Jewish areas, from the heartland of the Bar Kokhba Revolt, a religious and national movement. Many of the Greek documents were written close to the time when the revolt broke out—a revolt which was carefully prepared some years in advance. In fact, the very presence of their documents in the caves may demonstrate their owners' participation in the revolt. The writers of these documents cannot and should not be regarded as assimilated Jews.[135]

Conclusion

These last comments on Jewish law and society as reflected in the Greek documentary texts from the Judaean Desert are preliminary conclusions which sum up, for the reader's convenience, the author's observations in the commentaries to the individual documents. Once the entire documentary corpus from the Judaean Desert in the various languages has received its final publication, the time will be ripe for a more complete and balanced overview of the relationship between the documentary evidence and the rabbinic sources. However, the rabbinic sources are not the only background against which these documents should be assessed; one should not lose sight of the general environment in which they were written, namely the Roman Near East. Throughout the commentary parallels have been drawn between the Greek documents published here and similar documents written elsewhere in the Roman Near East. This approach is based on a firmly held belief that these papyri, although written by Jews, must be seen in the context of the papyrological evidence from the Roman Near East as a whole (including Egypt).[136] Although written in Greek, they hardly constitute evidence for the Hellenization of their writers. What they do show, though, is that Jewish society, as reflected in them, is part of a Near Eastern civilization which as a whole had absorbed the impact of Hellenism over the centuries, and yet retained its own multifarious culture, as formulated by A. Wasserstein:

---

[134] See Cotton, 'Ein Gedi Between the Two Revolts'.

[135] See Cotton, 'Cancelled Marriage Contract', 85f.

[136] For a general survey (excluding Egyptian papyrology) see Cotton, Cockle and Millar, 'Papyrology'.

published here and similar documents written elsewhere in the Roman Near East. This approach is based on a firmly held belief that these papyri, although written by Jews, must be seen in the context of the papyrological evidence from the Roman Near East as a whole (including Egypt).[136] Although written in Greek, they hardly constitute evidence for the Hellenization of their writers. What they do show, though, is that Jewish society, as reflected in them, is part of a Near Eastern civilization which as a whole had absorbed the impact of Hellenism over the centuries, and yet retained its own multifarious culture, as formulated by A. Wasserstein:

[136] For a general survey (excluding Egyptian papyrology) see Cotton, Cockle and Millar, 'Papyrology'.

Introduction to the Archive of Salome Komaïse Daughter of Levi

THE archive consists of seven documents: Nos. **12** (Aramaic), **60**, **61**, **62**, **63**, **64**, and **65** (all six in Greek).[1] Four documents and a fragment of a fifth document (No. **61** frg. b) were among the so-called Seiyâl collection: Nos. **60**, **61** frg. b, and **63** were formerly labelled XḤev/Se gr **5**, having all been assigned to the same plate in the Rockefeller Museum (Mus. Inv. 866; see Pl. XXXI); No. **64** was formerly XḤev/Se gr **1** (Mus. Inv. 869). To these we should add the Aramaic XḤev/Se ar **12** (Mus. Inv. 736). The other two documents, Nos. **62** and **65**, and three fragments of No. **61** (frgs. a, c, and d), came from other sources. No. **61** frgs. a, c, and d and No. **62** were found among Yigael Yadin's papers. The first was Mus. Inv. 3001 in the Shrine of the Book and was published in 1991 by H. M. Cotton.[2] Lines 1–20 of No. **62**, formerly known as XḤev/Se gr **7**, were published in 1988 by N. Lewis.[3] Finally, No. **65** was found in the 'Cave of Letters' in Naḥal Ḥever[4] and was published in 1989, together with the Greek part of the Babatha Archive, as P.Yadin **37**.[5] As pointed out in the GENERAL INTRODUCTION, the unity of this archive is the best proof that the 'Cave of Letters' in Naḥal Ḥever is the source of all the documents which belong to the archive.

The Archive of Salome Komaïse daughter of Levi shares many features with the Babatha Archive and complements in many respects that much larger archive. Like the Babatha Archive, this archive, too, revolves around the affairs of a Jewish family from Maḥoza,[6] a village in what used to be the Nabataean Kingdom and in 106 became the Roman province of Arabia. The Babatha Archive begins in 94 CE, before the annexation of the Nabataean Kingdom, and concludes in August 132, probably after the outbreak of the Bar Kokhba Revolt in Judaea.[7] The Salome Komaïse Archive covers the much shorter period from the end of January 125 to August 131. The presence of Nabataeans as witnesses (on the verso of Nos. **62** and **64**) and subscribers (No. **61** line 4) to the documents in the Salome Komaïse Archive demonstrates the

---

[1] Perhaps eight: a daughter of Levi (ברת לוי) is mentioned in No. **32** , and the date is given as 'year eight' which is likely to refer to the era of the province of Arabia, i.e. 22 March 113 to 21 March 114. Could No. **32** and, therefore, also 4Q**359** (see GENERAL INTRODUCTION) be part of the Archive of Salome Komaïse daughter of Levi? A serious objection is that the letters preceding ברת לוי cannot be made to yield the name Salome (שלם). Furthermore, the inclusion of this document in the archive would create a gap of more than twenty years between this document and the earliest document in the archive, but this is a much weaker objection.

[2] Cotton, 'Fragments'.

[3] Lewis, 'Jewish Landowner', 132–7.

[4] See Yadin, 'Expedition D—Cave of Letters', 231; Lewis, *Documents*, 3.

[5] Lewis, *Documents*, 130–33.

[6] On Maḥoza, see below.

[7] Millar, *Roman Near East*, 547.

same easy intercourse between Jews and Nabataeans that we witness in the Babatha Archive.[8] The Jews of the archives owned houses and orchards in the province of Arabia. Their successful integration into the Nabataean environment is emphasized by their use of non-Jewish legal instruments in their dealings with each other. In the two archives there are deeds of sale, petitions, land registrations, receipts, mortgages, promissory notes, and even marriage contracts—all bearing a striking resemblance to their Egyptian counterparts.[9] The frequent appeals in the Babatha Archive to the Roman governor, and the latter's accessibility and involvement in legal affairs between Jews,[10] reveals an aspect of Roman-Jewish relations not often in evidence.

All this makes the flight of the Jews from Arabia and their participation in the Bar Kokhba Revolt[11] all the more intriguing. It is true that the archives amply demonstrate that the Jews living in Arabia and in the province of Judaea belonged to a single Jewish society whose internal ties overrode provincial boundaries: these provincial boundaries were disregarded in their residence, marriages, and property holdings.[12] Close ties seem to have existed between Ein Gedi and Maḥoza: people from Ein Gedi reside in Maḥoza,[13] marry there,[14] and own property in both places.[15] But Ein Gedi was not the only place in Judaea to have ties with the Jews of Maḥoza: Salome Komaïse's second husband, Yeshuʿa son of Menahem, comes from the village of Soffathe[...] in the Peraea, which is part of the province of Judaea, albeit located in Transjordan (No. **65** line 4).

Like Babatha and her family, Salome Komaïse left her home in Arabia with her precious documents and probably perished in the Bar Kokhba Revolt. Neither Babatha nor Salome Komaïse retrieved their documents. The two women must have known each other since their families' properties were abutted by the same neighbours,[16] and the same witnesses signed their documents.[17]

Some external resemblances between the two archives should be pointed out: four of the documents in the Salome Komaïse Archive (Nos. **61**, **62**, **64**, and **65**)[18] are double

---

[8] The Nabataean ʿAbdobdas son of Illouthas is nominated by the *boulē* of the city of Petra as one of the two guardians of Babatha's orphaned child (P.Yadin **12**, 124 CE); Nabataeans serve as witnesses to many of the documents in the archive; cf. Bowersock, *Roman Arabia*, 75.

[9] See Wasserstein, 'Marriage Contract', 105ff.; Cotton, 'Guardianship'; Cotton, 'The Rabbis'; and MARRIAGE PRACTICES in No. **69**.

[10] Cotton, 'Guardianship', 106ff.

[11] As is suggested by the presence of their documents in the caves of Naḥal Ḥever.

[12] See Cotton, 'Cancelled Marriage Contract', 85–6 ('Appendix 1: The Jews of Arabia'), with Lewis, 'In the World of P.Yadin'.

[13] Note the frequent occurrence in the Babatha Archive of the expression 'an Ein-Gedian residing here', meaning Maḥoza, e.g. P.Yadin **18** lines 5–6 = lines 36–37; or 'an Ein-Gedian residing in Maḥoza', e.g. P.Yadin **19** lines 11–12.

[14] Judah son of Eleazar Khthousion from Ein Gedi married Babatha (P.Yadin **10**).

[15] See Cotton, 'Courtyard(s)' and 'Ein Gedi between the Two Revolts'.

[16] See COMMENTS on No. **64** line 11 = lines 32–33.

[17] See COMMENTS on No. **64** lines 44 and 47.

[18] Only the inner text of No. **65** survives; what remains of No. **61** is part of what was originally a double document.

documents.[19] The archive is trilingual: six documents are written in Greek and one in Aramaic (No. **12**). One of the Greek documents has an Aramaic subscription (No. **60** line 13), and both Aramaic and Nabataean are represented by signatures on the *verso* of Nos. **62** and **64**.

There is a certain inaccuracy in describing this archive as belonging to Salome Komaïse daughter of Levi: Nos. **60** and **62** belong to Sammouos son of Shimʿon, who, I believe, is to be identified as Salome Komaïse's first husband, mentioned in No. **63** line 2. No. **61** belongs to Salome's brother, who is described as dead in No. **63**; No. **63**, in its turn, was probably kept by the mother, Salome Grapte (or Gropte), in whose favour it had been made. Thus, only Nos. **64**, **12**, and **65** can rightly be claimed to belong to Salome Komaïse daughter of Levi, herself. Nevertheless, the documents belong to the same family, centred on the figure of Salome. Furthermore, one must remember that, unlike the Babatha Archive, these documents were not discovered in the course of a controlled archaeological excavation, and therefore we do not know whether they were found bundled together.[20]

Family Tree of Salome Komaïse Daughter of Levi

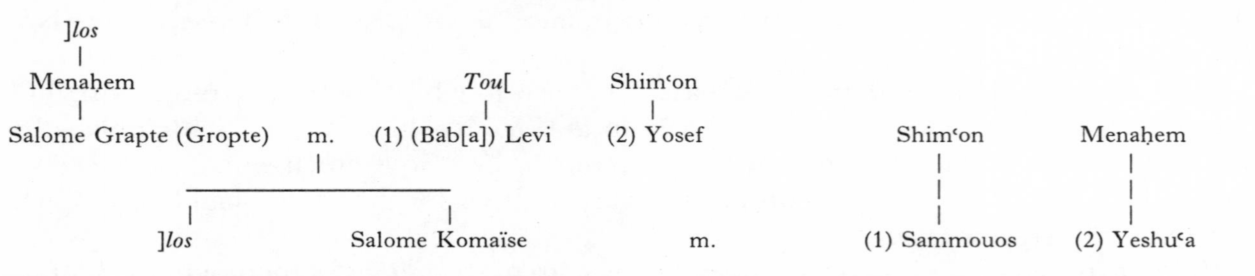

Contents of the Archive

The first document in the archive, No. **60**, is a receipt for tax (or rent) from 29 January 125. The addressee of the receipt, Menaḥem son of Iohannes, who also figures as one of the abutters to the family's property (No. **64** line 15 = lines 35–36), does not seem to be related to the family. The inclusion of of No. **60** in the archive is based on the identification of Sammouos son of Shimʿon, the middleman between the addressee of No. **60**, Menaḥem son of Iohannes, and the tax (or rent) collectors (No. **60** line 8), as Salome Komaïse's first husband of No. **63** line 2 ([Ϲαμμουο]ụ Ϲιμωνοϲ ἀνδρὸϲ α[ὐτῆ]ϲ). Admittedly, the restoration of the name Sammouos in No. **63** line 2 is somewhat problematic, since only the the last *upsilon* of Ϲαμμουου remains, and Shimʿon, the patronym, is a common name. Nevertheless, this would explain the presence of No. **60**, together with two other documents which belong to family

[19] See GENERAL INTRODUCTION and Lewis, *Documents*, 6ff.

[20] See Yadin, 'Expedition D—Cave of Letters', 231ff. for the circumstances in which the Babatha Archive was found.

members of Salome Komaïse, on the same plate (Mus. Inv. 866) in the Rockefeller Museum:[21] all three documents—nos. **60**, **61** (frg. b), and **63**—must have been found in the same place, brought to the Rockefeller Museum at the same time, and, therefore, put in the same plate.[22] Sammouos son of Shimʿon kept the receipt in order to prove his good faith, namely that he had given the money entrusted to him by Menaḥem son of Iohannes to the tax (or rent) collectors. Sammouos son of Shimʿon is also one of the abutters to the half courtyard in No. **64** of 9 November 129 (line 14 = line 35). Nothing is said there about his relations to Salome Komaïse, but this does not signify that the marriage had come to an end by that date, since there was no reason to refer to his relations to Salome in such a context (see below on No. **65**).

The next document which belongs to the family is No. **61**, a conclusion to a land declaration from the census of 127 held in Arabia by the Roman governor, Titus Aninius Sextius Florentinus.[23] The land declaration was submitted to the Roman authorities by Salome Komaïse's brother, whose name is lost. He does not write the subscription to his land declaration with his own hand, but uses the *chirocrista* (χειροχρήϲτηϲ), Onainos son of Saʿadalos (see No. **61** lines 3–4). The use of the *chirocrista*—the equivalent of the Egyptian ὑπογραφεύϲ,[24] and not of a guardian, proves that this was a case of illiteracy, rather than of minority.[25] The land declaration was subscribed by the Roman authorities on 25 April 127, and must, therefore, have been submitted by Salome's brother a few days before.[26] Thus the brother was still alive towards the end of April 127.

No. **62** is Sammouos son of Shimʿon's land declaration of 4 or 11 December 127, submitted in the same census, some seven months after the land declaration of Salome Komaïse's brother (No. **61**). Again, the inclusion of No. **62** in the archive is based on the identification of the declarant, Sammouos son of Shimʿon, as Salome Komaïse's first husband (see above, on No. **60**).

The next document in the archive, No. **63**, dated only by the year 127, reveals that Salome Komaïse's brother, the declarant of No. **61** (which is dated to 25 April 127), died before the year was out. This document is a deed of renunciation by Salome Komaïse in favour of her mother Salome Grapte (Gropte) regarding the properties left by Levi, her father, as well as those left by her brother. Thus we discover that Levi, the father, was also dead by the time the deed was written. I assume that the man to whom Salome Komaïse was married at that time and who serves as her guardian in the deed (No. **63** lines 1–2), is no other than Sammouos son of Shimʿon of Nos. **60** and **62**.

Two years later, on 9 November 129, the mother, Salome Grapte (Gropte), who in the meantime has married a man called Yosef son of Shimʿon, writes a deed of gift, No. **64**, in which she bestows on her daughter, Salome Komaïse, a date grove and half a courtyard including half of the rooms and the upper-storey rooms therein.

---

21 No. **61** belongs to her brother, and No. **63** belongs to her mother.

22 See GENERAL INTRODUCTION.

23 For the census, see INTRODUCTION to No. **61**.

24 For the role of the ὑπογραφεύϲ, see Youtie, 'ΥΠΟΓΡΑΦΕΥϹ'.

25 See Cotton, 'Subscriptions'.

26 As can be learnt from Babatha's land declaration, submitted on 2 December 127, and subscribed on 4 December (P.Yadin **16** line 9 and lines 37–8).

The next we hear of Salome Komaïse is on 30 January 131, in No. **12**, a receipt for dates in Aramaic which she receives from tax (or rent) collectors.

The last document from this archive is No. **65**, dated to 7 August 131. It is Salome Komaïse's marriage contract to her second husband, Yeshu'a son of Menaḥem, with whom she had been living in an unwritten marriage until then. Death or divorce will have terminated her marriage to Sammouos son of Shim'on, to whom she was still married after late April 127 (see above on No. **63**). If the cause was death, then it must have occurred sometime after 9 November 129, since Sammouos is still alive in No. **64**, where he is mentioned as one of the abutters to the half courtyard (line 14 = line 35). Divorce is less likely than death to be the cause for the termination of Salome's first marriage, since two of Sammouos's documents, Nos. **60** and **62**, were found together with the rest of her archive.

Personal Names

Several of the names that appear in these documents call for some note.

Levi was the father of Salome Komaïse and husband of Salome Grapte (Gropte); he was dead by 127 CE. His name is transliterated in the Greek documents variously, as Λειουου, No. **61** line 2; Ληο̣υ̣ε̣ι̣ο̣υ, No. **64** line 5 = line 24, and Ληουει—also the genitive—in No. **63** lines 1, 4, 8. In the Aramaic No. **12**, it occurs twice: שלם ברת לוי (line 1) and לוי אבוך (lines 6–7). בב before the name Levi in No. **12** line 6 could be a nickname. It does not occur together with Levi's name in any of the Greek documents. On the name Baba, see No. **64** ad lines 11 and 32–33.

An undated list of names from Naḥal Se'elim (34Se **5**) has 'Ιηcουc Ληουι̣ ἀδελφόc, 'Yeshuʿa son of Levi, brother'.[27]

The name Levi is attested in several Aramaic documents from the Judaean Desert. Eleazar son of Levi (אלעזר בר לוי) appears in a deed of sale, dated to the 14th of Iyyar (April/May), third year of the Bar Kokhba Revolt, i.e. 134 or 135 (No. **7** line 2). A deed of loan from Abi'or Cave, near Jericho, dated by the script to the end of the first century CE or to the beginning of the second, mentions a Naḥonia son of *the* Levi (נחו[נ]יא בר לויא).[28] Yehoḥanan son of Levi (יהוחנן בר לוי) is mentioned in Mur **74,** dated by the editor to before the first revolt.[29] Also from the first century (66–73/4 CE) is an ostracon from Masada bearing the words 'son of Levi' (בר לוי) and instructions for supplying bread.[30]

Salome, Cαλωμη, is the name of both mother and daughter. Cαλωμη renders the Hebrew/Aramaic name שלם/שלום—the most common female name at the time.[31] In the Aramaic document from her archive, No. **12** (as well as in the Greek No. **63**), only the

---

[27] Lifshitz, 'Greek Documents', 55, line 2. Josephus renders the name in Greek Ληιου (e.g. *B.J.* 2.575; 4.85); Λευιc (e.g. *B.J.* 2.642).

[28] Eshel and Eshel, 'Fragments', 278, line 4. See Naveh, *Stone and Mosaic*, nos. 1; 3; 80; 82; 104.

[29] The same date, according to the editor, as that of a list of names found on an ossuary lid at Bethphage, where the name Levi is written twice; see Milik, 'Couvercle', 78, lines 23, 24.

[30] Yadin and Naveh, *Masada* I, no. 577. See Rosenthal, 'Giv'at ha-Mivtar', 365–7, n. 128.

[31] See Ilan, 'Notes', 191–2; 198–9.

Γροπτη in No. **64**) are likely to have distinguished the homonymous mother and daughter from each other.[32] The name Grapte is attested in Josephus *B.J.* 4.567, as a relative of Izates King of Adiabene. The names Komaïse and Gropte are not otherwise attested, so far as I know.

Sammouos, שמוע, is not a common name. It is attested several times in the Aramaic documents from Elephantine: Kraeling 10 (= Porten and Yardeni, *TAD* II B3.11) line 19: שמוע בר פלוליה; Cowley 61–63 (= Porten and Yardeni, *TAD* II C3.13) line 59: שמוע; Cowley 22 (= Porten and Yardeni, *TAD* II C3.15) line 44: שמוע בר שלם; Cowley 12 (= Porten and Yardeni, *TAD* II C4.4) line 5: שמוע בר חגי. There is a Sammouos son of Menaḥem, שמוע בר מנחם, in the Babatha Archive (P.Yadin **14** lines 37, 46; P.Yadin **21** lines 17–18, 35).

The other names in the archive—Shimʿon, Menaḥem, Yosef, and Yeshuʿa—are among the most common Jewish names of the period. They occur in the Babatha Archive as well.

Maḥoza or Maḥoz ʿEglatain

Μαωζα of the Greek documents of the Salome Komaïse Archive is identical with Maḥoz ʿEglatain (מחוז עגלתין) of the Nabataean and Aramaic documents of the Babatha Archive.[33] Maḥoz ʿEglatain, 'the port (or city) of ʿEglatain', is sometimes abbreviated to Maḥoza (מחוזא),[34] i.e. 'the Port' or 'the City' by a process of *antonomasia*, as e.g. in *urbs Roma* becoming *Urbs*; *Glil Goyim* becoming *HaGalil* (Galilee), Portus Traiani becoming Portus.[35] Μαωζα of the Greek documents reproduces the Aramaic מחוזא. In the Greek name, the Aramaic definite article (i.e. the suffix, *'alep*) has become part of the name, and is no longer felt to be the definite article. Hence Μαωζα rather than ὁ Μαωζ.[36] In other words, the Greek transliterates the Aramaic rather than translates it.[37]

---

[32] See Hachlili, 'Names', 195.

[33] There is a full discussion in Cotton and Greenfield, 'Babatha's Patria'. For Maḥoz ʿEglatain, see XḤev/Se nab **1** (59–69 CE) frg. a. line 2 and frg. c, line 5, in Starcky, 'Contrat Nabatéen', 163–5. In A. Yardeni's new reconstruction of the text (kindly shown to me in advance of publication) these are now lines 12 and 15 respectively. Maḥoz ʿEglatain occurs also in P.Yadin **2** (99 CE) lines 2–3 = lines 20, 22; P.Yadin **3** (99 CE) lines 22–24; P.Yadin **6** (119 CE) line 4; P.Yadin **7** (120 CE) line 2 = line 32. See also XḤev/Ṣe nab **2** (c. 100? CE) lines 4–5 (interpreted for me by A. Yardeni), which perhaps does not belong to the Babatha Archive. Apart from P.Yadin **7**, all the papyri just cited are as yet unpublished. For P.Yadin **7**, see Yadin, Greenfield, and Yardeni, 'Deed of Gift'.

[34] Maḥoza occurs only once in the Aramaic and Nabataean documents—in P.Yadin **7** line 3 = line 33—but the context makes it clear that it is the equivalent of Maḥoz ʿEglatain; see Cotton and Greenfield, 'Babatha's Patria', 128–9.

[35] The suffix in Maḥoza (*ʾalep*) proves that Maḥoz ʿEglatain is the original name and not Maḥoz. In other words, ʿEglatain in the construct state was not added later in order to disinguish Maḥoz from another place called Maḥoz in another district, see Elizur, 'Place Names'.

[36] In the Greek documents, Μαωζα, as pointed out by Lewis (*Documents*, 20), is usually 'treated as a feminine singular', apart from P.Yadin **5**, where 'it is treated as a neuter plural', and P.Yadin **16** where 'it appears in both forms'.

[37] Cf. Βαγαλγαλα in P.Yadin **16** line 25, which renders בגלגלא. The latter means literally 'in the Galgala': the preposition 'in' (*bet*), as well as the definite article 'the' (the suffix *'alep*) have become part of the name in Greek; see Lewis, *Documents*, 70.

Maḥoza was a village, κώμη, as we learn from P.Yadin **12** (124 CE) lines 6–7.[38] Four out of the six Greek documents of the archive were written in Maḥoza (No. **60** line 6; No. **63** line 4;[39] No. **64** line 3; No. **65** lines 2–3).[40]

The village of Maḥoza/Maḥoz ᶜEglatain seems to have been composed of several units.[41] One of these was Galgala. In the Nabataean document P.Yadin **3** of 99 CE, Babatha's father buys from a Nabataean woman called ʾAbiᶜadan a date grove said to be situated in Galgala in Maḥoz ᶜEglatain: גנת תמריא די לאביעדן דא די מתקריה גה..א די בגלגלא די במחוז עגלתין, lines 23–24 = lines 2–3.[42] Again, among the date groves which Babatha declared in the census of 127 CE, there was one called 'Bagalgala', i.e. 'in the Galgala',[43] explicitly stated to be within the territory of Maḥoza: κῆπον φοινικῶνος ἐν ὁρίοις Μαωζων λεγόμενον Βαγαλγαλα, P.Yadin **16** lines 24–25. However, Galgala was not the only unit located in Maḥoza. In one of Bar Kokhba's Hebrew contracts, two men who now reside in Ein Gedi are said to come originally from the Luḥit in Maḥoz ᶜEglatain: 'Teḥinnah son of Simeon and Alma son of Judah both of the Luḥit in Maḥoz ᶜEglatain now resident in En-gedi' (P.Yadin **44**, 134 CE).[44] I suspect that Βηθφααραια (Bethphaaraia) of P.Yadin **16** line 30 may be another unit of Maḥoza.[45] What kind of village is Maḥoza/Maḥoz ᶜEglatain which contains both Galgala and Luḥit, and perhaps other units as well? It could be suggested that Maḥoza/Maḥoz ᶜEglatain was an important regional centre, or an agglomeration of once independent villages. But this explanation is somewhat hard to reconcile with Maḥoza/Maḥoz ᶜEglatain's obvious inferiority vis-à-vis Zoᶜar, in whose territory it is subsumed.[46]

The exact location of Maḥoza remains a puzzle. We know that it was included in the territory of Ẓoᶜar, which in its turn was part of the administrative district of the city of Petra.[47] Whether *maḥoz* means 'a port' or 'a city',[48] Maḥoza/Maḥoz ᶜEglatain lay on the

---

[38] Ἰαccούου Ἰουδαίου υἱοῦ Ἰαccούου κώμηc Μαωζα.

[39] Note, though, that Maḥoza is not explicitly named as the place of writing in No. **63** line 4, but see COMMENTS there on the expression [πάντεc Μα]ωζηνοι, and cf. No. **64** lines 5–6 = line 25: πάντεc οἰκοῦντες [ἐ]ν Μαωζαc, following the explicit ἐ̣ν̣ Μ̣α̣ω̣ζαc in line 4. There is no place name in the Aramaic document which belongs to this archive (No. **12**), but it is likely to have been written in Maḥoza.

[40] The two other documents, Nos. **61** and **62**, both land declarations, were written in the city of Rabbath-Moab.

[41] Cf. Kutscher, 'Ugaritica Marginalia', 11–13.

[42] Cf. P.Yadin **2**, of the same year, line 3 = line 22. This same date grove reappears in Babatha's land declaration of 127 CE, P.Yadin **16**: there is no doubt that it is one of the first two groves mentioned in P.Yadin **16**, since it is abutted by the same properties which abutted the date grove sold in P.Yadin **3**; see in detail Cotton and Greenfield, 'Babatha's Property', 216ff.

[43] See note 37, above.

[44] See Yadin, 'Expedition D—Cave of Letters', 251–2.

[45] κῆπον φοινικῶνοc ἐν ὁρίοιc Μαωζων λεγόμενον Βηθφααραια etc.

[46] Cf. No. **64** line 3: ἐ̣ν̣ Μ̣α̣ω̣ζαc τῆ̣ς̣ π̣ερὶ Ζ[ο]α̣ρ̣ω̣ν; this dependence is known from the Babatha Archive, see Lewis, *Documents*, 20–21.

[47] Cf. No. **62** line 12 and No. **65** lines 2–3. This fact too has been known already from the Babatha Archive, see INTRODUCTION TO THE GREEK DOCUMENTARY TEXTS.

[48] Kutscher, 'Ugaritica Marginalia'; see now Hoftijzer and Jongeling, *Dictionary*, 611.

seashore.[49] The proof is found in the two archives from Maḥoza. Babatha declares two date groves in Maḥoza, both named Algiphiamma, which is a Greek transliteration of Aramaic על גיף ימא, 'on the seashore': κῆπον φοινικῶνος ἐν ὁρίοις Μαωζων λεγόμενον Αλγιφιαμμα . . . γείτονες ὁδὸς καὶ θάλασσα κῆπον φοινικῶνος ἐν ὁρίοις Μαωζων λεγόμενον Αλγιφιαμμα . . . γείτονες μοσχαντικὴ κυρίου Καίσαρος καὶ θάλασσα (P.Yadin **16** lines 17–24). And indeed, the sea, or rather the seashore, is said here to be one of the abutters of these date groves.[50] Likewise, in No. **62**, Sammouos son of Shimʿon, Salome Komaïse's first husband, declares 'a field, called Arenoaratha, within the boundaries of the aforesaid Maḥoza' which is abutted by the sea: μέρος ἥμισυ χώρας ἐν ὁρίοις Μαωζων τῆς προγεγραμμένης λεγομένης Αρενοαραθα . . . γείτ[ον]ες Μαναῆς Μαναῆ καὶ θάλασσα, lines 14–17.

Another clue to the location of Maḥoza/Maḥoz ʿEglatain is that dates constitute the main, if not the only, product of the area: they are mentioned in land declarations,[51] deeds of gift,[52] and tax receipts.[53] Hence, we must look for a place with climatic and water conditions similar to those prevailing in Ẓoʿar[54] and Ein Gedi. The Ghor al-Ṣafi, south of the Dead Sea, with Wadi al-Ḥasa nearby,[55] would fit Maḥoza/Maḥoz 'Eglatain admirably. One may recall here Nelson Glueck's first impression of the Ghor al-Ṣafi area: ' . . . We pushed on to Ghōr eṣ-Ṣāfi near the south-eastern end of the Dead Sea. The waters of the Seil el-Qurāḥi, as the lower end of the Wādī el-Ḥesā is called, irrigate an extensive area, part of which is in a swampy state[56] . . . The large green fields of eṣ-Ṣāfi were a welcome relief after the waste stretches traversed from the time we left the plantations of el-Mezraʿah'.[57]

---

[49] Thus, an identification with Kh. Galgul (cf. Musil, *Arabia Petraea*, 365 and 381, n. 1) or with Kh. el-Gillime (cf. Abel, *Géographie*, 310, s.v. Eglaïm) is impossible since both are located inland. See the illuminating discussion of biblical ʿEglat (עגלת; Isa 15:5; Jer 48:34) in Schalit, 'Eroberungen'.

[50] In the Nabataean P.Yadin **3**, where one of these two groves is mentioned, the word used is רקקא (line 5 = line 27), i.e. 'shoals', a word used elsewhere for the shallow water near the shore of a lake or sea; cf. *b. Šabb.* 100b; *b. Erub.* 43a.

[51] P.Yadin **16** and No. **62**.

[52] P.Yadin **7** and No. **64**.

[53] No. **60** and No. **12**.

[54] Zoʿar is 'the city of palms', see *m. Yebam.* 16.7; see Broshi, 'Seven Notes', 233: 'The heat, the extreme low humidity and the abundant water are prerequisites for cultivating the date palm. The salinity . . . is no hindrance'; cf. ibid., 231–2.

[55] The 'great river', נהר רבא, and the 'water from the Wadi', מי ודיא, mentioned in P.Yadin **7** line 8 (= line 42) and line 43, may point to Wadi al-Ḥasa. Note also the 'desert', מדבר, as one of the abutters in P.Yadin **7** line 5.

[56] Cf. the רקקא in P.Yadin **3**, line 5 = line 27.

[57] *Explorations in Eastern Palestine* II (*AASOR* 15, 1935), 7.

60. XḤev/Se papTax (or Rent) Receipt from Maḥoza gr

Maḥoza, Arabia, 29 January 125 CE

(FIG. 27 AND PLS. XXXI–XXXII)

Preliminary publication: H. M. Cotton, 'Rent or Tax Receipt from Maoza', *ZPE* 100 (1994) 547–57, pl. XXXIIc; eadem, 'The Archive of Salome Komaïse Daughter of Levi: Another Archive from the "Cave of Letters"', *ZPE* 105 (1995) 174.

THIS document (*olim* XḤev/Se Gr. 5) is written against the fibres, which seems characteristic of papyri from the area. It is hard to know how much of the upper margin is lost. The verso is blank.

In the INTRODUCTION TO THE ARCHIVE OF SALOME KOMAÏSE DAUGHTER OF LEVI it was tentatively suggested that Sammouos son of Shimᶜon, the middleman in No. **60**, who is also the declarant of No. **62** and one of the abutters in No. **64** (line 14 = line 35), was Salome's first husband, whose name should be restored in No. **63** line 2. The presence of No. **60** in the archive is in this way fully accounted for: as the middleman between the addressee of No. **60**, Menaḥem son of Iohannes, and the tax or rent collectors, Sammouos kept the receipt in order to prove his integrity; the receipt proved that he did not misappropriate the sum of money entrusted to him by Menaḥem son of Iohannes. The other two people mentioned in No. **60** also appear in the deed of gift on behalf of Salome Komaïse (No. **64**). Reisha, who wrote the subscription to No. **60**, is most likely identical with Reisha son of Judah, the third name on the verso of the deed of gift (No. **64** line 44), especially if Ρεις is restored before 'son of Judah' in No. **60** line 3. Menaḥem son of Iohannes, the addressee of No. **60**, like Sammouos son of Shimᶜon, is one of the abutters of the half courtyard given in the deed of gift (line 15 = lines 35–36). It should be pointed out that not one of the three people in No. **60** appears in the Babatha Archive.

The form of the document includes many of the elements of Egyptian tax or rent receipts; see Wilcken, *Griechische Ostraka*, I, p. 103; Wallace, *Taxation*, 318ff.

This receipt shares five features with the Aramaic receipt from 131 CE (No. **12**): (1) the presence of more than one tax or rent collector who are described as 'colleagues' in both; (2) the dates: 29 and 30 January respectively; obviously, the tax or rent was collected at that time of year; (3) the doubtful word דמ̇י in line 3 of the Aramaic receipt is the construct-state of the word דמין, which is the exact equivalent of τιμή.[1] Thus lines 3–4 of the Aramaic receipt: קבלן מנך דמ̇י תמר̇י̇ן סאין עשר ותשע̇ וקב ופלג̇, 'We received from you the amount due (דמ̇י) for nineteen and a quarter *seʾah* of dates', are the exact equivalent of Ἀ̣πέ̣ς[χ]α̣μεν π̣[αρὰ coῦ] τειμὴν φο̣ί̣ν̣ι̣κ̣ο̣c of the Greek receipt. The expression דמ̇י תמר̇י̇ן suggests that an *adaeratio* took place, i.e. the nineteen and a quarter *seʾah* of dates were paid in cash—as is the payment in the Greek receipt—rather than in kind, even

[1] Τιμή is sometimes transliterated as טימי in Aramaic; see Sokoloff, *Dictionary*, 223.

though the sum is not specified; (4) it is very tempting to interpret the three vertical strokes with a horizontal stroke going through them, following the 'twenty' (עשרין), and the *waw* in line 8 of the Aramaic receipt, as standing for the digit 4, thus 'in the twenty-fourth year'. The parallel with the Greek receipt will then be complete: just as in the Greek receipt, where the tax or rent due for 'the eighteenth year of the province' is paid in the 'nineteenth year of the province', in the Aramaic receipt the tax or rent for 'the twenty-fourth year' is paid in the 'twenty-fifth year of the province' (lines 11–12); (5) the date in both receipts comes at the end. This is unlike all other Aramaic deeds from the Judaean Desert; it seems to follow the conventions of receipts in Greek.

Only four other receipts from the Judaean Desert are known to the present author:

1. P.Yadin **27**, from 19 August 132, which, like no. **60**, adopts the epistolary form (lines 1–11).[2] The subscription in Aramaic gives an abbreviated version of the receipt (lines 11–14); it is followed by its translation into Greek (lines 15–18).
2. A tiny fragmentary receipt on parchment from the second century CE, where it is possible that a translation into Greek follows the Aramaic acknowledgement.[3]
3. A broken ostracon from Masada from the 20s or 30s BCE, which might be either a receipt or a promissory note.[4]
4. P.Yadin **43** (132–3 CE), an Aramaic receipt for thirty-nine *denarii*, paid by Eliezer son of Samuel for a lease from Bar Kokhba. It is written by one of Bar Kokhba's *parnasim* (probably in ᶜEin Gedi), Ḥoron son of Ishmael, who is known also from P.Yadin **42** of the same date.[5]

It is hard to determine whether the payment here (and in the Aramaic receipt) is of tax or of rent. The term τιμή could be used for rent, even if the usual term for rent is φόρος.[6] Conversely φόρος could be used for tax,[7] and is certainly used in the latter sense in No. **62** (see frg. a line 16; frgs. c–m line 8).

The apparent presence of more than one revenue collector might suggest that No. **60** deals with a body of *conductores* on an imperial estate.[8] The existence of imperial properties in Maḥoza is known from P.Yadin **16** and from the deed of gift of Salome Komaïse daughter of Levi (No. **64**). P.Yadin **16** mentions a date grove owned by Babatha which borders the emperor's property and the sea, lines 23–24: γείτονες μοσχαντικὴ κυρίου Καίσαρος καὶ θάλασσα. This imperial property once belonged to the Nabataean kings, as is known from P.Yadin **2** and **3** from 99 CE, which state that a date grove which used to belong to Babatha's father is bordered by King Rabael's grove and a swamp: ולימינא גנת מראנא רבאל . . . מלך נבטו—'to the south the grove of our lord Rabael

---

[2] Βαβαθας Cίμω[ν]ος . . . Cίμωνι κυρτῷ Ἰωάνου Ἐγλα [τῆ]ς αὐτ[ῆ]ς Μαωζας χαίρι[ν] . . . ἀπ[έcχ]ον π[αρ]ά c[ο]υ ἰc λόγο[ν τρ]οφίων καὶ ἀμφιαζμοῦ τοῦ αὐτοῦ Ἰηcούου υ[ἱοῦ] μ[ου] ἀργυρίου δηναρίων [ἕξ] ἀ[π]ὸ μηνὸc Πανήμου πρώτη<c> τοῦ αὐτοῦ ἔτου<c> ἑβδόμου εἰκοστοῦ μέχρι Γορπι[αίο]υ τριακάδι, μηνῶν τελίων τρῖc (lines 4–11).

[3] See Misgav, 'Four Segments'.

[4] The beginnings of four lines read: ἔτου[c / ἔχω ..[/ Αλδη ..[/ ξ.....[; see Cotton, Geiger and Netzer, 'Greek Ostracon'.

[5] Yadin, 'Expedition D—Cave of Letters', 249.

[6] Rupprecht, *Quittung*, 30.

[7] Cf. introduction to P.Fay 60, 149 CE.

[8] On the three-tiered administration of imperial estates in Egypt, see Parássoglou, *Imperial Estates*, 52, 57; Kehoe, *Management and Investment*, 16ff.; for Africa, see Kehoe, *Economics of Agriculture*, 117–53. A general survey can be found in Crawford-Thompson, 'Imperial Estates'.

. . . king of the Nabataeans'. In No. **64** the Emperor's property abuts the date grove on the east: ἀνα[το]λῶν κῆπον κυριακὸν[9] καλούμενον Γανναθ Αββαιδαια, lines 9–10 = lines 30–31.

In Egypt, however, ordinary taxes were often collected by a group of people (see Wallace, *Taxation*, 286ff.). We have no information about the system of taxation which operated in Arabia before or after 106. The crucial question seems to be whether ὀφείλεις Κ[υ]ρίῳ Καίσαρι in lines 5–6 of the receipt could be used to describe the public purse, i.e. the ordinary taxes, or whether it signifies exclusively the emperor's private property. (See discussion in No. **64**, with reference to lines 28–30.)

In both receipts the tax or rent collectors are local people. This, according to S. Weingarten (*apud* Isaac, 'Tax Collection', 266 and n. 26 there), served for the central authorities as 'a built-in mechanism for verifying the census declarations'. People kept receipts in order to show them both to the tax collector (מוכס) as well as to the authority in charge of the latter (בעל המכס).[10]

Dates were the main product of the area, as we know from the Babatha Archive as well as from this document and others associated with Salome Komaïse daughter of Levi. This is known also from the literary sources: Ẓoʿar is the 'city of palms' according to *m. Yeb.* 16.7; for ʿEin Gedi and Jericho, see Pliny, *NH* 5.73 and 13.44 (= Stern, *Greek and Latin Authors*, 1:470 [no. 204], 491 [no. 214]). See the discussion in Broshi, 'Seven Notes', and Safrai, *Economy*, 138ff.

Date and Provenance

The document is dated by the consular year as well as by the provincial year, but not by the regnal year.[11] The Roman month and day are missing, while the Macedonian month and day are present. The Roman date formula given in lines 9–10 is unusual: ἐπὶ [ὑ]πάτων τῶν μετὰ ὑπατίαν Γλαβρίωνος [κ]αὶ Θηβανιανοῦ. Thus we are in the year 125 CE.

It is surprising to find this late formula here. The only likely reason for it is that the names of the eponymous consuls of the year had not yet reached this part of the Roman world. Something similar happened in the Arsinoïte nome of Egypt in 194: the names of the ordinary consuls of 194 were as yet unknown on 21 February of that year. Hence the dating formula: πρὸ θ̄ Καλανδῶν Μαρτίων ὑπάτοις τοῖς οὖσι, BGU I 326 (= *FIRA* III² no. 50 = MChr. 316) col. II line 11.

We can be sure, though, that in our receipt the μετὰ ὑπατίαν really means what it says: 'in the year after the consulate' and not just 'after the consulate', as it came to mean from the fourth century onwards. A glance at the abbreviation μ.τ.ὑ. in Bagnall and Worp, *Chronological Systems*, appendix D (pp. 103ff.) gives us a measure of how common this manner of dating had become from the fourth century onwards.

---

[9] Note that κῆπος κυριακός is a literal translation of the Nabataean גנת מראנא: in the transition to Roman rule, the name of the estate did not change.

[10] *T. Šabb* 8(9).11. Note that the Hebrew term for receipt is קשר מוכסין; in P.Yadin **43** line 7 we find קתרא דנן.

[11] See Lewis, *Documents,* 28 for 'the presence and the order of the several dates' in the Babatha Archive.

Although we do not know the method by which the provinces were informed of the names of the ordinary consuls for the coming year, it is likely that this was done soon after they became *designati*, and many months before they took office.[12] An indication of this can be found in P.Yadin **18** lines 29–30, where the *ordinarii* of 128 CE are recorded as P. Metilius Nepos II and M. Annius Libo—ἐ̣[πὶ ὑ]π̣άτων Πο̣υ̣[β]λ̣ε̣ί̣[ο]υ̣ Μετειλ̣ί̣[ου] Ν̣ε̣π̣ωνοϲ τὸ β̄ καὶ Μάρκου Ἀν̣ν̣ί̣ου Λίβωνοϲ. However, the first must have died before taking office and was replaced by L. Nonius Calpurnius Asprenas Torquatus II. The change, although unknown in Arabia on 5 April 128, was known in Egypt before the Kalends of April of that year, as we know from the 'Birth Certificate of Herennia Gemella', P.Mich. III, 166 (line 4) = *AE* 1939 309; cf. Salomies, 'Namengebung', 111 n. 18.[13]

Since by 29 January 125, the date of our receipt, the names of the ordinary consuls had been known for some time, the delay was much more than twenty-nine days.

Such locutions as found in lines 9–10 of No. **60**, caused by delays in transmitting the name of the eponymous magistrates from the centre to the periphery, are also known from the ancient Near East. Assyrian texts sometimes contain the following dating formula: 'eponymy: he who has taken over from PN', i.e. 'eponymy: he who came (after) PN' (Larsen, 'Unusual Eponymy-Datings', 15). A striking parallel occurs in a deed of sale from 651 BCE from Gezer in Palestine, where, on the back, we find: *Araḫ Siwanni ûmu sibâšēru lîm-mu ša arki D.P. Aššur-dura-uṣur D.P. bêl piḫati âl Bar-ḫal-zi*, 'month Sivan, day 17th eponymy which is after Assur-dûra-uṣur, prefect of Barḫalzu' (Macalister, *Gezer*, 1:25–9; Larsen, 'Unusual Eponymy-Datings', 22–3).

The document measures 8.5 x 9.5 cm.

Mus. Inv. 866
PAM 40.642

].θ.[ ]
]ε̣τ̣[ ]
.α[...]ϲ̣ Ιουδα κ̣αὶ ἑτα[ῖρ]ο̣ι̣ Μ[α]να[ημ̣ω̣]
Ι[ωα]ν̣ου χαίρι̣[ν]. Ἀ̣πέϲ̣[χ]α̣μεν π̣[αρὰ ϲοῦ]
τειμὴν φο̣ί̣ν̣ι̣κ̣ο̣ϲ οὗ ὀ̣φείλειϲ Κ̣[υ]ρ̣ίῳ̣
Καίϲαρι ἐν Μαώζᾳ̣ ἔτουϲ ὀκτωκαι-

[12] The precise timetable for the elections of the ordinary consuls for this period is unknown; see Mommsen, *Staastr.* I, 588f; Talbert, *Senate*, 343.

[13] Degrassi, *Fasti consolari*, 287, has a list of 'consolari designati che non entrarono in carica'. Cf. Duncan Jones, *Structure and Scale*, 7–29, for communication-speed in the Roman Empire.

δεκάτου, ἐξ ὧν ἀπειλήφαμεν παρὰ
ϲοῦ ἐ̣κ χερὸϲ Ϲ̣α̣μμούου Ϲίμωνοϲ μέ-
λεπτὰ πεντήκοντα ὀκτώ
λανεϲ τέϲϲαρε̣ϲ. Ἐγράφη ἐν Μαώζα̣ ἐπὶ
[ὑ]πάτων τῶν μετ̣ὰ̣ ὑ̣πατίαν Γλ̣α̣βρίωνοϲ
[κ]αὶ Θη̣βανιανοῦ, ἔ̣τ̣ο̣[υ]ϲ̣ ἐννεακαιδε̣[κάτ]ου
μ̣η̣ν̣ὸ̣ϲ̣ [Π]ε̣ρειτ̣ί̣ου τ[εϲϲα]ρ[εϲκ]α̣ιδε[κάτη̣]
רישה כתבה

4 χαίρειν ἀπέϲχομεν 5 τιμήν 8 χειρόϲ 8–9 μέλαναϲ 9 τέϲϲαραϲ 10 ὑπατείαν 12 Περιτίου

Translation

[Names and patronyms] [ ] son of Judah and colleagues to Menaḥem son of Iohannes greetings. We received from you the amount due for dates, which you owe to our Lord the Emperor in Maḥoza for the eighteenth year (of the province). On the account of which we have now received from you through Sammouos son of Shimʿon four blacks (and) fifty-eight lepta-units. Written in Maḥoza in the year of the consulate which comes after that of Glabrio and Thebanianus, the nineteenth year (of the province), the fourteenth day in the month of Peritios. Reisha wrote this.

Comments

Ll. 1–2 In *ZPE* 100 (1994) 551 it was suggested that the two lines are likely to have contained more names, perhaps also titles. This is very common in tax receipts from Egypt, e.g. WO 782: Παίων Παίου τελ(ώνηϲ) θηϲ(αυροῦ) ἱερῶν Νεφερῶϲ Πεχοίτο(υ) καὶ Πεκῦ(ϲιϲ) υἱὸ(ϲ) καὶ Παναμ(εὺϲ) ἄλλοϲ υἱὸ(ϲ) χα(ίρειν). Doubts arise when one recalls the opening of the Aramaic receipt (No. **12**) which this document so closely resembles: '*Ih*.. son of Thesha and my colleague (or colleagues?)' (יה.. בר תשה וחברי). If the same model is followed here, then no names preceded line 3. In that case it is hard to know what has been lost in these two lines.

L. 3 α[...]ϲ̣ Ιουδα. The likely identity of Reisha son of Judah of the deed of gift (No. **64** line 44: רישה בר יהודה) with the Reisha in line 13 of the present document makes it tempting to restore Ρειϲ or Ρειϲαϲ here. The Reisha who underwrote No. **60** (line 13 כתבה) is likely to be the senior person, and hence his name is likely to have appeared at the head of the document. The restoration of the name Reisha here will strengthen the case for believing that no names occurred in lines 1–2. However, the 'son of Judah' in line 3 may be a different person after all. Judah was a common patronym: more than one person in Maḥoza could have been 'son of Judah'.

L. 3 ἑται[ρ]ο̣ι̣. For ἑταῖροι in Egyptian receipts, see Stud.Pal. XX 153, line 2 and 170, line 2 (fifth-sixth centuries CE). Ἑταῖροι is parallel to חברי of the Aramaic receipt (No. **12**). Its restoration here makes this line completely parallel to line 1 of the Aramaic receipt (see COMMENTS ad lines 1–2). In Egyptian tax receipts, a name is sometimes followed by the title of the tax collecters, e.g. καὶ μ(έτοχοι) ἀπαιτ(ηταί) O.Tait 767 (148 CE); 771 (135 CE); 772 (138 CE); καὶ μ(έτοχοι) πράκτορεϲ O.Tait 834 (111 CE); 835 (116 CE); καὶ μ(έτοχοι) τελ(ῶναι) O.Tait 1021 (145 CE); καὶ μ(έτοχοι) ἐπιτ(ηρηταί) O.Tait 1023 (154 CE). The similarity to the Aramaic receipt makes the alternative suggestion, namely that ἑτα[ῖρ]οι may stand for ἕτεροι, less likely (see Gignac, *Grammar* 1:193 for interchange of ε and αι).

L. 4 χαίρι[ν] possibly χαίρει[ν]. This is epistolary style, as in P.Yadin **27** line 6.

L. 4 Ἀπέσ[χ]αμεν. For 2nd aorist formations with 1st aorist endings, see Gignac, *Grammar*, 2:340ff.; for our form, ibid., 342.5. In the Aramaic receipt, too, the verb of receiving the tax is in the plural, קבלן ('we received'), and signifies the plurality of collectors.

Ll. 4–5 For the formula ἀπέσχαμεν παρὰ σοῦ τιμήν, see Preisigke, *Wörterbuch*, *s.v.* ἀπέχω, where many examples of ἀπεσχήκαμεν τιμήν are cited. One could restore π[ρὸς] in line 4 and get πρὸς τειμήν, for which see P.Mich. III 173 (late third century BCE) lines 7–8: ὀφείλων μοι πρὸς τιμὴν ἐλάας; see also lines 23; 29; P.Münch. III 52 (second century BCE) lines 6–9: ὀφείλων γάρ μοι πρὸς τιμὴν οὗ ἠγοράκη παρ' ἐμοῦ οἴνου. The restoration παρὰ σοῦ τιμήν is better since it represents a parallel to lines 3–4 of the Aramaic receipt: קבלן מנך דמי תמרין.

L. 5 φοίνικος. Possibly φοίνεικος. Φοῖνιξ is used here as a collective noun for 'dates'; cf. P.Yadin **5a** col. i lines 7–11: ἔχ[ει]ν σε παρ' ἐμ[οὶ ἀργυρ]ίου μέ[λανας] χείλια . . . καὶ τειμῆς [ὀ]λύνθων κα[ὶ] τειμῆς οἴνου καὶ τειμῆς φοίνικος καὶ τε[ι]μῆς ἐλαίου κτλ.; P.Yadin **16** lines 17–20: κῆπον φοινικῶνος ἐν ὁρίοις Μαωζων λεγόμενον Αλγιφιαμμα . . . τελοῦντα φοίνικος συροῦ καὶ μείγματος σάτα δεκαπέντε.

L. 5 τειμὴν φοίνικος. This refers to the value of dates in money. See e.g. O.Tait II nos. 989–993: 'Receipts for τιμὴ οἴνου and eventually φοινίκων', ii–iii CE, nos. 994–1002: 'Receipts for τιμὴ φοινίκων', ii–iii CE. O.Tait II nos. 1003–1005 are receipts for τιμὴ δημοσίου φοίνικος, referring perhaps to a lease of an imperial date grove (but see Wilcken, *Griechische Ostraka*, I:310ff.). The absence of the amount of money after τὴν τειμήν in our document suggests that the whole sum has now been paid, although ἐκ πλήρους is missing; see e.g. BGU XI 2112; XV 2478, 2479 where ἐκ πλήρους occurs with τιμή without specifying the sum of money.

Ll. 6–7 Year 18 of the province is from 22 March 123 to 21 March 124, since the era of the province began in 22 March 106; see Brünnow and von Domaszewski, *Provincia Arabia*, III:303; Bowersock, 'Annexation', 39; idem, 'Report', 231.

L. 7 ἐξ ὧν must by *constructio ad sensum* refer to the τειμὴν φοίνικος. Since the full sum of money has been paid, this must be the last instalment. For payment of taxes in Egypt by instalments, see Wilcken, *Griechische Ostraka* I, pp. 140, 281, 567, 619; Wallace, *Taxation*, 296, 318f; Rupprecht, *Quittung*, 30–31. See COMMENTS to line 5 above on ἐκ πλήρους.

L. 8 Σαμμούου Σίμωνος. On Sammouos (שמוע) son of Shimʿon, see INTRODUCTION above and INTRODUCTION TO THE ARCHIVE OF SALOME KOMAÏSE DAUGHTER OF LEVI. A Sammouos son of Menaḥem is written in Greek letters in P.Yadin **14** line 37; P.Yadin **21** lines 17–18, and in Aramaic letters in P.Yadin **14** line 46 and P.Yadin **21** line 35.

Ll. 8–9 μέλανες (*scil.* μέλανας) here suggests a masc. form; see Gignac, *Grammar* 2:46 for nom. pl. -ες used for the acc. pl.; and ibid., 129 on μέλας. 'Blacks' appear in the Babatha Archive in all genders, see Lewis, *Documents*, 36.

The monetary unit 'blacks' occurs solely in the Greek documents from Naḥal Ḥever and nowhere else, as far as we know. 'Blacks' are silver coins, as we know from P.Yadin **5a** lines 7, 13–14; **5b** lines 4, 7. Whatever 'black money' may mean, its appearance in a tax or rent receipt and in two census returns (P.Yadin **16** and No. **62**) confirms beyond any doubt that it was an officially recognized unit, see Lewis, *Documents*, 36. Bowersock ('Babatha Papyri', 342) rightly regards the old Nabataean coinage as 'the obvious candidates' for these 'blacks'. There is sufficient evidence to believe that one 'black' equals half a *denarius*, see in great detail with bibliography on the Nabataean coinage Weiser and Cotton, 'Gebt dem Kaiser, was des Kaisers ist'; cf. Lewis, 'The Money Called Black'.

L. 9 For τέσσαρες instead of τέσσαρας, see Gignac, *Grammar*, 2:191. Perhaps the penultimate letter is *alpha*, not *epsilon*, and so τέσσαρας after all.

L. 9 The interlinear λεπτὰ πεντήκοντα ὀκτώ above the line belongs after τέσσαρες. *Lepta* are units of 'blacks'. The sum of fifty-eight *lepta*, unlike the thirty and forty-five *lepta* of P.Yadin **16** lines 20–21, 27–28, 32 and No. **62** line 17, does not support, even if it does not preclude, Lewis's conjecture that 'the monetary unit represented by the "blacks" was divided into sixty *lepta*' (*Documents*, 70).

Ll. 9–10 ἐπὶ [ὑ]πάτων τῶν μετὰ ὑπατίαν. I.e. 125 CE, in which the *ordinarii* were M. Lollius Paulinus D. Valerius Asiaticus Saturninus II and L. Epidius Titius Aquilinus; see P.Yadin **14** and **15**.

Ll. 10–11 μετὰ ὑπατίαν Γλαβρίωνος [κ]αὶ Θηβανιανοῦ. The full names of the consuls of 124 are M. Acilius Glabrio and C. Bellicius Flaccus Torquatus Tebanianus; see P.Yadin **12**.

L. 11 The year 19 of the province is from 22 March 124 to 21 March 125; see ad lines 6–7.

L. 12 The month of Peritios (Περίτιος) in Arabia is from 16 January to 15 February; see Samuel, *Chronology,* 177.

L. 13 Reisha (רישה) as a proper name is unattested as well as unlikely.[14] ריש in Aramaic means 'head'. Reisha means 'the head' as the *he* at the end stands for the definite article. Reisha could thus be a title or a nickname: 'the head', 'the chief', 'the boss'. Only two other cases where Rosh or Reisha could be a title or a nickname are known to the present author. In both of them, however, unlike in the present case, the nickname is affixed to the name rather than replacing it. There is a Rabbi Joshua son of Pathar Rosh, רבי יהשוע בן פתר ראש, in *b. Nazir* 56b (but see *t. Nazir* 5:1 with S. Lieberman, *Tosefta Ki-feshutah*, Part VII: *Order Nashim*, 557 for the variants). He was a contemporary of R. Meir and R. Eleazar son of Shammua, i.e. the third generation of Tannaim, in 130–160 CE. The other example is Joseph Reisha (יוסף ראשא) in *Midr. Lam. Rab.* 3.17 (= p. 130 [Buber]), who was a contemporary of R. Abbahu (of the third generation of Amoraim in Palestine; he was the head of the school of Caesarea, d. 309 CE), who lived in Bostra.

It is highly likely that this Reisha is to be identified with Reisha son of Judah (רישה בר יהודה) of the deed of gift, No. **64**. Both documents were written in Maḥoza within five years of each other. Although only a few letters have remained, the same hand may well have written the name in the two documents. However, if we assume that Reisha is a nickname or a title, and not a proper name, and that son of Judah (בר יהודה) is his name (a patronymic used as a name), then we are faced with an almost unparalleled case—as far as I know—of a title or nickname followed by a name: 'the chief, son of Judah'. The other case would be Hygros son of Levi (הגרס בן לוי), who appears in the list of officers in the Temple in *m. Šeqal.* 5.1, if indeed Hygros is a nickname (see Naveh, 'Nameless People', 110).

We must distinguish our case from the Reish (ריש) in the case of the famous Reish Lakish (ריש לקיש) of the second generation of Amoraim in Palestine, hence mid-third century CE. Since there is no definite article, it is hard to take it as a nickname. Although often found in the manuscripts without the symbol for an acronym, but with the *yod* (י) instead, it is nevertheless interpreted as an acronym and not as a nickname for R. Shimᶜon. If so, this is the sole instance for the use of the acronym as an independent name at the time; see Wasserstein, 'Good Man', 197–8.

The word רוש is found on a sarcophagus from Jerusalem; see Milik, 'Trois tombeaux', 246–8, no. 15 (fig. 15:2). Milik does not take it to be a name: 'il s'agirait du côté où se trouve le crâne'.

L. 13 כתבה means literally 'wrote this', but since the document is written in Greek it can hardly be taken literally: it must mean that Reisha underwrote the receipt, acknowledging thereby that the money has really been paid. It has the meaning of σεσημείωμαι in papyri from Egypt rather than that of ἔγραψα, see e.g. P.Oxy. III 485 (178 CE); IV 719 (193 CE); XII 1455 (275 CE); 1474 (216 CE) for the occurrence of both terms in the same document. There are other examples for the use of כתבה in this sense. In P.Yadin **20** (19 June 130), Besas son of Joshua and Julia Crispina attach their subscriptions to a document written in Greek by Germanus the *libellarius* (line 45): Besas does so in Aramaic and Julia Crispina in Greek. The first says: 'I acknowledge (מדא אנה) to you . . . that I will act and clear the title <according to> all that is written above. Besas son of Yeshuᶜa wrote it (כתבה)' (lines 41–42); whereas Julia Crispina writes in Greek: Ἰουλί{ι}α Κρισπεῖνα ἐπίσκοπος ὁμολογῶ συνκεχωρηκένε ἀκολούθως (line 43). The hand is not that of Germanus, but probably of Julia Crispina herself. There is no reason to assume that, unlike his female partner, Besas wishes to stress the fact that he himself wrote the subscription; thus the כתבה in his subscription adds nothing to the acknowledgement. The same seems to be true of the subscriptions to Mur **42** (134–5 CE), where the two administrators (פרנסים) who sent the message to the Head of Camp (רוש המחניה) certainly did not write it, despite the כתבה in their subscriptions (lines 8–9), as can easily be proved by the different hands: they are simply attesting responsibility for its

[14] 'Rosh' occurs once in the Hebrew Bible: Rosh (ראש) son of Benjamin son of Jacob (Gen 46:21).

contents. Milik's translation of כתבה as 'l'a (fait) écrire, l'a dicté (à un scribe professionnel)', *DJD* II, 158, is not literal but it captures the sense.[15] I suspect that 'Ḥoron son of Ishmael wrote this' in P.Yadin **43** line 8 has the same meaning of 'underwrote it', although it is written in the same language and the same hand as the rest of the receipt.

The fact that Reisha subscribes his name in Aramaic rather than in Greek is somewhat puzzling, if indeed he is to be identified with Reisha son of Judah, the Greek scribe of No. **64**. Still, this does not seem a strong enough argument to undermine the identification; see COMMENTS ad line 13 (above) and No. **64** line 44.

[15] See Naveh, *Sherd and Papyrus*, 106–7.

61. XḤev/Se papConclusion to a Land Declaration gr

Rabbath Moab, Arabia, 25 April 127 CE

(PLS. XXXI AND XXXIII)

Preliminary publication: H. M. Cotton, 'Fragments of a Declaration of Landed Property from the Province of Arabia', *ZPE* 85 (1991) 263–7, pl. IX; eadem, 'Another Fragment of the Declaration of Landed Property from the Province of Arabia', *ZPE* 99 (1993) 115–21, pl. XIIId; eadem, 'The Archive of Salome Komaïse Daughter of Levi: Another Archive from the "Cave of Letters"', *ZPE* 105 (1995) 176.

THE conclusion to a land declaration, No. **61** (*olim* XḤev/Se Gr. 5 + SHR 3001) is composed of two fragments, each with its own history. The larger fragment, frg. a, contains the middle and almost all of the right margin of lines 1–4. It was found among Yadin's papers, designated Inv. no. 3001 in the Shrine of the Book, and published in *ZPE* 85 (1991) 263–7. The other fragment, frg. b,[1] contains the left margin of lines 1–4 and almost all of lines 5–6, as well as blank space at the bottom. Frg. b belongs to the so-called Seiyâl group, and is one fragment in the museum plate formerly designated XḤev/Se Gr. **5** (see pl. XXXI). It was published together with frg. a in *ZPE* 99 (1993) 115–21. Two small fragments (frgs. c, d), also found on museum plate 3001 (see pl. XXXIII), seem to belong to the same papyrus; unlike the two larger fragments, their content shows that they belong to the body of the declaration and not to the conclusion. They are written by the same hand that wrote frgs. a and b. The conclusion includes two subscriptions, that of the declarant, X son of Levi, and that of the prefect Priscus. The fact that the body of the declaration, as well as the conclusion, containing two subcriptions by two different people, are both written by the same hand, and that the original subscription of the prefect in Latin was omitted,[2] proves that this is an official copy of the original land declaration, like P.Yadin **16**, which is written by the same hand throughout.[3]

The declarant of No. **61** is a 'son of Levi' (see λειουου in line 2). It is, therefore, very likely that he is the brother of Salome Komaïse, who is referred to as dead in No. **63**. From No. **63** line 3 we know that his name ended with *-los* or *-las*. He must have died in the course of the year 127, after making the declaration; this would account for the presence of the document in the archive. Elsewhere it was argued that he was not a minor, although he did not write his own subscription. The fact that he used the *chirocrista*, Onainos son of Saʿadalos, rather than a guardian, proves that he was illiterate.[4]

---

[1] Frg. b has now itself become two fragments.

[2] The original language of the declarant's subscription is not known: see COMMENTS.

[3] See Lewis, *Documents,* pl. 13: the scribe seems to have sharpened his pencil towards the end, which may explain Lewis's references to 'the hand of another writer' (p. 65) and '2nd hand' (p. 67).

[4] See Cotton, 'Subscriptions'.

Without No. **62** and P.Yadin **16** these fragments would have been without a context. The conclusion of No. **62**, the other land declaration, has not been preserved and therefore could not be used to place these fragments. The resemblance to the concluding formula in P.Yadin **16** lines 33–38 is indeed striking:

> Ἑρμηνεία ὑπογραφῆς· Βαβθα Cίμωνος ὄμνυμι τύχην κυρίου Καίcạρος καλῇ πίcτει ἀπογεγρạ́φθạι ὡ̣c προγέγραπ̣[τα]ι̣· Ἰ̣ουδάνης Ἐ̣λαζάρọυ̣ ἐπιτρọ́πευ[c]ạ καὶ ἔγραψα ὑπὲρ αὐτῆc· Ἑρμηνεία ὑπογραφῆc τοῦ ἐπάρχου· Πρεῖcκος ἔ̣παρχος ἱππέων ἐδεξάμην τῇ πρὸ μιᾶc νωνῶν Δεκεμβρίων ὑπατίας Γαλλικ̣[αν]ọῦ [καὶ Τιτιανο]ῦ̣.

Together with P.Yadin **16** and No. **62**, we have now three land declarations submitted at the same census in the Roman province of Arabia (see below, on DATE AND PROVENANCE). No other land declarations from the Roman world have survived. The Egyptian fourteen-year cycle census declarations involve only people and house property, never agricultural land.[5] The purpose of these land declarations was clearly to determine the rate of taxation (see Isaac, 'Tax Collection'). They illustrate neatly the *forma censualis* of *Dig*. 50.15.4. (On the provincial censuses in the imperial period, see Neesen, *Untersuchungen*; Brunt, 'Revenue'; Aichiniger, 'Zwei Arten?'.)

Priscus, a cavalry commander, is found here assisting the governor who conducted the census in Arabia. He is involved in accepting the declarations of the villagers in local centres, such as the *polis* of Rabbath-Moab. Another example of a cavalry officer accepting declarations is P.Lond. 904 = W.Chr. 202 (104 CE) lines 30–34 (edict of the prefect of Egypt): βούλομαι πάντας (who have a reason to stay in the city rather than return to the *chora*) ἀπογράφεcθαι παρὰ Βουλ ...[...][6] Φήcτῳ ἐπάρχω[ι] εἴλης. (For more examples of soldiers taking the census see Zwicky, *Verwendung*, 75–6 and Brunt, 'Revenue', 334. For army officers involved in civil duties in general see Zwicky, *Verwendung*, and MacMullen, *Soldier and Civilian*, chap. 3.[7])

Goodman, 'Babatha's Story', 172, draws attention to the fact that 'not even in the returns in the provincial census is there any sign of a role for the magistrates of the *polis* as is customarily reckoned normal'. For the respective roles of the provincial government and the city authorities in the assessment and collection of taxes in the province of Arabia, see Isaac, 'Tax Collection'.[8]

Date and Provenance

The conclusion to the land declaration, or rather the subscription of the prefect, Priscus, is dated only by the day of the month according to the Roman calendar. The year is missing, but can be recovered from the other two land declarations, P.Yadin **16**

[5] The basic study on which is still Hombert and Préaux, *Recherches*; see also Bagnall and Frier, *Demography*. Egyptian property returns, ἀπογραφαί, even if required by an official order, were not intended for the purpose of taxation (see Harmon, 'Egyptian Property'; Youtie, 'Review of A. M. Harmon'; and Préaux, 'Déclarations').

[6] H. Devijver, *De Aegypto*, no. 27 restores Βουλ[λατίῳ] in the lacuna.

[7] Wannemacher, 'Development', 177ff., mentioned in MacMullen, *Soldier and Civilian*, 62 n. 38, was not consulted by the present author.

[8] Cf. Lo Cascio, 'Census provinciale'.

and No. **62**—both of which refer to the census held in the Roman province of Arabia by the governor of the province, Titus Aninius Sextius Florentinus, in 127:

> ἐπὶ Αὐτοκράτορος Καίcαρος θεοῦ Τραιανοῦ Παρθικοῦ ụἱοῦ θεοῦ Νέρουα υἱωνοῦ Τραιανοῦ Ἁδριανοῦ Cεβαστοῦ ἀρχιερέως μεγίcτου δημαρχικῆc ἐξουcίαc τὸ δωδέκατον ὑπάτου τὸ τρίτον, ἐπὶ ὑπάτων Μάρκου Γα<ου>ίου Γαλλικανοῦ καὶ Τίτου Ἀτειλίου Ῥούφου Τιτιανοῦ πρὸ τεccάρων νωνῶν Δεκεμβρίων, κατὰ δὲ τὸν τῆc νέαc ἐπαρχείαc Ἀραβίαc ἀριθμὸν ἔτουc δευτέρου εἰκοcτοῦ μηνὸc Ἀπελλαίου ἑκκαιδεκάτῃ ἐν Ῥαββαθμωβοιc πόλει. ἀποτιμήcεωc Ἀραβίαc ἀγομένηc ὑπὸ Τίτου Ἀνεινίου Cεξcτίου Φλωρεντείνου πρεcβευτοῦ Cεβαcτοῦ ἀντιcτρατήγου (P.Yadin **16** lines 5–13; cf. No. **62** frg. a lines 4–12).

That the present declaration was submitted in the same census is clear from the presence of the cavalry commander, Priscus, who subscribed also the land declaration in P.Yadin **16** (see lines 36–39 there). There is a considerable interval, however, between the date of the subscription by the prefect in the present land declaration—25 April—and that in P.Yadin **16**—4 December 127 (lines 37–38: τῇ πρὸ μιᾶc νωνῶν Δεκεμβρίων ὑπατίαc Γαλλιḳ[αν]ọῦ [καὶ Τιτιανο]ῦ̣), two days after its submission on 2 December 127 (line 9).[9] In Cotton, 'Another Fragment', 121, it was suggested that the date of the present subscription could be either 25 April 128, i.e. almost five months after Babatha's land declaration or 25 April 127, i.e. more than seven months earlier than Babatha's. We now know that the declarant X son of Levi was dead already in the course of 127 (see No. **63**). Hence the date of the subscription is 25 April 127. The span of time separating the different declarations gives us some idea of the length of the census conducted in Arabia.

The place, Rabbath-Moab, is also missing in the present papyrus, but because of the presence of Priscus both here and in P.Yadin **16**, it can safely be posited. On the new *polis* of Rabbath-Moab, later Areopolis, see Bowersock, *Roman Arabia*, 87–8; Millar, *Roman Near East*, 418. Rabbath-Moab is northeast of Maḥoza (the declarant's *patria*, see INTRODUCTION TO THE ARCHIVE OF SALOME KOMAÏSE DAUGHTER OF LEVI), and far closer to it than to Petra (75 km from Rabbath-Moab to Maḥoza as against more than twice that distance from Rabbath-Moab to Petra). The latter, however, is said in Babatha's land declaration itself (as well as in that of Sammouos son of Shimʿon) to be the provincial subdivision to which Maḥoza belonged: Βαβθα . . . Μαωζηνὴ τῆc Ζοαρηνῆc περιμέτρου Πέτραc (P.Yadin **16** lines 13–14; cf. No. **62** frg. a line 12). Isaac ('Tax Collection', 260ff.) discusses the complicated problems raised by the fact that the three declarations from Arabia were not made in the city in whose territory the land was situated.

Frg. a measures 10.5 x 4 cm. Frg. b measures 16.5 x 6 cm. Frg. c measures 2.3 x 2.3 cm. Frg. d measures 3.5 x 2.8 cm.

Mus. Inv. 866; SHR 3001
IAA 350224; SHR 5962

---

9 No. **62** breaks off before the conclusion and thus we do not know when it was subscribed by the prefect; it was submitted, though, either on 4 or 11 December 127 (see lines 8–9 and COMMENTS ad loc).

Frg. a

1 *traces*

2]υ̣μι τυχην κυριου Καιϲα̣ροϲ κ[α]λη πιϲτει απο[

3]προγεγραπται μηθεν υποϲτειλαμενοϲ· ε̣[

4]υ Οναινου Σααδαλλου· Ερμην{ν}εια υπογραφη[

5 *traces*

Frg. b

1 μο[ ]ρ̣.[*traces*]

2 λειουου ομνυ̣[ ]

3 γεγραφθαι ωϲ .[ ]

4 χειροχρήϲτο[ ]

5 επαρχου πρειϲκοϲ υπαρχοϲ εδεξαμην προ επτα καλ[ ]

6 μαιων.

Frgs. a + b

1 μο[ ]ρ̣. *traces* λ̣ο̣ϲ̣

2 Λειουου ὄμνυ̣μι τύχην Κυρίου Καίϲα̣ροϲ κ[α]λῇ πίϲτει ἀπο-

3 γεγράφθαι ὡϲ προγέγραπται μηθὲν ὑποϲτειλάμενοϲ. ἐ̣[γράφη διὰ]

4 χειροχρήϲτου Οναινου Σααδαλλου. Ἑρμην{ν}εία ὑπογραφῆ[ϲ τοῦ]

5 ἐπάρχου. Πρεῖϲκοϲ ὕπαρχοϲ ἐδεξάμην πρὸ ἑπτὰ κα[λανδῶν]

6 Μαίων.

Frg. c

1]ἥμισυ[ ]

2 ἀπο]γραφῆ[c]

Frg. d

1 *traces*

2 c]πόρου ϵ.[ ]

3 ἥμι]cυ γεί[τονεc]

TRANSLATION

Frgs. a + b

I, [ ]*los* or [ ]*las* son of Levi, swear by the *tyche* of the Lord Caesar that I have in good faith registered as written above, concealing nothing. W[ritten by] the *chirocrista* Onainos son of Saʿadalos. Translation of the subscription of [the] prefect: I, Priscus prefect, received [this] six days before the Ka[lends] of May.

COMMENTS

Frgs. a + b

L. 1 At least the end of the itemized declaration occupied the first part of this line. The words ἑρμηνεία ὑπογραφῆc would have occupied its second half, if X son of Levi's, or rather the *chirocrista*'s, subscription was written in a language other than Greek, as in P.Yadin **16** line 37 and in line 4 below. It would be followed by the declarant's name.

L. 1 λ̣ο̣ç̣ or λ̣α̣ç̣. If the declarant is Salome Komaïse's dead brother of No. **63** line 7, then *-los* or *-las* should be restored at the end of line 1.

L. 2 Λειουου. On the name Levi, see INTRODUCTION TO THE ARCHIVE OF SALOME KOMAÏSE DAUGHTER OF LEVI.

L. 2 For the oath formulas in census returns from the fourteen-year census cycle in Egypt, see Hombert and Préaux, *Recherches*, 124–7, where the writers suggest that the presence or absence of the oath depends entirely on local custom.

L. 2 ὄμνυ̣μι τύχην Κυρίου Καίcα̣ροc. This particular form of the oath formula—even if we ignore the κ[α]λῇ πίcτει—is not found in Egyptian papyri, see Seidl, *Eid* I, 10ff., and the series of articles by Packman in 'Notes'; 'Further Notes', 258; 'Regnal Formulas'; 'Still Further Notes'.

L. 2 κ[α]λῇ πίcτει. I.e. *bona fide*. This expression is not found in Egyptian oath formulas. Bowersock (*Roman Arabia*, 88), citing the example of P.Yadin **16**, observes that the Jews in the new province of Arabia 'now had to swear by the fortune of the emperor'. Unfortunately we do not possess an example from Egypt of a Jew affixing an oath by the *tyche* of the Emperor to a census declaration, but that may be a coincidence: altogether there are two census declarations in the CPJ. In P.Hamb. I 60 = CPJ III 485 (90 CE) lines 20–23, a certain Pascheis son of Kapais and grandson of Sambatheios swears by the *tyche* of the emperor: [καὶ ὀμ]ν̣ύωι τὴν Αὐτοκράτοροc Καίcαροc Δομιτι[ανοῦ Cεβαcτο]ῦ Γερμανικοῦ τύχην <μὴ> ὑπάρχειν μοι [ο]ἰ̣κ̣[ίαν ἤ ἄλλα] ἔνγαια κα̣ὶ̣ μὴ ἔχειν με ἑτέρουc υἱο[ὺc ἤ ἄλλουc ἀ]ν̣απογράφ[ου]c ἔχω τῶν προγεγραμμένων. The other names in the document, all but one Egyptian, make it unlikely that this is a Jewish document. The exception, the grandfather's name, Sambatheios, which accounts for the inclusion of the papyrus in CPJ, may not be a Jewish name after all, and cannot be used as evidence for the Jewishness of its bearer.[10] In the census return submitted by a Jewish woman in P.Lond. III p. 25, no. 1119a = CPJ II 430 (105 CE), the bottom, where the oath might have stood, is missing. We have, however, an example of a Jew from the Fayyûm, Soteles son of Josepos, affixing an oath by the Emperor to the notification of his son's (Josepos's) death, which he is submitting to the authorities: Cωτέλης Ἰωcήπου ὁ πρωγεγραμένος ὀμνύω Αὐτοκράτορα Καίcα[ρα Νέρουαν] Τραιαν[ὸν] Cεβα[cτόν] BGU IV 1068 = CPJ II 427 lines 18–24 (101 CE). It is true that *tyche* is not mentioned here. However, the editors of CPJ are right to argue that this omission is not 'on account of the Judaism of Soteles', but to be explained as due to the fact that 'the Roman oath "by the genius of the Emperor" was not yet familiar in Egypt'.[11] At any rate, 'an oath by the Emperor presupposes his superhuman origin, which contradicts the principles of Judaism' (CPJ II, p. 214, on lines 18ff). It would seem that the Jews of the period were less conscious—even oblivious—of the religious implications, from the standpoint of a monotheistic Jewish theology, of an oath by the emperor or by his *tyche*. It is not necessary to assume that they felt coerced into using the formula. Babatha and X son of Levi swore by the *tyche* of the emperor as a matter of course. They simply followed local custom in this as well as in their other contacts with the authorities.

L. 3 μηθὲν ὑποcτειλάμενοc. The participle form establishes that the declarant is a man: in all likelihood the brother of Salome Komaïse (see INTRODUCTION). For the middle of the verb ὑποcτέλλω in census return attestations, see P.Oxy. II 246 lines 25–26 (66 CE): καὶ ὀμν[ύω] Νέρωνα Κλαύδιον Καίcαρ[α] Cεβαcτὸν Γερμανικὸν Αὐτοκράτορα μὴ ὑπεcτά[λθαι]; P.Oslo III 98.31–32 (132/33 CE); ἐπιδεδωκ(έναι) τὴν προκ(ειμένην) ἀπογρ(αφὴν) καὶ μηδὲν διεψεῦcθαι μηδὲ ὑπεcτάλθαι τι τῶι καθόλου. In both cases, its perfect infinitive follows the verb, whereas here it is the aorist participle. The Duke Data Bank gives no parallel for this construction in the papyri.[12] There is no parallel to the formula μηθὲν ὑποcτειλάμενοc in Babatha's subscription, see P.Yadin **16** lines 34–35. Obviously, there was no official subscription formula which the declarants in the province were obliged to follow.

L. 3 ἐ̣[γράφη διά]. ἐ̣[γράφη διὰ τοῦ], proposed in *ZPE* 99, 1993, 117, line 3, is perhaps too long.

L. 4 χειροχρήcτου. This is the earliest occurrence of the term χειροχρήcτηc in the Greek language. It is attested once in the fourth century CE, in Iamblichus, *V.P.* 161, where we find χειροχρήcτων τινῶν λόγων translated in the lexicons as 'manuals', 'handbooks'.[13] More telling is the entry in (spurious) Athanasius (*Quaest. ad Ant.* 88 = M. 28.652B), that the χειροχρήcτηc is ὁ τὰ ἀλλότρια πιcτευόμενοc ἐπὶ τῷ διαδοῦναι τοῖc πένηcιν, that is a kind of trustee. The idea of representing someone else brings us closer to the function fulfilled by the χειροχρήcτηc in the present document, but the latter's function was far more circumscribed. The χειροχρήcτηc here fulfilled the precise and specific legal function of writing a subscription in a case of illiteracy.[14] This function is not attested for the bearer of the title before the middle (perhaps the end) of the sixth century CE. At this late date it occurs in Latin letters in a group of papyri from Ravenna.[15] From the mid-eighth century it occurs again in this sense in Byzantine legal rules.[16] In the papyri from Egypt, this specific legal function is fulfilled by the ὑπογραφεύc.[17] We can see

[10] Cf. Tcherikover in CPJ I, 94–6; III, 43–57 and Horbury and Noy, *Jewish Inscriptions*, 127–8. In a lecture delivered in May 1996 at the Annual Conference of the Society for the Promotion of Classical Studies in Israel, held in Bar-Ilan University, N. Cohen made a good case for the non-Jewish origins of the name.

[11] So also Packman, 'Notes', 96.

[12] But cf. Plato, *Ap.* 24a.5–6: καὶ ὑμᾶc οὔτε μέγα οὔτε μικρὸν ἀποκρυψάμενοc ἐγω λέγω οὐδ' ὑποcτειλάμενοc.

[13] The apparatus (see Deubner-Klein, 1975, p. 91) mentions a suggestion by Reinesius to emend the text to πυθοχρήcτων; although rejected in modern editions, it demonstrates the rarity of the term.

[14] This function was obscured in the imprecise translations of the term as 'scribe' and '*scriba*, an *amanuensis*', in Cotton, 'Another Fragment', 117, 118.

[15] Tjäder, *Papyri Italiens* I nos. 16 ('um 600?'), line 34; 20 ('um 600?'), line 72; 27 ('mitte des 6. Jh.?'), line 1.

[16] *Nov.* 27.1–2 (797–802), K. E. Zachariä von Lingenthal, *Ius Graecoromanum* 1:48; *Ecloga legum* 5.2 (740 CE), ibid., 2:30.

[17] See Youtie, 'ΥΠΟΓΡΑΦΕΥC'.

how the term χειροχρήcτηc came into being in the periphrastic expression χεῖρα χρηcάμενοc παρὰ δεῖνοc in P. Oxy. L 3593 (238–44 CE, 'Instructions to a Rhodian Bank About a Slave Sale') lines 17–21 (cf. lines 45–50): Αὐ[ρῆλι]ο̣[c] Κ̣[υεῖντο]c̣ Εἰλάροṳ χίρα̣ [χ]ρ̣η̣[cάνενο]c̣ π̣αρ̣ὰ̣ Μά[ρκ]ο̣υ Αὐ‹ρηλίου› Εἰ̣ρ̣η̣[νίωνοc το]ῦ̣ κα̣ὶ̣ Διο[νυcί]ου Ῥοδί̣[ου διὰ τὸ ἐμὲ] ἀ̣γρ̣α̣μ̣α̣τ̣ο̣ν̣ ὑπάρχειν̣.[18] See the striking parallel above, No. **13** lines 9–12: שאלה כתב מתת ב[ר] שמעון ממרא ('She is borrowing the writing of Matat son of Shimʿon [who wrote] what she said'; and cf. Ingholt, 'Palmyrene Inscription', 106, lines 2–4 (214 CE): אשאלת כתב ידי ליוליס בר אורליס עגילו בר אפרהט בר חרי זבדבול בדילדי לא ידע ספר ('I have lent my hand to Iulius son of Aurelius ʿOgeilū, son of Afrahaṭ, freedman of Zabdiʾl, because he did not know writing'; see Cotton, 'Subscriptions' for a full discussion).

L. 4 For Ουαινοc, see Negev, *Personal Names*, no. 474. Ḥnynw son of Taymilahi is one of the abutters in P.Yadin **3** line 26. For Cααδαλλου, see Negev, *Personal Names*, nos. 1169–70, and Ustinova and Figueras, 'Funerary Inscription' (sixth century).

L. 4 ἑρμην{ν}εία. It is hard to see what it was the scribe intended; perhaps not a double *nu* after all.

Ll. 4–5 ἐπάρχου ... ὕπαρχοc. One expects ἑρμηνεία ὑπογραφῆ[c τοῦ] ἐπάρχου to be followed by ἔπαρχοc and not by ὕπαρχοc. The epsilon in ἐ̣πάρχου in P.Yadin **16** line 36 is a restoration. Nonetheless, he is called ἐπάρχου in our document too. Indeed, ἔπαρχοc was the usual Greek term for the cavalry commander, the *praefectus equitum* or *praefectus alae*. But ὕπαρχοc, too, meant *praefectus*; see Mason, *Greek Terms*, 13, 138–40, 155, 167. It is very puzzling to have both spellings in the same document, referring to the same person. Unless the scribe simply made a mistake or was not aware of the difference between ἔπαρχοc and ὕπαρχοc, a possible explanation for the different spellings could be that the *he* in Semitic languages could be used both to represent the epsilon of ἔπαρχοc (הפארכוס) as well as the aspiration of the *upsilon* in ὕπαρχοc; see Wasserstein, 'Aramaic Transcriptions', 205ff.[19]

Frgs. c + d
All of the terms in these two fragments appear in the other two land declarations, P.Yadin **16** and No. **62**, and thereby strengthen the case for regarding the fragments as part of a landed property declaration. However, if ἀπογραφῆc in frg. c line 2 belongs to the introduction (cf. P.Yadin **16** line 1 and lines 3–4; No. **62** frg. a lines 1, 3), it is hard to understand ἥμιcυ in the previous line. As for frg. d, it is hard to guess what comes after cπόρου in line 2; the *epsilon* which follows makes it impossible to restore κρειθῆc, which would have been attractive in view of P.Yadin **16** lines 18; 22; 25; 30; and No. **62** frg. a lines 16 and 20. In line 3 we should assume perhaps a sharp break between ἥμιcυ and γείτονεc: ἥμιcυ concludes the description of the yield of the lot and the tax it pays, whereas the γείτονεc commences the description of its abutters, as for example in P.Yadin **16** lines 21–24: κῆπον . . . τελοῦντα τῶν γεινομένων καθ' ἔτοc καρπῶν μέροc ἥμιcυ, γείτονεc μοcχαντικὴ κυρίου Καίcαροc καὶ θάλαccα.

---

[18] 'I, Aurelius Quintus son of Hilarus, having borrowed the handwriting of M. Aurelius Eirenion also called Dionysius, Rhodian, because I am myself illiterate'.

[19] Ὑπαρχία in P.Yadin **26** line 6 (ὅπου ἂν ᾖ ὑπ' αὐτοῦ ὑπαρχ̣[ί]α, lines 5–6) may well be a mistake for ἐπαρχία and can hardly be used as evidence that 'Arabia was divided into districts called *hyparcheiai*', as suggested by Isaac, 'Babatha Archive', 69. Admittedly, the passage still remains difficult to interpret. The late A. Wasserstein drew my attention to Epiphanius' Περὶ μέτρων καὶ cταθμῶν (late fourth century), where we have in the Greek text ἐπαρχία, and in the Syriac translation היפרכיא (see Dean, *Epiphanius' Treatise*, 117, pl. 77b). See the discussion of ὑπαρχεία in Koenen, 'Laudatio funebris'; cf. Naveh, 'Formal and Informal Spelling'.

62. XḤev/Se papLand Declaration gr

Rabbath Moab, Arabia, 4 or 11 December 127 CE

(PLS. XXXIV–XXXVII)

Preliminary publication of frg. a lines 1–20: N. Lewis, 'A Jewish Landowner from the Province of Arabia', *Scripta Classica Israelica* 8–9 (1985–8) 132–7 (no plate).

THIS is the land declaration (*olim* XḤev/Se Gr. 7) of Sammouos son of Shimʿon (frg. a line 12), Salome Komaïse's first husband (see INTRODUCTION TO THE ARCHIVE OF SALOME KOMAÏSE DAUGHTER OF LEVI, and No. **63** line 2), who is also the middleman between the addressee of No. **60**, Menaḥem son of Iohannes, and the tax (or rent) collectors (No. **60** line 8), as well as one of the abutters to the half courtyard in No. **64** of 9 November 129 (line 14 = line 35).

Sammouos son of Shimʿon declares land (fields and groves) which he owns in partnership with his brother, Ionathes. However, he gives only the size of his own half-shares and the taxes due on them: i.e. the fact that the land remained undivided[1] did not result in a joint declaration by the heirs. As an abutter to a neighbour's field or grove, the land owned in partnership by the two brothers would probably be described as κληρονόμοι Cιμωνος. This locution occurs often in the papyri from the Judaean Desert, and in the papyri from Egypt (see COMMENTS on No. **64** ad lines 10–11 and 32). The comparison of P.Yadin **7** (120 CE, line 12 = line 47: ירתי יוסף בר בבא) with No. **64** (129 CE, line 11 = lines 32–33: κληρονόμοι Ιωcηπος Βαβα) demonstrates that inherited land could remain undivided for years.[2]

The three land declarations, No. **62**, P.Yadin **16**, and No. **61**, were submitted by three different people from Maḥoza, on the occasion of the census conducted in the province of Arabia by its governor in 127. P.Yadin **16** is one of the best preserved papyri found by Yadin in the Cave of Letters in Naḥal Ḥever. The Cave of Letters in Naḥal Ḥever is also the source of the two other land declarations,[3] but these were not found in the course of a controlled excavation, a fact which accounts for their poor state of preservation: No. **61** preserves only the conclusion (i.e. the subscriptions) of a land declaration, while No. **62** lacks the conclusion with its subscriptions, as well as an incalculable part of the text.

Like P.Yadin **16** and No. **61**, No. **62** is also an authorized copy of the original declaration, which was posted and displayed in the basilica in the city of Rabbath-Moab.[4] Again, like P.Yadin **16**, it is a double document, with the inner text reduced to

---

[1] Witness the expression μετοχῆc τῆc πρὸc 'Ιωναθην in frg. a line 15; frg. b line 6; frgs. c–m lines 7, 11, and 15.

[2] For Egypt, see Kreller, *Erbrechtliche Untersuchungen* 63–75.

[3] See GENERAL INTRODUCTION.

[4] See INTRODUCTION to No. **61** and Cotton, 'Subscriptions', 31ff. For the need of the individual to obtain an authorized copy of his/her land declaration to show the tax collecting authorities see Isaac, 'Tax Collection', 265ff.

'a two-line notation repeating the opening formula of the outer text' (Lewis, *Documents*, 65). Frg. a, the largest surviving fragment, which contains the first 20 lines of text, was published by Lewis in 1988. The rest survived in larger and shorter fragments, some contiguous to each other, or nearly so. Including frg. a, 33 fragments have survived. A continuous text can be read in frg. b, but it is impossible to know where to place it. A body of continuous text is based on the combination of frgs. c, d, e, f, g, h, j, l, m, and x. Frgs. i and k also belong somewhere in this part of the text but the traces on them are too tiny to help in placing them. This body of continuous text is referred to as frgs. c–m. It is possible, but not entirely safe, to place frg. n before frg. b or before frgs. c–m. Frgs. o, p, q, r, s, t, u, v, w, y, and seven fragments caught in the frame could not be placed, and, like frgs. i and k, were not transcribed here.

In his edition of frg. a, Lewis observed that 'textual restorations are assured by identical language in P.Yadin **16**'. The restoration of a continuous text from the other fragments was facilitated both by the text of frg. a, published by Lewis and reproduced here with very slight alterations, as well by the existence of recurrent formulae for each separate entry of the land declaration. These formulae are:

1. μέρος ἥμιcυ;
2. χώραc or κήπου φοινικῶνοc or ἀμ[πελ];
3. ἐν ὁρίοιc Μαωζων;
4. τῆc προγεγραμμένηc or τῆc αὐτῆc;
5. λεγομένηc (i.e. χώραc) or λεγομένου (i.e. κήπου);
6. name of field or grove, etc.;
7. μετοχῆc τῆc πρὸc Ἰωναθην;
8. Cιμωνοc ἀδελφόν μου or τὸν προγεγραμμένον ἀδελφόν;
9. ὃ μέροc ἥμιcύ ἐcτιν cπόρου κρειθῆc cάτ- or κάβ- (ἡμικάβ- τετάρτου?); τελοῦν;
10. φόρου in 'blacks' and *lepta*,
    or:
    φοίνικοc cυροῦ or/and πατητοῦ or/and ναaρου cάτ- or κάβ- etc., sometimes with cτεφανικοῦ in 'blacks' and *lepta*;
11. γείτονεc
12. the first names and patronyms of the abutters, or 'road', 'sea', etc.

There are two new entries in frg. a, two new entries in frg. b, four or five new entries in frgs. c–m, and one, two, or no new entries on frg. n.[5] Thus, in what survives of the land declaration, there are altogether between eight and eleven entries, i.e. between eight and eleven pieces of land owned in partnership by the two brothers: there may have been more.

A comparison with other documents which contain similar information on land parcels may allow us to appreciate the size of the individual pieces of land owned by the brothers and the amount of taxes, both in kind and in money, on them.[6] Such information, though incomplete and limited, is available in No. **60** (receipt for tax or

[5] See COMMENTS ad loc.

[6] On this and what follows, see the pioneer study of Broshi in 'Seven Notes', 234–9, and Weiser and Cotton, 'Gebt dem Kaiser, was des Kaisers ist', 237ff.

rent from 125 CE), P.Yadin **16** (land declaration from 127 CE), No. **64** (a deed of gift from 129 CE), and No. **12** (a receipt from 131 CE).[7]

Table 1 attempts to convey the relations between size of land and the amount of tax (or rent), both in kind and in cash, on them. It seems that the inheritance of the two brothers, Sammouos and Ionathes sons of Shimʿon, was made up of small plots of land. Babatha's plots, declared in P.Yadin **16**, were generally much larger. The fact that each piece of land, in P.Yadin **16** as well as in Nos. **62** and **64**, has its own name (and thus, presumably, its own history), suggests that land was accumulated by one family over time.[8] There does not seem to be any constant ratio between the rate of tax and the size of land, in as far as we have these.[9] The only remarkable fact is the low rates paid by Βηθφααραια (P.Yadin **16** lines 30ff.) in contrast with the high rates paid by Χαφφουρα (No. **62** frgs. c–m lines 14ff.), which may be due to the quality of the soil and the resultant yields.[10] The monetary tax is variously described as τειμὴ φοίνικος (No. **60** line 5), φόρος[11] (e.g. No. **62** frg. a line 16), and sometimes στεφανικόν (e.g. P.Yadin **16** line 27).[12] The monetary tax seems to be loosely related to the size of land and the tax in kind. Our estimation of the tax is further hampered by our ignorance of the respective value of 'blacks' and *lepta*: how many *lepta* make up one 'black'?[13]

It is noteworthy that twenty-one years after the annexation of the kingdom of Arabia, as late as the census of 127 CE, the inhabitants were not required to declare the size of their land and its productivity in Roman units of measurement,[14] but could do so in their own local units of measurement. The amount of tax is given in terms of unit of volume: *kor* (κόρος), *seʾah* (σάτον), and *kab* (κάβος),[15] whereas the size of the individual fields is given in terms of *bet seʾah* and *bet kab* of barley, i.e the size of land sown by a *seʾah* or a *kab* of barley. There is much disagreement about the absolute values of these measurements.[16]

---

[7] To these should be added P.Yadin **21** and **22**; see below.

[8] See Broshi, 'Seven Notes', 240.

[9] The rates are in Αλγιφιαμμα (P.Yadin **16** lines 17ff.): 1:10; 1:6.66; and 1:0.86; Βαγαλγαλα (P.Yadin **16** lines 24ff.): 1:10; 1:10; and 1:1.1; Βηθφααραια (P.Yadin **16** lines 29ff.): 1:4.5; 1:3; and 1:0.42; Αρενοαραθα (No. **62** frg. a lines 14ff.): 1:0.96; Χαφφουρα (No. **62** frgs. c–m lines 7ff.): 1:1.1; and Χαφφουρα (No. **62** frgs. c–m lines 14ff.): 1:3.12; 1:3.12.

[10] Cf. Hyginus, *Constitutio limitum*, p. 168f. (Thulin).

[11] Indicated in the table by #.

[12] Indicated in the table by *; on the *stephanikon*, see COMMENTS ad frgs. c–m lines 17–18.

[13] See COMMENTS ad No. **60** lines 8–9 and line 9.

[14] Cf. Neesen, *Untersuchungen*, 30ff.

[15] A *kab* equals one sixth of a *seʾah*, i.e. six *kab*s make one *seʾah kor* equals thirty *seʾah*s.

[16] See Broshi in 'Seven Notes', 234–5 and Lewis, *Documents*, 69.

TABLE 1: *Land Units and their Taxes*

	Name of Grove	Size (*Bet Seʾah*)	Tax or Rent in *Seʾahs* on Dates[17]	Tax or Rent in *Seʾahs* on 'Splits'[18]	Monetary Tax or Rent * = στεφανικόν # = φόρος	Other Kind of Tax or Rent
No. **60**	—	—	—	—	4 blacks; 58 lepta	
P.Yadin **16**	Αλγιφιαμμα	1.5 *bet seʾah*	15 *seʾahs*	10 *seʾahs*	*1 black; 30 lepta	
	Αλγιφιαμμα	1/6 *bet seʾah*			none	half-share of the crops
	Βαγαλγαλα	3 *bet seʾah*	30 *seʾahs*	30 *seʾahs*	*3 blacks; 30 lepta	
	Βηθφααραια	20 *bet seʾah*	90 *seʾahs*	60 *seʾahs*	*8 blacks; 45 lepta	
No. **62**, Frg. a	Αρενοαραθα[19]	1.5 *bet seʾah*	none	none	# 1 black; 45 lepta	
	Χαφφουρα	—	—	—	—	
No. **62**, Frg. b	?	0.125 *bet seʾah*	—	—	—	
	Γανναθ ...χ.βαcα	less than 1 *bet seʾah*	—	—	—	
No. **62**, Frgs. c–m	Χαφφουρα	1 *bet seʾah*	none	none	# 1 black; 10 lepta	
	Γανναθ ..οραθ	—	unknown amount of Syrian dates	—	—	
	Χαφφουρα	0.08 *bet seʾah*	2.5 *seʾahs*	2.5 *seʾahs*	*unknown amount	
No. **64**	Γανναθ 'Αcαδαια	—	6 *seʾahs*	10 *seʾahs*	none	
No. **12**	—	—	none	none	none	19.25 *seʾahs* of dates, kind not specified

[17] Syian, mixed, and/or naʿaran dates are taxed together in the documents; on Syrian and naʿaran dates, see COMMENTS and frgs. c–m lines 12 and 17.

[18] Πατητόc in Greek, see frgs. c–m line 17.

[19] Admittedly, we do not know that this was a date grove.

One should also consider the two complementary contracts for the purchase of date crops: P.Yadin **21** and **22**, from 130 CE. The buyer of the crop of the three date groves (Γανναθ Φερωρα, Γανναθ Νικαρκος, and Γανναθ Μολχαιου) undertakes to pay forty-two talents of 'first' and 'second splits' and sixty-five *se'ahs* of Syrian and naʿaran dates. Failure to fulfill the terms of the contract will result in a fine of two *denarii* for each talent of 'splits', i.e. 84 *denarii*, and one 'black' for each *se'ah* (?) of Syrian and naʿaran dates, i.e. 65 'blacks'.

Date and Provenance

Lewis's observations about the date of No. **62** can be quoted here in full:

> There is a discrepancy between the Roman and the provincial dates. A similar discrepancy, but only of a single day, occurs in *P. Yadin* 14 and 15. Here the discrepancy is greater, *pro III id.* Dec. corresponding to 11 December, Appelaios 18th to 4 December. ν[ω]νῶν, which would reduce the discrepancy to one day (= 3 December), cannot be read here in place of ε̣[ἰ]δ̣ῶν because most of the *epsilon* and the right-hand corner of the *delta* are visible. It may seem that the 11 December date is confirmed by *trib. pot. XII* (lines 6–7), which began on the tenth of that month. That argument cannot be decisive, however, because *P. Yadin* 16, drawn up on 2 December, also has (incorrectly) *trib. pot. XII*. All that does emerge clearly is that more than twenty years after Rome's annexation of the province of Arabia local scribes were still having trouble equating the months and days of the old (Macedonian) and the new (Roman) calendar.[17]

Whether submitted on 4 or 11 December, No. **62** is much nearer in time to P.Yadin **16** than to No. **61**. The subscription to No. **61**, dated 25 April 127,[18] suggests that the land declaration itself was submitted a few days before, and thus much later than the other two land declarations (see DATE AND PROVENANCE in No. **61**).

On Rabbath-Moab, see DATE AND PROVENANCE in No. **61**.

TABLE 2: *Measurements of Transcribed Fragments (in cm)*

Frg	Width	Height	Frg.	Width	Height	Frg.	Width	Height
a	18.0	17.5	f	4.8	0.5	l	2.5	3.0
b	15.5	6.5	g	7.0	1.0	m	8.0	12.0
c	10.5	3.5	h	10.0	2.2	n	6.0	1.0
d	5.5	6.0	j	1.5	1.2	x	1.5	2.0
e	3.5	0.8						

[17] Lewis, 'Jewish Landowner', 135–6; see also Lewis, *Documents*, 57 ad P.Yadin **14** lines 2–4 = 17–20; and DATE AND PROVENANCE in No. **64** for a possibility of a three-day discrepancy between the Roman and the Macedonian calendars in lines 1–3)

[18] See DATE AND PROVENANCE in No. **61**.

Mus. Inv. Rockefeller
IAA 475782, 475784, 475980, 475982

Recto

Frg. a
Inner Text

1 ἐγγεγρ̣α̣μ̣μ̣έν̣ο̣ν καὶ ἀντιβεβλημένο̣ν̣ ἀντ̣ίγραφον ἀπογραφῆ̣ς̣ προκ̣ιμένης μεθ' ἐτ[έ]-

2 ρ̣ω̣[ν] ἐ̣ν̣ τ̣ῇ̣ ἐ̣ν̣θά̣δ̣ε̣ βασι[λι]κ̣ῆ̣ο̣ῦ̣ τ̣ὸ ἀ̣ν̣[τί]γρ̣α̣φον ὑ̣π̣οτέτακται.

Outer Text

3 ἐ̣[γγ]ε̣γρ[αμ]μ̣έ̣ν̣ο̣ν̣ καὶ ἀ̣ντιβεβ̣λ̣η̣μ̣ένον ἀντίγρα̣φον ἀπογραφῆς προκιμένης

4 μεθ' ἑτέρων ἐν τῇ ἐνθάδε βασιλικῇ, οὗ τὸ ἀντίγρα̣φον ὑ̣π̣ο̣τ̣έ̣τακται. ἐπὶ Αὐτ̣ο̣κρά-

5 τ̣[ο]ρος Καίcαρος, θεοῦ Τρα̣ι̣α̣ν̣ο̣ῦ̣ Π̣αρθικοῦ υἱοῦ, θεοῦ Νέρουα υἱωνοῦ, Τραιανοῦ

6 [Ἁδριανοῦ Cεβαcτοῦ, ἀρχιε]ρέ[ωc μεγίcτο]υ, δ̣η̣[μαρχ]ι̣κῆc ἐ̣ξ̣ο̣υ̣c̣ί̣α̣ς̣ τ̣ὸ̣ δ̣ω̣δ̣έ̣-

7 [κατον, ὑπάτου τὸ τρίτον, ἐ]π̣[ὶ ὑπάτων] Μά̣ρ̣κ̣ου Γα<ου>ίου Γαλλικανοῦ καὶ Τίτου Ἀ-

8 [τειλίου Ῥούφου] Τ̣[ιτ]ι̣[ανο]ῦ̣ πρὸ τριῶν ε̣[ἰ]δ̣ῶν Δ̣εκεμβρίων, κατὰ δὲ τὸν τῆc

9 ν̣[έαc] ἐ̣π̣α̣ρ̣χ̣ε̣ί̣α̣ς̣ Ἀ̣ραβίαc ἀ̣ριθμὸν ἔτ̣ο̣υ̣ς̣ δ̣ε̣υ̣τέρου εἰκοcτοῦ μηνὸς Ἀπελλαί-

10 ου ὀ̣κτοκαιδεκά̣[τῃ ἐν] Ῥαββαθμ̣ω̣βοιc πόλει, ἀποτειμ̣ήcεωc Ἀραβίαc ἀγομένηc

11 ὑ̣[πὸ Τ]ί̣τ̣[ο]υ̣ Ἀ̣[νεινίου Cεξτίου] Φ̣λ̣ω̣ρ̣ε̣ν̣τ̣είνο[υ] π̣ρ̣ε̣c̣βευτ̣ο̣ῦ̣ C̣ε̣βαcτ̣ο̣ῦ̣ ἀ̣ν̣τιcτρα-

12 τ̣ή̣γ̣ο̣υ. C̣α̣μ̣μ̣ο̣υ̣οc C̣ιμων[ο]c Μαωζηνὸc τῆc Ζοαρηνῆc περιμέτρου Πέτραc,

13 ο̣ἰ̣κῶν [ἐ]ν ἰδίοιc ἐν αὐτῇ Μαωζα̣, ἀπ̣ογράφομαι ἐμαυτὸν ἐτῶν τριάκοντ̣α̣

14 ...[..]η̣λ̣ν̣ι̣ο̣ν̣ [ἐ]ν̣ιαύcιον μέροc ἥμιcυ χώραc ἐν ὁρίοιc Μαωζων τῆc προ-

15 γ̣ε̣γραμμέν̣η̣c̣ λ̣ε̣γ̣ο̣μ̣έ̣νηc Αρενοαραθα μετ̣οχῆc τῆc πρὸc Ιωναθην Cιμωνοc

16 ὃ μέρ̣ο̣c ἥμιcύ ἐcτιν cπόρ̣ο̣υ̣ κρ̣ειθῆc cάτου ἑ̣[ν]ὸ̣c̣ κάβων τριῶ̣ν̣ τελοῦν φόρου μέ-

17 λαν ἓν λεπτὰ τεc̣c̣α̣ράκοντα̣ πέντε, γείτ̣[ον]εc Μαν̣α̣ηc Μαναη καὶ θάλαccα, μέ-

18 ροc̣ ἥμιcυ κ̣ήπου φοινικῶν̣οc ἐν ὁρ̣ί̣ο̣ι̣c̣ [Μ]αω̣ζων τῆc α̣[ὐ]τῆc λεγομένου Χαφ-

19 φ[ο]υ̣ρ̣α μ̣[ε]τ̣οχῆ[c τ]ῆ̣c̣ π̣ρὸc Ιω̣ν̣αθην C̣[ιμωνο]c̣ ἀ[δ]ε̣[λ]φόν μου ὃ μέροc ἥμιcύ ἐc-

20 [τι]ν cπόρου κ̣ρ̣ε̣[ι]θ̣ῆ̣[c] *traces of letters*

1; 3 ἐκγ- 10 ὀκτω-

Previous publication (Lewis, 'Jewish Landowner'):

1–2 ἑτ̣|[έρων] 2 βαcιλ̣ι̣κῆ̣ [ο]ὗ̣ ἀ̣ν̣τ̣ί̣γραφον 6 ἀρχιερέωc μεγίc]του 9 [νέαc ἐ]π̣α̣ρχεία̣[c] 10 ἀποτιμ̣ήcεωc 12 ......οc Cίμων[ο]c 14 ...[..]..ν̣ι̣ο̣ν̣ 18–19 Χαφ|φ[.]..α 19 C̣ί̣μ̣[ωνο]c 20 κ[ρ]ειθῆ[c]

Frg. n

1 [Ἰ]ωc̣ηπου, μ̣ε̣ροc ἥμιcυ ἀμ[πελῶνοc?

2 *traces*

Frg. b[19]

1 [μετοχῆς]

2 [τῆς πρὸς] Ιωναθην τὸν προ[γ]ε̣γρα̣μμ[έ]νο̣[ν ἀδελφόν, ὃ μέρος ἥμισύ ἐστιν]

3 [σπόρου κ]ρ̣ειθῆς ἡμικάβο̣υ τε[τ]άρτου̣ τ̣[ε]λ̣ο̣ῦ̣ν̣[

4 [γείτονες *? letters*]χεελ̣ανης Ϲ̣εδ̣αλλου καὶ Αβδ̣.[..]..[*? letters* , μέρος]

5 [ἥμισυ] κ̣ήπου φοινικῶνος ἐν ὁρίοις Μαωζω̣ν τῆς̣ [αὐτῆς λεγομένου]

6 [Γανν]α̣θ ...χ.βασα μετοχῆς τῆς πρὸς Ἰωναθη[ν τὸν προγεγραμμένον]

7 [ἀδελφόν, ὃ μέρος ἥμις]ύ̣ ἐς̣τιν σπ̣όρο̣υ κρειθ̣ῆς κάβ.[

Frgs. c–m (c, d, e, f, g, h, j, l, m, and x)[20]

6 μ[έρος ἥμισυ *c.15 letters* ἐν ὁρίοις] Μ̣α̣ω̣[ζ]ων τῆς αὐ̣τ̣ης λε̣γο̣[μέ-]

7 [ν]ο̣υ̣ Χαφφο̣υρα μετοχ̣[ῆς τῆς] π̣ρ̣[ὸς Ιωναθην τ]ὸ̣ν̣ π̣ρ̣ο̣γ̣εγραμ̣μέ[ν]ον
ἀδε̣[λ]φ̣όν,

8 ὃ̣ μ̣ε̣ρ̣ο̣ς̣ ἥμ̣ι̣[σύ] ἐστ[ιν] σπόρ[ου κρειθῆς σάτου ἑ]νὸς τελοῦν φόρου̣ μ̣έλαν ἓν
λ̣ε̣πτὰ

9 δέκα, γείτονες .α[*c.30 letters*]νου, [μ]έ̣ρος ἥμισυ

10 κήπου φοινικ̣[ῶνος ἐν ὁρίοις Μαωζων τῆς] α̣[ὐτ]ῆ̣ς λε[γ]ομέν̣ο̣υ Γανναθ̣ ..-

11 οραθ̣ μετ̣οχ[ῆς τῆς πρὸς Ἰωναθην τὸν πρ]ο̣γ[εγρ]α̣μ̣μ̣έ̣ν̣ο̣ν̣ ἀδε̣λ̣φόν, ὃ̣ μέ[ρο]ς

12 ἥμισύ ἐστιν ς̣[πόρου κρειθῆς *6–8 letters*] ἡ̣μίσους̣ τε[λο]ῦ̣ν φοίνικος συροῦ

13 [*c.20 letters?* γείτον]ε̣ς̣ Σαμμ̣οῦο̣ς̣ Μ̣αναη̣λ̣ο̣υ̣ καὶ Μ̣α̣ν̣αηλος Μα̣ν̣α-

---

[19] It is not certain where the lines begin. Another reconstruction could be:

1 [*c.8 letters* μετοχῆς τῆς πρὸς] Ἰωναθην τὸν προ[γ]ε̣γρα̣μμ[έ]νο̣[ν ἀδελφόν,]

2 [ὃ μέρος ἥμισύ ἐστιν σπόρου κ]ρ̣ειθῆς ἡμικάβο̣υ τε[τ]άρτου̣ τ̣[ε]λ̣ο̣ῦ̣ν̣[*6 letters*]

3 [γείτονες *? letters*]χεελ̣ανης Ϲ̣εδ̣αλλου καὶ Αβδ̣.[..]..[.]

4 [*c.7 letters* μέρος ἥμισυ] κ̣ήπου φοινικῶνος ἐν ὁρίοις Μαωζω̣ν τῆς̣ [αὐτῆς]

5 [λεγομένου Γανν]α̣θ ...χ.βασα μετοχῆς τῆς πρὸς Ἰωναθη[ν τὸν προγε-]

6 [γραμμένον ἀδελφόν, ὃ μέρος ἥμις]ύ̣ ἐς̣τιν σπ̣όρο̣υ κρειθ̣ῆς κάβ.[

[20] Lines 1-5 were not transcribed due to their extremely fragmentary state. However, their content is clear; see COMMENTS below.

14 ηλου, μέρος ἥ[μιcυ κ]ή̣που φο̣ινικ̣ῶν̣ο̣ς̣ ἐν̣ ὁ̣ρ̣ί̣οις Μαωζων τῆς αὐτῆς λε-

15 γομένου Χαφφο̣υρ̣[α] μετοχῆ[c] τ̣ῆ̣ς̣ πρ[ὸc] Ἰ̣ω̣ν̣α̣θ̣η̣ν̣ τ̣ὸ̣ν̣ προγεγραμμέ̣ν̣ο̣ν̣

16 [ἀδελ]φ̣ό̣ν̣ ὃ̣ μ̣έ̣ρ̣ο̣ς̣ ἥμ̣ι̣cύ̣ ἐ̣ς̣τ̣ι̣ν̣ ς̣π̣ό̣ρου {cπόρου} κ̣ρ̣ε̣ι̣θῆ̣ς̣ ἡμικάβου τελοῦν

17 φοίνικο̣c πατ̣ητοῦ ς̣άτα δύο κά̣β̣ο̣υ̣ς̣ τρεῖc, ναα̣ρου ς̣ά̣τα δύ̣ο̣ κά̣βουc τρ̣ε̣ῖ̣c
cτεφα-

18 νικο̣ῦ̣ [*traces of c.16 letters*] [γ]είτ̣ο̣νεc Ελα̣ζ̣α̣[ροc *c.23 letters*]

12 cυρίου

Verso
Frg. a[21]

1 והבאלהי בר עבׄדאל[הי] שהד

2 .... בר עותו שהד

3 Εὐτυ[χ.]c Αβδο̣ο̣βου

4 ......בׄרׄ[...] שׄהׄדׄ

5 ...בר ח[

Translation

Frg. a; Inner Text
Verified exact copy of a registration displayed amongst others in the basilica here, the copy of which follows.

Outer Text
Verified exact copy of a registration displayed amongst others in the basilica here, the copy of which follows. In the reign of Imperator Caesar divi Traiani Parthici filius divi Nervae nepos Traianus [Hadrianus Augustus pon]tifex maximus tribuniciae potestatis XII [consul III,] in [the consulship] of Marcus Gavius Gallicanus and Titus Atilius Rufus Titianus, three days before the ides of December, and according to the computation of the n[ew] province of Arabia year twenty-second month Apellaios the eighteenth, in the city of Rabbath-Moab, a census of Arabia being conducted by Titus A[ninius Sextius] Florentinus legatus Augusti pro praetore, I, Sammouos son of Shimʿon, of Maḥoza in the district of Ẓoʿar of the administrative region of Petra, domiciled in my own private property in the said Maḥoza, register myself, thirty years old, [as owner of?] a yearly half-share of a field, called Arenoaratha,

21 Transcriptions of the Nabataean names in lines 1, 2, 4, and 5 are given in Hebrew letters. The Nabataean signatures were read by A. Yardeni.

within the boundaries of the aforesaid Maḥoza, in partnership with Ionathes son of Shimʿon, which half-share is (the area) of sowing one *seʾah* three *kab*s of barley, paying as tax one 'black' and forty-five *lepta*, abutters (being) Manaēs son of Manaēs and the sea; half-share of a date grove within the boundaries of the said Maḥoza, called Ḥaffoura, in partnership with my brother Ionathes son of Shimʿon, which half-share is (the area) of sowing . . . of barley[. . .

Frg. n
[abutters being X and X] son of Joseph; a half-share of a vine[yard . . .

Frg. b
[in partnership with] the aforesaid [brother,] Ionathes, [which half-share is (the area) of sowing] half a *kab* and another quarter (of a *kab*) of barley, paying [. . . abutters (being)] Ḥeëlanes son of Sedallos and Abd[. . . , a half-share] of a date grove within the boundaries of the [said] Maḥoza, [called the Gar]den of [ ]...*ḥbasa*, in partnership with [the aforesaid brother] Ionathes [which half-share] is (the area) of sowing *kab* (or *kab*s) of barley[. . .

Frgs. c–m
[a half-share of a date grove (or a vineyard) within the boundaries] of the said Maḥoza, called Ḥaffoura, in partnership with [the aforesaid] brother [Ionathes,] which half-share is (the area) of sowing one [*seʾah* of barley], paying as tax one black and ten *lepta*, abutters being .*a*[. . . son of]*nos* (or]*nas*); a half-share of a date [grove within the boundaries of the] said [Maḥoza], called the Garden of [ ]*orath*, in partnership [with the] aforesaid brother, [Ionathes,] which half-share is (the area) of s]owing [ ] and a half [of barley,] paying [? of] Syrian dates, [the abut]ters (being) Sammouos son of Manaʾelos and [Man]aʾelos son of Manaʾelos; a half-share of a date grove within the boundaries of the said Maḥoza, called Ḥaffoura, in partnership with the aforesaid brother Ionathes, which half-share is (the area)] of sowing half a *kab* of barley, paying two *seʾah*s and three *kab*s of 'splits', two *seʾah*s and three *kab*s of naʿaran dates, and as *stephanikon* [ ] abutters (being) Elaza[ros . . .

Verso
Frg. a
1. Whbʾalhy son of ʿAbdʾal[hy,] witness.
2. .... son of ʿAwtw, witness
3. Eutyches (or Eutychos) son of 'Adoobos
4. ......son of [...,] witness
5. ...son of Ḥ[

COMMENTS

Frg. a
Ll. 1 and 3 ἐγγεγραμένον καὶ ἀντιβεβλημένον. The phrase renders the Latin *descriptum et recognitum*; see Lewis's comments and bibliography on the subject ad P.Yadin **12** lines 1 and 4, *Documents*, 50. In *FIRA* I^3 no. 76 lines 4–9, we have a description of how the individual obtained such a copy: 'M. Valerius M.f. Pol(lia) Quadratus vet(eranus) dimmissus honesta missione ex leg(ione) X Fretense testatus est se descriptum et recognitum fecisse ex tabula aenea, quae est fixa in Caesareo Magno . . . in pariete, in qua scriptum est, {et} id quod infra scriptum est'; the last phrase is rendered in Greek: ọῦ τὸ ἀ̣ν̣[τί]γρα̣φον ὑπο̣τέτακται (line 2 = line 4).

Ll. 1 and 3 ἀπογραφῆς. Here, as in P.Yadin **16**, in the sense of registration, see ἀπο̣γράφομαι ἐμαυτόν in line 13: 'I register myself'. It is used in the same sense in P.Yadin **24**, where, however, it does not refer to registration on the occasion of the census: ἐπιδὴ ἀπεγράψατο Ἰούδας Ἐλεαζάρο[υ Χθουςίωνος] ἀπογενομένου cου ἀνὴρ ἐπ' ὀνόματός cου ἐν τῇ ἀπ[ο]γραφῇ κήπους φοινικῶνος ἐν Μαωζᾳ (lines 4–6).[22]

Ll. 1–2 and 3–4. Cf. the similar but not identical formula in P.Yadin **16** lines 1–2 = 3–5: ἐγγεγραμμένον καὶ ἀντιβεβλημένον ἀντίγραφον πιτακίου ἀπογραφῆς προκειμένης ἐν τῇ ἐνθάδε βασιλικῇ, καὶ ἔςτιν ὡς ὑποτέτακται.

Ll. 4–7 There are, it appears, two other examples of the full form of Hadrian's imperial titulature in the papyri; in both of them the titulature appears in the nominative: SB III 6944 (two copies of an edict from 136 CE); P.Oslo III 78 (another copy of the same edict),[23] and P.Würzb. 9 (a letter to the city of Antinoopolis, between 130 and 135 CE).[24] A much shorter form of the imperial titulature occurs when it is part of the dating formula, as here, i.e following ἐπί.[25] Concerning the reason for the extended form of the imperial titulature on this occasion, see INTRODUCTION TO THE GREEK DOCUMENTARY TEXTS: 'The Calendar'.

Ll. 6–7 δη[μαρχ]ικῆς ἐξουςίας τὸ δωδε[κατον]. See DATE AND PROVENANCE to No. **62**.

Ll. 8–9 κατὰ δὲ τὸν τῆς ν[έας] ἐπαρχείας Ἀραβίας ἀριθμόν. For 'new' in the dating formula, see INTRODUCTION TO THE GREEK DOCUMENTARY TEXTS.

L. 11 Titus Aninius Sextius Florentinus is attested here for the first time as governor of Arabia. His predecessor, Ti. Iulius Iulianus Alexander, is attested for the first time as governor on 11–12 October 125 (P.Yadin **14** and **15**), and his successor, T. Haterius Nepos, is attested for the first time in Arabia on 17 November 130 (P.Yadin **23**). Titus Aninius Sextius Florentinus died in office, as his tomb in Petra, dedicated by his son, demonstrates (*CIL* III 87 = 14148^{10}; see *IGLS* XXI *Inscriptions de la Jordanie* IV, 51). His governorship fell approximately between 126/7 and 128/9.[26]

Ll. 12–13 Çαμμουος Çιμων[ο]ς Μαωζηνὸς τῆς Ζοαρηνῆς περιμέτρου Πέτρας οἰκῶν [ἐ]ν ἰδίοις ἐν αὐτῇ Μαωζᾳ. Identical phrasing is found in P.Yadin **16**: Βαβθα Cίμωνος Μαωζηνὴ τῆς Ζοαρηνῆς περιμέτρου Πέτρας οἰκοῦςα ἐν ἰδίοις ἐν αὐτῇ Μαωζᾳ (lines 13-14).

L. 13 ἀπογράφομαι ἐμαυτὸν ἐτῶν τριάκοντα. There is no parallel for this formula in P.Yadin **16**, where Babatha registers only land: ἀπογράφομαι ἃ κέκτημαι (line 15). The age of the declarant, whether male or female, was a standing element of the ἀπογραφὴ κατ' οἰκίαν in Egypt.[27] Lewis considers this to be 'no more than a stylistic variation in the declaration formula' ('Jewish Landowner', 136). Aichinger ('Zwei Arten?', 37) suggests that it was intended to distinguish Sammouos son of Shimᶜon from a homonym. 'With these two documents as the sole evidence [any] assumption must be regarded as at best speculative' (Lewis, 'Jewish Landowner', 136).[28]

L. 14 ...[..]ηλνιον. One expects here something like ἔχοντα or κεκτημένον, but the text defies any attempt at restoration.

L. 14 [ἐ]νιαύςιον. In the extant fragments of No. **62**, this is the only time that a half-share (μέρος ἥμιςυ) is described as 'annual'. It is hard to know if by 'annual' a lease is meant. In two other documents from this archive there may be a case of a lease from the emperor—at least, in both cases it is specified that payment is to be made to the emperor.[29] But, in both cases, it is impossible to determine whether

---

[22] Cf. ἀπογράφο[μαι] αὐτὰ [ἐν τῇ *c.8 letters* ἀπο]γρα[φῇ] (lines 11–12). On ἀπογραφή and ἀπογράφομαι in P.Yadin **24**, see Cotton, 'Deeds of Gift', 412 (Hebrew).

[23] See Oliver, *Greek Constitutions*, no. 88A, B, C.

[24] See Oliver, *Greek Constitutions*, no. 164; see Bureth, *Les Titulatures impériales*, 63.

[25] Cf. Bureth, *Les Titulatures impériales*.

[26] See Eck, 'Jahres- und Provinzialfasten', 1983, 163–6; 213; Sartre, *Trois études*, 81–2, nos. 4, 5, 6..

[27] Thus it is hard to accept Lewis's alternative suggestion 'that such a personal declaration was not required from Babatha because she was a woman' ('Jewish Landowner', 136).

[28] Lo Cascio, 'Census provinciale' infers from this discrepancy that women were not subject to the *tributum capitis*.

[29] No. **60** lines 5–6: τειμὴν φοίνικος οὗ ὀφείλεις Κ[υ]ρίῳ Καίςαρι; No. **64** lines 28–30: <ἣ> τελέςει καθ' ἔτος εἰς λόγον κυριακοῦ φίςκου . . . φοίνεικος πατητοῦ ςάτα δέκα καὶ ςυροῦ καὶ νααρου ςάτα ἕξ.

the payment mentioned is of rent or of taxes.[30] Be this as it may, if the date groves in Nos. **62** and **64** were on lease from the emperor, then 'tax' and 'rent' would, in any case, be indistinguishable. As for the status of the field in question here, the issue cannot be decided by the use of φόροϲ in line 16, since the term is used for both rent and tax.[31]

Ll. 14–17 Nothing in the text suggests that this μέροϲ ἥμιϲυ χώραϲ was a date grove. See COMMENTS ad frg. n.

L. 15 Αρενοαραθα. See COMMENTS on frgs. c–m lines 9–10.

L. 15 Ιωναθην Cιμωνοϲ. Ionathes son of Shimʿon does not appear elsewhere in the papyri from Naḥal Ḥever.

L. 16 φόρου. See COMMENTS ad line 14.

Ll. 16–17 μέλαν ἒν λεπτὰ τεϲϲ̣αράκοντ̣α̣ πέντε. On these monetary units, which occur also in the Babatha Archive, see COMMENTS ad No. **60** lines 8–9 and line 9. They occur again in No. **62** frgs. c–m lines 8–9.

L. 17 Μαν̣α̣ηϲ. The name appears not to be attested elsewhere.

L. 17 θάλαϲϲα. The sea, as is to be expected, is also one of the abutters of the two date groves called Αλγιφιαμμα in P.Yadin **16** lines 18–24; the Greek transliterates the Aramaic phrase על גיף ימא, 'on the seashore'. This is one of the clues for the exact location of Maḥoza; see 'The Archive of Salome Komaïse Daughter of Levi'.

Ll. 18–19 Χαφφ[ο]υ̣ρα. The name of the field is likely to come from the Semitic root חפר, i.e. 'to dig'. Two additional lots owned in partnership by the two brothers are called by the same name, see frgs. c–m lines 7 and 15. P.Yadin **44**, a deed of lease from 134 CE (unpublished), mentions twice 'a place called Haḥfir' (המקום שנקרה החפיר, lines 8–9, 11).

Frg. n

This small fragment contains the remnants of two entries. [Ι]ωϲ̣ηπου is the patronymic of the second neighbour of the land described in one entry, and thus the last word in it; μ̣έροϲ ἥμιϲυ ἀμ[is the beginning of the next entry. Frg. n could be a link between frgs. a and b, or between either of them and frgs. c–m; interpreted in this way, there are no new entries in this fragment. Alternatively, [Ι]ωϲ̣ηπου could be the last word of the last entry on frg. a (see lines 17–20) or of the second entry on frg. b (lines 4ff.), whereas μ̣έροϲ ἥμιϲυ ἀμ[constitutes a new entry, or vice versa: the patronymic is the last word of a lost entry and the next entry is the missing beginning of the first entry on frg. b or on frgs. c–m. Either of the last two reconstructions means that there are nine or ten entries in what survived of the land declaration.[32] A less likely suggestion is that frg. n contains the remnants of two lost entries. In that case there would be altogether ten or eleven entries in what survived of the land declaration.

L. 1 μ̣έροϲ ἥμιϲυ ἀμ[. 'Αμ[πελῶνοϲ] or ἄμ[πελου], or ἀμ[πέλικοῦ χωρίου] are all possible restorations. Although this is the only time that a vineyard is mentioned in the papyri from Arabia, there is no reason to suspect the reading in view of the fact that 'vine was cultivated on almost any arable land, from the ridges of the Galilean Heights to the Negev'.[33] The evidence of wine-presses in the Nabataean areas of the Negev in the Byzantine period, combined with that of the literary sources, as well as that of the Nessana papyri, fully bears out this statement.[34]

---

[30] See INTRODUCTION to No. **60** and excursus on No. **64** lines 28–30.

[31] See INTRODUCTION to No. **60**. The term φόροϲ occurs also in frgs. c–m line 8, but the term ἐνιαύϲιον, if it occurred, came in the lacuna in line 6.

[32] See COMMENTS on frgs. c–m line 1.

[33] Broshi, 'Wine in Ancient Palestine', 22–3.

[34] Mayerson, 'Wine and Vineyards'; Rubin, *The Negev*, 89–90.

Frg. b

L. 3 ἡμικάβο̣υ τε[τ]άρτου̣. 'Half a *kab* and another quarter (of a *kab*)', i.e. three quarters[35] of a *kab* or one-eighth of a *se'ah*. Babatha's smallest plot was one-sixth of a *se'ah*; see P.Yadin **16** line 22. However, this is only a μέρος ἥμιcυ; the undivided plot measured a quarter of a *se'ah*.

L. 4 χεε̣λανηc. Perhaps not the beginning of a name.

L. 4 Ç̣εδ̣αλλου. Cf. No. **61** line 4 Cααδαλου; Negev, *Personal Names*, nos. 1169–1170: **שעדאלהי**, **שעדאלה**.

L. 4 Αβδ̣.[. This could be the beginning of the name ʿAbdʾal[hy], attested in Nabataean letters, as the patronymic of the first witness on the verso: והבאלהי בר עבֿדֿאל[הי], Whbʾalhy son of ʿAbdʾal[hy]. Alternatively it could be the beginning of the name ʿAbdoobos, attested as the patronymic of the third witness on the verso: Εὐτυ[χ.]c Αβδο̣ο̣βου, Eutyches (or Eutychos) son of ʿAbdoobos. Other possible restorations, all based on the nomenclature found in the papyri from the Judaean Desert, are: (1) Αβδου, ʿAbdu,[36] attested in Nabataean letters in P.Yadin **16** line 39: עבדו בר מקימו, 'ʿAbdu son of Muqimu'; (2) עבדחרתת, ʿAbdḥaretat, attested in Nabataean letters in No. **64** line 47: תימדושרא בר עבדחֿרֿ[תת], 'Timadushra son of ʿAbdḥare[tat]', as well as in P.Yadin **2** and **3** (unpublished);[37] (3) עבדעבדת, ʿAbdʿobdath and (4) עבדאיסי, ʿAbdʾisay, both attested in Nabataean letters in P.Yadin **12** (124 CE) lines 14–15; (5) עבדעמנו, ʿAbdʿamnou or עבדעמיו, ʿAbdʿamiou, attested in Nabataean letters in P.Yadin **1** (94 CE; unpublished) and **2** (99 CE; unpublished); (6) finally, 'Αβδερευc, ʾAbdereus, attested in Greek letters in P.Yadin **12** line 16.

L. 6 [Γανν]α̣θ. This is a transliteration of Aramaic גנת, the construct-state of גנה 'garden' or as here 'orchard', meaning 'orchard of'; see COMMENTS ad No. **64** lines 8 and 27.

Frgs. c–m

L. 1 The traces on this line contained the concluding part of an entry, and the beginning of a new entry, continued in lines 2–5. Frgs. c–m may be a continuation of frg. a or of frg. b, in which case it contains only four new entries.

L. 2 [Μ]α̣ωζω[ν. Before Μ]α̣ωζω[ν, one can safely restore μέρος ἥμιcυ χώρας, or κήπου φοινικῶνος, or ἀμπελ- ἐν ὁρίοις—some of which occupied the second half of line 1. After Μ]α̣ωζω[ν came τῆς προγεγραμμένης] or τῆς αὐτῆς].

L. 3 [ἀ]δ̣ε̣λφ[όν]. Since this is the end of the line, it was preceded by: λεγομένης or λεγομένου (depending on whether χώρας, κήπου φοινικῶνος, or ἀμπελ- is restored before), followed by the name of the field and by μετοχῆς τῆς πρὸς Ἰωναθην τὸν προγεγραμμένον.

Ll. 4–5 These lines were occupied by the formulae describing the size of the field, date grove, or vineyard, the taxes on it, in kind or money, or both, and the names of two abutters.

Ll. 6–9 These lines contain a new entry.

L. 6 There is enough room to restore κήπου φοινικῶνος in the lacuna; this is further confirmed by λε̣γο̣[μεν]ο̣υ̣ in lines 6–7.

L. 8 φόρου̣. See COMMENTS ad frg. a line 14.

Ll. 8–9 μέλαν ἓν λ̣[ε̣]πτὰ δέκα. On the monetary units, see COMMENTS ad No. **60** lines 8–9; they occur in frg. a lines 16–17.

L. 9 .α[. Perhaps θά[λαcca] should be restored as the first abutter; see frg. a line 17.

Ll. 9–14 These lines contain a new entry.

Ll. 9–10 Γανναθ̣ ..ορaθ. Any association with Αρενοαραθα in frg. a line 15?

---

[35] For ἥμιcυ τέταρτον, see P.Hib. I 87 (256 BCE) line 8; O.Wilck. 1311 (2nd century CE) line 4.

[36] The Nabataean word for 'slave'; see Negev, *Personal Names*, nos. 782; 783; 798.

[37] Negev, *Personal Names*, no. 802.

L. 12 cυροῦ. On the spelling cυροῦ for cυρίου see Lewis ad P.Yadin **16** lines 19, 26, and 31, citing Gignac, *Grammar*, 1:302. Syrian dates are mentioned also in No. **64** line 30, P.Yadin **21** lines 14, 23, and P.Yadin **22** lines 16, 20.

Ll. 13–14 Cαμμοῦοϲ Μαναηλου καὶ Μαναηλοϲ Μαναηλου. Sammouos son of Mana'elos and Mana'elos son of Mana'elos are likely to be brothers, whose plots abut the date grove described here.

L. 13–14 Μαναηλου ... Μαναηλοϲ Μαναηλου. The name Mana'elos is a *compositum* of which the first element comes from the Semitic root מנה, 'to count', 'to weigh' and the second element, *-el* means God, as in Nathana'el, Ishma'el, Rabba'el. Mathna'el is restored in P.Yadin **3**, as one of the signatures on the verso, Mathna'el son of Letha: [מתנא]ל בר לתה. See a list of names ending in -ηλ in P.Oslo I 1 (4th century CE) col. vi lines 171–176 (= *Pap.Graec.Mag.* II 35).

L. 17 πατητοῦ. Here translated as 'splits', following Lewis ad P.Yadin **16** lines 20, 27, and 31. See COMMENTS ad No. **64** lines 29–30.

L. 17 *ναaρου*. The word is spelled here in the same way as in No. **64** line 30; P.Yadin **21** lines 14, 23; **22** lines 16; 20; it is spelled *νοαρου* in P.Yadin **16** lines 26, 31. See COMMENTS ad No. **64** line 30.

Ll. 17–18 cτεφανικοῦ. Despite Lewis (*Documents*, 70),[38] cτεφανικόν cannot mean 'crown money', *aurum coronarium*, in the technical and specific sense of the term. The *aurum coronarium* did not become an annual tax before the time of Elagabalus.[39] In a land declaration on the occasion of the taking of the census, cτεφανικόν must refer to an ordinary annual tax. I suggest, therefore, that cτεφανικόν was the tax-rate imposed on these date groves by the Nabataean kings and taken over later by the Roman government.[40] This hypothesis accounts fully for the fact that it is quoted in Nabataean currency, namely 'blacks'.[41] Nor is the term, whether coined by the Nabataeans or the Romans, inappropriate: cτεφανικόν, signifying that tax which was imposed by the kings.

L. 18 Ελαζα[ροϲ]. For Ελεαζαροϲ. It is spelled like this throughout the Babatha Archive.

Verso

Frg. a

L. 1 והבאלהי בר עבדאל[הי]. Whb'alhy son of ʿAbd'al[hy]. והבאלהי בר משלמו, Whb'alhy son of Meshalmw, is one of the witnesses on the verso of P.Yadin **3** (99 CE; unpublished). On the patronym, see above ad frg. b line 4.

L. 2 בר עותו .... . X son of ʿAwtw. חורו בר עותו, Ḥwrw son of ʿAwtw, is the scribe (ספרא) of P.Yadin **1** (unpublished) of 94 CE, and עזור בר עותו, ʿAzwr son of ʿAwtw, is the scribe of P.Yadin **2** and **3** (unpublished). See Negev, *Personal Names*, nos. 862–3; Cantineau, *Le Nabatéen* 2:128.

L. 3 Αβδοοβου. Perhaps one *omicron* is superfluous. See Cantineau, *Le Nabatéen* 2:126 עבד-[ה]בו.

---

[38] And Broshi, 'Seven Notes', 238.

[39] See Wallace, *Taxation*, 281–4; Neesen, *Untersuchungen*, 142–5; Millar, 'The *Fiscus*', 38–9; Wilcken, *Griechische Ostraka* I, 299–302. The cτεφανικόν is rarely mentioned before the late 2nd century CE: I was able to find only two examples of ὑπὲρ cτεφάνου Καίcαροϲ on ostraca, both from Claudius's time; see O.Wilck. 1376 and 1556. It is certainly not an ordinary tax.

[40] That the Romans reimposed taxes collected by their predecessors, once a territory became a Roman province (sometimes, but not always, using the same names), is too well known to need illustration.

[41] See COMMENTS ad No. **60** lines 8–9 and, in detail, Weiser and Cotton, 'Gebt dem Kaiser, was des Kaisers ist', 237ff.

63. XḤev/Se papDeed of Renunciation of Claims gr

Maḥoza, Arabia, between 25 April and 31 December, 127 CE

(PLS. XXXI AND XXXVIII)

Preliminary publication: H. M. Cotton, 'The Archive of Salome Komaïse Daughter of Levi: Another Archive from the "Cave of Letters"', *ZPE* 105 (1995) 177–83, pl I.

THIS papyrus (*olim* XḤev/Se Gr. 5) has survived in two fragments (frgs. a and b), between which is a lacuna of between 3 and 8 letters; approximately 7 or 8 letters on the left margin and perhaps as many as 26 letters on the right margin are lost (see reconstruction of lines 1 and 2). Lines 12 and following are preserved only on the right-hand fragment (frg. b). The verso is blank. The writing is across the fibres.

The recent death of the brother—perhaps also of the father—was the likely occasion for writing this deed. The brother was still alive on 25 April 127, when his land declaration was subscribed by the prefect Priscus (see No. **61**).

We cannot be certain about the nature of the controversy—παρῳχημέν[ης ἀμφιcβ]ητήcεωc (line 10)—which preceded the deed, but it is likely to have concerned the property left after the death of both father and son: [τ]ῶ̣ν καταλειφθέντω̣[ν ὑπὸ Λ]ηουει γενομένου ς̣υ̣[μβίου αὐτῆc . . . καὶ ὑπὸ + 4]λου γενομένου αὐ[τῆc υἱοῦ] ἀδελφοῦ δὲ τῆc ὁμ[ολογούcηc] (lines 6–7).

Καὶ ἡ [Cαλωμη Λ]ηουει, '*and* also Salome daughter of Levi' (line 4), may imply that there was a separate deed of renunciation of claims by another person; probably the mother, Salome Grapte, for her part, had written a deed of renunciation in favour of the daughter.[1]

This is a case of settlement (out of court) accompanied by an oath—ὅρκου ἐπ̣[ιδοθέντοc]. In the preliminary publication (*ZPE* 105) I described this document as 'a renunciation of claims' without citing any parallels and without attempting a more precise definition. We have in fact a close parallel in No. **13**. The wife renounces all claims against her former husband. Three times, in different variations, the phrase 'I have no claim against you' (כל מדעם לא איתי לי עמך) recurs. This Aramaic formula all but recalls the formula μηδένα λόγον ἔχειν πρὸc αὐτήν, repeated twice, or even three times, in the present document (lines 4, 8, 11). The formula recurs in the Nabataean P.Yadin **9**: ולא . . . עמך מנדעם לא זעיר [ולא שגיא] (lines 6–7, unpublished); however, due to its poor state of preservation, we cannot be sure that this is also a deed of renunciation of claims.

The presence of the formula μηδένα λόγον ἔχειν πρὸc δεῖνα and the taking of an oath, as well as the whole tenor of the present deed, permit us to assign the present document to a category of deeds known as διαλύcειc, although some of the elements of

[1] As the editor of P.Haun. III 57 rightly observes, 'Vergleichsverträge sind in der Regel gegenseitig' (p. 53).

the later διαλύϲειϲ are missing here.[2] Both Montevecchi and Taubenschlag point out that these deeds are rare in Ptolemaic and Roman times, but recur more frequently later.[3] Nevertheless there are two early examples from Egypt: BGU IV 1160 from 5 BCE and P.Ryl. II 180 from 124 CE; the latter is almost contemporary with the present document. Because of their extreme similarity it will be enough to cite the better preserved P.Ryl. II 180: the address 'Norbanus Orestes to Hermias son of Sabourion, greetings' (lines 1–2) is followed by an agreement: ὁμολογῶ μὴ ἐγκαλεῖν ϲοι μηδ' ἐγκαλέϲειν περὶ μηδενὸϲ πράγματοϲ ἁπλῶϲ περὶ ἐγγράπτου ἀγράφου ὑπὲρ τῶν ἔμπροϲθεν χρόνων μέχρι τῆϲ ἐνεϲτώϲηϲ ἡμέραϲ, μηδὲ ϲὲ ἐμοί (lines 2–8). The deed concludes with the date (lines 8–11). One immediately notices several differences between the two examples from Egypt and our document: (1) in the Egyptian documents the possibility of court proceedings is dismissed, although the issue to be kept out of court is not mentioned, whereas in our document nothing is said about the possibility of court proceedings, but the issue which occasioned the renunciation of claims is specified; (2) in the Egyptian documents—but not in ours—the renunciation clause is further modified by a clause which gives a time span: ὑπὲρ τῶν ἔμπροϲθεν χρόνων μέχρι τῆϲ ἐνεϲτώϲηϲ ἡμέραϲ; (3) our document mentions an oath like the later διαλύϲειϲ.[4] Most of the later διαλύϲειϲ are receipts;[5] a divorce settlement can be viewed as a special kind of receipt.[6] On occasion, the διάλυϲιϲ concerns a sale.[7] Finally, in a διάλυϲιϲ, a person may give up his claim to having been wronged and to have suffered some damage.[8]

Date and Provenance

What is left of the dating formula in line 15]ῦ καὶ Τίτ[allows for five possibilities: (1) the consuls of 112: Imp. Traianus VI and T. Sextius Africanus; (2) the consuls of 120: L. Catilius Severus Iulianus Claudius Reginus II and T. Aurelius Fulvus Boionius Arrius Antoninus;[9] (3) the consuls of 125: M. Lollius Paulinus D. Valerius Asiaticus Saturninus II and L. Epidius Titius Aquilinus;[10] (4) the consuls of 127: M. Gavius

---

[2] These deeds are called also ἀνεγκληϲία, ὁμολογία διαλύϲεωϲ, or διαλυτικὴ ὁμολογία.

[3] See Montevecchi, ***Papirologia***, 231–3: 'Transazioni'; Taubenschlag, ***Law***, 403–6: '***Transactio***'. Cf. Kaser, ***Römisches Zivilprozessrecht***, 481–2; Modrzejewski, 'Arbitration'.

[4] Perhaps the oath in this document is not, after all, part of the deed; see COMMENTS ad line 10.

[5] E.g. BGU II 408 (314 CE); III 941 (367 CE); P.Lips. 14 (391 CE); P.Lond. V 1717 (ca. 560 CE); P.Mich. XIII 659 (first half of vi century CE); P.Coll.Youtie II 94 (late vi–early vii century CE).

[6] E.g. P.Stras. III 142 lines 14–15 (391 CE); P.Ness. III 33 lines 23–28 (VI century CE).

[7] PSI XII 1228 lines 24–25 (188 CE); SB VIII 9763 (457–74 CE).

[8] P.Haun. III 57 (412–415? CE).

[9] In P.Yadin **7**, in Aramaic, the name is M. Aurelius Antoninus: מרקס אורליס אנטונינס.

[10] Cf. P.Yadin **14** lines 16–17 and **15** lines 1–2 = 14–15: ἐπὶ ὑπάτων Μάρκου Οὐαλερίου Ἀϲιατικοῦ τὸ $\overline{\text{B}}$ καὶ Τιτίου Ἀκουλείνου.

Squilla Gallicanus and T. Atilius Rufus Titianus;[11] (5) the consuls of 134: L. Iulius Ursus Servianus III and Titus Vibius Varus.

The year 112 is too early for the archive (but cf. INTRODUCTION TO THE ARCHIVE OF SALOME KOMAÏSE DAUGHTER OF LEVI, n. 1 on No. **32**), whereas 134 seems too late: it is hard to imagine that a Roman date would be used after the outbreak of the Bar Kokhba Revolt, which caused these women to leave their homes in the province of Arabia. The years 120, 125, and 127 are all possible: the other documents which belong to this archive date to 125 (No. **60**), 127 (Nos. **61** and **62**), 129 (No. **64**) and 131 (Nos. **12** and **65**). However, only the year 127 can fit the identification of the dead brother with the declarant of No. **61**, the land declaration, subscribed on 25 April 127.

Frg. a measures 5 x 2.2 cm; frg. b measures 8.7 x 3 cm.

Mus. Inv. 866
PAM 40.642; IAA 350226*, 350227

Frg. a–b

γηϲατο και ϲυνεγρ	ωμη Ληουει τ̣ο̣υ̣
υ̣ Ϲιμωνοϲ ανδροϲ α	ϲ τουδε του ...π̣ρ̣
η̣ν Μαναημο	λου θυγατερα ι̣δ̣ι̣α̣ν̣
ω̣ζηνοι και η	ηουει μηδενα λ
.α̣ εξ ονοματοϲ αυ̣	α̣λωμην την και
ω̣ν καταλειφθεντω̣	η̣ουει γενομενου ϲ̣υ̣
λου γενομενου αυ	αδελφου δε τηϲ ομ
α̣ ετι δε ομολογει η̣	η Ληουει μηδενα λ
ν̣ την και Γ̣ραπτην	η̣ κληρονομουϲ αυ
. παρωχημεν	ητηϲεωϲ ορκου επ̣
traces	.ε.. π̣ροϲ αυτην̣
	υμενηϲ ϲταϲα δ̣[ε

[11] In this order, for which see P.Yadin **16** lines 7–8: ἐπὶ ὑπάτων Μάρκου Γα<ιου>ίου Γαλλικανοῦ καὶ Τίτου Ἀτειλίου Ῥούφου Τιτιανοῦ; cf. No. **62** frg. a lines 7-8. This is not the order in which they are given in Degrassi, *Fasti consolari*, 37.

13 υτως καλως γενες̣

14 *vacat?* *vacat*

15 (m. 2) υ̣ και Τιτ

16 *vacat*

1 [ἐξωμολο]γ̣ήϲατο καὶ ϲυνεγρ[άψατο Ϲαλ]ωμη Ληουει τ̣ο̣υ̣[... ϲυμπαρόντοϲ αὐτῇ ἐπιτρόπου]

2 [*c.7 letters*]υ̣ Ϲιμωνοϲ ἀνδρὸϲ α[ὐτῆ]ϲ τοῦδε τοῦ {...}π̣ρ̣[άγματοϲ χάριν πρὸϲ Ϲαλωμην τὴν]

3 [καὶ Γραπτ]ην Μαναημο[υ *c.6 letters*]λου θυγατέρα, ἰ̣δ̣ί̣α̣ν̣ [δὲ μητέρα αὐτῆϲ *c.13 letters*]

4 [πάντεϲ Μα]ω̣ζηνοι· καὶ ἡ [Ϲαλωμη Λ]ηουει μηδένα λ[όγον ἔχειν *c.17 letters*]

5 [*c.8 letters*].α̣ ἐξ ὀνόματοϲ αὐ̣[τῆϲ πρὸϲ Ϲ]α̣λωμην τὴν καὶ [Γραπτην *c.19 letters*]

6 [*c.3 letters* περὶ τ]ῶ̣ν καταλειφθέντω̣[ν ὑπὸ Λ]ηουει γενομένου ϲ̣υ̣[μβίου αὐτῆϲ *c.13 letters* καὶ]

7 [ὑπὸ *c.4 letters*]λου γενομένου αὐ[τῆϲ υἱοῦ] ἀδελφοῦ δὲ τῆϲ ὁμ[ολογούϲηϲ *c.17 letters*]

8 [*c.7–8 letters*]α̣ ἔτι δὲ ὁμολογεῖ ἡ̣ [Ϲαλωμ]η Ληουει μηδένα λ[όγον ἔχειν *c.17 letters*]

9 [πρὸϲ Ϲαλωμη]ν̣ τὴν καὶ Γ̣ραπτην̣[*c.4–5 letters*]η̣ κληρονόμουϲ αὐ[τῆϲ περὶ *c.19 letters*]

10 [*c.7–8 letters*]. παρῳ̣χημέν[ηϲ ἀμφιϲβ]ητήϲεωϲ ὅρκου ἐπ̣[ιδοθέντοϲ *c.17 letters*]

11]....[.]. ..[.... ..... .].ε.. π̣ρὸϲ αὐτ̣ὴ̣ν̣[*c.26 letters*]

12 [*c.26 letters*]υμενηϲ ϲτᾶϲα δ̣[ὲ *c.25 letters*]

13 [πίϲτει ἐπηρωτήθη καὶ ἀνθωμολογήθη ο]ὕτωϲ καλῶϲ γενέϲ̣[θαι *vacat?*]

14 [*vacat?*] *vacat*

15 m. 2. [ἐπὶ ὑπάτων Μάρκου Γαουίου Γαλλικανο]ῦ̣ καὶ Τίτ[ου Ἀτιλίου Ῥούφου Τιτιανοῦ *vacat?*]

16 *[day and month? place?]* *vacat*

Translation

[Sal]ome daughter of Levi, the son of X (or: son of Tou[)?—[present with her as her guardian for the purpose] of this matter, her husband [Sammou]os(?) son of Shimᶜon—[acknow]ledged and agreed in w[riting], vis-à-vis Salome also (called) [Grapt]e daughter of Menaḥem, [son of *]los* (or *]las*), her own [mother . . . —all of them living in Ma]ḥoza: and also [(she) Salome] daughter of Levi has no [claims . . .] in her name [towards S]alome who is also (called) [Grapte . . . regarding] the properties left [by L]evi, her late hus[band . . . and by *]los* (or *]las*), her late [son] and brother of her who ag[rees . . .]. Likewise [Salom]e daughter of Levi agrees that she has no [claims . . . vis-à-vis Salom]e also (called) Grapte ... her heirs [regarding . . ., the cont]roversy which has now been solved, an oath having been gi[ven] . . . towards her . . . while standing firm (?) [. . . In good faith the formal question was asked and it was agreed in reply] that this was thus rightly done. [*vacat*]
(*second hand*) [In the consulate of Marcus Gavius Gallican]us and Tit[us Atilius Rufus Titianus] *vacat?* [day and month? place?] *vacat.*

Comments

L. 1 [ἐξωμολο]γήcατο καὶ cυνεγρ[άψατο]. The combination is not found in papyri from Egypt. It is attested, though, in four papyri written elsewhere in the Near East. It occurs first in two double documents on parchment from Persian Kurdistan—both recording the sale of a vineyard:[12] P.Avroman I (88 BCE), A, lines 7–8 = B, line 8 and P.Avroman II (22/1 BCE), A, lines 4–5 = B, lines 4–5.[13] Next we find it in a contract of re-marriage between Jews written in Bethbassi in the toparchy of Herodium in Judaea in 124 CE: Mur **115** (= SB X 10305) line 2 = line 21.[14] Finally, it is attested in a marriage contract from 232 CE between a soldier of the *Cohors Duodecima Palaestinorum* and a woman with a Latin name, concluded in a place called Qatna, probably on the River Chabur (in the Roman province of Mesopotamia): P. Dura 30 lines 6–8.[15] Might this expression be unique to the Aramaic speaking areas? See the COMMENTS to Mur **115** lines 2–3 (*DJD* II, p. 251); cf. Arzt, 'Ägyptische Papyri', 27ff.

L. 1 [Cαλ]ωμη Ληουει. See INTRODUCTION TO THE ARCHIVE OF SALOME KOMAÏSE DAUGHTER OF LEVI, and note that, in No. **63**, the nickname Komaïse does not occur.

L. 1 τ̣ο̣υ̣. This is either the article, followed in the lacuna by the name of the grandfather, or Τ̣ο̣υ̣[the beginning of a name without an article as in the inner text of P.Yadin **18** lines 4–5: Ἰούδα̣[τι υἱῷ] Ἀ̣ν̣α̣ν̣ίο̣υ̣ Ϲ̣ωμαλα; though the outer text reads: Ἰούδατι ἐπικαλουμένῳ Κίμβερι υἱῷ Ἀνανίου τοῦ Ϲωμ̣α̣λα (lines 34–5). If Τ̣ο̣υ̣[, one may suggest To(u)bias (cf. Bagatti and Milik, *Scavi*, 96, no. 33).

Ll. 1–2 [cυμπαρόντος αὐτῇ ἐπιτρόπου]υ̣ Cιμωνος ἀνδρὸς α[ὐτῆ]c. Cf. No. **64** lines 4–5: c̣υνπαρό̣ν̣τος̣ α̣ὐ̣τ̣[ῇ ἐ]πιτρόπο̣[υ τοῦδε τοῦ πρά]γ̣μ̣α̣τ̣ος χάριν Ιωcηπου Cιμωνος [ἀ]νὴρ αὐτῆc. On the use of ἐπίτροπος

[12] See Minns, 'Parchments'. For the third document in this lot, see Nyberg, 'Pahlavi documents'. On the exact locality, see Edmonds, 'Place Names'.

[13] See Minns, 'Parchments', 50–51, 53 on the expression.

[14] In the commentary (p. 251 ad lines 2–3) there is a reference to the present document: 'cette formule se rencontre . . . dans un pap. inédit du Désert de Juda'.

[15] ἐ̣[ξωμολογή]c̣α̣ν̣[το καὶ c]υνεγράψαντ̣ο̣ π̣[ρὸς ἀλλήλ]ους τῇ ἐνεcτώcῃ ἡμέρᾳ Αὐρήλιος Ἀλέ̣ξ̣ανδρος̣, cτ̣[ρ]ατ̣ιώτης c[πείρης τῆ]c̣ προγεγραμμ̣ένης, (ἑκατονταρχίας) Παπ̣ίο̣[υ] καὶ Αὐρηλία Μαρκελλεῖνα̣ Μαρκελλείνου, ο̣ἰ[κο]ῦ̣c̣α ἐν Κάτνῃ.

rather than κύριος to describe the guardian of a woman, see Wolff, 'Le droit', 279ff. and 'Römisches Provinzialrecht', 793ff. The usage was not unique to Arabia, since we find it also in No. **69** line 4: διὰ Βορκ.. Αγλα ἐπιτρόπ[ου] αὐτῆς τοῦδε τοῦ πράγμα[τος], which was written in Judaea.[16]

L. 2]υ. The υ cannot be the last letter of ἐπιτρόπου since all the names, so far, appear with patronyms, so that it would be strange not to have one here. Thus, Cιμωνος is the patronym of the husband of Salome (Komaïse); his personal name is lost in the lacuna; ἐπιτρόπου has already come in line 1, which makes this line much longer than the average length in No. **63**. In the INTRODUCTION TO THE ARCHIVE OF SALOME KOMAÏSE DAUGHTER OF LEVI, it was argued that Sammouos son of Shimʿon was Salome's first husband, and that his name should be restored in the lacuna here: [Cαμμουο]υ. It is restored in the TRANSLATION.

L. 2 τοῦδε τοῦ {...}πρ[άγματος χάριν]. See No. **64** lines 4–5 quoted above; P.Yadin **17** lines 4–5 = 22–23: cυνπαρόντ[ος α]ὐτῆ ἐπιτρόπου τοῦδε τοῦ πράγματος χάριν Ἰακώβου; P.Yadin **20** lines 25–27: διὰ ἐπιτρόπου αὐτῆς Ἰούδας ὃς καὶ Κίνβερ Ἀνανίου Ἠν[γ]αδηνοῦ τοῦδε τοῦ πράγματος χάριν; P.Yadin **31** line 4: πράγματος χά[ριν]. The examples quoted above suggest that we must have χάριν after πράγματος; the restoration of 26 letters brings it in line with the preceding one.[17]

Ll. 2–3 [Cαλωμην τὴν καὶ Γραπτ]ην. On the name, see INTRODUCTION TO THE ARCHIVE OF SALOME KOMAÏSE DAUGHTER OF LEVI. The *alpha* in Γραπτην in line 9 is certain, despite the spelling Γροπτη in No. **64** line 3.

L. 3 Μαναημο[υ]. The patronym is also present in No. **64** line 3.

L. 3]λου. This is the end of the grandfather's name.

L. 4 [πάντες Μα]ωζηνοι. Unless ἐν Μαωζα is lost in a lacuna, or comes in line 16, this expression seems to serve also for the place of writing.

L. 4 καὶ ἡ [Cαλωμη]. See INTRODUCTION. See P.Ryl. II 180 line 8: μηδὲ cὲ ἐμοί with the editor's comment: 'It is probably a reference to a parallel deed by which Hermias made a similar declaration'.

L. 4 μηδένα λ[ογον ἔχειν]. The phrase means 'to have no claim', 'not to have ground for action'; see LSJ s.v. λόγος IIIb. The phrase occurs in two documents of the Babatha Archive. Babatha summons Iulia Crispina, the *episcopos*[18] of the orphans of her late husband's brother, to the governor's court if she has any claim against her: καὶ εἴ τι λόγον ἔχις πρὸς ἐμὲ παρεδρεύειν ἐπὶ τὸν αὐτὸν Νέπωτα[ν] (P.Yadin **25** lines 61–63 = lines 26–27). The phrase occurs again in the exchange between Babatha and her second husband's other (or previous) wife, Miriam.[19] The latter replies to Babatha's charges of having seized everything in their late husband's house with a reminder that 'you (Babatha) have no claim against the said Judah regarding his estate' (μηδέναν λόγον ἔχιν cε πρὸς τὸν αὐτὸν Ἰούδαν περὶ τῶν ὑπαρχόντων αὐτοῦ, P.Yadin **26** lines 15–17). Its Aramaic equivalent—כל מדעם לא איתי לי עמך—occurs in No. **13** of 135 CE. In Egyptian papyri it occurs only rarely before the fourth century CE, e.g. PSI XII 1228, lines 24–25 (188 CE);[20] SB VI 9201, lines 23–24 (203 CE); P.Grenf. II 69 (265), lines 22–24. It is used in a similar context of renunciation of claims over an inheritance in the much later P.Col. VIII 237 (395 CE?): [κ]αὶ

[16] See COMMENTS ad loc.

[17] The syntax of the following two examples is different and therefore cannot be used as an argument against restoring χάριν: P.Yadin **14** lines 22–23: διὰ ἐπιτρόπου αὐτ[ῆc τ]οῦδε τοῦ πράγμ[ατοc] Ἰούδα Χθουcίωνοc; P.Yadin **15** lines 31–32: διὰ ἐπιτρόπου αὐτῆc τοῦδε τοῦ πράγματο[c Ἰούδου Χ]θουcίωνοc ὃc παρὼν ὑπέγραψεν.

[18] For the term, see Cotton, 'Guardianship', 97.

[19] Katzoff, 'Polygamy?', maintains, against Lewis's polygamy (*Documents*, 22–4), that Judah and Miriam had been divorced before Judah married Babatha. Lewis, 'In the World of P.Yadin', is probably right to argue contra Cotton, 'Cancelled Marriage Contract', 85–6, that Miriam too lived in Maḥoza, and not in ʿEin Gedi.

[20] Ἑρμηcίων Ἀπολλωνίου ὁμολογεῖ ἀπεcχηκέναι τὰς ὀφειλομένας αὐτῷ ὑπὸ τῆc Θατρῆτοc ἐκ τοῦ διελθόντοc κζ (ἔτουc) Φαμενὼθ ἀργυρίου δραχμὰc ἑκατὸν τεccαράκοντα ἐπὶ ὑποθήκῃ τῆc προκειμένηc δούληc, [πε]ρὶ ὧν μηδένα λόγον ἔχειν πρὸc αυτὴν μηδὲ πρὸc τὴν ὑποθήκην.

πρ[ὸς τ]ὼ ἀπεντεῦθεν μηδένα λόγον [ἔ]χιν ἐ[μὲ] πρὸς cαὶ περὶ μηδενὸς πράγματος [τὸ] cύνολον οὔτε περὶ κληρονομίας οὔτε [ἐ]ν̣γράφου οὔτε ⟦εν⟧ ἀγράφου, lines 9–15; cf. lines 19–20.[21]

Ll. 4–6 It is possible to offer a different reconstruction of lines 4–6 from that suggested in the text: καὶ ἡ [Cαλωμη Λ]ηουει μηδένα λ[όγον ἔχειν πρὸς τὰ κατηντηκότ]α ἐξ ὀνόματος αὐ̣[τοῦ (or αὐτῶν) εἰς C]α̣λωμὴν τὴν καὶ [Γραπτην ... ἀπὸ τ]ῶ̣ν καταλειφθέντω̣[ν] κτλ. The restoration of line 5 is based on P.Harr. I 74A (99 CE); P.Oxy. II 75 (129 CE); II 247 (90 CE); II 248 (80 CE); II 249 (80 CE); II 250 (61 CE?); II 481 (99 CE); II 482 (109 CE). E.g. P.Oxy. II 248 (80 CE) lines 6–12: [ἀπογράφομαι] τῶι υἱῶι μου Ἀμόιτι [Δημητρίου τοῦ] Cαραπίωνος τοῦ Θε̣[ωνος τῶν ἀπὸ τῆς αὐ]τῆς πόλεως . . . [τὰ κα]τηντηκότα [εἰς αὐτὸν ἐξ] ὀν[όματος] τοῦ μὲν πατρὸς ἐμο̣[ῦ αὐ]τ̣ο̣ῦ̣ [δὲ πάππου]. There are several problems with this restoration: αὐτοῦ or αὐτῶν (line 5), unlike αὐτῆς, has no antecedent, but looks forward to Levi, or to Levi and the brother, who will be mentioned only in lines 6–7; neither is πρὸς before [τὰ κατηντηκότ]α as attractive as [περὶ τ]ῶ̣ν καταλειφθέντω̣[ν] (line 6), which has now to be changed to [ἀπὸ τ]ῶ̣ν καταλειφθέντω̣[ν]; finally, the restoration of [πρὸς Cαλωμη]ν̣ τὴν καὶ Γραπτην̣ in line 9, which seems necessary, and the presence of πρὸς αὐτήν̣ in line 11, make it likely that the same construction appeared in line 5, namely [πρὸς C]α̣λωμην τὴν καὶ [Γραπτην].

L. 10].. Possibly *eta* stood after the lacuna.

L. 10 παρῳ̣χημέν[ης ἀμφιςβ]ητήcεως. The combination is not found elsewhere, but the reading is quite certain. Similar expressions are found, though, in two late διάλυcιc documents: Stud. Pal. XX 122 (*c.*438 CE), line 13: πάcης ἑκατέρῳ μέρει λυθείcης ἀμφιcβητήcεως; P.Haun. III 57 (412–415 CE?) lines 12–13: κατὰ τοῦτο πάcης τμηθείcης ἀμφιcβ̣η[τήcεω]c ἧc εἶχ̣ο̣ν πρόc cε.

L. 10 ὅρκου ἐπ̣[ιδοθέντος]. The collocation ὅρκον ἐπιδεδωκέναι is common in Egyptian papyri; I could not find it in the aorist passive, as proposed here, or the perfect passive: ὅρκου ἐπ̣[ιδεδομένου]. The oath must have preceded the deed. It seems reasonable to assume that it was demanded by the mother, Salome Grapte, and was taken by the daughter, Salome Komaïse, to ensure that there would be no further claims on her part. Once the oath was taken, the controversy was resolved: παρῳ̣χημέν[ης ἀμφιcβ]ητήcεως. In other words the oath is not part of the deed, as it seems to have become in the later διάλυcιc documents, but merely recorded in it as having been taken. On the oath in the later διάλυcιc documents, see Seidl, *Eid* II, 96ff.; Taubenschlag, *Law*, 405; Modrzejewski, 'Arbitration', 242.

L. 11]....[.]. ..[.... ..... .].ε.. π̣ρὸς αὐτήν̣. It is tempting to restore].....[.]. μη[δένα λόγον ἔ]χ̣ε̣ι̣ν̣. Admittedly, it is not easy to read the *nu* of ἔχειν. If this is the correct restoration, something like [ἔτι δὲ ὁμολογεῖ ἡ Cαλωμη Ληουει] should have come before. It is somewhat disconcerting that this follows the declaration that the oath has been taken and the controversy resolved. Nor does it fit the interpretation of the rest of the document.

L. 12 cτᾶcα δ̣[ὲ]. This is no doubt the participle of ἵcτημι in the sense of 'to stand firm' (see LSJ ἵcτημι B.II.2), as with cταθόντεc (i.e. cταθέντεc) in P.Yadin **20** line 14 = line 37. In *ZPE* 105, I read cτᾶcα α̣[, but I now accept the suggestion of D. Thomas to read δ̣[ὲ]; cf. P.Euphr. 6 line 20 = P.Euphr. 7 line 14, and comments *ad loc.* for further examples.

L. 13 [πίcτει ἐπηρωτήθη καὶ ἀνθωμολογήθη ο]ὕτωc καλῶc γενέc̣[θαι. This restoration of the stipulation is based on P.Yadin **17** lines 38–39; **18**, lines 27–28 = lines 66–67. A different restoration based on P.Yadin **20** lines 16–17 = line 40; **21** lines 27–28; **22** lines 29–30; No. **65** lines 13–14 yields: ο̣ὕ̣τω̣c̣ [κ]α̣λῶc γείνεcθαι πίcτεωc ἐπηρω̣[τημένηc καὶ ἀνθωμολογημένηc]. The latter restoration would, however, have spilled over to the left margin of line 14, but the right margin of that line, as we can see on frg. b, remained blank.

The stipulation in the Babatha Archive follows upon the πρᾶξιc clause or its equivalent, e.g. P.Yadin **17** (128 CE) lines 33–38 = lines 12–15: γε̣[νο]μένηc δὲ τῆc πράξεωc τῇ α̣ὐτῇ Βαβαθα̣ ἢ τῷ ὑπ<ὲρ> αὐτῆc προφ[έ]ροντι τὴν cυνγραφὴν ταύτην ἀπό τε Ἰούδου καὶ τῶν ὑ̣π̣αρχόντων αὐτοῦ πάντῃ πάντων, ὧν τε ἔχει καὶ ὧν ἂν ἐπικτήcηται κυρίωc τρόπ̣ῳ ᾧ ἂν αἱρῆται ο̣ πράccων τὴν εἴcπρα̣ξιν ποι̣εῖcθαι. πίcτει ἐπ̣ηρωτήθη καὶ ἀνθωμολογήθη [ταῦ]τ̣α̣ ο̣ὕτω[c] κ̣α̣λ̣ῶ̣[c γ]είνεcθαι; cf. P.Yadin **18** lines 24–28 = lines 62–67; **21** lines 26–

[21] See Rupprecht, *Quittung*, 16–17; 33; 49 n. 36; 52. His statement on p. 97: 'Die Wendung μηδένα λόγον ἔχειν begegnet zum ersten Mal im Jahre 265 [Grenf. II 69], sie tritt stets allein auf und nur in Quittungen', is not quite accurate.

27; cf. No. **65** lines 11–14. In P.Yadin **20** (130 CE), itself a concession of rights, the stipulation is subsequent to an undertaking of an obligation to defray all the costs of conducting a legal defence and clearing the property against counterclaims: ἐὰν δέ τις ἀντιπο̣[ι]ήσῃ τῆς προγεγραμμένης αὐλῆς, σταθόντες ἐκδικήσωμεν καὶ καθαροποιήσωμέν σοι ἀπὸ παντὸς ἀ̣ντ̣ι̣ποιουμένου ταῖς εἰδίαις ἀναλώμασιν κατὰ μηδὲν ἀντιλέγων, πίστεως ἐπερωτημέ̣[ν]ης κ̣α̣ὶ̣ ἀνθομολογημένης (lines 36–40 = lines 13–16).[22] It is thus possible that in this deed of renunciation the stipulation is subsequent to the undertaking of a similar obligation. This likelihood is increased if we read στᾶσα δ̣[ὲ] in line 12 and take it to express the same idea as σταθόντες in P.Yadin **20** line 14 = line 37. However that may be, it is unlikely at any rate that the stipulation would not have followed upon an obligation.[23]

L. 15 For dating by consular date only, with no provincial or regnal eras, and for the position of the date at the end of the document, see P.Yadin **25** lines 28–30 = lines 64–67; **26** lines 17–19. Note the same position in No. **60** lines 9–12.

L. 15]υ̣ καὶ Τίτ[. The *upsilon* is not certain. All that is left before καί is an upper stroke; it may be either what remains of an *upsilon* or the stroke following a number, in the latter case the reiteration of the consulate.

---

[22] For the stipulation in the papyri see Simon, *Stipulationsklausel*; for more on the subject, see D. Hagedorn ad P.Turner 22 (142 CE, Pamphylia), lines 6–7 and Lewis, *Documents*, 17–18.

[23] But see Mitteis, *Reichsrecht*, 486–7.

64. XḤev/Se papDeed of Gift gr

Maḥoza, 9 November 129 CE

(FIG. 27 AND PLS. XXXIX–XL)

Preliminary publication: H. M. Cotton, 'The Archive of Salome Komaïse Daughter of Levi: Another Archive from the "Cave of Letters"', *ZPE* 105 (1995), 183–207, pls. II–III.

THIS is a double document (*olim* XḤev/Se Gr. 1) in which the inner text and the outer text survived in two separate fragments, frgs. a and b.[1] There are differences between the inner and the outer texts (see TABLE 1).[2] On the verso of frg. b there are eight signatures.

The document contains an ordinary gift, not a gift in contemplation of death.[3] Neither condition for the latter exists here: '(1) a gift of property with the donor retaining usufruct for life, or (2) a gift of property which is finally irrevocable only on the donor's death'.[4] Here, the gift becomes effective from the moment the deed is made, ἀπὸ τῆς σήμερον (line 6) independent of the donor's death. As such, it is different from P.Yadin **19** (128 CE), which, for one half of the gift, depends on the death of the donor.[5] It also differs from P.Yadin **7** (120 CE, Aramaic), where Babatha's father, Shimʿon son of Menaḥem, gives to her mother, Miriam daughter of Yosef, everything he owns in Maḥoza to become hers after his death (lines 15ff.; 21ff.; 52ff.; 63ff.).[6]

Ordinary gifts, as well as gifts in contemplation of death, should be seen in the context of the law of succession in force in the societies reflected in these archives; they may very well have been conceived as remedies to the harshness or inflexibility of this law, seen, for example, in the barring of daughters and wives from the inheritance.[7]

There seems to be a close relationship between marriage, dowry, and the bestowal of gifts on daughters. Elsewhere it was suggested that P.Yadin **7** (120 CE)—the deed of

---

[1] On double documents, see INTRODUCTION TO THE ARAMAIC AND HEBREW DOCUMENTARY TEXTS and INTRODUCTION TO THE GREEK DOCUMENTARY TEXTS; Lewis, *Documents*, 6–10.

[2] Cf. P.Yadin **18**, **19**, and especially **20** with Lewis, *Documents*, 89.

[3] For examples from Egypt, see P.Oxy. II 273 = MChr. 221 (95 CE) and P.Grenf. II, 68 = *FIRA* III^2 no. 98 (247 CE, of which P.Grenf. II, 70 = MChr. no. 191 is a copy); for examples from Dura-Europus, see P.Dura, 17B (*c.*180 CE) and 18 (87 CE) with Welles, 'Dura Pergament 21'.

[4] See Yaron, *Gifts*, 1. 1

[5] See Katzoff, 'P. Yadin 19'; idem, 'Interpretation'.

[6] See Yadin, Greenfield, and Yardeni, 'Deed of Gift'.

[7] Cf. Yaron, *Gifts*, 155 on gifts in the context of the Jewish law of succession: 'Greater freedom in dispositions in contemplation of death tended to counteract, at least to a certain degree, the extreme preference accorded to the male by law'; cf. 33; 153. One notes that the attempts to assert the claims of the daughter over the nieces (*b. B. Bat.* 115b) and to give daughters equal share in property inherited from the mother (*b. B. Bat.* 111a) were defeated; see Yaron, *Gifts*, 154–5; idem, 'Acts'.

gift in favour of Babatha's mother—was written on the occasion of Babatha's marriage to her first husband, when Babatha herself received, in a deed of gift which has not survived, the orchards which she declares in P.Yadin **16** (127 CE). Having provided for his daughter, Babatha's father took proper measures to protect his wife in the event of his death.[8] P.Yadin **19** (16 April 128) is a deed of gift following upon a daughter's marriage: eleven days after the marriage of his daughter Shelamṣion to Judah son of Ḥananiah,[9] Babatha's second husband, Judah son of Eleazar Khthousion, gave Shelamṣion a gift of half a courtyard including half of the rooms and the upper-storey rooms therein in Ein Gedi; and she was to receive the second half after his death.[10] The circumstances of the drawing up of the deed of gift in favour of Salome Komaïse are unknown to us. She was married to Sammouos son of Shimᶜon[11] in 127 (see No. **63**), and on 7 August 131 a marriage contract was drawn up between her and Yeshuᶜa son of Menaḥem with whom she had been living in an unwritten marriage for some time (see No. **65**). It is possible that the deed of gift here is connected with her second marriage.

On the other hand, it could be argued that the writing of a deed of gift in this case, as well as in P.Yadin **19**, is connected with a second marriage of the parent. At the time Judah son of Eleazar was writing P.Yadin **19** for his daughter, Shelamṣion, he had already been married to his second (or other) wife, Babatha.[12] The same is true of Salome Grapte (or Gropte), whose first husband, Levi, the father of Salome Komaïse, was dead by 127 (see No. **63**); she is now married to her second husband, Yosef son of Shimᶜon. It is possible that both Judah son of Eleazar and Salome Grapte (or Gropte) wrote deeds of gift in favour of their daughters in anticipation of the birth of a male child who would deprive the daughter of the previous (or other) marriage of her right to inherit. Therefore, one cannot argue that the writing of a deed of gift in itself proves that daughters (and wives) could not inherit even if there was no male heir. Nevertheless, the existence of such instruments creates a strong presumption that this was so.

Elsewhere it was observed that the evidence of P.Yadin **23** and **24** suggests that the law of succession in force in the early second century (at least among the Jews) in the province of Arabia did not automatically grant a daughter the right to inherit from her parents, when in competition with sons of her father's brother. It thus differs from Jewish law in preferring the claims of the man's brother or his brother's children to

---

8 Cotton and Greenfield, 'Babatha's Property'.

9 The marriage contract is P.Yadin **18** of 5 April 128. See Wasserstein, 'Marriage Contract', 110–13, for the eleven days delay between the execution of the marriage contract and the drawing up of the deed of gift.

10 [δι]ἐ̣θ̣ε̣τ̣[ο Ἰο]ύ̣δ̣αϲ Ἐ̣λ[αζά]ρου Χθουϲ[ίω]ν̣ο̣ϲ̣ Ἠ̣νγ̣α̣δη̣[νὸ]ϲ̣ οἰκῶν ἐν Μαωζαϲ [Ϲελ]αμψιο̣ῦ̣ϲ θυ[γατ]ὲ̣ρ̣ π̣ά̣ν̣[τα τὰ ὑ]πάρ[χον]τ̣α αὐ̣[τ]ῷ̣ [ἐ]ν Ἠνγαδῆϲ ἥ[μιϲ]υ̣ α[ὐ]λ̣ῆϲ . . . . ἥμιϲυ οἰκοιμάτω̣ν̣ καὶ ὑπερῴαιϲ ἐνο[ῦ]ϲι . . . καὶ τ[ὸ] ἄλ̣λ̣ο̣ ἥμιϲυ τῆϲ αὐλῆϲ καὶ οἰκ̣ο̣ι̣μ̣ά̣των διέθετο̣ ..[. Ἰ]ο̣ύ̣δαϲ τ̣ῆ̣ αὐ̣[τ]ῆ̣ [Ϲελ]α̣μψιοῦ[ϲ] μετὰ τὸ αὐτὸ[ν] τε<λε>υτῆϲαι, lines 11–16; cf. lines 22–23.

11 See INTRODUCTION TO THE ARCHIVE OF SALOME KOMAÏSE DAUGHTER OF LEVI and COMMENTS ad No. **63** line 2.

12 Lewis assumed that he had not divorced Miriam, the wife mentioned in P.Yadin **26**, before contracting his marriage with Babatha (*Documents*, 22–4); this is now questioned by Katzoff, 'Polygamy?'. Whether Babatha was his second or other wife does not affect the argument presented here. Furthermore, it is not clear that his other or previous wife, Miriam, is Shelamzion's mother.

those of the daughter: Jewish law prefers the claims of children, whatever their sex, to those of a man's brother or his brother's children.[13] Like Jewish law, however, the legal system reflected in the archives from the Judaean Desert recognized a legal instrument which mitigated the rigour of rules of succession which were so prejudicial to women: the deed of gift.[14]

In marriage contracts from Egypt, gifts of immovables or slaves bestowed on the bride on the occasion of marriage are not of the same order as that part of the dowry described as φερνή, προῖξ, or παράφερνα:[15] they are described as προcφορά or πρόcδοcιc.[16] For example, PSI X 1117 is a marriage contract from the second century CE: after the groom acknowledges the receipt of φερνή and παράφερνα from the mother, the latter declares in line 18ff: [ὁ]μολογεῖ προcενηνοχέναι τῇ θυγατρὶ Θεναπύγχει <ἐν> προcφο[ρᾷ ?] κατὰ τήνδε τὴν ὁ(μολογίαν) ἀπὸ τοῦ νῦν ἐπ' ἀεὶ τήν τε ὑπάρχουcαν αὐτῇ . . . οἰκ[ί]αν etc. Sometimes a separate document was drawn up in which immovables and slaves were given to the bride on the occasion of her marriage. In P.Ryl. II 155 (138–61 CE) a mother gives her daughter property ἐν προcφορᾷ;[17] in P.Oxy. II 273 (= MChr. 221, 95 CE) the word προcφορά is absent, but the cession of property (cυνκεχωρηκέναι, line 10) by the mother is done in favour of her daughter (still a minor, line 13) and a Theon who is likely to be the latter's fiancé; in P.Vind.Worp 5 (169 CE) a woman registers property, which she received from her mother ἐν πρ[ο]cφορᾷ ἀν[α]φ[α]ιρέτῳ (line 9), on the occasion of her marriage (lines 34–36). P.Dura 17B (*c.*180 CE) records a gift of slaves by a father to his daughter who is already married.[18]

It is worth noticing that immovables are never included in the dowry or the ketubbah[19] in marriage contracts from Judaea and Arabia.[20] Nevertheless, the married women encountered in the Babatha Archive and in the present archive own real estate. Since, as we have seen, the law of succession reflected in these archives seems not to have automatically granted a wife the right to inherit from her husband nor a daughter the right to inherit from her parents when in competition with sons of her father's

---

13 Num 27:8: 'When a man dies leaving no son, his patrimony shall pass to his daughter. If he has no daughter, you shall give it to his brothers'; and again in *m. B. Bat.* 8.2: 'The son precedes the daughter, and all the son's offspring precede the daughter; the daughter precedes the brothers (of the deceased)'.

14 Cotton, 'Deeds of Gift'; cf. Yaron, *Gifts*, 153–60; idem, 'Acts', 29–45.

15 See Gernet, *Beiträge*, 19–32; Häge, *Ehegüterrechtliche Verhältnisse*, 250–89.

16 E.g. CPR I 24 = MChr. 288 (136 CE) lines 8ff., where, in addition to jewelry, the mother gives ἐν φερνῇ κατὰ προcφορὰν ἀναφαίρετον land and part of a house; P.Mich. V 343 (54–55 CE) is an acknowledgement of the receipt of a dowry: in addition to φερνή and παράφερνα, a gift of a slave is given ἐμ προcφορᾷ (line 6); PSI V 450 (ii/iii CE) col. I, lines 12–13; P.Ryl. II 154 (66 CE) line 10; line 20.

17 The editors suggest that this document might have accompanied a marriage contract or have been a substitute for a marriage settlement.

18 For some reason, in two marriage contracts in Greek from the Judaean Desert, προcφορά describes what is normally designated φερνή in Egyptian papyri; see P.Yadin **18** lines 7–8 = lines 39–40; No. **69** lines 5–6. But note that φερνή and προcφορά are used interchangeably for jewelry and clothes in P.Mil.Vogl. II 71 (161–80).

19 See discussion of MARRIAGE PRACTICES in No. **69**.

20 Cf. Mur **115**, **116**, P.Yadin **10**, **18**, Nos. **64**, **69** (Mur **20**, **21** are too fragmentary).

brother, we may safely assume that they acquired their property by way of deeds of gift, like the present one.[21]

Language

The Greek of No. **64** is singularly ungrammatical and non-idiomatic. The scribe pays no attention to case endings and gender.[22] His dependence on an Aramaic *Urtext*, whether this was actually present before him or merely in his mind, is, I believe, unparalleled in other Greek papyri coming from the Judaean Desert.[23] At times, the Greek is so poor that the text can be understood only when translated back into Aramaic. This is particularly true of lines 6–9 = lines 26–28, but almost the entire document can be translated literally, with no adaptation, into the original Aramaic, as I have attempted to do below.

The first column contains most of lines 1–15 of the inner text and lines 39–41 of the outer text. In the second column, placed so as to correspond to the Greek text, is the text in Aramaic translation, based on P.Yadin **7**, esp. lines 1–5 = lines 30–36; lines 14–16 = lines 50–54.

---

[21] See Cotton and Greenfield, 'Babatha's Property'; Cotton, 'Deeds of Gift'. For comparison with the situation in the Egyptian papyri, see Hobson, 'Women as Property Owners'; Rowlandson, *Landowners*, 160ff.

[22] See below, in the apparatus to the text.

[23] See Lewis, *Documents*, 13–16 for Semitisms in the Babatha Archive.

[ἐ]π̣ὶ ὑπά̣τ̣ω̣ν̣ Πο̣[πλ]ί̣ο̣υ̣ Ἰ̣ο̣υ̣[ο]υ̣εν̣τ̣ί̣ου Κέ̣λ̣ϲου τὸ β̄ κ̣α̣ὶ̣ Λ̣[ο]υ̣κ̣ί̣ο̣υ̣ Νηρατίου Μαρκέλλου τὸ β̄ . . . κατὰ τὸν ἀριθμὸν τῆϲ νέαϲ ἐπαρχείαϲ Ἀραβία]ϲ ἔτουϲ τετάρτου καὶ εἰκοϲτοῦ . . . ἐ̣ν̣ Μ̣α̣ω̣ζαϲ . . . Ϲα[λω]μ̣η̣ ἡ καὶ Γροπτη Μαναημου . . . Ϲαλωμη̣ [..] καὶ Κομα̣ϊϲη̣ Ληο̣υ̣ε̣ι̣ο̣υ θυγατρ̣ὸ̣ϲ̣ αὐτῆϲ πάντεϲ οἰκοῦντεϲ̣ [ἐ]ν Μαωζαϲ . . . ὁμολογῶ ἐνεν̣ο̣χ[έ]ν̣αι ϲ̣ο̣ι̣ ε̣ἰ̣ϲ̣ δόϲιν ἀπὸ τῆϲ ϲήμερον δόϲιν αἰωνίου τὰ ὑπάρχοντά μοι ἐν Μαωζαϲ ἃ εἴδη ὑποτεταγμένα κ̣ῆπον φοινεικῶνοϲ κ̣α̣λούμενον Γαννα̣θ Αϲαδαια ϲὺν ὕδατοϲ αὐτῆϲ ἐφ᾽ ἡ̣μερῶν ἑπτὰ εἰϲ ἑπτὰ ἡμέραν̣ τετάρτη̣ ἡ̣[μ]ι̣ω̣ρ<ί>αν μί̣α̣ν· ἧϲ γείτωνεϲ ἀνα[το]λῶν κῆπον κυρι̣α̣κὸν καλοῦ̣μ̣ενον Γανναθ Αββαιδαια δυϲμῶν κληρονό̣[μ]ο̣ι Αρεταϲ νότου ὁδὸϲ̣ βορρᾶ κληρονόμοι Ιωϲηποϲ Βαβα ϲ̣ὺ̣ν̣ εἰϲόδοιϲ καὶ ἐξ[ό]δοιϲ καὶ ϲυ̣γκ̣υ̣ρ̣ο̣ῦϲι πα[ντοίοιϲ] . . . ὁμοίωϲ καὶ ἥμ̣ι̣[ϲυ αὐλῆϲ ἀ]ν̣[ο]ι̣ω̣γημμέν̣ο̣ν̣ εἰϲ νότον ϲὺν οἰκοίματα δύο κ̣α̣ὶ ὑπερῴ̣ν ἕνα̣....α̣[.. ἧϲ γεί]τ̣ων̣εϲ ἀνατολῶν Ϲ̣α̣μ̣μ̣ωυοϲ Ϲιμωνοϲ δυϲμῶν Μαναημοϲ Ιω[ανν]ου ν̣ό̣τ̣ο̣υ̣ κ̣[λ]ηρ[ονό]μ̣ο̣ι̣ Ἰακώ̣[βου ..].[.]δ..[.] βορρᾶ [Ιω]ϲ̣η̣ποϲ . . .

על הפטית פובליוס יובנטוס קלסוס תנינותא ולוקיוס נרטיוס מרקלוס תנינותא . . . ועל מנין הפרכיה דא . . . שנת עשרין וארבע . . . במחוז עגלתין. שלום די . . . מתקריא גרפתא ברת מנחם . . . לשלום די מתקריא קומאיסה ברת לוי ברתה . . . די עמרין במחוזא. . . . אנא יהבת לכי מן יומא דנה ולעלם מתנת עלם דאיתי לי במחוזא . . . כדי כתיבין: גנת תמריא די מתקריא גנת חצדיה? אסאדיה? וענימיה יום ארבעה בשבת פלגות שעה. תחומיה למדנחא גנת מראנא די מתקריא גנת עבדיא ולמערבא ירתי חרתת ולדרומא אורחא ולצפונא ירתי יוסף בר בבא, מנעל ומנפק וכול די בה. וכות פלגות דרתא די פתיחא לדרומא ותרתי תוניא ועליתא די בה. תחומיה למדנחא שמוע בר שמעון ולמערבא מנחם בר יוחנן ולדרומא ירתי יעקב . . . ולצפונא יוסף . . .

ἔχειν τὴν π̣ρ̣ο̣[γ]εγραμμέ̣ν̣ην Κομαϊ[ϲην τὴν] προ̣γε̣γραμ̣μ̣ένην δόϲ[ι]ν κ̣υ̣ρίωϲ καὶ βεβ̣[αίωϲ] ε̣ἰ̣ϲ̣ τ̣ο̣ν ἅπαν[τα χρόνον]

תהוה קומאיסה . . . רשיה ושליטה במתנתא דא למחפר ולמעמקה ולמעבד בה כל די תצבה מן יומא דנה ולעלם.

The Aramaic and Nabataean signatures, as well as the deficient Greek of the scribe, demonstrate that despite the use of Greek, the people represented in this document can hardly be described as 'Hellenized'.[24] The resort to Greek is to be explained by the desire to make the deed of gift valid and enforceable in a Greek-speaking court, such as that of the governor of the province. Babatha, for example, as well as her opponents, were in the habit of approaching this court on their own initiative.[25] Another reason could be the need to deposit the deeds in a public archive, similar to what we know to have been the case in Egypt, where public archives were used to deposit private documents; having been registered there, these documents could later be produced in court as evidence.[26] We have a reference to such archives in P.Yadin **19**, a deed of gift from the Babatha Archive, which concludes with: 'And whenever Shelamzion

---

[24] See Wasserstein, 'Marriage Contract', 124ff.; cf. DATE AND PROVENANCE in the introductory remarks to No. **69**.

[25] See Cotton, 'Guardianship', 106ff.

[26] See Cockle, 'Archives', 116; see also Burkhalter, 'Archives'.

summons the said Judah he will register it with the public archives'.[27] Again, in a deed of concession of inherited property, Besas son of Yeshuᶜa and Julia Crispina promise Shelamzion to register with the 'public archives', at her expense, a courtyard in Ein Gedi which had belonged to her paternal grandfather.[28] In both cases, since the property is located in Ein Gedi, it is likely that the public archive which was located there operated in Greek. That similar archives existed in Arabia is clear from the fragmentary papyrus P.Yadin **24**, which tells us that Babatha's late husband had registered date groves in her name in the *apographe*.[29] *Apographe* here—as we can see from what follows—cannot refer to the census,[30] and thus must refer to an official registration of property, presumably in the public archives.

Date and Provenance

The deed of gift is dated by consular year as well as by provincial year, but not by the regnal year.[31] P. Iuventius Celsus T. Aufidius Hoenius Severianus II, L. Neratius Marcellus II were the ordinary consuls in 129 CE. The restoration of the Roman month of November in line 2 is based on the Δεῖου κ. in line 3. In Arabia, the month of Dios lasts from 18 October till 16 November.[32] If πέντε in line 1 is correct, then the date is the fifth day before the Ides of November, i.e. the ninth of November. In order to get a complete correspondence between the Roman and local calendars, κγ should be read after Δεῖου in line 3, i.e. 'the 23 of Dios'—but it is not certain that there is room for a letter between the *kappa* and ἐ̣ν̣ in line 3. Perhaps we should read only *kappa* and not κγ; in that case, there is a discrepancy of three days between the Roman and the local calendars. A discrepancy of one day between the two calendars exists in P.Yadin **14** and **15** (see Lewis, *Documents*, 57); there is a discrepancy of seven days in No. **62**.

Frg. a measures 9.4 x 17 cm. Frg. b measures 14.5 x 16.5 cm.

Mus. Inv. 869
PAM 42.205, 42.206

---

[27] ὅταν δὲ παρα̣νγείλει Cελα<μ>ψιοῦc τῷ αὐτῷ Ἰούδατι, τευχίζ{ζ}ει αὐτὴν διὰ δημοcίων, P.Yadin **19** lines 25–27.

[28] ταύτην δὲ τὴν αὐλὴν ὅπου ἂν βουληθῇc τευχίcω coι διὰ δημοc̣ίων, coῦ διδούcηc τὸ ἀνάλωμα, P.Yadin **20** lines 12–13 = 34–36.

[29] Lines 4–6: ἀπεγράψατο Ἰούδαc Ἐλεαζά̣ρο̣[υ Χθουcίωνοc] ἀ̣π̣ο̣γενομένου cου ἀνὴρ ἐπ' ὀνόματόc cου ἐν τ̣ῇ ἀπ̣[ο]γραφῇ κήπουc φοινικῶνοc ἐν Μαωζα̣.

[30] So Lewis, *Documents*, 105–7.

[31] The same in Nos. **60**, **65**, and P.Yadin **17**, **18**, **19**, **27**; see Lewis, *Documents*, 28.

[32] See Samuel, *Chronology*, 177.

Recto

Frg. a
Inner Text

1 [ἐ]π̣ὶ ὑπά̣τ̣ω̣ν̣ Πο̣[πλ]ί̣ο̣υ̣ Ἰ̣ο̣υ̣[ο]υ̣ε̣ν̣τ̣ίου Κέ̣λcου τὸ β̅ κ̣α̣ὶ̣ Λ̣[ο]υ̣κ̣ί̣ο̣υ̣ Νηρατίου
Μαρκέλλου τὸ β̅ πρὸ π̣έ̣ν̣τ̣ε̣

2 εἰδῶν [Νοουεμβρίων κατὰ τὸν ἀριθμὸν τῆc νέαc ἐπαρχείαc Ἀραβία]c ἔτουc
τετάρτου καὶ εἰκοc-

3 τοῦ Δ̣ε̣ί̣ου κ. ἐ̣ν̣ Μ̣α̣ω̣ζαc τῆ̣c̣ π̣ε̣ρ̣ὶ Ζ[ο]α̣ρ̣ω̣ν. Cα[λω]μ̣η̣ ἡ καὶ Γροπτη Μαναημου

4 cυνπαρό̣ν̣τ̣ο̣c̣ α̣ὐ̣τ̣[ῇ ἐ]πιτρόπο̣[υ τοῦδε τοῦ πρά]γ̣μ̣α̣τ̣οc χάριν Ιωcηπου Cιμ̣ω̣ν̣ο̣c̣

5 [ἀ]νὴρ αὐτῆc Cαλωμ̣η̣ [..] καὶ Κομα̣ϊcη Ληο̣υ̣ε̣ι̣ο̣υ θυγατρ̣ὸ̣c̣ αὐτῆc πάντεc
οἰκοῦντεc̣

6 [ἐ]ν Μαωζαc χ̣έ̣ρ̣ε̣ι̣ν̣. ὁμολογῶ ἐνεν̣ο̣χ[έ]ν̣αι c̣ο̣ι̣ ε̣ἰ̣c̣ δόcιν ἀπὸ τῆc cήμερον

7 δόcιν αἰωνίου τὰ ὑπάρχοντά μοι ἐν Μαωζαc ἃ εἴδη ὑποτεταγμένα·

8 κ̣ῆπον φοινεικῶνοc κ̣α̣λούμενον Γανν̣α̣θ Αcαδαια cὺν ὕδατοc αὐτῆc ἐφ'

9 ἡ̣μερῶν ἑπτὰ εἰc ἑπτὰ ἡμέρα̣ν̣ τετάρτη ἡ̣[μ]ι̣ω̣ρ<ί>αν μ̣ί̣α̣ν· ἧc γείτωνεc ἀνα-

10 [το]λῶν κῆπον κυρ̣ι̣α̣κὸν καλού̣μ̣ενον Γανναθ Αββα̣ιδαια δυcμῶν κληρον̣ό̣-

11 [μ]ο̣ι Αρεταc νότου ὁδὸ̣c̣ βορρᾶ κληρονόμοι Ιωcηποc Βαβα c̣ὺ̣ν̣ εἰcόδοιc καὶ
ἐξ[ό]-

12 δοιc καὶ cυ̣γ̣κ̣υ̣ρ̣ο̣ῦcι πα[ντοίοιc ὥ]c̣[τε] ἔχειν τὴν π̣[ρ]ο̣γεγραμμέ̣[νη]ν̣ Cαλωμη
ἡ κ[αὶ Κομα-

13 ϊ[cη]. ὁμοίωc καὶ ἥμ̣ι̣[cυ αὐλῆc ἀ]ν̣[ο]ι̣ω̣γμμέ̣ν̣ο̣ν̣ εἰc νότον cὺν οἰκοίματα δύο

14 κ̣α̣ὶ̣ ὑπερῷ̣ν ἐνα̣....α̣[.. ἧc γεί]τ̣ων̣εc ἀνατολῶν C̣α̣μ̣μωυοc Cιμωνοc δυc-

15 μῶν Μαναημοc Ιω[ανν]ου ν̣ό̣τ̣ο̣υ̣ κ̣[λ]ηρ[ονό]μ̣ο̣ι̣ Ιακω̣[βου ..].[.]δ..[.] βορρᾶ
[Ιω]c̣ηποc̣

16 [.] *traces of c.40 letters* κυρίωc καὶ βεβαίω[c *c.4 letters*]

17 [*c.26 letters*].. διοικ̣ε̣ῖ̣ν̣ [τρ]ό̣π̣ῳ̣ ᾧ̣ ἂ̣ν̣ [αἱρ]ῇ̣ πά[ντ]α̣ κ̣[ύρια]

Frg. b
Outer Text

traces

ἀνὴρ α̣ὐτ̣ῆ̣ς Ϲ̣αλωμη ἁ κ̣α̣ὶ Κ̣ο[μ]αϊ[c]η Ληουειου θυγατρὸc αὐτῆc
πάντεc οἰκοῦντεc ἐν Μα[ω]ζαc τὰ ὑπάρχοντα αὐτῆ̣c ἃ ε̣ἴ̣δη ἐ̣ν̣
[Μ]αωζαc ὑποτεταγμ<έν>α· κ̣ῆπον φοινεικώνων καλούμε-
ν̣ον Γ̣α̣νναθ Αcαδαια cὺν ὕδατοc του̣̂ αὐτοῦ κήπου ἐφ' [ἡ]μερῶν
ἑπτὰ εἰc ἑπτὰ ἡ̣μ̣έραν τετάρτη̣ ἡμιωρ<ί>αν μίαν <ἣ> τελέcει
καθ' ἔτοc εἰc λόγον κυριακοῦ φίcκου {καθ' ἔτοc} φοίνεικο̣c πατητοῦ cάτα δέκα καὶ cυροῦ καὶ νααρου cάτα ἕξ, ἧc γείτωνεc ἀ-
ν̣ατολῶν κῆπον κυριακὸν καλούμενον Γαννα̣θ Αββα̣ι-
δαια δυcμῶν κληρονό̣μοι Αρεταc νότου ὁδὸc βορρᾶ̣ [κλ]ηρονό-
μ̣οι Ιωcηποc Βαβα. ὁμ[ο]ί̣ωc καὶ ἥ̣μιcυ αὐλῆc ἀνοιω̣γμ̣[ένο]ν̣ ε̣ἰ̣c̣
ν̣ότον cὺν {ἥμιcυ} οἰκοίματα δύο καὶ ὑπερῴ̣ν ἐνο̣ῦ[cι] ἧ̣c̣ γείτ̣ω̣-
νεc ἀνατολῶν Ϲ̣αμμ̣ο̣υοc Cιμωνοc δυcμῶν Μ̣α̣ν̣α̣ημ̣ο̣c̣
Ι̣ω̣α̣ν̣ν̣ο̣υ̣ [νότου κλη]ρ̣ο̣ν̣ό̣μ̣ο̣ι̣ ...αγε̣ι̣ρ̣ο̣c̣.. βο̣ρρᾶ [Ι]ωc[ηπο]c
καὶ *traces of letters for the remainder of the line*
traces of c.21 letters οματα̣ καὶ κ̣α̣τ̣ο̣χῆc *traces of c.14 letters*
.αιο.[*c.5 letters*] ἔχειν τὴν π̣ρ̣ο̣[γ]εγραμμ̣έ̣ν̣ην Κομ̣αϊ[cην τὴν]
προ̣γε̣γραμ̣μένην δόc[ι]ν̣ κ̣υρίωc καὶ βεβ̣[αίωc] ε̣ἰ̣c̣ τ̣ὸ̣ν ἅπαν
[τα χρόνον]

3 Μαωζα̣ τῇ 5, 24 ἀνδρόc τῇ θυγατρί 6 ἐνηνοχέναι 6, 25 Μαωζα̣ χαίρειν 7, 26 Μαωζα̣ 8 ὕδατι αὐτοῦ 8–9, 27 ἀφ' ἡμερῶν 9, 28 εἰc ἑπτα ἡμέραc 9, 14, 30, 34–35 γείτονεc 10, 31 κῆποc κυριακόc καλού̣μενοc 11, 32–33 Αρετα Ιωcηπου 12 Cαλωμην 13, 33 ἀνεω̣γμένον 13, 34 οἰκήμαcι 14, 34 ὑπερῴοιc ἐνοῦcι (or: ὑπερῴ̣ω ἐνί) 26 φοινικῶνοc 29 κατ' ἔτοc 40–41 ἅπαν[τα]

Verso

Frg. a[33]

42 [שלם ברת מנחם על נפשה]

43 יה֯ו֯ס[ף בר שמעון ממרה]

44 רישה בר יהודה כת֯[בה]

45 מליך בר א○○○○[שהד]

46 ישוע בר יוחנן שה[ד]

47 תימדושרא בר עבדח֯ר֯[תת שהד]

48 יהוסף בר ש֯ול֯י֯ שהד

49 י֯[וה]ס֯ף בר ח֯נ֯[נ]יה֯ שה֯[ד]

Notes on Readings

Ll. 45, 47 The signatures on these lines are written in Nabataean; they have been transcribed here in Hebrew characters.

[33] The signatures were read by A. Yardeni.

TABLE 1: *Comparison of Inner and Outer Texts*

Line(s)	Inner Text	Outer Text	Line(s)
6	χ̣έρ̣ε̣ι̣ν̣	no equivalent	
6–7	ὁμολογῶ ἐνεν̣ο̣χ̣[έ]ν̣αι ς̣ο̣ι̣ ε̣ἰ̣ς̣ δόςιν ἀπὸ τῆς ςήμερον δόςιν αἰωνίου	no equivalent	
7	τὰ ὑπάρχοντά μοι ἐν Μαωζας ἅ εἴδη ὑποτεταγμένα	τὰ ὑπάρχοντα αὐτῆς ἅ ε̣ἴ̣δη ἐ̣ν̣ [Μ]αωζας ὑποτεταγμ<έν>α	25–26
8	κ̣ῆπον φοινεικῶνος . . . cὺν ὕδατος αὐτῆς	κ̣ῆπον φοινεικώνων . . . cὺν ὕδατος το̣ῦ αὐτοῦ κήπου	26–27
	no equivalent	<ἣ> τελέςει καθ' ἔτος εἰς λόγον κυριακοῦ φίςκου {καθ' ἔτος} φοίνεικο̣ς̣ πατητοῦ ςάτα δέκα καὶ ςυροῦ καὶ ναάρου ςάτα ἕξ	28–30
11–13	ς̣ὺ̣ν̣ εἰςόδοις καὶ ἐξ[ό]δοις καὶ ς̣υ̣γ̣κ̣υ̣ρ̣ο̣ῦςι πα[ντοίοις ὥ]ς[τε] ἔχειν τὴν π̣[ρ]ο̣γεγραμμ̣έ̣[νη]ν̣ Cαλωμη Κ̣ο̣[μαϊςη]	no equivalent (but see lines 39–40)	
13–14	ςὺν οἰκοίματα δύο κ̣α̣ὶ̣ ὑπερῷ̣ν̣ ἐνα̣....α̣[..	ςὺν {ἥμιςυ} οἰκοίματα δύο καὶ ὑπερῷν ἐνο̣ῦ̣[ςι]	34
	no equivalent	ἔχειν τὴν π̣ρ̣ο̣[γ]εγραμμ̣έ̣νην Κομ̣α̣ΐ̣[ςην τὴν] προ̣γ̣ε̣γραμμένην δός[ι]ν (but see lines 11–13)	39–40

TRANSLATION

(The inner text is written in Roman font; the outer text is written in italics; when the texts coincide, it is written in bold.)

Recto

In the second consulship of Publius Iuventius Celsus and Lucius Neratius Marcellus, the ninth [of November, according to the computation of the new province of Arabia] year twenty-four, on the twentieth (twenty-third?) of Dios in Maḥoza in the district of Ẓoʿar. Salome, who is also Gropte, daughter of Menaḥem, present with her as a guardian for the purpose of this matter, Yosef son of Shimʿon, **her husband, to Salome who is also Komaïse, daughter of Levi, her daughter, all of them living in Maḥoza,** greetings. I acknowledge that I have given you as a gift from this day and for ever my (*her*) **property in Maḥoza, which items are listed as follows: a date orchard called the Garden of Asadaia with** its *[the]* **water [allowance]** (*of that orchard*), **once a week on the fourth day, for one half-hour** *which will pay every year to the account of the fiscus of our Lord ten sata of 'splits', and six sata of the Syrian and the na'aran dates.* **The abutters on the east the orchard of our Lord [the Emperor] called the Garden of ʿAbbaidaia, on the west the heirs of Aretas, on the south a road and on the north the heirs of Yosef son of Baba.** Together with entrances and exits and all the existing appurtenances of every kind so that the above mentioned Salome Komaïse will hold [the gift written above]. **Similarly also half a courtyard which opens to the south with** (*half*) **two rooms and the upper storey room(s) therein. The abutters on the east Sammouos son of Shimᶜon, on the west Menaḥem son of Iohannes, on the south the heirs** of Jacob . . . **on the north Yosef** . . . *possession* . . . *that the above-mentioned Komaïse will hold the gift written above* **validly and securely** *for all [time]* . . . to manage in whatever manner she chooses to. Everything valid . . .

Verso:

42. [Shalom daughter of Menaḥem in person]
43. Yose[f son of Shimᶜon wrote for her]
44. Reisha son of Yehudah wr[ote ?]
45. Malik son of A...[, witness]
46. Yeshuᶜa son of Yoḥanan, wit[ness]
47. Timadushra son of ʻAbdḥare[tat, witness]
48. Yehosaf son of Shullai, witness
49. Y[ohe]saf son of Ḥana[n]iah, wit[ness]

COMMENTS

Frgs. a and b; recto; inner and outer texts

Ll. 1–4 These lines of the inner text = lines 18–23 of the outer text, which must be restored on the basis of the inner text.

L. 2 This line is heavily restored on the basis of the formula which appears in a land declaration from 127 from the Babatha Archive, namely the addition of *νέας* before ἐπαρχείας in the dating formula: κατὰ δὲ τὸν τῆς νέας ἐπαρχείας Ἀραβίας ἀριθμὸν ἔτους δευτέρου εἰκοστοῦ μηνὸς Ἀπελλαίου ἑκκαιδεκάτῃ (P.Yadin **16** lines 9–11). This dating formula continues down to 132—the latest dated document in the archive, P.Yadin 27.[34] It is also found in No. **62** (127 CE) and in No. **65** (131 CE). The exact wording used to restore the line here is taken from P.Yadin **19**, **20**, **21**, **22**, and **27**; see Wasserstein, 'Marriage Contract', 99–100; Lewis, 'World of P.Yadin', 35–6; INTRODUCTION TO THE GREEK DOCUMENTARY TEXTS; and Cotton, ''Η νέα ἐπαρχεία Ἀραβία'.

L. 3 Δ̣ε̣ί̣ου κ. ἐ̣ν̣ Μ̣α̣ωζας. There may not be enough room after the *kappa* for another letter. See above, DATE AND PROVENANCE, for a possible discrepancy between the Roman and local calendars.

L. 3 ἐ̣ν̣ Μ̣α̣ωζας τῆς π̣ερὶ Ζ[ο]α̣ρων. Nothing quite like this is found in the Babatha Archive, where we find the following variations: ἐ[ν] Μαω[ζοις τ]ῶ̣ν περὶ Ζ[οα]ρα (P.Yadin **5a** col. i lines 4–5); ἐν Μαωζα̣ περὶ Ζοαραν (P.Yadin **14** line 20; **15** lines 16–17 = line 3; **17** lines 2–3 = lines 19–20; **18** line 3 = 32); ἐν Μαωζα̣ περὶ Ζοορων (P.Yadin **25** line 28 = line 64); ἐ̣ν Μ̣α̣ω̣ζας τῆς πε[ρὶ Ζοα]ρα (P.Yadin **19** lines 10–11); ἐν Μαωζα̣ περιμέτρῳ Ζοορων (P.Yadin **20** line 4 = lines 22–23; **21** lines 5–6; **22** lines 5–6; **26** line 18); Βαβθα . . . Μαωζηνὴ τῆς Ζοαρηνῆς περιμέτρου Πέτρας (P.Yadin **16** lines 13–14). In No. **62** frg. a line 12 we find: Ϲ̣α̣μ̣μ̣ο̣υ̣[ο]ϲ Ϲιμων[ο]ϲ Μαωζηνὸϲ τῆϲ Ζοαρηνῆϲ περιμέτρου Πέτραϲ.[35]

L. 3 Ϲα[λω]μ̣η ἡ καὶ Γροπτη. Cf. No. **63** line 9: Γραπτη, and see INTRODUCTION TO THE ARCHIVE OF SALOME KOMAÏSE DAUGHTER OF LEVI on the nickname Grapte or Gropte.

L. 4 ϲυνπαρό̣ν̣τ̣ο̣ϲ α̣ὐ̣τ̣[ῇ ἐ]πιτρόπο̣[υ τοῦδε τοῦ πρά]γ̣μ̣α̣τ̣ο̣ϲ χ̣άριν. The identical expression is found in P.Yadin **17** (128 CE) lines 4–5 = lines 22–23: ϲυνπαρόντ̣[οϲ α]ὐτῇ ἐπιτρόπου το̣ῦ̣δε τοῦ π̣ρ̣ά̣γ̣μ̣α̣τ̣ο̣ϲ χ̣ά̣ριν Ἰακώβου; see COMMENTS on No. **63** lines 1–2 for the use of ἐπίτροποϲ rather than κύριοϲ to describe the guardian of a woman.

Ll. 4–5 and 24 Ιωϲηπου Ϲιμ̣ω̣ν̣ο̣ϲ [ἀ]νὴρ αὐτῆϲ. As we know from No. **63** line 6 (περὶ τ]ῶ̣ν καταλειφθέντω̣[ν ὑπὸ Λ]η̣ουει γενομένου ϲ̣υ̣[μβίου αὐτῆϲ]), Salome Grapte's first husband, Levi, had been dead at least since 127 CE.

[34] Cf. also P.Yadin **17**, **18**, **19**, **20**, **21**, and **22**.

[35] Cf. No. **65** lines 2–3: [ἐν Μαωζα̣ τῆϲ Ζο]αρανῆϲ .[...]...... Πέτραν, and COMMENTS ad loc.

Ll. 5 and 24 See INTRODUCTION TO THE ARCHIVE OF SALOME KOMAÏSE DAUGHTER OF LEVI on the nickname Komaïse.

L. 5 Ληουειου. For the spelling of Levi's name, see INTRODUCTION TO THE ARCHIVE OF SALOME KOMAÏSE DAUGHTER OF LEVI.

Ll. 5–6 and 25 πάντες οἰκοῦντες ἐν Μαωζας. For the expression, see No. **63** line 4: [πάντες Μα]ωζηνοι; P.Yadin **17** lines 5–6 = 24: πάντες ἐνθάδε (i.e. ἐν Μαωζα) κα[τ]αμένον[τε]ς; P.Yadin **16** lines 5–6 = 36–37; **21** lines 6–7: ἀμφότεροι οἰκοῦντες ἐν Μαωζα (cf. **22** lines 6–7); P.Yadin **27** lines 5–6: ἀμφότε[ροι τ]ῆ[ς] αὐτῆς Μαωζας.

L. 6 χέρειν. The word is found only in the inner text, presumably because the inner text is phrased in the subjective mode (ὁμολογῶ ἐνενοχ[έ]ναι ςοι . . . τὰ ὑπάρχοντά μοι, lines 6–7), unlike the outer text, which is phrased in the objective mode (τὰ ὑπάρχοντα αὐτῆς, line 25). The same distinction exists in the Babatha Archive: χαίρειν is used in those documents which are formulated in the 1st person, cf. P.Yadin **11** line 2 = line 14 (loan with hypothec); **20** line 6 = line 27 (concession of rights); **21** line 6 (purchase of a date crop); **22** line 7 (sale of date crop); **27** line 6 (receipt).

L. 6 ὁμολογῶ. The verb occurs in other deeds of gift: e.g. P.Dura 18 (87 CE) line 5 = lines 21–22: ἐξωμολογ[ής]ατο Νικάνω[ρ] ὁ αὐτὸς διδόναι . . . ; P.Grenf. II 68 = *FIRA* III^2 no. 98 (247 CE) line 4: ὁμολογῶ χαρίζεςθ[αι] ςοὶ χάριτ[ι ἀ]ναφεραίτῳ. Ὁμολογεῖ must have stood in the outer text in view of μοι, as against αὐτῆς in lines 7 and 25, respectively, see ad loc.

L. 6 ἐνενοχ[έ]ναι (instead of ἐνηνοχέναι). See Gignac, *Grammar*, 1:242f. for the interchange of *eta* and *epsilon* before a liquid; cf. προςενηνοχέναι in PSI X 1117 (ii CE), a marriage contract with προςφορά given by the mother of the bride: [ὁ]μολογεῖ προςενηνοχέναι τῇ θυγατρὶ Θεναπύγχει ‹ἐν› προςφο[ρᾷ ?] κατὰ τήνδε τὴν ὁ(μολογίαν) ἀπὸ τοῦ νῦν ἐπ' ἀεὶ τήν τε ὑπάρχουςαν αὐτῇ . . . οἰκ[ί]αν (lines 18f.).

L. 6 ἀπὸ τῆς ςήμερον. This confirms Lewis's restoration in P.Yadin **19** lines 20–23: ὥςτε ἔχειν τὴν προγεγραμμ[έ]νην Ϲελαμψιοῦ[ς] τὸ ἥμιςυ τῆς προγεγραμμένης αὐλῆς καὶ οἱ[κη]μ[ά]των ἀ[πὸ τῆς ςήμερον] cf. BGU I 316 (= MChr. 271, 359 CE, Askalon, deed of sale) lines 21–22: ἀπὸ τῆς ς[ήμερον] ἡμέρας καὶ εἰς ἀεί.[36]

Ll. 6–7 εἰς δόςιν ἀπὸ τῆς ςήμερον δόςιν αἰωνίου. The whole expression is probably an attempt to translate the Aramaic expression 'from this day and forever', found in Aramaic deeds; cf. No. **8a** lines 11–12: מן ימה דנה ולעלם; No. **50** line 13 (10): מן יומא דנה ולעלם (restored in No. **8** line 6). In Greek, one could expect e.g.: ἀπὸ τοῦ νῦν εἰς τὸν ἀεὶ χρόνον, as in P.Oxy. IX 1200 (266 CE) lines 16–17: ὁμολογῶ πεπρακέναι ςοι καὶ παρακεχωρηκέναι ἀπὸ τοῦ νῦν εἰς τὸν ἀεὶ χρόνον.

L. 7 δόςιν αἰωνίου. This seems to be a literal translation of the Aramaic construct state in the phrase מתנת עלם—'an eternal gift'; cf. the Aramaic deed of gift, P.Yadin **7** lines 2; 5; 14. The construct state is characteristic of Semitic rather than Indo-European languages.[37] In Greek one would say εἰς τὸν ἀεὶ χρόνον (P.Oxy. XXXIV 2722 lines 19–20) or ἐπ' ἀεὶ (PSI X 1117 line 20); μέχρ[ι] παντός (P.Grenf. II 68 line 7); or εἰς τὸν ἅπαντα χρόνον, as in No. **64** lines 40–41; cf. P.Oxy. XLVII 3638 lines 4–5; P.Mich. XV 719 line 6; P.Yadin **19** line 23; P.Dura 26 lines 14–15; P.Dura 18 line 7 = line 26 and P.Avroman, IA line 16 = IB line 16.

Ll. 7 and 25–26 In the inner text (line 7), τὰ ὑπάρχοντά μοι ἐν Μαωζας ἃ εἴδη ὑποτεταγμένα, one should understand ἐςτι with the participle: 'which items are listed as follows'. The word order in the outer text (lines 25–26)—τὰ ὑπάρχοντα αὐτῆς ἃ εἴδη ἐν [Μ]αωζας ὑποτεταγμ‹έν›α—is baffling.

Ll. 7 and 25–26 Note the 1st person in the inner text—τὰ ὑπάρχοντά μοι—and the 3rd person in the outer text—τὰ ὑπάρχοντά αὐτῆς. See line 6 on ὁμολογῶ.

Ll. 8 and 26 Φοινεικῶνος in the inner text (line 8) and φοινεικώνων in the outer text (line 26). The first form is attested in No. **62** frg. a line 18; frg. b line 5; frgs. c–m lines 10, 14: κήπου φοινικῶνος, and in the Babatha Archive: κῆπον φοινικῶνος in P.Yadin **16** lines 17, 21, 24, 29; καρπίαν φοινικῶνος κήπων in

[36] Cf. ἀπὸ τοῦ νῦν in PSI X 1117 (ii CE, a marriage contract) line 18; P.Grenf. II, 68 (= *FIRA* III^2 no. 98, a deed of gift, 247 CE) line 7.

[37] Cf. οἶκος αἰώνιος, 'house of eternity', i.e. 'grave', in *CIJ* 337 (Rome); בית עלמא in Aramaic (cf. Mur **20** line 7; see Hurvitz, 'בית קברות').

P.Yadin **21** line 8; **22** lines 7–8; χάριν κήπου φοινικῶνοϲ in P.Yadin **23** lines 5–6 and **24** lines 5–6. The expression seems to be a literal translation of the construct state in Aramaic: **גנת תמריא** 'orchard of dates'; cf. P.Yadin **7** line 5.[38]

Ll. 8 and 26–27 κῆπον . . . καλούμενον Γανναθ Αϲαδαια. Cf. line 10 (= lines 31–32): κῆπον κυρ̣ι̣ακὸν καλο̣ύ̣μενον Γανναθ Αββ̣α̣ιδαια. The other Greek documents use λεγόμενοϲ to express what is here expressed by καλούμενοϲ; cf. No. **62** frg. a lines 14–15: μέροϲ ἥμιϲυ χώραϲ . . . λ̣ε̣γ̣ο̣μ̣έ̣νηϲ Αρενοαραθα; lines 17–19: μέρο̣ϲ̣ ἥμιϲυ κ̣ήπου φοινικῶ̣ν̣οϲ ἐν ὁρ̣ί̣ο̣ι̣ϲ̣ [Μ]αω̣ζων τῆϲ α̣[ὐ]τῆϲ λεγομένου Χαφφ[ο]υ̣ρα; P.Yadin **21** lines 9–11: (date groves) λεγόμεναι Γ̣ανναθ Φερωρα καὶ Γανναθ Νικαρ{ι}κοϲ καὶ ἡ τρίτη λεγομένη τοῦ Μολχαίου (cf. P.Yadin **22** lines 10–11); P.Yadin **16**: κῆπον φοινικῶνοϲ ἐν ὁρίοιϲ Μαωζων λεγόμενον Αλγιφιαμμα (lines 17–18); κῆπον φοινικῶνοϲ ἐν ὁρίοιϲ Μαωζων λεγόμενον Βηθφααραια (lines 29–30); κῆπον φοινικῶνοϲ ἐν ὁρίοιϲ Μαωζων λεγόμενον Βαγαλγαλά (lines 24–25). In P.Yadin **3**, a Nabataean deed of sale from the Babatha Archive, we find: **גנת תמריא די לאביעדן די מתקריא גה..א די בגלגלא** 'A date grove which belongs to ʾAbiʿadan called Gh..a in the Galgala' (lines 2–3 = lines 23–24); and, in a deed of gift in Aramaic from the same archive, P.Yadin **7** in line 7 = line 39, we find: **אתרא די מתקרא כרבא נציב תמרין** 'a place called Karaba, a date grove'.

Ll. 8 and 27 Γανναθ. This is a transliteration of Aramaic **גנת**, the construct state of **גנה** ('garden', or, as here, 'orchard'), meaning 'orchard of'; cf. P.Yadin **21** lines 9–10; **22** lines 10–11: Γ̣ανναθ Φερωρα καὶ Γανναθ Νικαρ{ι}κοϲ; see below, lines 10 and 31–32: Γανναθ Αββ̣α̣ιδαια.

Ll. 8 and 27 Αϲαδαια. Is this **אסאדיה**? or **חצדיה**, perhaps derived from **חצד**, a kind of date mentioned in P.Yadin **46** line 5 (see *m.ʿAbod. Zar.* 1.5 with Yadin, 'Expedition D—Cave of Letters', 255–6).

Ll. 8 and 27 ϲὺν ὕδατοϲ. The water rights—'the times of permitted irrigation'—'formed part of the ownership of the garden',[39] as we learn from P.Yadin **2**, **3**, and **7** of the Babatha Archive, as well as from P.Yadin **42**, a deed of lease from Ein Gedi:[40] **וענימיה כדי חזא להון** 'and its water periods as proper and fit for them'. Dates need a great amount of water; in this rainless zone, it is supplied mainly, and often exclusively, by irrigation.[41] In the Aramaic deed of gift P.Yadin **7** line 43, we hear of the right to use water from the wadi once a week for half an hour (**ענימיה חד בשבת פלגות שעה מן מי ודיא**).[42] Two double documents on parchment from Avroman in Kurdistan from the first century BCE[43] specify water rights among other rights in a sale of vineyards, P.Avroman IA (88 BCE) lines 13–14: μετὰ ὕδατοϲ καὶ ἀκροδρύοιϲ καρποφόροιϲ τε καὶ εἰϲόδῳ καὶ ἐξόδῳ καὶ τοῖϲ ϲυνκυροῦϲιν εἰϲ αὐτὴν πᾶϲιν[44] P.Avroman IIA (22/1 BCE) line 7 (= IIB lines 7–8): ϲὺν εἰϲόδωι καὶ ἐξόδωι καὶ ὕδαϲι ὑπάρχουϲι μετὰ τῶν ϲυνκλήρων.

That water rights are conceived as part of the property is seen in the so-called *Tablettes Albertini*, where two adjacent pieces of land are sold together with water rights: 'particellas agrorum, id est bumas (vumas) duas sivi coerentes cum aquario de gemione superiore in quibus sunt amigdal(ae) arb(ores) tres, fici arb(ores) quatuor, pl(us) m(inus) sitecia arborem unam [cum aquari]o de flumine ascendente' (Dec. 493 or Jan. 494 CE, *FIRA* III^2 139 lines 5–9).[45] Water rights and access to a water source are mentioned in Jewish sources.[46] In the Mishna we read that the existence of a water source (a fountain) could influence the terms of a lease of an irrigated field (*m. B. Meṣ* 9.2; cf. *t. B. Meṣ.* 9.3–4). The division of a

---

[38] This will explain the tautology in κῆποϲ φοινικῶνοϲ.

[39] Yadin, 'Expedition D—Cave of Letters', 243.

[40] Yadin, 'Expedition D—Cave of Letters', 249, no. 42 = Cotton, Cockle, and Millar, 'Papyrology', no. 293.

[41] 'The irrigation arrangements at En-gedi—using the spring-waters which flowed down the slopes in specially made channels—were thus very carefully worked out, the water being allocated to every garden according to specific quotas' (Yadin, 'Expedition D—Cave of Letters', 249; cf. Yadin, 'Nabataean Kingdom', 232ff.).

[42] Yadin, Greenfield, and Yardeni, 'Deed of Gift', 385.

[43] Both were originally published by Minns, 'Parchments', 22ff. P.Avroman IA, with variant readings from IB, is published in Meyer, *Jur. Pap.*, no. 36.

[44] The water rights are not mentioned in the parallel part of the outer text, IB, lines 13–14; on water rights, see Minns, 'Parchments', 55–6.

[45] For interpretation, see Shaw, 'Lamasba', 81; ibid. for the reading *flumine ascendente*.

[46] I am grateful to Sh. Naeh, M. Kahana, and J. Garb for help with the Jewish sources.

field between heirs had to take account of the location of the water source, so that both fields would have access to it (see *b. B. Bat.* 12b).[47] On water rights in Egypt, see Taubenschlag, *Law,* 259–60. For irrigation of date groves in Egypt, see Hohlwein, 'Palmiers et Palmeraies', 11; 31ff.; Johnson, *Roman Egypt*, 20ff. Note also the fragmentary BGU III 899 and 890 of the Antonine period, which seem to be leases of olive groves with rights of irrigation: see Johnson, ibid., 82; cf. W. Habermann, *Die Wasserversorgung einer ägyptischen Metropole im kaiserzeitlichen Ägypten. Eine Neuedition von P.Land. III 1177* (forthcoming; I am grateful to the author for the information).

L. 8 αὐτῆc. The Greek pronoun in the inner text is influenced by the gender of the preceding Aramaic noun גנת, γανναθ; cf. P.Yadin **21** lines 9–10: λεγόμεναι and ἡ τρίτη λεγομένη; **22** lines 10–11; and Lewis, *Documents*, 97. The outer text of No. **64**, on the other hand, avoids the mistake by having τοῦ αὐτοῦ κήπου (line 27).

Ll. 8–9 and 27–28 ἐφ' ἡμερῶν ἑπτὰ εἰc ἑπτὰ ἡμέραν. This circumlocution conveys the notion of a 'week' (שבה) that we find in the Nabataean and Aramaic documents in the same context (P.Yadin **3** line 25; **7** lines 43, 46, and 47). It could be expressed in Greek by the word ἑβδομάc.

Ll. 9 and 28 τετάρτῃ. On the fourth day of the week. In the documents from Kurdistan, the day of the week is specified only in the inner text: κα[ὶ] τὸ ὕδωρ παρὰ ὀγδόην ἡμέρας τὸ ἥμιcυ [καὶ τ]ῆc ἐπαγωγῆc νυκτὸc τὸ ἥμιcυ (P.Avroman IA lines 26–28); but not in the outer text: ἕξει δὲ καὶ τὸ ὕδωρ τὸ ἐπιβάλλον αὐτῷ μέροc μ[ετὰ τῶ]ν cυν[κλ]ήρω[ν] (P.Avroman IB lines 27–28).

Ll. 9 and 28 ἡμιωρ<ί>αν. Cf. P.Yadin **3** line 25: 'one hour on the first day of the week'; P.Yadin **7** lines 43–44: 'half an hour on the first day of the week . . . '; lines 46–47: 'one hour on the fourth day of the week . . . and one hour on the night of the fourth with the heirs of Yosef son of Baba'. The allotment of water in units of hours is recorded in an extensive inscription from Lamasba in Numidia from the time of Elagabalus. This is a decree concerning a large-scale irrigation scheme in which the names of the possessors are followed by a timetable for using the water of the Aqua Claudiana (*CIL* VIII 18587). The formula runs: 'ex h(ora) I d(iei) VII Kal. Octobr. in h(oram) VS (quintum dimidiam) d(iei) eiusdem p(ro) p(arte) s(ua) h(oras) IIIIS (quattuor et) s(emis)'; or: 'ex h(ora)II noc(tis) III kal. Dec. in h(oram) X d(iei) pr(idie) kal. Dec. p(ro) p(arte) s(ua) h(oras) XX (viginti)'.[48]

Pliny the Elder tells us of palm growing in the oasis of Tacape in North Africa, where water is allotted in units of time: 'certis horarum spatiis dispensatur inter incolas' (Pliny, *NH* 18.188).[49] For other references to irrigation in units of time see Frontinus, *De Aquis* 9 '[Aquam Crabram Agrippa] possessoribus relinquendam credebat; ea namque est quam omnes villae tractus eius per vicem in dies modulosque certos dispensatum accipiunt'; *Dig.* 43.20.2 (Pomponius): 'Si diurnarum aut nocturnarum horarum aquae ductum habeam, non possum alia hora ducere quam qua ius habeam'; cf. 39.3.17pr. (Paulus); 43.20.5pr. (Iulianus); *CIL* VI 1261 (Rome, the Aventine) ; XIV 3676 (Tibur).[50]

Watering periods are mentioned several times in the Jewish sources: *m. Šeb.* 2.9; *t. Šeb.* 2.9; *t. Moʿed* 1.2; *b. Moʿed* 11b. For several fields using one water channel, see *t. B. Meṣ.* 11.21; *b. B. Qam.* 27b; *b. B. Meṣ.* 108a. Taking turns in using a common source of water supply is implied in *m. Giṭ* 5.8: 'The cistern nearest to a water channel is filled first—in the interests of peace' (cf. *b. Giṭ.* 60b).

See Introduction to O. Waqfa, §6, 'Le partage de l'eau' (pp. 20ff.) with nos. 61–62 there, on paying a tariff according to hours of irrigation.

Ll. 28–30 Notwithstanding its import, there is no equivalent in the inner text to the clause contained in lines 28–30 of the outer text (see TABLE 1). This may confirm once more the opinion that the outer text was written before the inner text (see Lewis, *Documents*, 9; 127). See the Excursus, below.

L. 28 τελέcει. We find both present and future tenses in the parchments from Kurdistan: P.Avroman IA lines 17–18 (cf. IB lines 17–18): τελῶντεc κατ' ἐνιαυτὸν κοινῇ τὰ γεγραμμένα ἐν τῇ παλαιᾷ cυνγραφῇ πάντα; P.Avroman IIA line 9 (= IIB line 9): τελέcουcι δὲ αἰεὶ κατ' ἐνιαυτ[ὸ]ν cκέλοc δραχμὴν

[47] See, in general, Patai, *The Water*, 72ff.; Irsai, 'Water Installations', 47ff.; Sperber, *Material Culture*, 29ff.

[48] For interpretation, see Shaw, 'Lamasba', 61–103.

[49] Cf. Pavis d'Escurac, 'Irrigation', 177ff.

[50] See White, *Roman Farming*, 157–60.

μίαν κτλ. The same verb is used in the land declarations to describe the payment of annual taxes: e.g. P.Yadin **16** lines 21–23: κῆπον φοινικῶνος ἐν ὁρίοις Μαωζων λεγόμενον Αλγιφιαμμα cπόρου κρειθῆc κάβου ἑνὸ<c> τελοῦντα τῶν γεινομένων καθ' ἔτοc καρπῶν μέροc ἥμιcυ, see lines 19; 22–23; 26; 30–31; No. **62** frg. a lines 16–17: ὃ μέρ̣ο̣c ἥμιcύ ἐστιν cπόρο̣υ̣ κρειθῆc cάτου ἑ̣[ν]ὸ̣c̣ κάβων τριῶ̣ν̣ τελοῦν φόρου μέλαν ἓν λεπτὰ τεc̣c̣α̣ράκοντα̣ πέντε; see frg. b line 3; frgs. c–m lines 8, 12. Note that the duties incumbent on the date grove (see below on lines 28–29) are conceived to be as much a part of the property as the water rights.

L. 29 On the false aspiration καθ' ἔτοc, see Gignac, *Grammar*, 1:135; cf. P.Yadin **16** line 23 (quoted above ad line 28).

L. 29 εἰc λόγον κυριακοῦ φίcκου. This tautology is apparently not found elsewhere; κυριακὸc λόγοc is the φίcκοc; see the Edict of Ti. Iulius Alexander, *CIG* III 4957 (= *OGIS* II 669 =*FIRA* I², no. 58): τῶν ὀφειλόντων εἰc τὸν κυριακὸν λόγον;[51] P.Amh. II 77 = WChr. 277 = Select Papyri 282 line 16: τῷ κυριακῷ λόγωι; P.Heid. N.F. II 221 (197–222?): ἔcχον παρὰ cοῦ ἃc δέδωκά cοι εἰc τιμὴν μηχανῶν δύο ἀργυ(ρίου) δραχμὰc διακοcίαc τοῦ κυριακοῦ λόγου. There are other variations: *CIG* II 2842 line 9: τῷ κυριακῷ φίcκῳ (Aphrodisias); BGU II 620 (iii century CE) line 15: ἐν τοῖc κυριακοῖc λόγο[ιc]. Cf. P.Dura 26 (= *FIRA* III², no. 138), a deed of sale from 227 CE: τοῦ ἠγορακότοc δειδοῦντοs πᾶν [τὸ] ἐπιβάλ̣λ̣[ο]ν̣ τῇ αὐτῇ χώρα̣ εἰc λόγ[ο]ν̣ κυ̣ρ̣ι̣α̣κ[ο]ῦ (sic! not κυ̣ρ̣ι̣α̣κ[ό]ν) (line 26).

L. 29 φοίνεικοc. Φοῖνιξ is used here as a collective noun for 'dates', cf. τειμὴν φο̣ί̣ν̣ι̣κ̣ο̣c, No. **60** line 5; P.Yadin **16** lines 17–20: κῆπον φοινικῶνοc ἐν ὁρίοιc Μαωζων λεγόμενον Αλγιφιαμμα . . . τελοῦντα φοίνικοc cυροῦ καὶ μείγματοc cάτα δεκαπέντε.

Ll. 29–30 πατητοῦ. This is a particularly juicy variety of dates which bursts open on the tree itself (see Pliny, *NH* 13.45, thus explained by Hohlwein, 'Palmiers et Palmeraies', 18–22, and followed by others); the ***patetos*** is mentioned in No **62** frgs. c–m line 17 and in P.Yadin **16** lines 20, 27, 31 (see Lewis, ***Documents***, 69–70), as well as in Egyptian papyri: P.Mich. XII, 657 lines 7–8; BGU XI, 2105 line 4; P.Wien.Boswink. 8 line 15; Manfredi, 'Affitto di un uliveto', 96 line 11.[52]

L. 30 cάτα. Cάτον is the Hebrew סאה, *se'ah*, a measure of volume estimated by some to be equal to 8.56 litres, and by others to 13 litres.[53] It is attested in Greek in No. **62** frgs. c–m line 17; P.Yadin **16** lines 18–20, 26, 30; **21** line 15; **22** line 17; Mur **97**; and in Hebrew in Mur **24B** line 17; **24K** col. 2; **30** line 14.

L. 30 cυροῦ. On the spelling cυροῦ for cυρίου see COMMENTS on No **62** frgs. c–m line 12. It is considered an inferior variety of dates (see Pliny, *NH* 13.48).

L. 30 ναaρου. The word is spelled here in the same way as in No **62** frgs. c–m line 17 and in P.Yadin **21** lines 14, 23; **22** lines 16, 20; whereas in P.Yadin **16** lines 26, 31, it is spelled νοαρου. 'Its name is derived from Naʿaran, north of Jericho, and also has several variants: Naaratha (LXX), Noorath (Eusebius, *Onomasticon*, 136, 24) and Neara (Josephus, *Ant.* XVII 340), with similar variants in talmudic literature' (Broshi, 'Seven Notes', 233).

Ll. 9 and 30 ῆc. The ῆc is influenced by the gender of the Aramaic γανναθ; see COMMENTS on αὐτῆc, in line 8.

Ll. 9 and 30 γείτωνεc. Whereas the Egyptian practice was to start with the neighbours on the south and then those on the north, in Palestine and Arabia, as well as in Dura-Europus, the neighbours are given in east-west-south-north order: cf. P.Yadin **11** lines 4–6 (= lines 17–19); P.Yadin **19** lines 17–18; P.Dura 26 (= *FIRA* III² no. 138) lines 15–17. The same order is found in Hebrew and Aramaic contracts: Mur **22** line 3 = lines 11–12; Mur **30** lines 3–4 = lines 16–17; No. **8** lines 4–5; No. **50** lines 3–4. See COMMENTS on No. **66** lines 3–4.

Ll. 9–10 and 30–31 ἀνα[το]λῶν . . . δυcμῶν. In Egyptian papyri we find ἀπηλιώτηc and λιβόc respectively.

Ll. 10 and 31 κῆπον κυριακὸν. On imperial properties in Maḥoza, see INTRODUCTION to No. **60**.

Ll. 10 and 31–32 καλούμενον Γανναθ Αββαιδαια. On καλούμενον, see above ad lines 8 and 26.

---

[51] Similarly BGU III 747 lines 16–17: [αἱ ἀ]παιτή[cε]ιc τῶν ὀφιλομέ[ν]ων τῷ κυριακῷ λ[ό]γῳ.

[52] See Broshi, 'Seven Notes', 232–3.

[53] See Broshi, 'Seven Notes', 234–5.

Ll. 10 and 31–32 Αββạιδαια. Possibly Αββẹιδαια. The name of the grove is derived from the Nabataean name ʿAbed or ʿAbda, or ʿAbdu meaning 'slave'; see Negev, *Personal Names*, nos. 782; 783; 798. For 'Abdu, see P.Yadin **16** line 39: 'Abdu son of Muqimu, witness' (עבדו בר מקימו שהד). The name implies that the grove once belonged to a Nabataean.

Ll. 10–11 and 32 κληρονόμοι Αρετας. Cf. below lines 11 and 32–33: κληρονόμοι Ιωcηπος Βαβα and line 15: κ̣[λ]ηρ[ονό]μ̣ο̣ι̣ Ιακω̣[βου; No. **66** line 4:]ν̣ [ν]ο̣του κληρονόμοι τῶν Κ.[; P.Yadin **16** line 28: γε̣ί̣τ̣ο̣ν̣ε̣[c κλ]η̣ρ̣ο̣ν̣όμοι Θηcαίου Cαβακα̣. The declarant of No. **62**, Sammouos son of Shimʿon , is one of two brothers holding properties in partnership (μετοχῇ) in Maḥoza. As abutters, they could be described as κληρονόμοι Cιμωνος, although they do not make a joint declaration. The appearance of heirs holding property together is very common in the papyri; see e.g. P.Oxy. IV 719 (193 CE) lines 16–17: ὧν γείτονες τῆς μὲν μιᾶς τοῦ αἰθρίου νότου εἴcοδος καὶ ἔξοδος βορρᾶ [κλ]ηρονόμων Διογᾶτος ἀπηλιώτου κληρονόμων Ὥρου λιβὸς δημοc[ί]α ῥύμη. For Latin documents, see e.g. *CIL* XI 1147 (the alimentary table from Veleia), col. I lines 14–15: adf(inibus) Ulvis Stolicinis fratribus et Vettis fratribus; col. V lines 28–29: adf(inibus) Antonis Sabino et Prisco, etc.

Ll. 11 and 32 Αρετας. The writer's carelessness about case endings makes him use this form for the genitive whereas usually it stands for the nominative; the genitive form would be Αρετα or Αρετου (see Gignac, *Grammar*, 2:12–14). In the Babatha Archive, we find Ιουδας (nominative) and Ιουδα (genitive) in P.Yadin **19** lines 11 and 23 respectively; P.Yadin **15** line 32: δι' ἐπιτρόπου μου Ιουδα; and'Ιουδου in P.Yadin **17** line 35. Aretas—חרתת—is a dynastic Nabataean name (Negev, *Personal Names*, no. 494).[54] According to Negev (p. 107), it was used by others as well. See Schürer, Vermes, and Millar, *History*, 1:574–86 on the names of the Nabataean kings.

Ll. 11 and 32–33 κληρονόμοι Ιωcηπος Βαβα. It should have been κληρονόμοι 'Ιωcηπου Βαβα. The scribe happens to be correct about Βαβα being used as the genitive of this name in Greek probably because it corresponds to the Aramaic form. These heirs are found in P.Yadin **7** from 13th July 120 CE—ירתי יוסף בר בבא—as neighbours to two pieces of land owned by Babatha's father (lines 6, 11 = lines 38, 45), with whom he also shares some water rights (P.Yadin **7** line 12 = line 47). Almost nine years after P.Yadin **7**, these heirs are still referred to as a single body of owners, i.e. the property remained undivided.[55]

Ll. 11 and 32–33 Βαβα. Baba—בבא—'father' is probably borrowed from Persian (see Nöldeke, *Beiträge*, 93); like other words describing kinship it could be used as a proper name (Nöldeke, 90–98: 'Verwandtschaftsnamen als Personennamen'). In No. **12** lines 6–7, בב לוי אבוך is translated 'papa Levi, your father', i.e. בב is understood as Levi's nickname; see COMMENTS ad loc. On the name Βάβας (בבא) in inscriptions and the sources, see Oren and Rappaport, 'The Necropolis in Maresha', 144.

Ll. 11–13 c̣ὺ̣ν εἰcόδοιc καὶ ἐξ[ό]δοιc καὶ cυγκ̣ύ̣ρ̣ουcι πα[ντοίοιc ὥ]c̣[τε] ἔχειν τὴν π̣[ρ]ο̣γεγραμμέ̣[νη]ν̣ Cαλωμη ἡ κ[αὶ Κομα]ϊ̣[cη]. These lines have no equivalent in the outer text which continues with ὁμοίωc καί in line 33.

Ll. 11–12 c̣ὺ̣ν εἰcόδοιc καὶ ἐξ[ό]δοιc. Identical phrasing can be found in P.Yadin **19** line 19; see also P.Dura 26 (= *FIRA* III² no. 138, 227 CE) lines 10–11: cὺν εἰcόδ[ῳ] καὶ ἐξόδῳ; cf. P.Avroman, IA and IB lines 13–14 and IIA line 7 = IIB lines 7–8. The pair may stand for a concrete passageway or for the legal right: see Taubenschlag, 'Das Recht auf εἴcοδοc καὶ ἔξοδοc'; *Law*, 256–9; Husson, *OIKIA*, 65–72. The same phrase occurs in Aramaic deeds (מעל ומפקה or מעלה ומפקה): No. **8** line 5; No. **8a** line 10; No. **50** line 6; P.Yadin **7** line 14 = line 50; Mur **25** line 3; see Broshi and Qimron, 'House Sale Deed', 209.

L. 12 καὶ cυγκ̣υ̣ρ̣οῦcι πα[ντοίοιc .]. Perhaps cυ̣ν̣κ̣υ̣ρ̣οῦcι, see line 4: cυνπαρό̣ν̣τ̣ο̣c. Although there is enugh room for παντοίοιc, πᾶ[cι......] cannot be excluded. Cf. τοῖc ἐνοῦcι παντοίοιc in P.Yadin **19** line 20.

L. 12 [ὥ]c̣[τε] ἔχειν τὴν π̣[ρ]ο̣γεγραμμέ̣[νη]ν̣ Cαλωμη ἡ κ[αὶ Κομα]ϊ̣[cη]. We should supply here τὴν προγεγραμμένην δόcιν, as in the outer text line 40, or τὴν προγεγραμμένην γανναθ, or τὸν προγεγράμμενον κῆπον. Cf. P.Yadin **19** lines 20–22: ὥcτε ἔχειν τὴν προγεγρα̣μ̣μ̣[έ]ν̣ην Cελαμψιοῦ[c] τ̣ὸ ἥμιcυ̣ τῆc προγεγραμμένηc αυλῆc καὶ οἰ[κη]μ̣[ά]τ̣ω̣ν̣.

---

[54] Cf. Wuthnow, *Semitische Menschennamen*, 25, 120, 143.

[55] Cf. Kreller, *Erbrechtliche Untersuchungen*, 63–75 on 'Die Erbgemeinschaft' in Egyptian papyri.

Ll. 13 and 33 See Gignac, *Grammar*, 1:275 (ε > οι) for ἀνοιωγμμένον instead of ἀνεωγμένον and Gignac, *Grammar*, 1:157–8 for the gemination of the *mu* in ἀνοιωγμμένον.

Ll. 14 and 34 ὑπερῷν. For the contraction of two /o/ vowels see Gignac, *Grammar*, 1:300. In the preliminary publication (*ZPE* 105), no accent was given, to indicate that we do not know what number or case is meant i.e. ὑπερῷ<ο>ν (to agree with cὺν οἰκοίματα δύο) or ὑπερῴ<ω>ν (to agree with αὐλῆc).

Ll. 14–15 and 33–34 The description of a half-courtyard with (half) two rooms and the rooms of the upper storey (ἥμιcυ αὐλῆc ἀνοιωγμμ[ένο]ν εἰc νότον cὺν {ἥμιcυ} οἰκοίματα δύο καὶ ὑπερῷν ἐνοῦ[cι], lines 33–34), closely resembles that of the half-courtyard in Ein Gedi given in a deed of gift to Shelamṣion daughter of Judah son of Eleazar, Babatha's second husband: ἥ[μιc]υ α[ὐ]λῆc . . . ἥμιcυ οἰκημάτων καὶ ὑπερῴαιc ἐνο[ῦ]cι (P.Yadin **19** lines 13–14). For the courtyard house, see Hirschfeld, *Palestinian Dwelling*, 57ff.

L. 34 The ἥμιcυ seems gratuitous.

L. 14 ἐνα....α[..]. Because of the *alpha* after the *nu* it is impossible to restore ἐνοῦcι read in the parallel line 34, or ἐνόντα, which the writer's grammar could easily tolerate. Perhaps ἒν α....α[..], which would agree with ὑπερῷν.

L. 34 ἧc. This refers to αὐλή, and is therefore restored also in line 14; however, it would be possible to restore οὗ there, referring to ἥμιcυ.

Ll. 14 and 35 The spelling Cαμμωυοc in line 14 must be a mistake for Cαμμουοc, as in line 35; cf. No. **62** frgs. c–m line 13; P.Yadin **14** line 37; **21** lines 17–18.[56] The restoration of the name Cαμμουοc in No. **63** line 2 identifies Sammouos son of Shimᶜon as Salome Komaïse's first husband. He is also the middleman between the addressee and the tax (or rent) collectors in No. **60** line 8; see INTRODUCTION TO THE ARCHIVE OF SALOME KOMAÏSE DAUGHTER OF LEVI.

Ll. 15 and 35–36 Μαναημοc Ιω[ανν]ου. Menaḥem son of Iohannes is the addressee of No. **60**; see lines 2–3.

L. 15 κ[λ]ηρ[ονό]μοι Ιακω[βου. There is enough space for a patronym for Jacob; cf. line 11 = lines 32–33: κληρονόμοι Ιωcηποc Βαβα. Jacob son of Yeshu'a appears as Babatha's guardian in P.Yadin **17** (21 February 128 CE) line 5 = lines 23–24 (Greek) and in lines 40–41 (Aramaic).

L. 36 The remaining letters between [κλη]ρονόμοι and βορρᾶ are not reconcilable with Ιακωβου, read in the inner text, line 15.

Ll. 15 and 36 [Ιω]cηποc. His patronym is likely to have followed.

Ll. 39–40 ἔχειν τὴν προ[γ]εγραμμένην Κομαϊcην τὴν προγεγραμμένην δόc[ι]ν. See above on lines 12–13 of the inner text.

Ll. 16–17 and 40–41 These lines should be restored from P.Yadin **19** lines 23–25 (overlapping words are given in bold): **κυρίω[c] [καὶ βε]βαίωc** εἰc **τὸν ἅπαντα** χρόνον, [οἰκ]οδομεῖν, ὑπερ<αίρ>ειν, ὑψεῖν, cκάπτειν, βοθάνειν, κτᾶcθαι, χρᾶcθαι, πωλεῖν, **διοικεῖν, τρόπῳ ᾧ ἂν αἱρῆ<τα>**, πάντα κύρια καὶ βέβαια: 'validly and securely for all time, to build, raise up, raise higher, excavate, deepen, possess, use, sell and manage in whatever manner she may choose, all valid and secure'. Cf. P.Dura 26 (deed of sale, 227 CE) lines 14–15: εἰc τὸ ἔχειν αὐτὸν κυρίωc καὶ βεβαίωc εἰc τὸν ἅπαντα χρόνον κτᾶcθαι χρᾶcθαι πωλεῖν δι[οι]κεῖν τρόπῳ ᾧ ἂν αἱρῆται.[57]

---

[56] Sammouos son of Menaḥem is a witness in P.Yadin **14** (lines 37, 46), and the guarantor to a legal transaction in P.Yadin **21** (lines 17–18, 35, see Lewis, *Documents*, 146). The same person must be the abutter to two plots that belonged to Babatha's father, described in P.Yadin **7** lines 9, 11 = lines 42, 45.

[57] The only other examples of the phrase κυρίωc καὶ βεβαίωc found in the Duke Data Base are: P.Bub. 13 (224 CE) lines 6–7: μένειν ἐμοί . . . [τούτων κράτηcιν καὶ κυριείαν ἐπὶ τὸ]ν ἀεὶ χρόνον κυρίωc καὶ βεβα[ίωc] P.Bub. 4 (221 CE), 23, lines 6–7: τῷ [μέ]νειν μοι τὴν κύρωcιν ἐμο[ὶ καὶ τοῖc ἀπ' ἐμοῦ μεταπαραλημψομέ]ν[οιc κυρίωc κ]αὶ βεβαίωc ἀναφαίρετ[ον ἐπὶ τὸν ἀεὶ χρόνον]. The phrase κύρια καὶ βέβαια appears many times, but only from the fourth century CE onwards. On the Hebrew equivalent שריר וקים, see Gulak, *Urkundenwesen*, 24ff.; cf. pp. 36–8 of the new edition in Hebrew.

Verso:

Ll. 42–49 There were eight signatures on the verso of this deed. The first two signatures belong to the subscription. The first signature, of which only traces are left, is likely to have been that of the mother, Salome Gropte, the donor, although she did not write it herself. The second signature is probably that of her husband and guardian, Yosef son of Shimᶜon , who signed for her—the traces of ink are compatible with his name. Reisha son of Judah, whose signature follows in the third line, is not a witness; what remains of the two letters after his name is not compatible with the Aramaic word for witness שהד; he is likely to be the scribe. The last five signatures belong to the witnesses. Five witnesses are found in Greek, Aramaic and Nabataean documents from the Judaean Desert, e.g. No. **9** (Aramaic, deed of sale) lines 28–32; No. **62** (Greek, land declaration, verso lines 1–5); No. **69** (Greek, marriage contract), verso, lines 1–5. For a general discussion of the five-witness document, see INTRODUCTION TO THE GREEK DOCUMENTARY TEXTS.

Ll. 42–43 The procedure proposed here for the subscription—one person signing for another and then adding his own name—is well attested in the papyri from the Judaean Desert. The expression על נפשה—'in person' (line 42)—implies that the principal 'was one of the parties to the deed',[58] even when he or she did not write the subscription himself or herself. It indicates his or her presence when the subscription was written, as is implied by 'at the request' of the principal and 'in his presence' in Greek subscriptions; cf. Ἐλεαζαρος Ἐλεαζαρου ἔγραψα ὑπὲρ αὐτῆϲ ἐρωτηθεὶϲ διὰ τὸ αὐτῆϲ μὴ ε<ἰ>δένα<ι> γράμματα, P.Yadin **15** lines 34–35.[59] We find the same procedure in No. **13** lines 9–12: שלמצין ברת יהוסף על נפשה שאלה כתב מׄתׄתׄ ב[ר] שמעון מׄמרא 'Shelamṣion daughter of Yehosaf in person. She is borrowing the writing of Matat son of Shimᶜon (who wrote) what she said'; see also Mur **18** lines 9–10 (with Yardeni's new reading): [זכ]ריה בר יהוחׄ[נן ע]ל נפשהׄ [כת]ב יהוסף ב[ר] מׄמרהׄ, 'Zakhariah son of Yehoḥanan [wrote] for himself. Yehosaf s[on of] wrote what he said'; cf. also No. **8a** lines 14–15; Mur **21** lines 21–24; Mur **24c** lines 19–20 (with Yadin, 'Expedition D—Cave of Letters', 253); P.Yadin **44** (Hebrew) lines 28–30.[60]

L. 44 רישה בר יהודה. Reisha son of Yehudah, or rather, the Chief son of Judah (see COMMENTS ad No. **60** line 13) should probably be identified with the tax (or rent) collector in Maḥoza in 125 (see No. **60** lines 1–2 with COMMENTS). The fact that he wrote an Aramaic subscription to the Greek receipt (No. **60** line 13) goes somewhat oddly with his being the scribe of No. **64**. However, this may account for the highly Aramaic flavour of the document; see above, LANGUAGE.

L. 45 מליך בר א[. Malik son of A[is a Nabataean. On the name, see Negev, *Personal Names*, no. 632; Wuthnow, *Semitische Menschennamen*, 70; 148; Cantineau, *Le Nabatéen* 2:114.

L. 46 ישוע בר יוחנן. Yeshuᶜa son of Yoḥanan. This name, written in the same illiterate hand, appears as a second witness in P.Yadin **20** line 47 dated 19 June 130 (see pl. 24 in Lewis, *Documents*). The first three letters of the patronym יוח are missing in P.Yadin **20** line 47, but we can now restore them safely, and correct the translation 'Yeshuᶜa son of Yeshuᶜa?' in Lewis, *Documents*, 92, to Yeshuᶜa son of Yoḥanan'.

L. 47 תימדושרא בר עבדחׄרׄ[תת]. Timadushra son of ᶜAbdḥare[tat] is a Nabataean. For Timadushra, where the second element stands for the Nabataean God Dushra, see Negev, *Personal Names*, no. 1217; Wuthnow, *Semitische Menschennamen*, 54; 175; Cantineau, *Le Nabatéen* 2:156. For ᶜAbdḥaretat, literally 'slave of Ḥaretat', see Negev, *Personal Names*, no. 802; Cantineau, *Le Nabatéen* 2:126. For Ḥaretat = Aretas, see above, ad lines 11 and 32. A woman, Thḥa daughter of ᶜAbdḥa[retat], is mentioned as one of the abutters to the orchard sold by a Nabataean woman, ᶜAbiᶜadan to Archelas, and a month later to Shimᶜon , Babatha's father in P.Yadin **2** line 4 = line 23; **3** line 26.

L. 48 יהוסף בר שולי שהד. Yehosaf son of Shullai, witness. The name Shullai appears as a patronym in No. **10** line 5: בר שולׄי כתבה ('son of Shullai wrote this'). The name is attested for Nabataeans as well: see

---

[58] Yadin, 'Expedition D—Cave of Letters', 252–4; cf. Lehmann, 'Studies', 65; Sijpesteijn, 'A Note', 49–50; Cotton, 'Subscriptions'.

[59] Cf. P.Dura 31 (204 CE) lines 53–54: Βαραναῖοϲ Λυϲίου ἐρωτηθεὶϲ ἔγραψα ὑπὲρ Ἄκοζζιϲ μητρόϲ μου; P.Euphr. 6 lines 32ff. = P.Euphr. 7 lines 26ff. (Syriac subscription to a Greek contract); see Youtie, 'ΥΠΟΓΡΑΦΕΥϹ', 211 and n. 26.

[60] Cf. P.Dura 28 (243 CE, Syriac) lines 20–23; verso lines 31–32, cf. Goldstein, 'Syriac Deed', 1–15.

the signature of והבדשׂרא בר שלי (*whbdšr*ʾ *br šly*) in P.Yadin **3** line 53. The name Shullai is rendered in Greek Cουλλαιοc; see COMMENTS ad No. **69** verso line 2, where Cου[λαι]οc Ε[λεαζ]αρου is a possible restoration.

L. 49 י[הו]סף בר חנ[נ]יה שהד. Yohesaf son of Ḥananiah, witness. On the spelling Yohesaf instead of Yehosaf see Naveh, 'Formal and Informal Spelling', 264–5. This is the name of a witness on six of the papyri from the Babatha Archive: it appears once in Greek letters—Ιωcηποc Ανανια—written by a scribe, P.Yadin **14** line 39 (11 or 12 October 125); six times we have his own signature in Aramaic: **14** line 48; **15** line 43 (11 or 12 October 125); **17** (21 February 128) line 49; **18** (5 April 128) line 79; **21** (11 September 130) line 33; **22** (11 September 130) line 40.

Excursus on Lines 28–30

> <ἣ> τελέcει καθ' ἔτοc εἰc λόγον κυριακοῦ φίcκου φοίνεικοc πατητοῦ cάτα δέκα καὶ cυροῦ καὶ ναaρου cάτα ἕξ: 'It (i.e. the date grove) will pay every year to the account of the *fiscus* of our Lord ten *sata* of 'splits', and six *sata* of the Syrian and the na'aran dates'.

Does the annual payment in kind 'to the account of the *fiscus* of our Lord' imply that the date grove given in gift was on lease from the emperor? And, similarly: does the expression ọφείλειc Κ̣[υ]ρ̣ίῳ Καίcαρι in No. **60** lines 5–6 imply that this receipt is for rent rather than for tax? In other words, were the date groves in Nos. **60** and **64** part of an imperial estate in Maḥoza or were they privately owned?

Several expressions suggest that we are dealing in No. **64** with private property: first, the use of the term τὰ ὑπάρχοντα, and, more particularly, τὰ ὑπάρχοντά μοι (αὐτῆc) ἐν Μαωζαc (lines 7 and 25), to describe the property given in gift.[61] Secondly, the presence of an imperial orchard, the κῆπον κυριακὸν καλούμενον Γανναθ Αββα̣ιδαια (lines 10 and 31–32), as one of the abutters of the date grove given in gift perhaps implies that the date grove given in gift is not a κῆποc κυριακόc. Thirdly, the fact that the date grove is said to be given as a gift forever—εἰc δόcιν ἀπὸ τῆc cήμερον δόcιν αἰωνίου (lines 6–7)—also points to private ownership.

Unfortunately, these reasonings are not as cogent as they appear to be at first sight. Land owned by the *fiscus* was exploited in different ways: between land leased to tenants and land worked by slaves under a *vilicus*, 'there was still an infinite range of local variations'.[62] It is possible, therefore, that a date grove described as κῆποc κυριακόc would be cultivated directly by the *fiscus*, whereas others would be leased to tenants—probably to hereditary tenants who would speak of it as their own property. There are examples of 'perpetual leaseholds' from other parts of the empire: in Egypt the lease of οὐcιακὴ γῆ could be transmitted to heirs.[63] An inscription attests hereditary leaseholds on an imperial estate in Lydia.[64] We also have the evidence of the North African inscriptions for 'perpetual leaseholds' held under the terms of the Lex

---

[61] See Preisigke, *Wörterbuch*, s.v. ὑπάρχω.

[62] Crawford-Thompson, 'Imperial Estates', 44ff.; cf. Flach, *Römische Agrargeschichte*, 82ff.

[63] On *Erbpacht*, see Kuhnke, *Οὐσιακὴ γῆ*, 99: 'Nach allem gibt es bei . . . οὐcιακὴ γῆ keine Eigentumsübertragung. Sie sind res extra commercium. Möglich ist allein eine Vergabe in Erbpacht', and see nn. 2 and 3 there; cf. Eger, *Zum ägyptischen Grundbuchwesen*, 32; Johnson, *Roman Egypt*, 74 on 'crown land', but this became imperial land in Roman times.

[64] Abbott and Johnson, *Municipal Administration*, no. 142, 200–250 CE.

Manciana: '[Qui in f(undo) Vill<a>e Magn<a>e Varia]n<a>e siv<e> Mappali<a>e Sig[<a>e ficetum olivetum vineas se]verunt severin[t, eis eam superficiem heredibus], qui e legitim[is matrimoniis nati sunt eruntve], testamento relinquere permittitur', *CIL* VIII 25902 (the Henchir-Mettich inscription), col. IV lines 2–6.[65] The *Tablettes Albertini* (*FIRA* III^2 139) prove that this was still true many years later, when private landlords replaced the emperor as the owner of these lands. Thus, the fact that the date grove is spoken of as privately owned and given as 'a gift forever' does not, in itself, force us to regard it as private property *strictu sensu*.

It may even be possible that we witness here the wholesale transfer of Nabataean terms of ownership. Two Nabataean deeds of sale of a date grove by a Nabataean woman, ᶜAbiᶜadan daughter of ᵓAftaḥ, dated to 99 CE, contain a clause about an annual and fixed share of the Nabataean king which is conceived to be as much a part of the property as the payment in lines 28–30 of No. **64** (see COMMENTS on line 28 above): חלק מראנא . . . לשנתא כות בה סאין עשרה, P.Yadin **2** lines 13–14 = line 37; P.Yadin **3** line 15 = line 41. The fact that the date grove is sold on the open market does not by itself prove that the grove was privately owned. Not enough is known about Nabataean legal practice to exclude the possibility that land leased from the king could be alienated. The Roman emperor stepped into such property without altering the terms of ownership and alienation of it: this land could be sold and given in gift as long as the fixed rent to the emperor was paid.

The fact that the annual payment is in kind rather than in cash could also be adduced as further support for the view that this deed involves the lease of imperial land and the annual payment of rent for it. However, the argument is not unassailable.

It is certainly true that, in Egypt, taxes on vineyard and agricultural land (which includes date groves) were all converted into money terms (*adaeratio*),[66] whereas in leases of date groves one finds both kinds of payment.[67] However, the two land declarations, No. **62** and P.Yadin **16**, demonstrate that in the province of Arabia, part of the annual taxes was paid, or at least estimated, in kind;[68] an *adaeratio* might have followed later, as is likely in the case of the tax mentioned in the Aramaic receipt (No. **12**). As pointed out in the introduction to No. **60**, the expression דמי תמרין in No. **12** lines 3–4 suggests that the nineteen and a quarter *seᵓah* of dates (קבלן מנך דמי תמרין סאין עשר ותשע וקב ופלג) were paid in cash—as was the payment in the Greek receipt (No. **60**)—rather than in kind, even though the sum is not specified. The same may have

---

[65] The quotation follows Flach's text, 'Inschriftenuntersuchungen', 480 (This paragraph defines the *usus proprius* of col. I, lines 9–10 of the Lex Manciana, cf. Flach, 'Inschriftenuntersuchungen', 445-6); cf. '<i>isque qui occupaverint possidendi ac fru<en>di{i} eredique suo relinquendi id ius datur quod e<s>t lege Ha<drian>a comprehensum de rudibus agris et iis, qui per X an<n>os continuos inculti sunt', *CIL* VIII 25943 (Ain Wassel inscription), col. I, lines 7–13 (Flach, 'Inschriftenuntersuchungen', 487); see Kehoe, 'Lease Regulations', 156–9; idem, *Economics of Agriculture*, 39; idem, *Management and Investment*, 50.

[66] Wallace, *Taxation*, 47ff.

[67] Hohlwein, 'Palmiers et Palmeraies', 65–74.

[68] See e.g. No. **62** frgs. c–m lines 14–17: μέροϲ ἥ[μιϲυ κ]ήπου φοινικῶνοϲ . . . τελοῦν φοίνικοϲ πατητοῦ ϲάτα δύο κάβουϲ τρεῖϲ, ναaρου ϲάτα δυο κάβουϲ τρεῖϲ; P.Yadin **16** lines 17–20: κῆπον φοινικῶνοϲ . . . τελοῦντα φοίνικοϲ ϲυρίου καὶ μείγματοϲ ϲάτα δεκαπέντε πατητοῦ ϲάτα δέκα; cf. the *Lex Portorii Asiae* from 62 CE in Engelmann and Knibbe, 'Das Zollgesetz', 25, lines 72–73 (*AÉ* 1989 681) for the *decuma* being paid in kind; see the general survey of taxation in money and kind in the Roman Empire in Duncan Jones, *Structure and Scale*, 187–98.

occurred in No. **64**: the φοίνεικος πατητοῦ cάτα δέκα καὶ cυροῦ καὶ ναρου cάτα ἕξ may have been converted into cash when actual payment took place. The Romans are likely to have inherited the evaluation, perhaps also the payment, of taxes in kind from the Nabataean kings, just as they seem to have inherited from them the tax designated *stephanikon*, whatever it represented.[69]

In support of the view that the payment in No. **64** was payment of tax, it should be noted that the verb τελεῖν used in No. **64** line 28 to describe the annual payment to the *fiscus* is used to describe the payment of annual tax in the two land declarations from Maḥoza: κῆπον φοινικῶνος ἐν ὁρίοις Μαωζων λεγόμενον Βαγαλγαλὰ cπόρου κρειθῆς cάτων τριῶν τελοῦντα φοίνικος cυροῦ καὶ νοαρου κόρον ἕνα πατητοῦ κόρον ἕνα cτεφανικοῦ μελαίνας τρεῖς λεπτὰ τριάκοντα, etc. (P.Yadin **16** lines 24–28); μέρος ἥμιcυ χώρας . . . τελοῦν φόρου μέλαν ἕν, etc. (No. **62** frg. a lines 16–17).

Assuming, for the moment, that No. **64** involves private property and not land leased from the emperor, and that there is nothing about the payment itself which cannot be reconciled with tax rather than rent, what are we to make of the straightforward implication of the text that the annual taxes went into the imperial *fiscus* rather than into the *aerarium*? Do we have here a clear exception to the claim that, in the first two centuries, the annual taxes—even from the imperial provinces—did not go into the imperial *fiscus*?[70] Are we to assume that No. **64** reflects one stage in a process in which the distinction between public and private revenues became blurred: i.e. the slow absorption of public income by the imperial financial administration? Against this, it could be said that we have here, no less than in the ọφείλειc Κ̣[υ]ρ̣ίῳ Καίcαρι in No. **60** lines 5–6, a case of 'loose terminology':[71] whoever wrote the deed of gift or the receipt was convinced that the monies belonged to the emperor. In other words, even if we could prove that the date grove was private property on which there was an annual tax in kind, we cannot use this text to record a stage in the process of the development of the imperial *fiscus* into the public chest any more than we can use for this purpose the evidence of the New Testament, where people speak about the annual taxes, κῆνcοc and φόροc, as being paid 'to the emperor'.[72]

[69] See P.Yadin **16** lines 17–32 with Cotton, 'Rent or Tax Receipt', 553 and Weiser and Cotton, 'Gebt dem Kaiser, was des Kaisers ist', 240–41.

[70] Millar, 'The *Fiscus*', 29ff. Millar mentions possible exceptions to his claim on pp. 40–41 and in *Emperor*, 623ff. See Alpers, *Nachrepublikanisches Finanzsystem*, 1–20 for a survey of opinions.

[71] Millar, *Emperor*, 625.

[72] To the question ἔξεcτι δοῦναι κῆνcον Καίcαρι; ἢ οὔ; (Matt 22:17) Jesus answers with the famous: Ἀπόδοτε οὖν τὰ Καίcαροc Καίcαρι (Matt 22:21; cf. Mark 12:14; 12:17; φόροc replaces κῆνcοc in Luke 20:22: ἔξεcτι ὑμᾶc Καίcαρι φόρον δοῦναι). See also Luke 23:2, where Jesus is charged with obstructing the payment of the tribute: κωλύοντα Καίcαρι φόρουc διδόναι.

65. XḤev/Se papMarriage Contract gr

Maḥoza, Arabia, 7 August 131 CE

(PL. XLI)

Preliminary publication: N. Lewis, *The Documents from the Bar Kokhba Period in the Cave of Letters. Greek Papyri,* (1989) 130–33, pl. 40; H. M. Cotton, 'The Archive of Salome Komaïse Daughter of Levi: Another Archive from the "Cave of Letters"', *ZPE* 105 (1995) 204–7.

NO. **65** is the inner text of a double document found by Yadin's expedition in a passage between chambers B and C in the Cave of Letters.[1] It was published by N. Lewis, with the Greek part of the Babatha Archive, as P.Yadin **37**, although Lewis recognized that it was not part of that archive.

The document has survived in three fragments. Frg. a 'preserve[s] the left half of the text'. Frg. b 'give[s] us a third of the right half'. A small frg. c cannot be placed. The verso is blank. Between fragments a and b 'there is a lacuna of some twenty letters. Although the hand gives an impression of skilled rapidity, the unattractive writing, in small letters produced with a thick pen that left many an ink blot, looks clumsy and crude. Reading and restoration of the text are materially assisted by formulaic language found also in other documents, most notably **18**' [i.e. P.Yadin **18**].[2]

To Lewis's description it might be added that difficulties of reading are increased by interlinear additions and lack of alignment in the bottom left part (lines 9ff.).[3]

Lewis read the name of the bride as Salome Komaïs (Cαλωμη Κωμαϊc). After the 'discovery' of Salome Komaïse's Archive among the Seiyâl collection, there is no longer any doubt that the marriage contract belongs to her. There is no difficulty in restoring the name Κομαϊcη (rather than Lewis's Κομαϊc) in lines 4 and 13, where Lewis read Κ̣ο̣[μαϊν] and Κομαϊ[c], respectively, before a lacuna. Lewis's Κομαϊc....[in line 15 is, in any case, incompatible with the immediately preceding τῆ̣ς̣ α̣ὐ̣τ̣ῆc. After Κομαϊc, and before the last surviving letters of the document, ϵπ,[4] there is space for (as well as faint traces of) two letters. I have therefore restored Κομαϊc̣[ηc] in line 15. Finally, the remaining ink stains in line 6, where Lewis read Κομα̣ϊ̣δ̣[ι], are incompatible with a *delta*, and one can safely restore Κομα̣ϊ̣c̣[η̣].[5]

---

[1] See Yadin, 'Expedition D—Cave of Letters', 231: 'In the connecting passage between [the second] chamber and the next chamber (C) we came upon . . . a Greek papyrus which formed the *interior* of a "tied" deed'; Lewis, *Documents*, 3.

[2] The citations are taken from the preliminary publication: Lewis, *Documents*, 130. There is no doubt, however, that what Lewis believed to be six fragments are in reality only two. However, at one point on the back a piece of glue strengthens the tenuous contact between two contiguous pieces of papyrus. There is no other sign of the papyrus having been tampered with in modern times.

[3] This was not caused by faulty conservation of the papyrus in recent times, as I had first believed.

[4] See Lewis, *Documents*, 133.

[5] See Cotton, 'The Archive of Salome Komaïse Daughter of Levi', 205 n. 97.

Lewis assumes that because No. **65** 'is expressed as the action of the groom in taking a wife . . . its structural form is that of the *ketubba*' (*Documents*, 130). He, therefore, restored εἰληφέναι in line 4, and in the commentary to line 3 he proposes to restore ἑκών before [ὡμολογήϲ]ạτο, which 'would render the Aramaic term used in such contexts, מן רעותה' (*Documents*, 132). Lines 3–5 according to Lewis should read: [ὡμολογήϲ]ạτο[6] Ἰηϲοῦϲ Μαναήμου τῷ[ν οἰκούντων ἐν κώ]μῃ Cοφφαθε[.]... π̣ẹρ̣ὶ πόλιν Λιουιάδοϲ τῆϲ π̣[*c.*10 letters εἰληφέναι C]ạλ̣ώμην κ̣αλọυμένην Κ̣ọ[μαϊν *c.*12 letters] γυ̣ṿαῖκα Μ̣[α]ωζηνήν. He translates as follows: 'Jesus son of Menahem, domiciled in the village of Soffathe . . . in the district of the city of Livias of the administrative region of P[ ] acknowledged of his own free will(?) that he has taken Salome also called Komaïs . . . a Maozene woman'.

In fact, in order to get the Aramaic formula Lewis has in mind—a predicate noun—something like 'as (wedded) wife' (εἰϲ γυναῖκα γαμετήν) should have followed 'that he has taken Salome also called Komaïs . . . a Maozene woman'.[7]

Be that as it may, Lewis's restoration of the opening lines of No. **65** echoes the opening of the Aramaic marriage contract between Jews written in Antinoopolis in 417 CE: אנה ש[מואל בר ס]מפט[י] [מן]סוס ושרי באנטינו אמר[ת ו]בעית מן דעתי מן צביוני למסב לי יאת מיטרא ברת לעזר מן אלכסנדריא וש[ריה] [באנט]ינו בתולתה לאתה,[8] 'I Samuel son of Sampati from [ ]*sos* and residing in Antinoos have spoken and requested, of my own mind and will, to take[9] Mitra daughter of Lazar from Alexandria and residing in Antinoos, a virgin, as my wife'—a formula frequently attested in the Palestinian ketubbah tradition.[10]

A part of a similar, but not identical, formula occurs in what remains of the opening lines of two almost contemporary Aramaic marriage contracts from the Judaean Desert. In Mur **20** (117 CE?) line 3 we read: [ד]י תהוא לי לאנתה כדין מ[ושה ויהודאי], 'that you will be my wife according to the law of Moses and the Jews';[11] only the last four words remain in P.Yadin **10** (125–128 CE) line 5:[12] [ ]לאנת[ה כדי]ן משה ויה[ו]דאי, but די תהוא לי can be safely restored before them.[13] We should note that the verb 'to take', the equivalent of Lewis's εἰληφέναι, is not used here—in contrast with the usage of the later marriage contract from Antinoopolis (see above); nor do we know what stood before 'that you will be my wife' in the two early Aramaic marriage contracts.

Mention should be made of lines 2–3 of P.Ent. 23 (= CPJ I 128, 218 BCE): [κατὰ τὸν νόμον π]ọλ̣ιτικὸν τῶν [Ἰου]δαίων ἔχειν με γυν[αῖκα].[14] The phrase has been taken to reproduce for a Greek audience the formula 'to be my wife according to the law of

---

[6] Lewis does not actually restore [ὡμολογήϲ]ạτο in the text, but see his commentary on line 3.

[7] Cf. Mur **115** lines 4–5: ὁμολογεῖ ὁ αὐτὸϲ Ἐλαῖοϲ Cίμ̣ω̣[νοϲ] ἐξ ἀνανεώϲεοϲ καταλλάξαι κ[αὶ] π̣ροϲλαβέϲθαι τὴν αὐ̣τ̣ὴν Cαλώ[μην Ἰω]άṿ[ο]υ Γ̣[αλγο]ṿλὰ ẹἰ̣[ϲ γυναῖ]κ̣α γαμετὴν.

[8] Sirat *et al.*, *Ketouba,* 21, lines 5–8 and discussion in 36ff.

[9] The verb למסב means, literally, 'to take'.

[10] The formula כלתה . . . למסב . . . אמרית/אמר מן דעתי/ה occurs in eleven out of thirty marriage contracts from the Cairo geniza collected by M. Friedman; see *Jewish Marriage,* 1:148–55; the earliest dates to 1023, see 2:38, lines 3–5.

[11] This is the revised reading of A. Yardeni.

[12] See Yadin, Greenfield, and Yardeni, 'Babatha's Ketubba', 85.

[13] See the restoration of the line in Yadin, Greenfield, and Yardeni, 'Babatha's Ketubba', 78 and discussion in 85ff. See also the restoration of No. **11** line 2.

[14] See the CONCLUSION to MARRIAGE PRACTICES in No. **69**.

Moses and the Jews' (די תהוא לי לאנתה כדין מושה ויהודאי) of the Jewish ketubbah recorded in the two Aramaic marriage contracts just cited.[15] This heavily restored passage can hardly be used as evidence for the currency of the formula in Jewish marriage contracts at the time (3rd century BCE) or later.[16]

Thus, there is no safe attestation for the existence of the formula as reconstructed by Lewis in the Aramaic ketubbah tradition prior to the fifth century CE.[17] With the exception of Mur **115** (124 CE), a contract of remarriage (see below), there is no parallel for the formula in any of the contemporary marriage contracts in Greek between Jews,[18] or in their Egyptian counterparts, which they, no less than No. **65**, closely resemble.[19] With the exception of contracts of the *ekdosis*, 'written contracts . . . never attest the establishment of marriage itself, but merely include a clause more or less detailed, concerning the personal relations of the couple, which follows acknowledgement of receipt of the dowry given in the form of a homologia' (Wolff, *Written and Unwritten Marriages*, 67). [20] All of them, therefore, to paraphrase Lewis, express the action of the groom.

The special circumstances of remarriage set Mur **115** apart from other marriage contracts in Greek between Jews. Having described the divorce in lines 3–4: Ἐπ<ε>ὶ πρὸ τοῦ cυνέβη τῷ αὐτῷ Ἐ̣λ̣α̣ίῳ Cίμωνος ἀπαλλαγῆναι καὶ ἀπολύειν Cαλώμην Ἰωανου̣ Γ̣α̣λ̣γυλ̣α, the groom resumes in lines 4–5 with the declaration of remarriage: *νυνεὶ* ὁμολογεῖ ὁ αὐτὸc Ἐλαῖοc Cίμ̣ω̣[νοc] ἐξ ἀνανεώcεοc καταλλάξαι κ[αὶ] π̣ροcλαβέcθαι τὴν αὐ̣τ̣ὴν Cαλώ[μην Ἰω]άν̣[ο]υ Γ̣[αλγο]υ̣λὰ ε̣ἰ̣[c γυναῖ]κ̣α γαμετήν.[21] It is doubtful whether we can use the remarriage formula in Mur **115** in support of Lewis's restoration of εἰληφέναι in line 4.

There is some difficulty in reconciling Lewis's restoration of lines 4–5 with the sequel in lines 5–6: Yeshuʿa son of Menaḥem's statement that he has taken Salome Komaïse to be his wife sits awkwardly with the most straightforward implication of lines 5–6, namely that the couple had been married for some time when No. **65** was drawn up.[22]

---

[15] E. Volterra, 'P. Ent. 23', 25: where the writer actually cites the variant, namely, 'according to the law of Moses and Israel', see No. **69**, n. 128.

[16] See Modrzejewski, 'Jewish Law', 85f. and Yadin, Greenfield, and Yardeni, 'Babatha's Ketubba', 87 n. 32.

[17] Or after the fifth century BCE: in three Aramaic marriage contracts between Jews from Elephantine we find in the opening lines the declaration of the groom that he came to the house of the person in charge of the bride and asked that she be given to him in marriage: אנא [א]תית לביתך למנתן לי [ל]ברתך מפטיה אנתו, Cowley 15 (= Porten and Yardeni, *TAD* II B2.6) line 3; cf. Kraeling 2 (= Porten and Yardeni, *TAD* II B3.3) line 3; Kraeling 7 (= Porten and Yardeni, *TAD* II B3.8) lines 4–5.

[18] Mur **116** (first half of ii CE); P.Yadin **18** (128 CE); and No. **69** (130 CE).

[19] See the many examples in COMMENTS to No. **69** and in the discussion of marriage practices there. It is quite true that the earliest Greek marriage contract, P.Eleph. 1 from 311 BCE, has a similar declaration in its opening lines: λαμβάνει Ἡρακλείδηc Δημητρίαν Κώιαν γυναῖκα γνηcίαν παρὰ τοῦ πατρὸc Λεπτίνου Κώιου καὶ τῆc μητρὸc Φιλωτίδοc, lines 2–5; but the formula never appears again in Greek marriage contracts written in Greek from Egypt.

[20] For a discussion of the dowry, see No. **69**, THE DOWRY, in MARRIAGE PRACTICES; cf. Allam, 'Aspects du mariage', 125.

[21] Καταλλάξαι κ[αὶ] π̣ροcλαβέcθαι, as the editor observes ad loc., is juxtaposed with the preceding ἀπαλλαγῆναι καὶ ἀπολύειν.

[22] This is not a serious objection since such a declaration is present in the renewal of an old marriage contract; see COMMENTS ad line 6.

However, as we shall see immediately, this is not the way Lewis interprets the relevant phrase in lines 5–6 of the document.

Lewis believes that 'Jewish custom is also reflected, in all probability, in the statement that the bridal pair are to live together henceforth ὡ[c κ]αὶ πρὸ τούτου τοῦ χρόνου (line 6), "as also before this time"'. He raises, only in order to dismiss it, the possibility that we have here a parallel to ἄγραφος γάμος, recorded in Egyptian papyri, a union which was 'sometimes later converted by a written contract into ἔγγραφος γάμος' (*Documents*, 130). Instead, he opts for an *interpretatio Hebraica*: 'Close as that parallel may be, however, . . . the expression "as also before this time" more likely implies that the bride and groom had been living together since the day of their betrothal, in keeping with a Jewish practice of the time when the bride was both an orphan and a minor' (*Documents*, 130).[23]

We now know a great deal more about Salome Komaïse: she was indeed an orphan in 131, but not a minor. Already in 127 (if not before), she had been married to Sammouos son of Shimᶜon,[24] who represented her in No. **63**. Yeshuᶜa son of Menaḥem of No. **65** is her second husband. In 129, her mother, Salome Grapte (Gropte), bestowed on her a date grove and half a courtyard in Maḥoza in a deed of gift (No. **64**), and in January 131, seven months before the present document, she received a receipt for dates from two tax (or rent)[25] collectors (No. **12**). Thus, putative minority cannot explain why Yeshuᶜa and Salome had been living together before the contract was drawn up, even if we assume that they followed Jewish customs—an assumption unwarranted by the marriage contract concluded between them, which cannot be described as a Jewish ketubbah, and in which the groom undertakes to follow Greek law and custom in providing for the wife and for the children to come: cὺν αἱρέcει τροφῆς [καὶ ἀμφιαcμοῦ αὐτῆc] τε καὶ τῶν μελλόντω[ν τέκ]νων νόμ[ῳ] [ἑλληνικ]ῷ καὶ ἑλλ[η]νικῷ τρόπῳ, lines 9–10.[26]

Lewis's interpretation has been branded 'apologetic'[27] in a discussion which interprets lines 5–6 of No. **65**, as restored by Lewis (cυμβιῶcαι τ[ὸν Ἰηcοῦν μετ'?] αὐτῆc ὡ[c κ]αὶ πρὸ τούτου τοῦ χρόνου), to be referring to 'premarital cohabitation', and claims, on the basis of No. **65**, that 'premarital cohabitation was a local practice particular to and common to Judaea'.[28] This radical approach[29] assumes no less than

---

[23] I could not find any rabbinic sources for the custom alleged by Lewis. The custom in Judaea (in contrast to Galilee) of entertaining the groom at his father-in-law's house after betrothal, and before marriage (as a result of which the husband loses a virginity claim, *m. Ketub.* 1.5), may be interpreted as 'life together before marriage'; but it has nothing to do with the wife being an orphan and a minor (see Ilan, 'Premarital Cohabitation', 256ff.). Jewish custom assumed that the young couple would settle down in a small house adjacent to that of the groom's father: *m. B. Bat.* 6.4: 'if a man received it from his fellow to build him a bridal-house (בית חתנות) for his son or a dower-house for his daughter'. I am grateful to Sh. Naeh and R. Klopstock for help with the rabbinic sources.

[24] See INTRODUCTION TO THE ARCHIVE OF SALOME KOMAÏSE DAUGHTER OF LEVI, and COMMENTS on No. **63** line 2.

[25] See discussion of lines 28–30 in No. **64.**

[26] See COMMENTS ad loc.

[27] Ilan, 'Premarital Cohabitation', 253; see Katzoff, 'Philo and Hillel', 46*f.

[28] Ilan, 'Premarital Cohabitation', 262.

[29] Ilan's claim to have a 'conservative approach' ('Premarital Cohabitation', 263) is inconsistent with her argument thus far.

the 'apologetic approach' that, by this time, there existed a coherent and operative Jewish system of law which had already become normative. In such a system, 'a man may not keep his wife even one hour without a ketubbah' (*b. B. Qam.* 89a, quoted in Ilan, 'Premarital Cohabitation', 254), and life together without a ketubbah must be branded 'premarital cohabitation' or 'sex out of wedlock'. As already pointed out, if we follow halakha, No. **65** is not the ketubbah which would turn 'premarital cohabitation' into a proper Jewish marriage.

Although the text in the crucial lines 5–6 is extremely lacunose, ὥϲτε αὐτοὺϲ and later ϲυμβιωϲ.. in line 5 followed by ὡ[ϲ κ]αὶ πρὸ τούτου τοῦ χρόνου in line 6, create a strong presumption for a case of unwritten marriage becoming a written one. The phrase ὡ[ϲ κ]αὶ πρὸ τούτου τοῦ χρόνου, which implies the continuation of life together, looks like a variation on the formulas καθότι καὶ πρότερον or καθὼϲ καὶ προεγάμουϲαν, common in such cases as an addition to the formula which speaks of life together, e.g.: ϲυνβιο[ύ]τωϲαν οὖν ἀλλήλοιϲ ὅ τε Ἑ[ρμῆϲ καὶ ἡ Ἰϲιδώρα ἀμέ]μπτωϲ καθότ[ι] καὶ πρότερον (BGU IV 1045 [= MChr. 282, 154 CE] lines 16–18);[30] or ϲυμβιούτοϲαν οὖν ἀλλήλοιϲ τῶν γαμούντων καθὼϲ καὶ προεγάμουϲαν (BGU I 183 [= MChr. 313, 85 CE] line 6). Ὥϲτε αὐτοὺϲ followed by ϲυμβιωϲ.. in line 5 excludes the restoration of something like ϲυνβιούτωϲαν οὖν ἀλλήλοιϲ ἀμέμπτωϲ οἱ γαμοῦντεϲ;[31] however, one may suggest something along the lines of BGU I 252 (98 CE) lines 6–7: μένειν οὖν αὐτοῖϲ τὴν ϲυμβιώϲιν [ἀμέμπτωϲ κ]αθότι καὶ πρότερον; or Stud.Pal. XX 5 (136 CE) lines 20–21: μένειν οὖν τοῖϲ γαμοῦϲι [τῷ τε Ϲουχάμμωνι καὶ τῇ Ἀφροδι]τοῦτι τὴν πρὸϲ ἀλλήλουϲ ϲυμβίωϲιν;[32] perhaps one can restore ϲυμβιώϲεωϲ χάριν of Mur **115** line 4, although its exact context was not preserved: Ἐπ<ε>ὶ πρὸ τοῦ ϲυνέβη τῷ αὐτῷ Ἐλαίω Ϲίμωνοϲ ἀπαλλαγῆναι καὶ ἀπολύειν Ϲαλώμην Ἰωάνου Γαλγουλα τὴ[ν..].[.]κ[..]λ[....].ηναι ϲ[υ]νβιώϲεοϲ χάριν νυνεὶ ὁμολογεῖ ὁ αὐτὸϲ Ἐλαῖοϲ Ϲίμω[νοϲ] ἐξ ἀνανεώϲεοϲ καταλλάξαι κ[αὶ] προϲλαβέϲθαι τὴν αὐτὴν Ϲαλώ[μην Ἰω]άν[ο]υ Γ[αλγο]υλὰ εἰ[ϲ γυναῖ]κα γαμετὴν (lines 3–5).

Lewis's original suggestion of ἄγραφοϲ γάμοϲ is, therefore, likely to be the correct interpretation of lines 5–6. Whatever its origins,[33] the institution is known to have existed outside Egypt. P.Dura 31 from 204 CE attests its existence in the village of Ossa, in what was then Syria Coele: Ναβουϲάμοαϲ Κόνωνοϲ τοῦ Ἀβιϲϲαίου καὶ Ἄκοζζιϲ Ϲελεύκου τοῦ Ἀβιϲϲαίου ἀμφότεροι δὲ τῶν ἀπὸ Ὄϲϲηϲ κώμηϲ, φάμενοι γεγενῆϲθαι

[30] Cf. P.Ryl. II 154 (66 CE) lines 18–20: ϲυμ[β]ιούτω[ϲαν ο]ὖν [ἑα]υτοῖϲ ἀλλήλο[ιϲ ο]ἱ γ[α]μοῦντεϲ ἥ τε Θαιϲάριον καὶ ὁ Χα[ι]ρήμων ἀμεμψιμοιρήτωϲ καθότι π[ρότ]ερον [ϲυ]νβίουν.

[31] This clause is by no means exclusive to marriage contracts attendant upon the conversion of an unwritten marriage into a written one: cf. P.Oxy. XII 1473 (3rd century CE) lines 10–11: ϲυνβιούτωϲαν οὖν ἀλλήλοιϲ οἱ γαμοῦντεϲ ἀμέμπτωϲ καθὰ καὶ πρότερον ϲυνεβίουν—remarriage after a divorce; SB XII 10924 lines 14–15: [Ϲ]υνβιούτωϲ[αν οὖν ἀλλήλ]οιϲ [ἥ]τε Τ[αμαρεῦϲ κ]αὶ Μύϲτηϲ καθότι κ[αὶ π]ρότερον ϲυν[ῆϲαν]—replacement of an old contract by another; P.Oxy. X 1273 lines 22–23; PSI X 1115 lines 16–17; PSI X 1116 lines 11–13; more examples in P.Hamb. III 220 ad lines 7–8; to which one should add P.Oxy. XLIX 3500 lines 5–7: ϲυνβιούτωϲαν οὖν ἀλλήλοιϲ οἱ γαμοῦντεϲ φυλάϲϲοντεϲ τὰ τοῦ γάμου δίκαια.

[32] Cf. the divorce formulae: ὁμολογοῦμεν ἀπεζεῦχθαι τῆ[ϲ] π[ρὸ]ϲ ἀλλήλουϲ ϲυμβιώϲεωϲ (P.Oxy. XXXVI 2770 [304 CE] lines 9–10) and ϲυν[ῆρ]ϲθαι τὴν πρὸϲ ἀλλήλων ϲυμ[βί]ωϲ[ιν] (P.Mil.Vogl. III 185 [139 CE] lines 13–14; cf. 184 lines 18–19).

[33] There is no need to enter here into a discussion of its origins; see Wolff, *Written and Unwritten Marriages*, 48ff., 83ff.; Taubenschlag, *Law*, 115ff.; Modrzejewski, 'P. Strass. 237', 152ff.

αὐτοῖϲ τὸν ϲυνοικυϲμὸν ἔτι πρότερον ἀγράφωϲ, τέκνα δὲ αὐτοῖϲ μὴ γένηται, δυϲαρετῆϲ δὲ νυνὶ τὴν ἑαυτῶν ϲιμβίουϲιν etc., lines 28–33 = lines 4–7.[34] The documentation of this institution in Jewish society is another instance of the remarkable degree of assimilation of this society to its environment, observed in many of the documents from the Judaean Desert.[35]

It is important to emphasize that the unwritten marriage, ἄγραφοϲ γάμοϲ, was, as its name implies, a marriage without a contract: it did not require a contract in order to become valid. Its legal validity was no different from that of the written marriage, the ἔνγραφοϲ γάμοϲ.'There was only one type of marriage, and it could be contracted by mere *de facto* union. If there were, in connection with this marriage, some points, especially with regard to property matters, which needed a special arrangement, a document could be drawn at any time, either at the beginning of the marital life or later. But a written contract neither modified the character of the union itself nor was essential to it' (Wolff, *Written and Unwritten Marriages*, 66–7).[36]

In the majority of cases, the receipt of a dowry constituted the occasion for drawing up a contract, thereby transforming the marriage from an ἄγραφοϲ into an ἔγγραφοϲ γάμοϲ,[37] though a dowry is found also in connection with an unwritten marriage: in BGU IV 1045 col. II lines 8–12, the husband acknowledges the φερνή he received long before: Ὁμολογῶ ἔχιν παρὰ τῆϲ πρ[ο]ούϲη καὶ ϲυνούϲη μοι ἀγρ[ά]φωϲ γυναικὸϲ Ἰϲιδώραϲ ἐφ' ἑαυτῆϲ ἔ[τ]ι πάλαι τὴν φερνήν.[38] However, the presence of the phrase 'on the present day' in lines 7–8 of No. **65** ([ἀπ]ε̣ϲχηκ̣[έν]αι παρ̣' α̣ὐτῆϲ τῇ [οὔ]ϲῃ ἡμέρᾳ τειμογ̣[ρ]αφίαν etc.) leaves no doubt that it is the receipt of a dowry which called forth the present contract.

[34] Note the mixture of Greek and Semitic elements in the names of the parties; see the introduction to the document in Welles *et al.*, *Dura-Europos* , 160–61.

[35] See the excellent exposition by Wasserstein, 'Marriage Contract', 117ff.; Cotton, 'Cancelled Marriage Contract', 64ff.; contra Katzoff, 'Marriage Formulas'; see COMMENTS ad lines 9–10.

[36] Cf. Modrzejewski, 'P. Strass. 237'; 145: 'Les documents en question constituent un règlement écrit des rapports patrimoniaux du mariage basé sur une liaison inécrite'.

[37] E.g. PSI I 36 (11–19 CE); P.Ryl. II 154 (68 CE); BGU I 183 (= M.Chr. 313, 85 CE); 251 (81 CE); 252 (98 CE); CPR I 28 (= M.Chr. 312, 110 CE); P.Mil.Vogl. II 71 (161–80 CE).

[38] Cf. col. I lines 10–11 and U. Wilcken, ***Archiv*** 3 (1904–6) 509; see also the formula ἅμα τῇ τοῦ γάμου ϲυνβιώϲει in P.Stras. IV 237 line 13 and P.Hamb. III 220 line 4, which, as the editors of P.Hamb. III 220 observe ad loc., shows 'dass der Ehemann die Mitgift schon längst erhalten hat'; PSI V 450 col. I (2nd century CE) is also an acknowledgement of an old dowry. In P.Lund VI 3 (= SB VI 9353, 140 CE), the groom undertakes to return (with an additional fine of half its value) the dowry which he now received unless he writes his wife in the future τοῦ γάμου ϲυγγράφη (line 11ff.).

SB XII 10924 (114 CE, first published by Kiessling, 'Zwei Papyrusurkunden', 243–5) and P.Mich. V 339 (46 CE) are acknowledgements of additions to a dowry. They each refer to a previously written contract whose terms are acknowledged as still valid (see SB XII 10924 lines 11–12 and P.Mich. V 339 lines 4–5); thus, they cannot be taken, as they often are, to be documents which turned unwritten marriages into written ones.

Date and Provenance

The document is dated by consular year as well as by provincial year, but not by regnal year.[39] For νέας in the phrase κατὰ δὲ τὸν τῆς [νέ]ας ἐ̣πα[ρχ]είας Ἀραβίας ἀριθμον, see INTRODUCTION TO THE GREEK DOCUMENTARY TEXTS.

On Maḥoza, where the marriage contract takes place, see INTRODUCTION TO THE ARCHIVE OF SALOME KOMAÏSE DAUGHTER OF LEVI.

The groom, Yeshuᶜa son of Menaḥem, comes from a village, whose name remains otherwise unattested, located in the administrative region of the *polis* of Livias in the Peraea: Ιηcουc Μαναημου τ[ῶν ἀπὸ κώμηc *c.*8 letters] Cοφφαθε̣[..].... π̣ε̣ρ̣ὶ πόλιν Λιουιάδοc τῆc Π̣[εραίαc].[40] Although it is impossible to restore οἰκῶν ἐν Μαωζα̣ (e.g. P.Yadin **19** 11–12) or ἐνθάδε καταμένων (e.g. P.Yadin **18** line 6 = line 37) in the appropriate place,[41] it is to be assumed that, at the time the contract was drawn, he resided in Maḥoza.[42] Thus, there is no need to puzzle with Lewis about the fact 'that this document was found in the same cave as the Babatha archive' (*Documents*, 132): nowhere is Yeshuᶜa son of Menaḥem 'specifically stated to have been domiciled'[43] in his village of origin, other than in Lewis's own restoration of line 3: Ιηcοῦc Μαναήμου τῶ̣[ν οἰκούντων ἐν κώ]μ̣η̣—which is not adopted in the present edition.

Frg. a measures 12.5 x 8.5 cm; frg. b measures 10.3 x 6.3 cm; frg. c (not transcribed) measures 4.3 x 2.2 cm.

Mus. Inv. 99
IAA 515168

[39] See Lewis, *Documents,* 28 for 'the presence and the order of the several dates' in the Babatha Archive, and INTRODUCTION TO THE GREEK DOCUMENTARY TEXTS.

[40] On Livias and the Peraea, see COMMENTS ad line 4.

[41] Unless, in the lacuna of line 5, ἐνθάδε καταμένων came after {ὥ̣c̣τ̣ε̣ α̣[ὐτοὺc}].

[42] As Katzoff neatly puts it: 'In these documents the absence of indication of residence elsewhere than in his *idia* is not conclusive evidence that the person resided in his *idia*', 'Polygamy?', 130 n. 12 (see examples there); this is further proved by Lewis in 'In the World of P.Yadin'.

[43] Lewis, *Documents*, 132.

Frg. a + b
Inner text

1 ἐπὶ ὑπάτ̣[ων] Ϲ̣ε̣ρ̣γ̣ί̣ο̣υ̣ Ὀκταουίου Λαίνα Ποντι[ανοῦ καὶ Μάρκου Ἀντων]ί̣ου
Ῥουφείνου πρὸ ἑπτὰ ε̣ἰ̣δ̣[ῶν Αὐγούcτων, κατὰ δὲ]

2 τὸν τῆc [νέ]αc ἐ̣παρ̣χ̣είαc Ἀραβίαc ἀριθμ̣ὸν ἔτο[υc ἕκτου καὶ εἰκοcτοῦ μην]ὸc
Λῴ[ο]υ̣ ἐ̣ν̣ν̣ε̣ακαιδεκ̣ά̣[τῃ ἐν Μαωζα τῆc Ζο-]

3 αρηνῆc .[...]...... Πέτραν μητρόπολιν τῆ̣[c Ἀραβίαc, *c.4 letters* ὡμολογήc]α̣το
Ιηcουc Μαναημου τ[ῶν ἀπὸ κώμηc *c.8 letters*]

4 Cοφφαθε̣[..].... π̣ε̣ρ̣ὶ πόλιν Λιουιάδοc τῆc Π̣[εραίαc *c.9 letters* πρὸc(?) Cαλ]ωμην
κ̣αλ̣ο̣υ̣μένην Κ̣[ομαϊcην Ληουειου τὴν]

5 γ̣υ̣ν̣αῖκα, Μ̣[α]ωζηνὴν ὥcτε αὐτο̣ὺc̣ {ὥ̣c̣τ̣ε̣ α̣[ὐτοὺc} *c.17 letters*].ετ̣....
cυμβιωc̣...[*c.14 letters*]

6 αὐτῇ^{c} ὡ̣[c κ]αὶ πρὸ τούτου τοῦ χρόνου ..[καὶ ὀφείλειν? *c.10 letters*]..... τῇ
αὐτῇ Κομα̣ι̣c̣[ῃ τὴ]ν̣ προῖ{ο}κα

ὁ αὐ]τὸc Ιηcουc̣

7 αὐτῆc ἀ[ρ]γ̣υρίου δηνάρια ἐνανήκο̣ντα ἕξ, [ἃ ὡμολογήcατο ὁ γήμαc
[ἀπ]ε̣cχηκ̣[έν]αι παρ̣' α̣ὐτῆc τῇ [οὔ]cῃ ἡμέρα̣

8 τειμογ̣[ρ]αφίαν κοcμίαc γυναικίαc ἐν ἀ̣[ργύρῳ καὶ χρυcῷ καὶ ἱμα]τιcμῷ καὶ
ἑταίροιc γυ[ναι]κίοιc ἀ̣ξι-

9 [οχρέαν] .....τ̣ο̣υ̣ ἀργυρίου, cὺν αἱρέcει τ̣ροφῆc̣ [καὶ ἀμφιαcμοῦ αὐτῆc] τ̣ε καὶ
τῶν μελ̣λόντ̣ω̣[ν τέκ]ν̣ω̣ν̣ ν̣ό̣μ̣[ῳ]

10 [ἑλληνικ]ῷ καὶ ἑλλ̣[η]ν̣ι̣κ̣ῷ τρόπῳ ἐ̣π̣ὶ τ̣ῆ̣c̣ τ̣[οῦ αὐτοῦ Ιηcουου πίcτεω]c καὶ
κινδύ̣ν̣ου πά̣ν̣[των ὑπα]ρ̣χόντων̣

αὐτοῦ

11 α̣ὐ̣τ̣ο̣ῦ̣ ὧ̣ν̣ τ̣ε ἔχει ἐν τ̣ῇ α̣ὐ̣τ̣ῇ π̣ατρίδι Ϲ̣οφφ[αθε... *c.7 letters* καὶ ὧν ἂν]
ἐπικτήcηται ...[*c.10 letters*]

12 c[*c. 6 letters* ἀπὸ] τοῦ αὐτο̣[ῦ Ἰ]η̣cουου καὶ ἐκ τ̣[ῶν ὑπαρχόντων αὐτοῦ πάντ]η̣ [....]........[....]c τρόπ̣ῳ ᾧ

13 ἂν̣ αἱ̣ρῆτ̣αι̣ ἡ αὐτὴ Κομαϊ[cη] ἢ̣ ὃ̣ς̣ [δι' αὐ]τῆc ἢ̣ [ὑπὲρ αὐτῆc πράccων τὴν εἴcπραξιν ποιεῖcθαι, περὶ τοῦ]

14 ο̣ὕτω̣ς̣ [κ]α̣λ̣ῶc γείνεcθαι πίc̣τεωc ἐπηρω̣[τημένηc καὶ ἀνθωμολογημένηc· cυμπαρόντοc *c.8 letters*]

15 Μα[ναημο]υ̣ ἐπιτρόπου τῆ[c αὐ]τ̣ῆc Κομαΐcη̣c̣. Ἐπ[ιγραφή? *letters?*]

7 ἐναν̣ήκον̣τα 8 τιμογραφίαν ἑτέροιc

Previous publication (as P.Yadin **37**):

1 δ]ε̣ 2–3 [Ζ]ο̣|αρηνῆc τ̣ῆ̣c π[ερὶ] 3 [*c. 12 letters*]α̣το 'Ιηcοῦc τ̣ῶ̣[ν οἰκούντων ἐν κώ]μ̣η̣ 4 Coφφαθε[.]... π̣[*c.10 letters* εἰληφέναι C]α̣λ̣ώμην Κ̣ο̣[μαϊν *c.12 letters*] 5 [*c.12 letters*]....... cυμβιῶcα̣ι̣ τ̣[ὸν 'Ιηcοῦν μετ'?] 6 αὐτῆc χρόνου τ̣α̣[*c.20 letters*] Κομαΐ̣δ̣[ι τὸ]ν 7 [καὶ ὡμολογήcατο] 8 ἐν ἀ̣ργ̣ύ̣[ρῳ] γυν̣[αι]κίοιc 8–9 α̣ξ̣ι̣|[ο]χ̣ρ̣έ̣α̣[ν] ..[..].τ̣ο̣υ̣ 9 –10 νόμ[ῳ] | ἑ̣[λλη]ν̣ικῷ ἐπὶ τῆc 11 αὐτοῦ ὧν̣ C̣οφφα[θε.. καὶ ἐνθάδε] 11–12 π̣ρ̣ά̣[ξεωc α]ὐ̣τ̣ῆ̣ | οὔc̣η̣ς̣ [κα]ὶ̣ α̣π̣ὸ̣ 12 ω̣c κ̣[υρίω]c 13 Κομαϊ[c].. δ̣ι̣' [α]ὐ̣τῆc 14 οὕτω̣ς̣ πίcτεωc [ἀνθωμολογημένηc. *c.20 letters*] 15 Μα[να]ή̣μ̣ο̣υ̣ τῆ̣ς̣ α̣ὐ̣τ̣ῆc Κομαΐc. ...[

TRANSLATION

In the consul[ship] of Sergius Octavius Laenas Pontia[nus and Marcus Anton]ius Rufinus, the seve[nth] of August, and according to the computation of the ne[w] province of Arabia year [twenty-six] on the nineteenth of month Loos, [in Maḥoza in the district of Z]oʿar [of the administrative region of] Petra, metropolis of Arabia, Yeshuʿa son of Menaḥem, from [the village] of Soffathe... in the district of the city of Livias of the administrative region of P[eraea . . . agreed with Sal]ome also called K[omaïse, daughter of Levi], his wife, who is from Maḥoza, [that they continue] life together . . . as also before this time . . . , [and that he owes?] the above-mentioned Komaïse, as her dowry, ninety-six denarii of silver, [which the bridegroom], the above-mentioned Yeshuʿa, [acknowledged] to have received from her on the present day, as the written evaluation of feminine adornment in sil[ver and gold and clo]thing and other feminine articles equivalent to the above-mentioned amount of money, (combined) with his undertaking to feed [and clothe both her] and her children to come in accordance with Greek custom and Greek manner upon [the above-mentioned Yeshuʿa's good faith] and on peril of all his [posses]sions, both those which he possesses in his home village of Soffathe... [and those which he has here(?) as well as those which he may in addition] acquire. [She has the right of execution both upon] the above-mentioned Yeshuʿa and [upon all(?)] his [validly] held possessions [everywhere], in whatever manner the above-mentioned Komaïse, or whoever [acts] through her or [for her, may choose to carry out the execution,] regarding this being thus rightly done, the formal question having in good faith been as[ked and acknowledged, in reply. X] son of Menaḥem, guardian of the above-mentioned Komaïse was present with her. Ad[dendum . . .].

COMMENTS

Ll. 2–3 [τῆϲ Ζο]αρηνῆϲ .[...]...... Πέτραν. Lewis's τῆϲ π[ερὶ] before Πέτραν does not fill all the missing letters; perhaps τὴν Πέτραν? Another formula, which cannot be made to fit in here, is used in No. **62** frg. a line 12: Ϲαμμουοϲ Ϲιμων[ο]ϲ Μαωζηνὸϲ τῆϲ Ζοαρηνῆϲ περιμέτρου Πέτραϲ, and in P.Yadin **16** lines 13–14: Βαβθα Cίμωνοϲ Μαωζηνὴ τῆϲ Ζοαρηνῆϲ περιμέτρου Πέτραϲ.

L. 3 μητρόπολιν τῆ[ϲ Ἀραβίαϲ]. Cf. P.Yadin **12** lines 8–9: ἐν Πέτρᾳ μητροπόλει τῆϲ Ἀραβ[ία]ϲ; cf. lines 1–2 (= lines 4–5): ἀπὸ ἄκτων βουλῆϲ Πετραίων τῆϲ μητροπόλεωϲ. For the title *metropolis*, see the inscription from an arch dedicated to Trajan in Petra in 114 CE: [ἡ τῆϲ Ἀραβίαϲ μη]τρόπολιϲ Πέτρα, *IGLS* XXI *Inscriptions de la Jordanie* IV 37.

L. 3 Ιηϲοῦϲ Μαναημου τ[ῶν ἀπὸ κώμηϲ]. Lewis had τῶ[ν οἰκούντων ἐν κώ]μῃ, drawing a parallel to P.Yadin **19** lines 11–12: Ἰο]ύδαϲ Ἐλ[αζά]ρου Χθουϲ[ίω]νοϲ Ἠνγαδη[νὸ]ϲ οἰκῶν ἐν Μαωζαϲ. This is hardly a convincing parallel, since οἰκῶν ἐν Μαωζαϲ is intended as a contrast to Ἠνγαδη[νὸ]ϲ: 'Judah son of Eleazar, also named Khthousion, from Ein Gedi, residing in Maḥoza'; see also P.Yadin **20** (130 CE), lines 4–5 = lines 23–24: Βηϲᾶϲ Ἰηϲούου Ἠνγαδηνὸϲ οἰκῶν ἐν Μαζρααᾳ ἐ‹πί›τροποϲ ὀρφανῶν Ἰηϲούου Χθουϲίωνοϲ. Οἰκῶν, in these documents, expresses the place of residence, not of origin. The restoration here is based on No. **69** line 5: Ακαβαϲ Μηειρω τῶν ἀπὸ κώμηϲ Ἰακείμων τ[ῆϲ Ζειφηνῆϲ]; P.Yadin **5**a col. i lines 5–6: ἐγὼ Ἰώϲηποϲ τοῦ Ἰωϲήπ[ου ἐπι]καλουμ[ένου] Ζαβούδο[υ] τῶν ἀπὸ Μαωζων; Mur **115** line 2: Ἐλεαῖοϲ Cίμωνοϲ τῶν ἀπὸ κ(ώμηϲ) Γαλωδῶν. It is hard to know what occupied the rest of the line.

Ll. 3–5 [ὡμολογήϲ]ατο Ιηϲουϲ Μαναημου . . . [πρὸϲ(?) Cαλ]ωμην . . . ὥϲτε αὐτοὺϲ (+ an infinitive in the lacuna in line 5). For the construction of the entire clause, see P.Yadin **17** lines 3–6 (= lines 21–25): ὡμολογήϲατο Ἰούδαϲ Ἐλεαζάρου τοῦ καὶ [Χ]θουϲίωνοϲ Ἀινγαδηνὸϲ πρ[ὸϲ] Βαβαθαν Cίμωνοϲ ἰδίαν γυναίκαν αὐτοῦ, . . . ὥϲτε τὸν Ἰούδαν ἀπε[ϲ]χηκέναι παρ' αὐτῆϲ etc.; cf. Mur **115** lines 2–3 ἐξωμολ[ογ]ήϲα[το καὶ ϲ]υνεγράψατο Ἐλεαοιϲ Cίμωνοϲ . . . πρὸϲ [Cα]λώμην [Ἰ]ωά[νου Γαλγ]ουλὰ προγενομέ[νην] αὐτοῦ Ἐλαίου ϲύνβιον; P.Dura 30 line 6: ἐ[ξωμολογή]ϲαν[το καὶ ϲ]υνεγράψαντο π[ρὸϲ ἀλλήλ]ουϲ τῇ ἐνεϲτώϲῃ ἡμέρᾳ Αὐρήλιοϲ Ἀλέξανδροϲ . . . καὶ Αὐρηλία Μαρκελλεῖνα Μαρκελλείνου.

L. 4 Cοφφαθε[..].... περὶ πόλιν. Since the name of the village is unattested, it is hard to know how many letters of the name are missing; perhaps three, if we assume that τῆϲ stood before περί. The name occurs again in line 11, before a lacuna.

L. 4 πόλιν Λιουιάδοϲ. On Livias in the Peraea, see Schürer, Vermes, and Millar, *History*, 2:176–8.

L. 4 Π[εραίαϲ]. That Π[εραίαϲ] should be restored here is convincingly argued by Isaac in 'Babatha Archive', 69: 'the only city named Livias in the wider region was in Peraia', and 'there was only one Peraia in the entire region'. Peraea, although located in Transjordan, was part of the province of Judaea, like Judaea proper, Galilee, and Samaria; see Schürer, Vermes, and Millar, *History*, 2:192ff. Lewis's argument that, since the document was written in the province of Arabia, τῆϲ Ἰουδαίαϲ should have followed, as in P.Yadin **16** line 16—'for which there is no room in the lacuna' (*Documents*, 132), could be countered with the assumption that Judaea in P.Yadin **16** line 16 is a geographical notion, Judaea proper, rather than the province.

Ll. 4–5 Κ[ομαϊϲην Ληουειου τὴν] γυναῖκα, Μ[α]ωζηνὴν. This genitive form of Levi's name is adopted from No. **64** line 5 (= line 24). An alternative restoration (perhaps too long for the remaining space) would be: Κ[ομαϊϲην Ληουει θυγατέρα], γυναῖκα, Μ[α]ωζηνὴν. The shorter, and undeclined form, of Levi's name, Ληουει, is based on No. **63** lines 1, 4, 8. In any case, γυναῖκα or τὴν γυναῖκα is translated here as 'his wife', since they have already been married for a while (see INTRODUCTION).

Ll. 5–6 ϲυμβιωϲ...[*c*.14 letters] αὐτῆϲ ὡ[ϲ κ]αὶ πρὸ τούτου τοῦ χρόνου. What remains of the clauses in these two lines makes it extremely likely that No. **65** is a contract that transforms an unwritten marriage into a written one; see INTRODUCTION for a discussion and attempts at reconstruction.

Ll. 6–9 These lines consist of the acknowledgement by the husband of the receipt of the dowry on the present day from his wife, and his admission of being indebted to her for its value in money; accordingly, they contain a description of the valuables of the dowry and their assessment in money. It must be observed, though, that, in comparison with other marriage contracts, this part of the contract is formulated in an inverse order—at least in the present attempt to reconstruct the text:[44] first comes the

[44] For the normal order, see No. **69** lines 5–9 with COMMENTS, and P.Yadin **18** lines 7–15 = lines 39–49.

acknowledgement of debt [καὶ ὀφείλειν?] . . . τῇ αὐτῇ Κομαιϲ[η τὴ]ν προῖ{ο}κα αὐτῆϲ; this is followed by the assessment of the dowry objects in monetary terms: ἀ[ρ]γυρίου δηνάρια ἐνανήκοντα ἕξ; at this point, only, comes the acknowledgement of receipt: [ἃ ὡμολογήϲατο ὁ γήμαϲ ὁ αὐ]τὸϲ Ιηϲουϲ [ἀπ]εϲχηκ[έν]αι παρ' αὐτῆϲ τῇ [οὔ]ϲῃ ἡμέρᾳ; finally, preceded by the term τειμογραφία (see below), comes a breakdown of the individual items of the dowry which, together, make up the above sum of money.

L. 6 [καὶ ὀφείλειν(?)]. The traces of letters before the dative τῇ αὐτῇ Κομαιϲ[η] are not compatible with ὀφείλειν, which therefore is likely to have come earlier, but not necessarily right at the beginning of the lacuna, as suggested in the restoration.

L. 6 προῖ{ο}κα. The same misspelling is in P.Yadin **18** line 15 (= line 49): εἰϲ λόγον προι{ο}κόϲ; another version in P.Yadin **21** line 11 ἀντὶ τῆϲ ϲῆϲ προ{ο}ικόϲ (cf. P.Yadin **22** line 10); see Lewis's explanation in *Documents*, 82 ad P.Yadin **18** lines 13–15 and 44–46. The correct spelling is found in Mur **115** line 6: εἰϲ λόγον προικόϲ and (heavily restored) in No. **69** line 6: εἰϲ λόγον προϲφορᾶϲ προικ[όϲ]; on προίξ see COMMENTS ad No. **69** line 6.

L. 7 τῇ [οὔ]ϲῃ ἡμέρᾳ. 'On the present day'. See INTRODUCTION for a discussion of the crucial importance of the phrase for the correct interpretation of No. **65**.

L. 8 τειμογ[ρ]αφίαν. Τιμογραφία is a rare term.[45] Outside the papyri from the Judaean Desert, it appears only once more, in an inscription from Didyma from the second century BCE:[46] [ἀπολογιϲμὸϲ τ]ῶν γεγονότων ἔργων ὑπὸ τῶν ἱερῶν [π]αίδων, κα[θότι τεθεικαν οἱ ἐγ]λογιϲταὶ τὰϲ τιμογραφίαϲ ἑκάϲτου τῶν ἔργων κατὰ [τὸν ἀνενηνεγμ]ένον ὑπ' αὐτῶν ἐπὶ τὸ νεωποιεῖον ἐγλογιϲμόν (*SEG* II 568 = *Didyma* II. *Die Inschriften* No. 40 lines 7–10).[47] However, it appears in P.Yadin **18** in the same context as in No. **65**, namely that of the evaluation of the valuables of the dowry: προϲφερομένην (i.e. the bride, Shelamṣion) αὐτῷ εἰϲ λόγον προϲφορᾶϲ κοϲμίαν γυναικιαν ἐν ἀργύρῳ καὶ χρυϲῷ καὶ ἱματιϲμῷ διατετειμημένην ἐν ἀλλή[λ]οιϲ, ὡϲ λέγουϲιν οἱ ἀμφότεροι, ἀξιοχρέαν εἶναι ἀργυρίου δηναρίων διακοϲίων, ἣν τειμογραφίαν ὡμολόγηϲεν ὁ γήμαϲ Ἰούδαϲ Κίμβερ ἀπειληφέναι παρὰ τῆϲ αὐτῆϲ Cελαμψιουϲ γυναικὸϲ αὐτοῦ διὰ χειρὸϲ παραχρῆμα παρὰ Ἰούδου πατρὸϲ αὐτῆϲ, lines 7–12 = lines 39–45 (with slight variations). Lewis translates ἣν τειμογραφίαν as 'which appraised value' (*Documents*, 80). It is translated here as 'written evaluation', since the connotation of 'γραφία' is always present in the many *composita* of the word.[48] There is no doubt that τιμογραφίαι, in the inscription from Didyma, refer to computations made in writing, of which the forecast of the budget (ἐγλογιϲμόϲ) was composed. The question remains: what did the husband receive in reality: a piece of paper, the actual valuables, or their monetary equivalent? The παράφερνα in Egyptian papyri, to which the items described here, as part of the προίξ, correspond, although said to be received by the husband, were there for the personal use of the wife during the marriage.[49]

L. 8 ἐν ἀ[ργύρῳ καὶ χρυϲῷ καὶ ἱμα]τιϲμῷ. Cf. No. **69** line 6; P.Yadin **18** lines 8–9 = lines 40–41.

Ll. 8–9 ἀξι[οχρέαν] .....του ἀργυρίου. τοῦ αὐτοῦ ἀργυρίου can be safely restored: 'equivalent to the above-mentioned amount of money', i.e. the ninety-six denarii of line 7.

Ll. 9–11 The undertaking of the husband to support the wife and any future children, accompanied by a liability clause which pledges his entire property—both that which he possesses at present as well as that which he will acquire in the future—as a guarantee, appears only in No. **65** and in P.Yadin **18**. In No. **69**, the obligation and the attendant liability clause are restricted to the upkeep of the wife only (see

---

45 There is no parallel in the Duke Data Bank. Note that the verb τιμογραφεῖν is used once in the Septuagint to translate the fixing of tax on land by assessment: ἐτιμογράφηϲεν τὴν γῆν τοῦ δοῦναι τὸ ἀργύριον ἐπὶ ϲτόματοϲ Φαραω (2 Kgs 23:25).

46 'Account of expenditure (ἀπολογιϲμόϲ) on works performed by the holy slaves, as it was laid down by the *eglogistai* in written computations (τὰϲ τιμογραφίαϲ) for each individual work, and in accordance with the forecast of the budget (ἐγλογιϲμόϲ) which they had deposited in the office in charge of temple building'.

47 Cf. LSJ, *s.v.* 'assessment of payment due'.

48 See Buck and Petersen, *Reverse Index*, 165–6.

49 See Mitteis, *Grundzüge*, 220–21; Häge, *Ehegüterrechtliche Verhältnisse*, 241ff; Talamanca, 'Gli apporti patrimoniali', 246ff.

lines 10–11). For more details, see No. **69**, MAINTENANCE OF THE WIFE and THE LIABILITY CLAUSE in MARRIAGE PRACTICES.

Ll. 9–10 ν̣ό̣μ̣[ῳ] [ἑλληνικ]ῷ καὶ ἑλλ[η]ν̣ι̣κ̣ῷ τρόπ̣ῳ. Only the first element, albeit in reverse order (ἑλληνικῷ νόμῳ), is attested in P.Yadin **18** line 16 = line 51. Nevertheless, in both contracts the expression appears in the same place: it follows the undertaking to provide for the wife and children, and precedes the liability clause.[50] We can be sure, therefore, that a single model was followed. The meaning of the expression ἑλλιηνικός νόμος in this context has been the subject of heated debate: custom or law? What precisely is meant by Greek custom or law? Whose custom or law? As Lewis points out, nowhere in the Roman Near East is the expression attested in any language, nor is there 'a single occurrence of the expression Ἑλλιηνικός νόμος in all the thousands of Greek papyri from Egypt' ('The World of P.Yadin', 40–41).

Nevertheless, it seems that Wasserstein is right to be less concerned with the precise meaning of the term, than with the highly significant evidence 'that the obligation to provide for the wife and the children to be born is taken upon himself by the [Jewish] husband in accordance with Greek νόμος. . . . There is visible here a remarkable degree of assimilation'. And yet, 'the assimilation noticed here is not necessarily an assimilation to Hellenism *tout court* but an assimilation to an environment that in spite of not being Hellenized uses Hellenic elements; and conversely, to an environment that in spite of using Hellenic elements, is not by virtue of that use to be thought of as Hellenized' ('Marriage Contract', 125). For a further discussion, see Katzoff in Lewis et al., 'Papyrus Yadin 18', 241ff.; Katzoff, 'Papyrus Yadin 18'; Geiger, 'Note'; Wasserstein, 'Documents from the Cave of Letters'; Wasserstein, 'Non-Hellenized Jews'; Katzoff, 'Marriage Formulas'.

L. 11 Ϲ̣οφφ[αθε... *c*.7 letters καὶ ὧν ἂν] ἐπικτήϲηται. Three letters followed Ϲοφφαθε to make up the name of Yeshuᶜa's village; see above ad line 4; Lewis's καὶ ἐνθάδε is, therefore, too long for the remaining space. However, assuming that we have here the same construction as in the liability clause of P.Yadin **18** lines 17–18 = lines 52–54, namely τε . . . καὶ . . . καὶ, then καὶ ὧδε can be restored in the lacuna. Thus, lines 10–11 should read: πά̣ν̣[των ὑπα]ρχόντων̣ α̣ὐ̣τ̣ο̣ῦ̣ ὧ̣ν̣ τ̣ε ἔχει ἐ̣ν̣ τῇ̣ α̣ὐ̣τ̣ῇ̣ π̣ατρίδι αὐτοῦ Ϲ̣οφφ[αθε... καὶ ὧδε, καὶ ὧν ἂν] ἐπικτήϲηται. The possession of property in Maḥoza will increase the likelihood that Yeshuᶜa son of Menaḥem resided in the village of Maḥoza when this contract was concluded; see DATE AND PROVENANCE.

Ll. 11–12 The *sigma* at the beginning of the line is very clear. Lewis's restoration of the end of line 11 and the beginning of line 12, which makes the latter begin with an *omicron* (π̣ρά̣[ξεωϲ α]ὐ̣τῇ̣ | οὔϲηϲ) is, therefore, very difficult; there is no doubt, though, that the πρᾶξιϲ clause was divided between the two lines.

Ll. 13–14 On the stipulation clause, see COMMENTS ad No. **63** line 13.

Ll. 13–15 Lewis, who assumes, as we have seen, that Salome Komaïse was a minor (see INTRODUCTION), suggests that the 'fact that the bride is represented by a guardian implies that her father, who would normally be giving her away (cf. [P.Yadin] **18**), was dead . . . or absent'. We now know that the father, Levi, had been dead at least since 127 CE (see No. **63** line 6). However, the presence of an *epitropos* is not occasioned by the bride's being underage.[51] Salome Komaïse, as was argued in the INTRODUCTION, was not a minor when No. **65** was written. As elsewhere in the Greek contracts from the

---

[50] P.Yadin **18** lines 15–18 = lines 49–54: ἀκολούθωϲ αἱρέϲει τροφῆϲ καὶ ἀμφιαϲμοῦ αὐτῆϲ τε καὶ τῶν μελλόντων τέκνων ἑλληνικῷ νόμῳ ἐπὶ τῆϲ τοῦ αὐτοῦ Ἰούδα Κίμβ[ε]ρο[ϲ] π̣ίϲτ̣εωϲ καὶ κ̣ινδύνου καὶ πάντων ὑπαρχόντων ὧν τε ἔχει ἐν τῇ α̣ὐ̣τ̣ῇ̣ [πα]τ̣ρ̣ί̣δ̣ι α̣ὐ̣τ̣ο̣ῦ̣ καὶ ὧδε καὶ ὧν ἐπικτήϲηται etc.

[51] Nor, for that matter, is the bride's being underage the explanation for the ἔκδοϲιϲ by the father in P.Yadin **18**: the practice of giving away the daughter by one or both parents is attested both in Palestine and in Egypt at this time; cf. Wasserstein, 'Marriage Contract', 109ff. and No. **69**, 'The Mother Gives Away the Bride' in MARRIAGE PRACTICES; contra Katzoff in Lewis, *et al.*, 'Papyrus Yadin 18', 240ff. and idem, 'Papyrus Yadin 18', 173f.

Judaean Desert,[52] the presence of the woman's *epitropos*[53] is to be interpreted as an expression of Romanization.[54]

Ll. 14–15 [cυμπαρόντος *c.*8 letters] Μα[ναημο]υ ἐπιτρόπου. The first name of the *epitropos* stood in the lacuna. It is tempting to restore here Ιηcουου (see line 10), and identify the guardian as the husband, Yeshuᶜa son of Menaḥem. This would clinch the argument that the couple had lived in an unwritten marriage until the writing of No. **65** (see INTRODUCTION). The temptation should be resisted, however, not because of the dubious claim that the husband in an unwritten marriage did not become his wife's guardian,[55] but because of the nature of the transaction here recorded, which excludes the husband as guardian. In support of his exclusion in such transactions one may cite P.Yadin **17**, where Babatha, attested here for the first time as being married to Judah son of Eleazar,[56] is 'assisted' by Jacob son of Yeshuᶜa, 'her guardian for the purpose of this matter': ὡμολογήcατο Ἰούδας Ἐλεαζάρου τοῦ καὶ [Χ]θουcίωνος Ἀινγαδηνὸς πρ[ὸς] Βαβαθαν Cίμωνος ἰδίαν γυναίκαν αὐτοῦ cυνπαρόντ[ος α]ὐτῇ ἐπιτρόπου τοῦδε τοῦ πράγματος χάριν Ἰακώβου Ἰηcοῦ (lines 3–5 = lines 21–24). P.Yadin **17** and No. **65** involve the husband and wife as the two opposing parties to a contract creating a state of obligation between them: the acknowledgement of a παραθήκη by Judah in P.Yadin **17** (τὸν Ἰούδαν ἀπεcχηκέναι παρ' αὐτῆς εἰς λόγον παραθήκης, etc., lines 24–25 = line 6) does not differ in essence from the acknowledgement of a dowry in No. **65** (see Lewis's introduction to P.Yadin **5** and **17**, *Documents*, 35, 71).[57]

Ll. 14–15 [cυμπαρόντος *c.*8 letters] Μα[ναημο]υ ἐπιτρόπου τῆ[ς αὐ]τῆς Κομαϊcης. Lewis rules out the formula διὰ τοῦ δεῖνος as being too short to fill the space. In fact, it is doubtful whether this formula is appropriate here. With one exception, I could find this formula only in documents in which the woman is the agent, and the guardian is, therefore, actively participating.[58] In No. **69** line 4, the mother gives her daughter in marriage διὰ Βορκ.. Αγλα ἐπιτρόπ[ου] αὐτῆς τοῦδε τοῦ πράγμα[τος χάριν]. In P.Yadin **14**, Babatha summons Iohannes son of Joseph, her son's guardian, to appear before the governor: παρήνγει[λεν Βαβαθα Cίμωνος τοῦ Μανα]ήμου; she does it through her guardian: διὰ ἐπίτροπου αὐτ[ῆς τ]οῦδε τοῦ πραγμ[ατος] Ἰουδα Χθουcίωνος, etc. (lines 21–23). Similarly, in P.Yadin **15**, she writes a deposition against her sons' guardians through her guardian: [ἐμαρ]τυροποιήcατο ἡ Βαβαθα ὡς προγέγραπται διὰ ἐπιτρόπου αὐτῆς τοῦδε τοῦ πράγματο[ς Ἰούδου Χ]θουcίωνος ὃς παρὼν ὑπέγραψεν (lines 31–32). In P.Yadin **22**, Babatha declares that she sells the date crop of three date groves to Shimᶜon son of Yeshuᶜa under certain term: [δι]ὰ ἐ[πιτρ]όπου αὐτῆς καὶ ὑπογράφαντος Ἰωά{α}νης Μαχχουθας (lines 28–29). She summons Julia Crispina to come before the governor in P.Yadin **25**: διὰ ἐπιτρόπου αὐτῆς Μαρας Ἀβ[δ]αλγου Πετραῖος (lines 46–47 = lines 14–15). Finally, in P.Yadin **27**, Babatha acknowledges the receipt of maintenance money for her orphaned son: [διὰ ἐπιτ]ρόπου αὐτῆς Βαβελις Μαναήμου (line 18).[59] In contrast, in P.Yadin **17**, where Babatha is entirely passive, the mere presence of the *epitropos* is recorded: ὡμολογήcατο Ἰούδας Ἐλεαζάρου [Χ]θουcίωνος Ἀινγαδηνὸς πρ[ὸς] Βαβαθαν Cίμωνος ἰδίαν γυναῖκαν αὐτοῦ, cυνπαρόντ[ος α]ὐτῇ ἐπιτρόπου τοῦδε τοῦ πράγματος χάριν Ἰακώβου Ἰηcοῦ, lines 3–5 = 22–24.

---

[52] They are absent from the Aramaic and Hebrew contracts; see INTRODUCTION TO THE GREEK DOCUMENTARY TEXTS.

[53] Not κύριος; see Wolff, 'Le droit', 279–83.

[54] Wolff, 'Römisches Provinzialrecht', 792–7.

[55] E.g. Mitteis, *Grundzüge*, 208; see Wolff, *Written and Unwritten Marriages*, 29 on the nature of the evidence in support of this claim.

[56] Not in an unwritten marriage; the marriage is recorded in P.Yadin **10**.

[57] This, probably, is the explanation for the presence of a κύριος other than the husband in P.Oxy. XLIX 3487 lines 2–3, and not the fact that the husband is described as τῶι cυνόντι μοι κατὰ [ν]όμους ἀνδρί, lines 4–5: here, too, there is a state of obligation between husband and wife.

[58] The exception is P.Yadin **20**, where Besas son of Yeshuᶜa and Julia Crispina concede a courtyard in Ein Gedi to Shelamṣion, the daughter of Babatha's second husband, who is said to act through her guardian: Cελαμcιοῦ Ἰούδου Ἠνγαδηνῇ διὰ ἐπιτρόπου αὐτῆς Ἰούδας ὃς καὶ Κίνβερ Ἀνανίου Ἠν[γ]αδηνοῦ τοῦδε τοῦ πράγματος χάριν (lines 25–27 = lines 5–6); on the document, see Cotton, 'Courtyard(s)'.

[59] Note that in P.Yadin **26** Babatha acts without a guardian.

The opposite rule, however, does not seem to hold: the formula διὰ τοῦ δεῖνος does not always occur in contracts in which the woman is the agent; here, too, the mere presence of the *epitropos* can be recorded. In No. **64**, the mother is writing a deed of gift in favour of her daughter, with her guardian merely present: Σα[λω]μη ἡ καὶ Γροπτη Μαναημου συνπαρόντος αὐτ[ῇ ἐ]πιτρόπο[υ τοῦδε τοῦ πρά]γματος χάριν Ιωσηπου Σιμωνος [ἀ]νὴρ αὐτῆς, lines 3–5. Nor is the formula διὰ τοῦ δεῖνος long enough to fill the lacuna in No. **63** lines 1–2, where the daughter renounces her rights vis-à-vis her mother; the text was thus restored with the mere presence of the guardian recorded: [ἐξωμολο]γήσατο καὶ συνεγρ[άψατο Σαλ]ωμη Ληουει τοῦ[... συμπαρόντος αὐτῇ ἐπιτρόπου + *8 letters*]υ Σιμωνος ἀνδρὸς α[ὐτῆ]ς τοῦδε τοῦ {...}πρ[άγματος χάριν].

In conclusion, it seems reasonable to restore here, where the wife is completely passive, the formula which conveys the mere presence of the guardian. Admittedly, the formula is out of place in lines 14–15; it should have come in line 5, when the wife was mentioned for the first time (see following *lemma*).

L. 15 τῆ[ς αὐ]τῆς Κομαΐσης. The formula normally reads: συμπαρόντος αὐτῇ τοῦ δεῖνος ἐπιτρόπου or συμπαρόντος αὐτῇ ἐπιτρόπου, τοῦ δεῖνος (see examples, in COMMENTS ad lines 14–15). The variation can be accounted for by the reason given before: the formula is out of place here; τῆ[ς αὐ]τῆς Κομαΐσης is a reminder that this is so.

L. 15 Ἐπ[ιγραφή? letters?]. This addendum occurs twice in the Babatha Archive. In P.Yadin **5**a col. ii line 14, Lewis suggests that 'the word introduces the lines that follow' (*Documents*, 40). In P.Yadin **22** line 30, the word ἐπιγραφή is followed by ἔτι δέ, an interlinear addition above line 16 of the document, thus affirming the authenticity of ἔτι δέ, there (so Lewis, *Documents*, 101). The latter explanation is attractive. However, unless the lines which follow ἐπιγραφή in P.Yadin **5**a col. ii have already been introduced as interlinear insertions in the text, it is hard to see how they could be authenticated by the preceding ἐπιγραφή. The suggested restoration of the rest of No. **65** line 15 assumes that a repetition of the interlinear insertions in the text, of which there are several, came after Ἐπ[ιγραφή]. It must be pointed out, though, that the authentication of interlinear additions to the inner text of a double document is not attested in the Babatha Archive. Germanus son of Judah, the scribe of P.Yadin **22–27**, left the interlinear insertions in the inner texts of P.Yadin **20** and **23**, both of them double documents, unmarked,[60] while authenticating the interlinear addition in P.Yadin **22**, as we have seen, which is not a double document. Unless we are to take him to task for inconsistency, it may be suggested that, although it is commonly assumed that the inner text was written after the outer text,[61] the insertions were deemed to have been authenticated by their presence in place in the outer text.

---

[60] As did the scribe of P.Yadin **15**, **17**, and **18**, Theënas son of Shimʿon.

[61] See Lewis, *Documents*, 8–9.

66. XḤev/Se papLoan with Hypothec gr

Philadelphia?, Arabia, 99 or 109 CE

(PL. XLII)

Preliminary publication: H. M. Cotton, 'Loan with Hypothec: Another Papyrus from the Cave of Letters?' *ZPE* 101 (1994) 53–60, pl I.

THIS deed is the largest fragment on museum inventory 732, a plate formerly designated XḤev/Se Gr. 3, which contains many fragments, some of which seem to belong to this deed but are hard to place since only traces of letters remain on them (see pls. XLVIII–XLIX). The upper and lower margins are preserved. The verso is blank. The writing is across the fibres, a feature which seems to be common to the Seiyâl collection. A strap of papyrus, 4 cm long, with ink stains and some writing on it, projects to the left in line 8. There is an ink stain on the far end of the strap, followed by some blank space. This is followed by three letters and again what looks like blank space, unless, of course, the vertical fibres, which by now have mostly rubbed away, contained writing. In the latter case, we can assume the loss of *c.*16 letters on the left of all the other lines. Two considerations, however, work against this assumption: (1) It seems reasonable to assume that the document started with ὑπατείας,[1] which would mean that only two letters are lost on the left-hand side of the first line. Since it is hard to believe that the first line was inset, we must assume that in all the other lines no more than two or three letters have been lost on the left.[2] (2) The larger blank space in line 8 looks like a real space, perhaps an inter-column space, in which case another column stood to the left of the document. It might even be suggested that a single word stood in line 8, whereas the rest of the left-hand margin remained blank. However, if very little was lost on the left side of the document, there must have been considerable loss on the right-hand side, as we shall see in the reconstruction of line 1. Finally, it may well be that this is a draft: the interlinear additions may point in this direction, as do the corrections of letters in lines 1 and 3 (see COMMENTS).

This papyrus was preliminarily (and erroneously) described as a 'rental deed'.[3] Despite the extensive gaps in the papyrus, once it was realized that this is a contract of loan, it was possible to reconstruct the deed from known formulae in this type of contract. For the formulae in contracts of loans on papyrus see Kühnert, *Kreditgeschäft*; Rupprecht, *Darlehen* and Montevecchi, *Papirologia*, 225–9. See also

---

[1] The evidence for ἐπὶ ὑπατείας is so slight (see P.Panop. 22 line 5; P.Oxy. I 42 line 8 is a restoration) and late that it is not considered here.

[2] On the other hand, it is possible that some such word as ἀντίγραφον and/or ἑρμηνεία came before; see P.Yadin **5a** col. i line 1 and Lewis, *Documents,* ad loc. The possibility that we could have had here something parallel to P.Yadin **25** line 64 (= lines 28–29): ἐ]πράχθη [ἐν] Μ̣αωζα̣ π̣ε̣ρ̣ὶ Ζ̣[οο]ρ̣ω̣ν̣ ὑπατίας etc. (cf. **26** lines 17–18) is ruled out, since it is not an opening formula.

[3] Cf. Tov with Pfann, *Companion Volume*, first edition (1993), 66; but see 2nd edition (1995), 66.

Wolfe, 'Contract', for a short summary of the distinct nature of the loan with hypothec.

Date and Provenance

A. Cornelius Palma Frontonianus was ordinary consul for the first time in 99 with Q. Sosius Senecio, and for the second time in 109 with P. Calvisius Tullus Ruso. It seems plausible that, like much of the Seiyâl collection, this document too originated in Arabia. If so, then the presence of a consular date indicates that, by the time of its composition, Arabia had become a Roman province. These considerations would put the document in Palma's second consulate in 109, making it the earliest dated papyrus in Greek from Arabia,[4] and one of the earliest attestations for the use of Greek after the annexation.[5] It supplements our information on the early history of the province by documenting the existence of financial ties between people from Philadelphia (ʿAmman), one of the cities of what used to be the Decapolis (see below), and some residents of what used to be the Kingdom of Nabataea.

On the other hand, unlike the other papyri belonging to the Seiyâl collection, there is no apparent evidence that we are in the Jewish and Nabataean milieu with which we have become familiar through the archives of Babatha and Salome Komaïse: there are no obvious Jewish or Nabataean names in this fragment, and consequently no evidence that the document was written in what was formerly the Nabataean kingdom and had now become the province of Arabia. We should never lose sight of the fact that this group of papyri was not found in the course of a controlled archaeological excavation, and there is even a remote possibility that Naḥal Ḥever and the Judaean Desert are not the provenance of this particular papyrus.

The presence of people from Philadelphia raises further questions as to place and date. Until the annexation of the Nabataean kingdom and the creation of the province of Arabia in 106, Philadelphia, like the rest of the Decapolis, was part of the province of Syria.[6] In 106, together with a few other cities of the Decapolis, it was incorporated into the newly created province of Arabia.[7] If the document was written in Philadelphia, we cannot rule out the possibility that it belongs to Palma's first consulate, i.e. 99. The fact that inscriptions in Philadelphia, as in other cities of the Decapolis, used the Pompeian era rather than consular dates,[8] does not exclude the possibility that consular dates were used in documents on papyrus; thus the use of a

---

[4] See Lewis' introduction to P.Yadin **5** dated to 2 June 110.

[5] It is contemporary with a bilingual (Nabataean and Greek) epitaph found in Madaba and published by Milik, 'Nouvelles inscriptions', 242–3, no. 6. The Greek reads, line 4: ἔτους τρίτου ἐπαρχείας; the Nabataean reads: בשנת תלת להפרך בסר, 'the third year of the governor of Bosra'. The earliest inscription dated by the province is in Nabataean, see Negev, 'Nabatean Inscriptions', 117–18, no. 11: אתבני שנת תרתין להפרכיא, 'built in the second year of the Province'. For the vexed question of the use of Greek in Nabataea before the annexation, see Millar, *Roman Near East*, 400ff.

[6] It was governed, perhaps, as a separate administrative unit; see Isaac, 'Decapolis'.

[7] Schürer, Vermes, and Millar, *History* 2:158 n. 388; Sartre, *Trois études*, esp. 45.

[8] See Schürer, Vermes, and Millar, *History* 2:125–58.

consular date in our document does not speak against its being written in Philadelphia.[9] However, if it was written in Philadelphia, the use of the Greek language and the consular date will hardly be striking.[10]

Finally, it is possible that the papyrus was written in the province of Judaea along with some of the other papyri which belong to the Seiyâl collection, with P.Yadin **11** from the Babatha Archive (written in ʿEin-Gedi), and the Murabbaʿat papyri. Here too we find the use of consular dates in private documents.[11]

The document measures 6 x 9 cm.

Mus. Inv. 732
PAM 42.209

top margin

ὑπ]ατϵίας Κορνηλίου Πάλμα̣[
]ι̣ας Βαχχίου Φιλαδϵλφ.[
δ]ϵδανισμένοι παρ' αὐτ̣ο̣[ῦ
].του
]ν̣ κληρονόμοι τῶν κ.[
]α̣ι τὸ̣ δὲ προγϵγραμμέν̣[ον
καὶ βουληθῇ ὁ δϵδ[ανικὼς
] χρόνῳ̣ τϵλέσϵι τοῦ ὑπϵ̣[
]α̣ι ἐξέσστω αὐτῷ̣ διακατ[
.*vacat?* ϵ̣λ̣ι̣ *vacat?* ὑ̣πο̣θήκην τῷ̣ δϵδανικότι̣[
].[*c.5 letters*].λαι..ο̣λ[

bottom margin

[9] It does speak against its being written in Philadelphia in Egypt, though, where we find no consular dates in Greek documents until the third century; see Lewis, *Documents,* 27, who also explains away the exceptions. However, the possibility that the debtor(s) come(s) from Philadelphia in Egypt cannot be excluded.

[10] See Schürer, Vermes, and Millar, *History* 2:155–8; Wenning, 'Dekapolis', 19–23 on Philadephia; Isaac, 'Decapolis', 72–4 reviews the inscriptions of four soldiers from Philadelphia recruited into the Syrian army as proof of the full integration of that city into the empire. As it happens, there are very few Greek inscriptions from Philadelphia; see Millar, *Roman Near East,* 411; Graf, 'Hellenization'; the whole volume of *Aram* 4 (in which Graf's article appears) is devoted to various aspects of the Decapolis.

[11] See No. **69**; Mur **114**; Mur **115**.

2 Βακχίου 7 ἐξέcτω

TRANSLATION

1. In the consulship of <A.> Cornelius Palma[and <P.> Calvisius Tullus (or <Q.> Sosius Senecio), they acknowledge
2.]*ias* son (or daughter) of Bacchius from Philadelphia [and X son of X that they have received from Y a sum of money?
3.]they have taken a loan from him [upon an hypothec, of a house(?) an orchard(?) whose abutters are . . .
4.]*n* on the south the heirs of K[they should pay the debt
5.].. mentioned before[and the interest? on such and such a date. And if they fail to pay it
6.]at the time that is fixed and the creditor wishes, he (the debtor) will pay [the interest for overtime
7.]and(?) let it be possible for him (the creditor) to take possession of[
8.]the hypothec [will be forfeit] to the creditor[
9.] [*traces of letters*]

COMMENTS

L. 1 If the year is 109, then we have to restore $\overline{\beta}$ after the name of Cornelius Palma as well as some of the elements of his colleague's name—P. Calvisius Tullus Ruso.[12] It is assumed that Calvisius's *praenomen* as well as the second *cognomen* of each consul ('Frontonianus' and 'Ruso') were omitted. If we were to include the two *cognomina* as well as the verb ὁμολογοῦcιν, a loss of approximately 53 letters (+ day and month?), all on the right-hand margin, must be allowed for—a very wide piece of papyrus if we add to it the length of the papyrus strap in line 8. This is less likely than the possibility that the abridged forms of the consuls' names were used. Therefore [ὑπ]ατείαc Κορνηλίου Πάλμα̣[τὸ $\overline{\beta}$ καὶ Καλουιcίου Τούλλου], a loss of 23 letters, may be restored in the first line. It is a mere coincidence, of course, that three years earlier, A. Cornelius Palma Frontonianus, as governor of Syria, annexed Arabia (Dio 68.14.5).[13] If the year is 99, we must restore the name of Q. Sosius Senecio: [ὑπ]ατείαc Κορνηλίου Πάλμα̣[καὶ Cωcίου Cενεκίωνοc]—a loss of 19 letters. In either case, the day and the month may have followed.

It is assumed that we have here a *homologia*, and therefore the verb ὁμολογεῖν must have stood before the name in line 1. Later on we learn that there was more than one debtor: see line 3: [δ]εδανιcμένοι and therefore ὁμολογοῦcιν may be restored. It follows that another name must have followed or, less likely, preceded that of]*ias* son of Bacchius, and that both are the debtors of line 3. Note, though, that the singular is used in line 6: τελέcει. The interchange in the writer's mind between plural and singular may also account for the fact that, in line 3, the final *iota* in [δ]εδανιcμένοι is corrected from *sigma*. The *homologia* form appears in the three known contracts of loan from the Judaean desert: P.Yadin **11** lines 2–3 = 14–15: ὁμολογῶ ἔχειν καὶ ὀφείλειν cοι ἐν δάνει ἀργυρίου . . . . P.Yadin **17** lines 3–6 = lines 21–5: ὡμολογήcατο Ἰούδαc . . . ὥcτε . . . ἀπε[c]χηκέναι παρ' αὐτῆc . . . ἀργυρίου . . .; Mur **114** lines 9–12: Ὁμολο[γῶ . . .]cοι ἀργυρίου . . . ἃ καὶ ἀπέcχον καὶ ἠρίθμημε.

L. 2]ι̣αc Βαχχίου. ']*ias* son (or daughter) of Bacchius'. The trace before αc seems to belong to this line rather than to the *delta* from the line below. It looks like the tail of an *iota* (see e.g. the first *iota* in line 7 and the last *iota* in line 8). If so, then [Ιου]δ̣αc is excluded. Endless possibilities exist (see Dornseiff, *Rückläufiges Wörterbuch,* 131ff.). Ὀνίαc is attested in the Babatha archive (see P.Yadin **5b** col. ii line 3: Ὀνίαc C̣ίμω[νοc]). There is no reason, though, in the absence of other evidence in the papyrus for a Jewish and Nabataean milieu, to restrict the restoration to names from this milieu.

L. 2 Βάκχιοc is a common Greek name, see Fraser and Matthews, *Lexicon,* 1:98, with an example of the spelling Βάχχ- from Euboia; see also Preisigke, *Namenbuch,* 70, 72; Foraboschi, *Onomasticon,* 75. For κχ becoming χχ, see Gignac, *Grammar,* 1:100, citing P.Gron. 2 line 1: Βαχχιάδοc.

---

12 *PIR*^{2} C 1411–12; in the *fasti* the cognomen Ruso is missing, see Vidman, *Fasti,* 47.

13 For his years as governor of Syria, see Eck, 'Jahres- und Provinzialfasten' 1982, 340ff.

L. 2 Φιλαδελφ.[. Φιλαδελφε̣[ύc] or Φιλαδελφε̣[ῖc] since both debtors could have come from Philadelphia. On the city of the Decapolis, Philadelphia, see INTRODUCTION.

L. 2 It is in this line that the clause ἔχειν or ἐcχηκέναι with παρὰ δεῖνoc with the sum of money borrowed must have come, since παρ' αὐτ̣ο̣υ in line 3 implies that the creditor has already been named.

L. 3 The left-hand stroke of a *mu* is corrected to form a *sigma* in [δ]εδανιcμένοι; the final *iota* in [δ]εδανιcμένοι is corrected from *sigma*; on the interchange from sing. to pl., see COMMENTS to line 1.

L. 3 παρ' αὐτο̣[ῦ] could be restored safely since the creditor in this document is certainly a single person as demonstrated by the participle of the verb δανείζειν in line 6: ὁ δεδ[ανικώc], and in line 8: τῷ δεδανικότι.

L. 4]ν̣ [ν]ό̣του κληρονόμοι τῶν κ.[. In the papyri from Arabia (as well as in those from Palestine and Dura-Europus), the neighbours are given in east-west-south-north order (e.g. No. **64** lines 9–10 = lines 30–31), whereas in Egypt the order is south-north-east-west. If the 'non-Egyptian' order was followed here, then the neighbours to the east and west will have been named in the preceding line. This would make it far too long. Perhaps there was variation in the order of abutters as in No. **8a** lines 8–9, where the order is south-east-north-west.[14] Another possibility is that fewer than four abutters are mentioned, as in land declarations, where only two abutters were named.[15] Be this as it may, I suggest that in lines 3–4 it was stated that the two debtors borrowed money from the creditor upon hypothec (ἐφ' ὑποθήκῃ), whose abutters are, etc.

L. 5 τ̣ὸ δὲ προγεγραμμέν̣[ον]. Scil. δάνειον or ἀργύριον or κεφάλαιον. However, the second letter in the line may be an *alpha* and not an *omicron* (i.e. τά) and thus perhaps τ̣ὰ δὲ προγεγραμμέν̣[α], as in P.Adler 4 lines 14–15: [ἀ]ποτίcω coι τὰ προγεγραμμέν̣α διπλᾶ, but the parallel is not exact. In either case, it could have been followed by something like καὶ τοὺc τόκουc. Because of δέ, the verb of paying back ἀποδότω—or rather ἀποδότωcαν—is likely to have followed τ̣ὸ προγεγραμμένον.[16] In view of what comes in the next line, it was at this point that the time of payment was fixed.

L. 6 χρόνῳ . . . τελέcει τοῦ ὑπε̣[. We may safely restore τοῦ ὑπε̣[ρπεcόντοc χρόνου τόκουc], or [τοὺc καθήκονταc τόκουc], as in P.Oxy. II 269 (57 CE) lines 8–12, esp. lines 9–10: (ἐκτείcω) . . . καὶ τοῦ ὑπε̣ρπεcόντοc χρ[ό]νου τοὺc καθήκονταc τόκουc. Disregarding for the moment the interlinear addition, the preceding clause can be restored along the lines of e.g. P.Grenf. II, 18 (127 BCE) lines 13–17: ἐὰν δὲ μὴ ἀποδῶcι ἐν τῷ ὡριcμένῳ χρόνῳ, ἀποτειcάτωcαν παραχρῆμα ἡμιόλιον καὶ τοῦ ὑπε̣ρπεcόντοc χρόνου τόκουc.[17] We find a somewhat different formula in Mur **114** lines 14–16: Ἐὰν δὲ μὴ ἀποδῶ τῇ ὡριcμέν[ῃ] προθεcμίᾳ, τελέcω coι τὸν ἐγ διατάγματοc τόκ[ον] μέχρι οὗ ἂν ἀποδῶ; as well as in P.Yadin **11** lines 7–8 = 22–23: κα̣ὶ ἐά̣ν̣ coι [μ]ὴ̣ ἀποδώcω τῇ ὡριcμένῃ προ[θ]ε̣cμίᾳ, καθὼc προγέγραπται τ[ὸ δίκα]ιον ἔc̣[ται] coι κτᾶcθ[αι χ]ρ̣ᾶcθ̣α̣ι̣ π[ωλ]ε̣ῖ̣ν̣ διο̣[ικεῖν τὴ]ν αὐτὴν ὑποθήκην. For τελέcει rather than τελέcουcιν see ad line 1.

The interlinear clause καὶ βουληθῇ ὁ δεδ[ανικώc] introduces a new element, absent from the model we have so far followed: it seems to modify the harshness of the protasis (ἐὰν δὲ μὴ ἀποδῶcι ἐν τῷ ὡριcμένῳ χρόνῳ) by leaving to the discretion of the creditor whether or not to carry out the so-called penalty clause.

L. 7]α̣ι ἐξέcτω αὐτῷ διακατ[. One could restore [κ]α̣ί but it is difficult to know what other phrase was linked to the foreclosure phrase which comes now. It is hard to decide whether we should restore

---

[14] But see INTRODUCTION to No. **8a** for previous reconstructions of the order of the abutters to the property sold in No. **8a**.

[15] E.g. P.Yadin **16** line 21 and No. **62** frg. a line 17. But note that only two were required by the 'census form', cf. *Dig.* 50.15.4: 'quos duos vicinos proximos habeat'.

[16] As in P.Adler 10 line 11: τὸ δὲ δάνειον τοῦτο ἀποδότω ὁ δεδανειcμένοc; it precedes the noun in P.Mich. III 190: ἀποδότω δὲ 'Αριcτοκλῆc Θεοκλῇ τὸ προγεγρα(μμένον) δά(νειον).

[17] See also P.Grenf. II 21 (113 BCE) lines 12–16, and I, no. 20 (127 BCE) lines 12–14; SB XIV 11284 (100–117 CE) lines 10–13; cf. P.Diog. 25 (132 CE) lines 10–12: [ἐὰν δέ τι πα]ραβαίνω, ἐκτείcω coι τὸ δ̣[άνειον cὺν ἡμιολίᾳ καὶ] τοῦ ὑπερπεcόντοc χρό[νου τοὺc τόκουc]; P.Oxy. II 269 (57 CE) lines 8–10: ἐὰν δὲ μ[ὴ ἀπ]οδ[ῶ]ι καθὰ γέγραπται ἐκτείcω coι τ[ὸ π]ρο[κ]είμενον κεφ[άλ]αιον μεθ' ἡμιολίαc καὶ τοῦ ὑπερπεcόντοc χρ[ό]νου τοὺc καθήκονταc τόκουc.

διακατ[οχῆ] or διακατ[έχειν], and impossible to take either of them in the technical sense of *possessio bonorum*.[18] I would, therefore, translate it in the general sense of 'to take possession of', 'to possess', as seems to be the sense in UPZ II 162 (117 BCE = MChr. 31 = Jur.Pap. 80), col. ix line 18.[19] Although the hypothec appears only in line 8, it seems reasonable that the διακατ[οχῆ] or διακατ[έχειν] refer to it. Unfortunately, all the examples of διακατέχειν with ὑποθήκη are late (vi century) and they all appear in an identical formula, which is seen most completely in SB XIV 11373 lines 4–6: ὁμολογῶ ἑκουςίως καὶ αὐθαιρέτως μεμιςθῶςθαι παρὰ τῆς cῆς εὐγενείας ἐφ' ὅςον χρόνον διακατέχεις τὴν γενομένην ςοι ὑποθήκην παρὰ Θεονίλλας Ἐπιφανίου ἀπὸ τῆς αὐτῆς πόλεως; cf. SB V 7519 (510 CE) lines 4–6; P.Stras. IV 248 (560 CE) lines 4–5; V 398 (553 CE) lines 5–8.

One may object to reading διακατ[οχῆ] or διακατ[έχειν] on the grounds that the gap between δια and κατ[suggests that they belong to two different words. If we were in Egypt, one could think of διὰ καταλογείου, e.g. P.Oxy. LI, 3638 lines 29–31: κυρία ἡ παραχώρηςις διςςὴ γραφεῖςα, ἥνπερ ὁπηνίκα ἐὰν αἱρῇ ποιήςομαί ςοι καὶ διὰ καταλογείου μηδὲν ἕτερον λαμβάνων παρὰ ςοῦ, τῶν τελῶν καὶ γραμματικῶν ὄντων πρὸς ςὲ τὴν Τετςεῖριν. This deed of cessation was to be deposited at the *katalogeion* 'a record office of legal judgements' in the charge of the *archidicastes*, chief justice, in Alexandria. 'This office acted as the place of "publication" δημοςίωςις, of private documents, whereby, through their registration there, they acquired the legal status so that they could be produced in court as evidence'.[20] Can we assume that an office bearing the same name operated in Arabia to register deeds of loan?[21]

Only three instances of the foreclosure formula beginning with ἐξεῖναι could be found: P.Mert. III 109 (ii CE) lines 3–4: [ἐὰ]ṿ δὲ μὴ ἀπ̣ο̣δῷ κ̣[αθὰ γ]έγραπται ἐξέ̣ς[τω τῷ Ὠφελᾶτι . . . ἐ]νβαδεύειν . . . [τὰ]ς̣ πρ̣ο̣κειμένας [ἀρούρας] καὶ κρατεῖν;[22] P.Oxy. XVII 2134 (*c*.170 CE) lines 24–25: ‹καὶ› ὁπόταν βούλῃ ἐξεῖναί ςοι τῆς ὑποθήκης κατοχὴν ποιήςαςθαι καὶ τῶν αὐτῶν ἀρουρ[ῶ]ν κατοχὴν ποιεῖςθ[αι]; and P.Oxy. III 506 (143 CE), line 49: ἐ̣ξόντος τῷ δεδανεικότι ὁπόταν αἱρῆται κατοχὴν [αὐτῶν .....]χίςα[ςθ]αι πρὸ τοῦ τῶν ἐνκτήςεων βιβλιοφυλακίου.

L. 8 Clearly, the forfeit of the hypothec to the creditor is envisioned here as well, but the context is unrecoverable.

The praxis-clause—cf. e.g. P.Oxy. XIV 1640 (252 CE) lines 8–9: τῆς πράξεως παρά τε ἐμοῦ καὶ ἐκ τῶν ὑπαρχόντων μοι πάντων—is missing, and cannot be read in the traces left from line 9. We find it even in loans guaranteed by hypothec; thus P.Yadin **11** (124 CE) lines 24–25: [καὶ ἡ πρᾶξις ἔςται ςοι καὶ τῷ παρά ςου κ]α̣ὶ ἄ̣λλῳ π̣α̣ν̣[τὶ] τῷ διά [ςο]υ̣ ἢ ὑ̣[πέρ ςο]υ̣ κυρ̣ίως̣ τ̣[οῦτο τὸ γράμμα προφέροντι, ἔκ τε ἐ]μοῦ καὶ ἐκ τῶν Ἐλαζάρου̣ πατρός μου ὑ̣παρχ̣[ό]ν̣των̣ [πάντῃ] π̣ά̣[ν]τ̣ω̣[ν], ὧ̣[ν κεκτήμεθα] κ̣α̣[ὶ ὧν ἐ]ὰ̣ν̣ ἐπικτηςώμ̣ε̣θ̣α̣ [π]ρ̣ά̣[ς]ς̣ο̣ν̣τι κ̣υ̣ρ̣[ί]ως.

[18] That is praetorian succession as opposed to κληρονομία = testamentary succession, see P.Meyer 23 (end of iv CE) ad line 3, p. 95; cf. Mason, *Greek Terms,* 36, where he gives as an example SB I 1010 (249 CE) = *FIRA* III^2, p. 183, a bilingual text which has in Latin: 'Rogo domine des mihi bonorum possessionem matris meae Aureliae . . . ex ea parte edicti quae legitimis heredibus bonorum possessionem daturum te polliceris'; and in Greek: Αἰτῶ τὴν διακατοχὴν τῶν τῆς μητρός μου.

[19] See Wilcken, UPZ II, p. 89: 'Διακατέχειν steht . . . als Äquivalent für κυριεύειν'; Meyer, Jur.Pap., p. 276: 'διακατέχειν hat in ptolemäischer Zeit die allgemeine Bedeutung "besitzen"'; it seems that we have here the same pre-Roman *allgemeine Bedeutung*. P.Tebt. I 88, line 16 given as an example for this general sense in Preisigke, *Wörterbuch* is apparently not a good example: the editors suggest that the διά of διακατέχειν is a mistake (see *ad loc.*). This general sense is also present in P.Dura 32 (254 CE, a divorce) line 9, where the husband declares that he restored to his wife everything that he had received from her: πά[ντα ὅςα παρ]ὰ αὐτῆς διακατεῖχεν (repeated in line 13 from the wife's point of view).

[20] The citations are from Cockle, 'Archives', 116; see also Burkhalter, 'Archives'.

[21] The consular dating rules out the possibility that the papyrus was written in Egypt and brought to Arabia (or Palestine) in modern or ancient times; cf. n. 9 above.

[22] See J. D. Thomas's introduction to P.Mert. III 109.

67. XḤev/Se papText Mentioning Timber gr

Ein Gedi?, before 127 or 128 CE ?

(PLS. XXXI AND XLIII)

THE fragment (*olim* XḤev/Se Gr. 5) contains twelve lines of text. Part of the left margin has been preserved. Since the date comes at the end of the document, and χαίρε̣ι̣ν̣ occurs in line 3, it is very likely that the first line of the fragment preserves the beginning of the document. The right and bottom margins have not been preserved. It is impossible to gauge the length of the lines. The verso is blank. A horizontal line between lines 10 and 11, marking a *paragraphos*, follows the date. The two last lines were written by a different hand.

The names Molimas (Molimos?) (line 1) and perhaps Onesimos (line 11), both Greek names[1], suggest an 'imperial' environment of freedmen on an imperial domain.[2] Combined with the reference to the felling or collection of timber in line 4 (ξυλ<ϵ>ία), one may wonder whether there is a connection to the balsam groves, cultivated by the imperial *fiscus* after the Great Revolt.[3] We know that even the pruned twigs of the balsam, the *xylobalsamum*, were exploited by the *fiscus* by being boiled down into perfumes; within the first five years following the subjection of Judaea, the *xylobalsamum* earned 800,000 sesterces for the *fiscus*.[4] Even the wood (*lignum*), of which the best kind was that resembling the boxwood, was valued because of its excellent scent.[5] To reinforce this hypothesis, it may not be amiss to cite one of Bar Kokhba's letters to two of his henchmen in Ein Gedi, since we may safely assume that Bar Kokhba took over the imperial domain in Ein Gedi. In P.Yadin **44** (unpublished),[6] there is a warning to prevent cattle from destroying the trees (lines 10–11); the warning is followed by the stricture: 'that no man should get near the *Lotem*' (lines 12–13). Again, one may legitimately think of the precious balsam groves. See below, DATE AND PROVENANCE.

---

[1] Admittedly the name Molimas (or Molimos) is not attested elsewhere.

[2] Cf. Theodotus, ἀπελεύθεροc βαcιλίccηc 'Αγριππείνηc, in Hachlili, 'Goliath Family', 33ff., who, despite the author's hesitations (ibid., 46), may well have been connected with the imperial balsam groves in Jericho; see Cotton and Eck, 'Staatsmonopol und seine Folgen', n. 12.

[3] For the balsam in Ein Gedi, see Josephus *Ant.* 9.7; Galen *De Antidotis* 1.4 = Stern, *Greek and Latin Authors* no. 391; Eusebius *Onom.* 86 (Klostermann); Hieron. *Comm. in Hiezechielem* 27:17 (PL XXV, col. 256); *b. Šabb* 26a; see Mazar, 'Inscription on the Floor of the Synagogue in En-Gedi', 20–21; with Lieberman, 'Preliminary Note'; for the cultivation of the balsam by the *fiscus*, see Cotton and Eck, 'Staatsmonopol und seine Folgen'.

[4] Pliny *NH* 12.118 = Stern, *Greek and Latin Authors* no. 213; cf. Cotton and Geiger, *Masada* II ad *Doc.Mas.* 725 and 749b.

[5] Pliny *NH* 12.119 = Stern, *Greek and Latin Authors* no. 213.

[6] Yadin, 'Expedition D', no. 8, pp. 44–5. I am grateful to A. Yardeni for allowing me to see a complete transcription of the text.

Date and Provenance

It is reasonable to assume that the name of the writer came first and that of the addressee second. Ein Gedi is more likely to be the addressee's provenance than the writer's, unless both parties came from Ein Gedi. Ein Gedi is described in lines 1–2 as a 'village of our lord Caesar': ['Εν]γαδων κυρίου κ[αίcαροc κώμηc]. The same title occurs in P.Yadin **11** of 6 May 124: ἐν Ἐνγαδοῖc κώμῃ κυρίου Καίcαροc (line 1 = line 12).[7] The reality behind the designation κώμη κυρίου Καίcαροc is far from clear.[8] Ein Gedi was destroyed in the Great Revolt.[9] The Babatha Archive bears witness to its revival in the first quarter of the second century, though it did not regain its former status as a centre of a toparchy (Josephus *B.J.* 3.55), but was incorporated into the toparchy of Jericho (P.Yadin **16** line 16). A detachment of a milliary cohort, under the command of a centurion, was stationed in Ein Gedi; its presence there is attested in P.Yadin **11** of 6 May 124.[10] It seems reasonable to assume that the balsam groves in Ein Gedi, over which the Romans fought pitched battles with the Jews in 68 CE,[11] were now under direct Roman exploitation and protection (see above). Perhaps no more than that is implied by the designation κώμη κυρίου Καίcαροc: 'the imperial possessions here were restricted to the famous balsam trees',[12] for notwithstanding the straightforward implication of the designation, κώμη κυρίου Καίcαροc, 'it is also a fact that there was private property in the village',[13] as attested in P.Yadin **11**, **19**, and **20**. The same seems to be true of the 'imperial village of BephPhoura' (κώμηc ΒηφΦούρηc κυριακῆc) in Syria Coele in the middle of the third century, as revealed in *P.Euphr.* 1 (28/8/245):[14] despite the designation κώμη κυριακή, the litigation before the provincial governor, described in the petition, concerns the possession (see νόμη, lines 12–13) of land (χώραc, line 6) in the village.[15]

In line 10, the day of the month, the Nonae of May, i.e. 7 May, has been preserved. The names of the consuls in the preceding line(s) cannot be recovered. A tentative

---

[7] The full context is ἐπὶ ὑπάτων Μανείου Ἀκειλίου Γλαβρίωνοc καὶ Τορκουάτου Θηβανιανοῦ πρ[ὸ] μιᾶc νωνῶν Μαίων ἐν Ἐνγαδοῖc κώμῃ κυρίου Καίcαροc, lines 12–13 (= line 1).

[8] The designation cannot be equated with 'Hadrianic Petra', as claimed by Lewis ('Babatha Archive', 244), which is merely an honorific title.

[9] Pliny *NH* 5.73 (= Stern, *Greek and Latin Authors*, no. 204): 'Infra hos (i.e. the Essenes) Engada oppidum fuit, secundum ab Hierosolymis fertilitate palmetorumque nemoribus, nunc alterum bustum'. The hypothesis that some of the refugees from Ein Gedi must have settled in Maḥoza helps to explain the close ties between families in Ein Gedi and Maḥoza so apparent in the Babatha Archive; see Cotton, 'Ein Gedi Between the Two Revolts'.

[10] On the cohors I Thracum milliaria in Ḥebron, see Speidel, 'Cohors I Thracum Milliaria', 170–72; Isaac, *Limits of Empire*, 137, 174, 430; Cotton, 'Courtyard(s)', 197–8. A Roman bath dated by the coins to this period has been excavated in Ein Gedi; see Mazar and Dunayevsky, 'En-Gedi. Third Season', 128–30; Mazar and Dunayevsky, 'En-Gedi. Fourth and Fifth Seasons', 142–3.

[11] Pliny *NH* 12.111–13 (= Stern, *Greek and Latin Authors*, no. 213).

[12] Isaac, 'Babatha Archive', 70.

[13] Isaac, ibid.; see Cotton, 'Courtyard(s)'.

[14] Ἰουλίῳ Πρείcκῳ τῷ διαcημοτάτῳ ἐπάρχῳ Μεcοποταμίαc διέποντι τὴν ὑπατείαν παρὰ Ἀρχώδου Φαλλαιου καὶ Φιλώτα Νιcραιαδου καὶ Ουορωδου Cυμιοcβαραχου καὶ Αβεδcαυτα Αβεδιαρδα ὄντων ἀπὸ κώμηc ΒηφΦούρηc κυριακῆc τῆc περὶ Ἀππάδαναν, lines 3–5; see Feissel and Gascou, 'Documents 1. Les pétitions', 71.

[15] See the editor's comments, 'Documents 1. Les pétitions', 83–4.

terminus ante quem is suggested by a number of considerations. In P.Yadin **16** of 4 December 127, Ein Gedi is not designated κώμη κυρίου Καίϲαροϲ. Judah son of Eleazar is said to come from κώμηϲ Αἰνγαδδων περὶ Ἱερειχοῦντα τῆϲ Ἰουδαίαϲ (lines 15–16). P.Yadin **16** is an authorized copy of a land declaration submitted at the census. It is precisely in such a formal document that one would expect the entire title of the place to be present.[16] By April 128, and possibly before that date, the Roman unit left Ein Gedi.[17] The title κώμη κυρίου Καίϲαροϲ, whatever its implications, may no longer have been in use. Thus 127, or rather 128, may be cautiously proposed as a *terminus ante quem* for the present papyrus.

The fragment measures 7 x 4 cm.

Mus. Inv. 866
PAM 40.642

Μ̣ολιμα̣ϲ̣..[*? letters* Εν]
γαδων Κυρίου Κ[αίϲαροϲ κώμηϲ
χαίρει̣ν̣. Αλλαϲ[
ξυλ̣ί̣αϲ ἧϲ ἐξαλ̣[
τα λ̣ύ̣ω καὶ κ.[
...α̣τιαϲ λεγο̣[
[...]τ̣ὴν δὲ ἡμε[
traces
traces
[. ν]ώ̣νων Μαίω[ν

---

[16] See INTRODUCTION TO THE GREEK DOCUMENTARY TEXTS on the official aspects of P.Yadin **16** and No. **62**.

[17] See Cotton, 'Courtyard(s)', 199 on the relationship between P.Yadin **11** and **19**.

m. 2

[...]ων cυνα.εc.[

[δην]ά̣ρια τριακόντ̣[α

4 ξυλείας

COMMENTS

L. 1 Μ̣ολιμα̣ς̣..[. The name is not attested; nor is Molimos, if the sixth letter is read as *omicron* and not *alpha*. Perhaps the letters which follow Μ̣ολιμα̣ς̣ belonged to the name, i.e. Μ̣ολιμα̣ς̣ is not the whole name. The name Μόνιμοc is attested,[18] but reading the third letter as *nu* is difficult.

Ll. 1–2 The first element of the name of Ein Gedi, which occupied the very end of line 1, should be restored as Εν-, i.e. Ενγαδων. In the Babatha Archive, the name is always spelled Ενγ-, not Εγγ-. This is so, not for the reason given by Lewis ('in recognition of the fact that the first two letters represent not the Greek prefix ἐν but the Hebrew word for a spring [עַין]', *Documents*, 20), but 'as the common deviation from what we think of as "conventional" spelling' (see Wasserstein, 'Documents from the Cave of Letters', 376 and n. 4 there). The combination -νγ instead of -γγ occurs in the Babatha Archive in purely Greek words.

Ll. 1–2 Ενγαδων. The declined form of the name Ein Gedi in the plural occurs also in the Babatha Archive; see Lewis, *Documents*, 20.

Ll. 1–2 It is likely that the phrase [τῶν ἀπὸ Εν]γαδων Κυρίου Κ[αίcαροc κώμηc] followed the name of the addressee; cf. No. **69** line 5: Ακαβαc Μηειρω τῶν ἀπ̣ὸ κ̣ώμηc Ἰακείμων; P.Yadin **5**a col. 1 lines 5–6: ἐ̣γὼ Ἰώcηπο̣ς̣ τοῦ̣ Ἰωcήπ[ου ἐπι]κ̣αλουμ[ένου] Ζαβούδο[υ] τῶ̣ν̣ ἀπὸ̣ Μαωζων; Mur **115** line 2: Ἐ̣λ̣ε̣α̣ῖοc Cίμωνοc τῶν ἀπ̣ὸ κ(ώμηc) Γαλωδῶν.

L. 2 Κυρίου Κ[αίcαροc]. See above, DATE AND PROVENANCE.

L. 4 ξυλίαc. 'Felling and carrying of wood', LSJ. This meaning is present in Plb. 21.39.12 and Jos. *B.J.* 6.153. However, in Plb. 3.42.3, as well as in SB XVI 12836,[19] it means 'felled wood', i.e. timber.

L. 4 ἧc ἐξαλ̣[. I cannot find a verb which takes the genitive as its object which would fit the context. Consequently, it is impossible to know the precise meaning of ξυλεία here; see preceding note.

L. 7 [...]τ̣ὴ̣ν δὲ ἡμε[. Either ἡμέ[ραν] or ἡμε[τέραν] can be restored.

Ll. 8–9 Perhaps the dating formula began already in line 8. The consuls' names preceded the [Ν]ώ̣νων Μαίω[ν]. Depending on the length of the lines in this document, the consular date may have been preceded by the regnal date.

L. 11 [...]ων cυνα.εc.[. Perhaps, instead of *alpha*, we should read *omicron*, followed by *nu*, and instead of *epsilon* and *sigma*, we should read *eta*, followed by *sigma*, of which only a trace remained: thus Ὀνήc̣[ιμοc] (Onesimos)—a well-attested name for slaves and freedmen; see Solin, *Namenbuch*, 2:914–9.

[18] Fraser and Matthews, *Lexicon* II:320.

[19] ἀ[πὸ δὲ τῆc] ξυλίαc δώcομέν coι ξύλ̣[ων] δέcμαc πεντήκον[τ]α̣, lines 27–29; see Sijpesteijn, 'Der Veteran Aelius Syrion', 211–15.

68. XḤev/Se papText Mentioning a Guardian gr

Province of Arabia

(PLS. XXXI AND XLIV)

THE document (*olim* XḤev/Se Gr. 5) contains two fragments of unequal size. It is impossible to place the fragments in any relationship to each other. The verso of both is blank. The much larger frg. a contains six incomplete lines, and perhaps traces of two more lines (lines 1 and 8). No margins have been preserved. It is impossible to know how much was lost of each margin. Lines 2–4 begin and end at approximately the same place in the left and right margins. From line 5, the document tapers in on both sides. Compared with lines 2–4, line 5 has lost approximately two letters on the left and three letters on the right; line 6 has lost approximately five letters on the left and four letters on the right; line 7 has lost approximately nine letters on the left and seven letters on the right. At the same time, the tear in the interior of the papyrus, which extends down to line 5, decreases from *c*.17 letters in line 2 to *c*.15 letters in line 3, *c*.8 letters in line 4, and *c*.5 letters (whose traces are seen) in line 5.

No reference to the date or provenance has been preserved, nor can the context of the papyrus be ascertained. However, the mention of dates in line 5 brings us to the familiar milieu of Maḥoza and its date groves, described so many times in the Babatha Archive and in the archive of Salome Komaïse daughter of Levi. The presence of a Nabataean *epitropos* in line 4 confirms that we are in the Roman province of Arabia.[1] The *epitropos* could be the guardian either of a woman or of a minor, since in the Greek documents from Arabia (as well as from Judaea), the term ἐπίτροπος is employed for both.[2]

Frg. a measures 11 x 8.5 cm; frg. b measures 1.5 x 2 cm.

Mus. Inv. 866
PAM 40.642

---

1 I.e. after the annexation of the kingdom; there are no Greek documents from the Nabataean kingdom.

2 See Wolff, 'Le droit', 279ff.; 'Römisches Provinzialrecht', 793ff. For Judaea, see COMMENTS ad No. **69** line 4.

Frg. a

1 *traces*

2].ιαϲ [*c.15 letters*] πλ..[

3].οϲαυ [*c.12 letters* ἐπί]τ̣ροποϲ̣[

4 ἐ]π̣ίτροπον α.[*c.6 letters*].μ̣ον Αβδομ̣[

5 δί]μ̣οιρον α.[.] φ[οι]νεικώ̣νω̣[ν

6 .....π]ρ̣ο̣ϲ̣η̣κόντων λεγομ̣ε̣[νων

7 ....].θαιν και.[

8 *traces?*

Frg. b

1] ..[

2]νχου

COMMENTS

L. 4 ἐ]π̣ίτροπον α.[*c.6 letters*].μ̣ον. Perhaps [ἐ]π̣ίτροπον ἀ̣[δελφὸν] ἐ̣μ̣όν, or ἄ[νδρα] ἐ̣μ̣όν. In either case, the *epitropos* would be the guardian of a woman (see INTRODUCTION). However, one expects ἀδελφόν or ἄνδρα μου, respectively. Thus, perhaps, a name Α̣[......].μον followed by 'Αβδομ̣[as a patronymic.

L. 4 Αβδομ̣[. For names derived from the Nabataean word for slave, see Negev, *Personal Names*, nos. 780–832; cf. COMMENTS ad No. **62** frg. b line 4.

L. 5 δί]μ̣οιρον. Perhaps [μέροϲ δί]μ̣οιρον should be restored, suggesting division of profits.

L. 5 φ[οι]νεικώ̣νω̣[ν]. In the other documents in this collection, as well as in the Babatha Archive, a date grove is designated tautologically κῆποϲ φοινεικῶνοϲ (see ad No. **64** lines 8 and 26). In No. **64** line 26, φοινεικώνων is a mistake for φοινεικῶνοϲ. Here, however, κῆποϲ does not precede φοινεικώνων; the latter may well be the plural of φοινικών.

69. XḤev/Se papCancelled Marriage Contract gr

Aristoboulias, Judaea, 130 CE

(PLS. XLV–XLVI)

Preliminary publication: H. M. Cotton, 'A Cancelled Marriage Contract from the Judaean Desert (XḤev/Ṣe Gr. 2)', *JRS* 84 (1994) 64–86, pls. I–II.

LIKE the other marriage contracts from the Judaean Desert, the marriage contract reproduced here (*olim* XḤev/Se Gr. 2) is also a double document—although very little is left of the inner text.[1] The papyrus has suffered extensive damage: it survives in nine fragments and it is worm-eaten. The largest fragment (frg. a) contains the three last lines of the inner text and sixteen lines of the outer text. The other fragments belong to the outer text. The text is written across the fibres, a feature which seems to be characteristic of double documents.[2] On the back of frg. a there are signatures of three witnesses, written across the fibres and crossed through; there are traces of more signatures on frg. a, as well as on the back of frg. e.

The marriage concluded in this document was terminated by death or divorce, as shown by the pen strokes crossing diagonally over the document, as well as over the signatures on the back, marking its cancellation. It must be stressed, however, that the use of crossing diagonal strokes (χιαϲμόϲ) does not, in itself, invalidate the document thus crossed. It is merely a visual representation of the fact that the document is no longer in force, so that it will no longer be used.[3] Presumably there was also a deed of divorce or a receipt for the return of the dowry.[4] In fact, the deed of divorce and the receipt may be combined in the same document. Thus, for example, in a deed of divorce from 96 CE (P.Oxy. II 266), the former wife acknowledges that in accordance with a contract of marriage, she has received the money she brought as dowry to her husband; this contract she now returns to him cancelled: ἧϲ τὴν ἐπίφορον (scil. ὁμολογίαν) αὐτόθεν ἀναδεδωκέναι [κεχιαϲμένην ε]ἰϲ ἀκύρωϲιν (lines 14–15).[5]

---

[1] On double documents see INTRODUCTION TO THE ARAMAIC AND HEBREW DOCUMENTARY TEXTS and INTRODUCTION TO THE GREEK DOCUMENTARY TEXTS and Lewis, *Documents*, 6–10.

[2] See n. 1.

[3] Rupprecht, *Quittung*, 80–81; see also list of cancelled documents in Maresch and Packman, Papyrologica Coloniensia, 75–8, ad no. 79.

[4] On acts of divorce on papyri, see Montevecchi, 'Ricerche', 20ff.; *Papirologia*, 205–7 (and the 'Addenda' to the *Papirologia*, 568); Rupprecht, *Quittung*, 43–9; for receipts, see e.g. P.Oxy. II 268 from 58 CE, where the widow and her daughter acknowledge receipt of the mother's dowry from the dead man's nephew (lines 7–9); the marriage settlement is now void: καὶ εἶναι ἄκυρον τὴν δηλουμένην τοῦ γάμου ϲυγχώρηϲιν (lines 12–13); cf. P.Lond. II 178 (145 CE); P.Oxy. IV 460; P.Col.Youtie II 67; P.Tebt. II 460. The Mishna also knows of a receipt (שובר) given to the husband once he pays the ketubbah, cf. *m. Ket.* 9.9; *m. Giṭ* 2.5; 8.8, and, in this volume, the INTRODUCTION to No. **13.**

[5] Cf. P.Oxy. II 362; 363; P.Lips. 27 (= M.Chr. 293, 123 CE).

In the preliminary publication, only the outer text of frg. a was transcribed and discussed. Here the inner text as well as frgs. b–f are transcribed. There are three additional small fragments with letters on them. It seems that frgs. b, c, and d belonged to the left-hand margin and frg. f to the bottom of the document. It is difficult to place the fragments so as to recover any continuous or coherent text. Nevertheless, the meaning and significance of the document are apparent from frg. a, the largest surviving fragment.

Date and Provenance

The marriage contract is dated by regnal and consular years to 130 CE. This combination of dating by regnal and consular dates is found also in Mur **115** written in Judaea, but it does not exist, as far as we can tell, in the documents from Roman Arabia, where we find the following variations: (1) consular, regnal and provincial years; (2) consular and provincial years; (3) only consular date (see INTRODUCTION TO THE GREEK DOCUMENTARY TEXTS and Lewis, *Documents*, 28). The month and day are missing.[6] The date of cancellation of our contract is unknown, except that it was after 130 CE. The Bar Kokhba Revolt, 132–5, may explain the preservation of the document. If so, the marriage did not last long. One may speculate, though, whether the cancellation had something to do with the revolt.

The marriage contract was written 'in Aristoboulias of Zeiphênê' (ἐν Ἀριςτοβουλιάδι τῆς Ζε̣ι̣φηνῆς). The location is not without interest. Zeiphênê is biblical Zif (זיף): the name stands both for a city[7] and for the adjoining desert.[8] It is into this desert (εἰς τὴν ἔρημον Ζιφῶν) that St. Euthymius wandered, according to his biographer, to see the caves where David hid from Saul.[9] While sojourning there, he succeeded in exorcising an evil spirit which had taken possession of the son of one of the headmen of the village of Aristoboulias (υἱὸς πρωτοκωμήτου τινὸς Ἀριςτοβουλιάδος).[10] This is, in fact, the only other attestation from antiquity for the Aristoboulias of our document.

The biblical city of Zif is identified with present-day Tel Zif,[11] a well-protected hill which rises seventy metres above its hilly surroundings (880 m), situated on the north-south road from Hebron to Carmel-Maʿon as well as on an important road which passes through the desert to the Dead Sea. Aristoboulias is generally identified with Khirbet Istabûl which lies not far from Tel Zif.[12] The presence of Aristoboulias in this

---

[6] The absence of a month and day is lamented by Benoit in one of the two references to this papyrus in *DJD* II: 'dans un autre pap. grec du désert de Juda (encore inédit) la 14e année d'Hadrien correspond aux consuls de l'an 130 ap. J.-C.; malheureusement le mois et le jour ont disparu' (p. 250).

[7] Josh 15:24, 55; 1 Chr 11:8; Jos. *Ant.* 8.246: Ζιφά. Zif is one of the four cities whose names appear on the LMLK stamps from Lachish all dated to *c.*700 BCE, see Tufnell, *Lachish*, 342ff.; Na'aman, 'Hezekiah'. I am grateful to Ts. Schneider for this information.

[8] 1 Sam 23:14-24; 26:2.

[9] Kyrillos of Skythopolis, *Vita Euthymii*, ed. E. Schwarz, 1939, 11.

[10] Ibid., 12.

[11] Kochavi, *Judaea,* 68, no. 178; Abel, *Géographie* II, 490.

[12] Abel, *Géographie* II, 490; Kochavi, *Judaea*, 70, no. 190, The aphaeresis (removal of initial letters) from Aristoboulias to Arabic Istabûl is the result of a familiar, well-attested process, viz. the metanalysis of the first

document should restore confidence in the Hasmonaean foundation suggested by M. Avi Yonah.[13]

The bridegroom in this document, Aqabas son of Meir, is said to come from κ̣ώμη Ἰακείμων. It seems possible to identify the place with Kh. Yuqin (also called Kh. Bani Dar) two and a half km north of Zif and three and a half km north of Aristoboulias.[14] The Aramaic No. **9** was written in Yaqum (ביקום) or Yaqim (ביקים), see *recto* line 1, and *verso* lines 2, 5.

The relationship between Aristoboulias and Yaqim/Yakum, on the one hand, and Zeiphênê, on the other, must be one of dependence (or hierarchy); presumably Zeiphênê was the capital of the administrative subdivision to which both Aristoboulias and Yaqim/Yakum belonged. The phrasing is all but identical to another marriage contract from Judaea: the present marriage contract is concluded ἐν Ἀριστοβουλιάδι τῆς Ζ̣ε̣ιφ̣ηνῆς and the groom Aqabas son of Meir is τῶν ἀ̣π̣ὸ κ̣ώμης Ἰακείμων τ̣[ῆς Ζειφηνῆς(?)], whereas the other contract was concluded ἐν Βαιτοβαισσαιας[15] . . . τ̣ο̣παρχείας Ἡρω̣δε̣ί̣ο̣[υ], and the groom, Eleaios son of Simon, is τῶν ἀπὸ κ(ώμης) Γαλωδῶν τῆς περὶ Ἀκραβ̣α̣τ̣τῶν οἰκῶν ἐν κώμῃ Βαιτοα̣ρδοις τῆς περὶ Γοφνοῖς (Mur **115**, lines 2–3). However, unlike Herodium, Akrabatta, and Gophna, which are well-known subdivisions of Judaea proper[16] and designated as toparchies, there is no information about Zif as a toparchy.

Idumaea, the subdivision to which Aristoboulias and Yaqim/Yaqum are most likely to have belonged, is absent from the list of toparchies in Pliny (as well as from all later evidence),[17] as is Ein Gedi. The reason may well be that Pliny's list reflects the conditions prevailing in Judaea after 70 CE.[18] At least for Ein Gedi, we know from a document from 127 CE that it ceased to function as a toparchy and was included in the subdivision of Jericho: '[Judah son of Eleazar] κώμης Αἰνγαδδῶν περὶ Ἱερειχοῦντα τῆς Ἰουδαίας' (P.Yadin **16** lines 15–16).[19] Both Mur **115** and P.Yadin **16** prove that the system of toparchies, i.e. the division of Judaea proper into districts which took their names from their capital villages,[20] remained virtually unchanged after the First Revolt.[21] Could Zif have given its name to what used to be the subdivision of Idumaea—or part of it—and become its centre, until replaced by Beth Govrin when the latter was given city status under Septimius Severus and its name was changed to

---

syllable as the Arabic article *al-* and its subsequent detachment from the body of the word (I am grateful to S. Hopkins for the linguistic explanation). On Aristoboulias and Zif (Ziph), see Tsafrir et al., *Tabula*, 67; 262.

[13] *Gazetteer*, 31, *s.v.* 'Aristoboulias'.

[14] Kochavi, *Judaea*, 64, no. 162 who identifies it with Biblical Haqqayin הקין, mentioned together with Maʿon, Carmel, Zif, and Yuta in Josh 15:57 (ibid. p. 29).

[15] The place-name Bethbassi also survives until now, see Abel, *Géographie* II, 269.

[16] All three appear both in Josephus's list, *B.J.* 3.54–5, and in that of Pliny the Elder, *NH* 5.70 = Stern, *Greek and Latin Authors*, 1, no. 204; see Stern's comparison of the two lists and their respective dates on pp. 475f. and, in great detail, in 'Pliny the Elder', cf. Schürer, Vermes, and Millar, *History*, 2:184–98; cf. Cotton, 'Administration'.

[17] Isaac, 'Babatha Archive', 68.

[18] Isaac, 'Babatha Archive', 68; contra Stern, 'Pliny the Elder', 227 (reprint p. 258), who thinks that Pliny's list reflects earlier conditions.

[19] See Isaac, 'Babatha Archive', 68.

[20] See Schürer, Vermes, and Millar, *History*, 2:190–93.

[21] Isaac, 'Babatha Archive', 67ff.

Eleutheropolis?[22] After this, as we know from Eusebius, Zif was included in the territory of Eleutheropolis,[23] to which what used to be Idumaea as well as other districts were subordinated.[24]

Comparing two provinces which had previously been two different kingdoms[25] calls for caution; nevertheless, the striking similarity in the phrasing of the relationship between Aristoboulias/Yaqim and Zif, on the one hand, and that between Maḥoza and Ẓoᶜar in the province of Arabia, on the other, is inescapable. The expression ἐ[ν] Ἀριcτοβουλιάδι τῆc Ζηφ̣ηνῆc (No. **69** line 3) is closely paralleled by ἐν Μαω[ζοιc τ]ῷ̣ν περὶ Ζ[οα]ρα;[26] ἐν Μαωζα̨ περὶ Ζοαραν;[27] ἐν Μαωζα̨ περὶ Ζοορων;[28] ἐν̣ Μ̣α̣ῳ̣ζαc τῆc πε[ρὶ Ζοα]ρ̣α;[29] ἐν Μαωζα̨ περιμέτρῳ̣ Ζοορων of P.Yadin.[30] In each case, one village is subsumed in the subdivision to which another village gave its name.[31]

This marriage contract takes us to a very definite part of Judaea: Yaqim (or Yaqum), Zif, and Aristoboulias are all located in the area south-east of Hebron, along the eastern ridge of the Hebron mountains and a well-preserved north-south road.[32] We may recall that Mur **43** possibly mentions the nearby Kaphar Barucha—present day Bani Naᶜim, two km north of Kh. Yuqim[33]—in a letter from the leader of the second Jewish Revolt: 'Shimᶜon son of Koseba to Joshuᶜa son of Galgala and the people of HaBaruk (הברך)'.[34] The identification of Joshuᶜa son of Galgala of Mur **43** with his homonym, the addressee of Mur **42**, 'Commander of the Camp' (רוש המחניה), means that there was a rebel camp in Kaphar Barucha.[35]

---

[22] The coins fix the era of the city to 199–200 (Spijkerman, 'Coins'). Schürer, Vermes, and Millar (*History*, 2:194 n. 39) suggest tentatively that 'the toparchy [of Idumaea] was administered from Beth Govrin': there is no evidence for this.

[23] 'A village (κώμη) in Daroma, in the territory of Eleutheropolis, eight miles east of Hebron', *Onom.*, 92.19–22 (ed. Klostermann); see map of Palestine, 'nach dem Onomasticon' attached to the back cover.

[24] For the territory of Eleutheropolis, see Jones, 'Urbanization', 83 and n. 1 there, and pl. VII; Abel, *Géographie*, 2:173. Presumably Eleutheropolis is the *polis* suggested by the title of Kynoros son of Diodotos on the bilingual ossuary from Khirbet Zif: Κύνωροc Διοδότου πρωτοπολείτηc, קנרוס בר דוטוס רש מרום, published by Rahmani, 'Bilingual'; see also Kutscher, 'Note', who takes רש מרום, the Aramaic equivalent of πρωτοπολείτηc, to mean 'head of masters'; contra Yadin, 'Note', who reads רש(ע)מרים and takes it to mean 'head of dwellers' (עמר 'dwell').

[25] There is no evidence for toparchies in Arabia.

[26] P.Yadin **5a** col. i lines 4–5.

[27] P.Yadin **15** lines 16–17 = line 3; **17** lines 2–3 = lines 19–20; **18** line 3 = line 32.

[28] P.Yadin **25** line 28 = line 64.

[29] P.Yadin **19** lines 10–11.

[30] P.Yadin **20** line 4 = lines 22–23; **21** lines 5–6; **22** lines 5–6; **26** line 18; **27** lines 3–4.

[31] See INTRODUCTION TO THE GREEK DOCUMENTARY TEXTS.

[32] The Banī Naᶜim–Zif Road, see Kochavi, *Judaea,* 67, no. 170.

[33] See Kochavi, *Judaea,* 62, no. 151 and p. 29. Kaphar Barucha is north of Zif and five km east of Hebron; cf. Abel, *Géographie*, 288; Kyrillos of Skythopolis, *Vita Euthymii*, 12; and see the description of the pilgrimage of St. Paula, Jerome, *Ep*. 108.11.

[34] See 3Q**15** (the Copper Scroll), XII 8 in *DJD* III, 298, and commentary on pp. 269 and 301. However, some read the *bet* as *kap*, i.e. not הברך but הכרך, i.e. 'the large city', maintaining that here the word has its original meaning of 'a fortress'; see Yevin, 'Documents', 105; cf. Ginsberg, 'Notes', 25; Naveh, *Sherd and Papyrus*, 108–9.

[35] See commentary on Mur **43** (*DJD* II). The Arabic placename is Kafar Barik; see Abel, *Géographie*, 2:269.

The southeast part of the Hebron hills, in which all these sites are located, is described as 'the South' by Eusebius (Δαρωμά)[36] and in Jewish sources (דרום).[37] It is located within the territorial boundaries of the Bar Kokhba Revolt, namely 'Judaea in the narrow and proper sense' (see map).[38] It is true that no man-made subterranean hiding complexes—the hallmarks of settlements which participated in the Revolt[39]—were found in this area. The reason is clear: the bedrock geology is quite different here and prevented their creation.[40] Instead, the Jewish inhabitants who lived here escaped into the caves of the Judaean Desert, where their documents were found. In fact, both this document and No. **9** prove the participation of people from Aristoboulias and Yaqim/Yaqum in the revolt.[41] This was a densely populated Jewish area, no less so than the northern and western parts of the Hebron hills and the *Shephelah* (the Judaean lowlands), where the hideouts were found.[42] Thus in 130 CE, the date of No. **69**, we are not only some two years away from the outbreak of the Bar Kokhba revolt, a revolt which was carefully prepared some years in advance,[43] but we are in the very area in which it was prepared and organized. No. **69** places us in what can justly be called the heartland of this national-religious resurgence. The fact that Jews wrote their marriage contract in Greek raises the same questions as do the Greek letters and documents of the officers of the Bar Kokhba revolt,[44] or the Greek ostraca of the *sicarii* who occupied Masada between 66 and 73 or 74 CE.[45] Factors other than the Hellenization of the writers may well have made the use of Greek obligatory, or at least desirable, in documents of a legal nature, for example the need to make them accessible (or valid?) in a non-Jewish court of law.[46] The Babatha Archive has taught us that the

---

[36] E.g. *Onomasticon*, p. 26, lines 10, 12; p. 68, line 19; p. 70, line 11; p. 78, line 21; p. 86, line 9; p. 130, line 12 (Klostermann).

[37] See Schwartz, *Jewish Settlement*, 38f.

[38] See Isaac and Oppenheimer, 'Revolt', 53–4; Kloner and Tepper, *Hiding Complexes*, 366–72. For the numismatic evidence, see Barag, 'Note'.

[39] See Kloner and Tepper, *Hiding Complexes*, 366–72; Isaac and Oppenheimer, 'Revolt', 42–3.

[40] See Kloner and Tepper, *Hiding Complexes*, 23–9 for the geological structure of the hideouts in the foothills of the Judaean hills.

[41] See GENERAL INTRODUCTION for the presumed provenance of No. **9** and the present papyrus; cf. Amit and Eshel, 'Bar Kokhba', 54–9.

[42] It is necessary to emphasize the Jewish character of the area before the revolt, since it has been mistakenly claimed that it became overwhelmingly Jewish only afterwards, when refugees from the northern parts of the Hebron hills and from Jerusalem moved there (Schwartz, *Jewish Settlement*, 98; 106f.; cf. Mor, *Bar-Kochba*, 146). Safrai, 'Settlement', 190–92 (Hebrew), is more cautious. A. Kloner has said (private conversation) that the archaeological evidence clearly shows continuous Jewish settlement in this area from the Second Temple Period until the Bar Kokhba Revolt.

[43] Dio 69.12.2-3; Isaac and Oppenheimer, 'Revolt', 49–52.

[44] Lifshitz, 'Papyrus grecs' (= SB VIII 9843–9844); idem, 'Greek Documents'; Sevenster, 'Greek?'.

[45] See Cotton and Geiger, *Masada* II, 113–27 (cf. pp. 9–10). The content of at least one group of Greek ostraca, nos. **772–7**, closely resembles the Aramaic ostraca, nos. **557–84**; see Yadin and Naveh, *Masada* I, 52–7. Both series contain delivery instructions, which no doubt reflect the rationing of food among the *sicarii* who occupied the fortress.

[46] See Cotton, 'Guardianship', 112; cf. Sevenster, 'Greek?', 155ff. on the official character of the Greek texts from Wadi Murabbaʿat.

use of Greek in legal documents does not reveal Hellenized Jews: their signatures and subscriptions in Aramaic prove the opposite.[47]

Frg. a measures 12.5 x 18.5 cm.

Mus. Inv. 870
PAM 42.207, 42.208

Recto

Frg. a
Inner Text

1]...[.]...[.].αθαι ϵ...[

2]....[.].τῆϲ κ̣λ̣ηρονομίαϲ[

3].....[.]....ναι λέγω *vacat*

Outer Text

1 Ἔτουϲ τϵϲϵρϵϲκαιδϵκάτου̣ Αὐ̣τ̣[ο]κράτο̣ρο̣ϲ Τ̣ρα̣ι̣[ανοῦ Ἁδριανοῦ Καίϲαροϲ Σϵβαϲτοῦ ἐπὶ ὑπά-]

2 τω̣ν Μάρκου Φλα‹ου›ί̣ου Ἄπρ̣ου κ̣αὶ Κο̣ίν̣τ{ι}ου Φαβί̣ο̣υ̣ [Κατουλλίνου *c.19 letters*]

3 ἐν Ἀριϲτοβουλιάδι τῆϲ Ζϵ̣ι̣φη̣νῆϲ ἐξέδϵτο Cϵλα.ϵ[*c.30 letters*]

4 δια̣̣ Βορκ.. Αγλ̣α ἐπ̣ιτρόπ̣[ου] α̣ὐτῆϲ τοῦδϵ τοῦ πράγμ̣α̣[τοϲ χάριν *c.22 letters*]

5 Ακαβαϲ Μηϵιρω τῶν ἀπ̣ὸ κ̣ώμηϲ Ἰακϵίμων τ̣[ῆϲ Ζϵιφηνῆϲ? *c.22 letters*]

6 αὐτῷ ϵἰϲ λόγον προϲφορᾶϲ πρ̣ο̣ι̣κ̣[όϲ] ἐ̣ν ἀργύ[ρῳ καὶ χρυϲῷ *c.15 letters* δηνάρια πϵν-]

7 τακόϲιαι οἵ ϵἰϲιν ϲτατῆρϵ̣[ϲ ἑκατὸν ϵἰκο]ϲιπϵ̣́[ντϵ *c.29 letters* παρ']

8 αὐτῆϲ ἀ̣πϵϲκηκέναι καὶ ἔχ[ϵιν].[...].[...]....[*c.33 letters*]

---

[47] Cf. Wasserstein, 'Marriage', 124ff.

9 δηνάρια πεντακόϲιαι παραχρῆμα διὰ χερὸϲ χω.[*c.23 letters* γυναῖκα]

10 γαμετὴν ἐφ’ ᾧ ἔϲται ἡ Ϲελαμπιουϲ τρεφομένη καὶ ἀμ̣φ̣[ιαζο]μ̣[ένη *c.13 letters* ἐπὶ τῶν ὑπαρ-]

11 χ̣όντων ὧν τε νῦν ἔχει̣ κ̣α̣ὶ̣ ὧ̣ν̣ ἂν ἐπικτήϲηται. Ἐὰν̣ δὲ ἀπογέν̣[ηται *c.13 letters*]

12 α..[...].......[....].[....].[...] ἀ̣ρϲ̣ε̣νικὰ ἢ ὡϲ ἂν̣ κ̣[λη]ρονόμου.[*c.19 letters*]

13 .[*c.15 letters*]...[τρε]φόμεναι κα̣ὶ̣ ἀμφιαζό̣μ̣ε̣ν̣αι...[*c.21 letters*]

14 *c.10 letters*]..[...].ϲα.α̣.δρεϲιν ἐὰν δὲ ὁ π̣ρ̣ο̣γ̣ε̣γραμμ̣[ένοϲ *c.17 letters*]

15 *c.8 letters*]....[..]......[..].. δη̣ν̣ά̣ρ̣ια πεντ[ακ]ό̣[ϲι]α̣ι̣ ..[*c.21 letters*]

16 *traces*

1 τεϲϲαρεϲκαιδεκάτου 3 ἐξέδοτο 6–7, 9, 15 πεντακόϲια 8 ἀ̣πεϲχηκέναι 9 χειρόϲ

Frg. b

1].ν μ...[

2 ..ε καὶ ποιη[

3 ερωτη........[

4 α..ια....ο̣υδε..[

5 .....κ[

6 *traces*

Frg. c

1 α.....[

2 ἔκ τε τοῦ Ακαβαϲ αν.[

3 καὶ..[

4 π.ατ.π[

5]μ̣[

Frg. d

1 *traces*

2 μεχρι̣ ἀ̣ποδώ̣[cεωc?

3 χωρὶ̣c πάcηc ὑ̣[περθέcεωc

4 *traces*

Frg. e

1].....ρ.[

2]απ.αρε[....]cυ.

3]. ηδε....[

4].οιc καὶ .[.........]ν Μαριαμ̣η̣[

5]...αλ̣υπαρ.....καὶ ὡμολό̣[γηcεν

6 παρὰ τῆc π]ρογεγραμμένη̣c̣ [

7]φει̣αc καὶ αι[

8]και[..].[

Frg. f

1]ωιμ..θω..[

2]επι τ....... [ἀ]κολ<ο>ύ̣θωc

3 .... γρ]άμματα c[

Verso

Frg. a

1 Ιωcηποc̣ Ϲ̣.[.]δ̣εμωνοc μάρ̣[τυc]

2 Cου...οc Ε[λεαζ]αρου μάρ[τυc]

3 Μ̣α̣ρω̣.ηc [.....] μάρτυc

4 *traces*

5 *traces*

TRANSLATION

Recto, Outer Text, Frg. a

1. In the fourteenth year of the Emperor Tra[jan Hadrian Caesar Augustus, in the consul-]
2. ship of Marcus Flavius Aper and Quintus Fabius [Catullinus . . .]
3. in Aristoboulias of the Zeiphênê. Sela.e[ ] gave in marriage[her daughter (?) Selampious . . .]
4. through Bork.. Agla, her guardian for this matter[. . .]
5. to Aqabas son of Meir from the village of Iaqim [of the Zephene . . . she bringing]
6. to him on account of bridal gift of the dowry(?) in sil[ver and gold . . . all appraised in money value as five]
7. hundred *denarii* which are the equivalent of [one hundred and twenty-fi]ve staters, [and the groom acknowledges]
8. to have received and to ho[ld from her . . .]
9. five hundred *denarii* forthwith by hand [. . .]
10. wedded (wife) so that Selampious is nourished and cloth[ed . . . upon the security of all his posse-]
11. ssions, both those which he has now and those which he will acquire. And in the event of the death of [. . .]
12. [ ] the male children or if heirs [. . .]
13. [ ] the daughters will be nourished and clothed [. . .]
14. [ ] and if he who is mentioned before [. . .]
15. [ ] five hundred *denarii* [. . .]
16. [ ]

Verso, Frg. a

1. Joseph son of S..demon, witness.
2. Sou[lai]os son of Eleazar, witness.
3. Maro.es ... witness.
4. [
5. [

COMMENTS

Recto, Inner Text

Frg. a

Ll. 1–3 These are the last three lines of the inner text. It ended after the word λέγω in line 3, as is clear from the blank space. We cannot assume that the inner text contained an identical or even a similar version of what is in the outer text. As we know from the Babatha Archive, double documents show great variation in the relationship between inner and outer texts: from a complete repetition of the outer text to a mere sentence (see Lewis, *Documents*, 8–9).[48] Thus, there is no guarantee that we have here the lines which stood at the end of the outer text as well.

L. 2 κ̣λ̣ηρονομίας[. Perhaps κ̣λ̣ηρονομία ε[. It could refer to the right of male children to inherit their mother's property, mentioned in the outer text in line 12.

[48] The evidence suggests that the outer text was written first, see Lewis, *Documents*, 9.

Recto, Outer Text

Frg. a

L. 1 The restoration of the imperial titulature is based on P.Yadin **14** lines 15–16; **15** line 1 = 14; **20** line 1 = lines 18–19; **21** lines 1–2; **22** lines 1–2; and Mur **115** line 1. The suggested restoration means that thirty-four letters have been lost in line 1. If the restoration is accepted, then we know the approximate length of a line and are able to calculate the loss in all the other lines.

L. 2 The restoration of the cognomen of the second consul as Κατουλλίνου[49] (i.e. Catullinus) does not correspond to the practice found in the Babatha Archive where it is rendered Κατηλίνου: P.Yadin **20** line 2 = line 19; **21** line 3; **22** line 3 (it is restored in P.Yadin **23** lines 20–21).[50] The Roman day and month followed, perhaps also the Macedonian month and day, as often found in the Babatha Archive (e.g. P.Yadin **14** lines 15–19; **15** lines 1–2 = lines 14–16). The space which needs to be allowed for the restoration of the month and day conforms to the loss calculated in line 1 and the suggested restoration of the imperial titulature there.

L. 3 On Aristoboulias and Zif, see INTRODUCTION.

L. 3 ἐξέδετο. For the formation of the 3rd person of the 2nd aorist middle of ἐκδίδωμι in -ετο instead of -οτο, see Gignac, *Grammar* 2:394. Many of his examples are, predictably, from marriage contracts.

L. 3 Cελα is the name of the mother; restored as Cελα[μ] it will give us the Aramaic word Shlam (שלם), the equivalent of the Hebrew Shalom (שלום), meaning 'peace'. Hebrew Shalom is a well-known female name. In two Aramaic papyri from this collection we find the name in its Aramaic spelling: שלם ברת שמעון (No. **8** line 12) and שלם ברת לוי (No. **12** line 1). The latter's name is transcribed Cαλωμη in the Greek documents from her archive, the normal way of rendering Hebrew Shalom in Greek (see Bagatti and Milik, *Scavi*, 81). Note, however, that in a deed of sale written in Hebrew (Mur **30**), the name of the woman is written twice as Shalom (שלום; lines 6 and 25), and once without the *waw* as שלם; the same is true of No. **8a**, a house-sale in Aramaic, where the wife's name is spelled once as שלם (line 12) and once as שלום (line 14). Thus the spelling שלם may not necessarily reflect an Aramaic rendering of the Hebrew name שלום, but perhaps only the Hebrew name written in defective spelling.[51] This consideration, combined with the fact that the name Shalom, spelled with or without the *waw*, is usually rendered in Greek Cαλωμη, may suggest that another name is behind the text here. The first four letters look like one of the Greek transliterations of the name Shelamṣion (שלמציון) but the *epsilon* after the missing *mu* does not occur elsewhere in the transcription of that name. If it is Shelamṣion, then mother and daughter have the same name, albeit transliterated differently: see Cελαμπιουc in line 10.[52]

L. 3 ε[. If the restoration Cελα[μ] is accepted, then this could be the beginning of the patronym.

L. 4 Βορκ.. The two uncertain letters may in fact be not two letters, but an *omega*. In line 5 we find another name in the genitive ending in an *omega*: Μηειρω. It is hard to know whether the name derives from the root ברך or ברק. The former is attested in No. **10** line 1, which has שמוקא בר ברוכא. Greek inscriptions from Egypt attest the names Βαραχίαc, Βορούχ (CPJ 3, no. 1438 = Horbury and Noy, *Jewish Inscriptions*, no. 15, late Roman), and Βαρχίαc (CPJ 3, no. 1454 = Horbury and Noy no. 43, 5 CE) for Jews—all from the root ברך, but also Βαράκου (Horbury and Noy no. 156, 78 BCE) which comes from the root ברק. Wuthnow, *Semitische Menschennamen*, 37 has Βορκαιος and Βόρκου (see also on pp. 132–3). An inscription on a tag from Masada, and thus before 73 or 74 CE, reads יהוא בר ברקי (Yadin and Naveh, *Masada*, I no. **398**)—Barqay meaning the 'morning star' (ibid.). An ossuary inscription from Jerusalem

---

[49] Alternatively: Κατυλλείνου, see *IGR* III 81; cf. *IGR* I 623 Κατυλλεῖνοc, a *libertus* of the emperor.

[50] All written by Germanus the λιβλάριοc (*sic*!), and likely to reflect, therefore, a spelling peculiar to him.

[51] For the spelling שלם, see Sukenik, 'Burial Cave', 92: שלם; Rahmani, 'Rock-cut Tombs', 104: שלמום, to be read as שלם followed by another name; Bagatti and Milik, *Scavi*, 88, no 19: שלם ברת עוי ('Salome daughter of ʿAwiy'?); 95, no. 31: שלם הגירת ('Salome the proselyte').

[52] On the names Shalom and Shelamṣion, see Bagatti and Milik, *Scavi*, 79–81; Mayer, *Jüdische Frau*, 106–7; 109–10; Ilan, 'Ossuary Inscriptions', 156–7.

attests the name Caφιρα Βορκεου (Puech, 'Inscriptions funéraires', 527, no. 39)[52a] . An Amora by that name is mentioned in the Palestinian Talmud: Bourqi, Bourqai (ברקאי, בורקי, *y. Yoma* 43.1; *y. Qidd.* 63.4; *y. ʿAbod. Zar.* 43.1). Josephus records a friend of Agrippa II called Βόρκιος (*B.J.* 2. 524; 526). On an altar from the Beqaʿ Valley in Lebanon we find a dedication by two brothers, Βορκεος καὶ Cαβας (*IGLS* VI 2962).[53]

L. 4 Αγλα. Could it be Εγλα? Cf. Ἰωάνης Ἔγλα, 'John son of Eglas', one of the guardians of Babatha's orphaned son, named thus in P.Yadin **12** line 8; **13** lines 21–2; **27** line 6, as well as in the Aramaic subscription of P.Yadin **15** line 33: יוחנה חברי בר עגלא. But in P.Yadin **14** line 23 and **15** lines 3–4 = line 18 it is Ἰωάνης Ἰωσήπου τοῦ Ἔγλα, 'Iohanes son of Joseph Eglas'. Eglas must have been Joseph's nickname, 'the Calf'.[54]

L. 4 δια . . . ἐπιτρόπ[ου] αὐτῆς τοῦδε τοῦ πράγμα[τος χάριν]. Cf. P.Yadin **14** line 22; **15** lines 31–2; see also P.Yadin **20** lines 25–7: διὰ ἐπιτρόπου αὐτῆς Ἰούδας ὃς καὶ Κίνβερ Ἀνανίου Ἐν[γ]αδηνοῦ τοῦδε τοῦ πράγματος χάριν; cf. No. **64** lines 4–5: συνπαρόντος αὐτ[ῆ ἐ]πιτρόπο[υ τοῦδε τοῦ πρά]γματος χάριν Ιωσηπου Cιμωνος [ἀ]νὴρ αὐτῆς.

The use of ἐπίτροπος to describe the guardian of a woman, whereas in Greek-speaking lands the traditional term was κύριος, is thus not peculiar to the Babatha Archive and to the province of Arabia, as assumed by H. J. Wolff.[55]

In the space left after the break would come the name of the bride, Cελαμπιους, followed or preceded by τὴν ἰδίαν θυγατέρα αὐτῆς or τὴν ἑαυτῆς θυγατέρα, cf. P.Yadin **18** lines 32–38 = lines 3–5: ἐξ[έδ]οτ[ο Ἰούδα]ς Ἐλεαζάρου τοῦ καὶ [Χθουσί]ων[ος C]ελαμψ[ι]ώνην τὴν ἰδίαν θυγατέραν αὐτοῦ παρθένον Ἰούδατι ἐπικαλουμένῳ Κίμβερι υἱῷ Ἀνανίου τοῦ Σωμαλα.

L. 5 Ακαβας. Aqabas occurs also on frg. c. The name is attested in Hebrew letters on several inscriptions from Palestine: ח[נני]ה כהנא רבא עקביא בריה 'Ḥa[nani]as the High Priest, ʿAqabia his son' is found on a sherd from Masada (Yadin and Naveh, *Masada*, I, no. **461**);[56] יועזר אקביה, 'Joʿezer ʾAqabiah' (spelled with *ʾalep*) is found written eight times in Hebrew letters in a first-century tomb in Jericho (Hachlili, 'Goliath Family', 48, 54). עקביה בן עליועיני, ʿAqabiah son of ʿElioenai, is attested in Hebrew letters in Egypt (CPJ 3, no. 1424 = Horbury and Noy, no. 3, early Ptolemaic?). In a Ptolemaic census list from Trikomia in Egypt the name Akabias in Greek letters—'Ακαβιας—appears twice.[57] In rabbinic sources we find: R. ʿAqabia (עקביא) son of Mahalalel in *m. ʾAbot* 3.1; *m. ʿEd.* 5.6f., perhaps father of R. Ḥananyah son of ʿAqabiah (עקביה, *c.*130–60 CE) in *m. Ket.* 8.1; R. Issi son of ʿAqabiah (עקביה, *c.*130–60 CE) is mentioned in *b. Pes.* 113b and *b. Yoma* 52b. The name Akabiah may be related to the name Aqiba. The most famous bearer of the name is R. ʿAqiba son of Joseph, who died in the Bar Kokhba Revolt.[58]

L. 5 Μηειρω. Hebrew מאיר. This is the name of one of the most famous rabbis who played a significant part in the formation of the Mishna (*c.*130–60 CE). Nonetheless, we are informed that the

---

[52a] The ossuary is now in the Biblisch-Archäologisches Institut of the Eberhard-Karls-Universität Tübingen, Oss. No. 252.

[53] Βουρκερου in *IGLS* VI 2973, also from the Beqaʿ, is said to be a diminutive of Βορκαιος, see ad loc.

[54] See Hachlili, 'Names', 203. Could the nickname refer to his place of origin, Maḥoz ʿAglatain, mentioned in Nabataean and Hebrew documents of the Babatha Archive? See Cotton and Greenfield, 'Babatha's Patria'.

[55] Wolff, 'Le droit', 279ff. and in 'Römisches Provinzialrecht', 795f.; but he is right to point out that this cannot be accounted for by the influence of the local language, since the Aramaic makes the distinction: the guardian of a woman is called אדון — κύριος: e.g. P.Yadin **15** line 37: יהודה בר כתושין אדון בבתה; whereas for the guardian of an orphan, the Aramaic borrowed the Greek term ἐπίτροπος: אפטרפא. Cf. P.Yadin **20** line 41; **27** line 12.

[56] Cf. ibid., no. 645: [ ]עק; the editors suggest that this is 'perhaps the beginning of the name ʿAq[avia] or ʿAq[iva]'.

[57] CPR XIII 4 (iii BCE) lines 50 and 155. The latter attestation (line 155) is not in the original publication but read by Clarysse, see 'Jews in Triakomia', 194.

[58] See Schürer, Vermes, and Millar, *History* II, 377–8. עקיבא (ʿAqiba) is attested on a tomb from Jerusalem. Milik, 'Trois tombeaux', 247, no. 13, fig 16:2; cf. *RB* 65, 1958, 409.

name 'does not appear in the Bible, nor in any reliable Jewish literary, or legible and datable epigraphical material before the Geonic period [i.e. seventh century]'.[59] Hence it has been suggested that it is a transcription of an Anatolian (Phrygian) name Μεῖρος, Μῖρος, and that Rabbi Meir belonged to the family of a proselyte from Asia Minor.[60] The Meir of our document, being the father of the groom, belongs to a generation earlier than the famous rabbi. In view of the other names in the document, the more likely assumption is that Meir, too, is a Jewish name. Perhaps we should lend more credence to the other attestations of the name in Josephus and the inscriptions.

L. 5 τῶν ἀπὸ κώμης Ἰακείμων. See Mur **115** line 2: Ἐλεαῖος Cίμωνος τῶν ἀπὸ κ(ώμης) Γαλωδῶν; P.Yadin **5a** col. i lines 5–6: ὁμολογῶ ἐγὼ Ἰώσηπος τοῦ Ἰωσήπ[ου ἐπι]καλουμ[ένου] Ζαβούδο[υ] τῶν ἀπὸ Μαωζων. For οἱ ἀπὸ κ(ώμης) see Preisigke, *Wörterbuch*, s.v. ἀπό, and Wilcken, *Grundzüge*, 43. On Yaqim or Yaqum see INTRODUCTION.

L. 5 If τ[ῆς Ζειφηνῆς] followed and προςφερομένην came at the very end of the line, about nine or ten letters are left unaccounted for; too few for πρὸς γάμου κοινωνίαν which is most attractive here (see P.Yadin **18** lines 6–7 = lines 38–39). One might suggest κατὰ (τοὺς) νόμους as in P.Yadin **18** before προςφερομένην: εἶναι τὴν Cελαμψιών[ην] Ἰούδατι Κίμβερι γυναῖκαν γαμετὴν πρὸς γάμου κ[οι]νωνίαν κατὰ τοὺς νόμους, προςφερομένην αὐτ[ῷ] εἰς λόγον προςφορᾶς κτλ. (lines 37–40 = lines 6–8).

L. 6 εἰς λόγον προςφορᾶς προικ[ός]. Προςφορά here means gold and silver dowry objects as can be seen from what follows. The same usage is found in P.Yadin **18** lines 39–40 = lines 7–8: προςφερομένην αὐτ[ῷ] εἰς λόγον προςφορᾶς κοςμίαν γυναικίαν ἐν ἀργύρῳ κα[ὶ] χρυςῷ καὶ ἱματιςμῷ. In P.Mil.Vogl. II 71 (Marcus Aurelius 161–80), φερνή and προςφορά are used interchangeably for jewelry and clothes.[61] An alimentary contract from 42 CE also records jewelry as προςφο(ραὶ) ἄνευ δ(ιατιμήςεως), P.Mich. II 121, recto, col. III, xii, line 3.[62] Thus there are at least four exceptions to G. Häge's claim that *prosphora* always means either slaves or landed property, and is fundamentally different from either *pherne* or *parapherna* in that it does not pass into the groom's hands but remains legally the property either of the wife or of the giver (Häge, *Ehegüterrechtliche Verhältnisse*, 250–89).[63]

L. 6 προικ[ός]. The reading is not certain; as far as I know the combination εἰς λόγον προςφορᾶς προικός is not attested elsewhere. The term προίξ for dowry appears in three other marriage contracts found in the Judaean Desert. In P.Yadin **18** lines 12–15 = lines 45–9 the groom undertakes 'to add to the dowry consisting of jewelry and clothes just mentioned (πρὸς τὰ τῆς προγεγραμμένης προςφορᾶς αὐτῆς) three hundred *denarii*, and everything together will go towards Shelamṣion's dowry (πάντα εἰς λόγον προικὸς αὐτῆς)'; Mur **115** lines 6–7: ὡμολό[γη]cεν ὁ αὐτὸς Ἐλαῖος Cίμωνος ἠριθμ[ῆςθαι] [*c*.34 letters] π[ρογε]γραμμ[ένα] ∠ς εἰς λόγον προικὸς παρὰ Cαλώμης Ἰωάν[ο]υ Γαλγο[υλ]α; No. **65** lines 6–7: . . . τῇ αὐτῇ κομαις[η τῇ]ν προῖ{ο}κα αὐτῆς.[64] Προίξ describes the dowry in Egyptian papyri as well, e.g. P.Lond. II 178 (145 CE, receipt for the return of part of the dowry), lines 20–2: ἀπέ[χω] τὰς τοῦ ἀργυρίου δράχμας τετρακοςίας εἰς τὸν λόγον τῆς προοικό μου; P.Oxy. XVII 2133 (late iii CE, a woman complains that her uncle did not give her a dowry): μηδέν μοι καθ' ὁνδήποτ' οὖν τρόπον εἰς λόγον προ[ι]κὸς (lines 15–16); P.Grenf. II 76 (305–6 CE), lines 13–14: [εἰς λό]γον προικός.[65]

---

[59] See Cohen, 'Rabbi Meir', 52–3, and especially nn. 7–8, where the epigraphical material is collected.

[60] Cohen, 'Rabbi Meir', 53–9.

[61] In line 7 the groom acknowledges that he has received from Tephrosaïs daughter of Eudaimon (ἐν προςφ[ορᾷ]) a dowry (τὴν φερνήν) in gold measured in the scales of Arsinoe etc.; in the case of a divorce he will return to her τὴν προκειμένην φερνήν (line 11); finally, the wife says that she wants to bring to her husband ἐν προςφορᾷ: jewelry and clothes (line 21ff).

[62] The editor objects that 'the term προςφοραί here is used to designate the objects elsewhere classed as *parapherna*' and therefore 'this may be a scribal error'.

[63] See Modrzejewski, 'Hellenistisches Ehegüterrecht', esp. 69; Gernet, *Beiträge*, 19–32; see also the very lucid presentation of Rowlandson, *Landowners*, 152f.

[64] Cf. P.Yadin **21** line 12 and P.Yadin **22** line 12 where προίξ refers to the ketubbah money of P.Yadin **10** line 16; see below 'The Dowry' in MARRIAGE PRACTICES.

[65] For προίξ and φερνή used interchangeably for dowry in the papyri, see Wasserstein, 'Marriage Contract', 106–7 n. 44.

L. 6 ἐ̣ν ἀργύ[ρῳ καὶ χρυcῷ]. In P.Yadin **18** lines 39–43 = lines 8–11 we read: προς̣φερομένην αὐτ̣[ῷ] εἰc λόγον προcφορᾶc κοcμίαν γυναικίαν ἐν ἀργύρῳ κα[ὶ] χρυcῷ καὶ ἱματιcμῷ διατετειμένην ἐν ἀλλήλοιc, ὡc λέγουcιν οἱ ἀμφότεροι, ἀξιοχρέαν εἶναι ἀργυρίου δη̣[ναρίων] διακοcίων. A shorter phrase expressing the money value of the gold and silver objects of the dowry would fit in the remaining space of 15 letters: ἐν διατιμήcει or ἐν cυντιμήcει (see Whitehorne, 'Valuation', 50–3).

Ll. 6–7 δηνάρια πεντακόcιαι οἵ εἰcιν cτατῆρε̣[c ἑκατὸν εἰκο]cιπέ̣[ντε. The restoration is quite certain as seen from lines 9 and 15. The conversion to staters (סלעין) is well attested in documents from the Judaean Desert, e.g. in Babatha's own Aramaic marriage contract to her second husband, P.Yadin **10**, the sums of money are given in these two denominations: 'the sum of four hundred *zuzin* which equal one hundred tetradrachms *slaʿin*' (lines 8–9).[66]

The acknowledgement by the groom now follows, as is clear from what comes in the following line. In P.Yadin **18** lines 10–11 = lines 43–4, the evaluation of the dowry objects is followed by: ἣν τειμογραφίαν ὡμολόγηcεν ὁ γήμαc Ἰούδαc Κίμβερ ἀπειληφέναι παρὰ τῆc αὐτῆc Cελαμψιοῦc γυναικὸc αὐτοῦ; similarly in Mur **115** lines 5–6: ἃ ὡμολό[γη]cεν ὁ αὐτὸc Ἐλαῖοc Cίμωνο̣c ἠριθμ[ῆcθαι....]. The repetition of the sum of money in line 9 excludes the use of relatives like ἣν τειμογραφίαν and ἅ here. Something like καὶ ὡμολόγηcεν Ακαβαc Μειρω παρ' would fit admirably the space of 28 letters left till the end of the line. In frg. e line 5 we read καὶ ὡμολό̣[γηcεν]; unfortunately, the fragment does not fit here.

L. 8 ἀ̣πεcκηκέναι = ἀ̣πεcχηκέναι; see Gignac, *Grammar*, 1:86.

L. 8 ἀ̣πεcκηκέναι καὶ ἔχ[ειν]. The repetition 'to have received and to hold' is not found in Greek marriage contracts from Egypt and may be influenced by the Semitic language of the writer.[67] Since the sum of money at which the dowry was evaluated appears in line 9, it seems reasonable to assume that the rest of this line contained exactly the same text as line 6, now seen from the point of view of the groom: εἰc λόγον προcφορᾶc προικὸc ἐν ἀργύρῳ καὶ χρυcῷ, valued at, etc.

L. 9 παραχρῆμα διὰ χερόc. Cf. P.Yadin **18** line 12 = line 45: διὰ χειρὸc παραχρῆμα. The expression is found in Egyptian marriage contracts as well, e.g. P.Mich. V 339 (46 CE) lines 1–3, where the groom acknowledges that he has received from the bride, Taorsenouphis daughter of Aphrodisios, as dowry (φερνήν) a hundred drachmas of marked silver παραχρῆμα διὰ χιρόc.[68]

L. 9 χω.[. Perhaps χωρ̣[ὶc πάcηc ὑπερθέcεωc], i.e. without delay.[69] The same phrase is also found in frg. d line 3.

L. 9 Were it not for the accusative γυναῖκα γαμετήν, it would be tempting to restore later on in the line some form of the verb ἐπιχορηγεῖν, such as ἐπιχορ[ηγείτω].[70] Still, the accusative might be accounted for by the example of BGU IV 1050 (= M.Chr. 286, 13 BCE) lines 12–14: ⟨ἐφ' ᾧ⟩ τὸν Διονύcιον ἀπεcχηκότα τὴν προκειμέμην φερνὴν τρέφειν καὶ ἱματίζειν τὴν Ἰcιδώραν ὡc γυναῖκα γα[μετὴν] κατὰ δύναμιν, where γυναῖκα γα[μετήν] is to be explained by the accusatives which preceded it. Otherwise,

---

[66] See Weiser and Cotton, 'Gebt dem Kaiser, was des Kaisers ist', 241 pp.

[67] See Benoit, *DJD* II, 252 ad Mur **115** lines 3–5: ἀπαλλαγῆναι καὶ ἀπολύειν . . . ἐξ ἀνανεώcεωc καταλλάξαι κ[αὶ] π̣ροcλαβέcθαι: 'Ces accouplements de termes ainsi que leur parallélisme antithétique ne manque pas de saveur sémitique'.

[68] ὁμολογῶι ἔχιν παρὰ τῆc . . . Ταορcενοῦφιc τῆc Ἀφροδιcίου παραχρῆμα διὰ χιρὸ̣c ἐξ οἴκου ἐν προcδόcι ἐφ' αὐτῆc φερνὴν ἀργυρίου ἐπιcήμου δραχμὰc ἑκατὸν; cf. CPR I 24 (= MChr. 288, 136 CE) lines 4–5: [ὁ μὲν Cουχάμ]μων ἔχειν παρὰ̣ [τ]ῆc Ἀφρο̣δ̣είτ̣η̣[c] ἐπὶ τῇ θυγατρὶ α̣ὐ̣τῆc Ἀφροδε̣ι[το]ῦτι Ἀμμωνίου παρ[θένῳ οὔcῃ παρ]αχρῆμα διὰ χε̣ι̣ρ̣ὸ̣c χρυcο̣ῦ δοκιμίου κτλ.; BGU V 1052, line 9; BGU V 1103, line 11; P.Lond. II 178, line 9; P.Hamb. III 220, line 4.

[69] Cf. SB VI 9353 (140 CE) line 21, where the groom promises to return the dowry without delay.

[70] Cf. P.Oxy. XLIX 3500 (iii CE) lines 8–9: ὁ δὲ [γαμῶ]ν καὶ ἐπιχορηγ[εί]τω τῇ γυναικὶ τὰ δέοντα πάντα κατὰ δ[ύ]ναμιν ('the husband is further to provide his wife with all necessities according to his means'); BGU IV 1045 (= MChr. 282, 154 CE) lines 18–19; P.Mil.Vogl. II 71 (161–80 CE) lines 9–10; P.Oxy. VI 905, line 10. The simple verb χορηγεῖν occurs too in the same context, cf. P.Oxy. X 1273 (260 CE) line 24: χορηγεῖ[τω] τῇ γυναικῖ τὰ δέοντα πάντα; cf. P.Oxy. XLIX 3491 (157/8 CE) lines 16–17.

one might tentatively suggest restoring ἔχειν[71] or εἶναι later in the line in order to account for the accusative (but see reservations in the next note).

Ll. 9–10 [γυναῖκα] γαμετήν. The expression, 'legitimate wife', 'wedded wife', is common in Greek marriage contracts from Egypt,[72] usually in the clause which stipulates that the husband is to provide for his wife (see ad line 9), and thus in the dative, e.g. P.Mil.Vogl. II 71 (161–80 CE): τοῦ Ἀμμων[ᾶτος] ἐπιχορηγ[οῦντος αὐτῇ τὰ δέον]τα πάντα καὶ τὸν ἱματισμὸν καὶ τὰ ἄλλα ὅσα καθήκει γυναικὶ γαμετῇ [κατὰ δύναμιν].[73]

The accusative γυναῖκα γαμέτην is found either in the context of the giving away of the bride, i.e. the *ekdosis*, or in the context of remarriage. As an example of the first, one may cite P.Yadin **18** lines 32–38 = lines 3–7: ἐξ[έδ]οτ[ο Ἰούδα]ς Ἐλεαζάρου τοῦ καὶ [Χθουσί]ων[ος Σ]ελαμψ[ι]ώνην τὴν ἰδίαν θυγατέραν αὐτοῦ παρθένον Ἰούδατι ἐπικαλουμένῳ Κίμβερι . . . εἶναι τὴν Σελαμψιών[ην] Ἰούδατι Κίμβερι γυναῖκαν γαμετὴν (cf. P.Giss. I. 2 (173 BCE, self-*ekdosis*) lines 8–12: Ἐξέδοτο ἑαυτὴν Ὀλυμπιὰς . . . Ἀνταίωι . . . [εἶναι] γυναῖκα γαμετὴν φερνὴν προσφερομένην κτλ.). As an example of the second, one may cite Mur **115** lines 4–5: ὁμολογεῖ ὁ αὐτὸς Ἐλαῖος Σίμω[νος] ἐξ ἀνανεώσεος καταλλάξαι κ[αὶ] προσλαβέσθαι τὴν αὐτὴν Σαλώ[μην Ἰω]άν[ο]υ Γ[αλγο]υλὰ εἶ[ς γυναῖ]κα γαμετὴν. The *ekdosis* in No. **69** came much earlier; nor have we here a case of remarriage. The explanation in the preceding note should, therefore, be preferred. See, also, the discussion in the INTRODUCTION to No. **65**.

L. 10 Σελαμπιους. It appears that this spelling is not attested elsewhere.[74] In the Babatha Archive the name is transliterated Σελαμψιοῦς and Σελαμψιώνη.[75]

Ll. 10–11 [ἐπὶ τῶν ὑπαρ]χόντων ὧν τε νῦν ἔχει καὶ ὧν ἂν ἐπικτήσηται. In the Babatha Archive the undertaking to feed and clothe the wife and children is followed by: ἐπὶ τῆς τοῦ αὐτοῦ Ἰούδα Κίμβ[ε]ρο[ς] πίστεως καὶ κινδύνου καὶ πάντων ὑπαρχόντων ὧν τε ἔχει ἐν τῇ αὐτῇ [πα]τρίδι αὐτοῦ καὶ ὧδε καὶ ὧν ἐπικτήσηται πάντῃ πά[ν]των κυρίω[ς] (P.Yadin **18** lines 16–18 = lines 51–53). Perhaps we should restore [ἐπὶ πάντων ὑπαρ]χόντων; thus either 13 or only 10 letters are missing between ἀμφ[ιαζο]μ[ένη and [τῶν or πάντων ὑπαρ]χόντων; not enough room for the whole formula just cited from the Babatha archive.[76]

L. 11 Ἐὰν δὲ ἀπογέν[ηται]. Because of the fragmentary condition of the lines, we cannot know from the immediate context whether the prior death of the husband or of the wife is envisioned here. What follows, however, namely the stipulation that male children will become heirs, makes it very likely, as will be shown in the discussion MARRIAGE PRACTICES, that the prior death of the wife is the subject of the conditional clause; the husband is the subject of a subsequent conditional clause in line 14: ἐὰν δὲ ὁ προγεγραμμ[ένος]. The same sequence is found in Mur **20**, **21**, and **116**.

L. 12 α..[...].......[....].[....].[...] ἀρσενικὰ ἢ ὡς ἂν κ[λη]ρονόμου.[. If the suggested restoration is correct, a reference to male children as heirs is made here.

L. 13 [τρε]φόμεναι καὶ ἀμφιαζόμεναι. I.e. the daughters. Ἔσονται can be restored before [τρε]φόμεναι by analogy with line 10: ἔσται ἡ Σελαμπιους τρεφομένη καὶ ἀμφ[ιαζο]μ[ένη.[77]

---

71 See Chariton, *Chaereas and Callirhoe*, 3.2.2: ἕξω σε γαμετήν with Geiger, 'Note'.

72 See Modrzejewski, 'Structure', 250 n. 76.

73 Cf. Stud.Pal. XX 5 lines 21–22 (136 CE): τοῦ Σουχάμμωνος ἐπαρκ[ο]ῦντος αὐτῇ τὰ [δέοντα πάντα καὶ τὸ]ν ἱματισμὸν καὶ τὰ ἄλλα ὅσα προσήκει γυναικὶ γαμετῇ κατὰ δύναμιν; BGU IV 1045 (= MChr. 282, 154 CE) lines 18–19; P.Giess. I 2, lines 15–17 (173 BCE); P.Gen. I 21, lines 1–2 (= MChr. 284, ii BCE); P.Tebt. I 104, lines 13–14.

74 See Ilan, 'Notes', 198–9.

75 Σελαμσιους is read on a first century ossuary from Jericho; see Hachlili, 'Goliath family', 42, no. 11a, figs. 31 and 33; see also Beyer, *Aramäische Texte*, 130; 711.

76 Perhaps a maintenance clause should be restored in the first part of Mur **115** line 7, since the rest of the line, as well as line 8, are occupied by the liability clause: κατὰ τοῦ αὐτοῦ Ἐλεαίου Σίμωνος ... καὶ κατὰ τῶν ὑπαρχόντων αὐτῷ. At the least, it is clear that his property is liable for the maintenance of the children.

77 In *DJD* II, 253 n. 5 (commentary on Mur **115**), there is a reference to line 13 of No. **69**, 'encore inédit'.

L. 14 [*c*.10 letters]..[...].cα.α.δρεcιν ἐὰν δὲ ὁ προγεγραμμ[ένος. I.e. the husband. The mention of the monetary sum of the dowry in the following line suggests the need to return the dowry, which will be caused either by divorce or by the death of the husband.

Frg. b

L. 3 ερωτη........[If the reading is correct, it is just possible that we have here part of the *stipulatio*: e.g. P.Yadin **20** line 40 = lines 16–17: πίcτεως ἐπερωτημέ[ν]ηc καὶ ἀνθομολογημένηc. It could have followed a πρᾶξιc clause, as in the marriage contract of Shelamṣion, daughter of Judah son of Eleazar Khthousion, Babatha's second husband, where we find both the *praxis* clause and the *stipulatio* at the end of the contract: εἰ δὲ μή γε, ἐκτίcει αὐτῇ τὰ προγεγραμμέν[α δηνάρ]ια πάντα διπλοῦν, καὶ τῆc πράξεωc γεινομένηc αὐτῇ ἀπό τε Ἰο[ύδου Κίμ]βε[ροc] ἀνδρὸc αὐτῆc καὶ ἐκ τῶν ὑπαρχόντω[ν] αὐτοῦ κυρίω[c], τρόπῳ [ᾧ ἂν] αἱ[ρ]ῆται ἢ ὃc [δ]ι' [α]ὐτῆc ἢ ὑπὲρ αὐτῆc πράccων τὴν εἴc[π]ρα[ξι]ν ποιεῖcθαι. πί[c]τει ἐπηρωτήθη κα[ὶ ἀνθω]μολ[ογ]ήθη ταῦτα οὕτω[c καλῶc] γείνεcθαι, P.Yadin **18** lines 23–28 = lines 60–67.

Frg. d

L. 2 μεχρι ἀποδώ[cεωc?] If this fragment came immediately after frg. a lines 14–16, it could be suggested that it refers to the return of the dowry to the wife in the event of the prior death of the husband. This may, therefore, be the clause found in other marriage contracts from the Judaean Desert, which allows the widow to stay in her husband's house and be supported out of his property until his heirs pay her back her dowry/ketubbah. This clause is fully preserved in Babatha's ketubbah, P.Yadin **10** 14–16: 'If I go to my eternal home before you, you will dwell in my house and be provided for from my estate until the time that my heirs wish to give you your ketubbah money'. In other words, the heirs have the right to expel her from her husband's house by paying back her dowry/ketubbah. Yadin, Greenfield, and Yardeni ('Babatha's Ketubba', 95) suggest that Mur **20** lines 7–11 and Mur **21** lines 14–6 can be restored to give the same meaning. But we may have here a different provision, that which is found in Mur **116** lines 8–12, where the widow is allowed to stay in her husband's house for as long as she wishes, and leave whenever she wishes: ἐὰν δὲ ὁ Αὐρήλιοc πρὸ [τ]ῆc Cαλώμηc τὸν βίον μεταλλάξει [τρ]αφήcηται ἡ Cαλώμη [κ]αὶ ἀμφιαcθ[ήc]εται ἐκ τῆc τοῦ Αὐρηλίου οὐcίαc ἐφ' [ὅc]ον ἂν θέλῃ χηρεύειν χρόνον. ἐ[ὰν] δὲ βουληθῇ με<τ>ὰ τὴν αὐτοῦ τε[λευ]τὴν ἀπεῖναι ἢ ἐὰν ἀνθ' ἑαυτῆ[c] ἀποπέμψῃ . . . .

L. 3 χωρὶc πάcηc ὑ[περθέcεωc]. Cf. frg. a line 9. This phrase, too, may refer to the return of the dowry.

Frg. f

Ll. 2–3 . . . ἀ]κολ<ο>ύθωc .... γρ]άμματα. This is the bottom of the document as the blank space below line 3 shows. The proximity of the two words to each other here indicates that we have here some version of the formula attested in P.Yadin **15** lines 34–35 (the whole context, lines 32–35, is cited): Βαβαθαc Cίμωνοc ἐμαρτυροποιηcάμη<ν> κατὰ Ἰωάνου Ἐγλα Ἀ<βδ>αοβδα Ἐλλουθα ἐπιτρώπων Ἠcοῦc υ<ἱ>ο<ῦ> μου ὀρφανοῦ δι' ἐπιτρόπου μου Ἰούδα Χαθουcίωνοc ἀκολ[ο]ύθωc τὲc προγεγραμμένεc ἐρέcαcιν Ἐλεάζαροc Ἐλεαζάρου ἔγραψα ὑπὲρ αὐτῆc ἐρωτηθεὶc διὰ τὸ αὐτῆc μὴ ε<ἰ>δένα<ι> γράμματα. The mother, represented by her guardian, was illiterate and had someone else subscribe for her: see Greenfield, 'Letters', 39–44; Cotton, 'Subscriptions'.

Verso

Frg. a

Ll. 1–3 All the witnesses whose signatures can be read sign in Greek as in Mur **115** (verso); only one of the witnesses signs in Greek in P.Yadin **18** line 76; no signatures are left in No. **65**.

L. 2 Cου...οc Ε[λεαζ]αρου. Cου[λαι]οc? Ε[λεαζ]αρου. The suggested restoration renders the name שולי Shullai, found in No. **10** line 5 in Aramaic: בר שולי כתבה, 'son of Shullai wrote this', and on the verso of No. **64** line 48 in Aramaic: יהוסף בר שולי שהד, 'Yehosaf son of Shullai, witness'. It has been suggested that this is a Nabataean name.[78] One may recall the powerful minister of the Nabataean realm, Syllaeus (Cυλλαῖoc, Jos. *Ant.* 16.220-225; *B.J.* 1. 487; 574f). A Nabataean inscription from Petra (mid-first century BCE or mid-first century CE) attests: '‘BDMNKW son of ʾKYS (Achaios) son of SLY (Syllaios) son of ‘TYH(W) who has made a tomb for himself and his descendants'.[79] It is also possible to restore Cου[μαι]oc. An Abdereus son of Soumaios serves as a witness in P.Yadin **12** line 16 and a Soumaios son of Ka[.]abaios serves as a witness in P.Yadin **19** line 34—both sign their names in Greek letters; both are Nabataeans.[80] Soumaios is restored as the name of the writer of one of the two Greek letters from Naḥal Ḥever from the time of the Bar Kokhba Revolt.[81] The letter implies that he could communicate in Greek only.[82] It has been suggested that he, too, was a Nabataean.[83] Whether we restore Cου[μαι]oc or Cου[λαι]oc, in view of the restoration of the patronym, Ε[λεαζ]αρου, our man seems to be a Jew.[84]

Marriage Practices

The Mother Gives Away the Bride

The αὐτῆc in line 4 shows that it is a woman, and in all likelihood the mother, who is giving (ἐξέδετο, line 3) her daughter in marriage. Similar examples are found in papyri from Egypt: P.Oxy. X 1273, lines 1–6: 'Aurelia Thaësis daughter of Eudaemon and Heraïs, of Oxyrhinchus, acting with Aurelius Theon also called Nepotianus . . . has given (ἐξέδετο) her daughter Aurelia Tausiris in marriage to the groom Aurelius Arsinoüs son of Tryphon and Demetria, of the said city, to whom the said giver contributes as the dowry of her said daughter, the bride, etc.'; P.Oxy. II 372 (74–5 CE) is reported to begin with ἐξέδοτο Ταοννῶφριc ('the mother of the bride', P.Oxy. II, p. 312); see also PSI X 1117 (ii CE), where the groom acknowledges the receipt of φερνή and παράφερνα from the mother, and the mother declares in lines 18ff.: 'I acknowledge that I have given my daughter Thenapynchis as dowry by the terms of this agreement a house that will be hers from this day and for ever, etc.'[85] There are examples of both parents giving away the daughter: BGU IV 1100 (time of Augustus), line 7: ἐγδέδονται . . . τὴν ἑαυτῶν θυγατέρα; P.Oxy. XLIX 3491 (157/8 CE), lines 1–2: ἐξέδοντο . . . τὴν ἀμφοτ(έρων) θυγ(ατέρα). The *ekdosis* remained a standard feature of the matrimonial institution, even when it lost its original meaning and was reduced to a mere formula.[86]

---

[78] Mussies, 'Personal Names', 252.

[79] Milik, 'Inscription bilingue', 143, and see p. 146 on the name.

[80] Obbink, 'Bilingual Literacy', 57.

[81] Lifshitz, 'Papyrus grecs', 240 (= Yadin, 'Expedition D', 42, no. 3 = SB no. 9843) line 1: Cου[μαῖ]oc; it could also be restored as Cου[λαῖ]oc, see Mussies, 'Personal Names', 252.

[82] Lines 11–15: ἐγράφη δ[ὲ] Ἑληνιcτὶ διὰ τ[ὸ ἀφορ]μὰc μὴ εὑρηθ[ῆ]ναι Ἑβραεcτὶ γ[ρά]ψαcθαι, Obbink's restoration and translation, 'Bilingual Literacy', 54–5; see also Howard and Shelton, 'Bar-Kochba', 102.

[83] Obbink, 'Bilingual Literacy', 57.

[84] Admittedly there is no safe evidence for the use of Nabataean names by Jews: in *CIS* II 219, ‘Omrath is the wife of a man who declares himself a Jew; it is not at all certain, though, that she, too, is Jewish; see Hirschberg, 'New Jewish Inscriptions', 144–5.

[85] For active participation of the mother in the marriage contract see e.g. P.Eleph. 1 (311 BCE) = Select Papyri I. 1 = M.Chr. 283; CPR I 24 (136 CE) = M.Chr. 288; P.Oxy. III 496 (127 CE) = M.Chr. 287 (the grandmother); BGU I 183 (85 CE) = M.Chr. 313; BGU I 251 (81 CE); P.Stras. IV 237 (142 CE).

[86] See Modrzejewski, 'Structure', 252; cf. Wolff, *Written and Unwritten Marriages*, 18; 25ff.; see the examples of *ekdosis* in the Roman period cited there on p. 17 n. 48. The use of ἐξέδοτο in P.Yadin **18** line 3 = lines 32–33, does

Rabbinic legal practice provides for Jewish mothers to give away their daughters in marriage when still underage—presumably because the father has died[87]—as is clear from *m. Ketub.* 6.6: 'If an orphan was given in marriage by her mother or her brothers with her consent, and they assign to her as her portion a hundred *zuz* or fifty, when she comes of age she may exact from them what should rightfully have been given to her'.[88] Minority is assumed also in the case of the father who betroths his daughter: 'A man may give his daughter in betrothal (מקדש) while she is still in her girlhood (נערה) either by his own act or by that of his agent' (*m. Qidd.* 2.1). Once she was of age, the girl could betroth herself.[89] Nothing, however, compels us to assume that this document followed rabbinic practice, if indeed by then rabbinic legal practice had gained the authority it later acquired. Thus, in the absence of other compelling reasons, we need not assume that the bride is a minor (see more below).[90]

The Dowry

In lines 5–7, the bride is said to be bringing with her a dowry in gold and silver evaluated at five hundred *denarii* or one hundred and fifty staters: [προcφερομένην] αὐτῷ εἰc λόγον προcφορᾶc πρ̣ο̣ι̣κ̣[ὸc] ἐ̣ν ἀργύ[ρῳ καὶ χρυcῷ . . . δηνάρια πεν]τακόcιαι οἵ εἰcιν cτατῆρε̣[c ἑκατὸν εἰκο]cιπέ̣[ντε]. The groom then acknowledges to have received this sum of money from her (or her mother's) hands, lines 7–9: [καὶ ὡμολόγηcεν Ακαβαc Μειρω παρ'] αὐτῆc ἀ̣πεcκηκέναι καὶ ἔχ[ειν] . . . δηνάρια πεντακόcιαι παραχρῆμα διὰ χε̣ρὸc. The acknowledgement of a dowry brought in by the bride or her relatives is common to all Greek marriage contracts between Jews from the Judaean Desert,[91] as it is to all Greek marriage contracts from Egypt.

1. Mur **115** lines 4–6: 'The same Eleaios son of Simon agrees to be reconciled and take again Salome daughter of Johannes Galgoula as wedded wife (ἐξ ἀνανεώcεωc καταλλάξαι κ[αὶ] π̣ροcλαβέcθαι[92] τὴν αὐτὴν Cαλω[μὴν Ἰω]άν̣[ο]υ Γ[αλγο]υ̣λὰ ε̣ἰ[c γυναῖ]κα γαμετήν) with a dowry of 200 drachmas which equal 50 Tyrians, which sum of money he acknowledges (ὡμολό[γη]cεν) to have been paid (ἠριθμ[ῆcθαι]) to him . . . the above written two hundred drachmas, on account of her dowry, by Salome (παρὰ Cαλώμηc) daughter of Johannes Galgoula'. The use of ὡμολό[γη]cεν,

not call, therefore, for an *interpretatio Hebraica*, given by R. Katzoff in Lewis, Katzoff, and Greenfield, 'Papyrus Yadin 18', 240–1, and in Katzoff, 'Papyrus Yadin 18', 173–4.

[87] See *t. Yebam.* 13.2 with S. Lieberman, *Tosefta Ki-Fshutah*: Part VI *Seder Nashim,* 1967, 153–4 (Hebrew).

[88] Cf. *m. Yebam.* 13.2.

[89] This is explicitly stated a few lines before, in the passage just quoted: 'A man may betroth (מקדש) a woman either by his own act or by that of his agent; and a woman may become betrothed either by her own act or by that of her agent'; cf. *m. Qidd.* 3.8.

[90] Cf. Wasserstein, 'Marriage Contract', 110ff.

[91] Mur **116** is too lacunose.

[92] The expression ἐξ ἀνανεώcεωc καταλλάξαι κ[αὶ] προcλαβέcθαι may well be an echo of the formula וחזר ופייסה ('he reconciled her') attested in later remarriage ketubbot, see Friedman, *Jewish Marriage*, 2:156 n. 3.

ἠριθμ[ῆcθαι][93] and παρὰ Cαλώμηc should leave us in no doubt as to the direction of the money: from the bride to the groom.[94]

2. In P.Yadin **18**, as in the present document, the direction of the goods from bride to groom is described twice: once from the point of view of the bride's father, 'Judah son of Eleazar . . . gave over Shelamṣion, his very own daughter . . . to Judah surnamed Cimber . . . to be a wedded wife . . . she bringing to him on account of dowry (προςφερομένην αὐτ̣[ῷ] εἰc λόγον προcφορᾶc) feminine adornment in silver and gold and clothing appraised . . . to be worth two hundred *denarii*' (lines 3–10 = lines 32–43); and then from the point of view of the groom: 'which appraised value [of 200 *denarii*] the bridegroom Judah called Cimber acknowledged (ὡμολόγηcεν) that he has received from Shelamṣion, his wife (ἀπειληφέναι παρὰ τῆς αὐτῆς Σελαμψιοῦς γυναικὸς αὐτοῦ), by hand forthwith from Judah her father and that he owes (ὀφείλειν) to Shelamṣion, his wife' (lines 10–13 = lines 43–46).
3. The occasion for writing No. **65**, as interpreted in the present publication,[95] is the receipt of a dowry by the husband, Yeshuᶜa son of Menaḥem, from his wife Salome Komaïse, thus transforming the marriage from an ἄγγραφοc into an ἔγγραφοc γάμοc. In fact, as specifically stated in the document, the dowry was given 'on the prsent day'. Despite the lacunose states of lines 3–8, there is no doubt that it is the husband, Yeshuᶜa son of Menaḥem, who acknowledges there that '[he owes(?)] the above-mentioned Komaïse as her dowry ninety-six denarii of silver . . . received from her on the present day, as the written evaluation of feminine adornment in silver and gold and clothing and other feminine articles equivalent to the above-mentioned amount of money':[96] [ὡμολήc]ạτο Ιηcουc Μαναημου . . . [καὶ ὀφείλειν? c.10 letters]..... τῇ αὐτῇ Κομạịc̣[η τῆ]ṿ προῖ{ο}κα αὐτῆc ἀ[ρ]γụρίου δηνάρια ἐνανήκο̣ṇτα ἕξ, [ἅ ὡμολογήcατο ὁ γήμαc ὁ αὐ]τὸc Ιηcουc̣ [ἀπ]ẹcχηκ̣[έν]αι παρ̣' ạὐτῆc τῇ [οὔ]cη ἡμέρạ τειμογ[ρ]αφίαν κοcμίαc γυναικίαc ἐν ạ̓[ργύρῳ καὶ χρυcῷ καὶ ἱμα]τιcμῷ καὶ ἑταίροιc γυ[ναι]κίοιc ạ̓ξι[οχρέαν] .....τọụ ἀργυρίου.

In two of the three Aramaic marriage contracts from the Judaean Desert[97]—Mur **21** and P.Yadin **10**—the husband acknowledges that he owes his wife the money of her ketubbah (כסף כתבתך, Mur **21** line 13; P.Yadin **10** line 16).[98] If, by 'the money of your ketubbah' the fictitious *mohar* is meant,[99] then it must be said that it is treated in the

[93] See Kühnert, 'Kreditgeschäft', 145, for the use of the verb ἠριθμῆcθαι in loans; cf. P. Dura 29 (251 CE, deposit) line 6: ἠριθμῆcθαι καὶ ἔχειν παρ' αὐτῆc ἐν παρακαταθήκῃ.

[94] This is a contract of remarriage; nevertheless, the groom acknowledges a new dowry, as in BGU IV 1101, lines 6–9 (a remarriage contract from 13 BCE); cf. P.Oxy. XII 1473, a remarriage contract from 201 CE, where there does not seem to be a new dowry (see the editor's introduction to the papyrus). For Jewish deeds of remarriage (המחזיר את גרושתו 'he who remarries his former wife'), see Friedman, *Jewish Marriage*, 2:155ff., no. 13, and Gulak, *Otsar Ha-Shtarot*, 42, no. 37.

[95] See INTRODUCTION to No. **65**; Lewis has a different interpretation; see his introduction to P.Yadin **37**.

[96] It is true that, in comparison with other marriage contracts, this part of the contract is formulated in an inverse order, see COMMENTS on No. **65** ad lines 6–9.

[97] Mur **20** and **21**, and P.Yadin **10**; on the latter, see Yadin, Greenfield, and Yardeni, 'Babatha's Ketubba', 75–99.

[98] P.Yadin **10** line 6: וקים <ע>לך עלי כסף זוזין ארבע מאה מה אנון צורין מאה.

[99] I.e. the rabbinic 'endowment pledge, the divorce payment' (Friedman, *Jewish Marriage*, 1:258), due to the wife upon the dissolution of the marriage; it replaced the biblical *mohar* which was an immediate payment, a bride-

very same way as what we may call the 'gentile' dowry is treated: the husband's entire property is put in lien to secure the return of that money on the dissolution of the marriage, and it is stipulated that the wife's sons will inherit the money, if she dies before the husband. However, there is nothing whatsoever in the text which compels us to think that 'the money of your ketubbah' is the rabbinic fictitious *mohar*, rather than the dowry of the Greek marriage contracts.[100]

Since in all these texts it is the dowry and not the ketubbah which is being acknowledged, it seems idle to dwell on the fact that the sum of two hundred *denarii* in P.Yadin **18** and Mur **115** tallies with the minimum ketubbah stipulated in Jewish sources as the bride-price of a virgin; it is merely a coincidence, as demonstrated by the five hundred *denarii* of our document and the ninety-six *denarii* of No. **65**. Nor is there a need to explain the discrepancy between the four hundred *zuzin* (= *denarii*) of Babatha's ketubbah in P.Yadin **10** and the one hundred *denarii* stipulated for a widow in rabbinic sources.[101] Finally, it is impossible to identify the three hundred *denarii* which the husband, Judah Cimber, adds to his wife's dowry (P.Yadin **18** lines 13–14 = lines 46–7) as the Jewish 'addition to the ketubbah'(תוספת כתובה),[102] since the first two hundred were not ketubbah but dowry brought in by the bride. If anything they are *donatio ante nuptias in dotem redacta.*[103]

Maintenance of the Wife

The undertaking to feed and clothe the wife is a recurrent element in marriage contracts in Greek from Egypt, and, as here, it often follows immediately upon the groom's acknowledgement of the receipt of the dowry (ἐφ' ᾧ ἔϲται ἡ Cελαμπιουϲ τρεφομένη καὶ ἀμ̣φ[ιαζο]μ̣[ένη]; line 10). We find it already in the earliest Greek marriage contract, P.Eleph. 1 (311 BCE), lines 2–5: λαμβάνει Ἡρακλείδηϲ Δημητρίαν Κῴαν γυναῖκα γνηϲίαν παρὰ τοῦ πατρὸϲ Λεπτίνου Κῴου καὶ τῆϲ μητρὸϲ Φιλωτίδοϲ . . . προϲφερομένην εἱματιϲμὸν καὶ κόϲμον (δραχμῶν) (χιλίων), παρεχέτω δὲ Ἡρακλείδηϲ Δημητρίαι ὅϲα προϲήκει γυναικὶ ἐλευθέραι πάντα. The 'freeborn wife' is later changed to 'wedded wife', cf. BGU IV 1050 (= M.Chr. 286, 13 BCE) lines 12–14: <ἐφ' ᾧ> τὸν Διονύϲιον ἀπεϲχηκότα τὴν προκειμένην φερνὴν τρέφειν καὶ ἱματίζειν τὴν Ἰϲιδώραν ὡϲ γυναῖκα γα[μετὴν] κατὰ δύναμιν. As has been shown ἐπιχορηγείτω cannot be safely restored in line 9 of No. **69**; consequently we cannot be sure that [γυναῖκα] γαμετήν of lines 9–10 is part of the maintenance clause; possibly the maintenance clause is restricted

gift to the wife's father. The traditional and almost universally accepted view is that the process reached its conclusion when Shimʿon b. Shetaḥ—who was active in the first half of the first century BCE—put a clause into the ketubbah that the husband's entire property is held liable for the payment of the *mohar*. The story is found in several versions in *b. Ketub.* 82b; *y. Ketub.* 8.11, 32b; *t. Ketub.* 12.1; see Friedman, *Jewish Marriage*, 1:257ff. and n. 71 for the sources; cf. Archer, *Jewish Woman*, 159–63.

[100] Bickerman ('Legal Interpretations', 212–15), in fact comes very close to suggesting that 'the money of the ketubbah' may refer to the dowry; cf. Satlow, 'Rabbinic *Ketubah*', 137ff. The documentary marriage contracts support Satlow's claim that 'the rabbinic *ketubah* payment was a rabbinic innovation of around the late first century CE', 146.

[101] Yadin, Greenfield, and Yardeni, 'Babatha's Ketubba', 89ff.; Friedman, 'Babatha's *Ketubba*' (I am grateful to M. Friedman for showing me his manuscript in advance of publication).

[102] Pace Katzoff, 'Papyrus Yadin 18', 242 and n. 35.

[103] See Wasserstein, 'Marriage Contract', 114; for *donatio ante nuptias* and marriage contracts, see the bibliography in Kuehn, 'New Papyrus'.

to ἐφ' ᾧ ἔϲται ἡ Ϲελαμπιουϲ τρεφομένη καὶ ἀμ̣φ[ιαζο]μ̣[ένη]. However, the combination of the maintenance formula and the expression 'as befits a wedded wife' is found in Babatha's Aramaic marriage contract (P.Yadin **10**), lines 9–10: 'with appropriate food and conjugal rights(?) and clothes befitting a freeborn woman', עם דין [לחמ]ך ופרשך וכסתך כ[א]נתה ברת חורין. It is striking to find here an echo of P.Eleph. 1 line 5 (cited above) with 'freeborn' rather than 'wedded' wife, unless, in this case, 'free', ברת חורין, means simply 'a married woman', 'a wife', as ἐλευθέρα does in later Greek.[104] The two Aramaic marriage contracts Mur **20** and **21** are too fragmentary at this point, but they mention the maintenance of the wife after the husband's death,[105] as does Mur **116**.[106]

There is only indirect evidence for the inclusion of the obligation to provide for the wife in rabbinic marriage contracts of the early mishnaic period.[107] It has been claimed that the maintenance clause was included in the Jewish ketubbah tradition under the influence of demotic marriage deeds.[108] In view of the persistence of the formula in Greek marriage contracts from Egypt from the late fourth century BCE onwards, there is no reason to exclude their influence as well.

The Liability Clause

In lines 11–12 we find a clause which earmarks the husband's entire property as security for his wife's maintenance: [ἐπὶ τῶν or ἐπὶ πάντων ὑπαρ]χ̣ό̣ντων ὧν τε νῦν ἔχε̣ι κ̣α̣ὶ ὧν̣ ἂν ἐπικτήϲηται. No such clause is found, as far as I know, in Greek marriage contracts from Egypt, where it is stated that the husband will provide for all that is necessary (τὰ δέοντα πάντα) according to his means (κατὰ δύναμιν or κατὰ δύναμιν τῶν ὑπαρχόντων). No such entailment is meant by the phrase found in P.Tebt. I 104 lines 16–18 (= M.Chr. 285, 92 BCE), which is used to restore the text in other marriage contracts (e.g. P.Gen. I 21 = M.Chr. 284, lines 2–3): [T]ὰ δὲ [δ]έοντα π̣[ά]ντα καὶ τὸν [ἱμ]ατιϲμὸν καὶ τἆλλα ὅϲα προϲήκει γυναικὶ γαμετῇ παρεχέϲθω Φιλίϲκοϲ 'Απολλωνίαν ἐνδημῶν καὶ ἀποδημῶν κατὰ δύναμιν τῶν ὑπαρχόντων αὐτοῖϲ, especially since, later on (lines 24–27), it is stated that unless the husband does provide for the wife's clothing and nourishment, as promised, he will have to return the dowry immediately. Nor is it the case, when the maintenance clause is explicitly included in the rabbinic marriage contract, that the husband's property is placed in lien to it.[109] The only exception—apart from No. **69**, P.Yadin **18** and No. **65**—is the Jewish marriage contract of 417 CE from Antinoopolis, written in Aramaic and containing many Greek words transcribed in Hebrew letters.

[104] See Feissel, 'Notes'; Drescher, 'Eleuthera'. See the late SB I 4658 (Arsinoe, 323–642 CE) lines 10–13: ὃν καὶ ἐγγυούμεθα ἑτοίμωϲ ἡμᾶϲ ἔχειν παραϲκευάϲαι αὐτὸν φιλιοθῆναι τῇ [αὐ]τοῦ γαμετῇ Μαρίᾳ καὶ θάλπειν αὐτὴν ὡϲ ἄξιό[ν ἐϲτι]ν τῶν ἐλευθέρων γυναικῶν.

[105] Mur **20** line 10:] ומתזנה ומכסיא 'she will be fed and clothed' i.e. after his death; Mur **21** line 15: ומתזנה [מנ נכסי] כל ימי[ן] די תהין ית[ב]א ב[י]ת די ארמלו, 'and be nourished [from my possessions] all the days that you will [be in] the house of your widowhood'.

[106] Mur **116** line 9: 'Εὰν δὲ ὁ Αὐ̣ρ̣ἑ̣λ̣ι̣οϲ πρὸ̣ τῆϲ Ϲαλώμηϲ τὸν βίον μεταλλάξε̣ι̣ [τρ]αφήϲηται ἡ Ϲαλ̣ώ̣μη [κ]α̣ὶ̣ ἀ̣μ̣φιϲαϲθ[ήϲ]εται ἐκ̣ τῆϲ τοῦ Αὐρηλίου ο̣ὐϲίαϲ, 'And if Aurelius dies before Salome, she will be fed and clothed'.

[107] See Friedman *Jewish Marriage*, 1:167ff. for the halakhic sources. In *m. Ketub.* 4.4, it is said explicitly that 'the husband is obliged to feed his wife', but no date can be assigned to this ruling.

[108] Geller, 'New Sources'.

[109] See Friedman, *Jewish Marriage*, 1:167–78.

In this contract, known as the Ketubbah from Cologne, the husband's possessions are said to guarantee the feeding and clothing of the wife.[110]

The liability clause, which pledges the husband's entire property to guarantee the upkeep of the wife, sets this marriage contract (as well as P.Yadin **18**, No. **65** and the much later Ketubbah from Cologne) apart from all other Jewish marriage contracts, as well as from Greek marriage contracts from Egypt. In marriage contracts from the Judaean Desert[111] and in Greek marriage contracts from Egypt,[112] the liability clause is used simply to guarantee the return of the dowry in the event of a divorce or death. It serves the same purpose in the rabbinic ketubbah, where it guarantees the payment of the postponed bride-money (viz. the fictitious *mohar*).[113] However, in demotic marriage contracts from Egypt we find that 'the husband repeatedly pledges everything he possesses and will acquire as security for honouring the obligations which he has taken upon himself by a deed drawn up in view of a marriage'.[114] The similarity to demotic contracts extends even to the particular wording used to apply the liability clause not only to the property possessed by the husband at the time of concluding the contract, but also to property acquired after its conclusion. In the demotic P.Mich. inv. 4526 (Philadelphia, 199 BCE), we find almost a translation of lines 10–11 of our document: 'Everything that I possess and that I shall acquire is security for your above-mentioned food-and-clothing allowance'.[115] This phrase is common to Jewish contracts from the Judaean Desert, both marriage contracts and contracts of sale or debt, in both Greek and Aramaic.[116]

Provisions for Male and Female Children

Lines 11–13 might have clarified many issues concerning the different rights of male and female children had they been better preserved. It is clear, though, that, as a result of the prior death of one partner, probably the wife, the male children are to become heirs, probably of her dowry. It is not certain whether the wife's prior death is also the condition for the next stipulation, namely that female children will be nourished and clothed—presumably until they get married—or whether that stipulation is

---

[110] Sirat et al., *Ketouba,* 20–1, lines 23–25: ויהוון אחריין [ו]ער[בין] למזונין ולתכסין; cf. pp. 13 and 57f.

[111] This is true at least in those in which the final clause has been preserved. It can be restored in Mur **20** lines 11–12. It is contained in the *praxis* clauses in Mur **115** lines 16–18 and P.Yadin **18** lines 21–27 = lines 57–66; see Yadin, Greenfield, and Yardeni, 'Babatha's Ketubba', 96 on P.Yadin **10**.

[112] E.g. P.Eleph. 1 = M.Chr. 283 = Sel.Pap. I.1 (311 BCE) lines 12–13; P.Tebt. III 1052 lines 19–22; P.Ryl. II 154 (66 CE) lines 33–35; P.Oxy. X 1273 (260 CE) lines 35–36; P.Oxy. II 237 (186 CE). In fact, it is a standing feature of all bills of debt; see Kühnert, 'Kreditgeschäft', *passim.*

[113] See Friedman, *Jewish Marriage*, 1:451ff.; Koffmahn, *Doppelurkunden*, 68f. The phrasing is: 'All properties which I have are surety and guarantee for your ketubbah' (כל נכסין דאית לי אחראין וערבאין לכתובתיך; *t. Ketub.* 12.1; cf. *m. Ketub.* 4.7).

[114] Pestman, *Marriages*, 115; see ibid. 115–17; 133–6.

[115] See Lüddeckens, *Aegyptische Eheverträge*, 148–51, no. 4D; cf. Pestman, *Marriage*, 115ff.

[116] Marriage contracts: P.Yadin **18** lines 16–18 = lines 51–54; **37** lines 10–11, quoted above ad lines 9–10, in both as part of the guarantee of upkeep. In Mur **115** line 17 it seems to be part of the guarantee of the return of the dowry: ἐκ τῶν ὑπαρχό[ντων αὐ]τ̣ῳ [ὧν δ]ὲ ἔχει καὶ ὧν ἂν ἐπ[ι]κτ̣[ήσηται]; Mur **20** line 12 (Aramaic); other contracts: P.Yadin **11** lines 10–11 = lines 25–27; **17** lines 12–15 = lines 34–37; Mur **114** lines 19–21 (Greek); Mur **18** line 8; Mur **26** line 6; Mur **30** lines 23–24; No. **8** line 6; No. **49** line 11 (Aramaic). See Friedman, *Jewish Marriage*, 1:452 and nn. 5–6 for this liability formula in the Jewish sources.

independent of it. It seems to be independent of it in the other documentary marriage contracts between Jews (see below).[117] These clauses are amongst the so-called 'court stipulations' (תנאי בית דין) of the Jewish ketubbah,[118] i.e. 'tacit conditions, binding upon all, even if not written in a specific marriage contract'.[119]

The specific clauses distinguishing between male and female children as heirs to their mother's property are so far attested only in the Jewish ketubbah tradition,[120] apparently already in the early mishnaic period. The phrase הבנים ירשו והבנות יזונו, 'the sons inherit and the daughters are provided for' (*m. Ketub.* 4.6), is said there to have been expounded on by R. Eleazar b. Azaryah, a second generation Tanna (90–130 CE), so that such a practice must have existed for a while. We read in *m. Ketub.* 4.10–11: 'If he had not written for her: "Male children which you will have by me shall inherit thy ketubbah besides the portion which they received with their brethren", he is still liable (thereto), since this is a condition enjoined by the court. (If he had not written for her:) "Female children which you will have by me shall dwell in my house and receive maintenance from my goods until they marry husbands", he is still liable (thereto), since this is a condition enjoined by the court'.[121] The distinction between the rights of sons and daughters is attested in different ways in all four marriage contracts from Wadi Murabbaʿat, in both Aramaic and Greek. However, the clauses are curiously absent from the two Greek marriage contracts from Arabia, P.Yadin **18** and No. **65**.[122] The order of the relevant clauses in the four documents, concerning provisions for children in the case of the prior death of the wife, and sometimes without reference to it, varies:

1. the heavily restored Mur **20** lines 7–9 (Aramaic) seems to state that if the wife predeceases her husband, the sons will inherit her ketubbah, while the daughters will be provided for;
2. according to Mur **21** lines 10–14 (Aramaic), the daughters will stay in the father's house and be provided for; if the wife predeceases her husband, the sons will inherit her ketubbah and whatever else belongs to her;
3. according to Mur **115** lines 8–14 (Greek), the children will be provided for; if the husband dies first, the widow will be provided for; if the wife dies first, the sons will inherit (her dowry);
4. in Mur **116** lines 4–6 (Greek), the daughters will be provided for and given in marriage; if the wife dies first, the sons will inherit her dowry, etc.

---

[117] The condition of the wife's prior death is also absent from *m. Ketub.* 4.11 (cited in the text), which provides for the daughters' maintenance. In this, as well as in what follows, I rely on the detailed discussion in Friedman, *Jewish Marriage*, 1:356–91.

[118] *M. Ketub.* 4.6–12.

[119] Friedman, *Jewish Marriage*, 1:15. Friedman maintains there that 'Some of them reflect similar marital obligations elsewhere in the ancient Near East'.

[120] A recently published Idumaean marriage contract singles out male children as heirs (line 6), but probably to their father's property; see Kloner and Eshel, 'Aramaic Ostracon', esp. 494–5 and 501. The element *kos* in their names—the Idumaean God—demonstrates that the parties involved are not Jewish.

[121] Cf. *m. Ketub.* 13.3.

[122] Only the inner part of No. **65** has been preserved. It is possible , therefore, that the outer text contained these clauses, but it is not very likely since the two contracts from Arabia resemble each other in many respects, see COMMENTS on No. **65**.

In Babatha's Aramaic marriage contract (P.Yadin **10**), after a space of two lines which are now almost completely obliterated and which may have contained a reference to the prior death of the wife and the stipulation that her male children will inherit her dowry, it is stipulated that the daughters will stay in the father's house and be fed from his property until taken by husbands (lines 14–15).

It seems that the provision concerning male children as heirs to their mother's property entered Jewish law under the influence of other Near Eastern traditions, where—unlike the case in Jewish law—the wife's children were her heirs.[123] The provision certainly contravenes the biblical law of inheritance which made the husband sole heir to his wife's property; upon his death, all his sons, including those from another woman, would divide his property equally between them.[124] Thus, the provision for sons to inherit their mother's dowry/ketubbah was meant to protect sons in polygamous marriages against the loss of part of their mother's property to sons of another woman.[125] This can be seen in a Greek marriage contract from the Judaean Desert: [ἐὰν δὲ ἡ Cαλώμη πρὸ τοῦ Αὐρηλίου] τὸν βίον μ[ε]τ̣α̣λλάξει υ̣[ἱοὺ]ς̣ οὓς ἂν ἕ̣ξε̣ι̣ ἀπ̣' α̣ὐ̣τ̣[οῦ . . . κληρονομήcουcιν] τὴν φ̣ερνὴν κ̣α̣ί τὰ πρ[ογε]γραμμένα̣ [*c*.40 letters] τ̣ῆ̣ς̣ τ̣οῦ Αὐρη̣λ̣ί̣ου ο̣ὐ̣[c]ί̣ας π̣ᾶ̣c̣α̣[ν κλ]ηρονομί̣αν μ̣εθ' ὧν ἂν̣ ἕξωcιν ἀ̣[δ]ελφῶν (Mur **116** lines 4–8).

The stipulation that the daughters are to be fed and clothed may have replaced an earlier one which provided for all children to be fed and clothed from the father's property.[126] The original situation is reflected in one of the marriage contracts from Murabbaʿat: καὶ τέκνων̣ αὐ̣τ̣ῆc οὓc ἔ[χ]ει κ̣α̣ι̣ ο̣[ὓc ἂν] cχῇ ἀπ' αὐτοῦ υἱ̣ο̣ὺc ἢ θυγατέραc ο̣ὓ̣c ἔχ[*c.* 20 letters] οὓc ἂν cχῇ ἀπ' αὐ[τ]οῦ τραφήc̣ονται κ̣α̣ί ἀ̣μ̣φ̣ιαcθήc[ον]ται ἐκ τ̣[ῶ]ν̣ ὑ[παρ]χόντων τῷ αὐτῷ Ἐλε̣α̣[ί]ῳ̣.(Mur **115** lines 8–10), as well as in the two marriage contracts from Arabia, both of which use an almost identical terminology: ἀκολούθωc αἱρέcει τροφῆc καὶ ἀμφιαcμοῦ αὐτῆc τε καὶ τῶν μελλόντων τέκνων ἑλληνικῷ νόμῳ (P.Yadin **18** lines 16–17 = lines 49–51); cὺν αἱρέcει τροφῆ̣c [καὶ ἀμφιαcμοῦ αὐτῆc] τ̣ε καὶ τῶν μελ̣λόντ̣ω[ν τέκ]ν̣ω̣ν̣ ν̣ό̣μ̣[ῳ ἑλληνικ]ῷ καὶ ἑλ̣λ̣[η]ν̣ι̣κ̣ῷ τρόπῳ (No. **65** lines 9–10).[127] This is not the place to enter into the intricate explanation of the reasons for the change which limited the maintenance clause to daughters only. It may well have been a consequence of the introduction of the provision in favour of male sons vis-à-vis their mother's property.

The provision which singles out sons as heirs to their mother's property is present, then, in six of the eight marriage contracts (both in Aramaic and in Greek) between Jews from the Judaean Desert,[128] regardless of whether the mother's property is described as dowry, about which it says explicitly that she brought it with her, or whether it is called her ketubbah.[129] Finally, it should be pointed out that even when

---

[123] See Friedman, *Jewish Marriage*, 1:380ff. and nn. 5–6 on p. 381.

[124] Friedman, *Jewish Marriage*, 1:382.

[125] See Falk, 'Inheritance'.

[126] Friedman, *Jewish Marriage*, 1:369.

[127] Cf. the heavily restored P.Oxy. XLIX 3491 (157/8 CE) lines 16–17: καὶ χορειγείτω ὁ γ[α]μῶν [τῇ γαμουμ(ένῃ)] καὶ τοῖc [ἐ]ξ [ἀλλήλ(ων) τέκνοιc τὰ δέο]ντα κατὰ δύναμιν.

[128] Mur **20**, **21**, **115**, **116**, P.Yadin **10** and the present document.

[129] As was pointed out above in the discussion of the dowry, this may well stand for her dowry.

taking into consideration the fragmentary condition of some of the documentary evidence surveyed here, one may detect a lack of uniformity regarding this clause in contemporaneous documentary marriage contracts between Jews, which suggests that the stipulation had not yet adopted its final and normative form.

Conclusion

There is no doubt that the marriage contract published here is between Jews who lived in Judaea on the eve of the outbreak of the Bar Kokhba Revolt. Nevertheless it must be stated that this is not a Jewish document, if by that we mean the presence of explicit formulae which would place it firmly within a Jewish framework and which would impose on it the sanction of Jewish law,[130] such as we find in the opening lines of two of the contemporary Aramaic marriage contracts. There, in Mur **20** (117 CE?), the groom declares: [את]י תהוא לי לאנתה כדין מ[ושה ויהודאי] '[you] will be my wife according to the law of M[oses and the Jews]', and in P.Yadin **10** line 5 (125–8 CE), Judah son of Eleazar, Babatha's second husband, declares that he is taking her לאנת[ה כדי]ן משה ויה[ו]דאי 'for a wife [according to the la]w of Moses and the Jews'.[131]

P.Ent. 23 = CPJ I 128 (218 BCE) is often cited in this context as proof for the existence of a Jewish marriage law in Egypt at the time. However, the heavily restored line 2 of the papyrus—[κατὰ τὸν νόμον π]ο̣λ̣ιτικὸν τῶν ['Ιου]δαίων ἔχειν με γυν[αῖκα]—can hardly sustain such an interpretation. The editors of CPJ are rightly sceptical about the deductions to be drawn from such a poorly preserved text, since 'no trace of any mention of Jewish law concerning marriage can be found in the remaining parts of the papyrus'; moreover, this will be 'the only instance in the Greek papyri of Jewish national law being applied to the legal life of members of the Jewish community'.[132]

No statement about the 'law of Moses and the Jews' is made in our papyrus. There is no room to insert it where it should traditionally have appeared, even if we allow for some fluidity.[133] It is not as though the formula could not be expressed in Greek. Moreover, the formula is not absent from our contract only, but also from the other marriage contracts between Jews written in Greek. No trace of it can be found in Mur **115**, P.Yadin **18**, or No. **65**. The claim that the Greek phrase κατὰ τοὺϲ νόμουϲ in P.Yadin **18** lines 32–39 = lines 3–7 [134] replaces the traditional Jewish formula cited above

---

[130] Friedman, *Jewish Marriage*, 1:163–4.

[131] See also the restoration to No. **11** line 2; note that in Yadin, Greenfield, and Yardeni, 'Babatha's Ketubba', 79, line 5, the word ויה[ו]דאי is translated 'Judaeans', rather than 'Jews'. 'According to the law of Moses and the Jews' is the earlier formula: it was later replaced by 'according to the law of Moses and Israel'; see Friedman, *Jewish Marriage*, 162ff.; cf. Flusser and Safrai, 'In the Image', 453–6.

[132] CPJ I, p. 238; cf. ibid. (*Prolegomena*), 33–4; see also II, 4–5; cf. Cotton, 'Guardianship', 105. It is regrettable that those who cite the papyrus fail to point out that this is a heavily restored text, e.g. Falk, *Introduction*, 286; cf. Modrzejewski, 'Jewish Law', 85–6.

[133] See Friedman, *Jewish Marriage*, 1:155–67.

[134] The full context is: ἐ̣ξ[έδ]ο̣τ[ο 'Ιούδα]ϲ̣ Ἐ̣λ̣ε̣αζάρου τοῦ καὶ [Χθουϲί]ω̣ν[οϲ C]ελαμψ[ι]ώ̣νη̣ν̣ τὴ̣ν ἰδίαν θυγατέραν αὐτο̣ῦ παρθ̣έ̣ν̣ο̣ν 'Ιοὐ̣δατι ἐπικαλουμένῳ̣ Κίμβερι υἱῷ̣ 'Ανανίου τοῦ Ϲ̣ω̣μ̣α̣λα, ἀμφότεροι ἀπὸ̣ κ̣ώ̣μ̣ηϲ 'Αινγαδῶν τῆϲ 'Ιου̣δαία[ϲ] ἐνθάδε καταμένοντ̣[εϲ], ε̣ἶ̣ν̣α̣ι̣ τ̣ὴν Ϲ̣ε̣λ̣αμψιών[ην] 'Ιούδατι Κίμβερι γυνα̣ῖκαν γαμετὴν π̣ρ̣ὸϲ γάμου κ̣[οι]νωνίαν κατὰ τοὺϲ νόμουϲ.

is, of course, unfounded.[135] This 'most conventional Greek phrase' means no more than what it says.[136]

The marriage contract published here—like other Greek marriage contracts between Jews—is not a Greek translation of an Aramaic ketubbah. It is an independent legal instrument with a spirit of its own: not only the Greek language but the entire ethos and diplomatics of the Greek marriage contract have been adopted by the contracting parties, as I have tried to show by the parallels to marriage contracts from Egypt, referred to throughout this survey.[137] Furthermore, there is nothing specifically Jewish about this marriage contract, apart from the clauses concerning the distinction between male and female children, for which, until now, no parallels from the surrounding region have been found. It is quite true that some of the clauses found in the Greek marriage contracts discussed here have halakhic parallels, as has been seen in the commentary. Nevertheless, it would be methodologically unsound to claim that, because the documents reflect halakhic rules familiar to us from tannaitic literature, these rules should be described as Jewish. The fact that there are many points of resemblance between Greek marriage contracts from Judaea and Arabia and contemporary marriage contracts from Egypt suggests that the traditions which came to be crystallized in the final redaction of the Mishna by the end of the second century were not uniquely Jewish. It is not so much that our documents reflect the halakhah, but, rather, that the halakhah was not created *in vacuo*: it reflects mixed local traditions which were later absorbed into Judaism.[138] Once they received halakhic sanction, they could be described as Jewish, but not before. With this document, we are still in the period of flux.[139]

---

[135] Katzoff in Lewis *et al.*, 'Papyrus Yadin 18', 241; he retracted later: Katzoff, 'Papyrus Yadin 18', 173; cf. Katzoff, 'Marriage Formulas'. The phrase is now attested in an unpublished marriage contract from Bostra (P. Bostra 2) dated to the third century CE in connection with the dowry; but the context is unclear. I am grateful to J. Gascou for showing me the text.

[136] See Wasserstein, 'A Marriage Contract, 113.

[137] The argument that a marriage contract written in Greek was valid in a Jewish court is irrelevant: it does not make it a Jewish document, as Katzoff ('Papyrus Yadin 18', 176) seems to imply.

[138] Goodman, *State and Society*, 13; 159ff. See the penetrating remarks of Wasserstein in the conclusion of 'Marriage Contract', 121–30, and the INTRODUCTION TO THE GREEK DOCUMENTARY TEXTS.

[139] See Yaron, 'Mesadah', 438; 454–5.

70. XḤev/Se papUnidentified Fragment A gr

(PLS. XXXI AND XLVII)

THIS is a small fragment (*olim* XḤev/Se Gr. 5), measuring 2.7 x 1.5 cm. The only complete word which can be read is τ]έccαρε̣[c, 'four', in line 3.

Mus. Inv. 866
PAM 40.642

1]....[

2]ει θηc[

3 τ]έccαρε̣[c

4].τελω̣[

5].ουκα[

71. XḤev/Se papUnidentified Fragment B gr

(PLS. XXXI AND XLVII)

THIS is a small fragment (*olim* XḤev/Se Gr. 5), measuring 2.5 x 1.3 cm.

Mus. Inv. 866
PAM 40.642

ϲ̣αδωραι.[

..]..αι αρ[

72. XḤev/Se papUnidentified Fragment C gr

(PLS. XXXI AND XLVII)

THIS is a small fragment (*olim* XḤev/Se Gr. 5), measuring 3 x 1.2 cm.

Mus. Inv. 866
PAM 40.642

]δ̣ι̣ω Θεοδώρου[

]μενω Νεελα[

COMMENTS

L. 1 δ̣ι̣ω. Perhaps *sigma*: ς̣ι̣ω. This may be the last part of a name followed by the patronymic Theodoros.

L. 1 Θεοδώρου. A Θεω̣δ̣ώ̣ρ̣ος̣ υἱὸς̣ Μ[...]ί̣ου μάρ(τυς) is one of the witnesses on the verso of P.Yadin **11**.

L. 2]μενω. Perhaps [καλου]μένῳ or [προγεγραμ]μένῳ should be restored before the name, Νεελα[.

73. XḤev/Se papEnd of a Document gr

106–107 or 109 CE

(PL. XLVII)

THIS fragment of a papyrus (*olim* XḤev/Se Gr. 4) has suffered considerable damage. It preserves *c*.8–10 letters, along the left margin, of the last six lines of a document. The beginning of the text is lost, the vertical fibres on which it was written having disintegrated. The four legible words in lines 4–6 belong to the dating formula, which came at the end of the document. The document seems to be dated by regnal as well as by consular year. Since this type of dating appears both in documents from Arabia and from Judaea, we cannot know the provenance of the fragment (see INTRODUCTION TO THE GREEK DOCUMENTARY TEXTS). For the placing of the date at the end of the document, see Nos. **60** lines 9–12; **61** lines 5–6; **63** line 15; and P.Yadin **12** lines 10–11; **23** lines 20–22; **24** lines 28–30 = lines 64–66; and **26** lines 18–19.

The fragment measures 8 x 4.5 cm.

Mus. Inv. 731
PAM 42.356

traces [
δ.ω *c.5 letters* [
ἐνδεκάτου ...[
Γ̣ερμανικοῦ. [
traces [
καὶ Πουβλί̣[ου

Comments

Ll. 2–6 A possible reconstruction of these lines is:

ἔτους]
ἑνδεκάτου [Αὐτοκράτορος Καίcαρος Νέρουα Τραιανοῦ Cεβαcτοῦ]
Γ̣ερμανίκοῦ [Δακικοῦ]
[ἐπι ὑπάτων Αὔλου Κορνηλίου Πάλμα τὸ β̅]
καὶ Πουβλί̣[ου Καλουιcίου Τούλλου]

L. 3 ἑνδεκάτου. Trajan's eleventh *tribunicia potestas* fell between 10 December 106 and 9 December 107.[1] If his regnal year in Judaea or Arabia was identical with the year of his *tribunicia potestas*, then the regnal year clashes with the consular date in line 6, namely 109 CE (see ad loc.). However, if Trajan's regnal years in Judaea or Arabia were counted from the time of Nerva's death, i.e. 27 or 28 January 98, then his eleventh year would fall between 27 or 28 January 108 and 27 or 28 January 109, i.e. an overlap of almost one month between the regnal year in line 3 and the consular date in line 6. 109 is the only year in which an eleventh regnal year of Trajan could coincide with that of a *consul ordinarius* whose *praenomen* is Publius (see καὶ Πουβλί̣[ου] in line 6).

Ll. 3–6 The suggested restoration, Αὐτοκράτωρ Καῖcαρ Νέρουαc Τραιανόc Cεβαcτόc Γερμανικὸc Δακικόc, 'is one of the most common series of titles of Trajan' (Sijpesteijn, 'Imperial Titles', 179–80); more than 180 examples are listed by Bureth, *Les Titulatures impériales*, 51–2.[2]

L. 4 Γ̣ερμανικοῦ. The title Germanicus excludes Hadrian, who shunned the triumphal titles in his titulature; see Kneissl, *Die Siegestitulatur*, 91–6; for the exceptions mentioned by Bureth, *Les Titulatures impériales*, 63, see Van't Dack, 'Les formulae des empereurs', 886–7, and Sijpesteijn, 'Imperial Titles', 181–2.

Ll. 4–5 In the Greek documents from the Judaean Desert, if a regnal year appears in the first place, the consular date comes in the second place, and the provincial year in the third (see Lewis, *Documents*, 28 and Introduction to the Greek Documentary Texts). Thus the provincial year could not have occupied the space between Δακικοῦ and ἐπι ὑπάτων or ὑπατείαc, even if there was enough room; neither can we expect here, in this most ordinary dating formula, a fuller titulature of the emperor.[3] It is unlikely that the day and the month occupied the space, since they usually follow the consuls' names. Admittedly, it is hard to see where they could have fitted in line 6. What could have come between Δακικοῦ and ἐπι ὑπάτων or ὑπατείαc must remain a puzzle.

L. 6 καὶ Πουβλί[ου]. The *praenomen* of the second consul points to the year 109, when the *ordinarii* were Aulus Cornelius Palma Frontonianus II and Publius Calvisius Tullus Ruso. This can harmonize with Trajan's eleventh regnal year (see ad line 1: ἑνδεκάτου) only if the latter differed in Arabia or Judaea from the year of his *tribunicia potestas*. Otherwise, one must postulate a discrepancy between the regnal and consular dates in this document. Note that 109 is also one of two possible dates for No. **66**.

---

[1] See Kienast, *Kaisertabelle*, 123.

[2] Theoretically, one might think of Domitian; however, his eleventh year, 91–2, seems too early for the collection here; nor does it coincide with that of a *consul ordinarius* whose *praenomen* is Publius.

[3] See No. **69** line 1; P.Yadin **14** line 1 = lines 15–16; **15** line 1 = line 14; **20** line 1 = lines 18–19; **21** lines 1–2; **22** lines 1–2. The fuller titulature occurs only in the two land declarations, No. **62** frg. a lines 4–7 and P.Yadin **16** lines 5–7. The latter is better preserved: ἐπὶ Αὐτοκράτοροc Καίcαροc θεοῦ Τραιανοῦ Παρθικοῦ υ̣ἱ̣οῦ θεοῦ Νέρουα υἱωνοῦ Τραιανοῦ Ἁδριανοῦ Cεβαcτοῦ ἀρχιερέωc μεγίcτου δημαρχικῆc ἐξουcίαc τὸ δωδέκατον ὑπάτου τὸ τρίτον.

APPENDIX

DOCUMENTARY TEXTS
ALLEGED TO BE FROM
QUMRAN CAVE 4

Introduction to the 'Qumran Cave 4' Documentary Texts

AMONG the hundreds of manuscripts attributed to Qumran cave 4 is a collection of texts in Aramaic, Hebrew, and Greek that are non-literary in character. The decision to append these documentary texts to the XḤev/Se documents was made on the basis of several factors.

1. Although these nineteen texts were labelled 4Q**342–348**, 4Q**351–354**, and 4Q**356–361**[1] at the time of their acquisition, their source is unclear. It is believed that they were purchased from Bedouin who attributed them to cave 4.

2. The discovery by the present editor that one of the Qumran fragments (4Q**347**) is in reality a part of a document from the Wadi Seiyal collection (No. **32**), brought into question the attribution of its provenance as Qumran cave 4. It is highly unlikely that two fragments of a single deed would be found in two such distant locales.

3. The genre of this set of documentary texts, a collection of letters, deeds, and accounts, is unparalleled among the Qumran manuscripts of proven cave 4 provenance, which as a group are literary in nature. See, however, the very fragmentary 6Q**26–29**.

4. The cursive script utilized in these texts sets them apart from the other Qumran manuscripts.

5. Recent Carbon-14 dating of 4Q**342** and 4Q**344** yielded dates well into the late first and early second centuries CE, long after the settlement at Khirbet Qumran was abandoned.[2]

6. 4Q**359** bears the name מתת בר חזק (Mattat son of Ḥazaq) and should probably be linked to No. **7** in the XḤev/Se collection, a deed of sale drawn up by an individual named חזק בר מתת (Ḥazaq son of Mattat), who may be a relative, perhaps a son, of the individual named in 4Q**359**.

Though a provenance outside of Qumran cave 4 cannot be conclusively demonstrated for the majority of the texts, the weight of the Carbon-14 dating of 4Q**342** and **344** and the links between 4Q**347** and **359** and Nos. **32** and **7**, together with the desire to present the documentary texts from 'Qumran cave 4' as a single corpus, resulted in the decision to include them as an appendix in the present volume.

Description of the 'Qumran Cave 4' Documentary Texts

The group includes fragments of twelve documents written on hide and of seven documents (in addition to 4Q**347**) written on papyrus. Five of these (4Q**352**, **352a**, **353**,

[1] 4Q**350**, written on the verso of 4Q**460** (Narrative Work and Prayer), and 4Q**355**, written on the verso of 4Q**324** (Calendrical Document C[c]) will be published in *DJD* XXXVI.

[2] The result of the tests carried out at the Arizona Accelerator Mass Spectrometry Facility yielded the following 1σ dates: for 4Q**342**, 14–115 CE, for 4Q**344**, 72–127 CE. 4Q**345** which dates earlier on the basis of both C-14 testing (1σ: 373–171 BCE) and palaeography, is an exception in this list. See A. J. T. Jull, D. J. Donahue, M. Broshi, and E. Tov, 'Radiocarbon Dating of Scrolls and Linen Fragments from the Judean Desert', *ʿAtiqot* 28 (1996) 1–7.

358, **360a**) are written along the fibres and one (4Q**359**) is written across the fibres. 4Q**345**, the only deed in this group which has remnants of a date, is torn after the name of the month; the year and era are missing. The documents differ from each other in their handwriting; on a palaeographical basis most of them belong to the Herodian period (late first century BCE to 70 CE).

The fragments in Aramaic include a deed of sale (4Q**346**); a debt acknowledgement (4Q**344**); a letter (4Q**342**); an account (4Q**351**); and two unclassified documents (4Q**346a**; 4Q**360a**). The fragmentary state of a number of documents prevents determining whether their language is Aramaic or Hebrew. These include seven accounts (4Q**352–354** and **356–358**), a double deed of unclear nature (4Q**345**), and a document which is apparently a deed (4Q**359**). The Hebrew document (4Q**348**) is a double deed containing the Hebrew words כוהן גדול (high priest) and names of seven or eight people. The precise nature of this unique deed cannot be determined due to its fragmentary state. Fragments of two letters in an early Nabataean script (4Q**343**), whose contents are unclear, are also included in this collection.

Two indecipherable fragments, one apparently in a Semitic script (4Q**360b**) and one in Greek script (4Q**361**), are not transcribed but are included in the plates.

342. 4QLetter? ar

(FIG. 28 AND PL. LIV)

4Q**342** is written on hide. Its maximal measurements are 4.8 x 6.2 cm. Although remains of four lines of text have survived, only single words can be identified and the nature of the document remains unclear. The words כל מה די in line 2 and perhaps די in line 4 indicate that the language is Aramaic. Apart from these words, the names Yehudah and ʾElʿazar are mentioned in line 3; these are among the most common names of the late Second Temple period up to the end of the Bar Kokhba revolt. If the reading of the name ʾElishuaʿ in line 4 is correct, it is the only appearance of that name in the non-literary documents from the Judaean Desert (cf. 2 Sam 5:15; 1 Chr 14:5).

There are no remains of script on the verso.

Palaeography

The handwriting is a Jewish cursive from around the early first century CE. The average height of the letters is about 4 mm. The spacing between the lines varies from 7 to 9 mm. Carbon-14 testing of this document yielded a 1σ date of 14–115 CE.[1]

Mus. Inv. 602
PAM 43.404*, 43.405*

1]◦חוה{ו/י}א◦◦◦[

2]◦{כי/בן} כל מה די עב[ד

3]◦[ ]◦ יהודה ואלעזר [

4]◦ח̊◦{י/ו}דע לאלישוע די◦[

TRANSLATION

1.] . . . [
2.] . . . all that di[d
3.] . . . [. . .] . . . Yehudah and ʾElʿazar [
4.] . . . to ʾElishuaʿ(?) . . . [

[1] See A. J. T. Jull, D. J. Donahue, M. Broshi, and E. Tov, 'Radiocarbon Dating of Scrolls and Linen Fragments from the Judean Desert', *ʿAtiqot* 28 (1996) 1–7.

343. 4QLetter nab

(FIG. 28 AND PL. LV)

THIS is a fragment of a letter written on hide in an early Nabataean script. Its maximal measurements are 9.2 x 7.5 cm. Remains of nine lines have survived on the recto. Six lines are partially preserved on the verso, with a space of two lines before the last line, which contains only one word. The script on the back is perpendicular to that on the front. The right and lower margins survive on both the front and the back, while on the latter the large left margin also partly survives. Although a large part of the text is legible, it remains unclear as a whole. The Nabataean name *Sʿdlhy* appearing in line 14 is well known from numerous documents and inscriptions.

Palaeography

The script reflects an early phase in the evolution of the Nabataean script, perhaps from the middle of the first century BCE. The letters are relatively large, their average height being about 0.5 cm. The average space between the lines is also about 0.5 cm. *ʾAlep* appears in two forms: the traditional three-stroke *ʾalep* occurs once at the end of a word (הוא, line 6); the later, looped form—characteristic of the Nabataean script but also appearing in late Aramaic and early Jewish scripts—appears in the medial position. A transitional form, with the loop still open at its bottom, appears once in final position (ואהוא, line 9). *Yod* has a typical Nabataean form, produced with a large stroke slanting down to the left on top of a lower stroke which curves down to the right and back to the left. An earlier stage in the evolution of *yod* toward that form appears in an Idumaean ostracon written in a late Aramaic script and dated to 176 BCE.[1] The forms of the other letters resemble those in the Jewish semi-cursive script from the late Hasmonaean period.

Mus. Inv. 601
PAM 41.687, 42.078, 43.402*, 43.403*

---

[1] Kloner and Eshel, 'Aramaic Ostracon'.

Recto

1 [ ]°°°[

2 °°° א̇נ̇ה̇[ ]מנה י°[

3 °°°[ ]°נ°° בה̇[

4 ש/על°°°ו̇ך̇ ו̇[ ]איך °[

5 ותנתנון °[ ]מ̇ע̇[?]לם/ה °°°[

6 א̇חי הוא מ̇ן שמר̇י̇[

7 לא ויעבב/ך לידיך הו̇[

8 בי̇ת̇ה ואתרה בא[

9 ואהוא מחשב/ך לכון במ̇[

(bottom margin)

Verso

10 מ̇°°°[

11 מן °°°ו̇ן̇ ע/ש°°°°°°°°[ ]°[(?)

12 ובא̇יש ע̇ביד̇[

13 והבו עם שמ̇ע̇[ו]ן ו̇[

14 שעדלהי

(space of two lines)

15 ע̇מ̇ה̇ו̇ן̇

(bottom margin?)

Translation

Recto

(beginning missing)

1. [. . .] . . . [
2. . . . I[. . .]from him/her(?) . . . [
3. . . . [. . .] . . . [

4. . . . [. . .] . . . [
5. and you will give . . . [. . .] . . . [
6. my brother was of . . . [
7. no, and he will deliver(?) into your hands . . . [
8. his/the house and his/the place in . . . [
9. and I will be suspecting(?) you/. . . to you in . . . [

Verso

(beginning missing?)

10. . . . [
11. from . . . [
12. and evil was done[
13. and give with Shimᶜ[o]n and[
14. *Sᶜdlhy*

(space of two lines)

15. with them(?)

Unidentified Fragments

Two small fragments, also in a Nabataean script of the same type but perhaps written by another person, are found on the same plate. They apparently belong together, but not to the document described above. They contain the remains of three lines. No script appears on their back. The words בית אפק in line 2 may be a place name, not known from literary sources.

Frgs. a + b

1]◦א◦יאׄ[ ]◦ באדני◦[ ]
2]◦א ◦◦[ ]ת בית אפׄק
3]כי אׄ[ ]עׄיני א◦[
4]◦◦[

Translation

1.] . . . [. . .] . in the ears of[?]
2.] . . . [. . .] . Beit ᵓAphek
3.] . . . [. . .]the eyes of/my eyes . . . [
4.] . . . [

344. 4QDebt Acknowledgement ar

(FIG. 29 AND PL. LVI)

THIS fragment is the remnant of a promissory note in Aramaic of unknown provenance, written on hide. Its maximal measurements are 7.1 x 3.1 cm. The nature of the deed is indicated by the words עמי אנה in line 2. Five lines of text and two lines of signatures have survived. The text is torn on the right and perhaps on top, and it is difficult to know how much is missing. It is also difficult to determine whether it was a tied document or a simple document, since the signatures are written on the recto of the deed rather than the verso, but perpendicular to the text (from top to bottom), and not parallel to it (the hole before the first name might have been from a tie). Promissory notes of this type are usually simple documents (see Mur **18**[1] and No. **49**). The back of the fragment is covered with paper applied for reasons of preservation, but there does not seem to be any writing on the verso.

Palaeography

The script is a tiny cursive, and most of the letters are difficult to identify. On the basis of the script, the deed would not seem to predate the end of the Herodian period. Carbon-14 testing of this manuscript yielded a 1σ date of 72–127 CE.[2] The fragment is too small to enable a reconstruction of the deed.

Mus. Inv. 602
PAM 41.686, 43.404*, 43.405*

]]סף לש הוו[ם/מ/זז]°°°°[ש/א]לפי °[[1

]]עמי אנה אלעזר בר הסף[[2

]]°°ן שבעה [כם/ום/בם]°°°[[3

]]°° °[שטם/קתה] מה °°ל °°°°°[[4

] תשלמתא מן נ]כסי ודי אקנה לקבל<ד>ך 5

---

[1] Benoit et al., *DJD* II, 101.

[2] See A. J. T. Jull, D. J. Donahue, M. Broshi, and E. Tov, 'Radiocarbon Dating of Scrolls and Linen Fragments from the Judean Desert', *ʿAtiqot* 28 (1996) 1–7.

אלעזר בר יהוסף על נפשה כתב[ה] 6

[ ]יהוס[ף] 7

]○[ ]○○○○[ ] 8

TRANSLATION

(beginning missing?)

1. [. . .] . . . [. . .]
2. [. . .]with me, I, ᵓElᶜazar son of <Ye>hosef[. . .]
3. [. . .] . . . seven . . . [. . .]
4. [. . .] . . . [. . .]
5. [. . . the payment from] my [p]roperty and (from) whatever I shall acquire, according to that.
6. ᵓElᶜazar son of Yehosef, for himself he wrote [it].
7. [. . .] Yehose[f . . .]
8. . . . [. . .] . . . [. . .]

(continuation missing?)

COMMENTS

L. 1 The division of the words in this line is not clear, and it is difficult to decide between several possible readings for most of the letters. The fourth letter from the left, which appears to be a *lamed*, could also be a long letter descending from the previous line.

L. 2 עמי אנה. These are key words for identifying the type of the deed. This may be an abbreviated form of איתי לך עמי אנה, 'you have with me, I', i.e. 'there is something of yours with me', 'I owe you'. Accordingly, we may identify this as a promissory note which was written by the borrower whose name appears in the continuation of the line. The combination עמי אנה appears e.g. in Mur **18** 3, and its Hebrew equivalent, עמי אני, in No. **49** 5.

L. 2 אלעזר בר הסף. This person is both the writer of the deed and the borrower. His name appears again as a signature (see line 6). Here, the name of his father is written with a ligature, and the first few letters are not clear.

L. 3 In this line, the sum of the loan was apparently given. The letters after שבעה are written over an erasure, or they themselves were erased. The usual form for such a bill is: (amount) כסף זוזין/דינרין, followed by (amount) די המון סלעין, i.e. the amount is first given according to the smaller unit of currency, and then according to the larger.[3] This is the practice in the majority of deeds from the Judaean Desert, though sometimes the amount is given according to only one unit of currency.[4] The reading here is difficult.

L. 4 The reading of this line is difficult.

L. 5 נ]כסי ודי אקנה לקבל<ד>ך. The reading of this line is clear and follows the usual formula for a promissory note. This is the guarantee clause, according to which the property of the borrower, and anything that he might acquire in the future, will serve as a guarantee, for the debt, and will be paid to the lender in the event that the loan is not paid back (cf. in a promissory note from Murabbaᶜat[5] תשלמתא מנכסי ודי אקנה לקובלדך, 'the payment from my property and from whatever I shall buy according

---

[3] See e.g. No. **50** בכסף זוזין שבעין ותמניה די המון סלעין תשע עסרה ותקל חד, or without the words די המון (e.g. No. **49** כסף זוזין ארבעה סלע אחת).

[4] Thus e.g. the larger currency unit is not indicated in No. **7** 4 בכסף דנרין עשרה ותרין.

[5] Mur **18** 7–8.

to that'; in Hebrew deeds from Naḥal Ḥever, the words לעמת ככה appear as equivalents of לקבלדך).[6] It might, therefore, be possible also to restore here the beginning of the line with תשלמתא מן/מ־.

Ll. 6–7 The signatures are written perpendicular to the text, as is the norm for double deeds; however, they are written on the recto, as is the norm for simple deeds. Such a combination of forms is attested also in a fragment of another double deed, in Hebrew (see 4Q**348**, below), but not in other deeds from the Judaean Desert known to the present editor, and so this clearly represents a different custom.

L. 6 אלעזר בר יהוסף. See above, line 2. Both names are among the most common in the Herodian and Late Herodian periods, and are found e.g. on ossuaries, on ostraca from Masada, and in documents from Wadi Murabbaʿat and Naḥal Ḥever.[7]

L. 6 על נפשה כ̇ת̇ב̇[ה], 'for himself he wrote [it]'.[8] This is the normal form for the signatures of the parties mentioned in the deed (unlike witnesses, who write שהד or עד).

L. 7 The remains of two more signatures appear near the lower, torn edge. The first may possibly read יהוס[ף].

---

[6] See e.g. P.Yadin **45** 29–30 וקים עלי לעומת ככה.

[7] According to the evidence, the most common names in this period are Shimʿon, ʾElʿazar, Yehoḥanan and Yehosef; their preponderance is apparently due to the influence of the names of the Hasmonaeans.

[8] In the Elephantine deeds appears the expression בכפי נפשה, 'by his own hands', *TAD* B2.7 (Cowley 13) 17–18 כתב מחסיה בכפי נפשה; B4.3 (Cowley 3) 21 כתב הושע בכפי נ[פשה].

345. 4QDeed A ar or heb

(FIG. 29 AND PL. LVI)

FIVE or six tiny, joined fragments form the remains of the right side of a double deed, perhaps a deed of sale, written in a semi-cursive hand on hide. The provenance of the document is not known. Its maximal measurements are 9.7 x 3 cm. The remains of nine lines from the upper version of the deed have survived, including parts of the first and last lines. The remains of ten lines have survived from the lower version. The writing is difficult to decipher, and the present editor could not identify the content of the deed. The word מן in line 12 perhaps suggests that the language of the deed was Aramaic (although in this period the particle מן could also appear in a Hebrew text[1] and the particle -מ could appear in an Aramaic text).[2] The upper and right margins of the deed remain, though it is difficult to estimate the document's width, since the text is unclear and it is impossible to reconstruct its formulation. According to the script, it would be possible to date it to approximately the middle or late 1st century BCE (a radiocarbon examination of this document dates it very early, the 1σ dates are 373-171 BCE).[3] The back of the document has been covered with paper which was attached for purposes of preservation; the paper covers the signatures (which appear in a photograph taken before the paper was attached).

Mus. Inv. 602
PAM 42.446, 43.404*, 43.405*

Recto
Upper Version

ב◦◦◦ באלול שׁ]נת [

]צׄ[אׄהׄוא ◦[[

] [

◦◦◦◦◦[[

---

1 See e.g. P.Yadin **44** 2 מן רצונם.

2 See e.g. Mur **18** 8 מנכסי.

3 Jull *et al.*, 1–7.

5 בכסף קדלר [ ]

6 ישוע אמר איך ◦◦נ[ ]

7 ◦◦◦◦◦◦◦◦◦[ ]

8 ◦◦נשׁ◦◦◦◦[ ]

9 ◦◦ס◦א◦[ ]

Lower Version

10 ב◦◦◦ [באלול]

11 ◦◦[ ]

12 מן ◦◦◦◦[ ]

13 ◦◦ ידבע ◦[ ]

14 שטר מ◦[ ]

15 [ ]ל[ ]

16 ◦[ ]◦[ ]

17 ◦◦◦◦[ ]

18 ◦ך ו[ ]

19 ◦◦[ ]ל[ ]

Verso

20 ה[ו]שעיה בר[ ]◦◦ על נפש[ה כתבה]

21 ישמעאל בר ש[מ]עון ממרא

TRANSLATION

Recto

Upper Version

1. On the . . . of Elul, y[ear . . .,]
2. . . . [. . .]
3. [. . .]
4. . . . [. . .]
5. for 30 silver q(uarters)/*d*(*enarii*)[. . .]
6. Yeshuaʿ said, as . . . [. . .]

7. . . . [. . .]
8. . . . [. . .]
9. . . . [. . .]

Lower Version
10. On the . . . [of Elul, . . .]
11. . . . [. . .]
12. of/from . . . [. . .]
13. . . . [. . .]
14. deed (of?) . . . [. . .]
(remains of five more lines)
(continuation missing)

Verso
20. H[o]shaᶜyah son of[. . .] . . ., for [him]self [he wrote it].
21. Yishmaᶜᵓel son of Shi[m]ᶜon, at his word.

COMMENTS

L. 1 ב°°° באלול שׂ[נת. The day of the month is not clear, but the remains suggest בחדא. Another possibility is that the day is written in numerals, perhaps four elements written with ligatures. Unfortunately, the date is broken and it is impossible to know the year or period. In most of the deeds *lamed* appears before the name of the month, rather than *bet* as here.[4]

Ll. 2–4 The reading of these lines is doubtful.

L. 5 בכסף ד̇/ר̇ ל̇ר. The letter signifying the unit of currency, a *dalet* for דינרין or *reš* for רבעין, is more similar to *reš* than to *dalet*. Logically, we would assume that any amount more than three 'quarters' would be given according to the larger unit of currency, while here the sum of thirty is given. If רבע was the name of a unit of currency (perhaps signifying a quarter of a *zuz* or of a *denarius*),[5] it would then be possible that the letter is a *reš* (and perhaps the equivalent amount in the larger currency was given immediately afterward, as we find in several documents from the Judaean Desert: . . . כסף זוזין . . . די המון סלעין; cf. 4Q**344** COMMENTS on line 3).

L. 6 ישׂוע. If the reading is correct (the second letter resembles a *ṣade* more than a *šin*), this is perhaps the patronym. The name ישוע is found in the Herodian period (e.g. on ossuaries as well as on sherds from Masada[6]) and also in the post-Herodian period (e.g. in signatures on documents from Naḥal

[4] See e.g. Mur **20** 1 [ב]שבעה לאדר and, on the other hand, P.Yadin **10** 1 (to be published) [בת]לתה באדר; see Yadin, Greenfield and Yardeni, 'Babatha's Ketubba'.

[5] The *denarius* was a Roman unit of currency (equivalent to the Greek drachma). In Aramaic and Hebrew deeds from Wadi Murabbaᶜat and Naḥal Ḥever זוז and דינר appear interchangeably as equal in value, a quarter of a סלע (the equivalent of the tetradrachma) or half of a שקל (see e.g. the sum defined as *zuzin* in No. **50** 7, and as *dinarin* in No. **7** 4, and in a Hebrew deed [P.Yadin **44** 20–21 [דינרין ששה עשר שהם סלעים ארבע]). The use of the *denarius* in Judaea apparently began close to the beginning of the period of Roman rule. The Jews adopted the use of Aramaic numerals together with the Aramaic script while under Persian rule. The *zuz* appears already in Elephantine documents from the Persian period (see e.g. *TAD* B3.4 [Kraeling 3] 6). In an ostracon discovered recently in Shuᶜafat (1138 35/91; unpublished) *dalet* appears as an abbreviation for דינר, together with *mem* (מעה, equivalent to the Obolos) and *pe* (פלג = half).

[6] See e.g. the name ישוע on a sarcophagus from Jerusalem (Avigad, 'Jewish Tombs') and on an ostracon from Masada (no. 457; Yadin and Naveh, *Masada* I, 36 and pl. 29).

Ḥever[7]); it is also the name of the first husband of Babatha and of their son). The words after the name are not clear.

Ll. 7–9 The lines are unclear.

L. 10 The lower version of the deed begins at this point, and the script is larger. The remains of the date are not clear.

Ll. 11–13 The words on these lines are not clear, except for מן in line 12.

L. 14 שטׄר מ◦[. We may perhaps reconstruct שטר מז[בנה] ('deed of sale'), though this expression does not appear in deeds from the Judaean Desert and the letter after *mem* does not resemble *zayin*. The remains of the second word are too scanty to enable its identification. If we assume that the deed is written in Hebrew, it may be possible to reconstruct שטר מכׄ[ר. The word מכר appears in a Hebrew deed from Wadi Murabbaᶜat (Mur **30**)[8] and שטרא[9] appears e.g. in another fragmentary deed (Mur **28**).[10]

Ll. 15–19 Only isolated letters remain in these lines. The rest of the deed is missing.

Ll. 20–21 The signatures are on the verso of the deed, written vertically downwards, as was the practice in double deeds.[11]

L. 20 הׄ[ו]שעיה בר[ ]◦◦. This is the signature of one of the parties. The name is not clear. It is also difficult to say whether the remnants of the father's name could be ישוע, which appears on the recto. The present editor has not found other occurrences of the name הושעיה on documents from this period.[12]

L. 20 על נפש[ה כתבה], '[Wrote it] for himself'. The reconstruction is according to deeds from Wadi Murabbaᶜat, Naḥal Ḥever, and elsewhere (see above, 4Q**344**). This is undoubtedly the first signature on the verso, and it is that of the writer of the deed.

L. 21 ישׄמעאל בר ש[מ]עׄוׄן. ישמעאל is not a common Jewish name, though it is attested in finds from the Herodian period (e.g. on a bowl from Jerusalem: ישמעאל בר פלטא שמעון מן ירושלם[13]) as well as from the post-Herodian period.[14] The letters *ᶜayin* and *waw* in the patronym are not clear. שמעון was among the most popular names from the Hasmonaean period until the end of the post-Herodian period.

L. 21 ממרׄאׄ/ה. This term appears when a person does not sign by himself, but someone else signs in his name. This word appears in deeds in Aramaic, usually without the *ʾalep* of the root.[15] The Hebrew equivalent is מאמרו. The remains of the last letter resemble *ʾalep*, though the possessive suffix in Aramaic is usually a *he* (see e.g. ממרה in No. **8a**; מן ממרה in Mur **21**[16]). In No. **13** 12, ממרא appears with an *ʾalep*. From the script, it would seem that the deed and both of the signatures were written by the same hand.

---

[7] ישוע appears e.g. in the signature on P.Yadin **20**, verso line 2, etc.

[8] מכר appears e.g. in Mur **30** (Milik, *DJD* II, 118) 16, 17, 22, 24, 28.

[9] שטר with the meaning of a legal document began to be used in Aramaic in approximately the third century BCE. In the Elephantine documents, ספר is used with this meaning. שטר appears in both singular and plural forms in a document from Egypt from the third century BCE (*TAD* C3.28 90–102 [= Cowley 81 14–26]).

[10] Mur **28** 10.

[11] On the practice of signing the deeds, see the INTRODUCTION TO THE ARAMAIC AND HEBREW DOCUMENTARY TEXTS.

[12] It is doubtful whether הושע appears, as Milik reads, in Mur **6** 7 ◦ושע[. The name הושעיה (and its various forms: אושעיה, הושע, עשוא) appears in Aramaic documents from Egypt from the Persian period (especially predating the end of the fifth century BCE).

[13] Hachlili, 'Jerusalem Family'.

[14] ישמעאל appears in a number of deeds from the Judaean desert, e.g. Mur **2** 1, and in several unpublished documents from Naḥal Ḥever: P.Yadin **8** 10; **42** 2, 11 (the same man also in P.Yadin **43** 4, 8); **54** 4; and **63** 6.

[15] Cf. the signatures on Hebrew P.Yadin **44** 29 מאמרו, compared with ממרה on line 30.

[16] Mur **21** 24 (the signature is on the verso of the deed; Milik reads מן ◦◦יה).

346. 4QDeed of Sale ar

(FIG. 30 AND PL. LVII)

4Q**346** consists of seven small fragments, apparently from a deed of sale written on hide in Aramaic. The largest, frg. a, comes from the lower right corner of the document and measures about 6.2 x 5.5 cm. It preserves remains of six lines of text, as well as part of the right and lower margins. Frgs. d, e, and g consist of remains of one line each, whereas frgs. b, c, and f comprise remains of two lines each. There are no remains of script on the verso.

The nature of the document may be determined by the words די יצבה in frg. a 2, which may be part of the ownership clause of a deed of sale or any conveyance of property, and by the words ודי אקנה in line 4, which are part of the guarantee clause. Shimʿon (line 3) and Menashe (line 6) apparently are the names of the parties to the transaction. The *lamed* preceding the name Menashe may indicate that he is the purchaser.

Palaeography

The handwriting is a semi-formal Jewish script of the early Herodian period (late 1st century BCE). The letters are large, with an average height of approximately 5 mm, and the average spacing between the lines is approximately 4 mm. Several letters are palaeographically significant for the dating of this document.

Bet is formed without a tail at the lower right corner.

The roof of *he* is a wavy stroke, slanting slightly down to the right, with its left downstroke already starting at the roof and descending almost vertically and parallel to the right downstroke.

Yod has a thickened, almost triangular top, made with a convex upper stroke and a horizontal lower stroke.

The horn and the roof of *mem* are formed as one stroke, which joins the top of the right downstroke. The letter also appears in a triangular form (line 3), which is attested in a few documents from the early Herodian period.

The *ʿayin* is unique; it is very small, and formed by two tiny parallel downstrokes.

The *ṣade* is still long, with a short, horizontal base.

Mus. Inv. 603
PAM 43.407

Frg. a

]° מן °[למעבד] 1

בה כל]די יצבה °[2

] שמען מן כל [מן נכסי 3

ודי אקנה מ[ן יומא דנה ועד עלם 4

ושׄ°°[5

למנשה לׄשׄ°[6

TRANSLATION

1. [. . .] . . . of/from . . . [. . . to do]
2. [with it anything]that he desires . . . [. . .]
3. [. . .] Shim^con from all [. . . from my property]
4. and (from anything) that I shall acquire fr[om today and forever. . . .]
5. and . . . [. . .]
6. to Menashe and . . . [. . .]

Frg. b

]הׄ °°[1

]°בׄ°[2

Frg. c

Two illegible lines

Frg. d

]°ך וכל °[1

TRANSLATION

1.] . . . and all . . . [

Frg. e

]◦תה מן ◦[1

TRANSLATION

1.] . . . from/of . . . [

Frg. f

Two illegible lines

Frg. g

] בׄתר צ[1

TRANSLATION

1.] after . . . [

346a. 4QUnidentified Fragment A

(FIG. 30 AND PL. LVII)

THIS fragment of hide, measuring 1 x 14.4 cm, bears the top of letters of one line, in a formal script of the late Hasmonaean or the early Herodian periods. The first word may be read חשבן (account). However, the reading is not certain, and the remains of the text are too fragmentary to enable its decipherment.

Mus. Inv. 603
PAM 43.407

ר י ע
חשון אלה◦◦קת ◦◦◦] [◦◦◦◦ ל◦◦◦◦◦ל ◦◦◦ 1
ב

348. 4QDeed B heb?

(FIG. 29 AND PL. LVIII)

THIS is a fragment of a tied, double deed, written on hide, of unknown provenance. Its maximal measurements are 17.8 x 4.7 cm. From the upper version of the deed, remains of nine lines survive in a tiny, cursive script which is almost impossible to read. The remains of nine lines from the lower version have also survived. This version is written in a Herodian calligraphic cursive. The remains of three lines of signatures have survived between the upper and lower versions, perpendicular to the text. The language of the deed is apparently Hebrew. Since the context is unclear, it is impossible to determine the nature of the deed, though it appears to be unlike other deeds that have survived from that period. The surviving part of the text consists mainly of names: those include יהוסף, שמעון, אלעזר and יהוחנן, all of which are among the most common names in documents from the end of the Herodian and post-Herodian periods. Despite the temptation which the name offers, אלעזר בר שמעון, mentioned here, should most probably not be identified with the leader of the Second Revolt. The names מתתיה and חוני (?) are less common, and were in vogue primarily in the Hasmonaean and Herodian periods. All of these names are also found in priestly families. There is no reason to bar the possibility that this deed deals with matters of priests or of the priesthood, although the only support for such an assumption is the words כוהן גדול in line 12 (if that reading is correct). Based upon the script, the date of the deed would not seem to be earlier than the middle of the Herodian period; perhaps it is from the end of that period.[1] Paper has been attached to the back of the document for reasons of preservation. From the photographs taken prior to the attachment of this paper (a transparent tape covered the back in the photograph), it is difficult to determine whether there were any remains of writing on the verso. Most, if not all, of the marks that can be seen in the photograph are in fact marks from the recto which are now also visible from the back.

Mus. Inv. 602
PAM 41.686, 43.404*, 43.405*

[1] See the discussion on cursive Jewish script in Yardeni, 'Cursive Script', 264–343.

Recto
Upper Version

1]מׄנׄחׄ[ם]◦ל◦◦ ◦◦ח◦◦ בׄרׄ אׄלׄ[עזר
2]ל֯ ◦◦◦ ◦◦[ ]◦◦◦ ◦◦◦ ◦◦◦◦◦ ◦◦◦◦ [
3]ר֯ ◦◦◦[ ]◦◦ א◦ה◦◦[
4]◦ל◦◦◦◦◦◦◦ [ ]ל[ ]◦◦ע בׄ[
5]◦◦◦◦◦ ושׄמׄעׄוׄן ◦◦◦◦◦◦◦ל◦[
6]◦◦◦ ◦◦◦◦ ◦◦◦◦◦◦◦◦◦ ◦◦ ◦◦◦[
7]ן א◦◦◦◦ ◦◦אקׄ◦◦ ◦◦◦◦◦◦◦◦ ◦◦[
8]◦◦◦◦◦◦◦◦[ ]ל[ ]ל◦◦ר◦◦◦ [
9]◦◦ ◦◦◦◦◦יׄהׄוׄחׄנׄן בר יׄהׄוׄסׄףׄ ◦[
10–12 *(signatures?)*

Lower Version

13]◦◦◦◦◦וׄס כׄוהן גׄדול ◦◦◦[
14 בר י]הוסף מתתיה בר שמעון אלעזר [בר
15 בר] חׄנן אלעזר בר שמעון בר חׄוׄנׄיׄ ◦[
16]◦ ב[ר י]הוחנן יהוסף בר ◦◦◦◦[
17]◦מלה פתחנׄוׄ ◦◦◦ [ ]◦◦ מנׄשׄ[ה
18]שמעון משוק הקׄוׄרׄוׄת ◦◦ח◦◦ ◦◦[
19]◦◦◦◦ה למ◦◦ה[ ]◦◦להׄ[ ]◦◦[
20]◦ בׄמ◦צׄ◦ה אׄ◦◦[
21]◦◦◦◦◦[

TRANSLATION

Upper Version

1. Menaḥe[m(?) . . .] . . . son of ʾEl[ʿazar(?)
2.]20 . . . [. . .] . . . [
3.]10 . . . [. . .] . . . [
4.] . . . [
5.] . . . and Shimʿon . . . [
6.] . . . [
7.] . . . [
8.] . . . [. . .] . . . 10(?)[
9.] . . . Yehoḥanan son of Yehosef (?) . . . [

10–12. (signatures?)

Lower Version

13.] . . . *os* High Priest . . . [. . .
14. . . . son of Ye]hosef, Mattatyah son of Shimʿon, ʾElʿazar [son of . . .
15. son of] Ḥanan, ʾElʿazar son of Shimʿon, son of Ḥoni . . . [
16.] . . . so[n of Ye]hoḥanan, Yehosef son of . . . [
17.] . . . we have opened (?) . . . [. . .] . . ., Menash[eh(?) . . .
18.]Shimʿon from the Beam Market/street, . . . [
19.] . . . [. . .] . . . [
20.] . . . [
21.] . . . [

COMMENTS

Ll. 1–9 These lines are written in an extreme cursive and the text is difficult to decipher, except for a couple of letters and perhaps the ligatures of the name שמעון in line 5 and יהוחנן (?) בר יהוסף in line 9. These names are very common in the Herodian and post-Herodian periods and they appear in many documents with ligatures reminiscent of this document. There are signs or letters between lines 7 and 8, close to the torn left edge.

Ll. 10–12 Traces of three lines of signatures are found between the upper and the lower versions, written perpendicular to the text; the direction of the signatures is not clear (cf. above, 4Q**344**). If one attempts to read downwards from the top (see the INTRODUCTION for the discussion of the practice of signing a document), it is difficult to identify shapes of letters, except perhaps the letter *lamed* in line 2. Except for 4Q**344**, we have no such examples of signatures perpendicular to the text in the body of the deed, so that it is difficult to draw any conclusions.

L. 13 This is the first line of the lower version of this double deed. The remains of the first word are difficult to read except for the *samek* at the end. The three preceding letters, formed as short vertical strokes, could be read as *waw*, *yod*, *reš* or *dalet*. Due to the *samek* at the end of the word, this would seem to be a personal name; the ending *-os* (-וס) is common in Greek names. A single spot of ink is all that is left of the letter next to the tear on the right. The second and third letters are apparently written with ligatures; the first might be a *bet*, *kap*, *pe*, or some other letter. Several possible names could be suggested, though the main problem in identifying the name lies in the following two words.

L. 13 כוהן גדול. The reading is almost certain. If these words are indeed found here they are in Hebrew, even though the names are followed by the Aramaic word בר. No combination of the letters before this produces the name of a high priest known to us from historical or literary sources. Unfortunately, the letters following these words are also unreadable. While the first line of a deed usually contains the date, it is difficult here to know whether these words indeed indicate the date or whether they are part of something else.

L. 14 בר י]הוסף מתתיה בר שמעון אלעזר [בר. These are the remains of the names of three people.

L. 15 בר] חנן אלעזר בר שמעון בר חוֹני ◦[.[2] At least two, or perhaps three, people are mentioned here: חוני is likely the grandfather of אלעזר בר שמעון, though perhaps he is someone else whose name is not given, and who is known by his father's name.[3]

L. 16 ב]ר י[הוחנן יהוסף בר ◦◦◦◦[. These are the remains of the names of two people. In lines 14–16 only the remains of names have survived, referring to seven or eight people. It is unusual to find such a large number of names in the body of a deed.[4]

L. 17 The words on this line are not clear, but they do not appear to be personal names.

L. 18]שמעון משוק הקוֹרוֹת ◦◦ח◦ ◦◦[. It is difficult to determine whether שמעון is the name of the man or of his father. שמעון (or his son) is here identified by his place of origin: משוק הקוֹרוֹת. The prefix מ- on the word שוק, along with the definite article ה- on the word קורות, may suggest that the language of the deed is Hebrew. The three letters following the *qop* are identical in form: all are comprised of a single downward stroke. Again, there are several possible readings: *waw*, *yod*, *dalet*, *reš* and perhaps also *zayin*. It is also possible to read הקריות. The name שוק הקורות 'beam market/street' or שוק העצים 'Timber Market/street' was the name of a district in Jerusalem and is mentioned by Josephus[5] as the district set fire to by Cestius Gallus in the twelfth year of the reign of Nero (66 CE). Accordingly, the origin of the man is apparently Jerusalem, despite the fact that the attribution of origin is usually to the city, and not to a district within the city.[6] The letters after this are not clear, though we may possibly read מנחם בר[.

Ll. 19–20 The words on the three remaining lines are difficult to decipher, despite the fact that most of the letters seem to be readable. The letter before the second *mem* is attached to it by a ligature. It could be *yod*, *nun*, *ᶜayin*, or perhaps another short letter. Another possibility is that this is not a letter followed by a *mem*, but a *ṣade*, though the shape is not unequivocal and there is no other *ṣade* in the text with which to compare it. The letter which follows could equally be *dalet*, *yod*, or *reš*.

L. 21 Only spots of ink from the ends of letters have survived and they are difficult to identify.

---

[2] The first *nun* in the name חנן is very long. A somewhat similar form in the name יהוחנן can be found on a sherd from Masada (Yadin and Naveh, *Masada* I, pl 45, no. 556, line 1).

[3] See Naveh, 'Nameless People?', 108–23.

[4] In a Hebrew deed from Naḥal Ḥever (P.Yadin **44**), dealing with the leasing of land, five individuals are mentioned who are involved in a single transaction.

[5] Josephus *J.W.* 2.19.4 (Δοκῶν ἀγοράν).

[6] The words מן ירושלם appear in a signature in No. **50** 19. Two Hebrew deeds from Wadi Murabbaᶜat were apparently written in Jerusalem in 135 CE (see Mur **29** 9 and **30** 8). See also the promissory note from the second year of the reign of Nero (55 CE) in which are mentioned the residents of בכסלון and כפר סגנה, settlements which were apparently close to Jerusalem (Mur **18** 3, 4).

351. 4QAccount of Cereal A ar

(FIG. 30 AND PL. LIX)

4Q351 measures approximately 3.5 x 3.8 cm. It is written on hide and is probably a fragment from an account of cereal. Two columns are partially preserved, each containing the remnants of two lines, written in a semi-formal, early Herodian script. Line 1 consists of a personal name, perhaps Yehoḥanan. In line 2 חנטין ('wheat') appears, as well as a *qop* which stands for קבין (a measure of grain as well as of liquids), followed by four unit marks, designating the number four. Line 3 contains traces of one unidentifiable letter. A line may be missing between lines 3 and 4. At the beginning of line 4, a *qop* again appears, followed by traces of two unit marks, which apparently were followed by additional unit marks, but the rest has torn away. No script appears on the verso.

Mus. Inv. 603
PAM 43.407

Col. i

י]הוחנ◦[? 1

]חנטין ק //// 2

Col. ii

◦] 3

ק //] 4

352. 4QpapAccount of Cereal B ar or heb

(FIG. 31 AND PL. LIX)

4Q**352** comprises three papyrus fragments of an account of cereal. Frg. a, the largest of the three, measures approximately 11.7 x 1 cm. It bears the remains of nine lines containing Aramaic numerals and a *kap*, which apparently stands for *kor* (a dry measure often used for grain, e.g. כורין in Mur **24B** 15, **D** 16, **E** 12; Mur **44** 3; and sometimes for dates: e.g. כ in P.Yadin **21** 36; כרין in P.Yadin **22** 33). Frg. b contains the remains of three similar lines. Frg. c measures approximately 3 x 0.8 cm. It bears traces of signs in script from three lines, written parallel to the fibres. On two of them the Aramaic numeral for ten appears, indicating that it is a fragment of an account.

Mus. Inv. 184
PAM 43.406

Frg. a

1 [ר̇//]
2 [///\ כ]
3 [// כ]
4 //] כ \
5 /]/ כ\
6 /]/ כ \
7 /]/ כ \
8 //] כ \
9 //] כ \

Frg. b

]כ ◦[
◦כ ◦[
◦כ [

Frg. c

]◦[
]ר ◦[
]ר [

352a. 4QpapAccount A ar or heb

(FIG. 31 AND PL. LIX)

FIVE small papyrus fragments have survived from this document. The largest fragment, which is from the upper left corner of the document, measures approximately 2.5 x 2.8 cm. Only numerals have survived on all of the fragments, written parallel to the fibres. The fragments were originally placed beside 4Q**352** on the museum plate, but it seems that they do not belong together. No letter has survived that could indicate the nature of the account.

Mus. Inv. 184
PAM 43.406

Frg. a

))\)) o[1

Frg. b

((\))o[1

o[2

Frg. c

]((\))o[1

o[2

Frg. d

]◦◦ 1

Frg. e

]◦[1

]◦◦◦[2

353. 4QpapAccount of Cereal or Liquid ar or heb

(FIG. 30 AND PL. LX)

A small papyrus fragment, measuring approximately 2.5 x 2.8 cm, is all that remains of this document. It bears the letter *qop*, standing for קבין (a measure of grains as well as of liquids), and four unit marks designating the number four. This is apparently a fragment from the left side of an account of cereal or liquid.

Mus. Inv. 184
PAM 43.406

]◦ ק ////

354. 4QAccount B ar or heb

(FIG. 30 AND PL. LX)

4Q**354** measures approximately 2.1 x 2.7 cm. Remains of one line have survived on this hide fragment. It consists only of Aramaic numerals designating the number 7 or 17 (the first sign is not clear), suggesting that it was an account of some kind. No script appears on the verso.

Mus. Inv. 603
PAM 43.407

[א 𐡘𐡘𐡘𐡘𐡘𐡘𐡘

356. 4QAccount D ar or heb

(FIG. 30 AND PL. LX)

4Q**356** measures approximately 2.5 x 3.6 cm. Remains of two lines of text have survived on this hide fragment, which is written in a semi-cursive hand. Only single letters are legible and the reading is doubtful. The Aramaic numerals in line 2 suggest that this was an account of some kind. No script appears on the verso.

Mus. Inv. 603
PAM 43.407

]שאׄר◦◦ ◦[1

]מן עׄלימׄאׄ ר ר// [2

357. 4QAccount E ar or heb

(FIG. 30 AND PL. LX)

4Q**357** measures approximately 2.6 x 1.8 cm. Remains of two lines have survived on this hide fragment. The Aramaic numerals appearing in both lines suggest that this was an account, but the document is too fragmentary to allow its classification. No script appears on the verso.

Mus. Inv. 603
PAM 43.407

]◦ 𐡘𐡙 א◦[1

]𐡛𐡜𐡜 ◦[2

358. 4QpapAccount F? ar or heb

(FIG. 30 AND PL. LX)

4Q**358** measures approximately 5.2 x 1.8 cm. Remains of four lines have survived, written along the fibres in a cursive hand. Numerals appearing in line 3 represent the number 300, thus suggesting that its subject was money, perhaps *zuzin* (= drachmas). It may be a fragment of a deed or of an account. The remains are too scanty to enable further classification of the document. One should note the form of the numeral 100 (as indicated by the three units preceding it) which very much resembles the numeral 10, but for the addition of an extra, short stroke above its left side.

Mus. Inv. 184
PAM 43.406

[◦◦] 1

[◦ לק◦] 2

[///ה◦] 3

[◦◦◦] 4

359. 4QpapDeed C? ar or heb

(FIG. 30 AND PL. LX)

4Q**359** consists of two small papyrus fragments that apparently are not contiguous. Remains of two lines survive on frg. a, while frg. b contains remains of a single line only. Frg. a measures approximately 1.5 x 2.4 cm. The script is a Herodian or post-Herodian cursive hand, written across the fibres. The height of the *ḥet* is approximately 4 mm. Although the fragments seem to belong to one document, they display different variants of *ḥet* and *taw*. This may indicate that at least one of them is a signature, perhaps that of the individual whose name appears on frg. a. The name reads 'Mattat bar Ḥazaq'. It is worth mentioning that the name 'Ḥazaq bar Mattat' appears in a deed of sale from the Bar Kokhba period, No. **7**. It is therefore tempting to suggest that these fragments (and perhaps also other fragments in that group) may have been found (by Bedouin) at the same place as the so-called Naḥal Ṣeʾelim fragments (apparently in a cave in Naḥal Ḥever), and not in Qumran cave 4.[7]

Mus. Inv. 184
PAM 43.406

Frg. a

]מתת בר חזק[1

]∘[ ]∘∘[ ]∘[2

Frg. b

ז
ד
]∘חת ר∘[1
ו
י

[7] See No. **7**, above, the GENERAL INTRODUCTION, and the INTRODUCTION to the Appendix.

360a. 4QpapUnidentified Fragments B ar

(FIG. 31 AND PL. LXI)

SEVENTEEN small papyrus fragments, partly joined together and written along the fibres in an early, formal Herodian script, remain of this document. The letters are large (the *ḥet* measures approximately 6 mm in height). The nature of the text is unclear. The word דבחי ('sacrifices of') suggests that it is a literary text. Three fragments apparently join together, yielding remains of four lines of text. Another fragment may perhaps be placed above the joined fragments, and still another perhaps continues the last line on the left. Two other fragments, bearing remains of two lines, may perhaps also be joined together. The remaining fragments were tentatively placed or grouped together.

Mus. Inv. 184
PAM 43.406*

Frg. a

]ן וׄחוׄ°[1

Frgs. b + c

]°שב{כׄיׄ}בׄוׄ[1
]לׄנא [2

Frg. d

]°ר°[1
]שגיא[2

Frg. e

[הי֯א]

Frg. f

[רנא ◦]

Frgs. g + h

[◦ ◦◦א◦ן֯ דבחי]

[ר

Frg. i

] ◦◦[

Frg. j

[שפל֯נ◦]

Frg. k

]◦◦ ◦◦◦◦ [

Frg. l

[מ]

Frg. m

]∘∘[1

Frg. n

]∘ ח[1

]∘ [2

Frg. o

]כ [1

Frg. p

]∘ ∘[1

]עמ[2

]ל[3

Frg. q

]א[1

Collation Table of Present and Previous Sigla

The following table contains a list of the documents appearing in this volume, together with their previous sigla, in the event that either the numbers or the names have been changed since the publication of the official list.[1]

I. XḤev/Se Aramaic and Hebrew Documents

Present Sigla:		Previous Sigla:	
XḤev/Se **7**	Deed of Sale A ar (134 or 135 CE)		pap contract ar
XḤev/Se **8**	pap Deed of Sale B ar and heb (135 CE)		pap contract heb and ar (Kefar Baru)
XḤev/Se **8a**	pap Deed of Sale C ar (134 CE)		pap contract ar (Kefar Bario ?)
XḤev/Se **9**	pap Deed of Sale D ar		pap deed ar
XḤev/Se **9a**	pa Unclassified Fragment A ar	**9**	
XḤev/Se **10**	pap Receipt for Payment of a Fine? ar		pap deed ar
XḤev/Se **11**	pap Marriage Contract? ar		pap deed
XḤev/Se **12**	pap Receipt for Dates ar (131 CE)		pap deed
XḤev/Se **13**	pap Waiver of Claims? ar (134 or 135 CE)		pap confirmation of divorce ar
XḤev/Se **14**	pap Fragment of a Deed ar?		(cancelled)
XḤev/Se **15**	pap Unclassified Fragments B		(cancelled)
XḤev/Se **16-17**	pap Unclassified Fragments C-D	**16, 17**	deed of rental, deed
XḤev/Se **18**	pap Unclassified Fragment E		deed
XḤev/Se **19**	pap Unclassified Fragment F		deed
XḤev/Se **20**	(cancelled)		
XḤev/Se **21**	pap Deed of Sale E ar		pap deed of sale ar
XḤev/Se **22**	pap Deed of Sale F? ar		pap unclassified document
XḤev/Se **23**	pap Deed of Sale G ar		pap deed
XḤev/Se **24**	pap Deed A ar		pap deed
XḤev/Se **24a**	pap Deed B ar		pap deed

[1] E. Tov with the collaboration of S. J. Pfann, *The Dead Sea Scrolls on Microfiche, Companion Volume* (2d rev. ed.; Leiden, 1995).

XḤev/Se **25**	pap Deed C ar		pap deeds
XḤev/Se **26**	pap Text Dealing with Deposits and Barley ar		pap deed
XḤev/Se **27**	pap Deed D ar		frgs. of pap deeds
XḤev/Se **28**	pap Unclassified Fragment G ar		frgs. of pap deeds
XḤev/Se **29**	pap Unclassified Fragments H		pap deed
XḤev/Se **30**	pap Letter to Shimʿon ben Kosibah		pap letter to Shimʿon bar Kokhba
XḤev/Se **31**	pap Deed E ar		pap unclassified
XḤev/Se **32**	pap Deed F ar (+4Q347)		pap unclassified
XḤev/Se **33**	pap Unclassified Fragment I ar		pap unclassified
XḤev/Se **34**	pap Deed G ar		pap unclassified
XḤev/Se **35**	pap Unclassified Fragment J ar		pap unclassified
XḤev/Se **36**	pap Unclassified Fragment K		pap unclassified
XḤev/Se **37**	pap Deed H ar?		pap unclassified
XḤev/Se **38**	pap Unclassified Fragments L		pap unclassified
XḤev/Se **39**	pap Unclassified Fragment M		pap unclassified
XḤev/Se **40**	pap Unclassified Fragment N		pap unclassified
XḤev/Se **41**	pap Unclassified Fragment O		pap unclassified
XḤev/Se **42**	pap Unclassified Fragment P		pap unclassified
XḤev/Se **43**	pap Unclassified Fragment Q		pap unclassified
XḤev/Se **44**	pap Unclassified Fragment R		pap unclassified
XḤev/Se **45**	pap Unclassified Fragment S		pap unclassified
XḤev/Se **46**	pap Unclassified Fragment T		pap unclassified
XḤev/Se **47a**	pap Unclassified Fragment U	**47**	pap unclassified
XḤev/Se **47b**	pap Unclassified Fragment V	**47**	pap unclassified
XḤev/Se **47c**	pap Unclassified Fragment W	**47**	pap unclassified
XḤev/Se **47d**	pap Unclassified Fragments X	**47**	pap unclassified
XḤev/Se **47e**	pap Unclassified Fragment Y	**47**	pap unclassified
XḤev/Se **47f**	pap Unclassified Fragment Z	**47**	pap unclassified
XḤev/Se **47g**	pap Unclassified Fragment AA	**47**	pap unclassified
XḤev/Se **47h**	pap Unclassified Fragment BB	**47**	pap unclassified
XḤev/Se **48**	(cancelled)		
XḤev/Se **49**	Promissory Note (133 CE)	**50**	pap promissory note on parchment ar
XḤev/Se **50**	pap Deed of Sale H ar (= part of Mur 26)	**49**	pap deed of land sale ar

II. XḤev/Se Greek Documents

Present Sigla:		Previous Sigla:	
XḤev/Se **60**	pap Tax (or Rent) Receipt from Maḥoza gr	Gr. **5**	pap rent or tax receipt
XḤev/Se **61**	pap Conclusion to a Land Declaration gr	Gr. **5**	pap census declaration
XḤev/Se **62**	pap Land Declaration gr	Gr. **7**	pap property census gr
XḤev/Se **63**	pap Deed of Renunciation of Claims gr	Gr. **5**	pap unclassified frags.
XḤev/Se **64**	pap Deed of Gift gr	Gr. **1**	pap double contract; deed of gift
XḤev/Se **65**	pap Marriage Contract gr	P.Yadin **37**	
XḤev/Se **66**	pap Loan with Hypothec gr	Gr. **3**	
XḤev/Se **67**	pap Text Mentioning Timber gr	Gr. **5**	pap unclassified frags.
XḤev/Se **68**	pap Text Mentioning a Guardian gr	Gr. **5**	pap unclassified frags.
XḤev/Se **69**	pap Cancelled Marriage Contract	Gr. **2**	pap double contract; marriage contract
XḤev/Se **70**	pap Unidentified Fragment A gr	Gr. **5**	pap unclassified frags.
XḤev/Se **71**	pap Unidentified Fragment B gr	Gr. **5**	pap unclassified frags.
XḤev/Se **72**	pap Unidentified Fragment C gr	Gr. **5**	pap unclassified frags.
XḤev/Se **73**	pap End of a Document gr	Gr. **4**	pap deed
XḤev/Se **74-169**	pap Unidentified Fragments gr	XḤev/Se sem	pap unclassified frags. sem, gr?
Ḥev/Se? **1-58**	pap Unidentified Fragments gr		

III. Documents Alleged to Be from Qumran Cave 4

Present Sigla:		Previous Sigla:	
4Q**342**	Letter? ar		letter in Judeo-Aram.
4Q**343**	Letter nab		
4Q**344**	Debt Acknowledgement ar		debt acknowledgement
4Q**345**	Deed A ar or heb		sale of land ar
4Q**346**	Deed of Sale ar		sale of land ar
4Q**346a**	Unidentified Fragment A	4Q**346**	
4Q**347**	pap Deed F ar (= part of XḤev/Se 32)		pap act ar
4Q**348**	Deed B heb?		act regarding ownership
4Q**351**	Account of Cereal A ar		account of cereal sem
4Q**352**	pap Account of Cereal B ar or heb		pap account of cereal sem
4Q**352a**	pap Account A ar or heb	4Q**352**	
4Q**353**	pap Account of Cereal or Liquid ar or heb		pap account of cereal sem
4Q**354**	Account B ar or heb		account of cereal ? sem
4Q**356**	Account D ar or heb		account of money
4Q**357**	Account E ar or heb		account of money sem
4Q**358**	pap Account F? ar or heb		pap account of money sem
4Q**359**	pap Deed C? ar or heb		pap list of people ar
4Q**360a**	pap Unidentified Fragments B ar		(PAM 43.406; inv. 184; no previous 4Q number)
4Q**360b**	Unidentified Fragment C		(PAM 43.407; inv. 603; no previous 4Q number)
4Q**361**	Unidentified Fragment gr		scribbles on papyrus

BIBLIOGRAPHY

Abbreviations of journals and series follow the conventions of the *Année Philologique* and the *Journal of Biblical Literature.*

Abel, *Géographie*
M. Abel. *Géographie de la Palestine*, vol. 2. Paris, 1938.

Abbott and Johnson, *Municipal Administration*
F. F. Abbott and A. Ch. Johnson. *Municipal Administration in the Roman Empire*. Princeton, 1926.

Abramson and Ginsberg, 'Aramaic Deed'
S. Abramson and H. L. Ginsberg. 'On the Aramaic Deed of Sale of the Third Year of the Second Jewish Revolt'. *BASOR* 136 (1954) 17–19.

Aharoni, 'Expedition B'
Y. Aharoni. 'Expedition B'. *IEJ* 11 (1961) 11–24.

Aichinger, 'Zwei Arten?'
Anna Aichinger. 'Zwei Arten des Provinzialcensus? Überlegungen zu neupublizierten israelischen Papyrusfunden'. *Chiron* 22 (1992) 35–45.

Aimé-Giron, *Textes*
N. Aimé-Giron. *Textes araméens d'Égypte*. Cairo, 1931.

Allam, 'Aspects du mariage'
S. Allam. 'Quelques aspects du mariage dans l'Égypte ancienne'. *JEA* 67 (1981) 116–35.

Alon, *Jews in Their Land*
G. Alon. *The Jews in Their Land in the Talmudic Age (70-640 C.E.)*. Jerusalem, 1980.

Alpers, *Nachrepublikanisches Finanzsystem*
M. Alpers. *Das nachrepublikanische Finanzsystem. Fiscus und Fisci in der frühen Kaiserzeit*. Berlin and New York, 1995.

Amit and Eshel, 'Bar Kokhba'
D. Amit and H. Eshel. 'The Bar Kokhba Revolt in the Southern Hebron Hills'. In *Settlement and Security in the Southern Hebron Hills in Ancient Times*, edited by Z. Safrai and I. Levine, pp. 54–9. Ramat Gan, 1994 (Hebrew).

Amit and Eshel, 'Tetradrachm'
D. Amit and H. Eshel. 'A Tetradrachm of Bar Kokhba from a Cave in Naḥal Ḥever'. *Isr. Num. Jour.* 11 (1990–91) 33–5.

Archer, *Jewish Woman*
L. J. Archer. *Her Price is Beyond Rubies: The Jewish Woman in Graeco-Roman Palestine*. Sheffield, 1990.

Arzt, 'Ägyptische Papyri'
P. Arzt. 'Ägyptische Papyri und das Neue Testament. Zur Frage der Vergleichbarkeit von Texten'. *Protokolle zur Bible* 6 (1997) 15–29.

Assaf, *Shetaroth*
S. Assaf. *The Book of Shetaroth (Formulary) of R. Hai Gaon*. Supplement to *Tarbiz*, vol. I, 3. Jerusalem, 1930 (Hebrew).

Avi-Yonah, *Gazetteer*
M. Avi-Yonah. *Gazetteer of Roman Palestine*. Qedem 5. Jerusalem, 1976.

Avigad, 'Burial Vault'
N. Avigad. 'The Burial Vault of a Nazirite Family on Mount Scopus'. *ErIsr* 10 (1971) 41–9.

Avigad, 'Inscribed Ossuaries'
N. Avigad. 'A Depository of Inscribed Ossuaries in the Kidron Valley'. *IEJ* 12 (1962) 1–12.

Avigad, 'Jewish Tombs'
N. Avigad. 'Jewish Rock-Cut Tombs in Jerusalem in the Judean Hill-Country'. *ErIsr* 8 (1967) 119–42.

Avigad and Yadin, *Genesis Apocryphon*
N. Avigad and Y. Yadin. *A Genesis Apocryphon.* Jerusalem, 1956.

Bagatti and Milik, *Scavi*
P. B. Bagatti and J. T. Milik. *Gli scavi del 'Dominus Flevit'.* Vol. 1: *La necropoli del periodo Romano.* Jerusalem, 1958.

Bagnall, *Egypt*
R. S. Bagnall. *Egypt in Late Antiquity.* Princeton, 1993.

Bagnall and Frier, *Demography*
R. S. Bagnall and B. W. Frier. *The Demography of Roman Egypt.* Princeton, 1994.

Bagnall and Worp, *Chronological Systems*
R. S. Bagnall and K. A. Worp. *The Chronological Systems of Byzantine Egypt.* Zutphen, 1978.

Barag, 'Note'
D. Barag. 'A Note on the Geographical Distribution of Bar-Kokhba Coins'. *Isr. Num. Jour.* 4 (1980) 30–3.

Barthélemy, *Devanciers*
D. Barthélemy. *Les devanciers d'Aquila.* VTSup 10. Leiden, 1963.

Barthélemy, 'Redécouverte'
D. Barthélemy. 'Redécouverte d'un chaînon manquant de l'histoire de la Septante'. *RB* 60 (1953) 18–29.

Ben Sasson, 'Fragments'
M. Ben Sasson. 'Fragments from Saadya's *Sefer Ha-edut VeHashetarot*'. *Annual of the Institute for Research in Jewish Law* 11–12 (1984–6) 135–278 (Hebrew).

Benoit *et al.*, *DJD* II
P. Benoit, J. T. Milik et R. de Vaux. *Les Grottes de Murabbaʿat. DJD* II. Oxford, 1961.

Beyer, *Aramäischen Texte*
K. Beyer. *Die aramäischen Texte vom Toten Meer.* Göttingen, 1984.

Beyer, *Ergänzungsband*
K. Beyer, *Die aramäischen Texte vom Toten Meer*: *Ergänzungsband.* Göttingen, 1994.

Bickerman, 'Legal Interpretations'
E. Bickerman. 'Two Legal Interpretations of the Septuagint'. In *Studies in Jewish and Christian History,* vol. 1, pp. 201–24. Leiden, 1976.

Birnbaum, 'Kephar Bebhayu'
S. A. Birnbaum. 'The Kephar Bebhayu Conveyance'. *PEQ* 88–9 (1956–57) 108–32.

Bowersock, 'Annexation'
G. W. Bowersock. 'The Annexation and Initial Garrison of Arabia'. *ZPE* 5 (1970) 37–47.

Bowersock, 'Babatha Papyri'
G. W. Bowersock. 'The Babatha Papyri, Masada and Rome'. *JRA* 4 (1991) 336–44.

Bowersock, 'Report'
G. W. Bowersock. 'A Report on Arabia Provincia'. *JRS* 61 (1971) 219–42.

Bowersock, *Roman Arabia*
G. W. Bowersock. *Roman Arabia.* Cambridge, Mass., and London, 1983.

Bowman and Rathbone, 'Cities and Administration'
A. Bowman and D. Rathbone. 'Cities and Administration in Roman Egypt'. *JRS* 82 (1992) 107–27.

Broshi, 'Seven Notes'
M. Broshi. 'Agriculture and Economy in Roman Palestine: Seven Notes on the Babatha Archive'. *IEJ* 42 (1992) 230–40.

Broshi, 'Wine in Ancient Palestine'
M. Broshi. 'Wine in Ancient Palestine: Introductory Notes'. *Israel Museum Journal* 3 (1984) 21–40.

Broshi and Qimron, 'House Sale Deed'
M. Broshi and E. Qimron. 'A House Sale Deed from Kefar Baru from the Time of Bar Kokhba'. *IEJ* 36 (1986) 201–14.

Broshi and Qimron, 'I.O.U.'
M. Broshi and E. Qimron. 'A Hebrew I.O.U. Note from the Second Year of the Bar Kokhba Revolt'. *JJS* 45 (1994) 286–94.

Broshi and Qimron, 'Shṭar'
M. Broshi and E. Qimron. 'I.O.U. Note from the Time of the Bar Kokhba Revolt', *ErIsr* 20 (1989) 256–61 (Hebrew).

Brünnow and von Domaszewksi, *Provincia Arabia* III
R. E. Brünnow and A. von Domaszewski. *Die Provincia Arabia,* vol. III. Strasbourg, 1909.

Brunt, 'Revenue'
P. A. Brunt. 'The Revenue of Rome'. In *Roman Imperial Themes*, pp. 324–46; 531–40. Oxford, 1990.

Buck and Petersen, *Reverse Index*
C. D. Buck and W. Petersen. *A Reverse Index of Greek Nouns and Adjectives*. Hildesheim and New York, 1970.

Bureth, *Les Titulatures impériales*
P. Bureth. *Les Titulatures impériales dans les papyrus, les ostraca et les inscriptions d'Égypte (30 a.C.–284 p.C.)*. Brussels, 1964.

Burkhalter, 'Archives'
F. Burkhalter. 'Archives locales et archives centrales en Égypte romaine'. *Chiron* 20 (1990) 191–216.

Cantineau, *Le Nabatéen*
J. Cantineau. *Le Nabatéen*, vol. 1: Paris, 1930. Vol. 2: Paris, 1932.

Clarysse, 'Jews in Triakomia'
W. Clarysse. 'Jews in Triakomia'. In *Proceedings of the 20th International Congress of Papyrologists Copenhagen, 23–29 August, 1992*, edited by A. Bülow-Jacobsen, pp. 193–203. Copenhagen, 1994.

Cockle, 'Archives'
W. E. H. Cockle. 'State Archives in Graeco-Roman Egypt from 30 BC to the Reign of Septimius Severus'. *JEA* 70 (1984) 106–22.

Cohen, 'Rabbi Meir'
N. G. Cohen. 'Rabbi Meir, a Descendant of Anatolian Proselytes'. *JJS* 23 (1972) 51–9.

Cotton, 'Administration'
H. M. Cotton. 'Some Aspects of the Roman Administration of Judaea/Syria-Palaestina with Special Emphasis on the Documents from the Judaean Desert'. In *Lokale Autonomie und römische Ordnungsmacht in den kaiserzeitlichen Provinzen vom 1.–3. Jh.* Kolloquien des Historischen Kollegs, edited by W. Eck. Munich (forthcoming).

Cotton, 'Another Fragment'
H. M. Cotton. 'Another Fragment of the Declaration of Landed Property from the Province of Arabia'. *ZPE* 99 (1993) 115–21.

Cotton, 'Cancelled Marriage Contract'
H. M. Cotton. 'A Cancelled Marriage Contract from the Judaean Desert (XḤev/Se Gr. 2)'. *JRS* 84 (1994) 64–86.

Cotton, 'Courtyard(s)'
H. M. Cotton. 'Courtyard(s) in Ein-Gedi: P.Yadin 11, 19 and 20 of the Babatha Archive'. *ZPE* 112 (1996) 197–201.

Cotton, 'Deeds of Gift'
H. M. Cotton. 'Deeds of Gift and the Law of Succession in Archives from the Judaean Desert', *ErIsr* 25 (1996) 410–15 (Hebrew); for an English version see 'Deeds of Gift and the Law of Succession in Archives from the Judaean Desert'. *Akten des 21. Internationalen Papyrologenkongress, 13.–19. August 1995, Arch. für Pap. Beiheft.* (forthcoming).

Cotton, 'Ein Gedi between the Two Revolts'
H. M. Cotton. 'Ein Gedi between the Two Revolts in the Light of the Documents from the Judaean Desert'. *Scripta Classica Israelica* (forthcoming).

Cotton, 'Fragments'
H. M. Cotton. 'Fragments of a Declaration of Landed Property from the Province of Arabia'. *ZPE* 85 (1991) 263–7.

Cotton, 'Guardianship'
H. M. Cotton. 'The Guardianship of Jesus Son of Babatha: Roman and Local Law in the Province of Arabia'. *JRS* 83 (1993) 94–108.

Cotton, ''Η νέα ἐπαρχεία 'Αραβία'
H. M. Cotton. ''Η νέα ἐπαρχεία 'Αραβία: The New Province of Arabia in the Papyri from the Judaean Desert'. *ZPE* 116 (1997) (in press).

Cotton, 'Loan with Hypothec
H. M. Cotton, 'Loan with Hypothec: Another Papyrus from the Cave of Letters?', *ZPE* 101 (1994) 53–60.

Cotton, 'Rabbis'
H. M. Cotton. 'The Rabbis and the Documents'. In *The Jews in the Graeco-Roman World*, edited by Martin Goodman. Oxford (forthcoming).

Cotton, 'Rent or Tax Receipt'
H. M. Cotton. 'Rent or Tax Receipt from Maoza'. *ZPE* 100 (1994) 547–57.

Cotton, 'Subscriptions'
H. M. Cotton. 'Subscriptions and Signatures in the Papyri from the Judaean Desert: The χειροχρήϲτηϲ'. *JJP* 25 (1996) 29–40.

Cotton, 'The Archive of Salome Komaïse Daughter of Levi'
H. M. Cotton. 'The Archive of Salome Komaïse Daughter of Levi: Another Archive from the "Cave of Letters"'. *ZPE* 105 (1995) 171–208.

Cotton, Cockle, and Millar, 'Papyrology'
H. M. Cotton, W. Cockle and F. Millar. 'The Papyrology of the Roman Near East: A Survey'. *JRS* 85 (1995) 214–35.

Cotton and Eck, 'Staatsmonopol und seine Folgen'
H. M. Cotton and W. Eck. 'Ein Staatsmonopol und seine Folgen: Plinius, *Naturalis Historia* 12,123 und der Preis für Balsam'. *RhM* (in press).

Cotton and Geiger, *Masada* II
H. M. Cotton and J. Geiger. *Masada*, Vol. II: *The Latin and Greek Documents*. Jerusalem, 1989.

Cotton, Geiger, and Netzer, 'Greek Ostracon'
H. M. Cotton, J. Geiger and E. Netzer. 'A Greek Ostracon from Masada'. *IEJ* 45 (1995) 274–7.

Cotton and Greenfield, 'Babatha's Patria'
H. M. Cotton and J. C. Greenfield. 'Babatha's Patria: Maḥoza, Maḥoz ʿEglatain and Ẓoʿar'. *ZPE* 107 (1995) 126–34.

Cotton and Greenfield, 'Babatha's Property'
H. M. Cotton and J. C. Greenfield. 'Babatha's Property and the Law of Succession in the Babatha Archive'. *ZPE* 104 (1994) 211–24.

Cowley
A. Cowley. *Aramaic Papyri of the Fifth Century B.C.* Oxford, 1923.

Crawford-Thompson, 'Imperial Estates'
D. J. Crawford-Thompson. 'Imperial Estates'. In *Studies in Roman Property*, edited by M. I. Finley,

pp. 57–70. Cambridge, 1976 (Abridged version in *The Roman World,* vol. 2, edited by J. Wacher, pp. 555–67. London and New York, 1987).

Crisci, 'Scritture greche'
E. Crisci. 'Scritture greche palestinesi e mesopotamiche (III secolo A.C.–III D.C.)'. *Scrittura et Civiltà* 15 (1991) 125–83.

Crisci, *Scrivere Greco*
E. Crisci. *Scrivere Greco fuori d'Egitto.* Papyrologia Florentina XXVII (1996).

Cross, 'Samaria Papyrus 1'
F. M. Cross. 'Samaria Papyrus 1: An Aramaic Slave Conveyance of 335 B.C.E. Found in the Wâdī ed-Dâliyeh', *ErIsr* 18 (1985) 7*–17*.

de Ruggiero, *DE*
Dizionario Epigraphico di antichità romana.

de Vaux, 'Fouille'
R. de Vaux. 'Fouille au Khirbet Qumrân'. *RB* 60 (1953) 83–106.

Dean, *Epiphanius' Treatise*
J. E. Dean, ed. *Epiphanius' Treatise on Weights and Measures.* Chicago, 1935.

Degen, 'Die aramäischen Ostraka'
R. Degen. 'Die aramäischen Ostraka in der Papyrussammlung der österreichischen Nationalbibliothek'. *NESE* (1978) 33–66.

Degrassi, *Fasti consolari*
A. Degrassi. *I fasti consolari dell' impero romano.* Rome, 1952.

Devijver, *De Aegypto*
H. Devijver. *De Aegypto et exercitu Romano; sive, Prosopographia militiarum equestrium, quae ab Augusto ad Gallienum seu statione seu origine ad Aegyptum pertinebant.* Leuven, 1975.

Dobson, 'Women as Property Owners'
D. Dobson. 'Women as Property Owners in Roman Egypt'. *TAPhA* 113 (1983) 311–21.

Dornseiff, *Rückläufiges Wörterbuch*
F. Dornseiff. *Rückläufiges Wörterbuch der griechischen Eigennamen.* Berlin, 1957.

Drescher, 'Eleuthera'
J. Drescher. ''Ελεύθερα once more'. *Bull. Société Archéol. Coptique* 20 (1969–70) 251–9.

Drijvers, *Inscriptions*
H. J. W. Drijvers. *Old Syriac (Edessean) Inscriptions.* Leiden, 1972.

Duncan Jones, *Structure and Scale*
R. Duncan Jones. *Structure and Scale in the Roman Economy.* Cambridge, 1991.

Eck, 'Consules Ordinarii und Consules Suffecti'
W. Eck. 'Consules Ordinarii und Consules Suffecti als eponyme Amtsträger'. In *Epigrafia. Actes du Colloque international d'épigraphie latine en mémoire de Attilio Degrassi, Rome, 27-28 Mai 1988*, pp. 15–44. Rome, 1991.

Eck, 'Jahres- und Provinzialfasten'
W. Eck. 'Jahres- und Provinzialfasten der senatorischen Statthalter von 69/70 bis 138/9'. *Chiron* 12 (1982) 281–362; 13 (1983) 147–237.

Edmonds, 'Place Names'
C. J. Edmonds. 'The Place Names of the Avroman Parchments'. *BSOAS* 14 (1952) 478–82.

Eger, *Zum ägyptischen Grundbuchwesen*
O. Eger. *Zum ägyptischen Grundbuchwesen in römischer Zeit.* Leipzig and Berlin, 1909.

Elizur, 'Place Names'
Y. Elizur. 'Place Names of Two Words in the Arabic Nomenclature and in the Bible'. In *Proceedings of the Tenth World Congress of Jewish Studies, Jerusalem 1989,* Div. D, vol. 1, pp. 21–8. Jerusalem, 1990 (Hebrew).

Engelmann and Knibbe, 'Das Zollgesetz'
H. Engelmann and D. Knibbe. 'Das Zollgesetz der Provinz Asia'. *Epigraphica Anatolica* 14 (1989).

Eshel and Eshel, 'Fragments'
E. Eshel and H. Eshel. 'Fragments of Two Aramaic Documents Which Were Brought to Abiʾor Cave during the Bar Kokhba Revolt'. *ErIsr* 23 (1992) 276–85.

Eshel and Misgav, 'Ketef Yeriḥo'
H. Eshel and H. Misgav. 'A Fourth Century B.C.E. Document from Ketef Yeriḥo'. *IEJ* 38 (1988) 158–76.

Falk, 'Inheritance'
Z. Falk. 'The Inheritance of the Daughter and the Widow in the Bible and the Talmud'. *Tarbiz* 23 (1952) 9–15 (Hebrew).

Falk, *Introduction*
Z. Falk. *Introduction to Jewish Law of the Second Commonwealth.* Leiden, 1978.

Feissel, 'Notes'
D. Feissel. 'Notes épigraphiques'. *BCH* 107 (1983) 601–18.

Feissel and Gascou, 'Documents'
D. Feissel et J. Gascou. 'Documents d'archives romains inédits du Moyen Euphrate (IIIe siècle après J.-C.)'. *Comptes-rendus de l'Académie des Inscriptions* (1989) 534–61.

Feissel and Gascou, 'Documents 1. Les pétitions'
D. Feissel and J. Gascou. 'Documents d'archives romains inédits du Moyen Euphrate (IIIe siècle après J.-C.) 1. Les pétitions (P.Euphr 1 à 5)'. *Journal des Savants* (1995) 65–119.

Feissel and Gascou, 'Documents 2. Les actes de vente-achat'
D. Feissel et J. Gascou. 'Documents d'archives romains inédits du Moyen Euphrate (IIIe siècle après J.-C.) 2. Les actes de ventes-achat (P.Euph. 6 à 10)'. *Journal des Savants* (in press).

Feliks, *Agriculture*
Y. Feliks. *The Agriculture in the Land of Israel in the Time of the Bible, the Mishna and the Talmud.* 2d ed. Jerusalem, 1990 (Hebrew).

FIRA^2
S. Riccobono, ed. *Fontes Iuris Romani Antejustiniani.* 2d ed. Florence, 1941–43.

Flach, 'Inschriftenuntersuchungen'
D. Flach. 'Inschriftenuntersuchungen zum römischen Kolonat in Nordafrika'. *Chiron* 8 (1978) 441–92.

Flach, *Römische Agrargeschichte*
D. Flach. *Römische Agrargeschichte.* Munich, 1990.

Flusser and Safrai, 'In the Image'
D. Flusser and Sh. Safrai. 'In the Image of the Form of His Likeness (בצלם דמות תבניתו)'. In *Isaac Leo Seeligman Volume* 2, pp. 453–61. Jerusalem, 1983 (Hebrew).

Foraboschi, *Onomasticon*
D. Foraboschi. *Onomasticon alterum papyrologicum. Suppl. al Namenbuch di F. Preisigke.* Milan, 1967–71.

Fraenkel, *Fremdwörter*
S. Fraenkel. *Die aramäischen Fremdwörter im Arabischen.* Hildesheim, 1962.

Fraser and Matthews, *Lexicon*
P. M. Fraser and E. Matthews. *A Lexicon of Greek Personal Names.* Vol. 1: *The Aegean Islands, Cyprus, Cyrenaica.* Oxford, 1987. Vol. 2: *Attica.* Edited by M. J. Osborne and S. G. Byrne. Oxford, 1994.

Freeman, 'The Era of the Province of Arabia'
Ph. Freeman. 'The Era of the Province of Arabia: Problems and Solution'. In H. I. MacAdam, *Studies in the History of the Roman Province of Arabia,* British Archaeological Reports 295 (1986) 38–46.

Friedman, 'Babatha's *Ketubba*'

M. A. Friedman. 'Babatha's *Ketubba*: Some Preliminary Observations', *IEJ* 46 (1996) 55–76.

Friedman, *Jewish Marriage*
M. A. Friedman. *Jewish Marriage in Palestine*: *A Cairo Geniza Study*, vols. 1–2. Tel Aviv and New York, 1980–1.

Geiger, 'Note'
J. Geiger. 'A Note on *P.Yadin* 18'. *ZPE* 93 (1992) 67–8.

Geller, 'New Sources'
M. J. Geller. 'New Sources for the Origin of the Rabbinic Ketubah'. *HUCA* 49 (1978) 227–45.

Gernet, *Beiträge*
E. Gernet. *Beiträge zum Recht der Parapherna.* Münchener Beiträge zur Papyrusforschung und antiken Rechtsgeschichte 38 (1954).

Gignac, *Grammar*
F. Th. Gignac. *A Grammar of the Greek Papyri of the Roman and Byzantine Periods*, vols. 1–2. Milan, 1976–81.

Gilliam, 'Sale of a Slave'
J. F. Gilliam. 'The Sale of a Slave through a Greek *Diploma*'. *JJP* 16–17 (1971) 63–70.

Ginsberg, 'Notes'
H. L. Ginsberg. 'Notes on the Two Published Letters to Jeshua Galgolah'. *BASOR* 131 (1953) 25–7.

Goldstein, 'Syriac Deed'
J. Goldstein. 'The Syriac Deed of Sale from Dura Europos'. *JNES* 25 (1966) 1–15.

Goodman, 'Babatha's Story'
M. Goodman. 'Babatha's Story'. *JRS* 81 (1991) 169–75.

Goodman, *State and Society*
M. Goodman. *State and Society in Roman Galilee, A.D. 132–212.* Totowa, New Jersey, 1983.

Graf, 'Hellenization'
D. Graf. 'On Hellenization and the Decapolis'. *Aram* 4 (1992) 1–47.

Greenfield, 'Azatiwada'
J. C. Greenfield. 'Notes on the Azatiwada (Karatepe) Inscription'. *ErIsr* 14 (1978) 74–7 (Hebrew).

Greenfield, 'Babylonian/Aramaic'
J. C. Greenfield. 'Babylonian/Aramaic Relations'. In *Mesopotamien und seine Nachbarn*, vol. 2, edited by H. Nissen and J. Regner, pp. 471–82. Berlin, 1982.

Greenfield, 'Defension Clause'
J. C. Greenfield. 'The "Defension Clause" in Some Documents from Naḥal Ḥever and Naḥal Ṣeʾelim', *RevQ* 15 (1991–92) 467–71.

Greenfield, 'Infinitive'
J. C. Greenfield. 'The Infinitive in the Aramaic Documents from the Judean Desert'. In *Studies in Hebrew and Other Semitic Languages Presented to Chaim Rabin*, edited by M. Goshen-Gottstein, S. Morag, and S. Kogut, pp. 77–81. Jerusalem, 1990 (Hebrew).

Greenfield, 'Legal Terminology'
J. C. Greenfield. 'Studies in the Legal Terminology of the Nabatean Funerary Inscriptions'. In *Henoch Yalon Memorial Volume*, pp. 64–83. Ramat Gan, 1974 (Hebrew).

Greenfield, 'Letters'
J. C. Greenfield. '"Because He/She Did Not Know Letters": Remarks on a First Millennium C.E. Legal Expression'. *JANES* 22 (1993) 39–44.

Greenfield, 'Naḥal Ṣeʾelim'
J. C. Greenfield. 'The Texts from Naḥal Ṣeʾelim' (Wadi Seiyal)'. In *The Madrid Qumran Congress*: *Proceedings of the International Congress on the Dead Sea Scrolls, Madrid 18–21 March 1991*, vol. 2, edited by J. Trebolle Barrera and L. Vegas Montaner, pp. 661–5. Leiden, 1992.

Greenfield and Sokoloff, 'Qumran Aramaic'
J. C. Greenfield and M. Sokoloff. 'The Contribution of Qumran Aramaic to the Aramaic Vocabulary'. AbrN Sup 3: *Studies in Qumran Aramaic* (1992) 78–98.

Gulak, *Otsar Ha-Shtarot*
A. Gulak. *A Collection of Legal Deeds Used in Israel* (*Otsar Ha-Shtarot*). Jerusalem, 1926 (Hebrew).

Gulak, *Towards a Study*
A. Gulak. *Towards a Study of the History of Jewish Law in the Talmudic Period*, vol. 1. Jerusalem, 1929 (Hebrew).

Gulak, *Urkundenwesen*
A. Gulak. *Das Urkundenwesen im Talmud*. Jerusalem, 1935. Rev. Hebrew ed., השטרות בתלמוד, supplemented by R. Katzoff. Jerusalem, 1994.

Hachlili, 'Goliath Family'
R. Hachlili. 'The Goliath Family in Jericho: Funerary Inscriptions from a First-Century A.D. Monumental Tomb'. *BASOR* 235 (1979) 31–66.

Hachlili, 'Jerusalem Family'
R. Hachlili. 'A Jerusalem Family in Jericho'. *BASOR* 230 (1978) 45–56.

Hachlili, 'Names'
R. Hachlili. 'Names and Nicknames of Jews in Second Temple Times'. *ErIsr* 17 (1984) 188–211 (Hebrew).

Häge, *Ehegüterrechtliche Verhältnisse*
G. Häge. *Ehegüterrechtliche Verhältnisse in den griechischen Papyri Ägyptens bis Diokletian*. Cologne and Graz, 1968.

Handbuch der Orientalistik, edited by B. Spuler, vol. I.4: *Iranistik*. Leiden and Cologne, 1958.

Harding, *Index*
G. L. Harding. *An Index and Concordance of Pre-Islamic Arabian Names and Inscriptions*. Toronto, 1971.

Harmon, 'Egyptian Property'
A. M. Harmon. 'Egyptian Property-Returns'. *YClS* 4 (1934) 135–234.

Hirschberg, 'New Jewish Inscriptions'
H. Z. Hirschberg. 'New Jewish Inscriptions in the Nabataean Sphere'. *ErIsr* 12 (1978) 142–8.

Hirschfeld, *Palestinian Dwelling*
Y. Hirschfeld. *Palestinian Dwelling in the Roman and Byzantine Period*. Jerusalem, 1995.

Hobson, 'Women as Property Owners'
D. H. Hobson. 'Women as Property Owners in Roman Egypt', *TAPA* 113 (1983) 311–21.

Hoftijzer and Jongeling, *Dictionary*
J. Hoftijzer and K. Jongeling. *Dictionary of the North-West Semitic Inscriptions* (*Handbuch der Orientalistik*), vols. 1–2. Leiden, 1995.

Hohlwein, 'Palmiers et Palmeraies'
N. Hohlwein. 'Palmiers et Palmeraies dans l'Égypte romaine'. *Études de Papyrologie* 5 (1939) 1–74.

Hombert and Préaux, *Recherches*
M. Hombert and Cl. Préaux. *Recherches sur le recensement dans l'Égypte Romaine* (P. Bruxelles Inv. E. 7616). Papyrologica Lugduno-Batava 5 (1952).

Horbury and Noy, *Jewish Inscriptions*
W. Horbury and D. Noy. *Jewish Inscriptions of Graeco-Roman Egypt*. Cambridge, 1992.

Howard and Shelton, 'Bar-Kochba'
G. Howard and J. C. Shelton. 'The Bar-Kochba Letters and Palestinian Greek'. *IEJ* 23 (1973) 101–2.

Hurvitz, 'בית קברות'
A. Hurvitz. 'בית קברות and בית עולם: Two Funerary Terms in Biblical Literature and Their Linguistic Background'. *Maarav* 8 (1992) 59–68.

Husson, *OIKIA*
G. Husson. *OIKIA: Le vocabulaire de la maison privée en Égypte d'après les papyrus grecs*. Paris, 1983.

Ilan, 'Divorce Bill'
T. Ilan. 'Notes and Observations on a Newly Published Divorce Bill from the Judaean Desert'. *HThR* 89 (1996) 195–202.

Ilan, 'Notes'
T. Ilan. 'Notes on the Distribution of Jewish Women's Names in Palestine in the Second Temple and Mishnaic Periods'. *JJS* 50 (1989) 186–200.

Ilan, 'Ossuary Inscriptions'
T. Ilan. 'New Ossuary Inscriptions from Jerusalem'. *Scripta Classica Israelica* 11 (1991–2) 149–59.

Ilan, 'Premarital Cohabitation'
T. Ilan. 'Premarital Cohabitation in Ancient Judaea: The Evidence of the Babatha Archive and the *Mishnah* (*Ketubbot* 1:4)'. *HThR* 86 (1993) 247–64.

Ingolt, 'Palmyrene Inscription'
H. Ingholt. 'Palmyrene Inscription from the Tomb of Malkû'. *Mélanges de l'Université Saint Josèphe* 38 (1962) 99–119.

Irsai, 'Water Installations'
O. Irsai. 'The Discussion of Water Installations and Aqueducts in Rabbinical Literature—Characteristics and Terminology'. In *The Aqueducts of Ancient Palestine*, edited by D. Amit, Y. Hirschfeld and J. Patrich, pp. 47–55. Jerusalem, 1989 (Hebrew).

Isaac, 'Babatha Archive'
B. Isaac. 'The Babatha Archive'. *IEJ* 42 (1992) 62–75.

Isaac, 'Decapolis'
B. Isaac. 'The Decapolis in Syria: A Neglected Inscription'. *ZPE* 44 (1981) 67–74.

Isaac, *Limits of Empire*
B. Isaac. *The Limits of Empire: The Roman Army in the East*. Oxford, 1990. 2d rev. ed. Oxford, 1992.

Isaac, 'Tax Collection'
B. Isaac. 'Tax Collection in Roman Arabia: New Evidence from the Babatha Archive'. *Mediterranean Historical Review* 9 (1994) 256–66.

Isaac and Oppenheimer, 'Revolt'
B. Isaac and A. Oppenheimer. 'The Revolt of Bar Kokhba: Ideology and Modern Scholarship'. *JJS* 36 (1985) 33–60.

Johnson, *Roman Egypt*
A. Ch. Johnson. *Roman Egypt to the Reign of Diocletian. Economic Survey of Ancient Rome*, vol 2. Baltimore, 1936.

Jones, *Cities*
A. H. M. Jones. *The Cities of the Eastern Roman Provinces*. 2d ed. Revised by M. Avi-Yonah. Oxford, 1971.

Jones, 'Urbanization'
A. H. M. Jones. 'The Urbanization of Palestine'. *JRS* 21 (1931) 78–85.

Jull *et al.*
A. J. T. Jull, D. J. Donahue, M. Broshi, and E. Tov, 'Radiocarbon Dating of Scrolls and Linen Fragments from the Judean Desert', *ʿAtiqot* 28 (1996) 1–7.

Kaser, *Römisches Zivilprozessrecht*
M. Kaser. *Das römische Zivilprozessrecht*. Munich, 1966.

Katzoff, 'Interpretation'
R. Katzoff. 'An Interpretation of P. Yadin 19 etc.'. In *Proceedings of the 20th International Congress of Papyrologists Copenhagen, 23–29 August, 1992*, edited by A. Bülow-Jacobsen, pp. 562–5. Copenhagen, 1994.

Katzoff, 'Marriage Formulas'
R. Katzoff. 'Greek and Jewish Marriage Formulas'. In *Classical Studies in Honor of David Sohlberg*, pp. 223–34. Ramat Gan, 1996.

Katzoff, 'Papyrus Yadin 18'
R. Katzoff. 'Papyrus Yadin 18 Again: A Rejoinder'. *JQR* 82 (1991) 171–6.

Katzoff, 'P. Yadin 19'
R. Katzoff. 'P. Yadin 19: A Gift after Death from the Judaean Desert'. In *Proceedings of the Tenth World Congress of Jewish Studies, Jerusalem 1989*, Div. C, vol. 1, pp. 1–8. Jerusalem, 1990 (Hebrew).

Katzoff, 'Philo and Hillel'
R. Katzoff. 'Philo and Hillel on Violation of Betrothal in Alexandria'. In *The Jews in the Hellenistic-Roman World. Studies in Memory of Menahem Stern*, edited by A. Oppenheimer, I. Gafni, and D. Schwartz, pp. 39*–57*. Jerusalem, 1996.

Katzoff, 'Polygamy?'
R. Katzoff. 'Polygamy in P. Yadin?' *ZPE* 109 (1995) 128–32.

Kaufman, 'Median Cubit'
A. Kaufman. 'Determining the Length of the Median Cubit'. *PEQ* 116 (1984) 120–32.

Kehoe, *Economics of Agriculture*
D. P. Kehoe. *The Economics of Agriculture on Roman Imperial Estates in North Africa*. Göttingen, 1988.

Kehoe, 'Lease Regulations'
D. P. Kehoe. 'Lease Regulations for Imperial Estates in North Africa. Part 2'. *ZPE* 59 (1985) 151–72.

Kehoe, *Management and Investment*
D. P. Kehoe. *Management and Investment on Estates in Roman Egypt during the Early Empire*. Bonn, 1992.

Kienast, *Kaisertabelle*
D. Kienast. *Römische Kaisertabelle. Grundzüge einer Kaiserchronologie*. 2d ed. Darmstadt 1996.

Kiessling, 'Zwei Papyrusurkunden'
E. Kiessling. 'Zwei Papyrusurkunden aus der Giessener Sammlung'. In *Proceedings of the 12th International Congress of Papyrologists*, pp. 243–7. Toronto, 1970.

Kloner and Eshel, 'Aramaic Ostracon'
A. Kloner and E. Eshel. 'An Aramaic Ostracon of an Edomite Marriage Document from Maresha, dated 176 B.C.E.'. *Tarbiz* 63 (1994) 485–502 (Hebrew).

Kloner and Tepper, *Hiding Complexes*
A. Kloner and Y. Tepper. *The Hiding Complexes in the Judaean Shephelah*. Jerusalem, 1987 (Hebrew).

Kneissl, *Die Siegestitulatur*
P. Kneissl. *Die Siegestitulatur der römischen Kaiser. Untersuchungen zu den Siegerbeinamen des ersten und zweiten Jahrhunderts, Hypomnemata* 23. Göttingen, 1969.

Kochavi, *Judaea*
M. Kochavi, ed. *Judaea, Samaria and the Golan, Archaeological Survey 1967–1968*. Jerusalem, 1972 (Hebrew).

Koenen, 'Laudatio funebris'
L. Koenen. 'Die "laudatio funebris" des Augustus für Agrippa'. *ZPE* 5 (1970) 235–41.

Koffmahn, *Doppelurkunden*
E. Koffmahn. *Die Doppelurkunden aus der Wüste Juda*. Leiden, 1968.

Kornfeld, *Grabinschriften*
W. Kornfeld. *Jüdisch-aramäische Grabinschriften aus Edfu*. Wien, 1973.

Kornfeld, 'Graffiti'
W. Kornfeld. 'Neues über die phönikischen und aramäischen Graffiti in den Tempeln von Abydos'. *Anzeiger der phil.-hist. Klasse der österreichischen Akademie der Wissenschaften* 115 (1978) 193–204.

Kraeling
E. G. Kraeling. *The Brooklyn Aramaic Papyri*. New Haven, 1953.

Kreller, *Erbrechtliche Untersuchungen*
H. Kreller. *Erbrechtliche Untersuchungen auf Grund der gräko-ägyptischen Papyrusurkunden*. Leipzig, 1919.

Kuehn, 'New Papyrus'
C. A. Kuehn. 'A New Papyrus of a Dioscorian Poem and Marriage Contract P.Berol Inv. No. 21334'. *ZPE* 97 (1993) 103–15.

Kühnert, 'Kreditgeschäft'
H. Kühnert. 'Zum Kreditgeschäft in den hellenistischen Papyri Ägyptens bis Diokletian'. Ph.D. dissertation, University of Freiburg in Breisgau, 1965.

Kuhnke, *Οὐσιακὴ γῆ*
H. Chr. Kuhnke. *Οὐσιακὴ γῆ. Domänenland in den Papyri der Prinzipatszeit*. Ph.D. dissertation, University of Cologne, 1971.

Kunkel, 'Doppelurkunde'
W. Kunkel. 'Zur gräko-ägyptischen Doppelurkunde'. In *Studi in onore Salvatore Riccobono*, pp. 414–33. Palermo, 1936.

Kutscher, *History of Aramaic*
E. Y. Kutscher, with the assistance of H. Natan. *The History of Aramaic (Part 1)*. Jerusalem, 1973 (Hebrew).

Kutscher, 'Note'
E. Y. Kutscher. 'Note on the Title רש מרום'. *IEJ* 22 (1972) 117.

Kutscher, *Studies*
E. Y. Kutscher. *Hebrew and Aramaic Studies*. Jerusalem, 1977.

Kutscher, 'Ugaritica Marginalia'
E. Y. Kutscher. 'Ugaritica Marginalia'. *Leshonenu* 34 (1970) 5–19 (Hebrew).

Lapin, 'Early Rabbinic Civil Law'
H. Lapin. 'Early Rabbinic Civil Law and the Literature of the Second Temple Period'. *Jewish Studies Quarterly* 2 (1995) 149–83.

Lapin, 'Palm Fronds'
H. Lapin. 'Palm Fronds and Citrons: Notes on Two Letters from Bar Kosiba's Administration'. *HUCA* 64 (1993) 111–35.

Larsen, 'Unusual Eponymy-Datings'
M. T. Larsen. 'Unusual Eponymy-Datings from Mari and Assyria'. *Revue d'Assyriologie et d'Archéologie orientale* 68 (1974) 15–24.

Lehmann, *Essays and Journeys*
M. R. Lehmann. *Essays and Journeys*. Jerusalem, 1982 (Hebrew).

Lehmann, 'Studies'
M. R. Lehmann. 'Studies in the Murabbaʿat and Naḥal Ḥever Documents'. *RevQ* 4 (1963–4) 53–81.

Levine, 'Comparative Perspectives'
B. A. Levine. 'Comparative Perspectives on Jewish and Christian History'. *JAOS* 99 (1979) 81–6.

Levine, 'Formulary'
B. A. Levine. 'On the Origins of the Aramaic Legal Formulary of Elephantine'. In *Christianity, Judaism, and Other Greco-Roman Cults: Studies for Morton Smith at Sixty*, vol. 3, edited by J. Neusner, pp. 37–54. Leiden, 1975.

Levine, 'Mulūgu/Melûg'
B. A. Levine. 'Mulūgu/Melûg: The Origins of a Talmudic Legal Institution'. *JAOS* 88 (1969) 271–85.

Lewis, 'Babatha Archive'
N. Lewis. 'The Babatha Archive: A Response'. *IEJ* 44 (1994) 241–6.

Lewis, *Documents*
The Documents from the Bar Kokhba Period in the Cave of Letters: Greek Papyri, edited by N. Lewis; *Aramaic and Nabatean Signatures and Subscriptions*, edited by Y. Yadin and J. C. Greenfield. Jerusalem, 1989.

Lewis, 'In the World of P.Yadin'
N. Lewis. 'In the World of P.Yadin: Where did Judah's Wife Live?', *IEJ* 46 (1996) 256–7.

Lewis, 'Jewish Landowner'
N. Lewis. 'A Jewish Landowner from the Province of Arabia'. *Scripta Classica Israelica* 8–9 (1985–8) 132–7.

Lewis, 'The Money Called Black'
N. Lewis. 'Again, the Money Called Black'. In *Classical Studies in Honor of David Sohlberg*, pp. 399–410. Ramat Gan, 1996.

Lewis, 'World of P.Yadin'
N. Lewis. 'The World of P.Yadin'. *BASP* 28 (1991) 35–41.

Lewis *et al.*, 'Papyrus Yadin 18'
N. Lewis, R. Katzoff and J. Greenfield. '*Papyrus Yadin* 18'. *IEJ* 37 (1987) 229–50.

Lidzbarski, 'Aramäischer Brief'
M. Lidzbarski. 'Ein aramäischer Brief aus der Zeit Ašurbanipals'. *Zeitschrift für Assyriologie* 31 (1917/18) 193–202.

Lieberman, 'Editor's Notes'
S. Lieberman. 'Editor's Notes'. In *Henoch Yalon Memorial Volume*, pp. 556–9. Ramat Gan, 1974 (Hebrew).

Lieberman, 'Preliminary Note'
S. Lieberman. 'A Preliminary Note to the Inscription on the Floor of the Synagogue in En-Gedi'. *Tarbiz* 40 (1970) 24–6 (Hebrew).

Lifshitz, 'Greek Documents'
B. Lifshitz. 'The Greek Documents from Naḥal Ṣeelim and Naḥal Mishmar'. *IEJ* 11 (1961) 53–61.

Lifshitz, 'Greek Documents from the Cave of Horror'
B. Lifshitz. 'The Greek Documents from the Cave of Horror'. *IEJ* 12 (1962) 201–7.

Lifshitz, 'Papyrus grecs'
B. Lifshitz. 'Papyrus grecs du désert de Juda'. *Aegyptus* 42 (1962) 240–58.

Lo Cascio, 'Census provinciale'
E. Lo Cascio. 'Census provinciale, imposizione fiscale e amministrazoni cittadine nel Principato'. In *Lokale Autonomie und römische Ordnungsmacht in den kaiserzeitlichen Provinzen vom 1.–3. Jh.* Kolloquien des Historischen Kollegs, edited by W. Eck. Munich (forthcoming).

Loewenstamm, 'Alalakh'
S. E. Loewenstamm. 'Notes on the Alalakh Tablets'. *IEJ* 6 (1956) 217–25.

Loewenstamm, 'Parallels'
S. E. Loewenstamm. 'In Which Texts May We Look for Parallels to Ugaritic Literature?' In *Henoch Yalon Memorial Volume*, pp. 212–20. Ramat Gan, 1974 (Hebrew).

Lüddeckens, *Aegyptische Eheverträge*
E. Lüddeckens. *Aegyptische Eheverträge*. Wiesbaden, 1960.

MacAdam, *Studies*
H. I. MacAdam. *Studies in the History of the Roman Province of Arabia*. British Archaeological Reports 295 (1986).

Macalister, *Gezer*
R. A. S. Macalister. *The Excavation of Gezer*, vol. 1. London, 1912.

MacMullen, *Soldier and Civilian*
R. MacMullen. *Soldier and Civilian in the Later Roman Empire*. Cambridge, Mass., 1963.

Maier, *L'épiscopat*
J. L. Maier, *L'épiscopat de l'Afrique Romaine, Vandale et Byzantine*. Rome, 1973.
Manfredi, 'Affitto di un uliveto'
M. Manfredi. 'Affitto di un uliveto'. *YClS* 28 (1985) 95–9.
Maresch and Packman, Papyrologica Coloniensia
K. Maresch and Z. M. Packman, eds. *Papyri from the Washington University Collection, Part 2*. Papyrologica Coloniensia 18. Opladen, 1991.
Mason, *Greek Terms*
H. I. Mason. *Greek Terms for Roman Institutions*. Toronto, 1974.
Mayer, *Jüdische Frau*
G. Mayer. *Die jüdische Frau in der hellenistisch-römischen Antike*. Stuttgart, 1987.
Mayerson, 'Wine and Vineyards'
Ph. Mayerson. 'The Wine and Vineyards of Gaza in the Byzantine Period'. *BASOR* 262 (1986) 75–80; also published in *Monks, Martyrs, Soldiers and Saracens. Papers on the Near East in Late Antiquity (1962-1993)*, pp. 250–55. Jerusalem, 1994.
Mazar, 'Inscription on the Floor of the Synagogue in En-Gedi'
B. Mazar. 'The Inscription on the Floor of the Synagogue in En-Gedi: Preliminary Survey'. *Tarbiz* 40 (1970) 18–23 (Hebrew).
Mazar and Dunayevsky, 'En-Gedi. Third Season'
B. Mazar and I. Dunayevsky. 'En-Gedi. Third Season of Excavations. Preliminary Report'. *IEJ* 14 (1964) 121–30.
Mazar and Dunayevsky, 'En-Gedi. Fourth and Fifth Seasons'
B. Mazar and I. Dunayevsky. 'En-Gedi. Fourth and Fifth Seasons of Excavations. Preliminary Report'. *IEJ* 17 (1967) 133–43.
Meyer, Jur. Pap.
P. M. Meyer. ed. *Juristische Papyri*. Berlin, 1920.
Milik, 'Acte de vente'
J. T. Milik. 'Acte de vente d'une maison, daté de 134 après J.C.'. *Biblica* 38 (1957) 264–8.
Milik, 'Couvercle'
J. T. Milik. 'Le couvercle de Bethphagé'. In *Hommages à A. Dupont-Sommer*, pp. 75–94. Paris, 1971.
Milik, 'Deux documents'
J. T. Milik. 'Deux documents inédits du désert de Juda'. *Biblica* 38 (1957) 245–68.
Milik, 'Inscription bilingue'
J. T. Milik. 'Une inscription bilingue nabatéenne et grecque à Pétra'. *ADAJ* 21 (1976) 143–51.
Milik, 'Note additionnelle'
J. T. Milik. 'Note additionnelle sur le contrat juif de l'an 134 après J.-C.'. *RB* 62 (1955) 253–4.
Milik, 'Nouvelles inscriptions'
J. T. Milik. 'Nouvelles inscriptions nabatéennes'. *Syria* 35 (1958) 227–51.
Milik, 'Travail'
J. T. Milik. 'Le travail d'édition des manuscrits du Désert de Juda'. In *Volume de Congrès, Strasbourg, 1956*. VTSup 4 (1957) 17–26.
Milik, 'Trois tombeaux'
J. T. Milik. 'Trois tombeaux juifs récemment découverts au sud-est de Jerusalem'. *Liber Annuus* 7 (1956–7) 232–67.
Milik, 'Un contrat'
J. T. Milik. 'Un contrat juif de l'an 134 après Jésus-Christ'. *RB* 61 (1954) 182–90.
Millar, *Emperor*
F. Millar. *The Emperor in the Roman World*. London, 1977.
Millar, *Roman Near East*
F. Millar. *The Roman Near East, 31 BC–AD 337*. Cambridge, Mass., 1993.

Millar, 'The *Fiscus*'
F. Millar. 'The *Fiscus* in the First Two Centuries'. *JRS* 53 (1963) 29–42.

Minns, 'Parchments'
E. H. Minns. 'Parchments of the Parthian Period from Avroman in Kurdistan'. *JHS* 35 (1915) 22–65; and plates in *New Palaeographical Society*, 2nd ser., vol. I.3 (1915) nos. 51–2.

Misgav, 'Four Segments'
H. Misgav. 'Four Segments of Inscribed Parchments from the Judaean Desert'. *Michmanim* 7 (1994) 37–40 (Hebrew).

Misgav, 'Jewish Courts'
H. Misgav. 'Jewish Courts of Law as Reflectd in Documents from the Dead Sea'. *Cathedra* 82 (1996) 17–24 (Hebrew).

Mitteis, *Grundzüge*
L. Mitteis and U. Wilcken. *Grundzüge und Chrestomathie der Papyruskunde*, vol. II.1. Leipzig and Berlin, 1912.

Mitteis, *Reichsrecht*
L. Mitteis. *Reichsrecht und Volksrecht in den östlichen Provinzen des römischen Kaiserreichs*. Leipzig, 1891.

Modrzejewski, 'Arbitration'
J. Mélèze Modrzejewski. 'Private Arbitration in the Law of Graeco-Roman Egypt'. *JJP* 6 (1952) 239–56.

Modrzejewski, 'Hellenistisches Ehegüterrecht'
J. Mélèze Modrzejewski. 'Zum hellenistischen Ehegüterrecht im griechischen und römischen Ägypten'. *Zeitschrift der Savigny-Stiftung für Rechtsgeschichte (Rom. Abt.)* 87 (1970) 50–84.

Modrzejewski, 'Jewish Law'
J. Mélèze Modrzejewski. 'Jewish Law and the Hellenistic Legal Practice in the Light of Greek Papyri from Egypt'. In *An Introduction to the History and Sources of Jewish Law*, edited by N. S. Hecht *et al.*, pp. 75–99. Oxford, 1996.

Modrzejewski, 'P. Strass. 237'
J. Mélèze Modrzejewski. 'Note sur P. Strass. 237'. *EOS* 43 (1957; *Symbolae Taubenschlag*, vol. 3) 139–54.

Modrzejewski, 'Règle de droit'
J. Mélèze Modrzejewski. 'La Règle de droit dans l'Egypt ptolémaïque'. In *Essays in Honor of C. Bradford Welles*, Amer. Stud. in Pap. 1 (1966) 125–73.

Modrzejewski, 'Structure'
J. Mélèze Modrzejewski. 'La Structure juridique du mariage grec'. In *Scritti in Onore di O. Montevecchi*, edited by E. Bresciani *et al.*, 1981, pp. 231–68 (also published in *Symposium 1979*: *Vorträge zur griechischen und hellenistischen Rechtsgeschichte*, edited by P. Dimakis, pp. 37–71. Cologne and Vienna, 1983).

Montevecchi, *Papirologia*
O. Montevecchi. *La Papirologia*. Milan, 1973.

Montevecchi, 'Ricerche'
O. Montevecchi. 'Ricerche di sociologia nei documenti dell'Egitto greco-romano II: I contratti di matrimonio e gli atti di divorzio'. *Aegyptus* 16 (1936) 3–83.

Mor, *Bar-Kochba*
M. Mor. *The Bar-Kochba Revolt*: *Its Extent and Effect*. Jerusalem, 1991 (Hebrew).

Muraoka, 'Notes'
T. Muraoka. 'Notes on the Aramaic of the Genesis Apocryphon'. *RevQ* 8 (1972) 7–51.

Musil, *Arabia Petraea*
A. Musil. *Arabia Petraea*. Vol. 1: *Moab*. Vienna, 1907.

Mussies, 'Greek in Palestine'
G. Mussies. 'Greek in Palestine and the Diaspora'. *The Jewish People in the First Century*, vol. 2, edited by S. Safrai *et al.*, pp. 1040–64. Amsterdam, 1976.

Mussies, 'Personal Names'
G. Mussies. 'Jewish Personal Names in Some Non-Literary Sources'. In *Studies in Early Jewish Epigraphy*, edited by J. W. van Henten and P. W. van der Horst. Leiden, 1994.

Naᶜaman, 'Hezekiah'
N. Naᶜaman. 'Hezekiah's Fortified Cities and the LMLK Stamp'. *BASOR* 261 (1986) 5–24.

Naveh, 'Formal and Informal Spelling'
J. Naveh. 'On Formal and Informal Spelling of Unpronounced Gutturals'. *Scripta Classica Israelica* 15 (1996; *Studies in Memory of Abraham Wasserstein*, vol. 1) 263–7.

Naveh, 'Marginalia'
J. Naveh. 'Marginalia on the Deeds from Kefar Baro'. In *Studies in Hebrew and Other Semitic Languages Presented to Chaim Rabin*, edited by M. Goshen-Gottstein, S. Morag, and S. Kogut, pp. 231–4. Jerusalem, 1990 (Hebrew).

Naveh, 'Nameless People'
J. Naveh. 'Nameless People'. *IEJ* 40 (1990) 108–23.

Naveh, *Sherd and Papyrus*
J. Naveh. *On Sherd and Papyrus*. Jerusalem, 1992 (Hebrew).

Naveh, *Stone and Mosaic*
J. Naveh. *On Stone and Mosaic*. Jerusalem, 1978 (Hebrew).

Naveh, 'Synagogue Inscriptions'
J. Naveh. 'The Aramaic and Hebrew Inscriptions from Ancient Synagogues'. *ErIsr* 20 (1989) 302–10 (Hebrew).

Neesen, *Untersuchungen*
L. Neesen. *Untersuchungen zu den direkten Staatsabgaben der römischen Kaiserzeit*. Bonn, 1980.

Negev, 'Nabatean Inscriptions'
A. Negev. 'Nabatean Inscriptions from ᶜAvdat (Oboda)'. *IEJ* 13 (1963) 113–24.

Negev, *Personal Names*
A. Negev. *Personal Names in the Nabatean Realm*. Qedem 32. Jerusalem, 1991.

Nöldeke, *Beiträge*
Th. Nöldeke. *Beiträge zur semitischen Sprachwissenschaft*. Strasbourg, 1904.

Nyberg, 'Pahlavi documents'
H. S. Nyberg. 'The Pahlavi Documents from Avroman'. *Le Monde Oriental* 17 (1923) 182–230.

Obbink, 'Bilingual Literacy'
D. Obbink. 'Bilingual Literacy and Syrian Greek'. *BASP* 28 (1991) 51–7.

Oliver, *Greek Constitutions*
J. H. Oliver. *Greek Constitutions of Early Roman Emperors from Inscriptions and Papyri*. Philadelphia, 1989.

Oppenheimer, 'Urbanization'
A. Oppenheimer. 'Urbanization and City Territories in Roman Palestine'. In *The Jews in the Hellenistic-Roman World. Studies in Memory of Menahem Stern*, edited by A. Oppenheimer, I. Gafni, and D. Schwartz, pp. 209–26. Jerusalem, 1996.

Oren and Rappaport, 'The Necropolis in Maresha'
D. Oren and U. Rappaport. 'The Necropolis in Maresha'. *IEJ* 34 (1984) 114–53.

Packman, 'Further Notes'
Z. Packman. 'Further Notes on Texts with the Imperial Oath'. *ZPE* 90 (1992) 258.

Packman, 'Notes'
Z. Packman. 'Notes on Papyrus Texts with the Roman Imperial Oath'. *ZPE* 89 (1991) 91–102.

Packman, 'Regnal Formulas'
Z. Packman. 'Regnal Formulas in Document Date and in the Imperial Oath'. *ZPE* 91 (1992) 61–76.

Packman, 'Still Further Notes'
Z. Packman. 'Still Further Notes on Papyrus Documents with the Imperial Oath'. *ZPE* 100 (1994) 207–10.

Parássoglou, *Imperial Estates*
G. M. Parássoglou. *Imperial Estates in Roman Egypt*. Amer. Stud. in Pap. 18 (1978).

Patai, *The Water*
R. Patai. *The Water*. Jerusalem, 1936 (Hebrew).

Pavis d'Escurac, 'Irrigation'
H. Pavis d'Escurac. 'Irrigation et vie paysanne dans l'Afrique du Nord antique'. *Ktema* 5 (1980) 177–89.

Pestman, *Marriage*
P. W. Pestman. *Marriage and Matrimonial Property in Ancient Egypt*. Leiden, 1961.

Polotsky, 'Greek Papyri'
H. J. Polotsky. 'The Greek Papyri from the Cave of the Letters'. *IEJ* 12 (1962) 258–63.

Polotsky, 'Three Documents'
H. J. Polotsky. 'Three Greek Documents from the Family Archive of Babatha'. *ErIsr* 8 (1967) 46–51.

Porten and Yardeni, *TAD*
B. Porten and A. Yardeni. *Textbook of Aramaic Documents from Ancient Egypt*, vols. 1–3. Jerusalem, 1986–94.

Préaux, 'Déclarations de propriété foncière'
Cl. Préaux. 'Déclarations de propriété foncière dans l'Égypte romaine'. *Chronique d'Égypte* 10 (1935) 393–6.

Preisigke, *Namenbuch*
F. Preisigke. *Namenbuch*. Heidelberg, 1922.

Preisigke, *Wörterbuch*
F. Preisigke *et al. Wörterbuch der griechischen Papyrusurkunden aus Ägypten*, vols. 1–3. Berlin, 1925–1931. Vol. 4: Berlin, Marburg and Wiesbaden, 1944–93.

Puech, 'Inscriptions funéraires'
E. Puech. 'Inscriptions funéraires palestiniennes: Tombeau de Jason et ossuaires'. *RB* 90 (1983) 481–533.

Rabinowitz, 'Some Notes'
J. J. Rabinowitz. 'Some Notes on an Aramaic Contract from the Dead Sea Region'. *BASOR* 136 (1954) 15–16.

Rahmani, 'Bilingual'
L. Y. Rahmani. 'A Bilingual Ossuary Inscription from Khirbet Zif'. *IEJ* 22 (1972) 113–6.

Rahmani, 'Rock-Cut Tombs'
L. Y. Rahmani. 'Jewish Rock-Cut Tombs in Jerusalem'. *Atiqot* 3 (1961) 93–120.

Rosén, 'Sprachsituation'
H. Rosén. 'Die Sprachsituation im römischen Palästina'. In *Die Sprachen im römischen Reich der Kaiserzeit* (Beihefte der Bonner Jahrbücher 40, 1980) 215–39.

Rosenthal, 'Giv^cat ha-Mivtar'
E. S. Rosenthal. 'The Giv^cat ha-Mivtar Inscription'. *Perakim* 2 (1969–74) 335–80 (Hebrew).

Rowlandson, *Landowners*
J. L. Rowlandson. *Landowners and Tenants in Roman Egypt*. Oxford, 1996.

Roxan, *Roman Military Diplomas*
M. Roxan. *Roman Military Diplomas 1954-1977*. London, 1978.

Rubin, *The Negev*
R. Rubin. *The Negev as a Settled Land*. Jerusalem, 1990 (Hebrew).

Rupprecht, *Darlehen*
H. A. Rupprecht. *Untersuchungen zum Darlehen im Recht der Graeco-Aegyptischen Papyri der Ptolemäerzeit*. Münchener Beiträge zur Papyrusforschung und antiken Rechtsgeschichte 51 (1967).

Rupprecht, *Quittung*
H. A. Rupprecht. *Studien zur Quittung im Recht der graeco-aegyptischen Papyri*. Munich, 1971.

Sachau, *Papyrus und Ostraka*
E. Sachau. *Aramäische Papyrus und Ostraka*. Leipzig, 1911.

Safrai, *Economy*
Z. Safrai. *The Economy of Roman Palestine*. London and New York, 1994.

Safrai, *Jewish Community*
Z. Safrai, *The Jewish Community in the Talmudic Period*, Jerusalem, 1995 (Hebrew).

Safrai, 'Settlement'
Z. Safrai. 'The Bar Kokhba Revolt and its Effect on Settlement'. In *The Bar-Kokhva Revolt: A New Approach*, edited by A. Oppenheimer and U. Rappaport, pp. 182–214. Jerusalem, 1984 (Hebrew).

Safrai, 'Village'
Z. Safrai. 'The Village in the Time of the Mishnah and the Talmud'. In *Nation and History: Studies in the History of the Jewish People*, edited by M. Stern, pp. 173–95. Jerusalem, 1983 (Hebrew).

Salomies, 'Namengebung'
O. Salomies. 'Zur Namengebung der Konsuln in den handschriftlich überlieferten Konsulverzeichnissen für die Zeit 15–284 n. Chr.'. *Arctos* 26 (1992) 105–16.

Samuel, *Chronology*
A. E. Samuel. *Greek and Roman Chronology, Handbuch der Altertumswissenschaft*, vol. I.7. Munich, 1972.

Sartre, *Trois études*
M. Sartre. *Trois études sur l'Arabie romaine et byzantine*. Coll. Lat. 60 (1982).

Satlow, 'Rabbinic *Ketubah*'
M. Satlow. 'Reconsidering the Rabbinic *Ketubah* Payment'. In *The Jewish Family in Antiquity*, edited by Sh. J. D. Cohen, pp. 133–51. Brown University, 1993.

Schalit, 'Eroberungen'
A. Schalit. 'Die Eroberungen des Alexander Jannäus in Moab'. In *Theokratia. Jahrbuch des Institutum Judaicum Delitzschianum* I, 1967–69 (1970) 3–50 (in Hebrew, *Er Isr* I [1951] 104–21).

Schubart, *Griechische Paläographie*
W. Schubart. *Griechische Paläographie*. Munich, 1925.

Schürer, Vermes, and Millar, *History*
E. Schürer, G. Vermes, and F. Millar. *The History of the Jewish People in the Age of Jesus Christ (175B.C.–A.D.135)*, vols. 1–3. Edinburgh, 1973–87.

Schwartz, *Jewish Settlement*
J. Schwartz. *Jewish Settlement in Judaea after the Bar-Kochba War until the Arab Conquest 135 C.E.–640 C.E.* Jerusalem, 1986 (Hebrew).

Schwartz, 'Remarques'
J. Schwartz. 'Remarques sur des fragments grecs du Désert de Juda'. *RB* 69 (1962) 61–3.

Segal, 'Hebrew IOU'
P. Segal. 'The Hebrew IOU Note from the Time of the Bar Kochba Period'. *Tarbiz* 60 (1990) 113–18 (Hebrew).

Seidl, *Eid* I
E. Seidl. *Der Eid im römisch-ägyptischen Provinzialrecht*, vol. I. Münchener Beiträge zur Papyrusforschung und antiken Rechtsgeschichte 16 (1933).

Seidl, *Eid* II
E. Seidl. *Der Eid im römisch-ägyptischen Provinzialrecht*. vol. II. Münchener Beiträge zur Papyrusforschung und antiken Rechtsgeschichte 24 (1935).

Sevenster, 'Greek?'
J. N. Sevenster. *Do You Know Greek?* NovTSup 19 (1968).

Shaw, 'Lamasba'
B. D. Shaw. 'Lamasba: An Ancient Irrigation Community'. *Antiquités Africaines* 18 (1982) 61–103.

Sijpesteijn, 'A Note'
P. J. Sijpesteijn. 'A Note on P. Murabbaʿat 29'. *IEJ* 34 (1984) 49–50.

Sijpesteijn, 'Der Veteran Aelius Syrian'
P. J. Sijpesteijn. 'Der Veteran Aelius Syrian', *BASP* 21 (1984) 211–20.

Sijpesteijn, 'Imperial Titles'
P. J. Sijpesteijn. 'Further Remarks on Some Imperial Titles in the Papyri'. *ZPE* 45 (1982) 177–96.

Simon, *Stipulationsklausel*
D. Simon. *Studien zur Praxis der Stipulationsklausel.* Münchener Beiträge zur Papyrusforschung und antiken Rechtsgeschichte 48 (1964).

Sirat, *Papyrus*
C. Sirat. *Les papyrus en caractères hébraïques, trouvés en Égypte.* Paris, 1985.

Sirat *et al.*, *Ketouba*
C. Sirat, P. Cauderlier, M. Dukan, and M. A. Friedman. *La Ketouba de Cologne: Un contrat de mariage juif à Antinoopolis.* Papyrologica Coloniensia 12. Opladen, 1986.

Sokoloff, *Dictionary*
M. Sokoloff. *A Dictionary of Jewish Palestinian Aramaic.* Ramat Gan, 1990.

Solin, *Namenbuch*
H. Solin. *Die Griechischen Personennamen in Rom. Ein Namenbuch.* Berlin and New York, 1982.

Speidel, 'Cohors I Thracum Milliaria'
M. P. Speidel. 'A Tile Stamp of Cohors I Thracum Milliaria from Hebron/Palestine'. *ZPE* 35 (1979) 170–72.

Sperber, *Material Culture*
D. Sperber. *Material Culture in Eretz-Israel during the Talmudic Period.* Jerusalem, 1993.

Spijkerman, 'Coins'
A. Spijkerman. 'The Coins of Eleutheropolis'. *Studi Biblici Franciscani, Liber Annuus* 22 (1972) 369–84.

Starcky, 'Contrat Nabatéen'
J. Starcky. 'Un contrat Nabatéen sur papyrus'. *RB* 61 (1954) 161–81.

Stern, *Greek and Latin Authors*
M. Stern. *Greek and Latin Authors on Jews and Judaism,* vols. 1–3. Jerusalem, 1974–84.

Stern, 'Pliny the Elder'
M. Stern. 'Pliny the Elder's Description of Eretz Israel and the Administrative Division of Judaea at the End of the Second Temple Period'. *Tarbiz* 37 (1978) 215–29. Reprinted in *Studies in Jewish History: The Second Temple Period,* edited by M. Amit, I. Gafni, and M. D. Herr, pp. 246–60. Jerusalem, 1991 (Hebrew).

Sukenik, 'Burial Cave'
E. L. Sukenik. 'A Jewish Burial Cave on the Northern Slope of Naḥal Qidron, near Kfar Shiloah'. In *S. Krauss Festschrift,* pp. 87–93. Jerusalem, 1936 (Hebrew).

Sukenik, 'Hypogeum'
E. L. Sukenik. 'A Jewish Hypogeum near Jerusalem'. *JPOS* 8 (1928) 113–21.

Szubin and Porten, 'Life Estate'
H. Z. Szubin and B. Porten. 'A Life Estate of Usufruct: A New Interpretation of Kraeling 6'. *BASOR* 269 (1988) 29–45.

Talamanca, 'Gli apporti patrimoniali'
M. Talamanca. 'Gli apporti patrimoniali della moglie nell'Egitto greco e romano'. *Idex* 2 (1971) 240–82.

Talbert, *Senate*
R. J. A. Talbert. *The Senate of Imperial Rome*. Princeton, 1984.

Taubenschlag, 'Das Recht auf εἴcοδοc καὶ ἔξοδοc'
R. Taubenschlag. 'Das Recht auf εἴcοδοc καὶ ἔξοδοc in den Papyri'. *Arch. f. Pap.* 8 (1927) 25–33.

Taubenschlag, *Law*
R. Taubenschlag. *The Law of Greco-Roman Egypt in the Light of the Papyri 322 B.C.–640 A.D.* 2d ed. Warsaw, 1955.

Teixidor, 'Deux documents syriaques'
J. Teixidor. 'Deux documents syriaques du IIIe siècle après J.-C., provenant du Moyen Euphrate'. *Comptes-rendus de l'Académie des Inscriptions* (1990) 144–63.

Teixidor, 'Un document syriaque'
J. Teixidor. 'Un document syriaque de fermage de 242 ap. J.-C.'. *Semitica* 41-2 (1993) 195–208.

Tjäder, *Papyri Italiens I*
J. O. Tjäder. *Die nichtliterarischen lateinischen Papyri Italiens aus der Zeit 445–700*, vol. I. Lund, 1955.

Tov, *Prophets Scroll*
E. Tov. *The Greek Minor Prophets Scroll from Naḥal Ḥever (8ḤevXIIgr)*. *DJD* VIII. Oxford, 1990.

Tov with Pfann, *Companion Volume*
E. Tov with the collaboration of S. J. Pfann. *The Dead Sea Scrolls on Microfiche, Companion Volume.* 1st ed. Leiden, 1993. 2d rev. ed. Leiden, 1995.

Tsafrir *et al.*, *Tabula*
Y. Tsafrir, L. di Segni, and J. Green, eds. *Tabula Imperii Romani*: *Iudaea, Palaestina, Maps and Gazetteer*. Jerusalem, 1994.

Tufnell, *Lachish*
O. Tufnell. *Lachish* 3: *The Iron Age*. London, 1953.

Turner, 'Recto and Verso'
E. G. Turner. 'The Terms Recto and Verso. The Anatomy of the Papyrus Roll', *Actes du XVe Congrès International de Papyrologie, Brussels-Leuven, 29 August–3 September 1977*, edited by J. Bingen and G. Nachtergael, pp. 7–71. Brussels, 1978.

Ustinova and Figueras, 'Funerary Inscription'
Y. Ustinova and P. Figueras. 'A New Greek Funerary Inscription from Beer-Sheva'. *Atiqot* 28 (1996) 167–70.

Van't Dack, 'Les formulae des empereurs'
E. Van't Dack. 'La papyrologie et l'histoire du Haut-Empire: les formulae des empereurs'. *ANRW* II.1 (1974) 857–88.

Vidman, *Fasti*
L. Vidman. *Fasti Ostienses*. Prague, 1982.

Volterra, 'P.Ent. 23'
E. Volterra. 'Intorno a P.Ent. 23'. *JJP* 15 (1965) 21–8.

Wallace, *Taxation*
S. L. Wallace. *Taxation in Egypt from Augustus to Diocletian*. New York, 1938.

Wannemacher, 'Development'
W. L. Wannemacher. 'The Development of the Imperial Civil Officia during the Principate'. Ph.D. dissertation. University of Michigan, 1940.

Wasserstein, 'Aramaic Transcriptions'
A. Wasserstein. 'A Note on the Phonetic and Graphic Representation of Greek Vowels and of the Spiritus Asper in the Aramaic Transcription of Greek Loanwords'. *Scripta Classica Israelica* 12 (1993; *Raʿanana Meridor Volume*) 200–208.

Wasserstein, 'Documents from the Cave of Letters'
A. Wasserstein. 'Lewis, Yadin and Greenfield, *Documents from the Cave of Letters*'. *JQR* 84 (1993) 373–7.

Wasserstein, 'Good Man'
A. Wasserstein. 'A Good Man Fallen among Robbers'. *Tarbiz* 49 (1979–80) 197–8 (Hebrew).

Wasserstein, 'Marriage Contract'
A. Wasserstein. 'A Marriage Contract from the Province of Arabia Nova: Notes on Papyrus Yadin 18'. *JQR* 80 (1989) 93–130.

Wasserstein, 'Non-Hellenized Jews'
A. Wasserstein. 'Non-Hellenized Jews in the Semi-Hellenized East'. *Scripta Classica Israelica* 14 (1995) 111–37.

Weiser and Cotton, 'Gebt dem Kaiser, was des Kaisers ist'
W. Weiser and H. M. Cotton. 'Gebt dem Kaiser, was des Kaisers ist: Die Geldwährungen der Griechen, Juden, Nabatäer und Römer im syrisch-nabatäischen Raum unter besonderer Berücksichtigung des Kurses von Sela^{c}/Melaina und Lepton nach der Annexion des Königreiches der Nabatäer durch Rom'. *ZPE* 114 (1997) 237–87.

Welles, 'Dura Pergament 21'
C. B. Welles. 'Dura Pergament 21. Hypothek und Exekution am Euphratufer im I. Jahrhundert n. Chr.'. *Zeitschrift der Savigny-Stiftung für Rechtsgeschichte (Rom. Abt.)* 56 (1936) 99–135.

Welles *et al.*, *Dura-Europos*
C. B. Welles, R. O. Fink, and J. F. Gilliam. *The Excavations at Dura-Europos, Final Report,* vol. V.I: *The Parchments and Papyri*. New Haven, 1959.

Wenning, 'Dekapolis'
R. Wenning. 'Die Dekapolis und die Nabatäer'. *ZDPV* 110 (1994) 1–35.

White, *Roman Farming*
K. D. White. *Roman Farming*. London, 1970.

Whitehorne, 'Valuation'
J. E. G. Whitehorne. 'The Valuation of Gold Dowry Objects in Papyri of the Roman Period'. *Arch. f. Pap.* 32 (1986) 49–53.

Wilcken, *Griechische Ostraka*
U. Wilcken. *Griechische Ostraka aus Aegypten und Nubien,* vol. I. Leipzig and Berlin, 1899.

Wolfe, 'Contract'
E. R. Wolfe. 'A Contract of Loan with Mortgage'. In *Collectanea Papyrologia: Texts published in Honor of H. C. Youtie*, vol. 1, edited by A. E. Hanson, pp. 305–8. Bonn, 1976.

Wolff, 'Le droit'
H. J. Wolff. 'Le droit provincial dans la province romaine d'Arabie'. *RIDA* 23 (1967) 271–90.

Wolff, *Recht der griechischen Papyri*
H. J. Wolff. *Das Recht der griechischen Papyri Ägyptens in der Zeit der Ptolemaeer und des Prinzipat*. Vol. 2: *Organisation und Kontrolle des privaten Rechtsverkehrs*. Handbuch der Altertumswissenschaft X.5.2. Munich, 1978.

Wolff, 'Römisches Provinzialrecht'
H. J. Wolff. 'Römisches Provinzialrecht in der Provinz Arabia'. *ANRW* II.13 (1980) 763–806.

Wolff, *Written and Unwritten Marriages*
H. J. Wolff. *Written and Unwritten Marriages in Hellenistic and Post Classical Roman Law*. Philological Monographs published by the American Philological Association, no. 9. Haverford, 1939.

Wolff, 'Zur Geschichte der Sechszeugendoppelurkunde'
H. J. Wolff. 'Zur Geschichte der Sechszeugendoppelurkunde'. In *Akten des XIII. Papyrologenkongresses, Marburg/Lahn, 2.–6. August 1971*. Münchener Beiträge zur Papyrusforschung und antiken Rechtsgeschichte 66 (1974) 469–79.

Wuthnow, *Semitische Menschennamen*
H. Wuthnow. *Die semitischen Menschennamen in griechischen Inschriften und Papyri des Vorderen Orients*. Leipzig, 1930.

Yadin, *Bar Kokhba*
Y. Yadin. *Bar Kokhba. The Rediscovery of the Legendary Hero of the Second Jewish Revolt*. London, 1971.

Yadin, 'Expedition D'
Y. Yadin. 'Expedition D'. *IEJ* 11 (1961) 36–52.

Yadin, 'Expedition D—Cave of Letters'
Y. Yadin. 'Expedition D—The Cave of the Letters'. *IEJ* 12 (1962) 227–57.

Yadin, 'Nabataean Kingdom'
Y. Yadin. 'The Nabataean Kingdom, Provincia Arabia, Petra and En-Geddi in the Documents from Naḥal Ḥever'. *Phoenix. Ex Oriente Lux* 17 (1963) 227–41.

Yadin, 'Note'
Y. Yadin. 'A Note on the Bilingual Ossuary Inscription from Khirbet Zif'. *IEJ* 22 (1972) 235–6.

Yadin, Broshi and Qimron
Y. Yadin, M. Broshi and E. Qimron. 'שטר של מכירת בית בכפר ברו מימי בר כוכבא'. *Cathedra* 40 (1986) 201–13 (Hebrew).

Yadin, Greenfield, and Yardeni, 'Babatha's *Ketubba*'
Y. Yadin, J. C. Greenfield, and A. Yardeni. 'Babatha's *Ketubba'*. *IEJ* 44 (1994) 75–99.

Yadin, Greenfield, and Yardeni, 'Deed of Gift'
Y. Yadin, J. C. Greenfield, and A. Yardeni. 'A Deed of Gift in Aramaic Found in Naḥal Ḥever: *Papyrus Yadin* 7'. *ErIsr* 25 (1996) 383–403 (Hebrew).

Yadin, Greenfield, Yardeni, and Levine, *The Documents*
Y. Yadin, J. C. Greenfield, A. Yardeni, and B. Levine. *The Documents from the Bar Kokhba Period in the Cave of Letters*. Vol. II: *Hebrew, Aramaic and Nabatean Documents* (forthcoming).

Yadin and Naveh, *Masada* I
Y. Yadin and J. Naveh. *Masada*. Vol I: *The Aramaic and Hebrew Ostraca and Jar Inscriptions*. Jerusalem, 1989.

Yardeni, 'Cursive Script'
A. Yardeni. 'The Aramaic and Hebrew Documents in Cursive Script from Wadi Murabbaʿat and Naḥal Ḥever, and Related Material: A Palaeographic and Epigraphic Examination'. Ph.D. dissertation. Hebrew University of Jerusalem, 1991.

Yardeni, 'Jewish Aramaic'
A. Yardeni. 'New Jewish Aramaic Ostraca'. *IEJ* 40 (1990) 130–52.

Yardeni, 'Receipt'
A. Yardeni and J. C. Greenfield. 'A Receipt for a Ketubba'. In *The Jews in the Hellenistic-Roman World, Studies in Memory of Menahem Stern*, edited by A. Oppenheimer, Y. Gafni, and D. Schwartz, pp. 197–208. Jerusalem, 1996 (Hebrew).

Yaron, 'Acts'
R. Yaron. 'Acts of Last Will in Jewish Law'. *Recueils de la Société Jean Bodin pour l'Histoire Comparative des Institutions* 59 (1992) 29–45.

Yaron, *Gifts*
R. Yaron. *Gifts in Contemplation of Death in Jewish and Roman Law*. Oxford, 1960.

Yaron, *Introduction*
R. Yaron. *Introduction to the Law of the Aramaic Papyri*. Oxford, 1961.

Yaron, *Law*
R. Yaron. *The Law of the Elephantine Documents*. Jerusalem, 1961 (Hebrew).

Yaron, 'Mesadah'
R. Yaron. 'The Mesadah Bill of Divorce'. *Studi in onore di E. Volterra* 6 (1971) 433–55.

Yaron, 'Note'
R. Yaron. 'Note on a Judaean Deed of Sale of a Field'. *BASOR* 150 (1958) 26, (a).

Yevin, 'Documents'
S. Yevin. 'Documents from Wadi Murabbaʿat'. *Atiqot* 1 (1955–6) 83–93 (Hebrew).

Youtie, 'ΑΓΡΑΜΜΑΤΟΣ'
H. C. Youtie. 'ΑΓΡΑΜΜΑΤΟΣ: An Aspect of Greek Society in Egypt'. *HSCPh* 75 (1971) 161–76.

Youtie, 'Because They Do Not Know Letters'
H. C. Youtie. '"Because They Do Not Know Letters"'. *ZPE* 19 (1975) 101–8.

Youtie, 'ΥΠΟΓΡΑΦΕΥϹ'
H. C. Youtie. 'ΥΠΟΓΡΑΦΕΥϹ: The Social Impact of Illiteracy in Graeco-Roman Egypt'. *ZPE* 17 (1975) 201–21.

Youtie, 'Review of A. M. Harmon'
H. C. Youtie. 'Review of A. M. Harmon, "Egyptian Property Returns", *YClS* 4 (1934) 135–234'. *AJA* 40 (1936) 282–4.

Zwicky, *Verwendung*
H. Zwicky. *Zur Verwendung des Militärs in der Verwaltung der römischen Kaiserzeit*. Zurich, 1944.

INDICES TO THE ARAMAIC AND HEBREW DOCUMENTARY TEXTS

THESE indices refer to all the Aramaic and Hebrew words occurring in the texts covered by this volume, together with their respective contexts. All independent words are covered, thus excluding the attached morphemes א-, -ב, -ה-, -כ, and -ל. The indices were prepared by S. and C. Pfann. The volume's editor has reviewed the indices, and the lemmatizations and readings reflect her preferences.

SIGLA

/	beginning of line
//	beginning of column
א̊	possible letter
א̇	probable letter
א̭	supralinear insertion
{א}	erasure
>א<	modern editor's deletion
<א>	modern editor's addition
[א]	reconstructed letter

Index 1: Months

אדר

3 1 ... לאדר

3 8 ... לא]דר

3a 1 //בעסר[ה\ין] לא̇ד\יר

איר

7 1 //בארבעה עשר לאיר

7 7 /בארבעה לאיר

3a 1 //בעסר[ה\ין] לא̇ד\יר

אלול

11 1]∘∘∘ לאלול שנת תמ̇נה [

4Q345 1 /ב∘∘∘ באלול ש̇]נת

כסלו

32 1 לכס]לו שנת תמ̇נה ב∘[

49 1 [בע]סרין לכסלו

סיון

13 1 //בעשרין לסיון

שבט

12 10 /ביום ע̇ש̇ר̇ה וח / מ̇ש̇ה̇ בשבט/

Index 2: Names of Persons and Peoples

Index 3: Geographical Terms

Index 4: Greek Words

Index 5: Signatures in Greek Script

A. Personal Names

50 d+e, 24v	Ευ[....
50 d+e, 24v	]Ẹυ̣[

B. Common Words

50 d+e, 25v	χειρ

Index 6: Hebrew Words

30 3	אב	/ אבה חבי\ובי שלם /
30 7	אח	/ שנטרפו אח∘
23 6	אם	ולעלם ואם/
49 10	אם	[וא]ם לא לא יתקים לי
49 9	אמ"ר	שאפרך בכל זמן שת/[ומ]ר לי
49 5	אני	עמי אני יהוסף בן / חנניה
49 7	אנ(י)	תסלע הזוא אנמקבל / המך
49 12	אש (= יש)	וקים עלי / כול שאש על השטר הזא/
8 e–k,10	את	[אח]לף לך ת[שטר הזה]
49 9	(א)ת	ואשה את השטר הזא/
30 8	בין	/ולא היינו מן בין להם
49 11	בית	והתשלם/ [מן]ביתי ומן נכסי
7 2	בן	מן בני ירשאל
8 1	בן	על ימי שמעון בן כוסבה נשי ישר[אל]
8 e–k,3	בן	[שקניתי מיהוס]ף בן[רובן]
13 14	בן	/משבלה בן שמעון עד//
30 1	בן	//לשמעון בן כוסבא נסי/
30 2	בן	/ישראל מן שמעון בן מתניה\ם/
30 9	בן	ש[לם] /שמעון בן מתנה/
49 2	בן	על ידי שמעון בן / כוסבא נשיא ישראל
49 4	בן	איתודי / יהודה בן יהודה סרטא
49 5	בן	עמי אני יהוסף בן / חנניה
49 14	בן	[יהוס]ף בן חנניה על / [נפש]ה כתביה/
49 15	בן	/מנחם בן [...] עד/
49 17	בן	/יהודה בן יהו∘[ ] עד//
49 2	גאלה	שנת שתין/ [ל]גאלת ישראל
4Q**348** 13	גדול	כוהן גדול
8 c-d,2	דלת	[ה]דלת[ות והמפ]תח
49 13	הו\יד(?)	ואחתם בהו\ידי כזא/
30 4	הי"ה	/ידוע יהיה לך
30 8	הי"ה	/ולא היינו מן בין להם
49 8	הם (= מן)	תסלע הזוא אנמקבל / המך
8 e–k,6	הן	[שה]ן סלעין תשע
49 9	זא	אשה את השטר הזא/
49 12	זא	קים עלי / כול שאש על השטר הזא/
49 13	זא	אחתם בהו\ידי כזא/
49 7	זוא	סלע הזוא אנמקבל / המך
49 8	זמן	שאפרך בכל זמן שת/ [ומ]ר לי
8 9	חדר	דר שפתוח/ [למערב]
8 e-k,10	חל"ף	אח]לף לך ת[שטר הזה]
8 10	חלק	חלקי בחצר
8 e–k,2	חלק	חלקי במע[רב]
8 10	חצר	חלקי בחצר
8 e–k,3	חצר	ב]מזרח הח[צר]
49 13	חתם	אחתם בהו\ידי כזא/
30 7	טר"ף	שנטרפו אח∘
49 2	יד	על ידי שמעון בן / כוסבא נשיא ישראל
30 4	יד"ע	ידוע יהיה לך
49 12	אש (= יש)	קים עלי / כול שאש על השטר הזא/
4Q**348** 13	כוהן	כוהן גדול
49 8	כל	שאפרך בכל זמן שת/ [ומ]ר לי
49 12	כל	קים עלי / כול שאש על השטר הזא/
30 8	לא	ולא היינו מן בין להם
49 10 (bis)	לא	וא]ם לא לא יתקים לי
8 9	מזרח	החדר] ש[פ]תוח למזרח
8 b,1	מזרח	מז]רח מן ...
8 e–k,3	מזרח	ב]מזרח הח[צר]
8 7	-מ	מכול חרר ותג[ר]
4Q**348** 18	-מ	שמעון משוק הקורות
30 2	מן	/ישראל מן שמעון בן מתניה\ם/
30 8	מן	/ולא היינו מן בין להם
49 8	הם (= מן)	תסלע הזוא אנמקבל / המך
49 11	מן	והתשלם/ [מן]ביתי ומן נכסי
8 e–k,7	מעלן	מעלן וירשה]
8 11	מערב	[במ]ערב/
8 e–k,2	מערב	בחלקי במע[רב]

Reference	Word	Context
l,1	מערב	[מע]רב
c-d,2	מפתח	[ה]דלת[ות והמפ]תח
49 11	נכס	והתשלם/ [מן]ביתי ומן נכסי
0 1	נסי (= נשיא)	//לשמעון בן כוסבא נסי/
49 9	נש"א/נש"ה	ואשה את השטר הזא/
49 3	נשיא	על ידי שמעון בן / כוסבא נשיא ישראל
a,16	עד	/שמעון בר יהוסף עד/
.3 13	עד	∘∘∘∘ בר שמעון עד/
.3 14	עד	/משבלה בן שמעון עד//
49 15	עד	/מנחם בן [...] עׄדׄ/
49 17	עד	/יהׄודה בן יהו∘[ ] עׄדׄ//
49 2	על	על ידי שמעון בן / כוסבא נשיא ישראל
49 11	על	וקים עלי / כול שאש עׄלׄ השטר הזא/
49 12	על	וקים עלי / כול שאש עׄלׄ השטר הזא/
49 14	על	[יהוס]ף בן חנניה על / [נפש]ה כתביה/
b,2	עם	... עמי\ו
9 1	עסרין (= עשרין)	[בע]סרין לכסלו
9 8	פר"ע	שאפרך בכל זמן שת/ [ומ]ר לי
9	פת"ח	[החדר] ש[פ]תוח למזרח
8 9	פת"ח	חדר שפתוח/ [למערב]
4Q348 17	פת"ח	פתחנׄוׄ
49 7	קב"ל	תסלע הזוא אנמקבל / המך
8 2	קורה	]ודרת בית קורה בכפר ברו
49 10	קי"ם	[וא]ם לא לא יתקים לי
49 11	קי"ם	וקים עלי / כול שאש עׄלׄ השטר הזא/
8 e–k,7	רש"י	]מעלן וירשה[
8 9	-ש	[החדר] ש[פ]תוח למזרח
8 9	-ש	חדר שפתוח/ [למערב]
8 e–k,9	-ש	[מ]כול חרר[ותגר] שי[בואוך]
30 7	-ש	/שׄנׄטׄרׄפׄוׄ אׄחׄ∘
49 8	-ש	שאפרך בכל זמן שת/ [ומ]ר לי
49 8	-ש	שאפרך בכל זמן שת/ [ומ]ר לי
49 12	-ש	וקים עלי / כול שאש עׄלׄ השטר הזא/
8 8	שנה	שנת [תל]ת לחרות ישראל[
49 1	שנה	שנת שתין/ [ל]גאלת ישראל
49 1	שתין	שנת שתין/ [ל]גאלת ישראל
49 10	תשלם	והתשלם/ [מן]ביתי ומן נכסי

Index 7: Aramaic Words

Reference	Word	Context
2 7	אב	/ ד\עי\∘ עׄמׄך מׄן בב לׄוׄי / אבוׄך
4	אבן	אבניה ושׄ[ ]ה דׄי חטיה
a 7	אבן	אבניה ושרית[א]ודגריא
1 3	אבן	אבניה כותליא שריתׄאׄ /
3	או	הנ חסיר או יתר לזבנה[
0 5	או	אׄם חׄ[סיר א]ו / [י]תׄיר לזבנה
0 8	אורח (= ארח)	צפונא אורחא
2 1	אח	אׄחׄוך / יׄחׄ∘∘ בׄרׄ תשׄה
6 3	אח	] ∘אׄחד\ך סערין טבן /
0 8	אח	דרומא / אפתלמים ופרׄדׄיון אחה
Q343 6	אח	/ אׄחי הוא מׄן שמרׄיׄ[
6 3	אחד(?)	] ∘אׄחד\ך סערין טבן /
6	אחראי	אחראין וערבין למקימה /
8	אחראי	וא[חר]אׄיׄן וערׄבׄ[י]ן
3 4	אחראי	ארׄחאׄיׄן וערבין /
4a 2	אחראי	[ודי] אׄקׄנׄה אׄ[חראין
0 14	אחראי	אחראין ו[ערבין]
a 11	אחרי	ואנה אחׄרׄיׄ וערב ל[ך]
0 19	אחריא	/ אחריא וערבה
3	אחרן	ירתה מתת בר אבי ואחרׄנׄן
4	(א)חרן	מד[נח]ה / ארחה וחׄ[רנין
4	(א)חרן	מערבה יהוד]הׄ זבנה ו[ח]רנין[
4	(א)חרן	דרומה] ארח∘ יׄ[ר]תי צפן וחרנין
9 4	(א)חרן	צפונה ירת[י]צפׄן וחׄ[רנין]
9 15	(א)חרן	[מ]דׄ[נ]חה ארחא וחרנין
9 16	(א)חרן	[יר]תי צפן וחרנין
21 3	אחרן	/ די\ודׄיׄ ואחר[נ]יׄן
33 1	אחרן	]סימניא לאוחרן
33 2	אחרן	סימניא [?]אוחרן
50 7	אחרן	מערבא / חׄוׄני ואחרנין
4Q345 6	איך(?)	/ ישׄוע אׄמׄרׄ אׄיׄךׄ
7 6	ית (= אית)	דׄיתה רׄשׄוׄ מן כל אנש
8a 5	איתי	/ ורשה לא איתי לך ›לך‹ עמי
8a 10	איתי	ורשה לא / איתי לך עמׄיׄ
8a 12	איתי	דנה מלין לאיתי / לי ולעלם
9 8	איתי	ודי אי]תי לי
13 3	איתי	]∘לאׄ אׄיתי[
13 8	איתי	ל[א] אׄיׄתׄיׄ לי עמךׄ
24a 1	איתי	אׄיתׄיׄ לׄיׄ יׄומא דׄנה ע[מך
50 14	איתי	וכל די איתי לי ודי אקנה
8 6	איתי	וכול די איתׄיׄ לי ודי אקנה
32 3	אכף(?)	]מסמרא ש\אכפׄ רב∘[
26 5	אלה(?)	]∘ אלה ו\יתקבל /
8 4	אלך	]∘ אׄלך
8 7	אלך	/ [ולמרק]א אתריה[אל]ך
21 3	אלך	אׄתׄ[ר]יא אלך[ב]תחומיהון

Reference	Word	Context
21 7	אלך	באת[ריא]אלך
26 4	אלך	] פקדנה אלך נתן /
23 6	אם	ולעלם ואם /
50 5	אם	אם ח[סיר א]ו / [י]תיר לזבנה
8 1	אמ"ר	אמר לשאול בר חרשה מן תמן[
8 7	אמ"ר	ובזמן די תמרון לי
8a 2	אמ"ר	אמר לאלעזר בר אלעזר שטר\יא /
9 1	אמ"ר	אמר / ליהודה
50 22	אמ"ר	[ובזמן די] / תאמר לנה
4Q**345** 6	אמ"ר	/ ישוע אמר איך
7 5	אנה	ואנה חזק בר מתת וסרה ברת ימ[
7 8	אנה	אנה חזק בר מת[ת
7 9	אנה	/ אנה לך ית
8 3	אנה	... בחלקי[ ]ואנה ב° [
8 5	אנה	ותקלי כספה אנה מקבל דמין גמרין
8 6	אנה	ואנה יהונתן מזבנה
8a 3	אנה	אנה מן רעותי >יומא דנה<
8a 10	אנה	אנ>ת<ה חדד /
8a 11	אנה	ואנה אחרי וערב ל[ך]
8a 12	אנה	ואנה שלם ברת שמעון אנ[תת]חדד
9 2	אנה	אנה מרעותי יומה דנה
9 6	אנה	וכס[פ]ה אנה מקבל דמין גמרין
9 13	אנה	אנה מרעותי יומה ד[נה]
11 3	אנה	ל]מפרעה ואנה מקב[ל
13 4	אנה	/ אנה שלמצין ברת יהוסף קבשן /
13 10	אנה	וקים עלה / אנה שלמצין
22 7	אנה	ואנה
23 3	אנה	ואנה / [מזבנה]
23 5	אנה	אנה לך יום /
24a 2	אנה	ואנה
50 11	אנה	וכספא אנה מקבל דמין /
50 13	אנה	ואנה / או°°°°ס מזבנה
4Q**343** 2	אנה	אנה[ ]מנה
4Q**344** 2	אנה	]עמי אנה אלעזר בר הסף[
9a 3	אנחנה	] אנחנה הנון\הכול שתין /
21 6	אנחנה	ואנחנה [מ]קב[לין] דמין גמירין
21 12	אנחנה	] אנחנה מן /
50 a,2r	אנחנה	]אנחנה /
7 6	אנש	דיתה רשו מן כל אנש
7 2	אנת	אנת אלעזר בר לוי השפי מן בני ירשאל
7 6	אנת	מן] / קדמך אנת אלעזר
13 5	אנת	עמך אנת אלעזר בר חנני[ה]
13 8	אנת	א[נת] / אלעזר
8a 12	אנתה	ואנה שלם ברת שמעון אנ[תת]חדד
50 18	אנתה	... אנתת[...
7 1	ארבעה	// בארבעה עשר לאיר
7 7	ארבעה	בארבעה לאיר שנת תלת[לחרת ישראל
9 4	ארח	ד[נח]ה / ארחה וח[רנין
9 4	ארח	רומה] ארח° י[ר]תי צפן וחרנין
9 15	ארח	מ]ד[נ]חה ארחא וחרנין
50 8	אורח (= ארח)	צפונא אורחא
9 21	את"א(?)	י יתנך על אתרה דנה
50 20	את"א(?)	.. י]תנכן[...
8 4	אתר	נחמי אתריה[אלך]
8 7	אתר	[ולמרק]א אתריה[אל]ך
9 2	אתר	בנ[ת] לכ לאתרה דלי
9 3	אתר	ת]חומי אתרה דך
9 5	אתר	אתרה דך בתחו[מה]
9 8	אתר	למשפיה ולמקימה אתרה
9 9	אתר	על אתרה[דנן]
9 14	אתר	לאת[רה]
9 16	אתר	אתרה דך בתחו[מה]
9 20	אתר	א]ת[ר]ה
9 21	אתר	י יתנך על אתרה דנה
9 22	אתר	°אתרה דנן /
21 3	אתר	את[ר]יא אלך[ב]תחומיהון
21 7	אתר	את[ריא]אלך
21 d,1	אתר(?)	ת]רה °°[
50 6	אתר	תחומי אתרא דך
50 8	אתר	אתרא דך בתחומה / ובמצרה
50 12	אתר	באתרא דך
4Q**343** 8	אתר	ביתה ואתרה בא[...
4Q**343** 12	באיש	ובאיש עביד[
12 6	בב	ד\עי\° עמך מן בב לוי / אבוך
9 9	בטלה	זקן ובטלה ד[י יתנך]
9 21	בטלה	זקן וב]טלה
50 20	בטלה(?)	ן כל חרר [ו]תגר ובטלן[
7 4	בי	רתה ובתיה ותרעיה
8 2	בי	ביתה[דילי]ודרת בית קורה בכפר ברו
8 2	בי	ביתה[דילי]ודרת בית קורה בכפר ברו
8 2	בי	לגו ביתה רבה דך
8 3	בי	מע]לת תרעה דביתה די זבנת
8 4	בי	מערבה דרת בית מנו\י רבתה
8a 3	בי	לבתה דילי /
8a 4	בי	י תפתחנה לגה בתך /
8a 7	בי	זבן בתה דך
8a 8	בי	נחמא בתה דך[
8a 11	בי	כז]בן בתה דך
8a 13	בי	זבן בתה דך ולעלם
4Q**343** 8	בי	ביתה ואתרה בא[...
9 14	בית זרע	ית [זר]ע חנט[י]ן
50 5	בית זרע	ית [ז]רע חנטין

אתֿרה דך בתחׄו[מה]	דך	**9** 5
זב]נה דך	דך	**9** 7
תרה דך בֿתחׄו[מה]	דך	**9** 16
חומי אתרא דך	דך	**50** 6
תרא דך בתחומה / ובמצרה	דך	**50** 8
ך זבנת לכן	דך	**50** 10
אתרא ˻דך˼	דך	**50** 12
למרקא ולקימא זבנה דך	דך	**50** 15
בנ[ת] לכ לאתרה דלי	דל (= דיל)	**9** 2
תקלי כספה אנה מקבל דמין גמרין	דמין	**8** 5
סלעין תרתן דמין גמרין	דמין	**8a** 6
בכֿס[פ]ה אנה מקבל דמין גמרין	דמין	**9** 6
מין גמרׄיׄ[ן]	דמין	**9** 18
קבלן מנך דמׄי\צמׄי / תמרׄין	דמין(?)	**12** 3
אנחנֿה [מ]קב[לין] דמין גמירין	דמין	**21** 6
כספא אנה מקבל דמין /	דמין	**50** 11
אנה] / זבנת לך יומה דנה	דנה	**8** 2
אחלף לך שטרה דנה כדי חזה /	דנה	**8** 7
אנה מן רעותי ›יומא דנה‹	דנה	**8a** 3
בנת לך ימה דנה	דנה	**8a** 3
[מ]ן ימה דנה ולעלם	דנה	**8a** 11
ן ימה דנה / ולעלם	דנה	**8a** 11
נה מלין לאיתי / לי ולעלם	דנה	**8a** 12
כ[תב]א דנה פֿשיט וחתס\מו בגוה	דנה	**8a** 14
אנה מרעותי יומה דנה	דנה	**9** 2
אנה מרעותי יוׄמׄהׄ דׄ[נה]	דנה	**9** 13
י יתנך על אתרה דנה	דנה	**9** 21
מן יומא] / דנה ועד לעלם	דנה	**21** 9
שטרה דנׄהׄ[	דנה	**21** e,2
איתׄי לׄי יׄומא דׄנה ע[מך	דנה	**24a** 1
י הוא מן קדמת דנה	דנה	**50** 7
מן יומא דנה ולעלם	דנה	**50** 13
מן יומה] / דנן ועד עלם	דנן	**7** 5
מן יומה דנן / [ולעלם]	דנן	**9** 7
מן יומה דנ[ן]	דנן	**9** 20
אתֿרה דנן /	דנן	**9** 22
נן דׄ[י] / הוא לך מנה	דנן	**13** 6
עקׄובֿ[בר]שמען בר דקנה	דקן	**9** 1
בניה ושרית[א]ודגריא	דרג(?)	**8a** 7
דרתה ובתיה ותרׄעׄיה	דרה	**7** 4
ביתהׄ[דילי]ודרת בית קורה בכפר ברו	דרה	**8** 2
ודנחיתה דׄרׄתֿאׄ[	דרה	**8** 3
ודנחה דרתה[	דרה	**8** 4
מערבה דרת בית מנׄו\י רבתה	דרה	**8** 4
די פתיח צפן לגה דרתי	דרה	**8a** 4
בגו דרתה	דרה	**8a** 5
נזקׄן ובֿטׄלהׄ ד[י יתנך]	די	**9** 9
וכל זמן די ת[מר]	די	**9** 10
]∘נבֿא רבֿה כדי חזה /	די	**9** 11
די בת[חומה]	די	**9** 14
תרעה]דׄיׄ מעל ומ[פק]	די	**9** 16
די יתנך על אתרה דנה	די	**9** 21
[פ]רׄעׄ[ן]תשלם די ל[	די	**9** 21
] ... די תהוין לי לׄ[אנתה	די	**11** 2
/ ד\עי\∘ עׄמׄך מׄן בב לׄוׄיׄ / אבוׄךׄ	די(?)	**12** 6
/ די הוית בעלה מן קדמת	די	**13** 6
דנן דׄ[י] / הוא לך מנה	די	**13** 6
כֿול די על כֿ[ת]בֿ /	די	**13** 10
די המון / סלעין חמש עשרה	די	**21** 5
וׄכל ד[י]	די	**21** 9
]∘ די מן עלה ∘[	די	**21** e,1
די בה	די	**22** 5
די בתׄ∘∘[	די	**22** 6
]למׄעׄבֿדׄ בהׄ כֿול די תצֿבֿהׄ	די	**23** 3
]ודי אקנה	די	**23** 4
די אסתד\רדׄ	די	**24a** 3
די הוא מן קדמת דנה	די	**50** 7
תאניא וכל די בה ודי חזא עלה	די	**50** 9
תאניא וכל די בה ודי חזא עלה	די	**50** 9
מעלא ומפקא כדי / חזא	די	**50** 9
בכסף זוזין שבעין ותמניה די המון /	די	**50** 10
די מן עלא	די	**50** 12
כל די יצבון	די	**50** 13
וכל די איתי לי ודי אקנה	די	**50** 14
וכל די איתי לי ודי אקנה	די	**50** 14
... די ...	די	**50** 16
[ר]ש[א]ין זבניה די מן עלא[	די	**50** 23
כל מה די עב[ד	די	4Q**342** 2
מן נ]כֿסי ודי אקנה לקבל‹ד›ך /	די	4Q**344** 5
[כל]די יצבה	די	4Q**346a** 2
/ ודי אקנה מ[ן ...	די	4Q**346a** 4
לבתה דילי /	דיל	**8a** 3
זבנ[ת] לכ לאתרה דלי	דל (= דיל)	**9** 2
/ בכסף דנרׄין עשרה ותרין	ד(י)נר	**7** 4
לגו ביתה רבה דך	דך	**8** 2
דך זׄבֿנׄ[ת]לך[	דך	**8** 5
דך זבנת לך	דך	**8a** 5
בזבן בתה דׄךׄ	דך	**8a** 7
תחמא בתה דך[	דך	**8a** 8
[בז]בן בתה דך	דך	**8a** 11
בזבן בתה דך ולעלם	דך	**8a** 13
[ת]חׄומי אתרה דך	דך	**9** 3

Text	Lemma	Reference
] ∘אׂחד\ך סערין טבן /	טב	**26** 3
פ]לגות טׂבׂא[	טב	**32** 5
ויעבד/עבר לׂידיך	יד	4Q**343** 7
/ והבו עם שמׂעׂ[ו]ן	יה"ב	4Q**343** 13
על ימי שמעון בן כוסבה נשי ישר[אל]	ים (= יום)	**8** 1
[אנה] / זבנת לך יומה דנה	יום	**8** 2
אנה מן רעותי ›יומא דנה‹	יום	**8a** 3
זבנת לך ימה דנה	ים (= יום)	**8a** 3
/[מ]ן ימה דנה ולעלם	ים (= יום)	**8a** 11
מן ימה דנה / ולעלם	ים (= יום)	**8a** 11
אנה מרעותי יומה דנה	יום	**9** 2
מן יומה דנן / [ולעלם]	יום	**9** 7
אנה מרעותי יוׂמׂהׂ דׂ[נה]	יום	**9** 13
מן יומה דנ[ן]	יום	**9** 20
/ ביום עׂשׂרׂה וח/מׂשׂהׂ בשבט /	יום	**12** 9
אנה לׂךׂ יום /	יום	**23** 5
אׂיתׂי לׂי יׂומא דׂנה ע[מך	יום	**24a** 1
מן יומא דנה ולעלם	יום	**50** 13
ירתה מתת בר אבי ואחרנׂן	ירת	**7** 3
דרומה] ארח∘ יׂ[ר]תי צפן וחרנין	ירת	**9** 4
צפונה ירת[י]צפׂן וׂחׂ[רנין]	ירת	**9** 4
יהו[דה] / זבנה ויר[תוהי]	ירת	**9** 7
קדמךׂ וׂ[קד]םׂ / ירׂתׂ[י]ך	ירת	**9** 9
[יר]תי צפן וחרנין	ירת	**9** 16
קדמך וקדם ירתיך	ירת	**9** 20
/ יהוסף זבנה וירת[ו]הי	ירת	**21** 7
י]רׂתׂךׂ	ירת	**23** 5
/ לעלם רשאין זבניא ... וירתהן	ירת	**50** 12
זבניא ... וירתהן	ירת	**50** 13
קדמׂ[כן]וקדם ירתכׂ[ן	ירת	**50** 15
[וקדם] / ירׂתכן	ירת	**50** 20
דׂיתה רׂשׂוׂ מן כל אנש	ית (= אית)	**7** 6
/ אנה לך ית	ית	**7** 9
דׂיתב בׂכׂפׂרׂ[	ית"ב	**7** 2
הנ חסיר או יתר לזבנה[	ית"ר	**9** 3
אׂם חׂ[סיר א]וׂ / [י]תׂיר לזבנה	ית"ר	**50** 6
[מ]עלה ומפקׂה כדי חזה	כדי	**8** 5
אחלף לך שטרה דנה כדי חזה /	כדי	**8** 7
כדי חזה	כדי	**9** 5
]∘נבׂא רבׂה כדי חזה /	כדי	**9** 11
מעלא ומפקא כדי / חזא	כדי	**50** 9
אבניה כותליא שריתׂאׂ /	כותל	**21** 3
דׂיתה רׂשׂוׂ מן כל אנש	כל	**7** 6
וכול די איתׂי לי ודי אקנה	כול (= כל)	**8** 6
מכול חרר ותג[ר]	כול (= כל)	**8** 7
כול די בה /	כול (= כל)	**8a** 7

Text	Lemma	Reference
ל די תצבה	כל	**9** 7
ל חרר ותגר	כל	**9** 9
כל זמן די ת[מר]	כל	**9** 10
ל צׂבׂת כל מדעם	כל	**13** 9
ול די על כׂ[ת]בׂ /	כול (= כל)	**13** 10
כל ד[י]	כל	**21** 9
כל [	כל	**21** d,2
למׂעׂבדׂ בהׂ כׂול די תצׂבׂהׂ	כול (= כל)	**23** 3
למׂעׂבדׂ בה כׂ[ל	כל	**32** 2
אניא וכל די בה ודי חזא עלה	כל	**50** 9
ל די יצבון	כל	**50** 13
כל די איתי לי ודי אקנה	כל	**50** 14
ן כל חרר [ו]תגר ובׂטלׂן[	כל	**50** 20
ל מה די עב[ד	כל	4Q**342** 2
.. שמעׂן מן כל ...	כל	4Q**346a** 3
כל	כל	4Q**346** d,1
בכסף דנרׂין עשרה ותרין	כסף	**7** 4
תקלי כספה אנה מקבל דמין גמרין	כסף	**8** 5
כסף / זוזין די המוׂן תמניא	כסף	**8a** 5
כסף זוזׂין עשר[ין] / ותמניה	כסף	**9** 5
כסׂ[פ]ה אנה מקבל דמין גמרין	כסף	**9** 6
ך בכסף זוזין שתין	כסף	**21** 5
כסף זוזין שׂבׂעׂיׂן ∘[ ]∘ מן ...	כסף	**25** 4
כסף זוזין שבעין ותמניה די המון /	כסף	**50** 10
כספא אנה מקבל דמין /	כסף	**50** 11
בכסף	כסף	4Q**345** 5
יתב בׂכׂפׂרׂ[	כפר	**7** 2
הונתן בר עלי מן כפר ברו	כפר	**8** 1
כפ]רׂ ברו	כפר	**8** 1
תונה[די פ]תיח למדנחה	כפר	**8** 2
כפר בׂריו /	כפר	**8a** 1
ן כפר בריו	כפר	**8a** 2
תב[ ] / אלעזר בר מתׂתׂאׂ ממרה /	כת"ב	**8a** 14
ת]בה /	כת"ב	**9a** 1
בר שׂולׂיׂ כתבה //	כת"ב	**10** 5
תד\ח∘∘ כתבה //	כת"ב	**12** 13
ול די על כׂ[ת]בׂ /	כת"ב	**13** 10
הוס]ף בן חנניה על / [נפש]ה כתביה/	כת"ב	**49** 14a
ל [נפ]שה כתבה /	כת"ב	**50** 26
ש∘∘ כתב ספריא /	כת"ב	**50** 29
אלעזר בר יהוסף על נפשה כׂתׂבׂ[ה]	כת"ב	4Q**344** 6
כ[תב]א דנה פׂשיט וחתס\מו בגוה	כתב	**8a** 14
ל נפשה שאלה כתב /	כתב	**13** 11
ורשה לא איתי לך ›לך‹ עמי	לא	**8a** 5
רשה לא / איתי לך עמׂי	לא	**8a** 9
לא מעל ול[א] מפק עלי	לא	**8a** 10

7 3	מערב	ולמערבה
8 2	מערב	ולעליתה די פתיח[ה] למׄ[ערבה]
8 4	מערב	מערבה דרת בית מנׄו\י רבתה
8a 9	מערב	מערבא [ח]דד מזבנה
9 15	מערב	מערבה יׄהודה / [זב]נה
50 6	מערב	מערבא / חׄוני ואחרנין
8 4	מפתח	ודשיה ומפתחהׄ
21 4	מפתח	ותרעא ומפתחא
50 9	מצר	אתרא דך בתחומה / ובמצרה
50 15	מר"ק	/ למרקא ולקימא זבנה דך
50 19	מר"ק	לׄמרקא ולקימׄ[א]
9 10	נכס	[פר]ען תשלמתה מן נכ[סי]
50 21	נכס	ותשלמתא מן נכסי[נה]
4Q**344** 5	נכס	מן נ]כׄסי ודי אקנה לקבל‹ד›ך /
9 9	נזק	נׄזקׄן ובׄטלהׄ ד[י יתנך]
8 5	נפ"ק	[מ]עלה ומפקׄה כדי חזה
8a 10	נפ"ק	ולא מעל ול[א] מפק עלי
9 5	נפ"ק	תרעה די]מעל ומפק לכ לאת∘תׄרׄ
9 16	נפ"ק	תרעה]דׄ׳ מעל ומ[פק]
21 5	נפ"ק	מעלה / ו[מפ]ק[ה]
34 a–b,3	נפ"ק	מפק[ ]מׄן
50 9	נפ"ק	מעלא ומפקא כדי / חזא
8 e,1v	נפש	על נפש[ה כתבה]
8a 14	נפש	שלום[בר]ת שמעון על נפשה
8a 15	נפש	/ חדד בר יׄהׄ[ו]דה על‹נ›פשה
9 26	נפש	ע]ל נפשׄ[ה כתבה
13 11	נפש	על נפשה שאלה כתב /
50 26	נפש	]עׄל [נפ]שה כתבה /
4Q**344** 6	נפש	/ אלעזר בר יהוסף על נפשה כׄתׄבׄ[ה]
4Q**345** 20	נפש	/ הׄ[ו]שעיה בר[ ]∘∘ על נפש[ה כתבה]
8 1	נשי(א)	על ימי שמעון בן כוסבה נשי ישר[אל]
13 2	נשיא	נ[שי]א ישראל /
4Q**343** 5	נת"ן	/ ותנתנון
26 4	נתן(?)	] פקדנה אלך נתן /
9 3	סאה	בית זרע חנטי]ן סאין תלת
9 14	סאה	[ס]אין תלת הן /
12 4	סאה	סאין עשר / ותשׄע
50 5	סאה	סאין תלת וקבין תלתה
24a 3	סדר(?)	די אסתד\רׄד
33 1	סימן	]סימניא לאוחרן
33 2	סימן	סימניא [?]אוחרן
8 5	סלע	[די המו]ן סל[ע]ין תשע
8a 6	סלע	וסלעין תרתן דמין גמרין
9 17	סלע	סׄל[עין שבע]
10 3	שלע (= סלע)	/ שׄלעין חמש אפופסאב∘[
21 6	סלע	די המון / סלעין חמש עשרה

21 b+f,2	סלע	סל]עין חמש עשרה
50 11	סלע	סלעין תשע עסרה ותקל חד לחוד
26 3	סערה	∘אחד\ך סערין טבן /
50 29	ספר	ש∘∘ כתב ספריא /
9 7	עב"ד	מקנה ולמז[ב]נה ול[מ]עׄבד בׄהׄ
9 19	עב"ד	]ל[מ]זׄ[בנה ו]לׄ[מ]עבד בה
23 3	עב"ד	לׄמׄעׄבׄד בהׄ כׄול די תצׄבׄהׄ
31 2	עב"ד	לׄמׄעׄבׄד בה כׄ[ל
50 13	עב"ד	מקנה ולמזבנה / ולמעבד בה
4Q**342** 2	עב"ד	ל מה די עב[ד
4Q**343** 12	עב"ד	ובאיש עׄביׄדׄ[
4Q**343** 7	עב"ד/עב"ר	יעבד/עבר לׄידיך
7 5	עד	ן יומה] / דנן ועד עלם
21 9	עד	ן יומא] / דנה ועד לעלם
8a 16	עד	שמעון בר יהוסף עד /
13 13	עד	∘∘∘ בר שמעון עד /
13 14	עד	משבלה בן שמעון עד //
21 4	עומקא	קרקעא עומקא ורומ[א]
4Q**343** a+b,3	עין	ניני ∘[
8 1	על	ל ימי שמעון בן כוסבה נשי ישר[אל]
8a 10	על	לא מעל ול[א] מפק עלי
8a 14	על	לום[בר]ת שמעון על נפשה
8a 15	על	תב[ ] / חדד בר יׄהׄ[ו]דה על ‹נ›פשה
9 9	על	ל אתרה[דנן]
9 21	על	י יתנך על אתרה דנה
9 26	על	]ל נפשׄ[ה כתבה
13 9	על	ל צׄבׄת כל מדעם
13 9	על	קים עלה / אנה שלמצין
13 11	על	ל נפשה שאלה כתב /
50 9	על	אניא וכל די בה ודי חזא עלה
50 17	על	קים ע[לי]
50 26	על	ל [נפ]שה כתבה /
4Q**344** 6	על	אלעזר בר יהוסף על נפשה כׄתׄבׄ[ה]
4Q**345** 20	על	הׄ[ו]שעיה בר[ ]∘∘ על נפש[ה כתבה]
13 10	על(א)	ול די על כׄ[ת]בׄ /
50 12	עלא	י מן עלא
50 23	עלא	ש[א]ין זבניה די מן עלא[
21 e,1	עלה	די מן עלה ∘[
8 2	עליה	עליתה די פתיח[ה] למׄ[ערבה]
8 5	על"ל	]עלה ומפקׄה כדי חזה
8a 10	על"ל	לא מעל ול[א] מפק עלי
9 5	על"ל	רעה די]מעל ומפק לכ לאת∘תׄרׄ
9 16	על"ל	רעה]דׄ׳ מעל ומ[פק]
21 4	על"ל	עלה / ו[מפ]ק[ה]
50 9	על"ל	עלא ומפקא כדי / חזא
7 5	עלם	ן יומה] / דנן ועד עלם

Text	Root	Ref.
קדמך וקדם ירתיך	קדם	**9** 20
קדמך וקדם ירתיך	קדם	**9** 20
מ]ן קדמי[	קדם	**22** 1
קדמ[כן]וקדם ירתכן[	קדם	**50** 15
קדמ[כן]וקדם ירתכן[	קדם	**50** 15
/ די הוית בעלה מן קדמת	קדמה	**13** 6
די הוא מן קדמת דנה	קדמה	**50** 7
אחראין וערבין למקימה /	קי"ם	**8** 6
למשפיה ולמקימה אתרה	קי"ם	**9** 8
וקים עלה / אנה שלמצין	קי"ם	**13** 9
ומקים	קי"ם	**24a** 3
/ למרקא ולקימא זבנה דך	קי"ם	**50** 15
וקים ע[לי]	קי"ם	**50** 17
למרקא ולקימ[א]	קי"ם	**50** 19
וכול די איתי לי ודי אקנה	קנ"י	**8** 6
ודי אקנה[לק]בל[דך]	קנ"י	**8** 7
ותש[למ]תה ודי נקנה לוקבלך /	קנ"י	**8a** 13
למקנה ולמז[ב]נה ול[מ]עבד בה	קנ"י	**9** 7
[ודי אק]נה לקבלדך	קנ"י	**9** 10
למקנה ולמזבנה[	קנ"י	**21** 8
]ודי אקנה	קנ"י	**23** 4
[ודי] אקנה א[חראין	קנ"י	**24a** 2
למקנה ולמזבנה / ולמעבד בה	קנ"י	**50** 12
וכל די איתי לי ודי אקנה	קנ"י	**50** 14
מן נ]כסי ודי אקנה לקבל<ד>ך /	קנ"י	4Q**344** 5
/ ודי אקנה מ[ן ...	קנ"י	4Q**346a** 4
די מתקרה / ח[ק]ל פרדסה[	קר"י	**9** 2
... וקרקעא	קרקע	**8a** 8
/ קרקעא עומקא ורומ[א]	קרקע	**21** 4
לגו ביתה רבה דך	רב	**8** 2
]∘נבא רבה כדי חזה /	רב	**9** 11
מערבה דרת בית מנו\י רבתה	רבה	**8** 4
למב[נה] / ולהרמא	רו"ם	**21** 8
/ קרקעא עומקא ורומ[א]	רום	**21** 4
אנה מן רעותי >יומא דנה<	רעו	**8a** 3
אנה מרעותי יומה דנה	רעו	**9** 2
אנה מרעותי יומה ד[נה]	רעו	**9** 13
/ ורשה לא איתי לך >לך< עמי	רשה	**8a** 5
ורשה לא / איתי לך עמי	רשה	**8a** 9
דיתה רשו מן כל אנש	רשו	**7** 6
לעלם רש[י שאול / זבנה]	רש"י	**8** 5
לעלם רשי / אלעזר	רש"י	**8a** 6
לעלם ר\דשי\ר ושלט	רש"י	**9** 6
לעלם רשי /	רש"י	**21** 6
/ לעלם רשאין זבניא ... וירתהן	רש"י	**50** 12
[ר]ש[א]ין זבניה די מן עלא[	רש"י	**50** 23
על נפשה שאלה כתב /	שא"ל	**13** 11
∘[י המון סלעי]ן ש[ב]ע להוד	שבע	**9** 6
שבעה	שבעה	4Q**344** 3
סף זוזין שבעין ∘[ ]∘ מן ...	שבעין	**25** 4
בכסף זוזין שבעין ותמניה די המון /	שבעין	**50** 10
∘ט שבקין ותרכ[ין]	שב"ק	**13** 7
/ אלעזר בר שמעון שהד /	שהד	**8a** 17
/ יהודה בר יהודה שהד //	שהד	**8a** 18
בר יהוסף ש[הד]	שהד	**9** 31
שהד	שהד	**9** 32
]שהד /	שהד	**9a** 8
ש]הד	שהד	**21** a,1v
יהוח]נן שה[ד	שהד	**21** e,1v
בר א]לעזר שה[ד]	שהד	**22** 16
בר יה]וסף שהד ב∘[	שהד	**22** 17
בר]יהודה שה[ד]	שהד	**22** 18
]בר י]הוסף שהד //	שהד	**22** 19
ש]הד //	שהד	**26** 9
/ישוע בר יהדה שהד/	שהד	**49** 16
ש]הד מן הקר∘[?]	שהד	**50** 28
]שהד מן חברן /	שהד	**50** 31
שותפותי\ו∘∘[	שותפו	**32** 6
אחלף לך שטרה דנה כדי חזה /	שטר	**8** 7
אחלף] / לך ש[טרא דנה]	שטר	**9** 11
שט]רה ∘∘[	שטר(?)	**21** d,1
∘ שטרה דנה[	שטר	**21** e,2
ואשה את השטר הזא/	שטר	**49** 9
וקים עלי / כול שאש על השטר הזא/	שטר	**49** 12
נחלף לכן ש[טרא דנה]	שטר	**50** 22
/ שטר	שטר	4Q**345** 14
אמר לאלעזר בר אלעזר שטר\יא /	שטרא(?)	**8a** 2
מסמרא ש\אכפ רב∘[	שכף(?)	**32** 3
לעלם ר\דשי\ר ושלט	של"ט	**9** 6
∘ם שלמת לכ\הון [	של"ם	**9a** 6
/אבה חבי\ובי שלם/	שלם	**30** 3
ש[לם] /שמעון בן מתנה/	שלם	**30** 8
/ שלעין חמש אפופסאב∘[	שלע (= סלע)	**10** 3
לשם[שמ]עון בר [כסבה נשיא ישראל]	שם	**7** 1
/ לשם שמע[ו]ן בר כסבה	שם	**13** 2
שנת תלת לחרת ישראל	שנה	**7** 1
/ בארבעה לאיר שנת תלת[לחרת ישראל	שנה	**7** 7
... לאדר שנת תלת לחרות ישראל	שנה	**8** 1
שנת [תל]ת לחרות ישראל[	שנה	**8** 8
שנת תלת לחרת ישראל	שנה	**8a** 1
/ שנת עשרין ותרתין	שנה	**10** 4
]∘∘∘ לאלול שנת תמנה [	שנה	**11** 1

12 7	שנה	בשנת / עשׂ֯ר[י]ן
12 11	שנה	/ שנת עשרין / וח[מ]ש להפרכ[יה]
13 1	שנה	שנת תלת לחרת ישראל /
32 1	שנה	לכס]לו שנת תמ֯נה ב◦[
4Q345 1	שנה	/ ב◦◦◦ באלול שׁ֯[נת
9 8	שפ"י	למשפיה ולמקימה אתרה
7 2	שפי	אנת אלעזר בר לוי השפ֯י מן ב֯נ֯י ׳֯רשאל
8a 7	שרי	אבניה ושרית[א]ודגריא
21 3	שרי	אבניה כותליא שריתׁ֯א֯ /
8 5	שתה	[בכסף]ז֯ו֯ז֯י֯ן֯[תלתי]ן ושתה[
9a 3	שתין	] אנחנה הנון\הכול שת֯י֯ן֯ /
21 5	שתין	לך בכסף זוזין שתין
50 9	תאנה	תאניא וכל די בה ודי חזא עלה
8 7	תגר	מכול חרר ותג[ר]
9 9	תגר	כל חרר ותגר
50 20	תגר	מן כל חרר [ו]תגר וב֯טל֯ן[
8 2	תוא	לתונה[די פ]תיח למדנחה
8 3	תחום	ב֯ת֯ח֯ומ֯ה מן מדנחה֯[
8 4	תחם (= תחום)	תחמי אתריה[אלך]
8a 8	תחם (= תחום)	תחמא בתה דך[
9 3	תחום	[ת]ח֯ומי אתרה דך
9 5	תחום	/ את֯ר֯ה דך בתח֯ו֯[מה]
9 14	תחום	די בת[חומה]
9 16	תחום	אתרה דך ב֯ת֯ח֯ו֯[מה]
21 3	תחום	א֯ת֯[ר]יא אלך[ב]תחומיהון
22 8	תחום	בתחומי◦◦◦◦◦
22 12	תחום	בתחומי◦◦◦◦◦
50 6	תחום	תחומי אתרא דך
50 8	תחום	אתרא דך בתחומה / ובמצרה
7 1	תלת	שנת תלת לחרת ישראל
7 7	תלת	/ בארבעה לאיר שנת תלת֯[לחרת ישראל
8 1	תלת	... לאדר שנת תלת לחרות ישראל
8 8	תלת	שנת [תל]ת לחרות ישראל[
8a 1	תלת	שנת תלת לחרת ישראל
9 3	תלת	בית זרע חנטי]ן סאין תלת
9 14	תלת	[ס]אין תלת הן /
13 1	תלת	שנת תלת לחרת ישראל /
50 5	תלת	סאין תלת וקבין תלתה
50 5	תלת	סאין תלת וקבין תלתה
8 5	תלתין	[בכסף]ז֯ו֯ז֯י֯ן֯[תלתי]ן ושתה[
8 1	תמן	אמר לשאול בר חרשה מן ת֯מ֯ן[
8a 3	תמן	/ מן תמן
9 2	תמן	מן ת]מן
9 13	תמן	מ֯[ן]ת֯מן
11 1	תמנה	]◦◦◦ לאלול שנת תמ֯נה [
32 1	תמנה	לכס]לו שנת תמ֯נה ב◦[
8a 6	תמניא/ה	בכסף / זוזין די המ֯ון תמניא
9 6	תמניא/ה	בכסף זוז֯ין עשר[ין] / ותמניה
12 4	תמר	]קבלן מנדד\צמ֯׳֯ / תמר֯י֯ן֯
8 5	תקל	ותקלי כספה אנה מקבל דמין גמרין
50 11	תקל	/ סלעין תשע עסרה ותקל חד לחוד
7 4	תרין	/ בכסף דנר֯י֯ן עשרה ותרין
13 7	תר"ך	גט שבקין ותרכ[ין]
7 4	תרע	דרתה ובתיה ותר֯ע֯י֯ה
8 3	תרע	מע]לת תרע֯ה דביתה די זבנת
21 4	תרע	ותרעא ומפתחא
10 4	תרתין	/ שנת עשרין ותרתין
8a 6	תרתן	וסלעין תרתן דמין גמרין
9 21	תשלם	[פ]ר֯ע֯[ן]תשלם די ל[
50 21	תשלמתא/ה	ותשלמתא מן נכסי[נה]
8a 13	תשלמתא/ה	ו֯תש֯[למ]ת֯ה ודי נקנה לוקבלך /
9 10	תשלמתא/ה	[פר]ען תשלמתה מן נכ[סי]
8 5	תשע	[די המו]ן סל[ע]ין תשע
12 5	תשע	סאין עשר / ותשע֯
50 11	תשע	/ סלעין תשע עסרה ותקל חד לחוד

INDICES TO THE GREEK DOCUMENTARY TEXTS

Index 1: Emperors and Regnal Years

Index 2: Consuls and Other Roman Officials

A. Consuls

B. Other Roman Officials

Index 3: Provincial Years

ἔτους ὀκτωκαιδεκάτου No. **60** 6–7

ἔτο[υ]ς ἐννεακαιδε[κάτ]ου No. **60** 11

κατὰ δὲ τὸν τῆς ν[έας] ἐπαρχείας Ἀραβίας ἀριθμὸν ἔτους δευτέρου εἰκοστοῦ No. **62** a,8–9

[κατὰ τὸν ἀριθμὸν τῆς νέας ἐπαρχείας Ἀραβία]ς ἔτους τετάρτου καὶ εἰκοστοῦ No. **64** 2–3

[κατὰ δὲ] τὸν τῆς [νέ]ας ἐπαρχείας Ἀραβίας ἀριθμὸν ἔτο[υς ἕκτου καὶ εἰκοστοῦ] No. **65** 1–2

Index 4: Months and Days

A. Roman Months

Δεκέμβριος
  Δεκεμβρίων No. **62** a,8
Μαῖος
  Μαίων No. **61** a+b,6
  Μαίω[ν] No. **67** 10

B. Roman Days

εἰδοί
  ε[ἰ]δῶν No. **62** a,8
  εἰδῶν No. **64** a,2r
  εἰδ[ῶν] No. **65** 1
καλάνδαι
  κα[λανδῶν] No. **61** a+b,5
νῶναι
  [ν]ώνων No. **67** 10

C. Macedonian Months

Ἀπελλαῖος
  Ἀπελλαίου No. **62** a,9-10
Δῖος
  Δείου No. **64** a,3r
Λῷος
  Λῴ[ο]υ No. **65** 2
Περίτιος
  [Π]ερειτίου No. **60** 12

Index 5: Personal Names

Index 6: Geographical Terms

A. Provinces, Districts, and Cities

B. Villages

C. Orchards (Date Groves)

Index 7: Religious Terms

(see also Index 14)

Index 8: Official and Military Terms and Titles

(see also Index 14)

Index 9: Legal Terms

(see also Index 14)

Index 10: Units of Measure

A. Measures

B. Money

Index 11: Taxes

(see also Index 14)

Index 12: Non-Greek Words

A. Latin

B. Aramaic

Index 13: Signatures in Aramaic and Nabataean Script

A. Personal Names

B. Common Words

Index 14: Greek Words

SUBJECT INDEX TO THE GREEK DOCUMENTARY TEXTS

FIGURES

Fig. 1

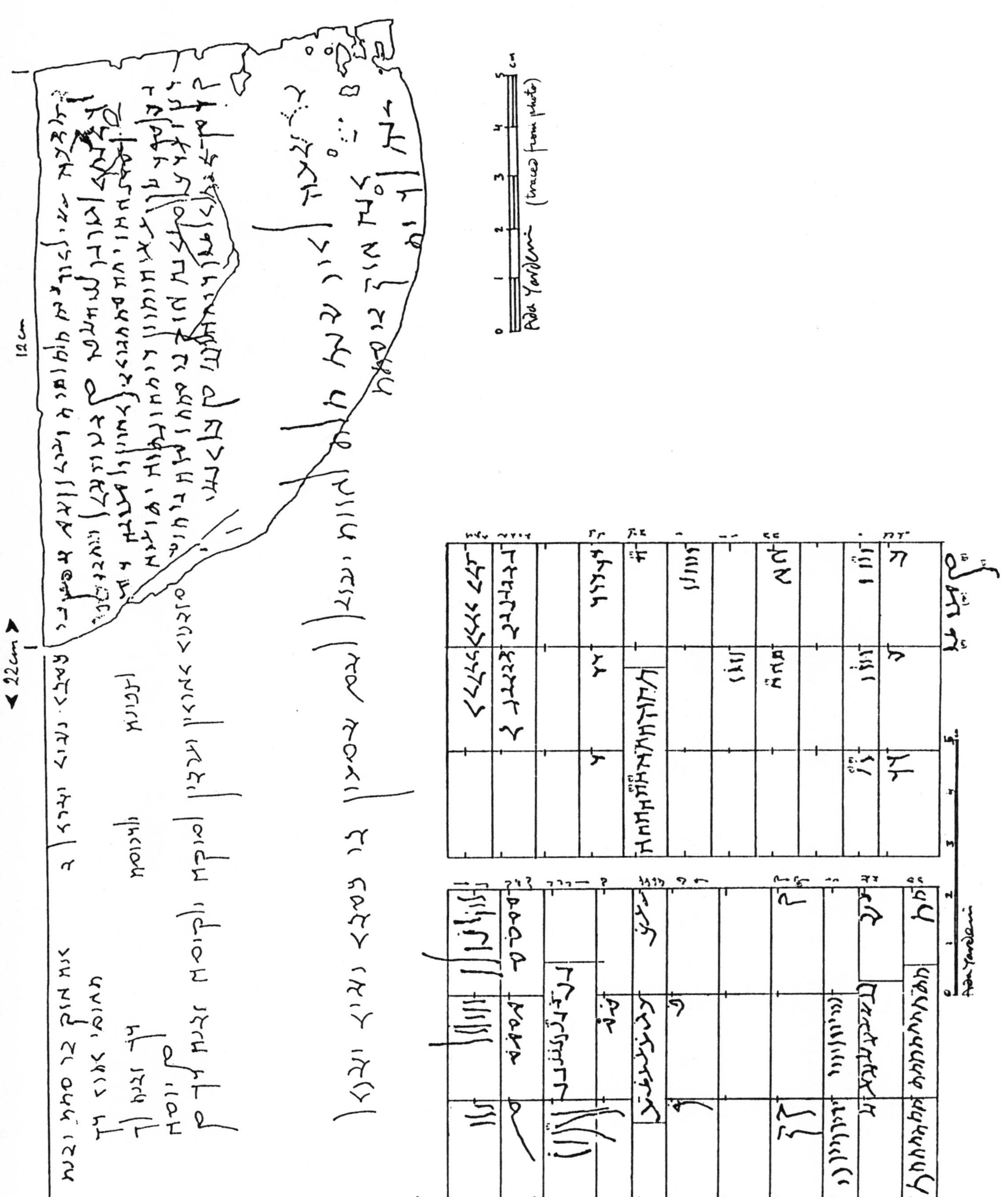

XḤev/Se 7 (Mus. Inv. 889)

Fig. 2

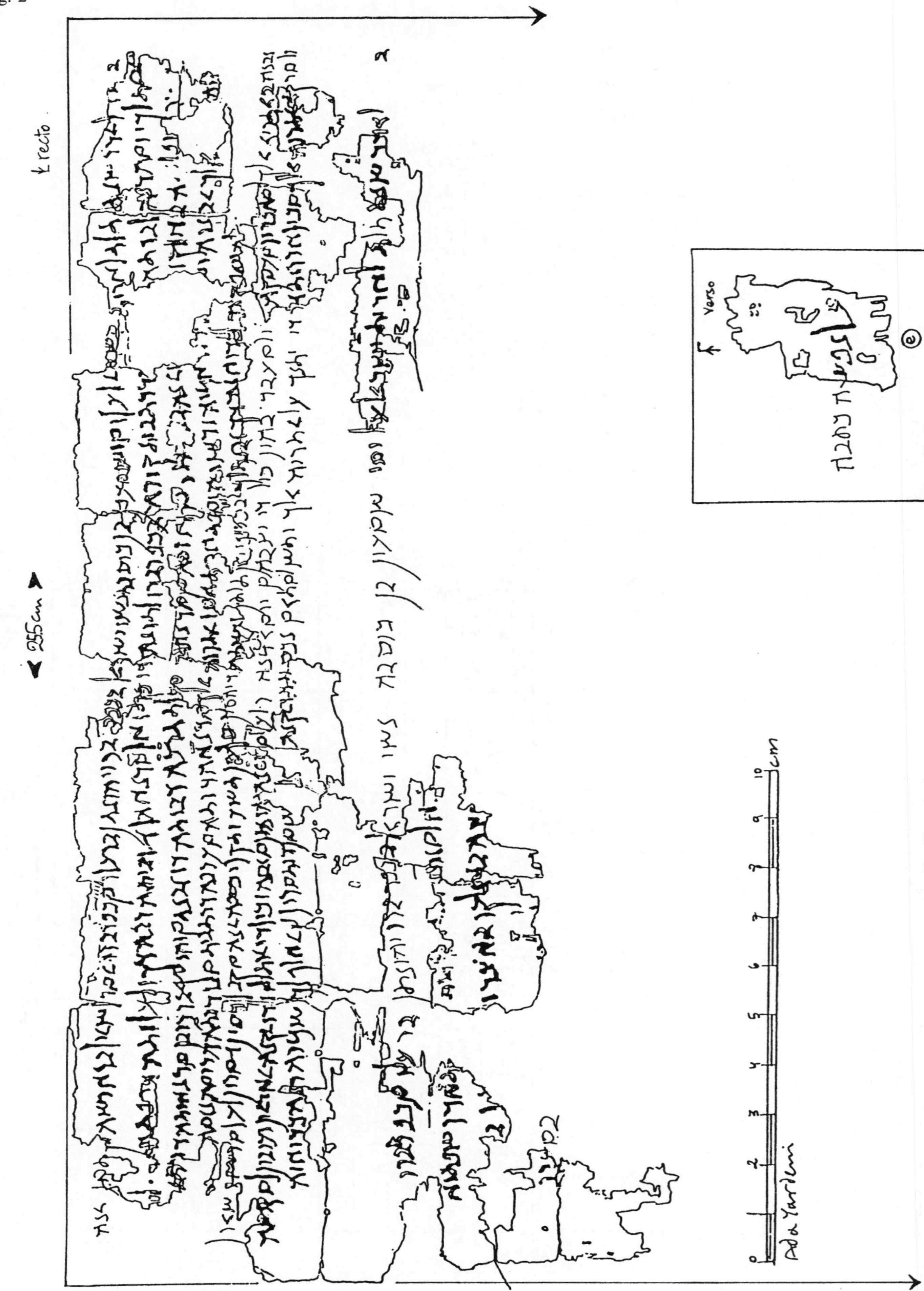

XḤev/Se 8 (Mus. Inv. 542, 734, 735, 736)

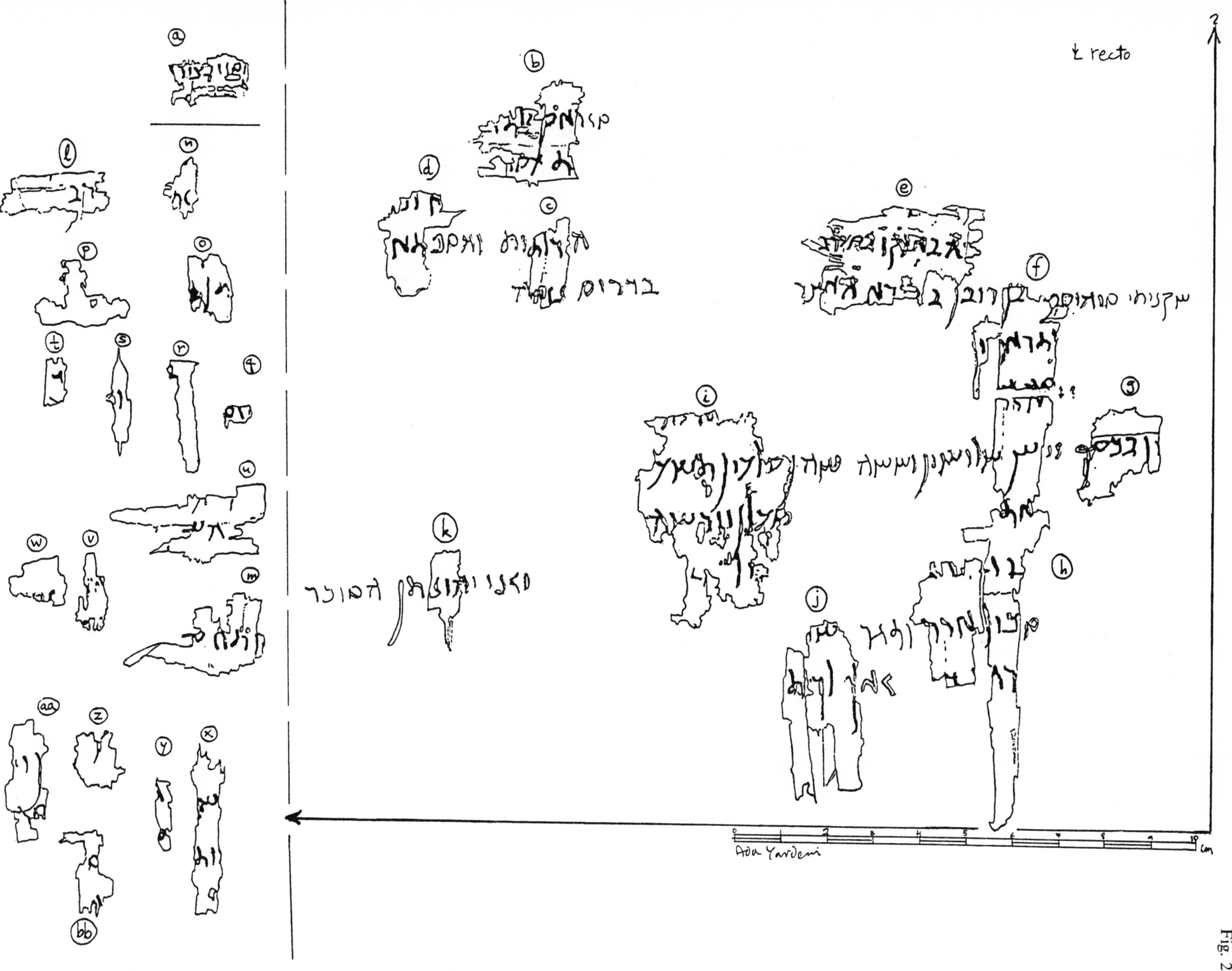

Fig. 2

Fig. 3

Ada Yardeni

cm

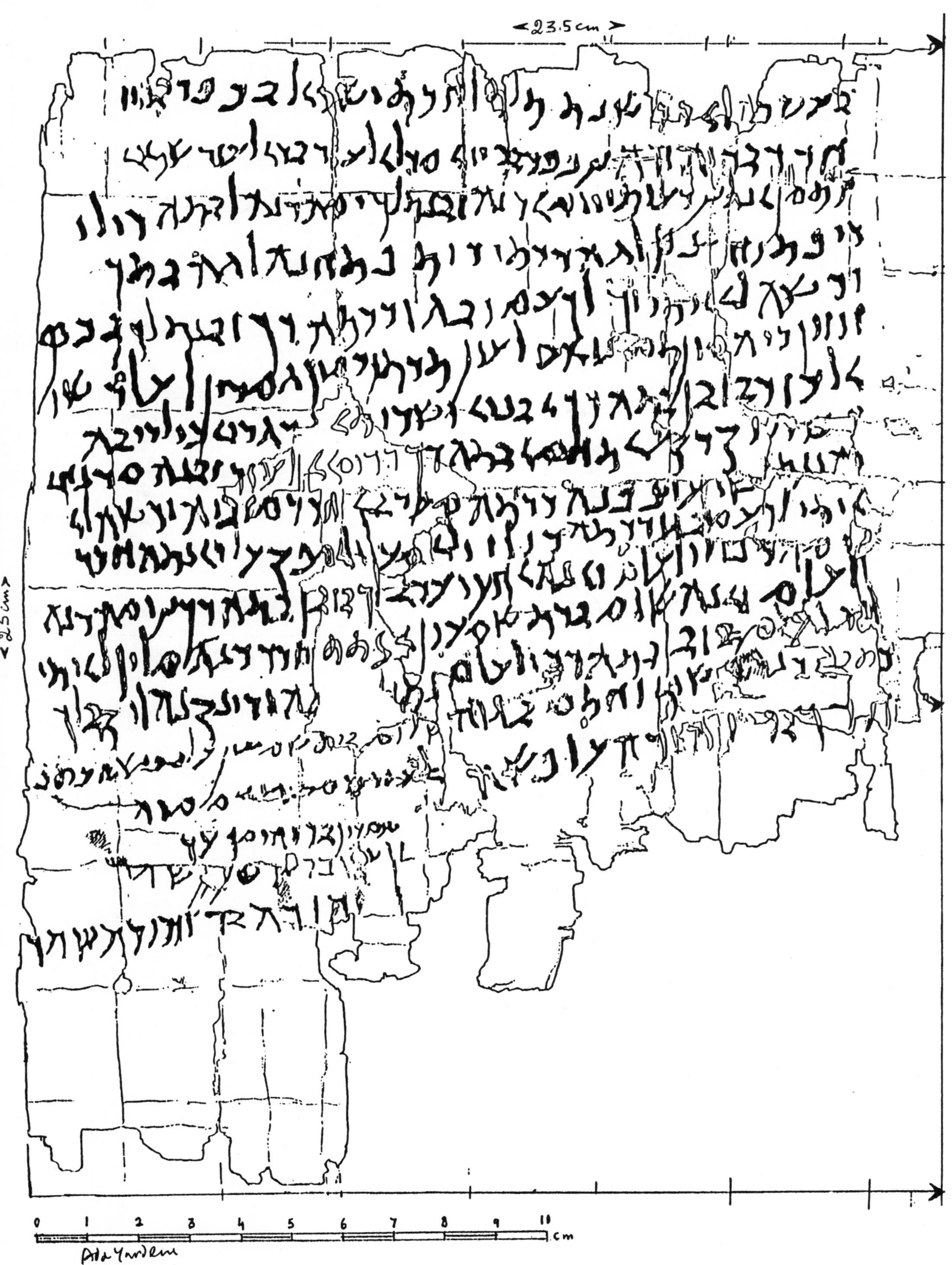

XḤev/Se 8a (SHR 72–560)

Fig. 5

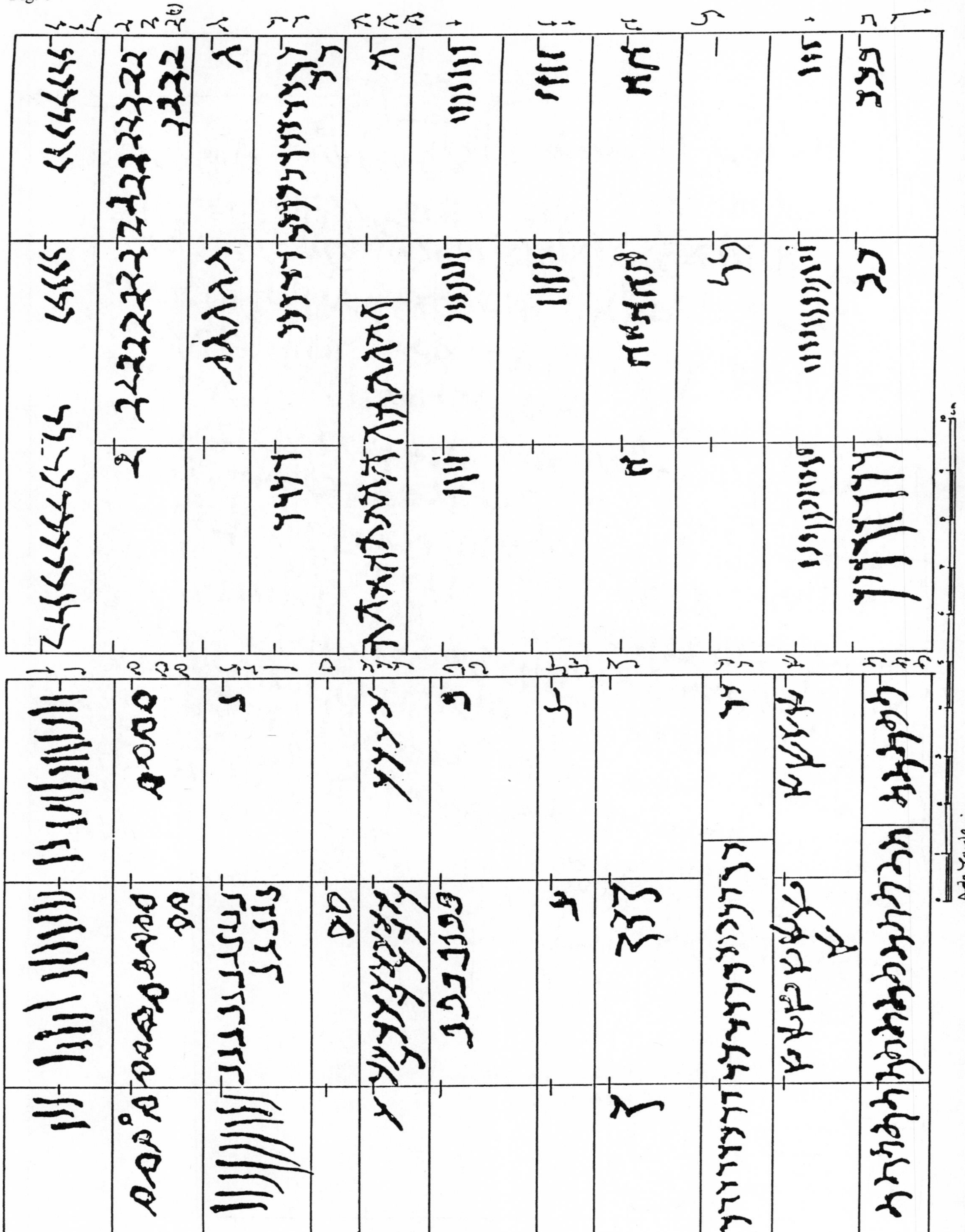

Ada Yardeni

XḤev/Se 8a (SHR 72–560)

Fig. 6

Verso

0 1 2 3 4 5 6 7 8 9 10 cm

Ada Yardeni

XḤev/Se 9 (Mus. Inv. 543)

Fig. 7

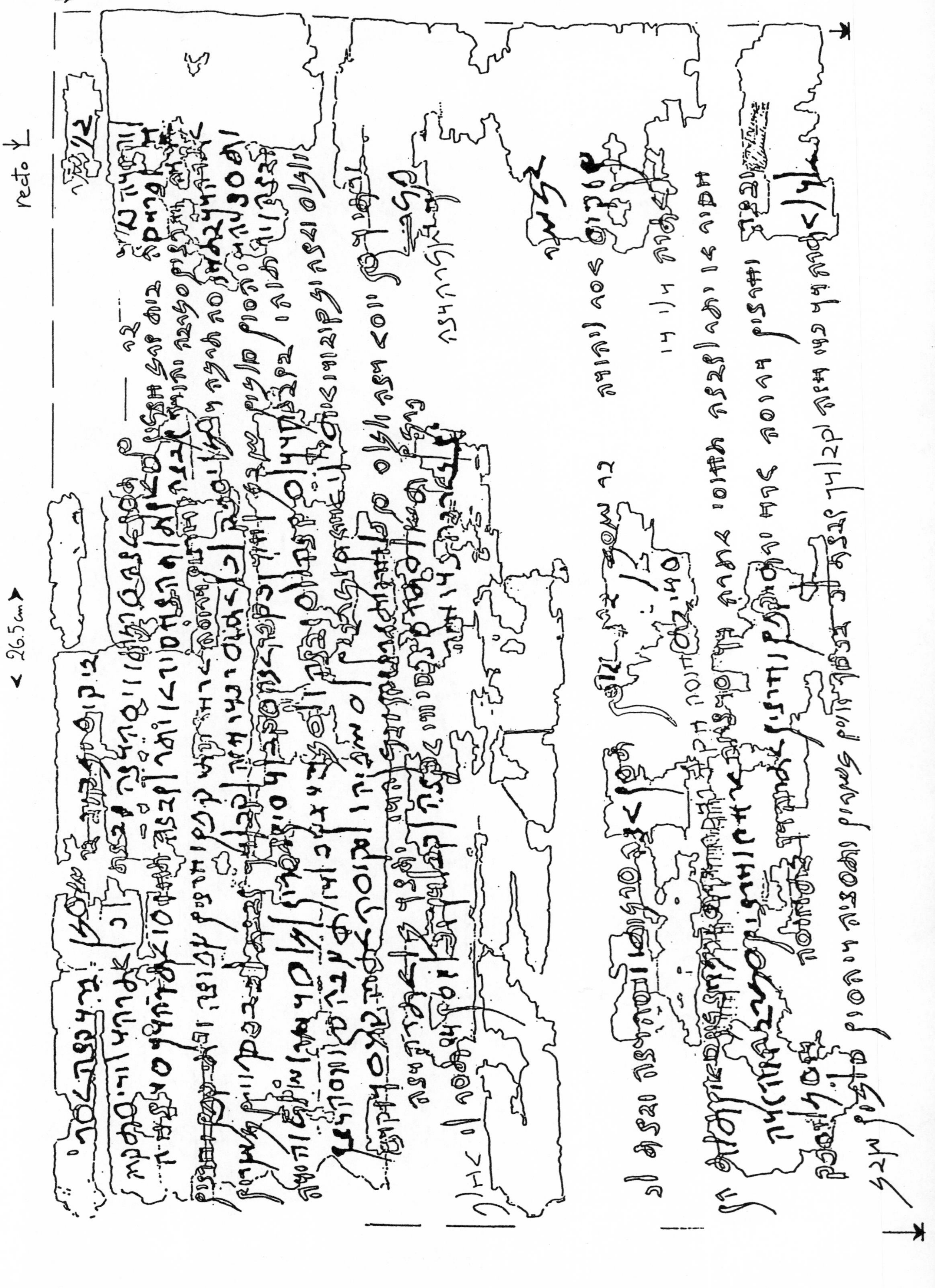

recto

26.5 cm

Fig. 7

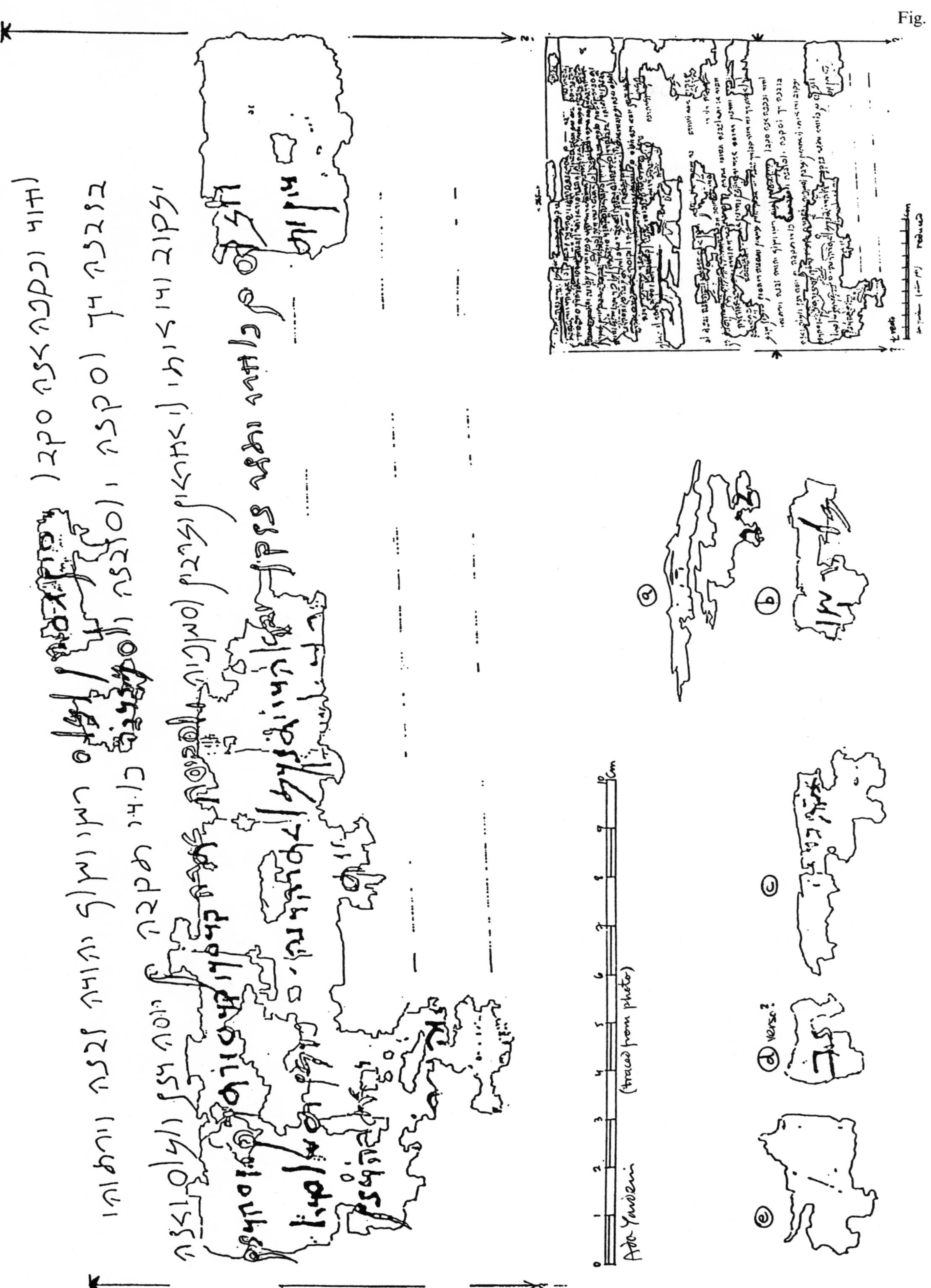

XḤev/Se 9 (Mus. Inv. 543)

Fig. 8

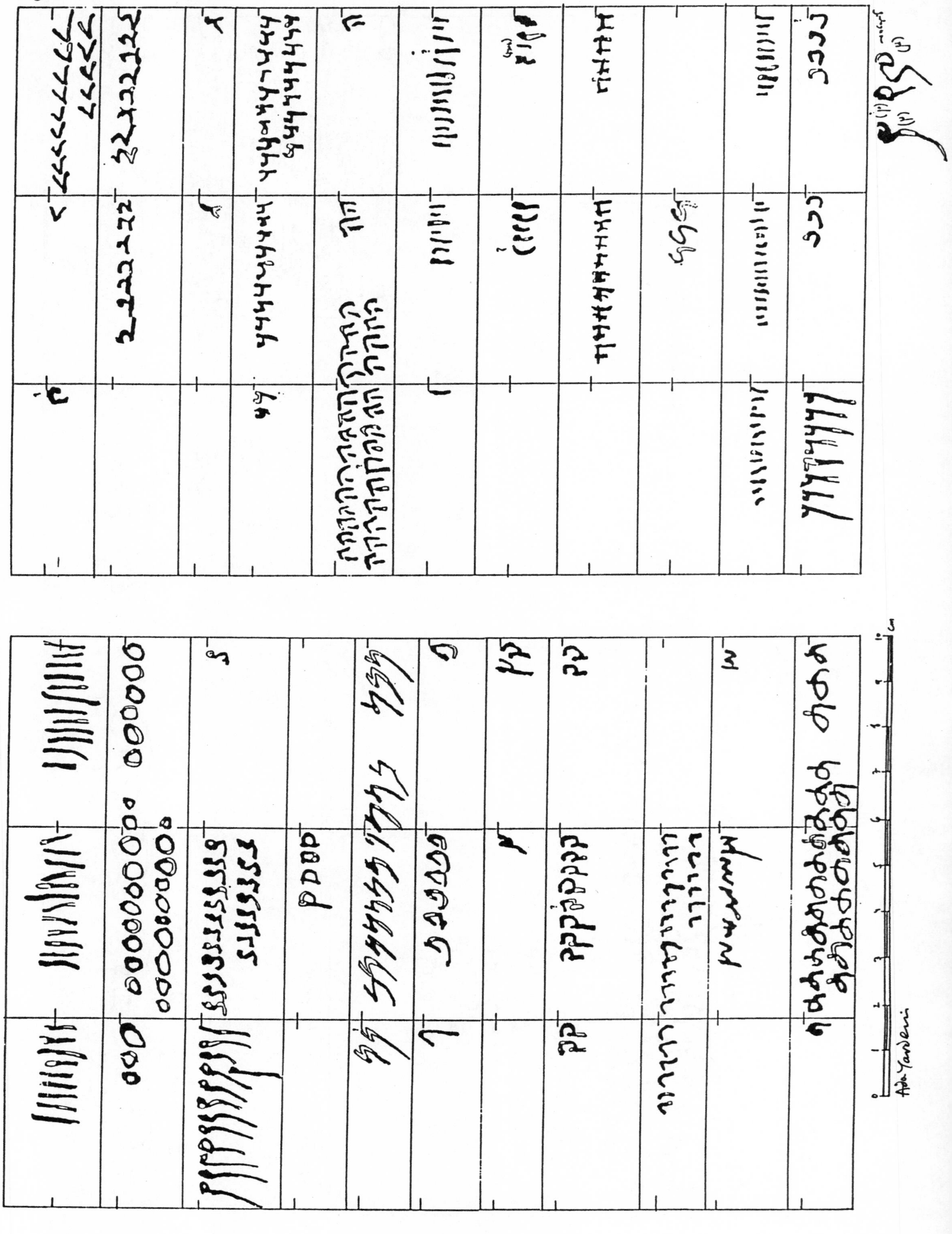

Ada Yardeni

XḤev/Se 9

Fig. 9

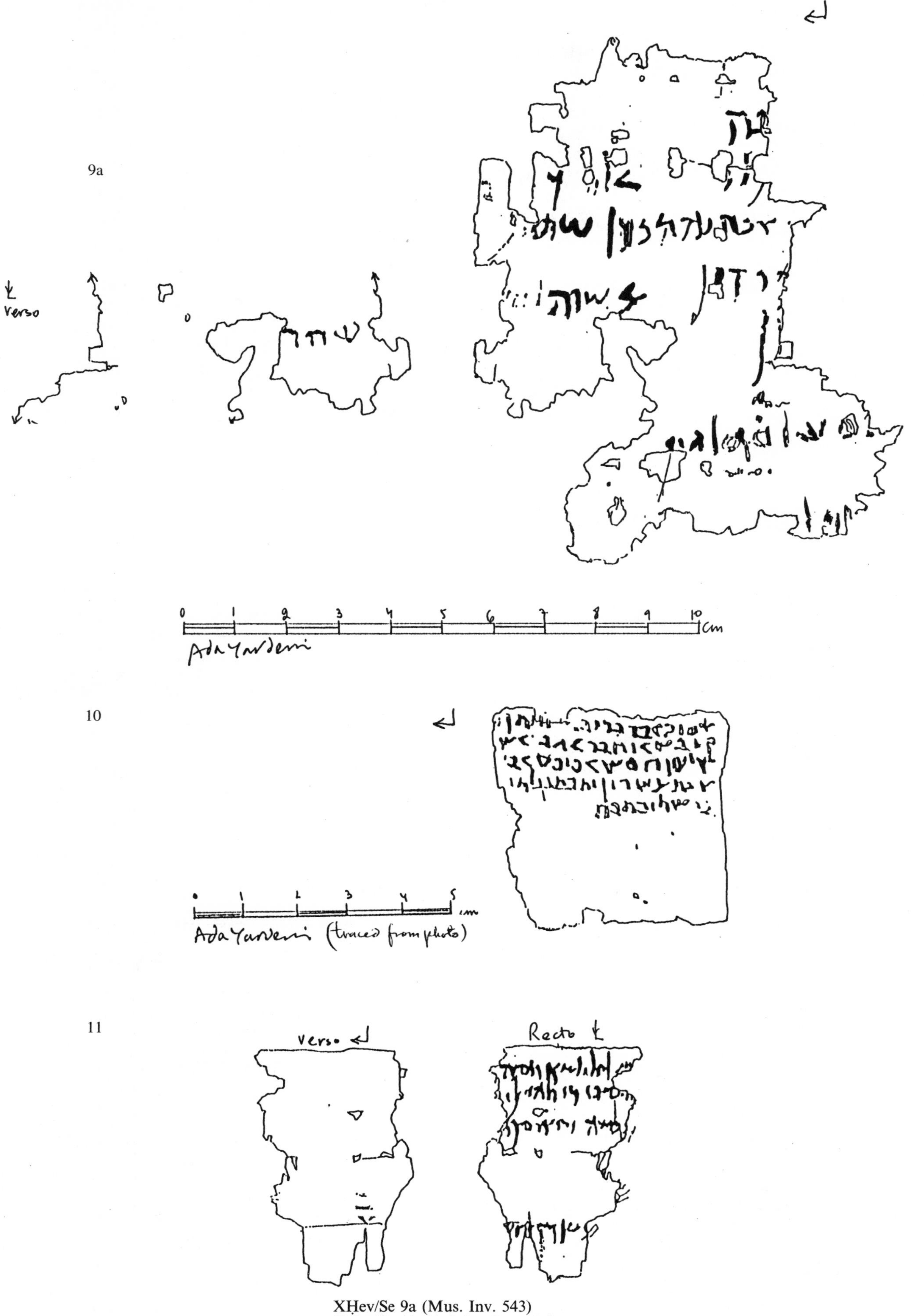

XḤev/Se 9a (Mus. Inv. 543)
XḤev/Se 10–11 (Mus. Inv. 736)

Fig. 10

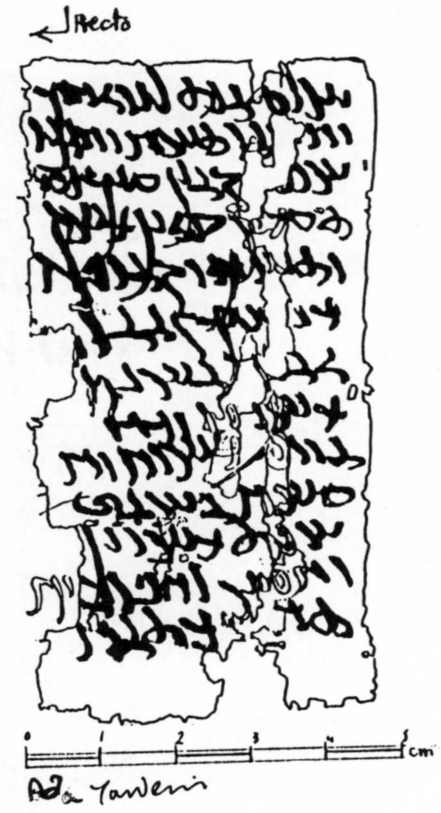

Ada Yardeni

XḤev/Se 12 (Mus. Inv. 736)

Fig. 11

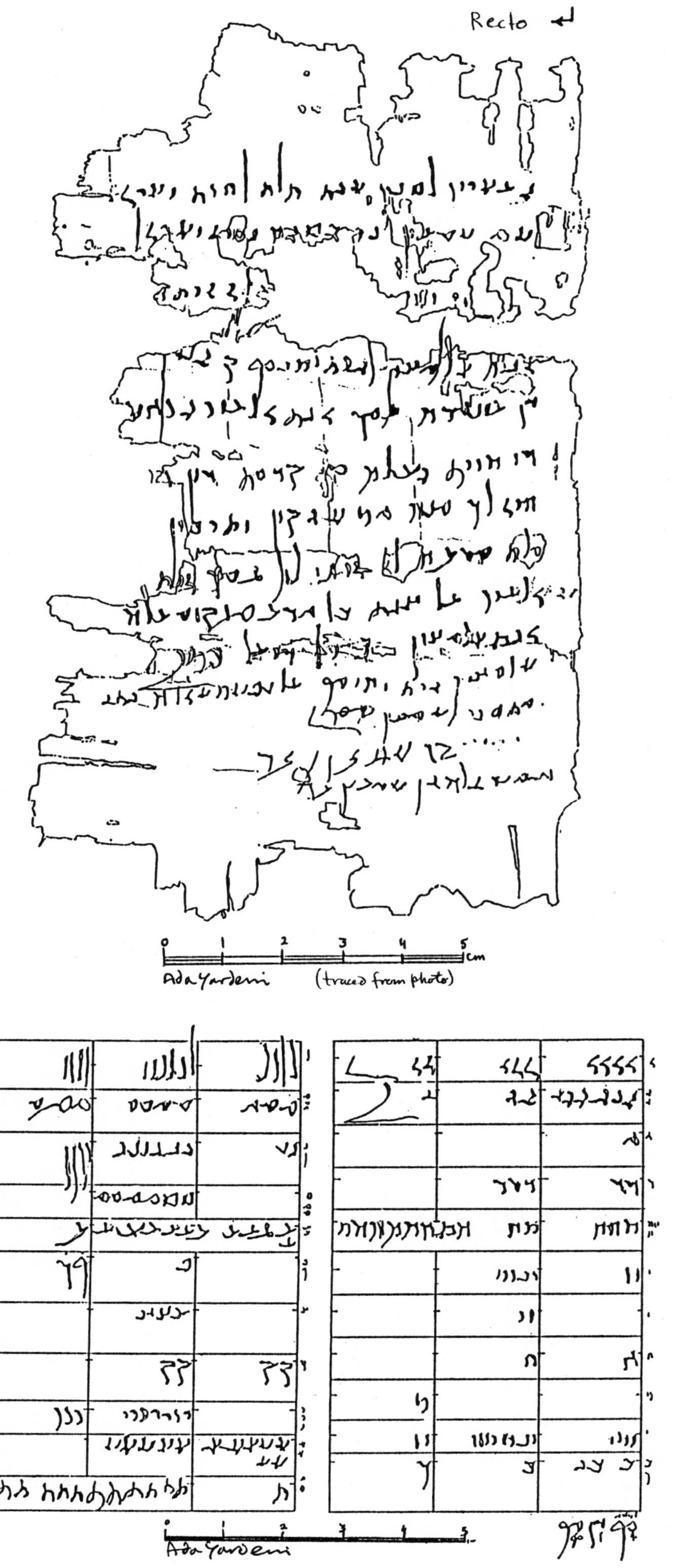

XḤev/Se 13 (Mus. Inv. 736)

Fig. 12

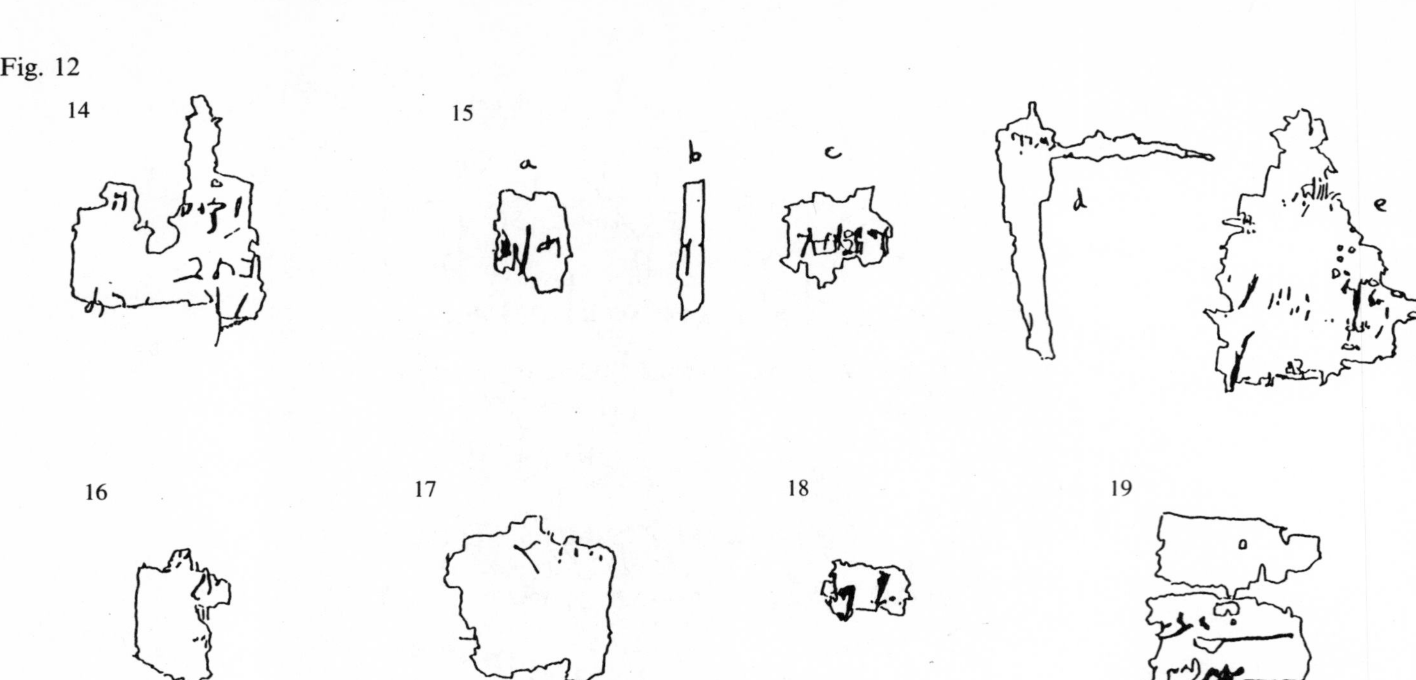

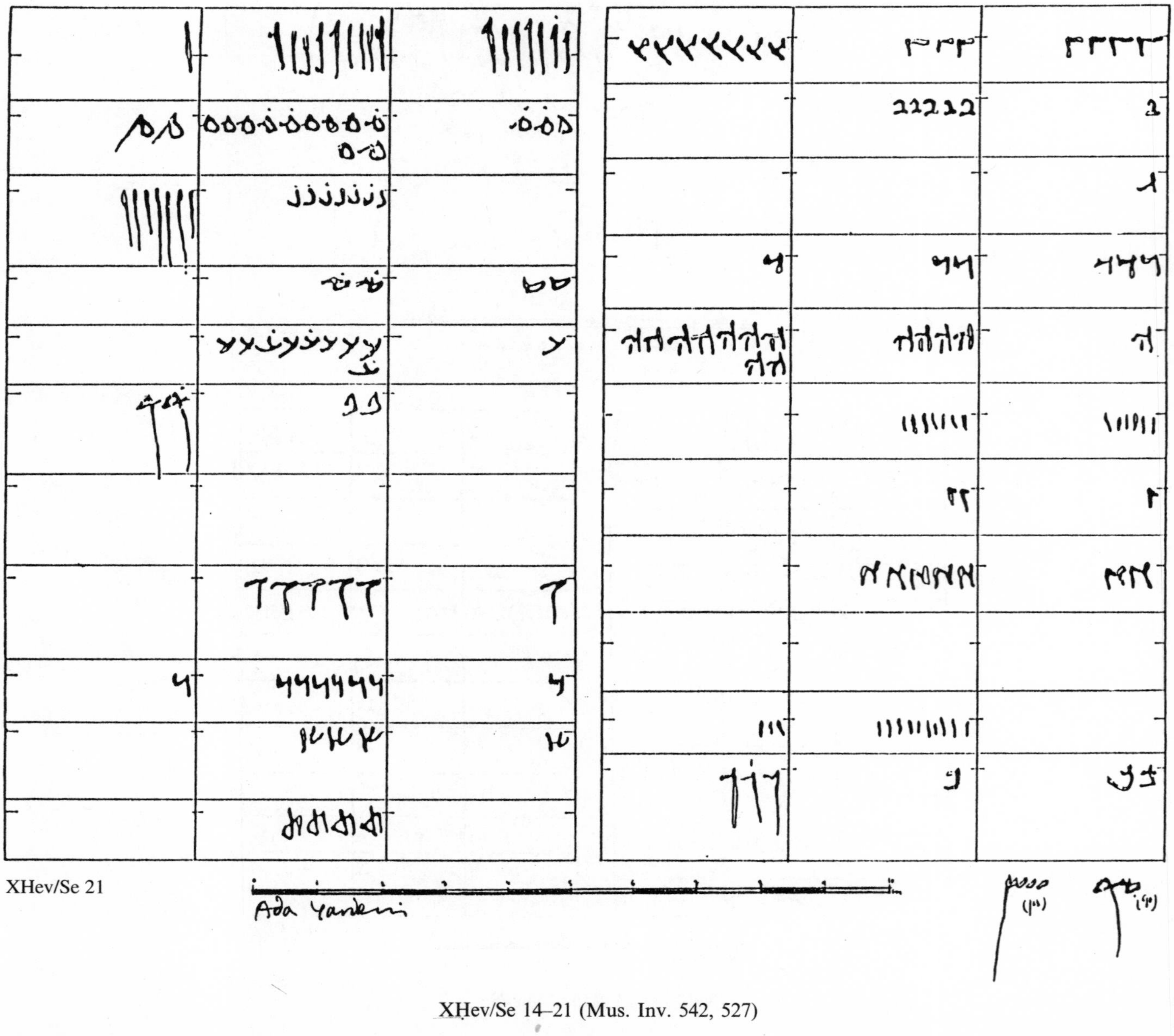

XHev/Se 21

Ada Yardeni

XHev/Se 14–21 (Mus. Inv. 542, 527)

Fig. 13

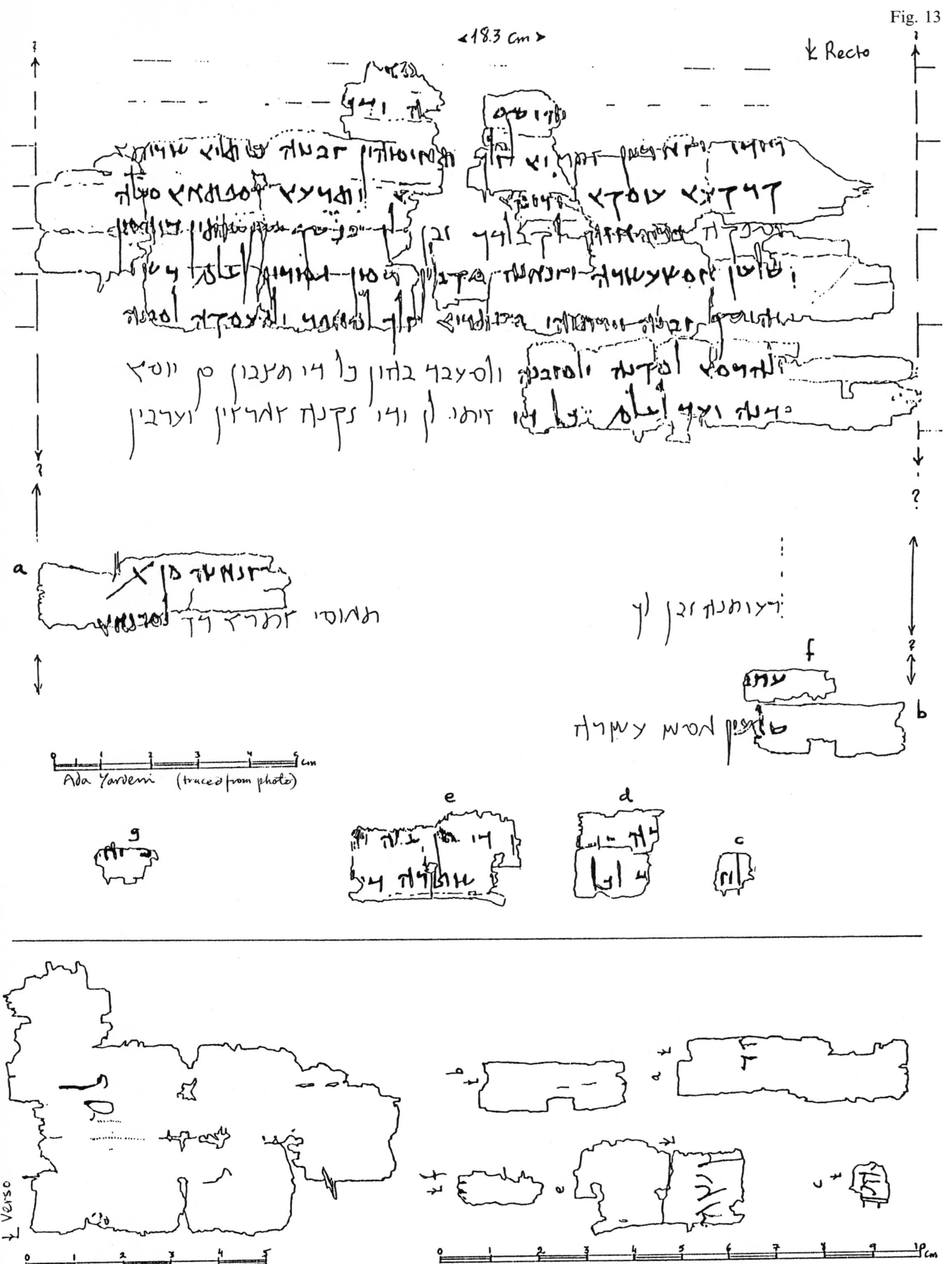

XḤev/Se 21 (Mus. Inv. 527)

Fig. 14

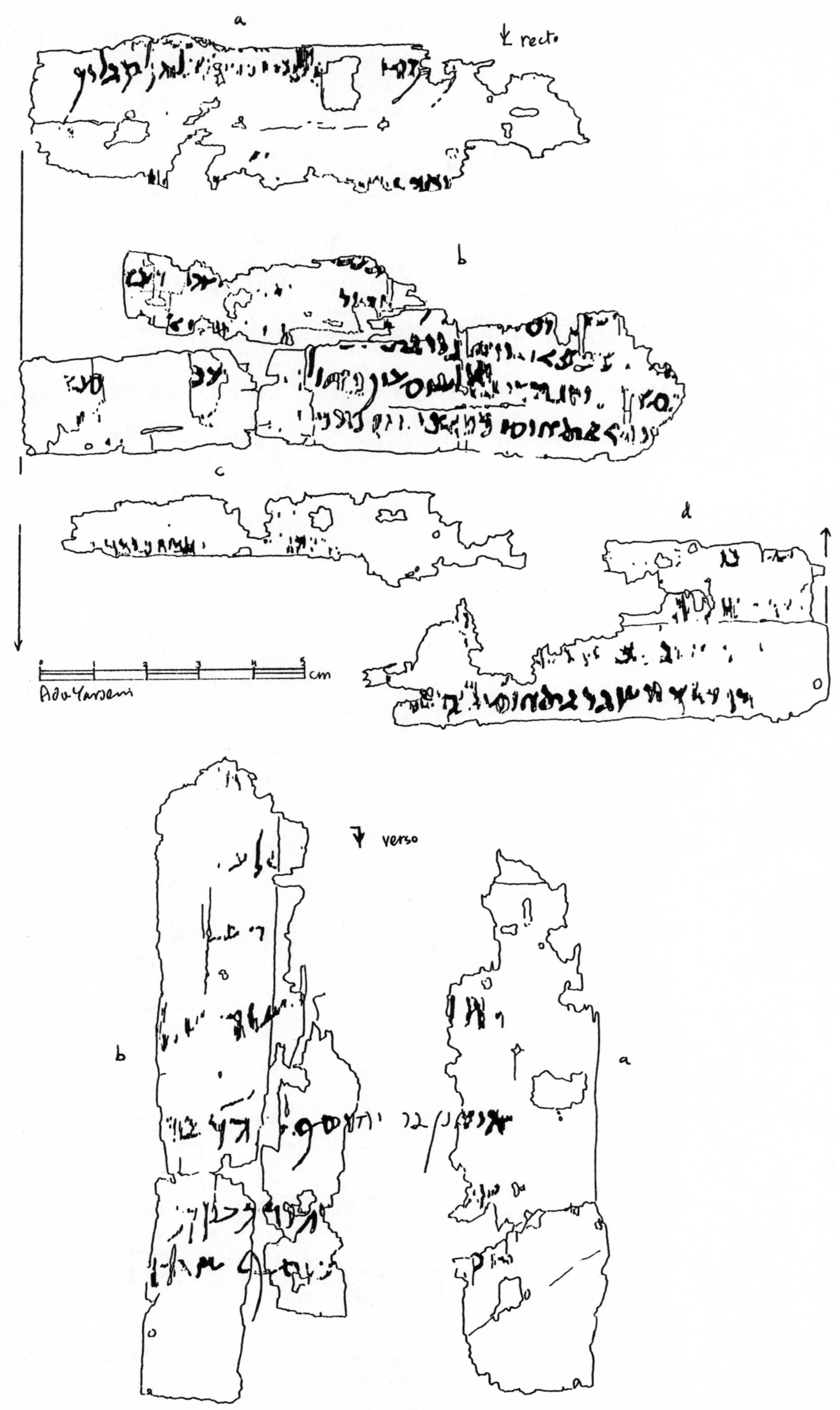

XḤev/Se 22 (Mus. Inv. 735)

23

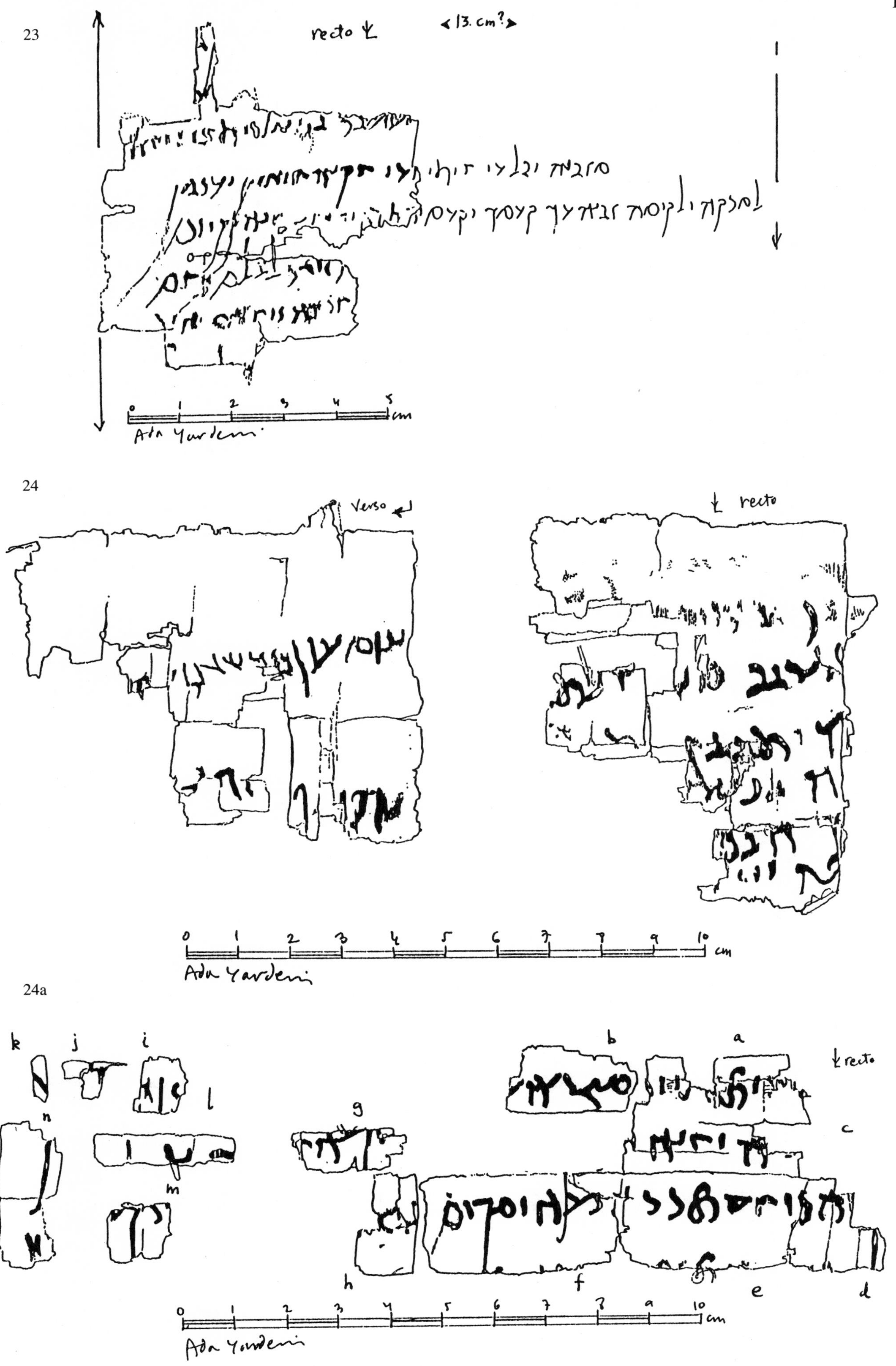

XḤev/Se 23–24a (Mus. Inv. 536)

Fig. 16

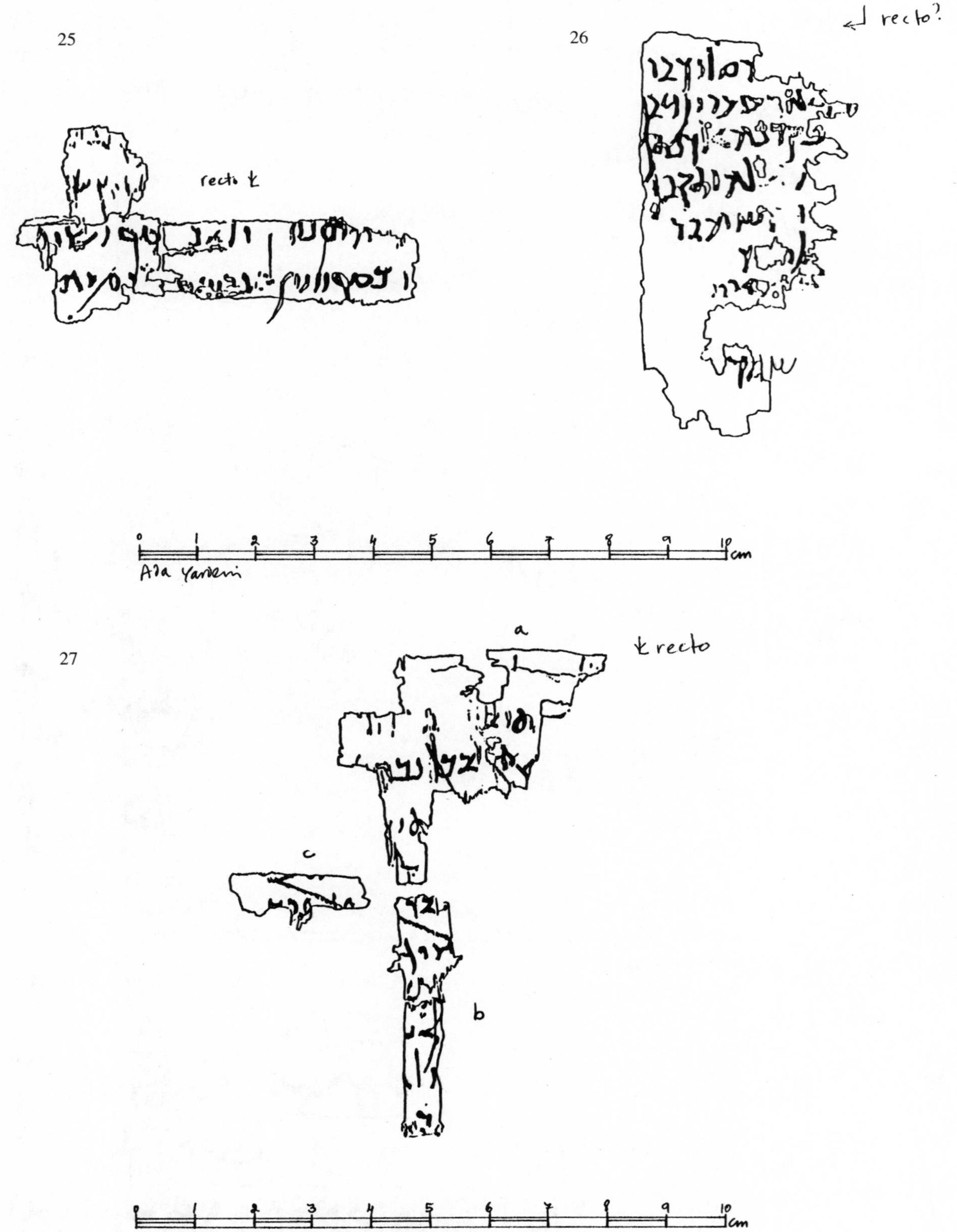

XḤev/Se 25–27 (Mus. Inv. 542)

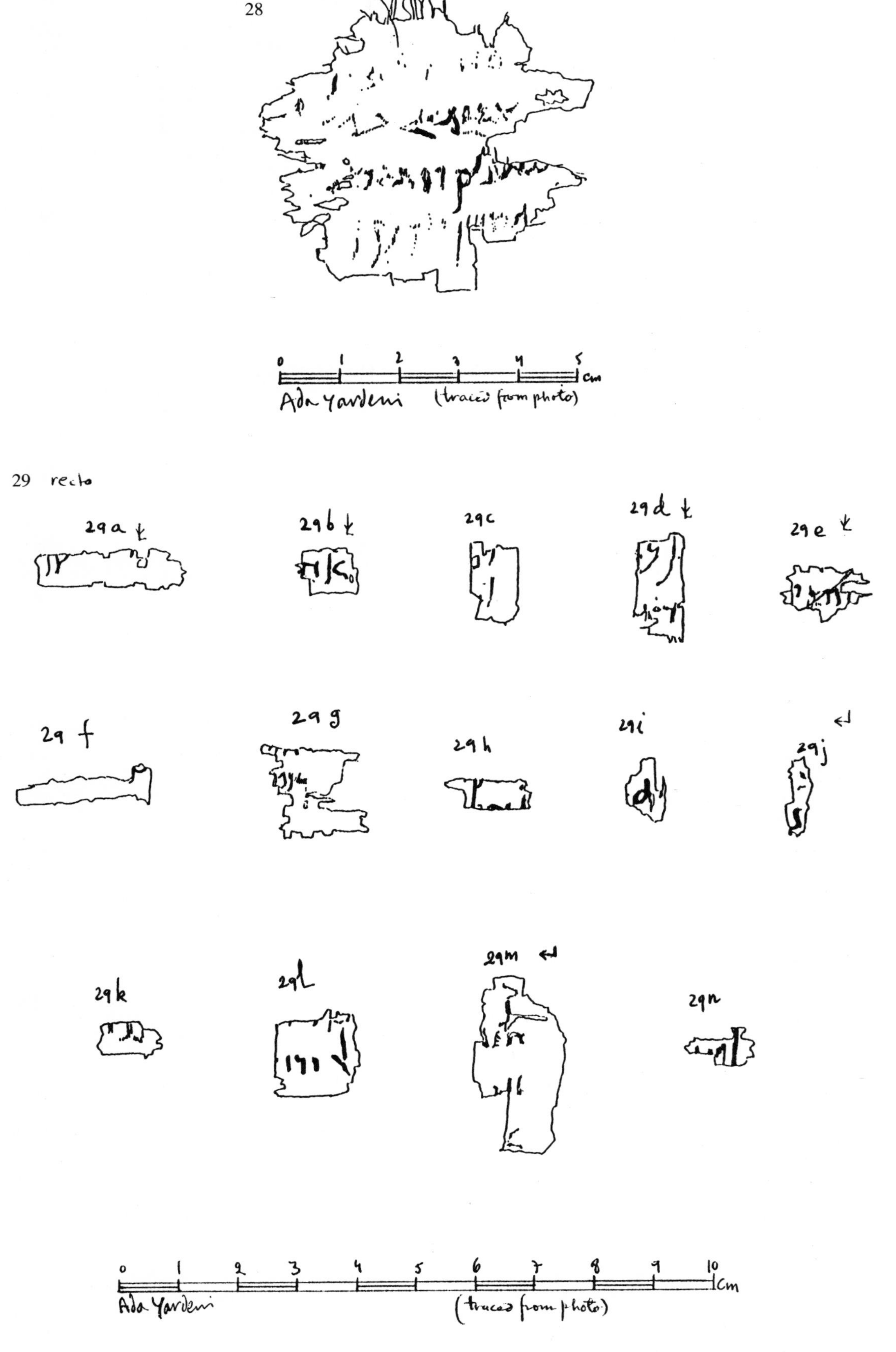

XḤev/Se 28 (Mus. Inv. 536)
XḤev/Se 29 (Mus. Inv. 732, 733)

Fig. 18

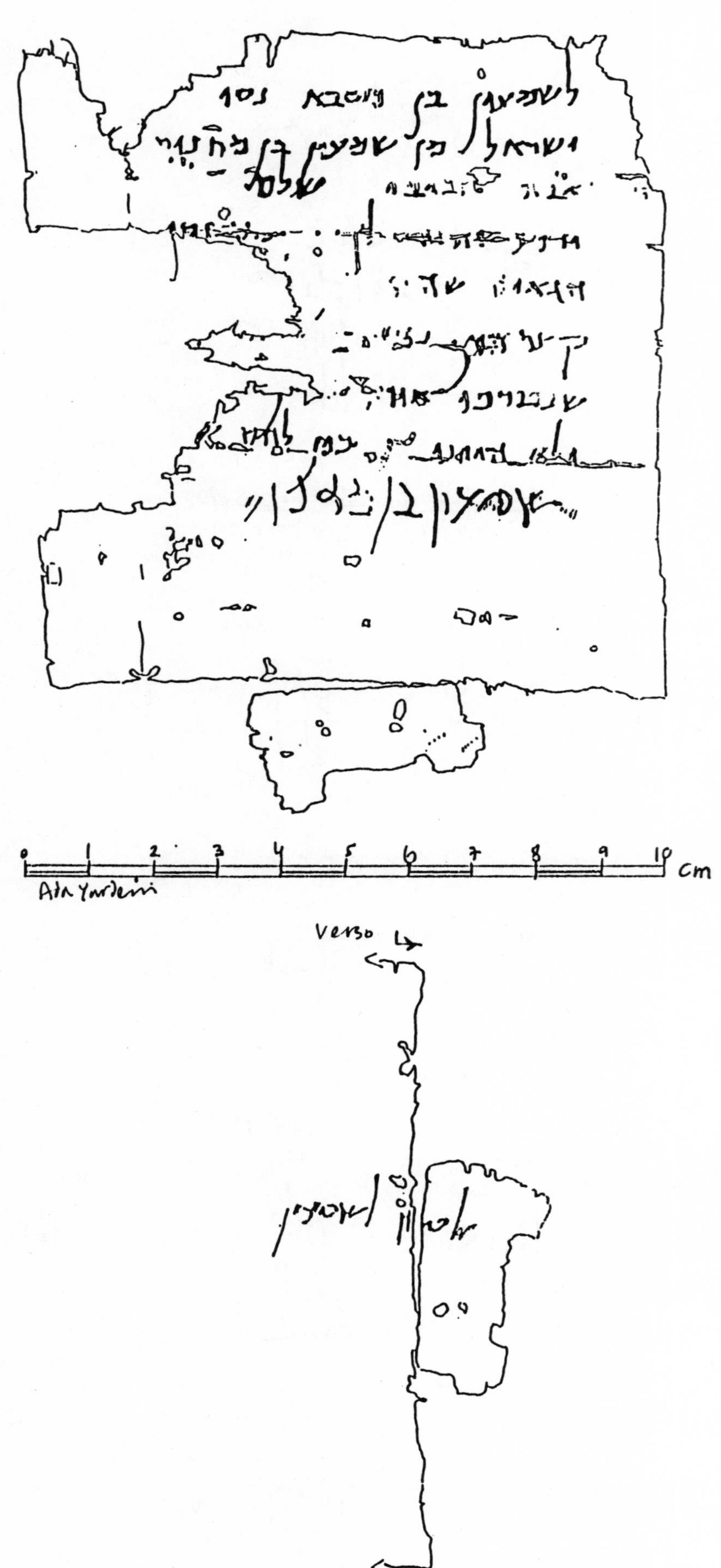

XḤev/Se 30 (Mus. Inv. 542)

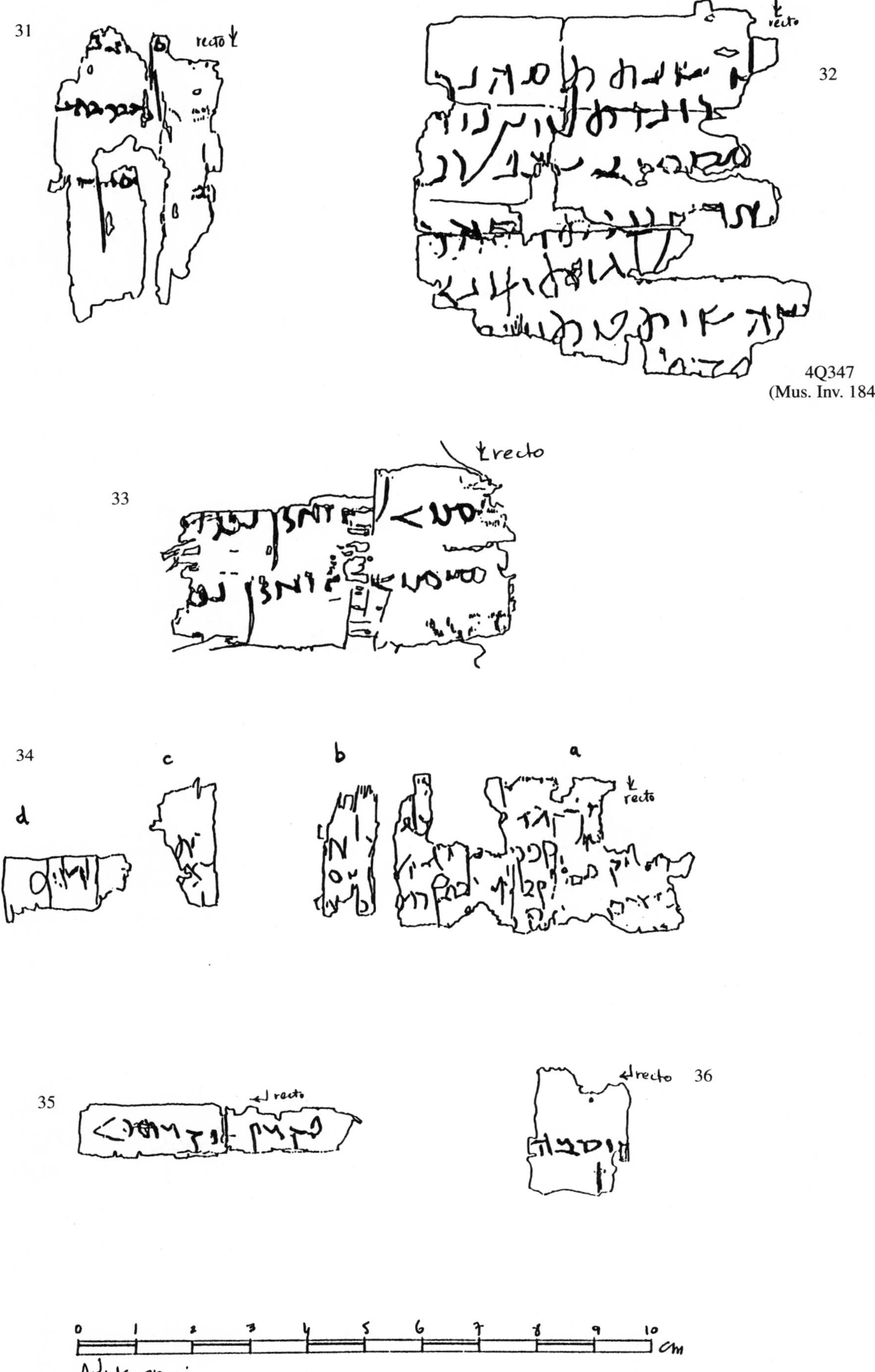

XḤev/Se 31–36 (Mus. Inv. 734, 184)

Fig. 20

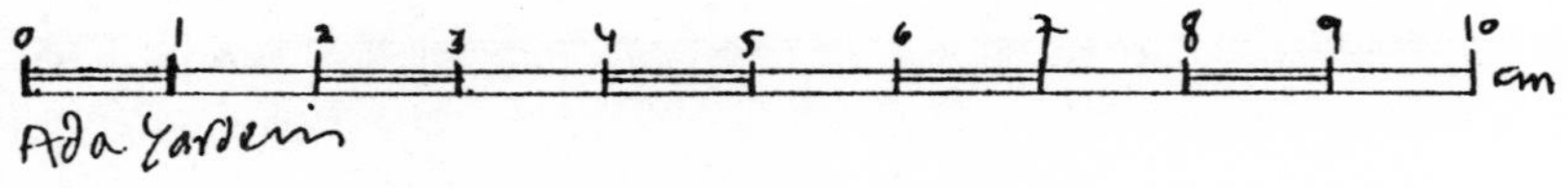

XḤev/Se 37 (Mus. Inv. 734)
XḤev/Se 38–41 (Mus. Inv. 865)

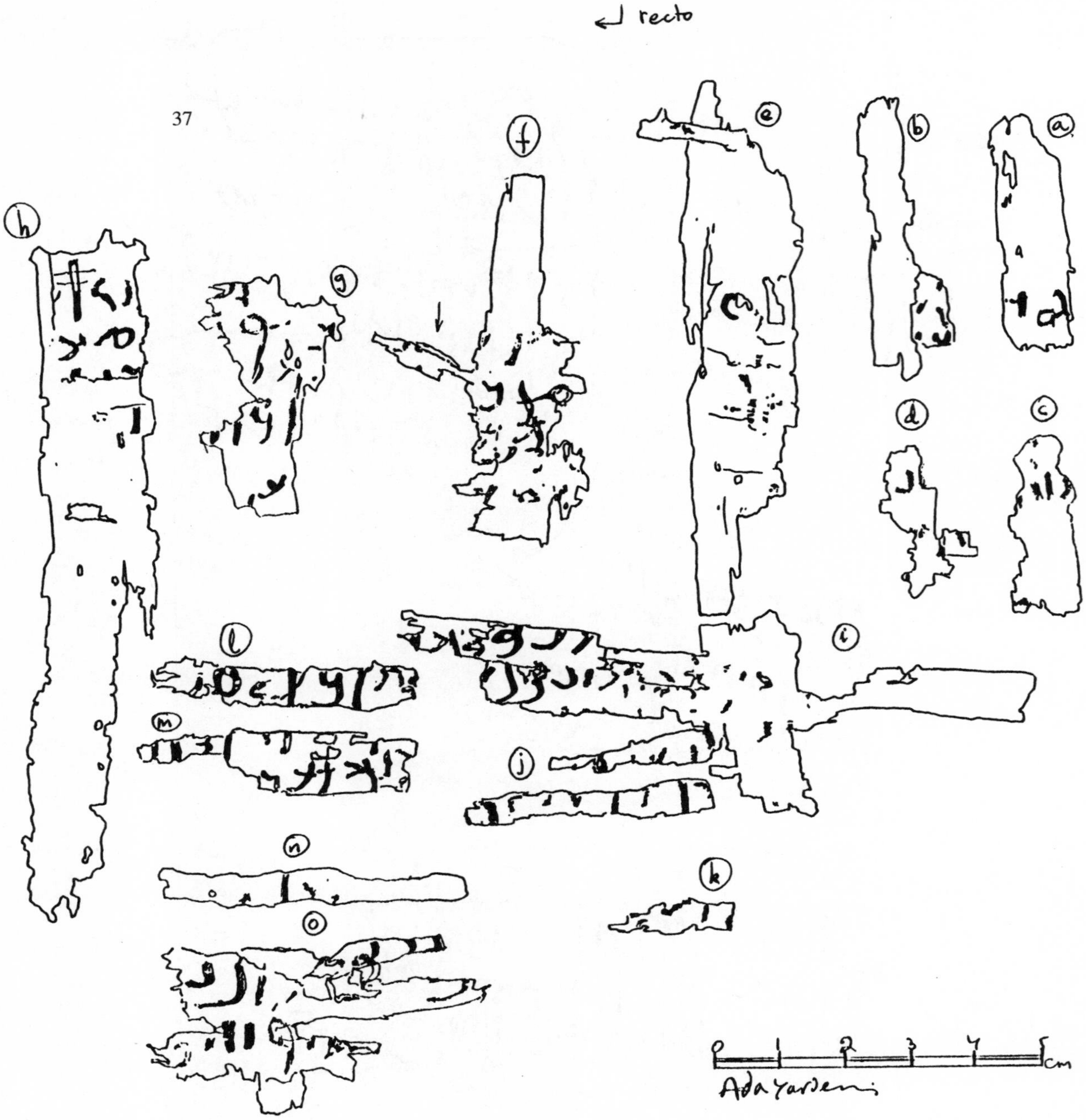

XḤev/Se 42–47h (Mus. Inv. 865)

Fig. 22

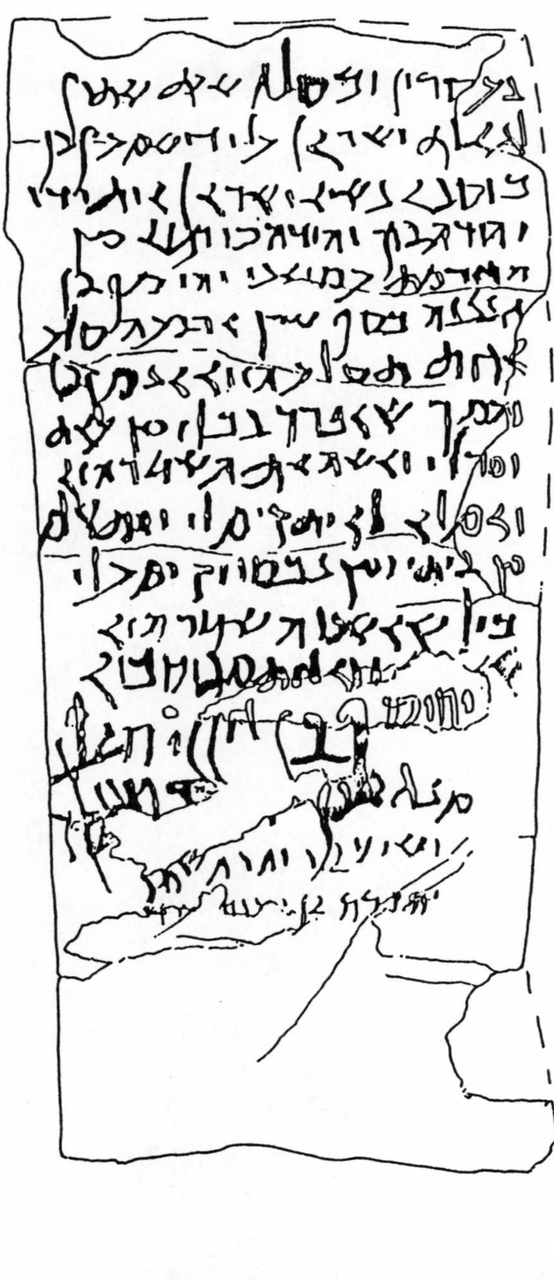

XḤev/Se 49 (Private Collection)

Fig. 23

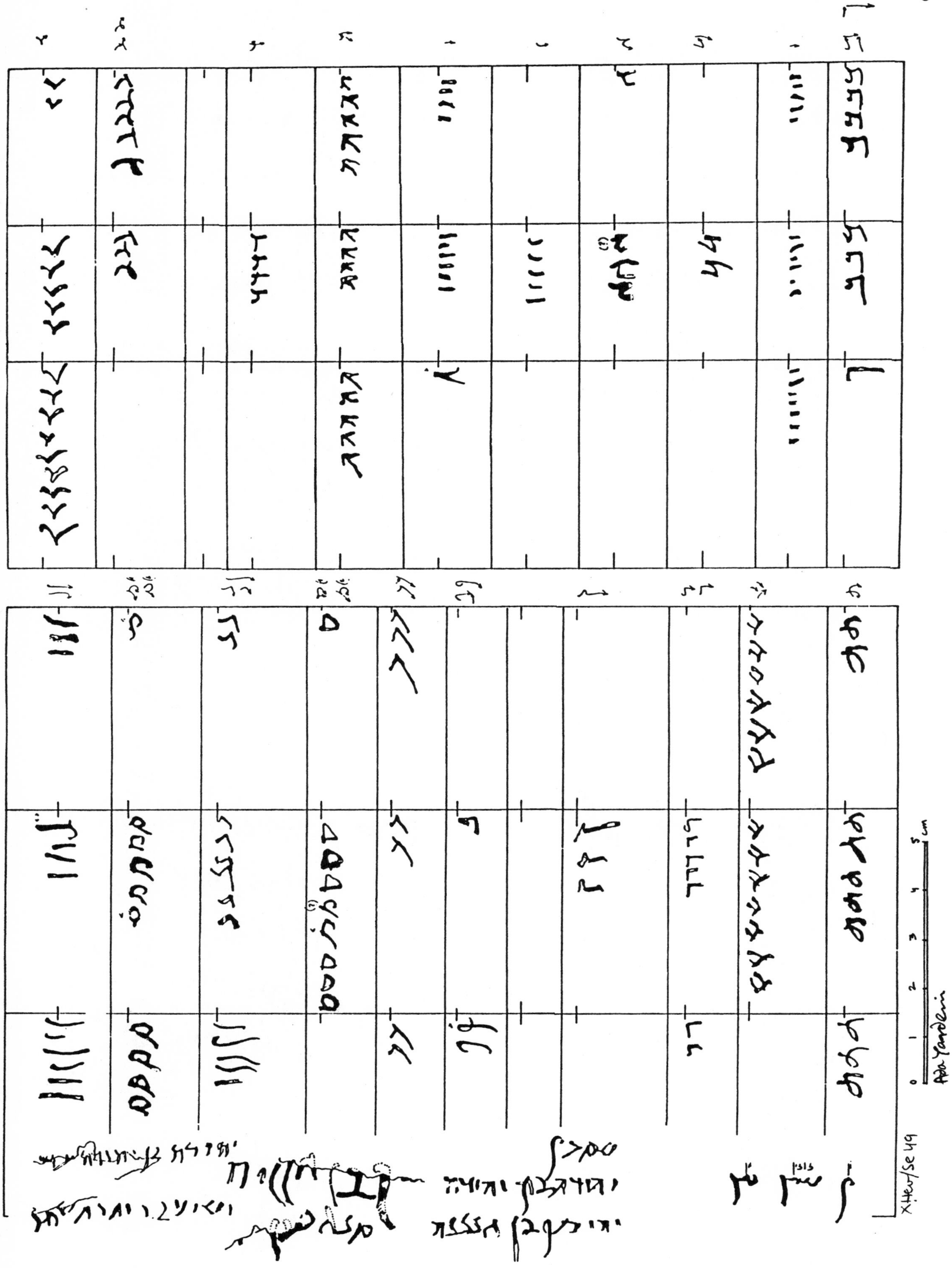

XḤev/Se 49

Fig. 24

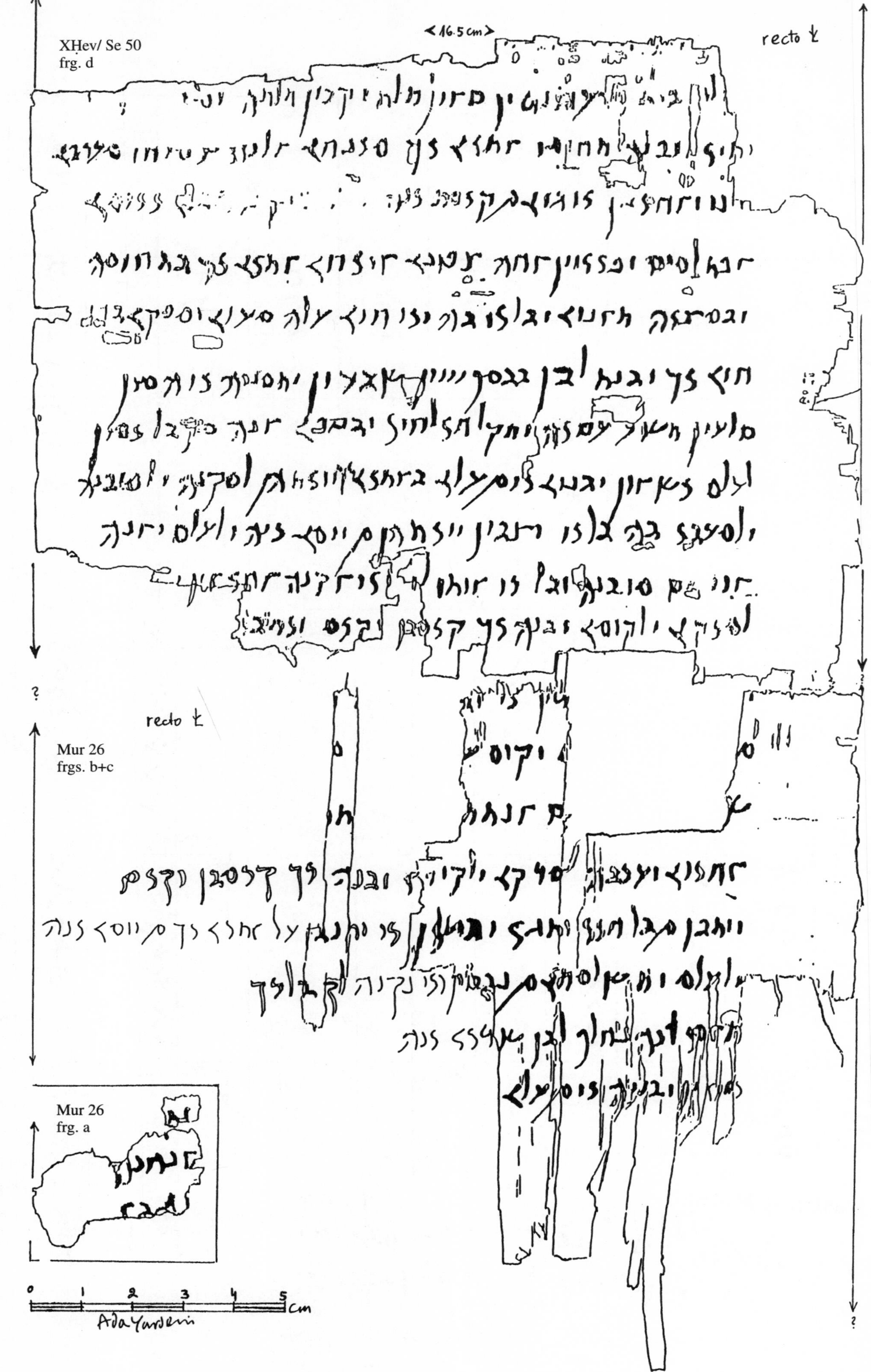

16.5 cm
XḤev/ Se 50
frg. d
recto
recto
Mur 26
frgs. b+c
Mur 26
frg. a
0 1 2 3 4 5 cm
Ada Yardeni

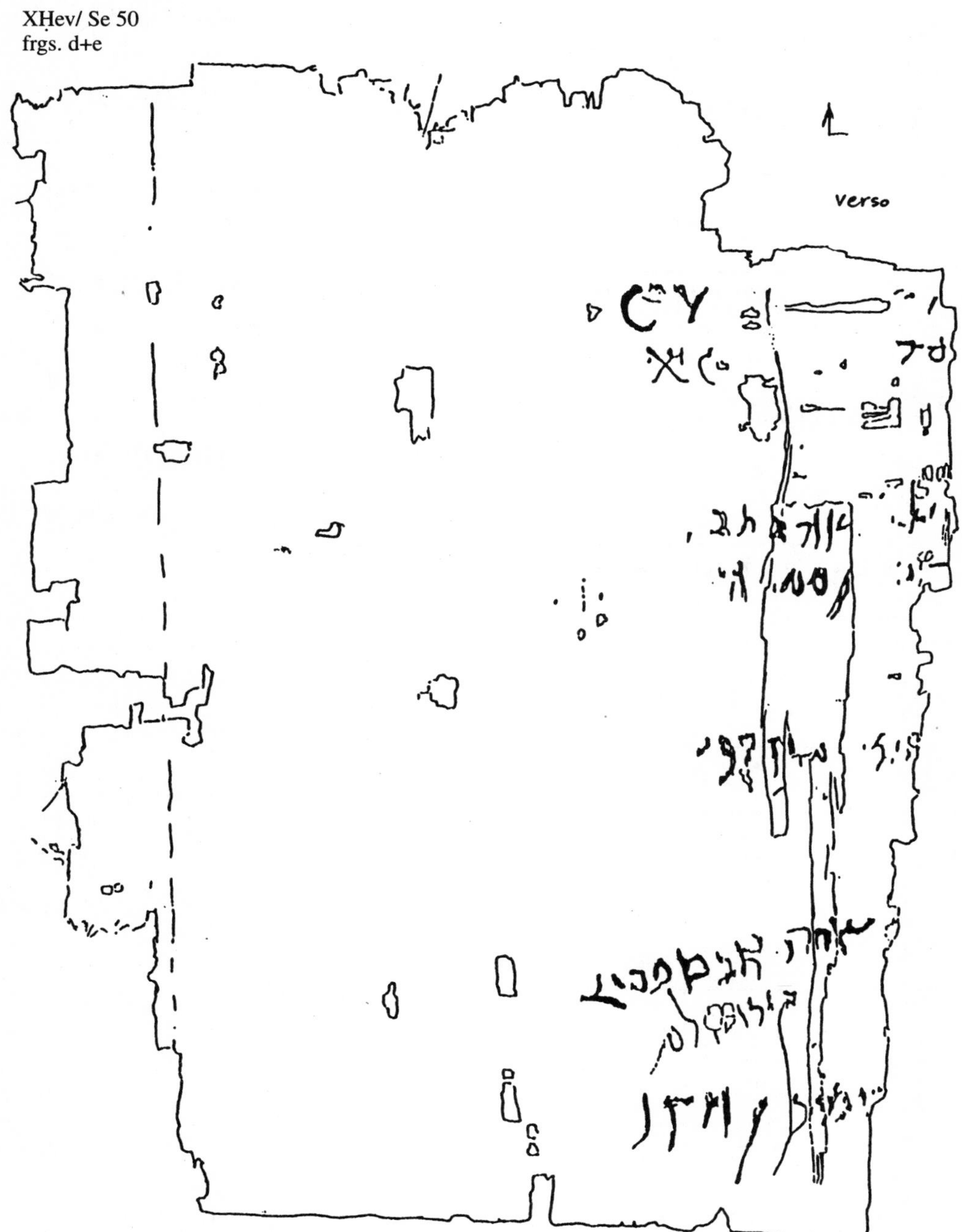

XḤev/Se 50 + Mur 26 (Mus. Inv. 725 + BTS 7163)

Fig. 26

0 1 2 3 4 5 6 7 8 9 10 cm

Ada Yardeni

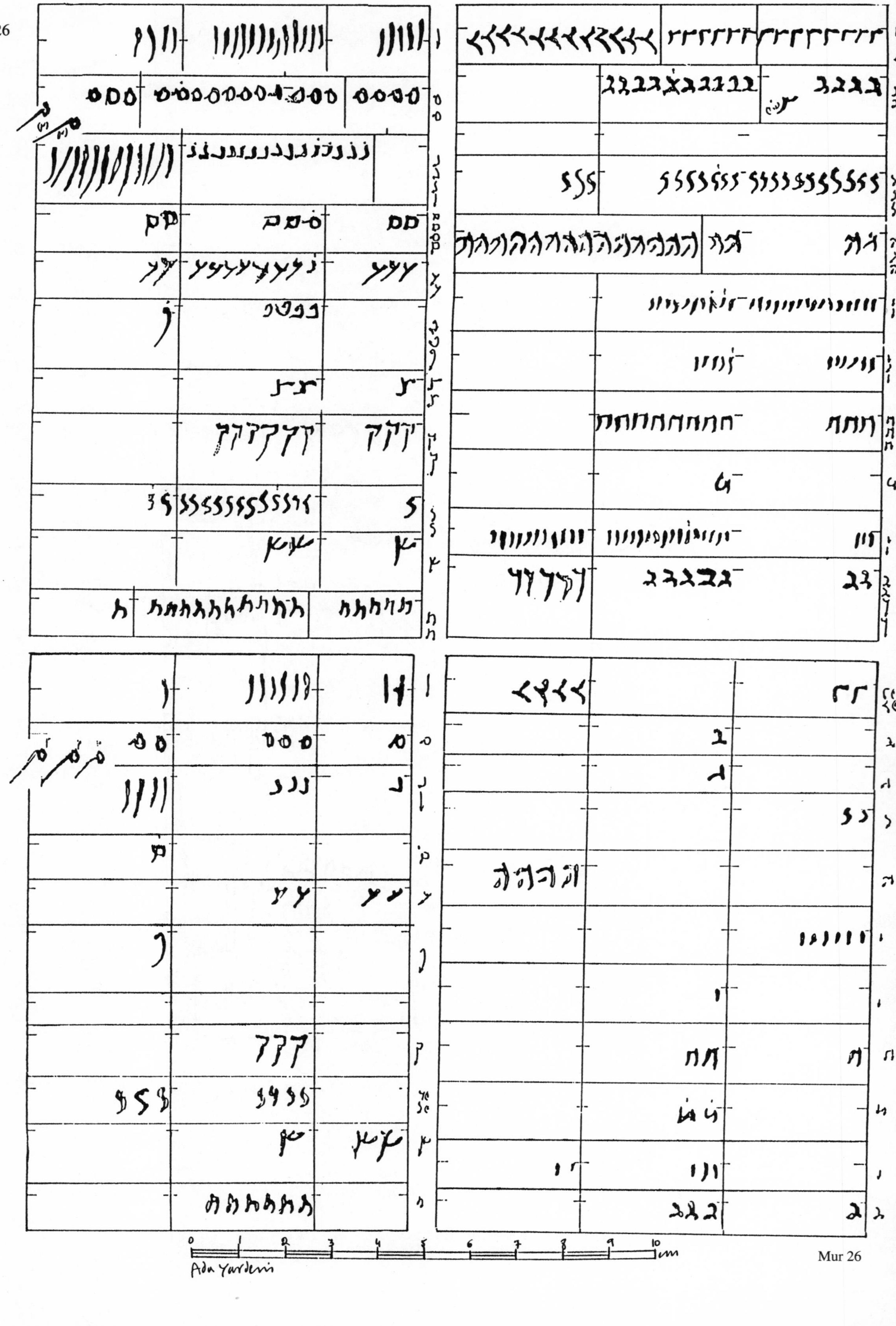

Mur 26

Fig. 27

64

60

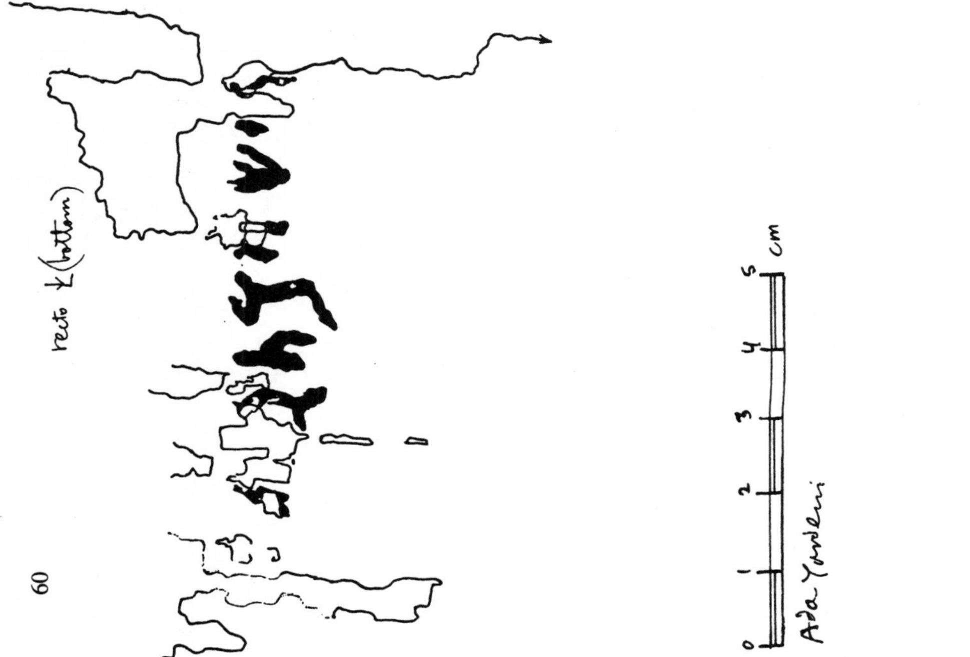

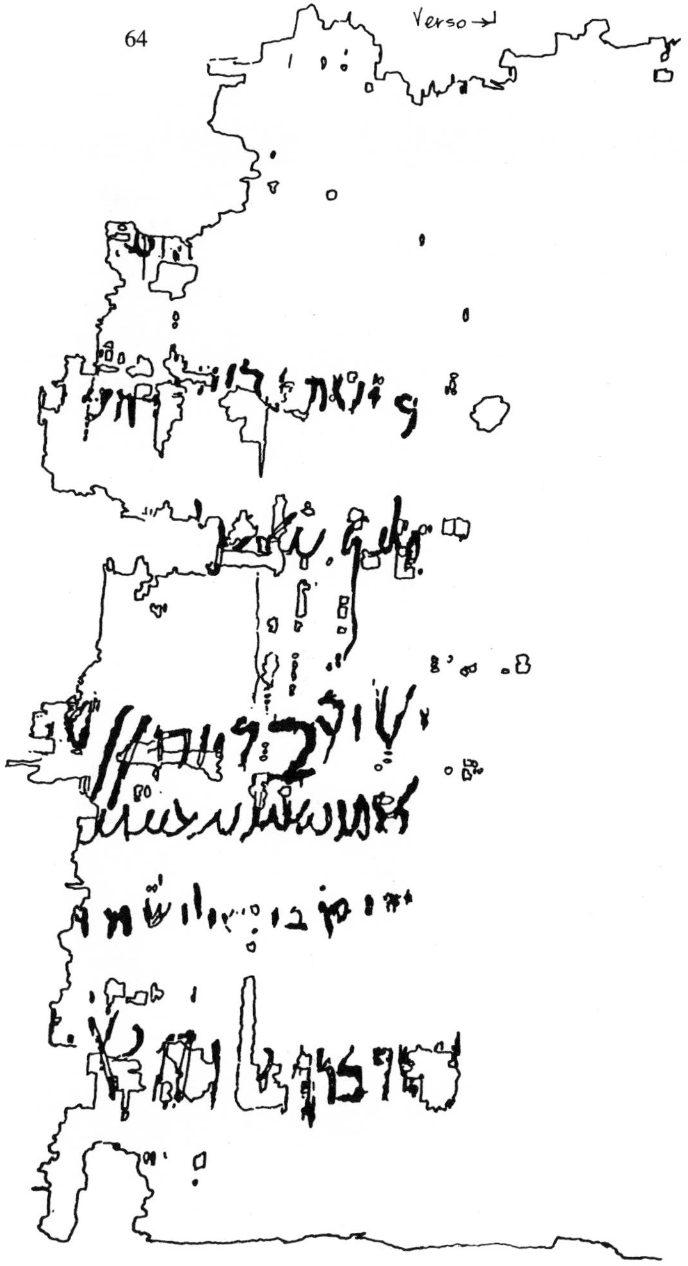

XḤev/ Se 60 (Mus. Inv. 866)
XḤev/ Se 64 (Mus. Inv. 869)

Fig. 28

342

343

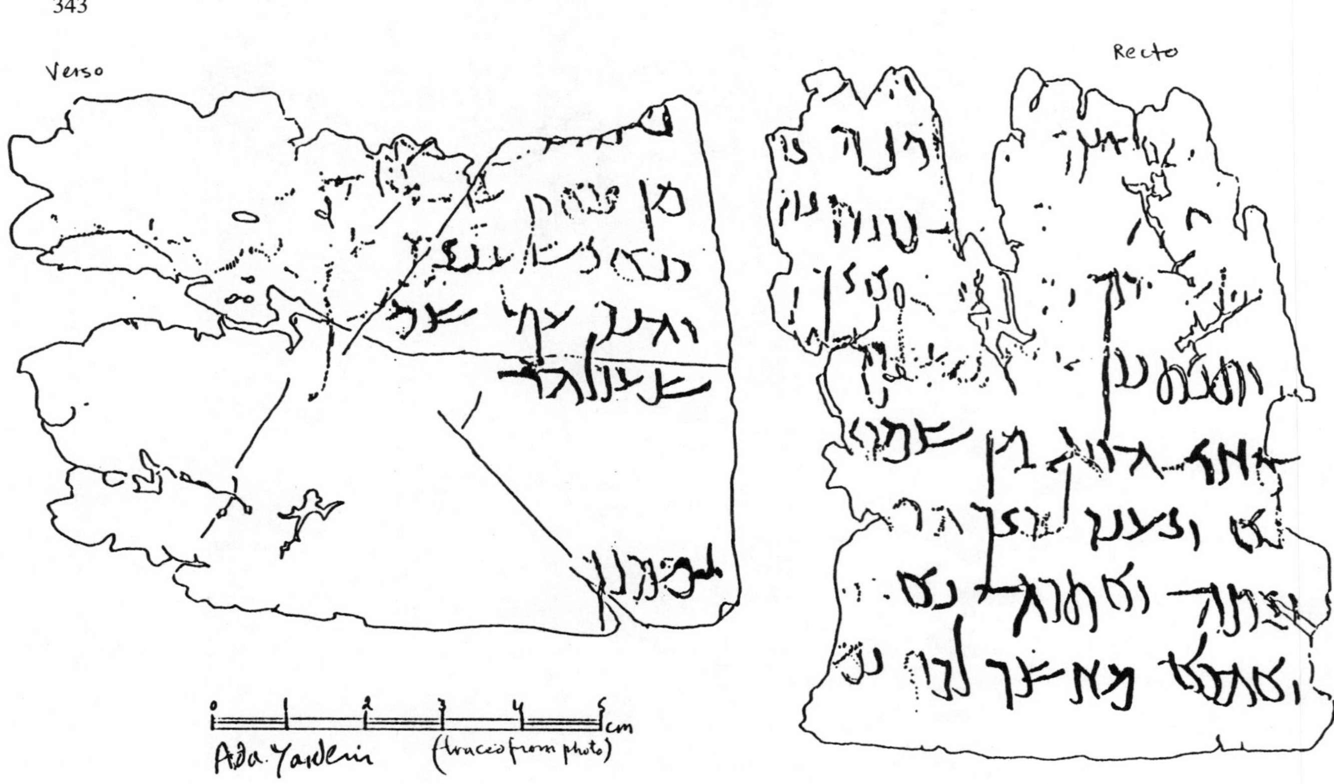

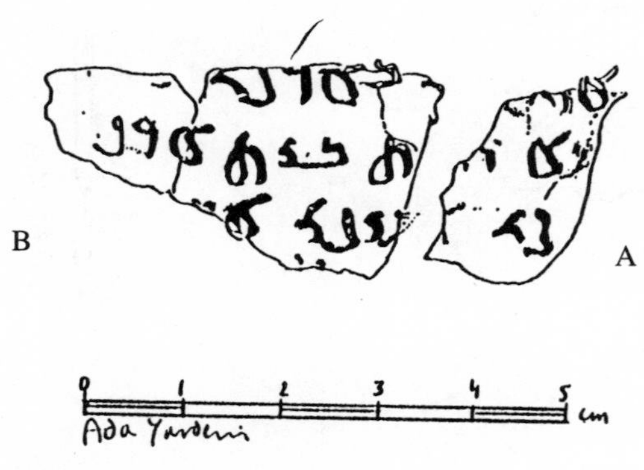

4Q342 (Mus. Inv. 602)
4Q343 (Mus. Inv. 601)

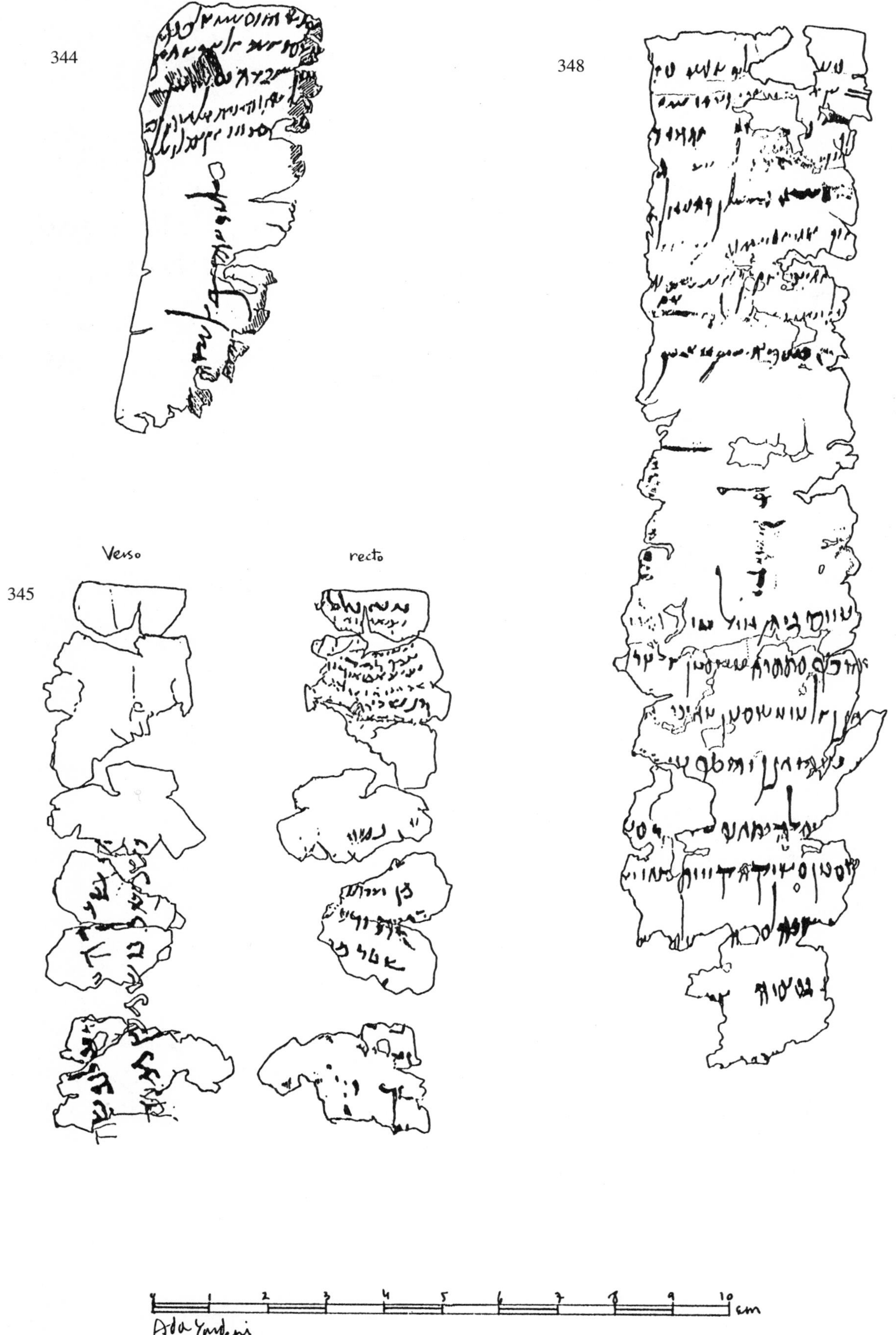

4Q344, 345, 348 (Mus. Inv. 602)

Fig. 30

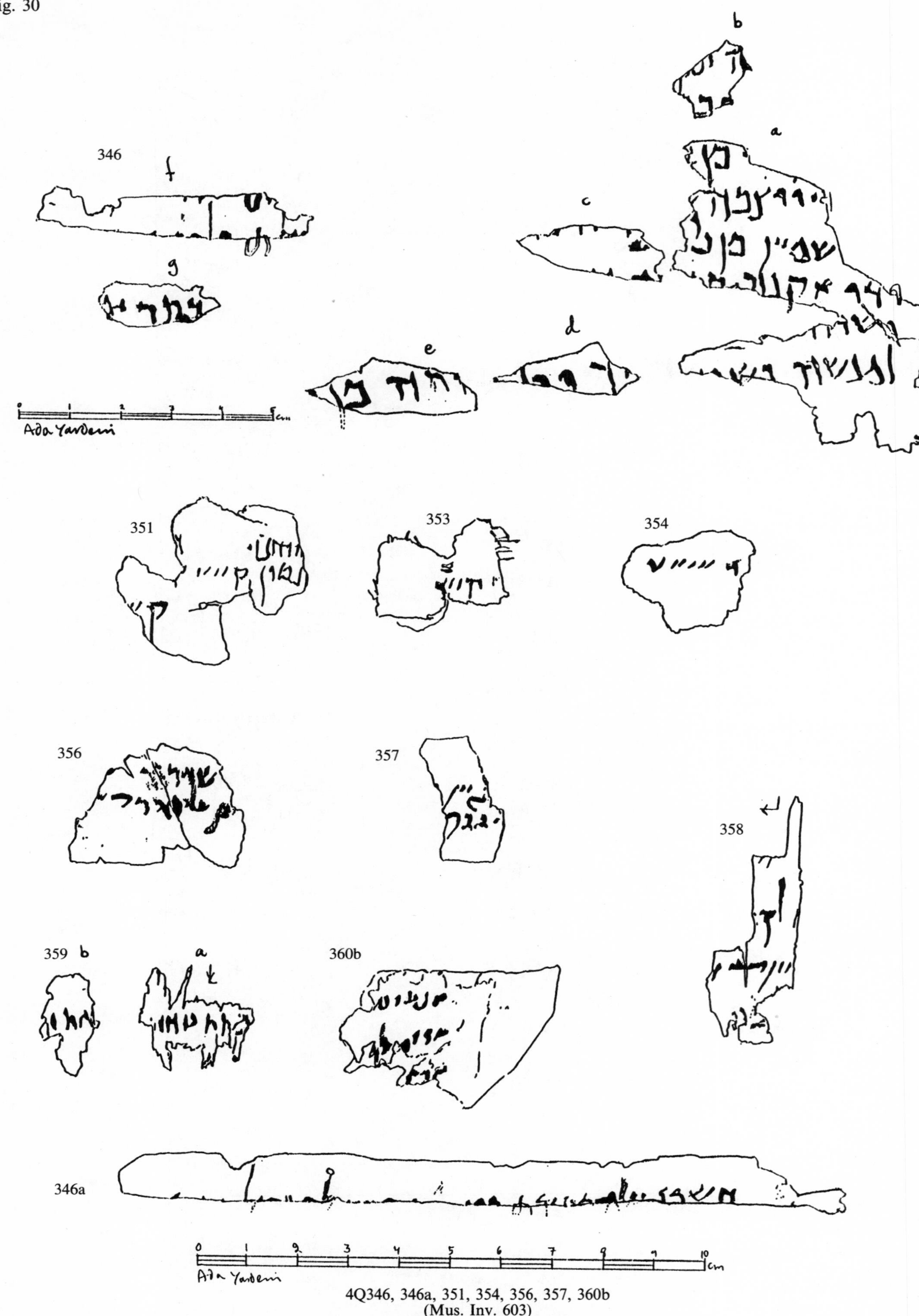

4Q346, 346a, 351, 354, 356, 357, 360b
(Mus. Inv. 603)
4Q353, 358, 359 (Mus. Inv. 184)

Fig. 31

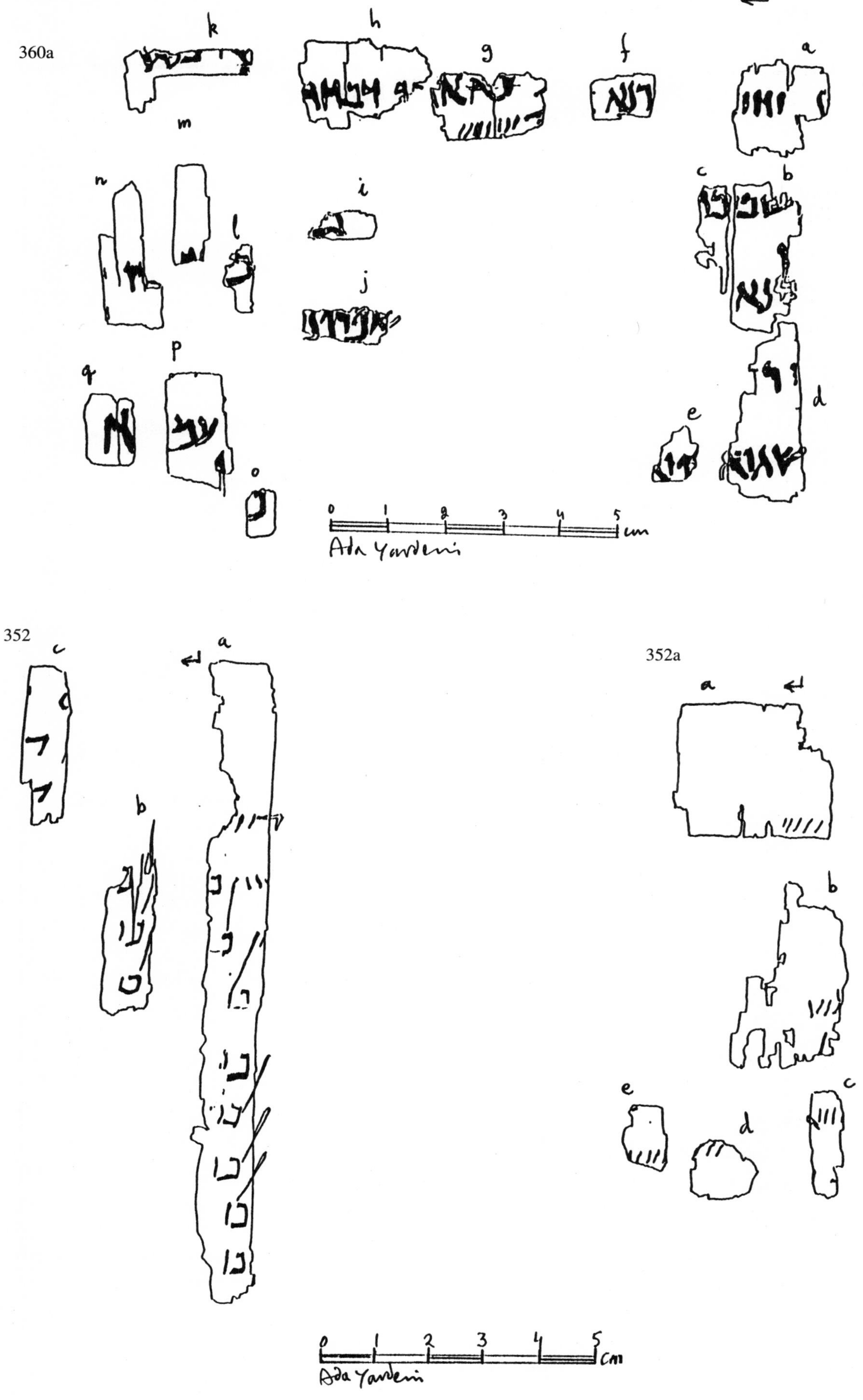

4Q352, 352a, 360a, (Mus. Inv. 184)

Fig. 32

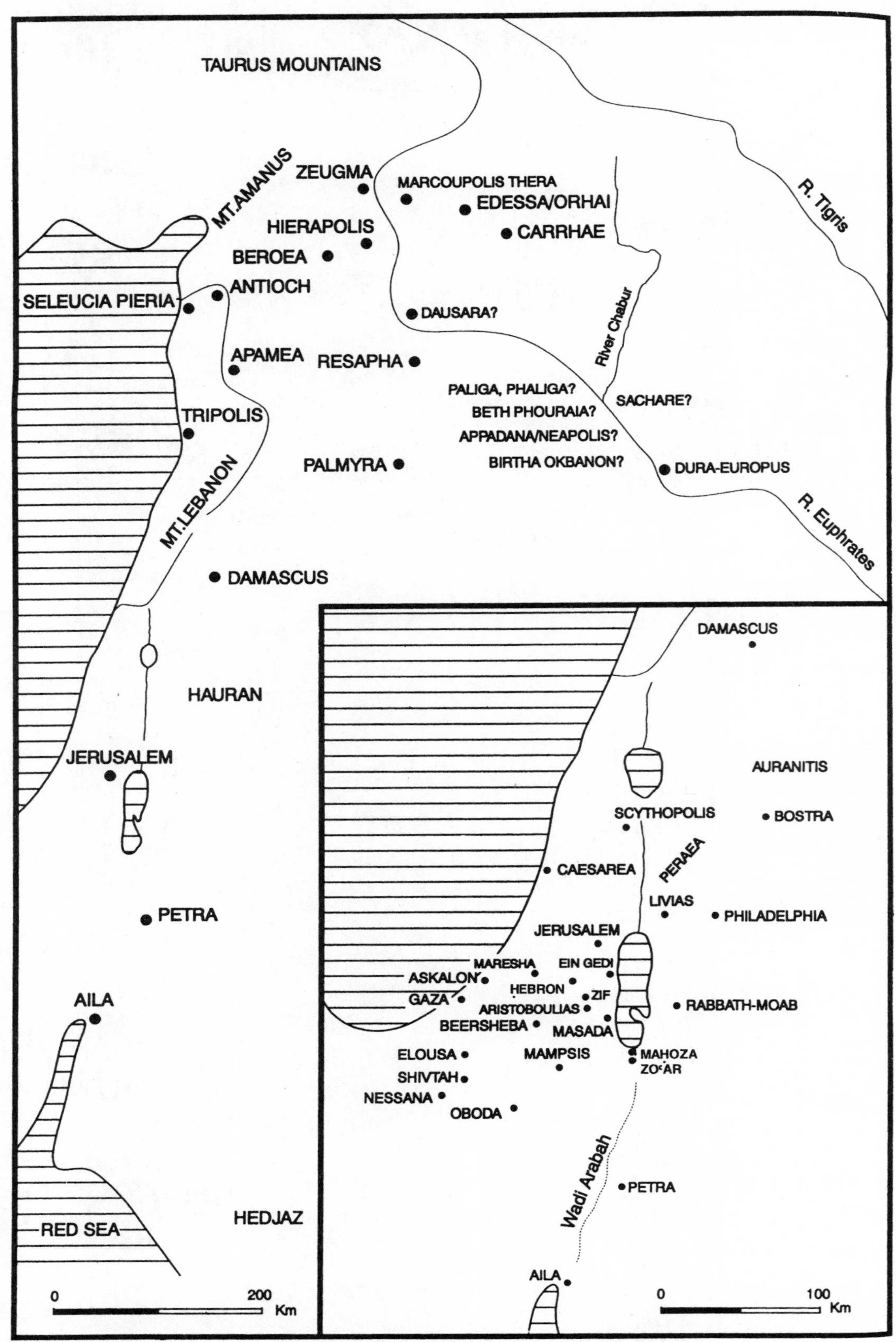

THE ROMAN NEAR EAST
Sites Mentioned in Documents
(Copied with permission from: H. M. Cotton, W. E. H. Cockle, and F. B. G. Millar, 'The Papyrology of the Roman Near East: A Survey', *JRS* [1995] 216)

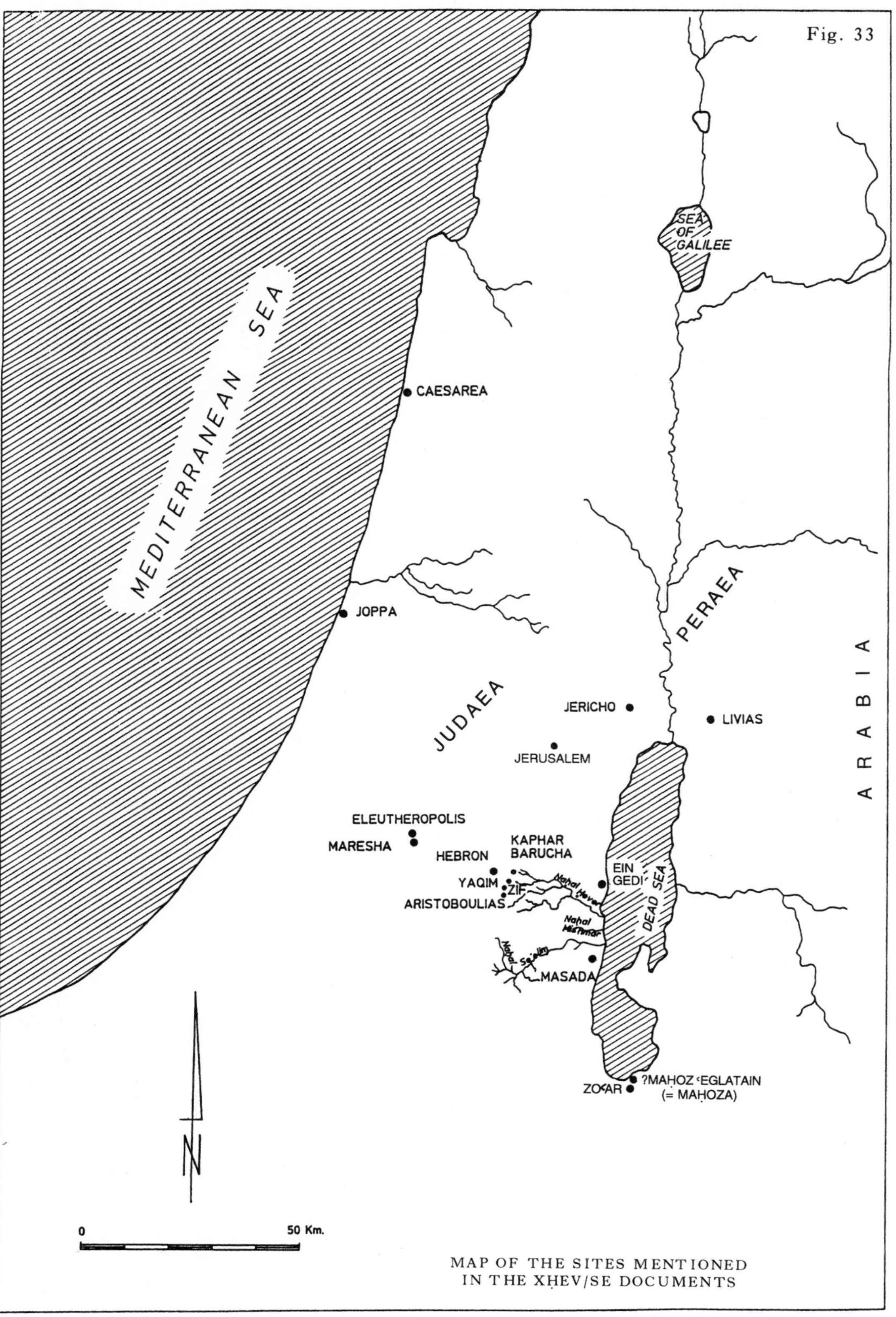

MAP OF THE SITES MENTIONED
IN THE XḤEV/SE DOCUMENTS

recto

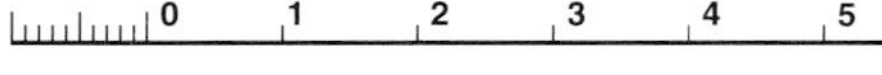

verso

7. XḤev/Se Deed of Sale A ar (134 or 135 CE)
IAA 440115(r), 449726(v); Mus. Inv. 889

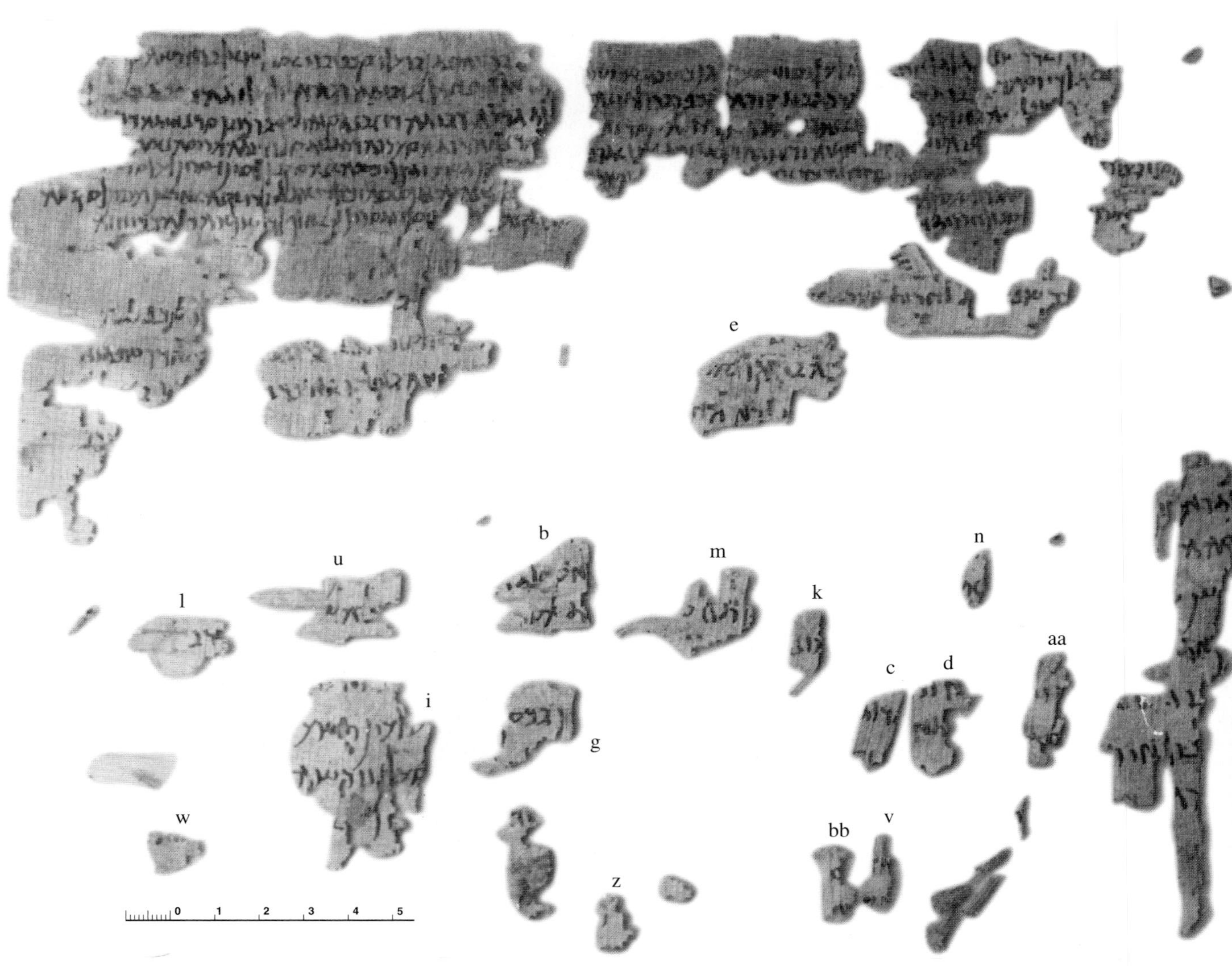

8. XḤev/Se papDeed of Sale B ar and heb (135 CE)
Mus. Inv. 533
Photograph: Yardeni

8a. XḤev/Se papDeed of Sale C ar (134 or 135 CE)
SHR 72–560; Mus. Inv. 651

d
e
b

c

a

recto

9. XḤev/Se papDeed of Sale D ar
IAA 445123; Mus. Inv. 543

PLATE V

verso

d

verso

9. XḤev/Se papDeed of Sale D ar
IAA 445125: Mus. Inv. 543

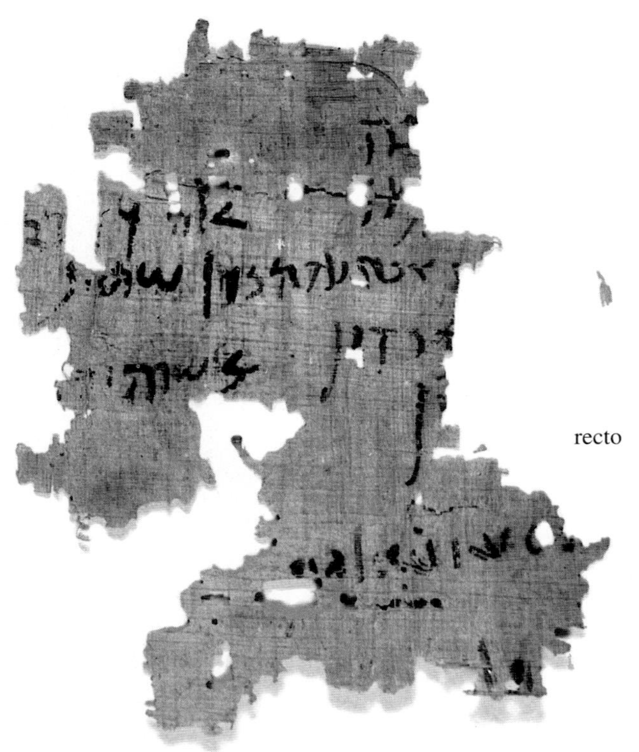

recto

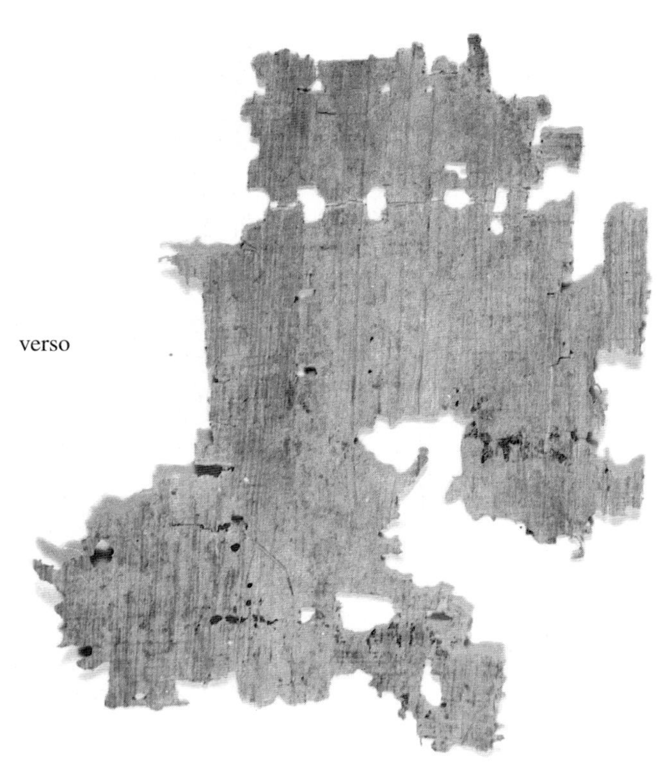

verso

9a. XḤev/Se papUnclassified Fragment A ar
IAA 445123(r), 445125(v); Mus. Inv. 543

verso 10 recto

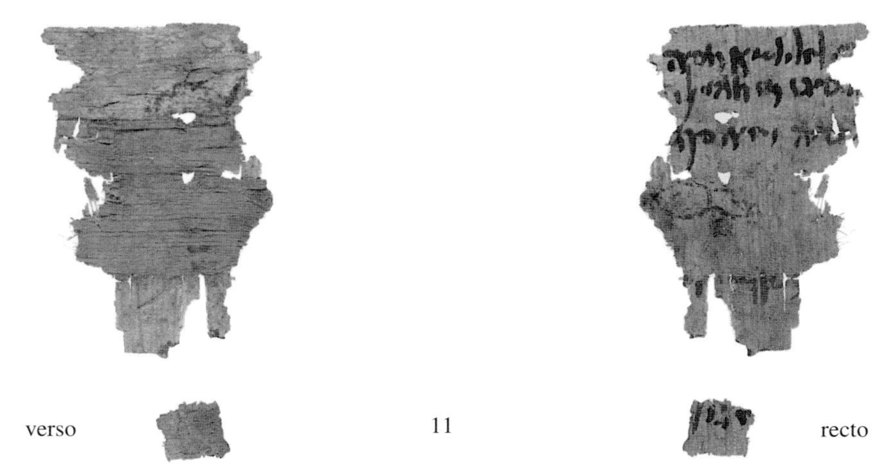

verso 11 recto

10. XḤev/Se papReceipt for Payment of a Fine? ar
11. XḤev/Se papMarriage Contract? ar
IAA 449734(r), 449737(v); Mus. Inv. 736

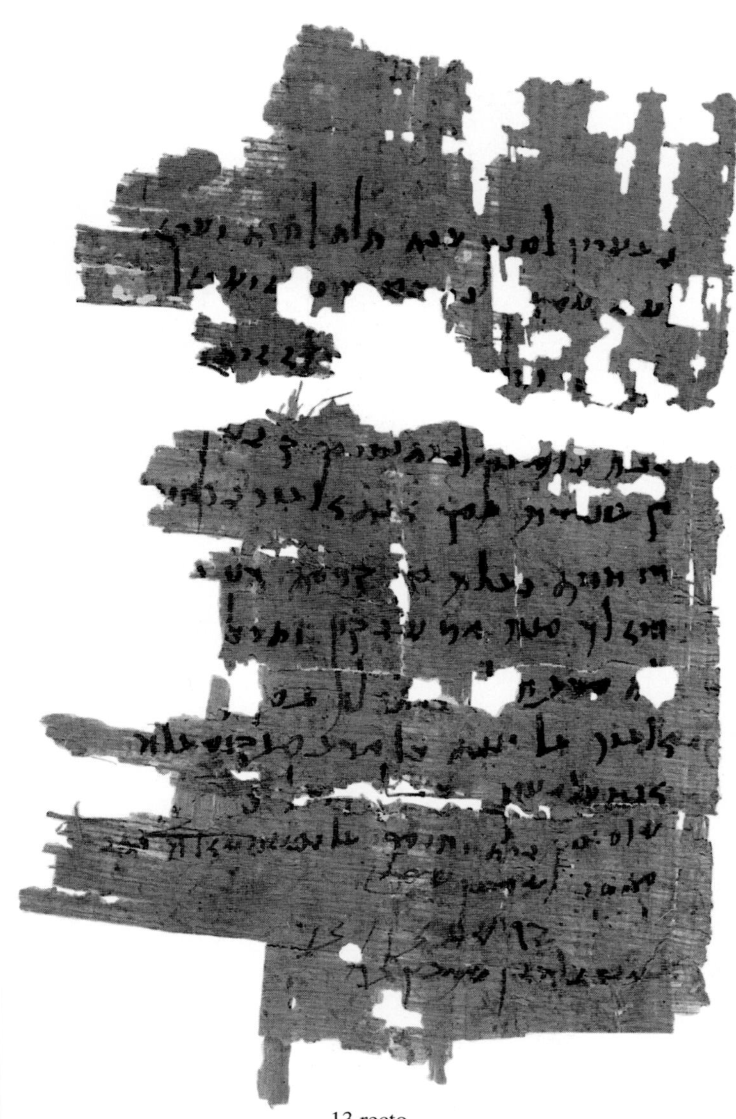

13 recto

12 recto

12. XḤev/Se papReceipt for Dates ar (131 CE)
13. XḤev/Se papWaiver of Claims? ar (134 or 135 CE)
IAA 449734; Mus. Inv. 736

12 verso

13 verso

12. XḤev/Se papReceipt for Dates ar (131 CE)
13. XḤev/Se papWaiver of Claims? ar (134 or 135 CE)
IAA 449737; Mus. Inv. 736

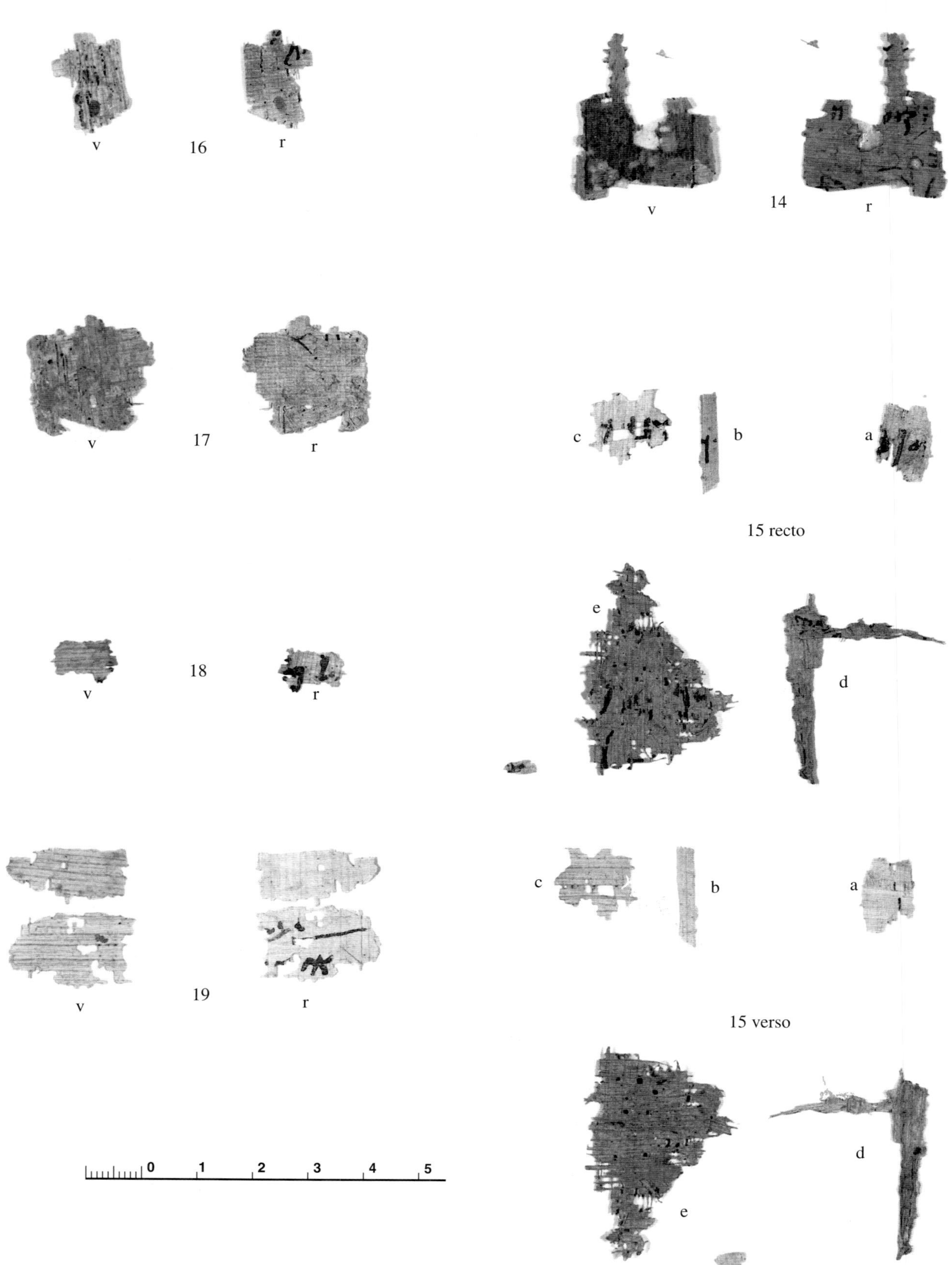

14. XḤev/Se Fragment of a Deed ar?
15–19. XḤev/Se papUnclassified Fragments B–F
IAA 445132(r), 445134(v); Mus. Inv. 542

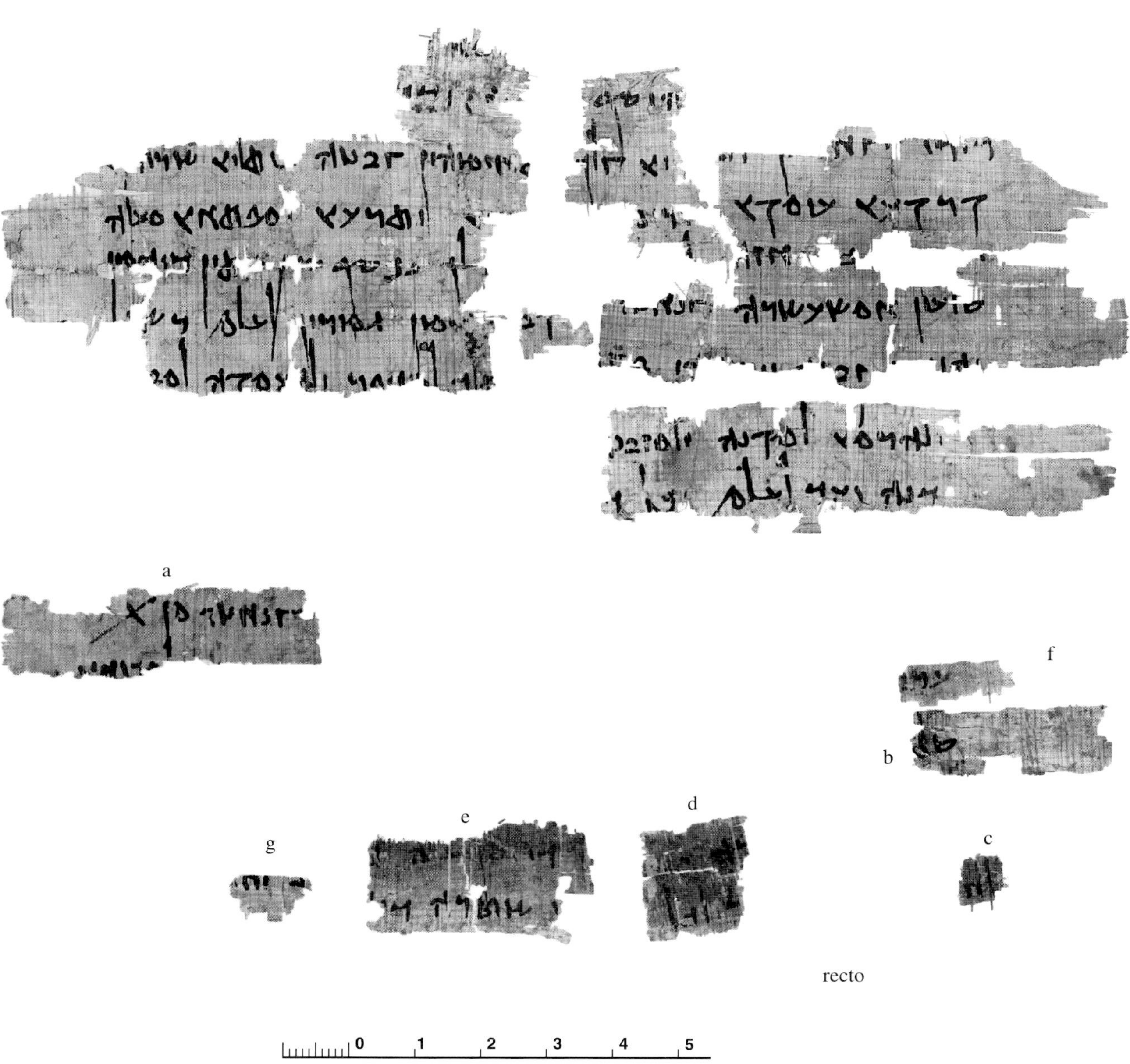

21. XḤev/Se papDeed of Sale E ar
IAA 449728; Mus. Inv. 527

21. XḤev/Se papDeed of Sale E ar
IAA 449729; Mus. Inv. 527

recto

22. XHev/Se papDeed of Sale F? ar
IAA 541677(r), 541678(v); Mus. Inv. 735

verso

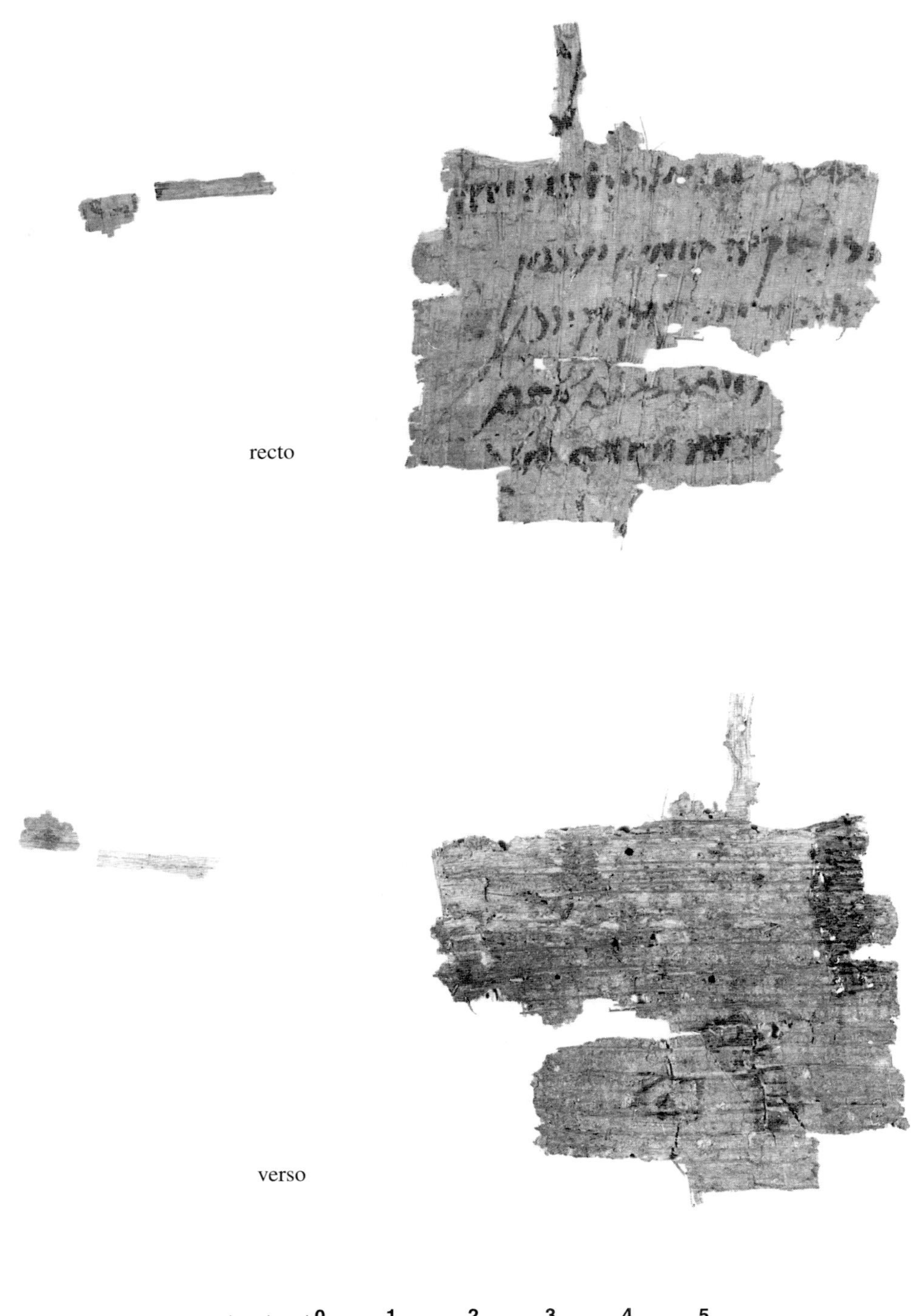

recto

verso

23. XḤev/Se papDeed of Sale G ar
IAA 445119(r), 445122(v); Mus. Inv. 536

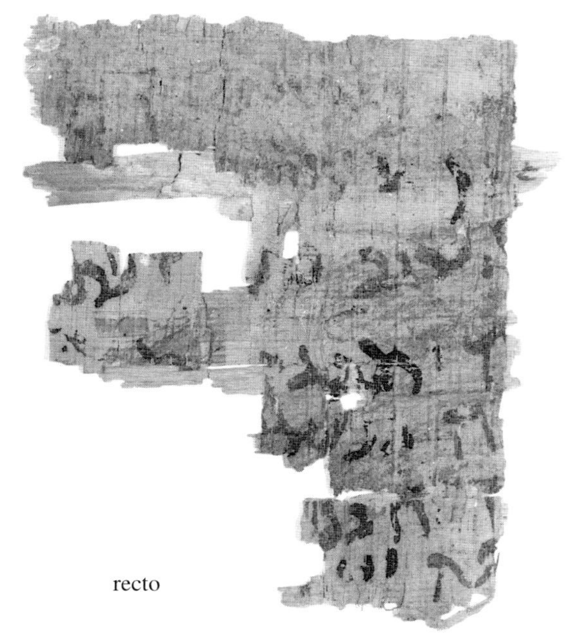

recto

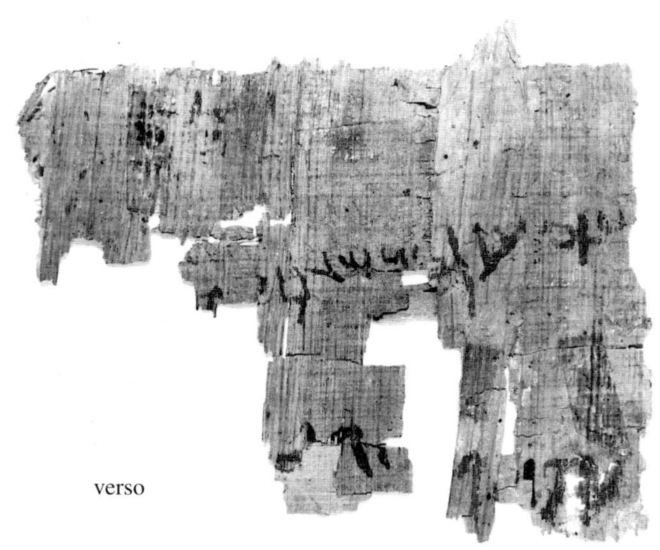

verso

24. XḤev/Se papDeed A ar
IAA 445119(r), 445122(v); Mus. Inv. 536

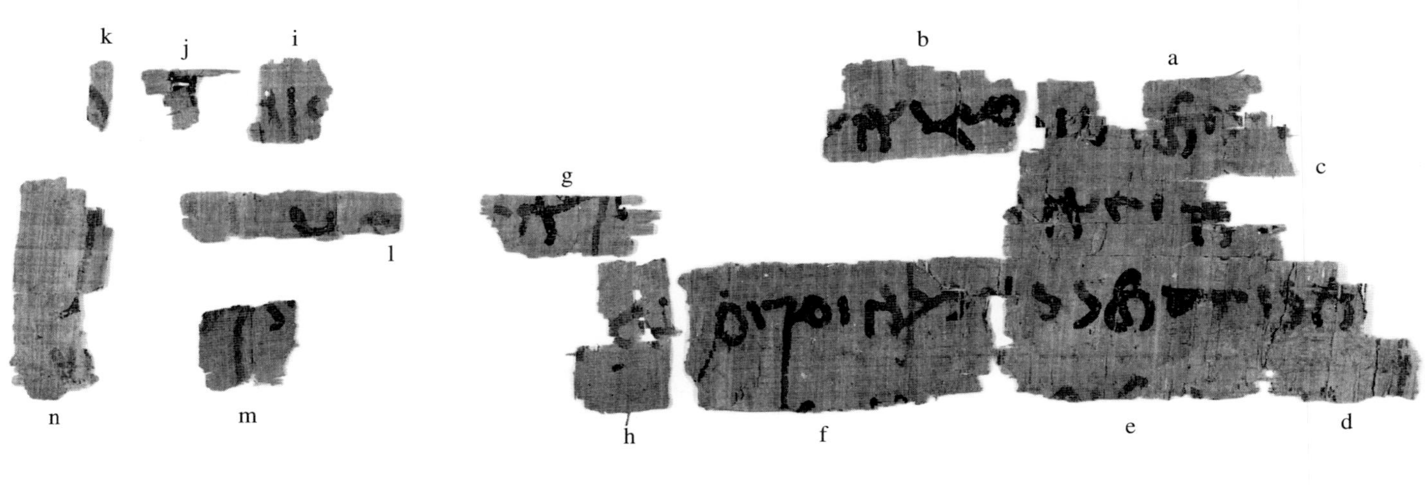

recto

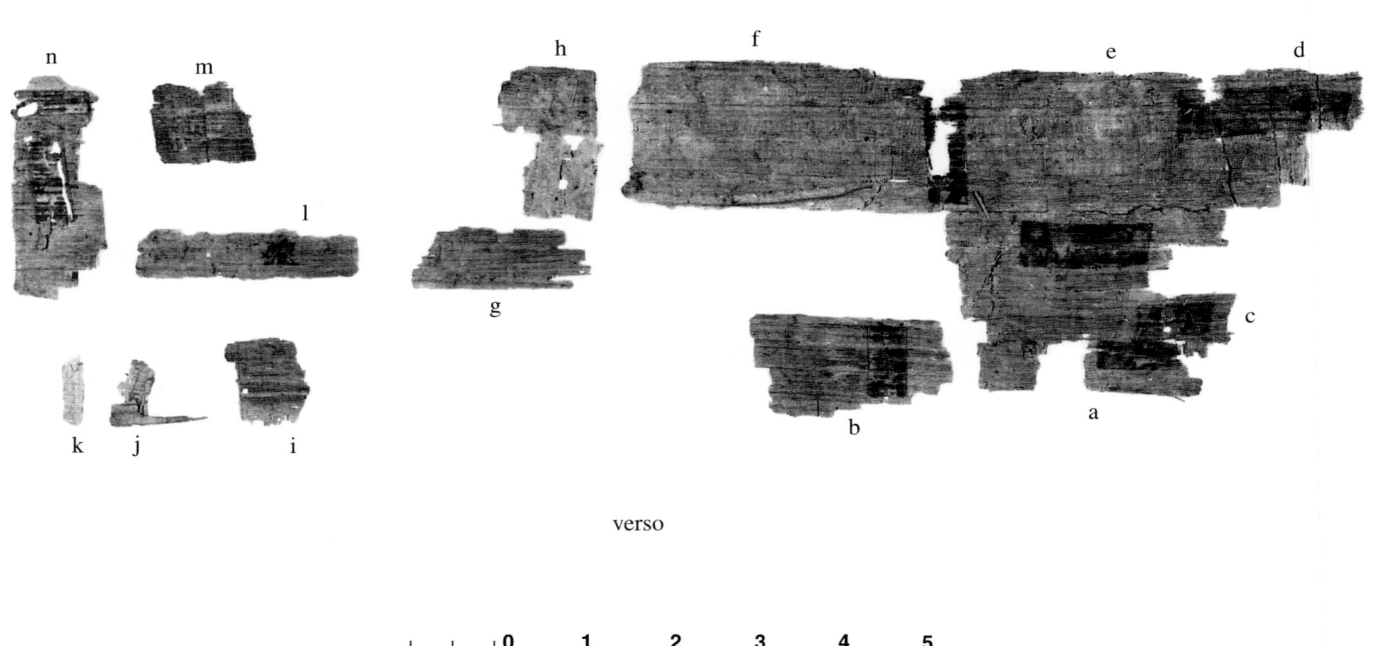

verso

24a. XḤev/Se papDeed B ar
IAA 445119(r), 445122(v); Mus. Inv. 536

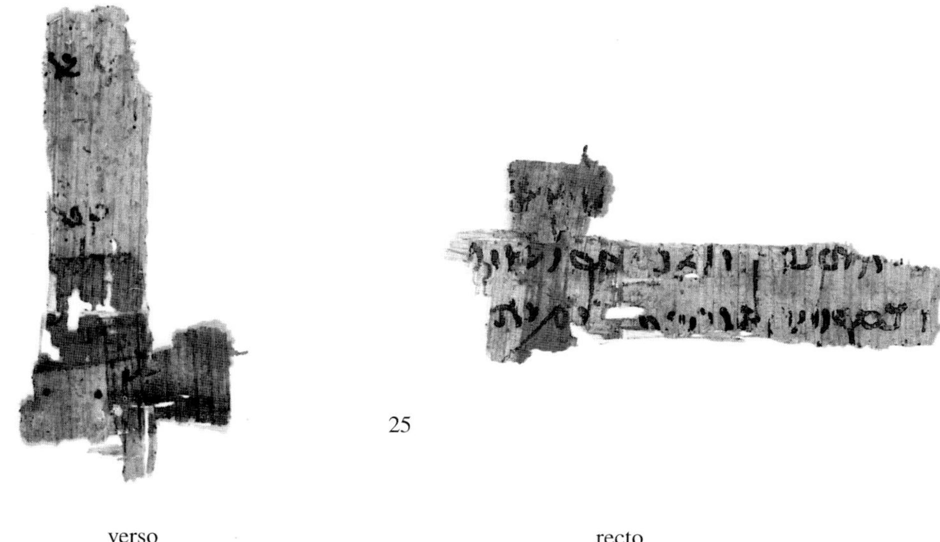

25

verso recto

26

25. XḤev/Se papDeed C ar
26. XḤev/Se papText Dealing with Deposits and Barley ar
IAA 445132(r), 445134(v); Mus. Inv. 542

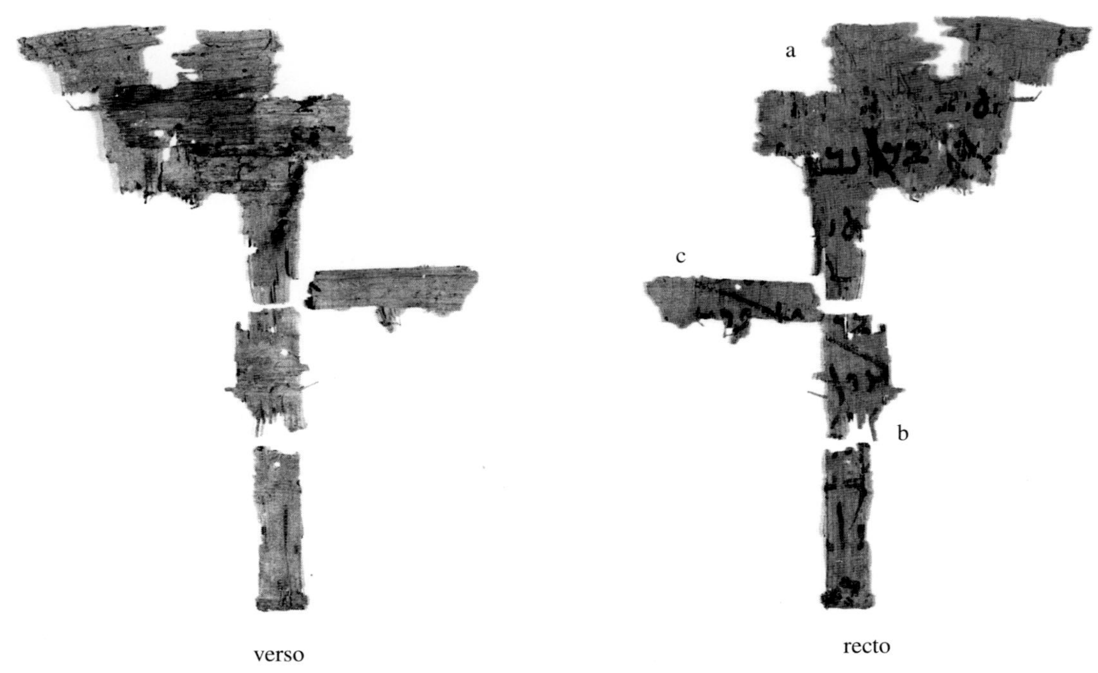

27. XḤev/Se papDeed D ar
IAA 445132(r), 445134(v); Mus. Inv. 542

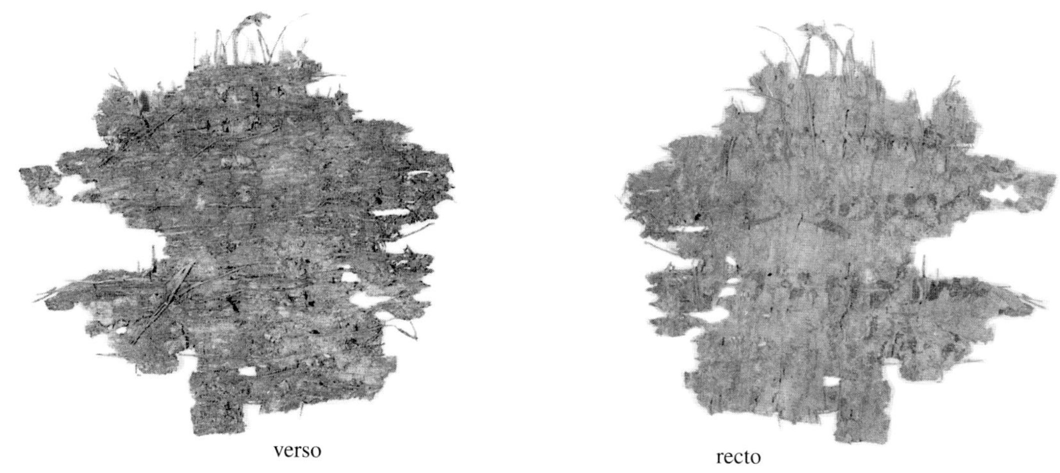

28. XḤev/Se papUnclassified Fragment G ar
IAA 445119(r), 445122(v); Mus. Inv. 536

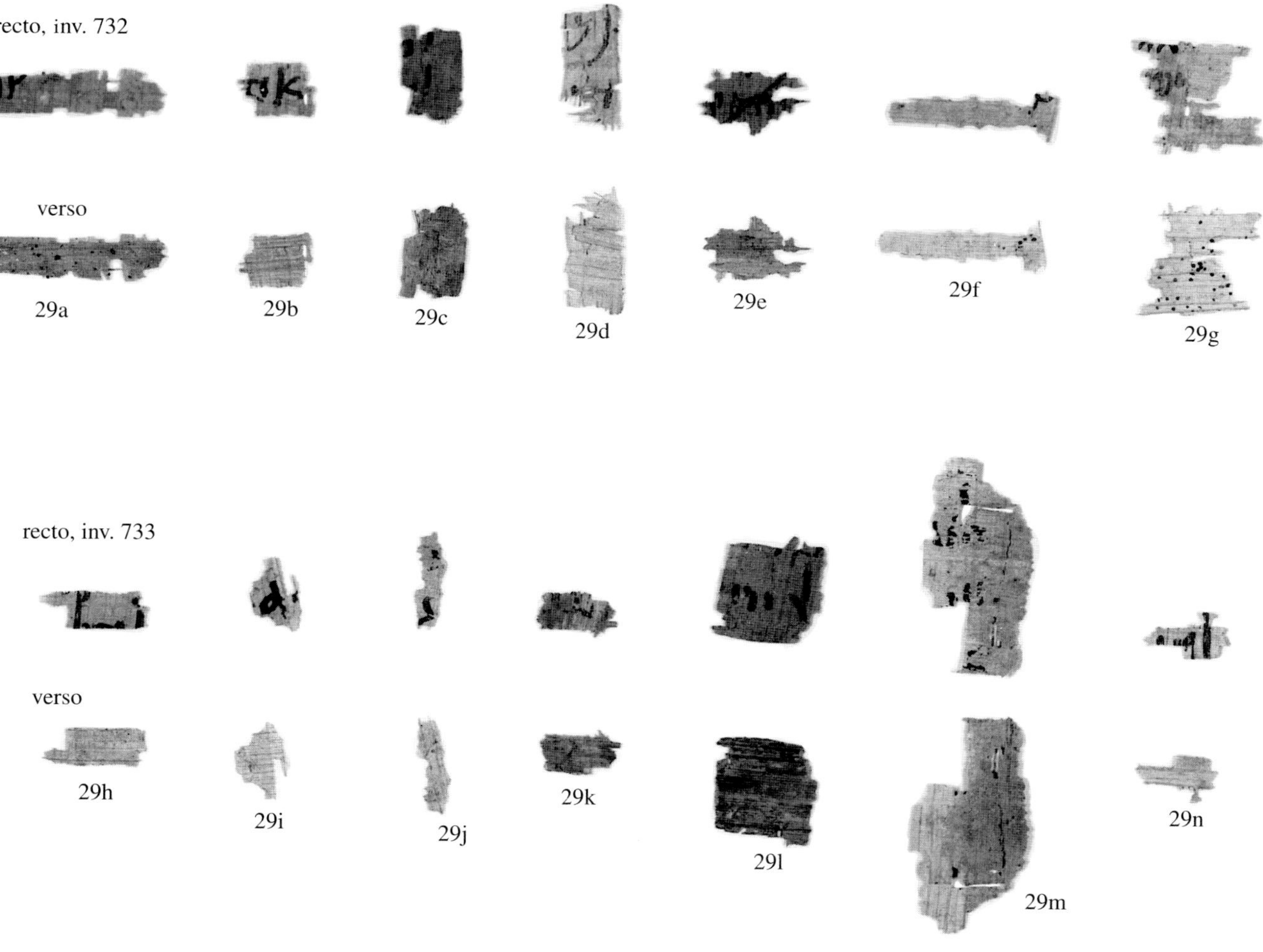

29. XḤev/Se papUnclassified Fragments H
IAA 445132(r), 445134(v); Mus. Inv. 732, 733

verso

recto

30. XHev/Se papLetter to Shim'on ben Kosibah
IAA 445132(r), 445134(v); Mus. Inv. 542

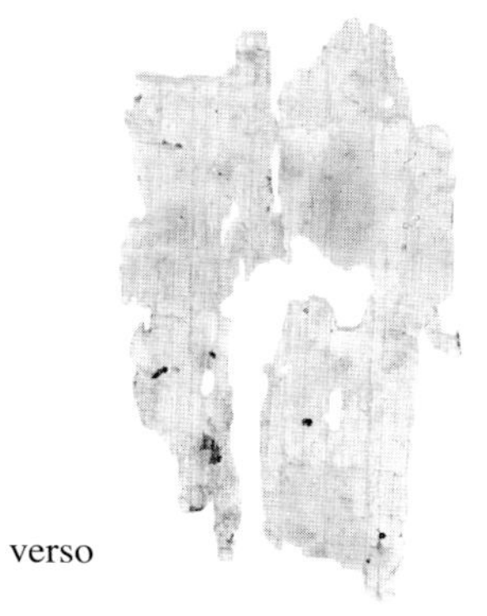

verso

recto

31. XḤev/Se papDeed E ar
IAA 445135(r), 445137(v); Mus. Inv. 734

verso

recto

4Q347
(43.406)
(Inv. 184)

32. XḤev/Se papDeed F (+ 4Q**347**) ar
IAA 445135(r), 445137(v); Mus. Inv. 734
PAM 43.406; Mus. Inv. 184

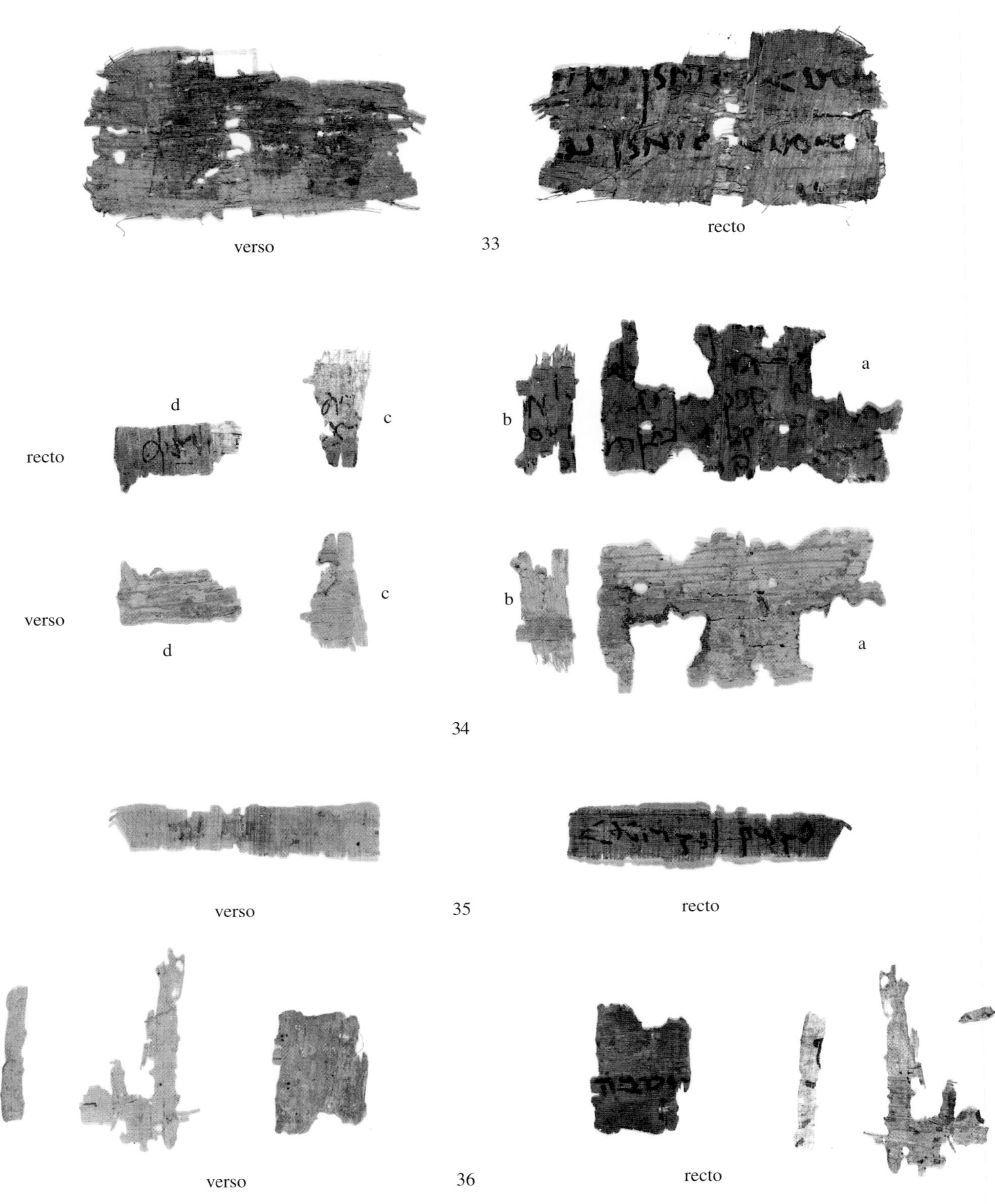

33. XḤev/Se papUnclassified Fragment I ar
34. XḤev/Se papDeed G ar
35. XḤev/Se papUnclassified Fragment J ar
36. XḤev/Se papUnclassified Fragment K
IAA 445135(r); 445137(v); Mus. Inv. 734

37. XḤev/Se papDeed H ar?
IAA 445135(r); Mus. Inv. 734

verso

0 1 2 3 4 5

37. XḤev/Se papDeed H ar?
IAA 445137(v); Mus. Inv. 734

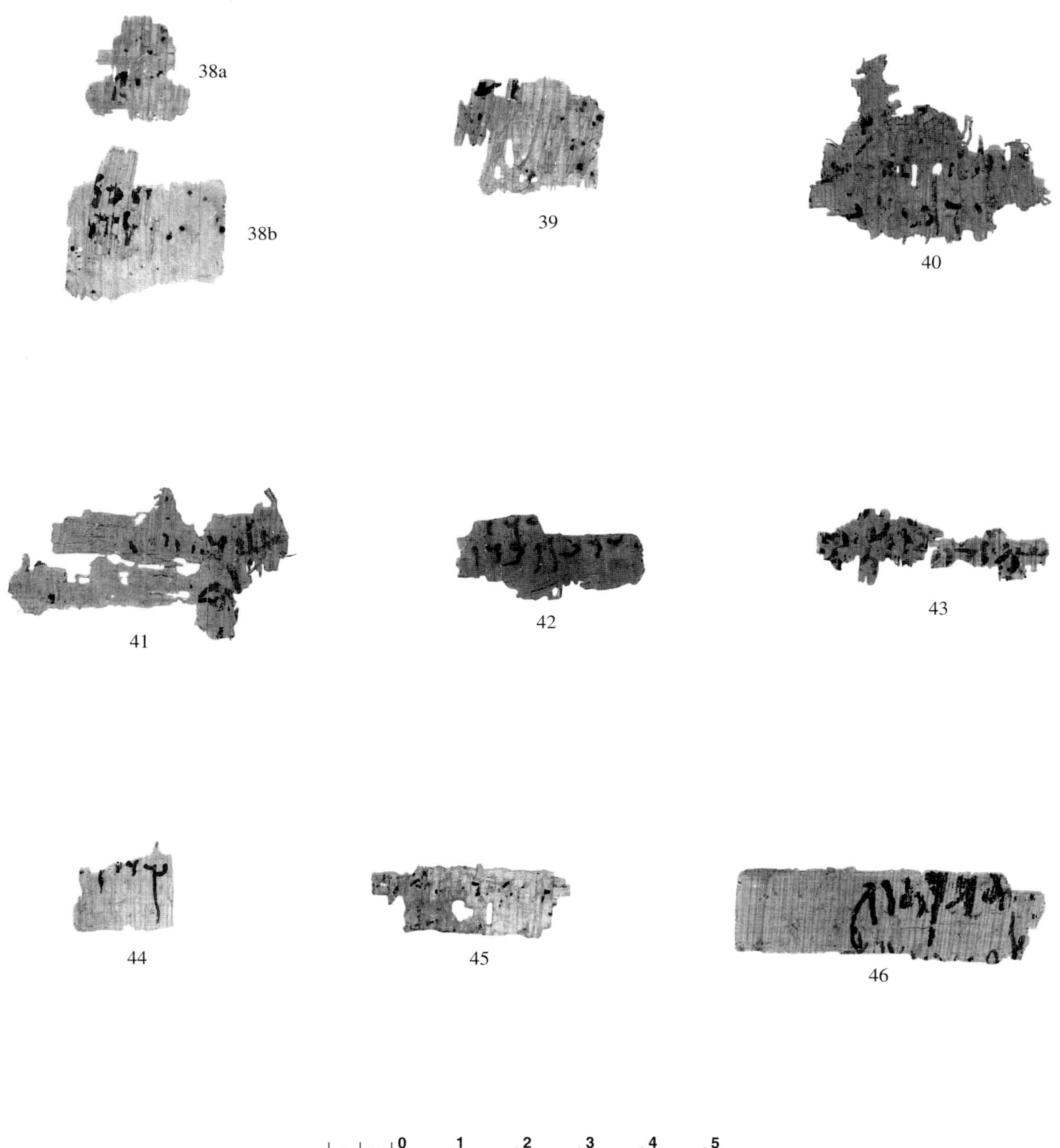

38–46. XḤev/Se papUnclassified Fragments L–T
IAA 445127; Mus. Inv. 865

47a–47h. XḤev/Se papUnclassified Fragments U–BB
IAA 445127; Mus. Inv. 865

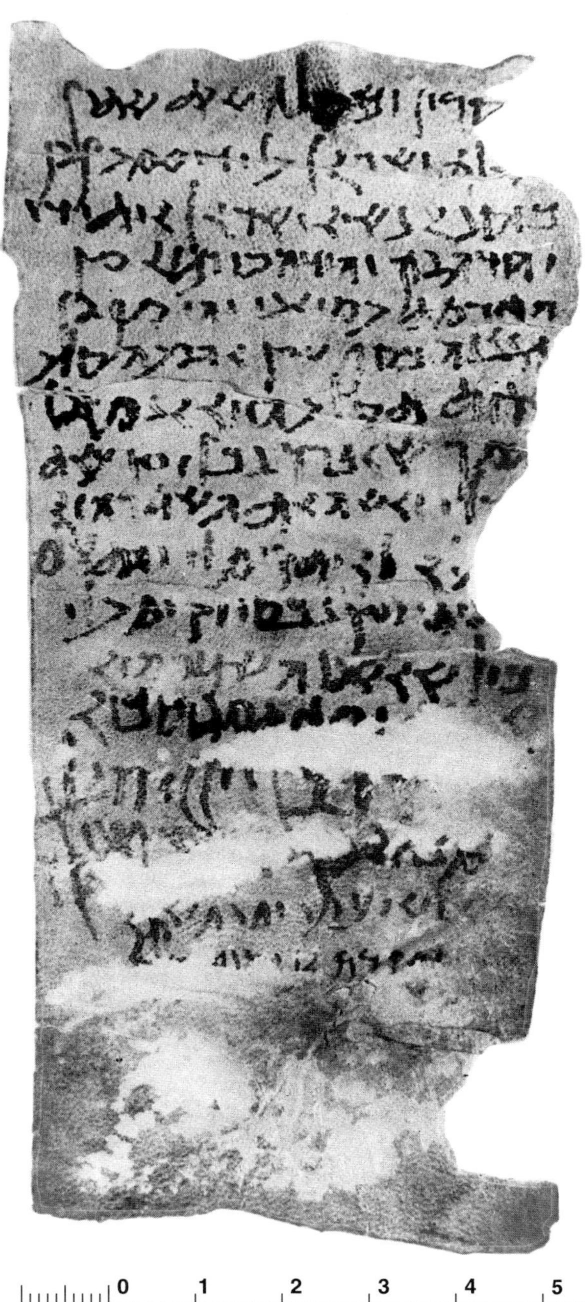

49. XHev/Se Promissory Note (133 CE)
Private Collection

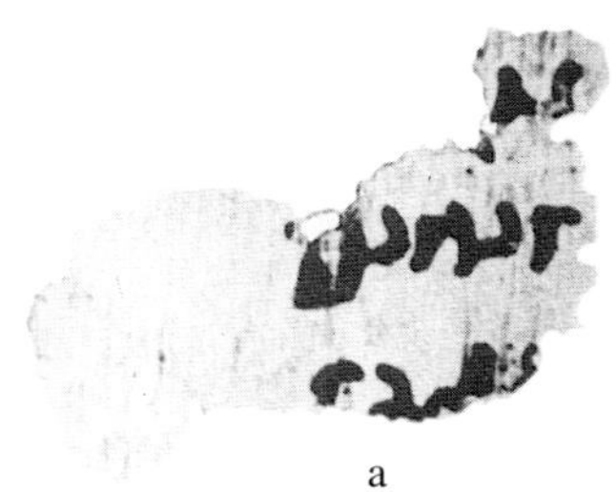

a

Mur 26
(Inv. 725)

recto

d

XḤev/Se 50
(BṪS 7163)

recto

0 1 2 3 4 5

XḤev/Se **50** + Mur **26**. papDeed of Sale H ar
Mus. Inv. 725; BTS 7163

Mur 26
(Inv. 725)

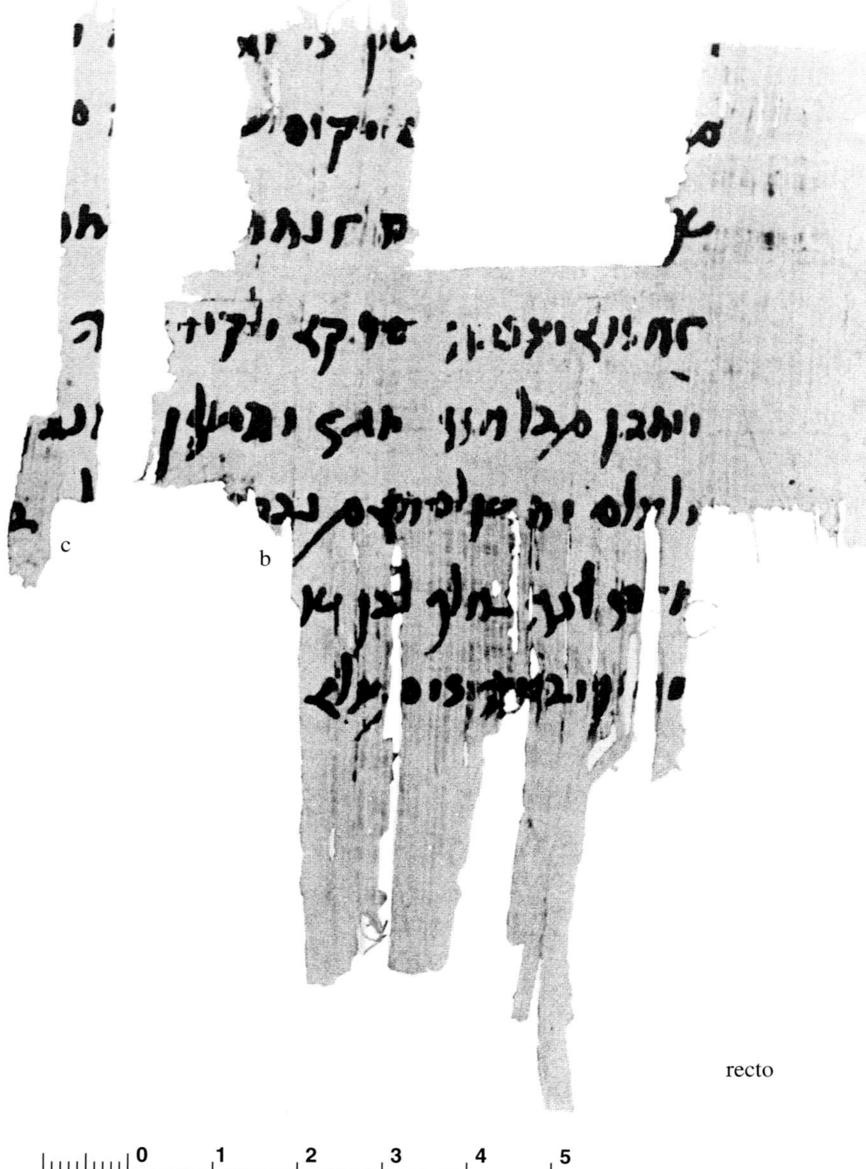

XḤev/Se **50** + Mur **26**. papDeed of Sale H ar
Mus. Inv. 725; BTS 7163

XḤev/Se 50, frg. d
(BTS 7163)

verso

Mur 26, frg. e
(553494)
(inv. 725)

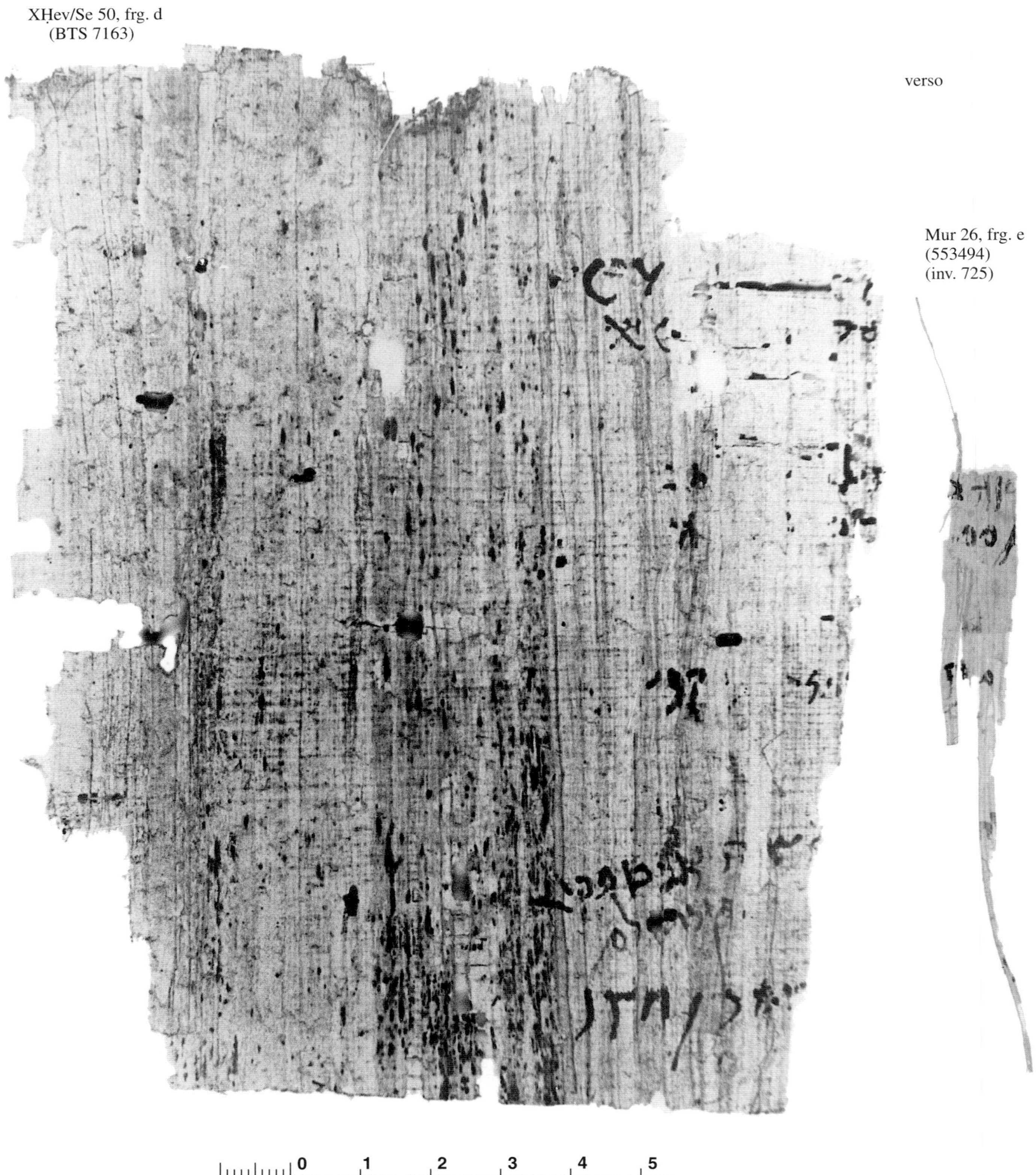

0 1 2 3 4 5

XḤev/Se **50** + Mur **26**. papDeed of Sale H ar
IAA 553494; Mus. Inv. 725; BTS 7163

(See Fig. 25 for a precise depiction of the relationship of frg. e to frg. d, which could not be illustrated here due to the differing scales of the photographs.)

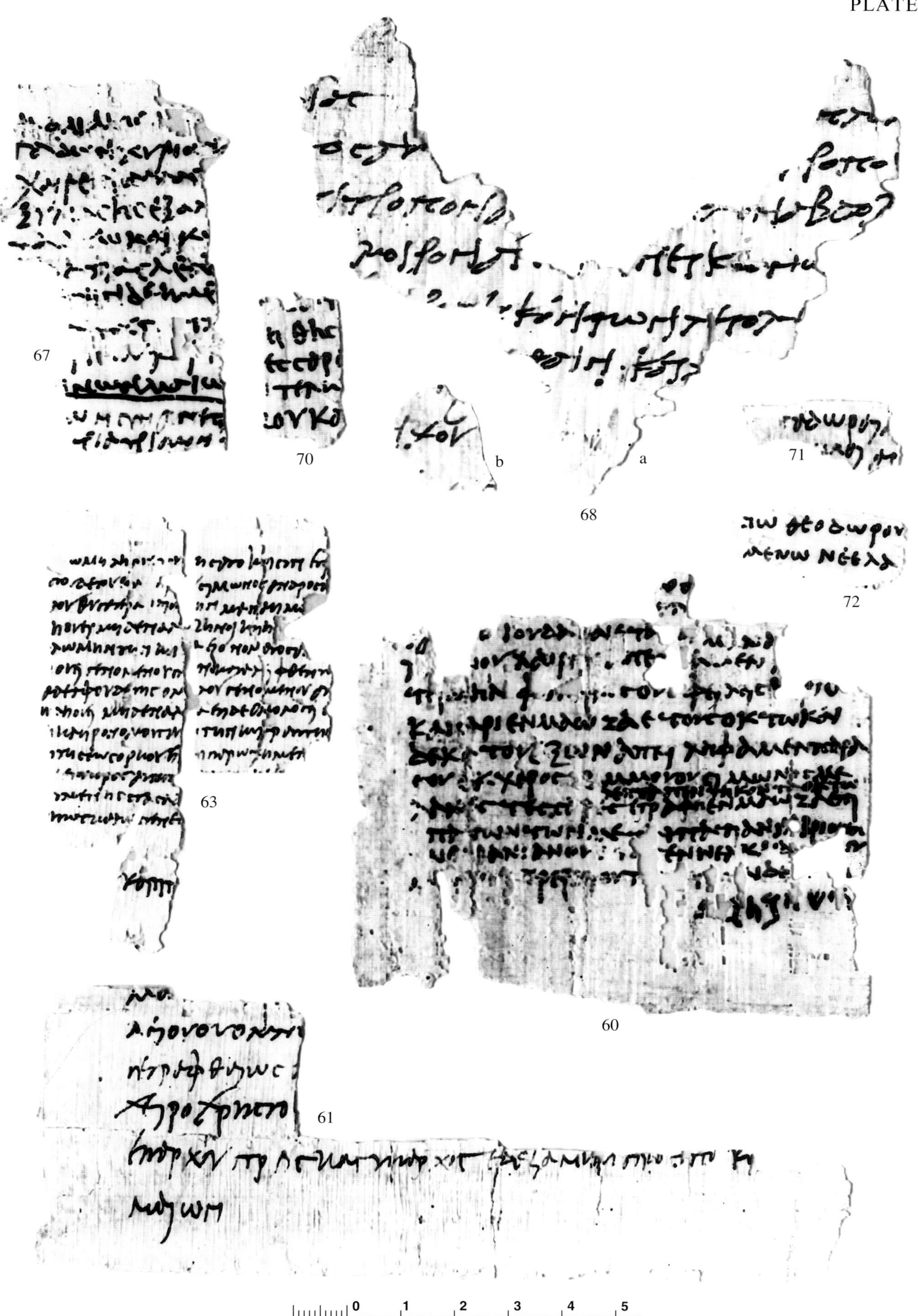

PAM 40.642; Mus. Inv. 866
(*olim* XḤev/Se Gr 5)

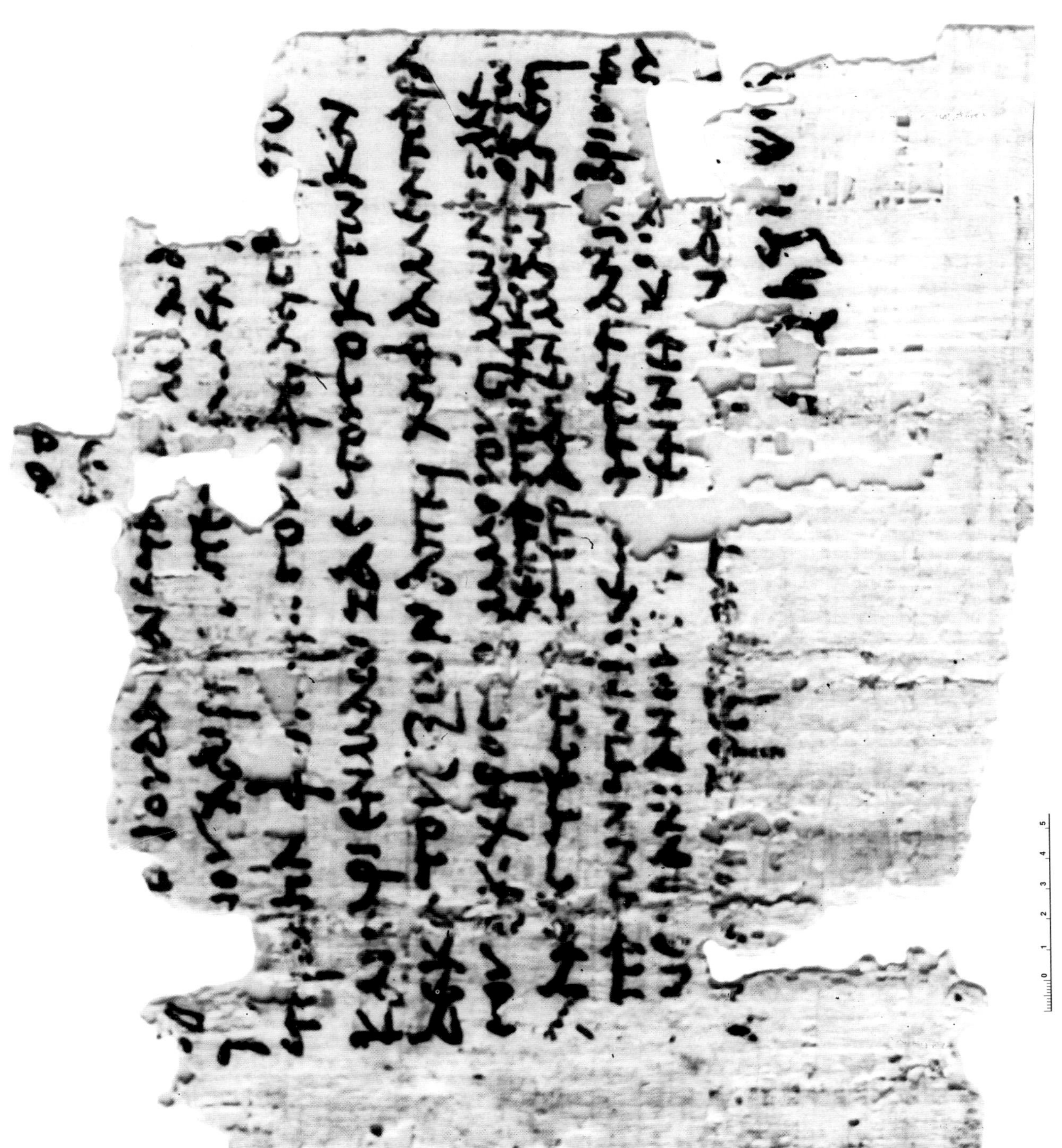

60. XḤev/Se papTax (or Rent) Receipt from Maḥoza gr
PAM 40.642; Mus. Inv. 866

a

b

0 1 2 3 4 5

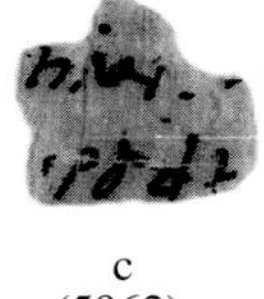

c
(5962)

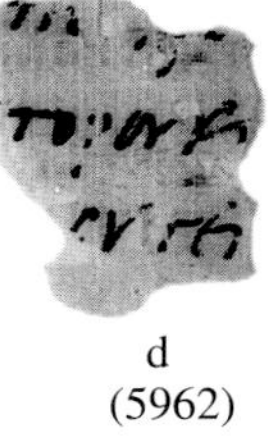

d
(5962)

61. XḤev/Se papConclusion to a Land Declaration gr
IAA 350224; SHR 5962; Mus. Inv. 866; SHR 3001

a

recto

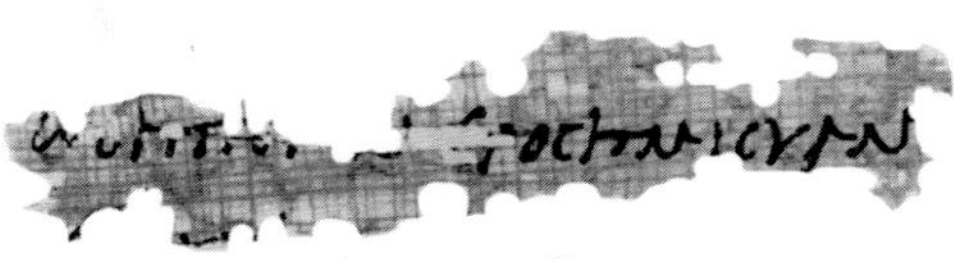

0 1 2 3 4 5

n

62. XḤev/Se papLand Declaration gr
IAA 475982; Mus. Inv. Rockefeller

b

0 1 2 3 4 5

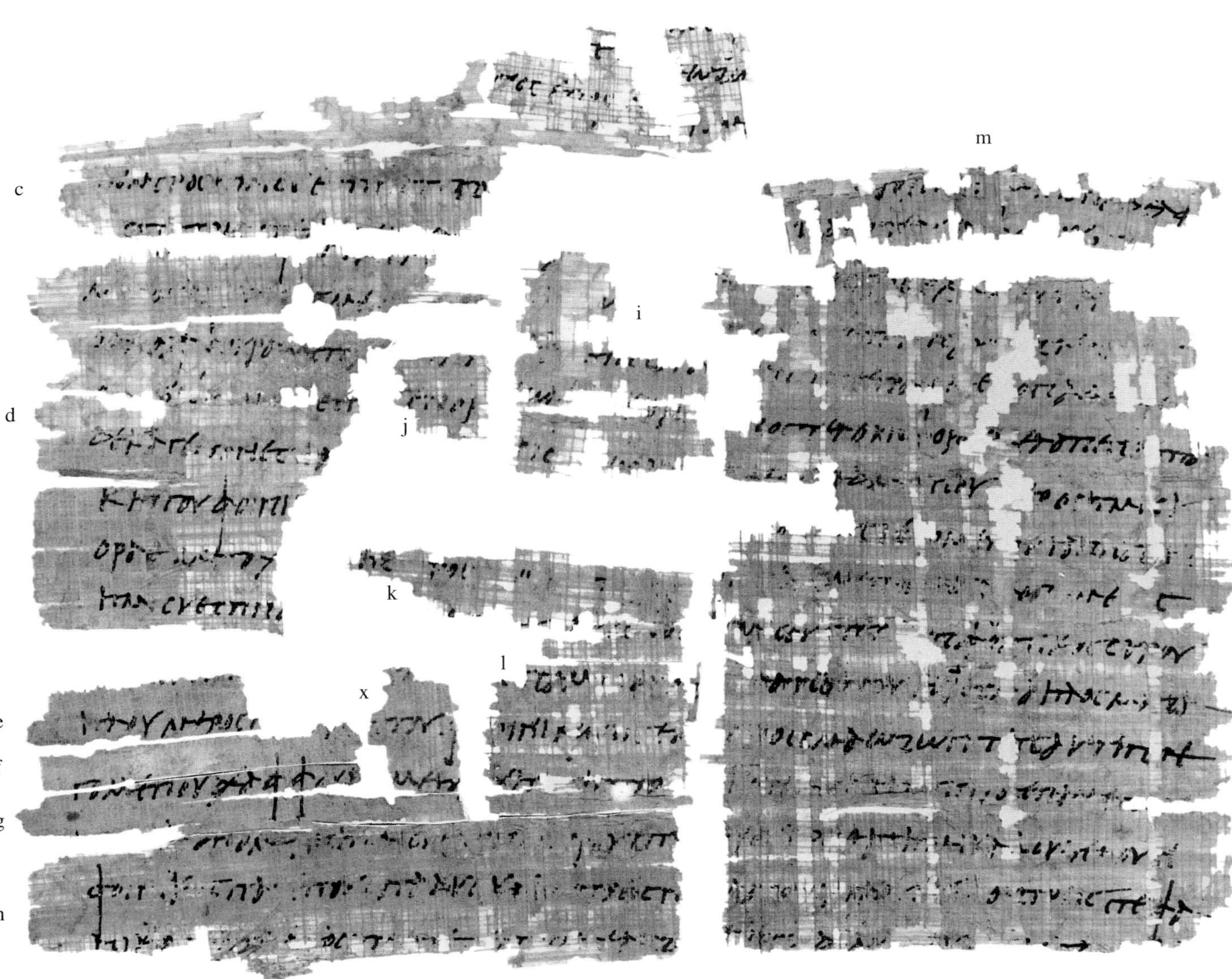

recto

62. XḤev/Se papLand Declaration gr
IAA 475980; Mus. Inv. Rockefeller

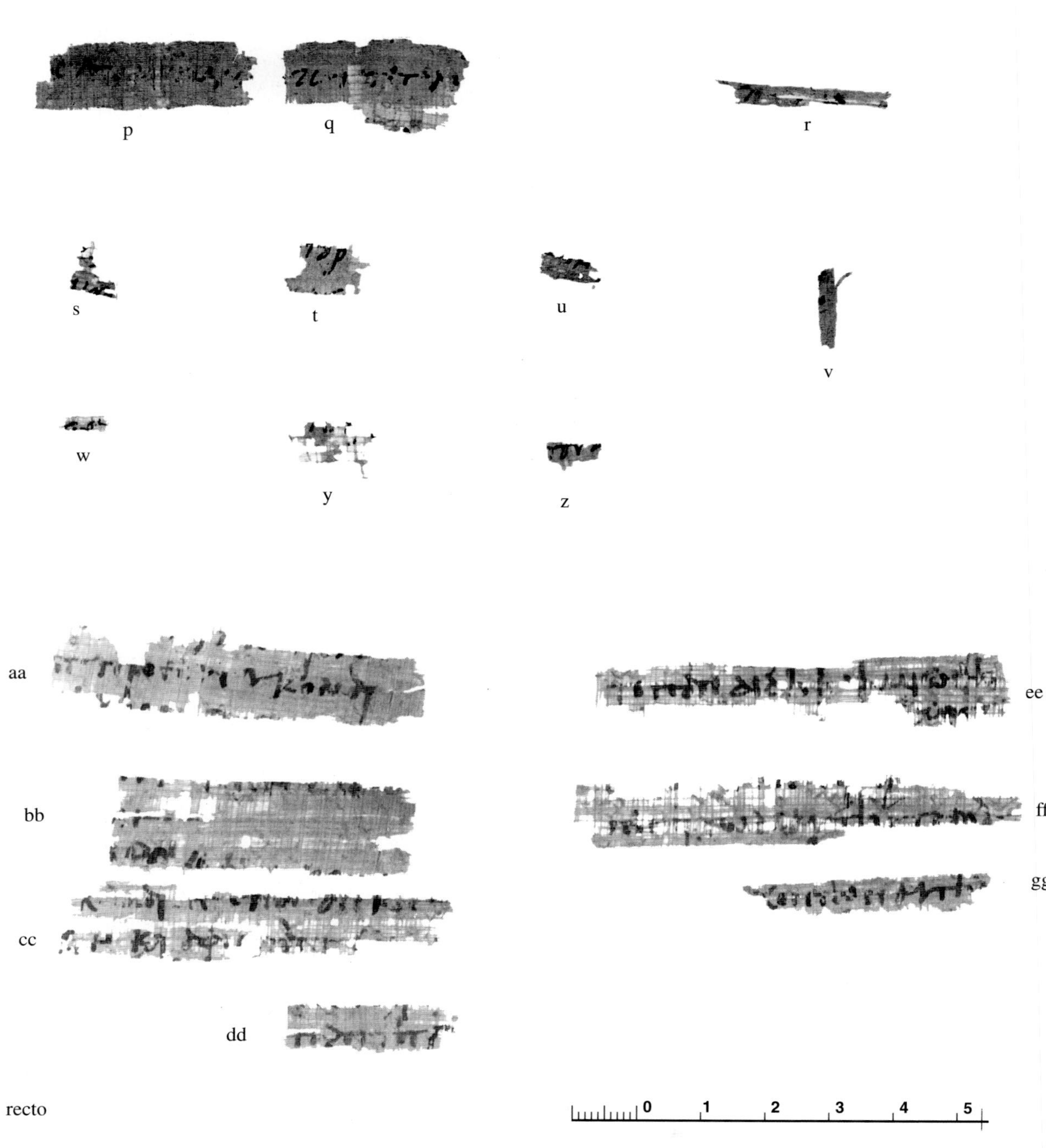

62. XḤev/Se papLand Declaration gr
Frgs. p–z, IAA 475980; Mus. Inv. Rockefeller
Frgs. aa–gg, IAA 475784

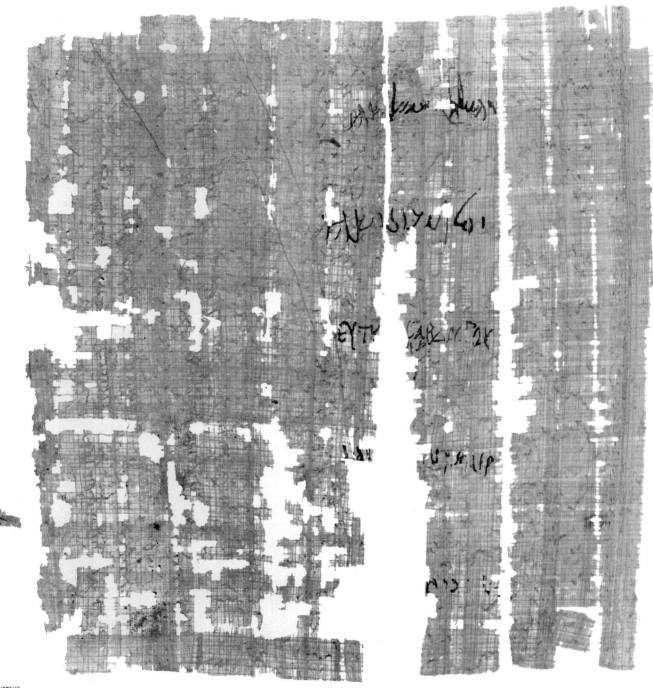

verso

62. XḤev/Se papLand Declaration gr
IAA 475782; Mus. Inv. Rockefeller

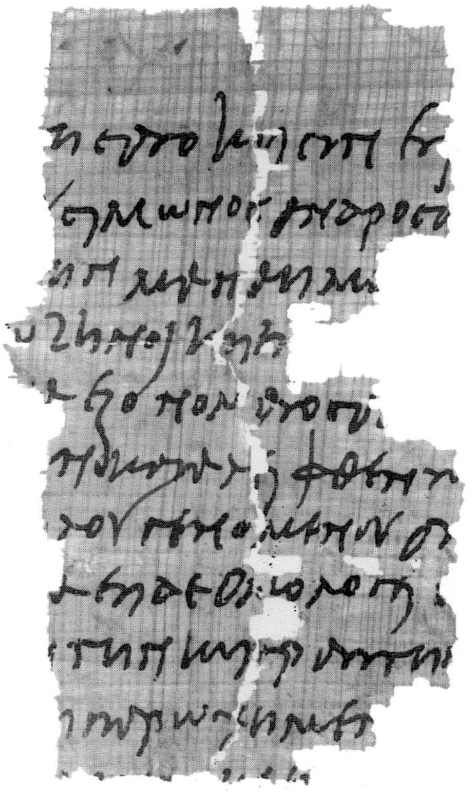

a

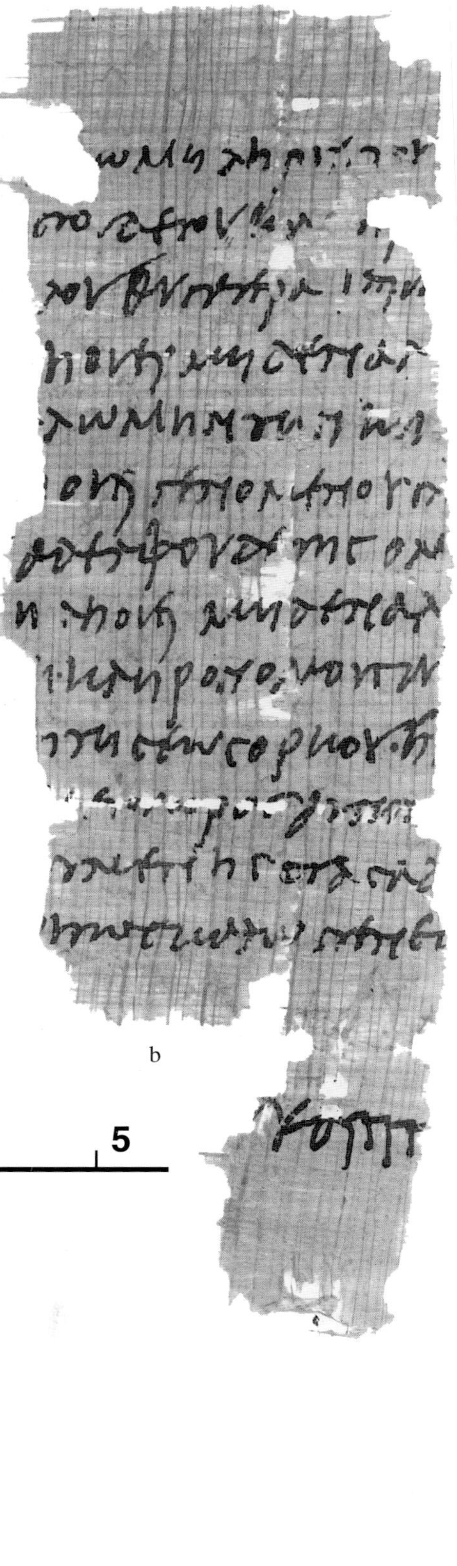

b

0 1 2 3 4 5

63. XḤev/Se papDeed of Renunciation of Claims gr
IAA ????; Mus. Inv. 866

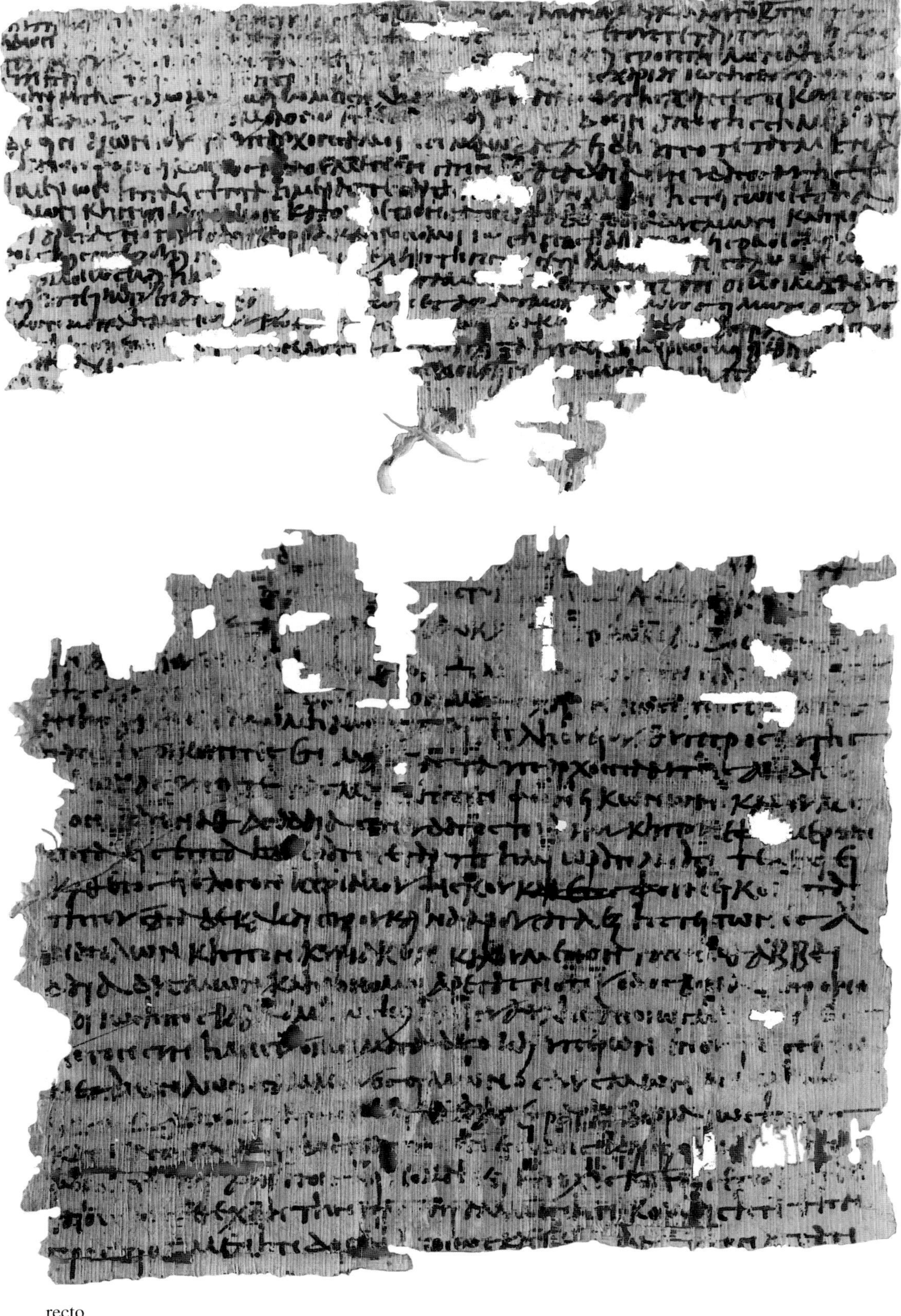

recto

64. XḤev/Se papDeed of Gift gr
PAM 42.205; Mus. Inv. 869

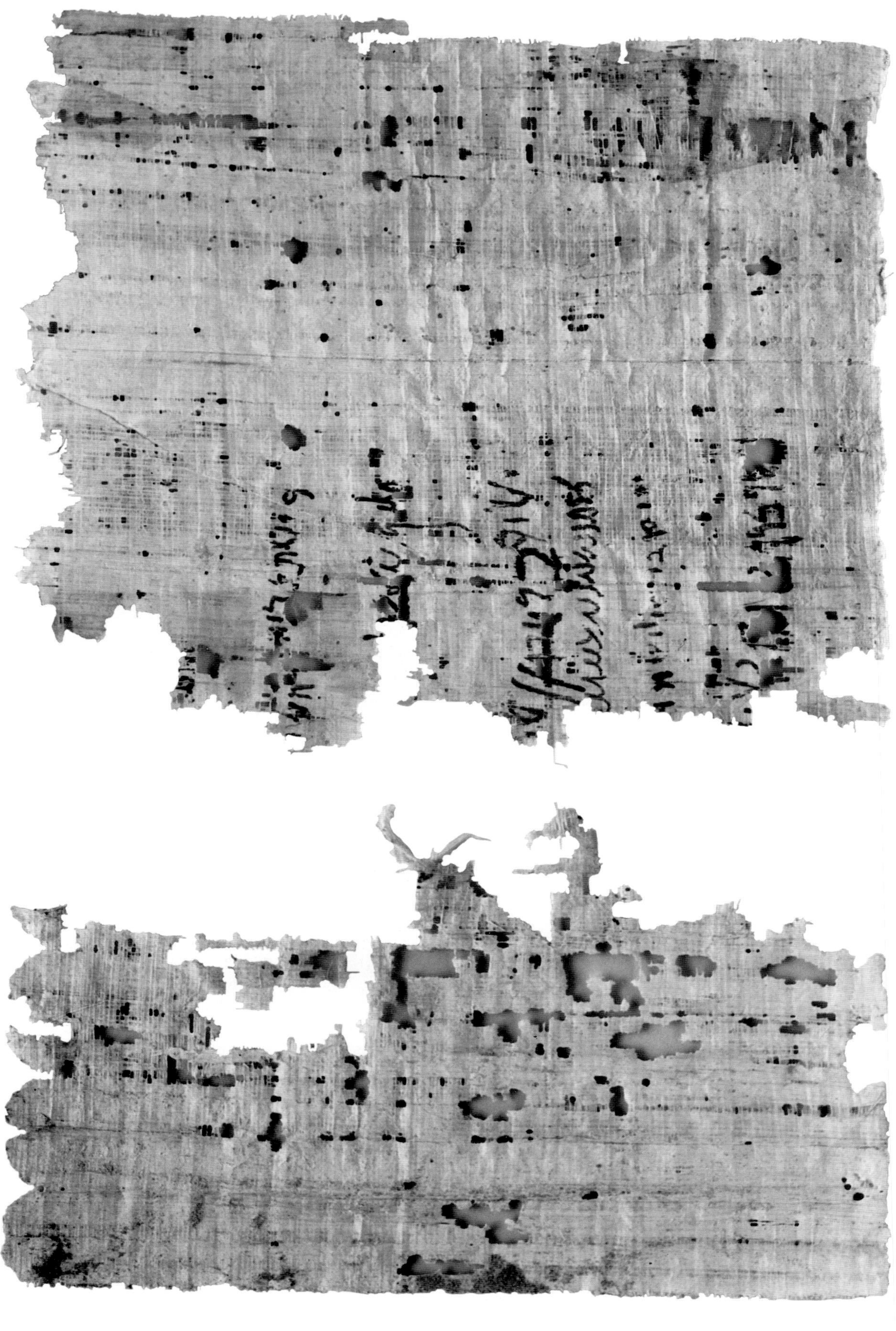

verso

64. XḤev/Se papDeed of Gift gr
PAM 42.206; Mus. Inv. 869

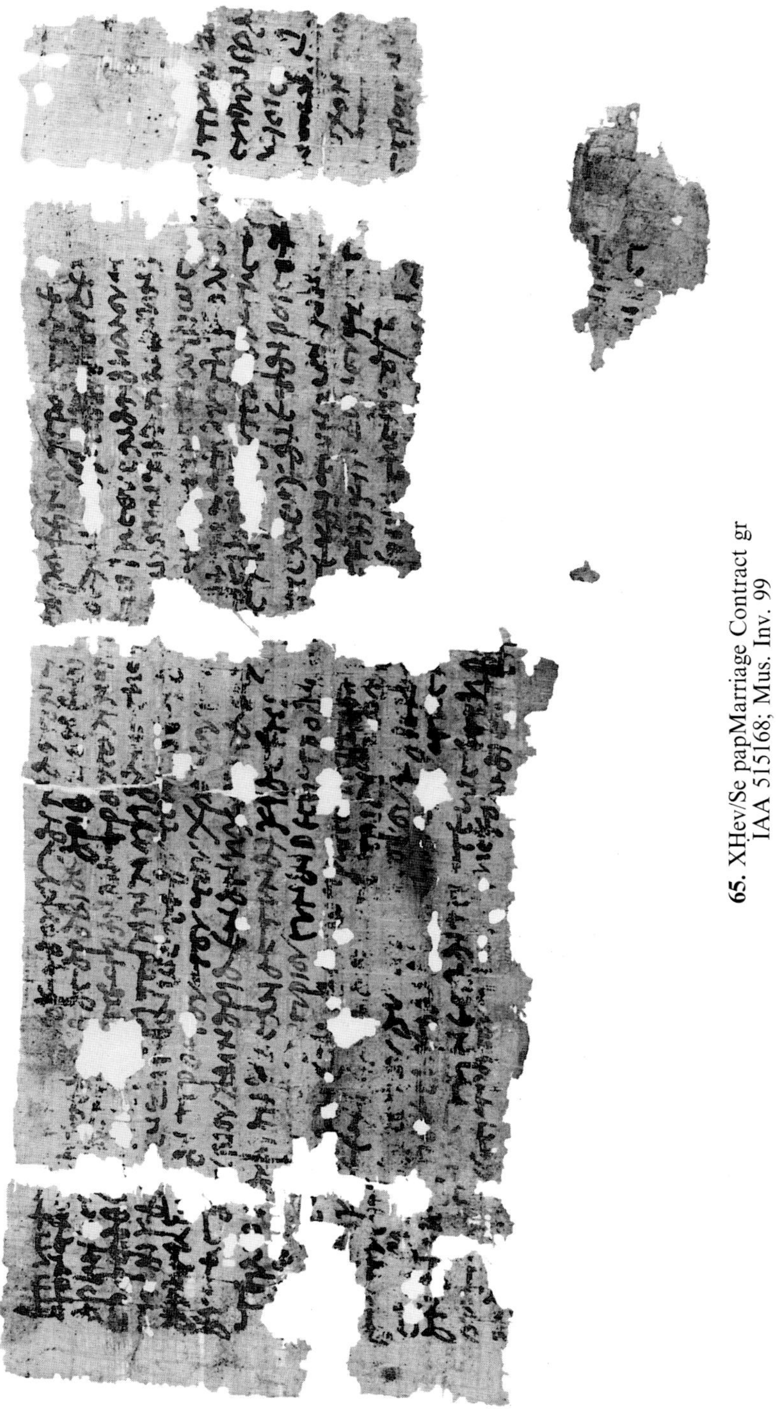

65. XḤev/Se papMarriage Contract gr
IAA 515168; Mus. Inv. 99

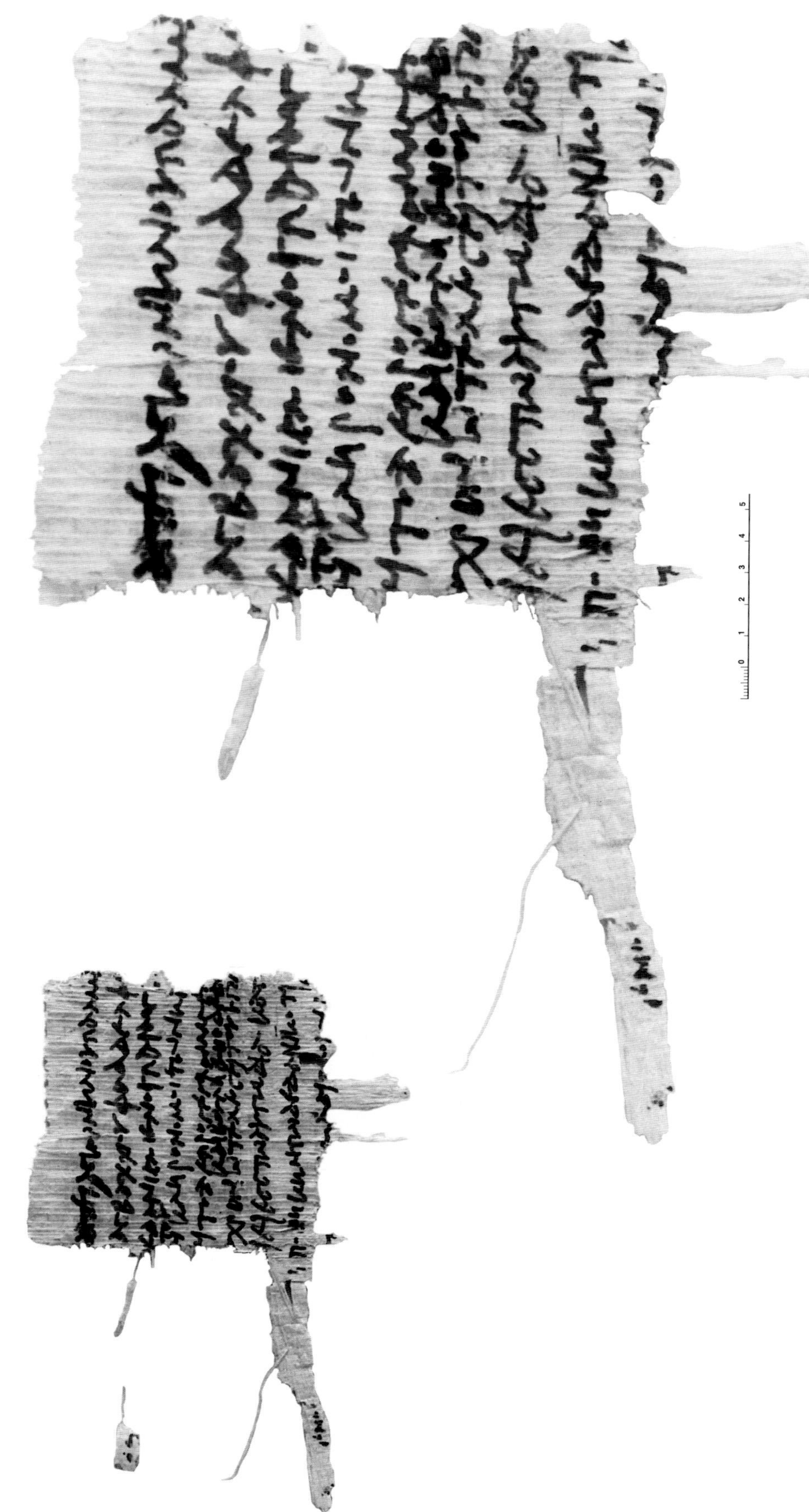

66. XḤev/Se papLoan with Hypothec gr
PAM 42.209; Mus. Inv. 732

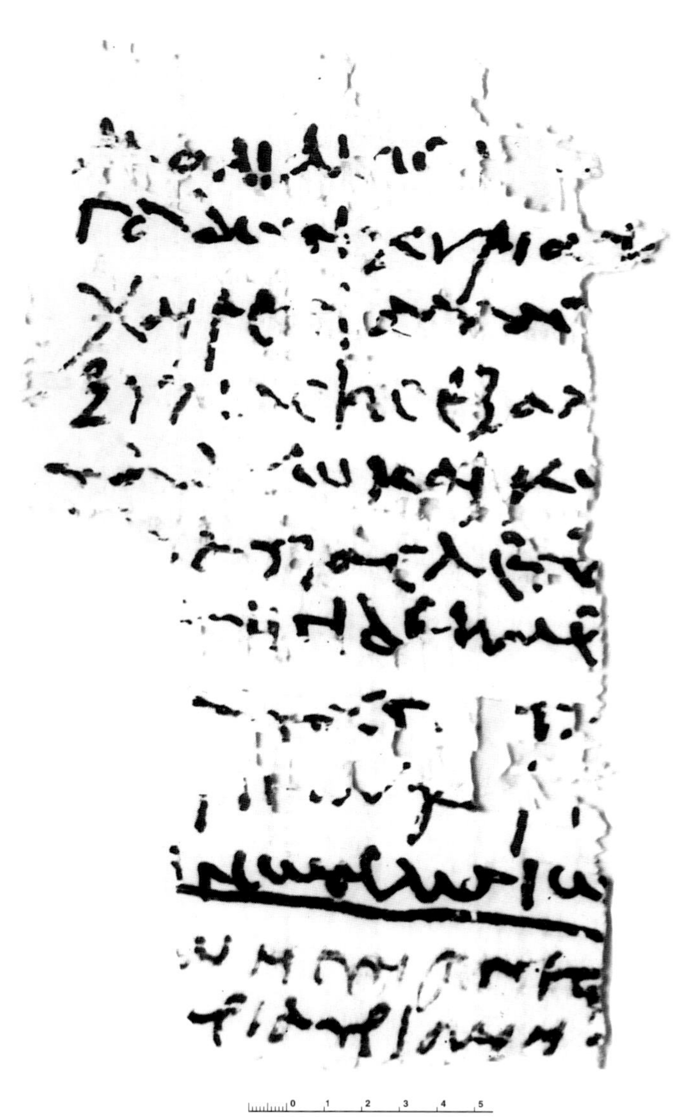

67. XḤev/Se papText Mentioning Timber gr
PAM 40.642; Mus. Inv. 866

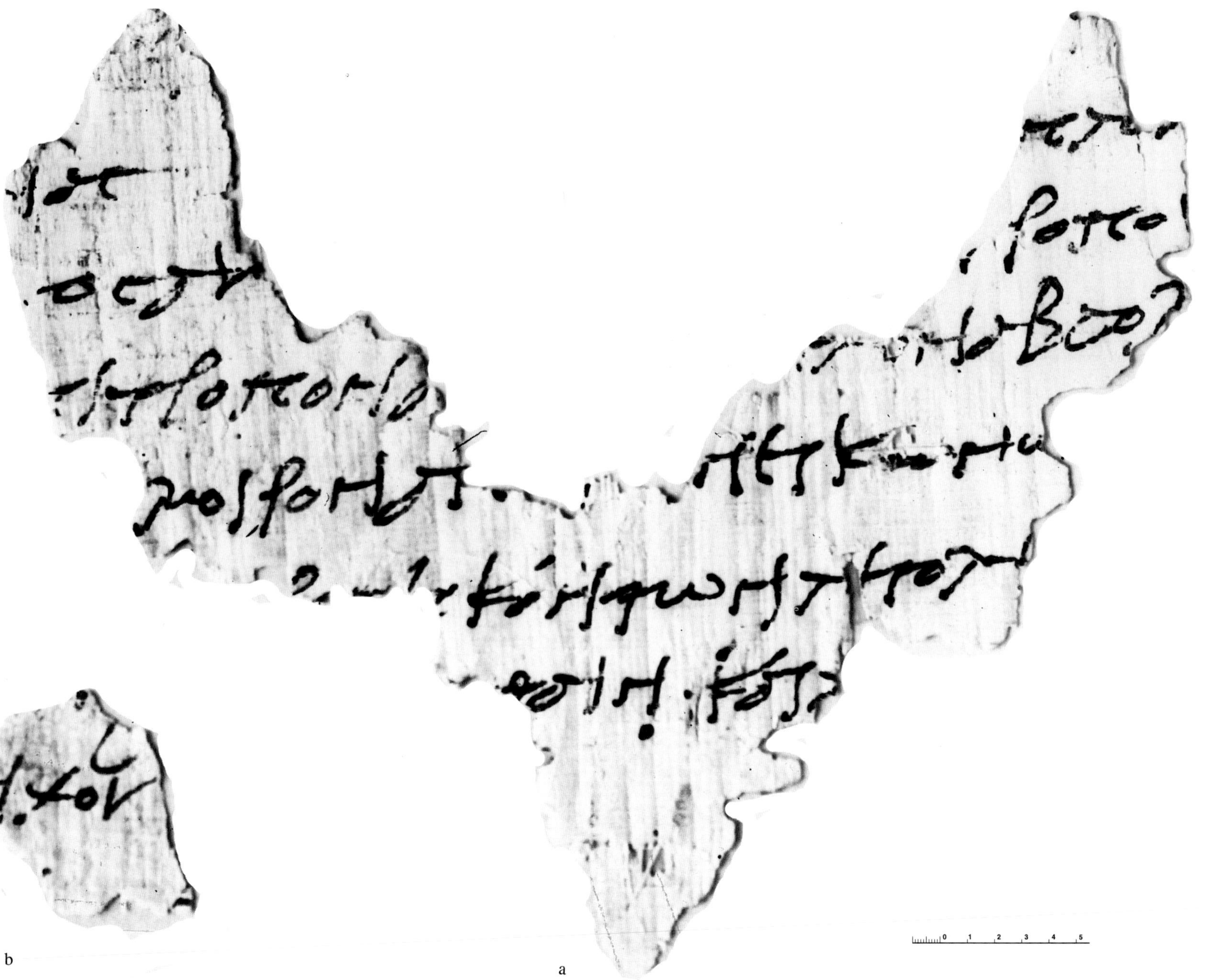

b

a

68. XḤev/Se papText Mentioning a Guardian gr
PAM 40.642; Mus. Inv. 866

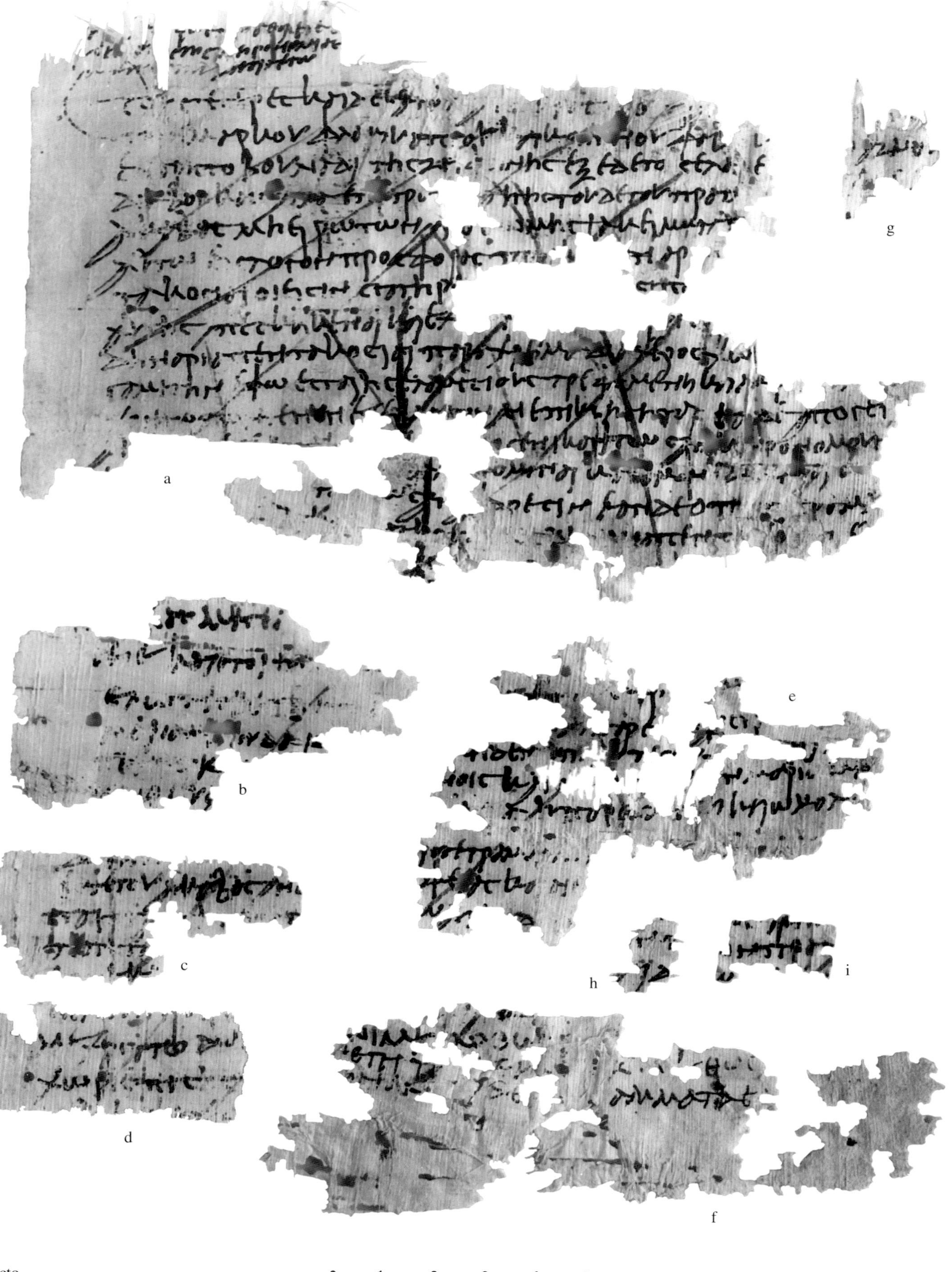

recto

69. XḤev/Se papCancelled Marriage Contract gr
PAM 42.207; Mus. Inv. 870

verso

69. XḤev/Se papCancelled Marriage Contract gr
PAM 42.208; Mus. Inv. 870

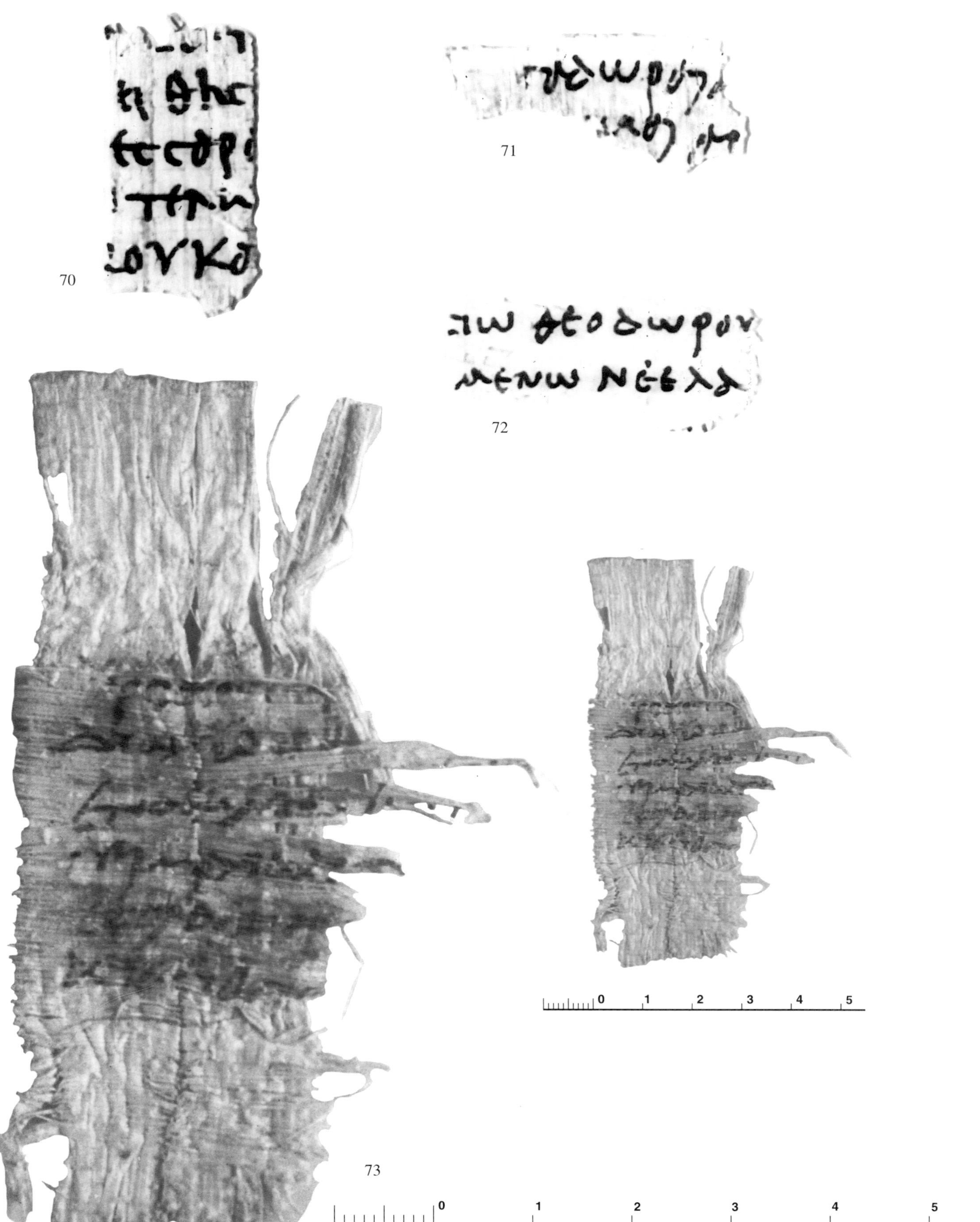

70–72. XḤev/Se papUnidentified Fragments A–C gr
PAM 42.642; Mus. Inv. 866
73. XḤev/Se papEnd of a Document gr
PAM 42.356; Mus. Inv. 731

74–139. XḤev/Se papUnidentified Fragments gr
PAM 42.209; Mus. Inv. 732

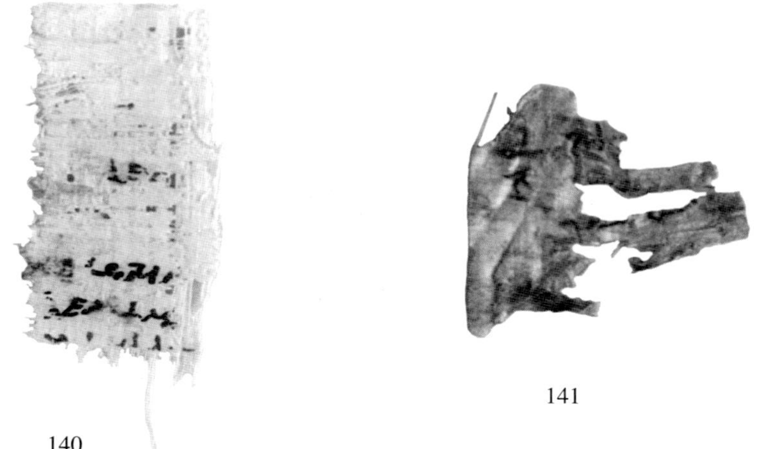

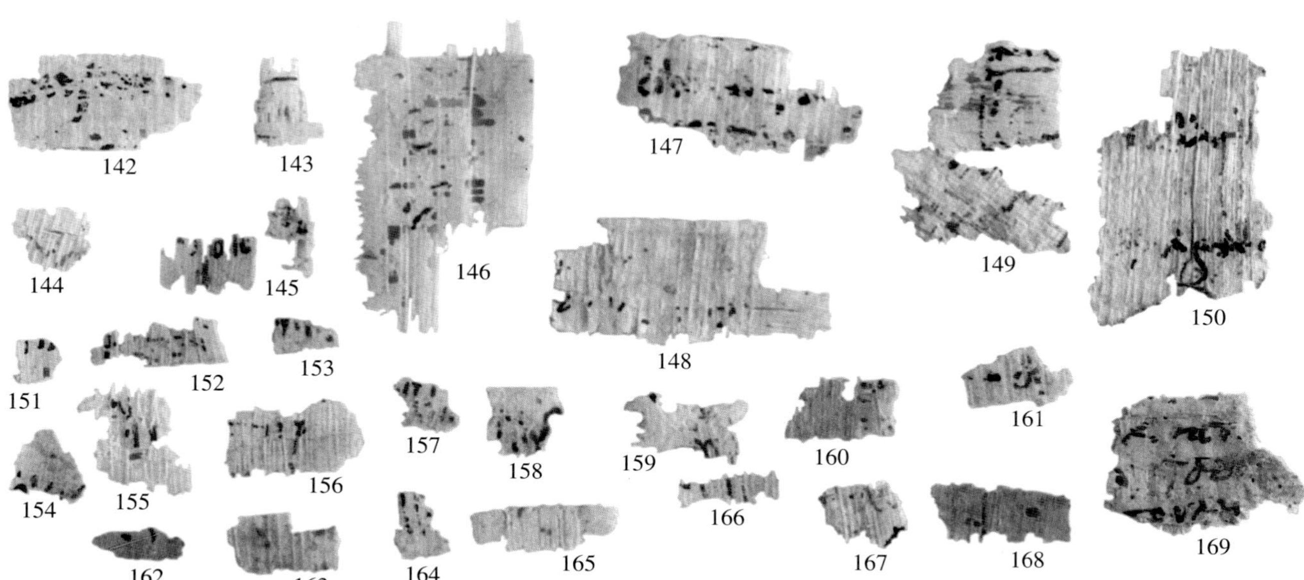

140–169. XḤev/Se papUnidentified Fragments gr
PAM 42.356; Mus. Inv. 731

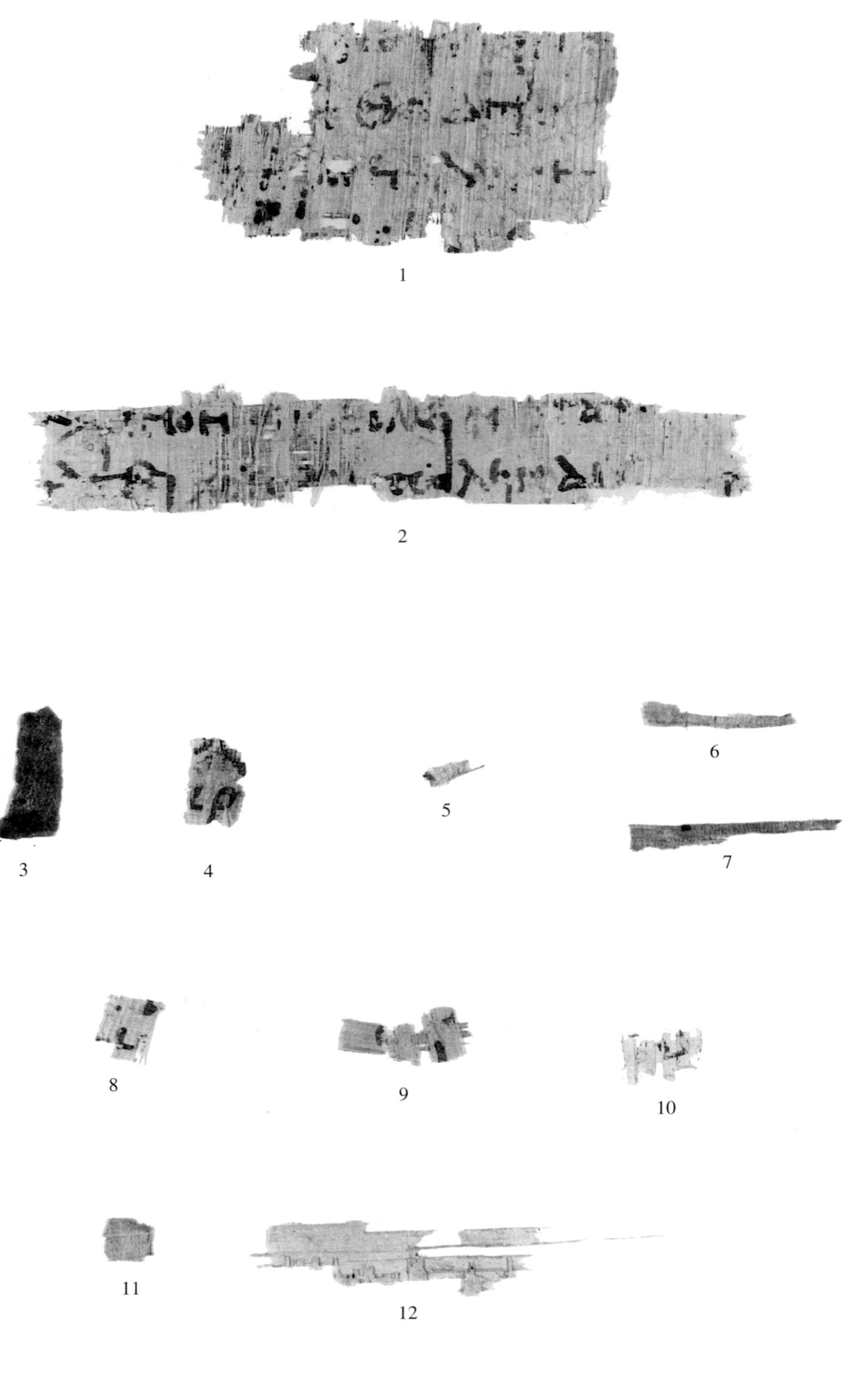

1–12. Ḥev/Se? papUnidentified Fragments gr
SHR 5962; Mus. Inv. 3001

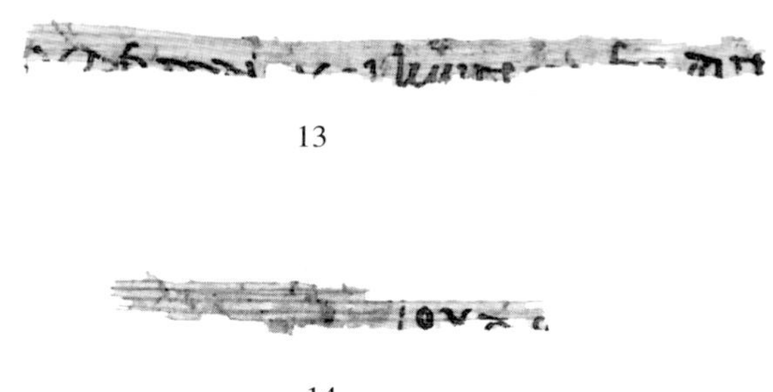

13-14. XḤev/ Se? papUnidentified Fragments gr
IAA 508034; Mus Inv. 3004

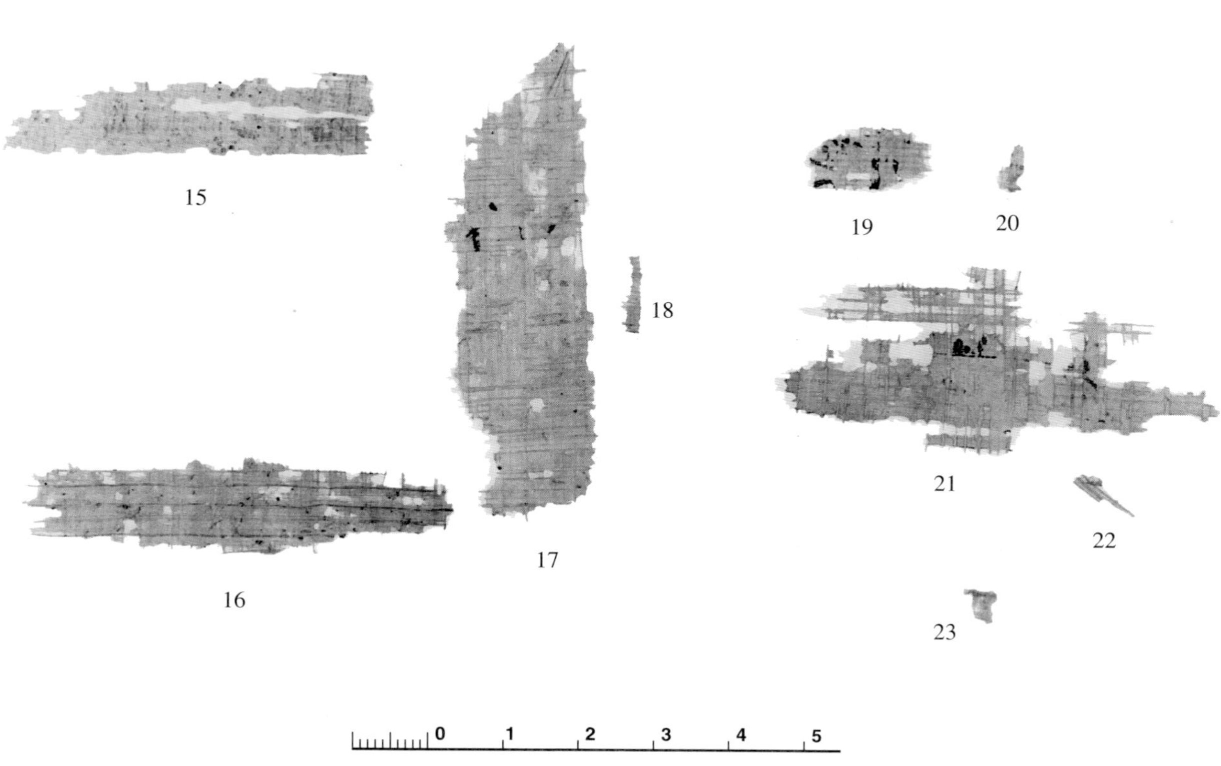

15–23. Ḥev/Se? papUnidentified Fragments gr
IAA 508036; Mus. Inv. 3005

24–35. Hev/Se? papUnidentified Fragments gr
IAA 508038; Mus. Inv. 3006

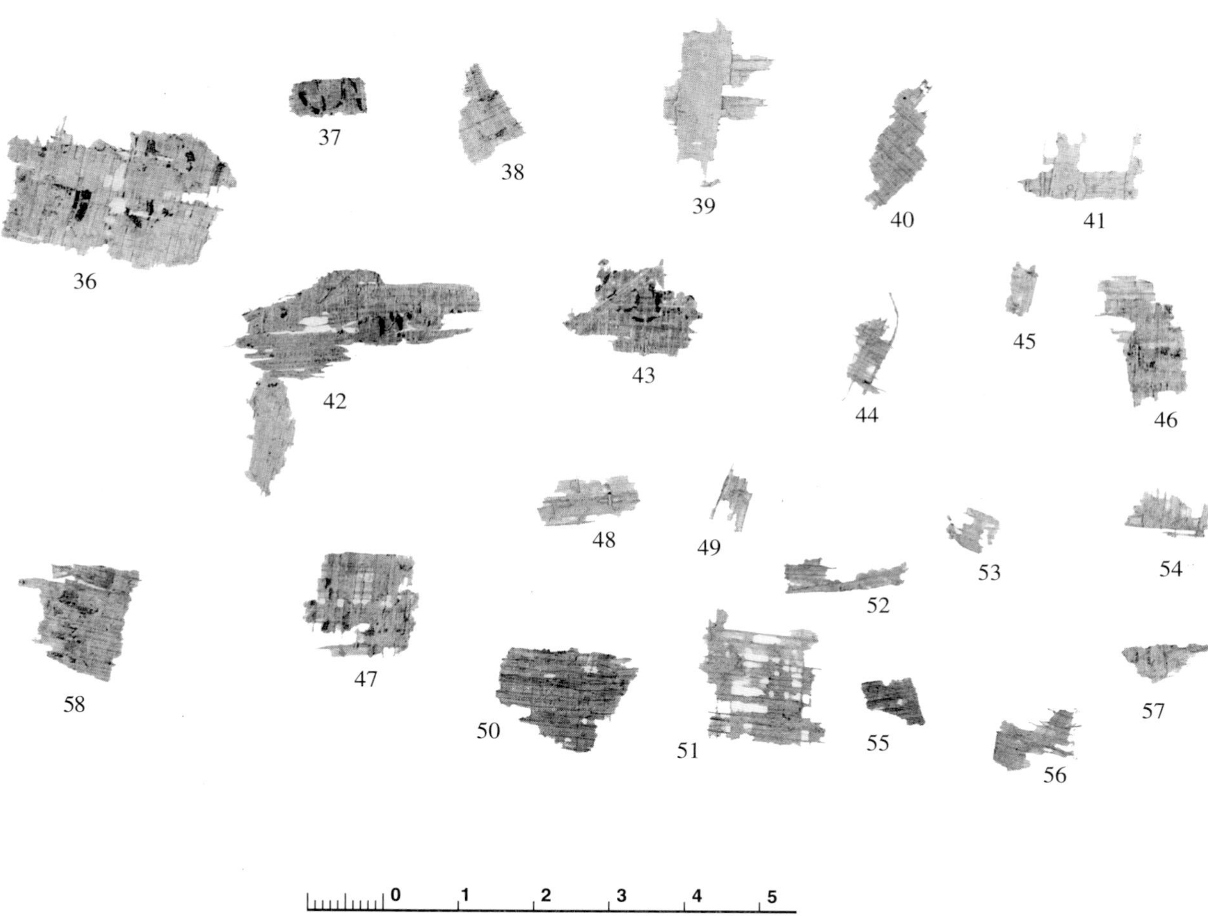

36–58. Ḥev/Se? papUnidentified Fragments gr
IAA 508046; Mus. Inv. 3007

recto

verso

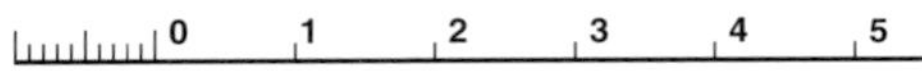

342. 4QLetter? ar
PAM 43.404(r), 43.405(v); Mus. Inv. 602

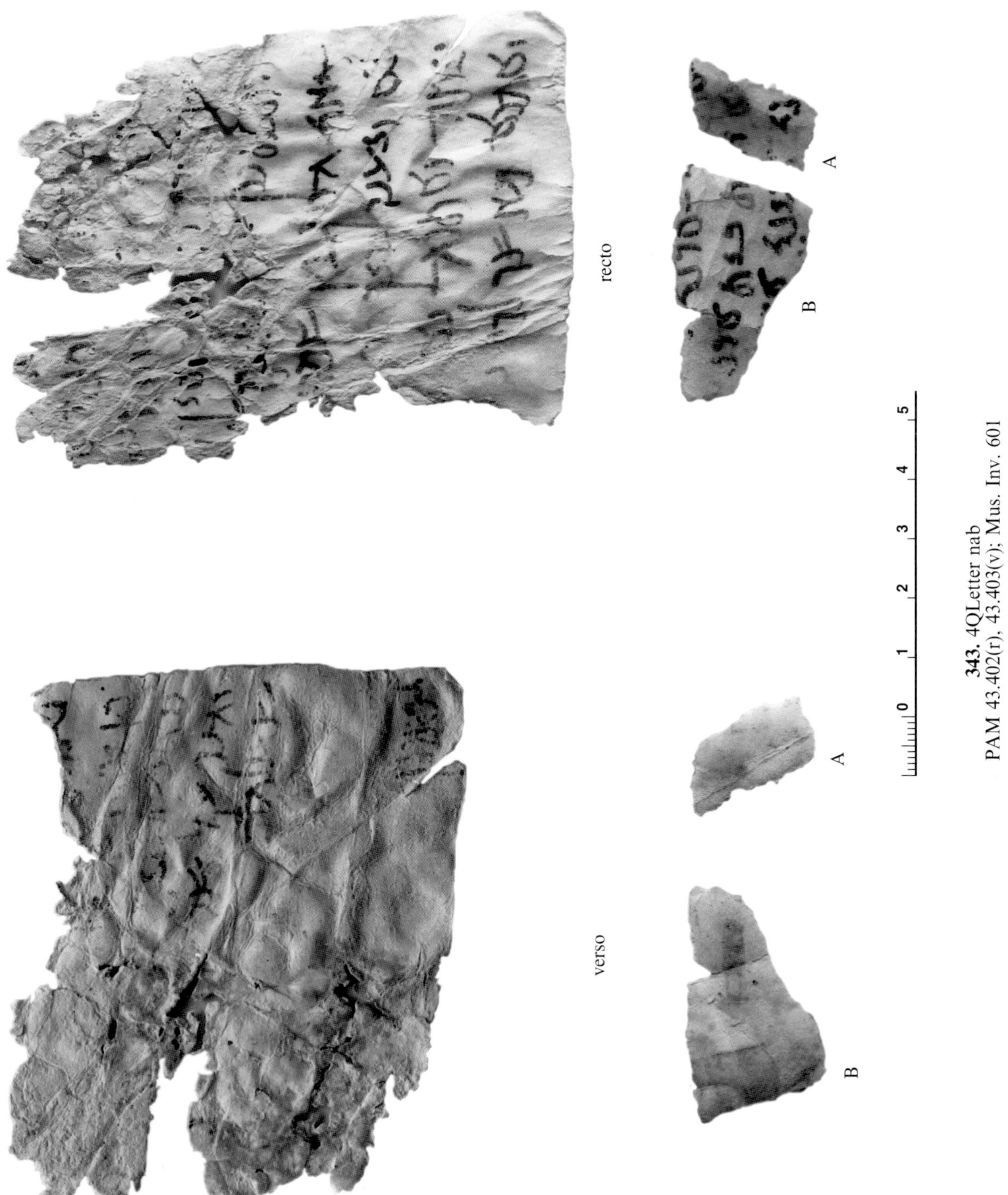

343. 4QLetter nab
PAM 43.402(r); 43.403(v); Mus. Inv. 601

344

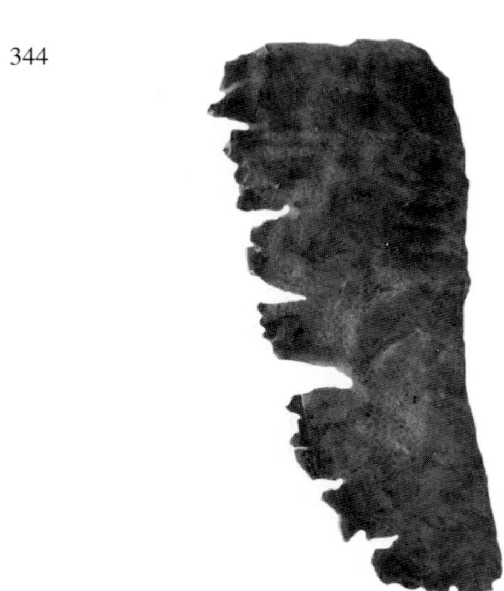

verso

recto

345

verso

recto

344. 4QDebt Acknowledgement ar
345. 4QDeed A ar or heb
PAM 43.404(r), 43.405(v); Mus. Inv. 602

346

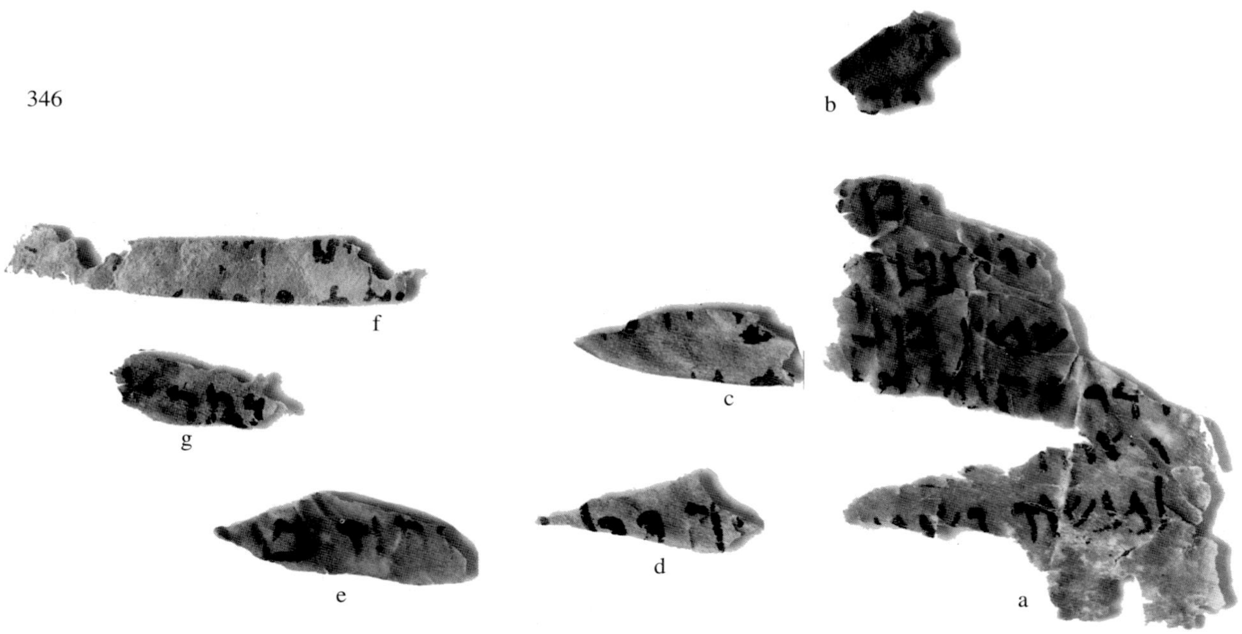

346a

0 1 2 3 4 5

346. 4QDeed of Sale ar
346a. 4QUnidentified Fragment A
PAM 43.407; Mus. Inv. 603

verso

recto

348. 4QDeed B heb?
PAM 43.404(r), 43.405(v); Mus. Inv. 602

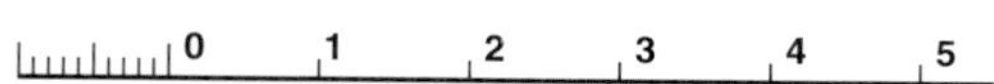

351. 4QAccount of Cereal A ar
PAM 43.407; Mus. Inv. 603

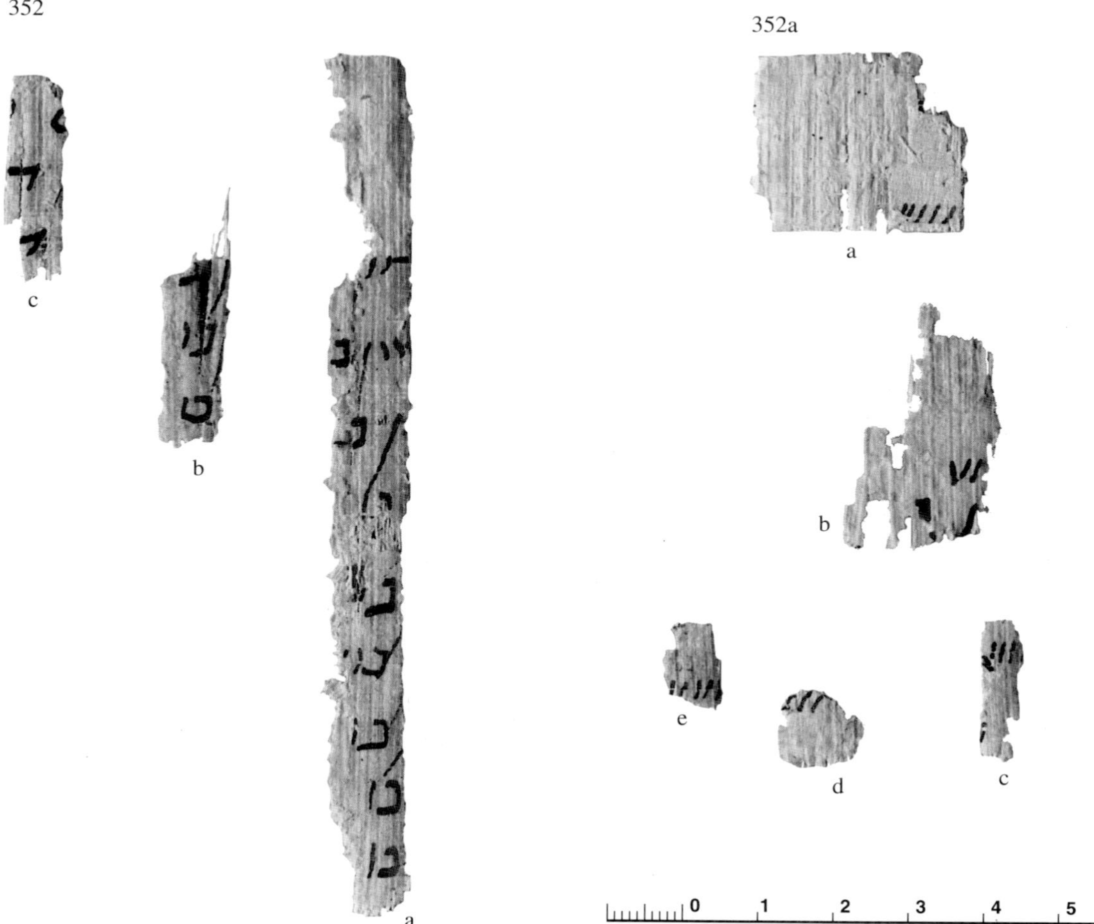

352. 4QpapAccount of Cereal B ar or heb
352a. 4QpapAccount A ar or heb
PAM 43.406; Mus. Inv. 184

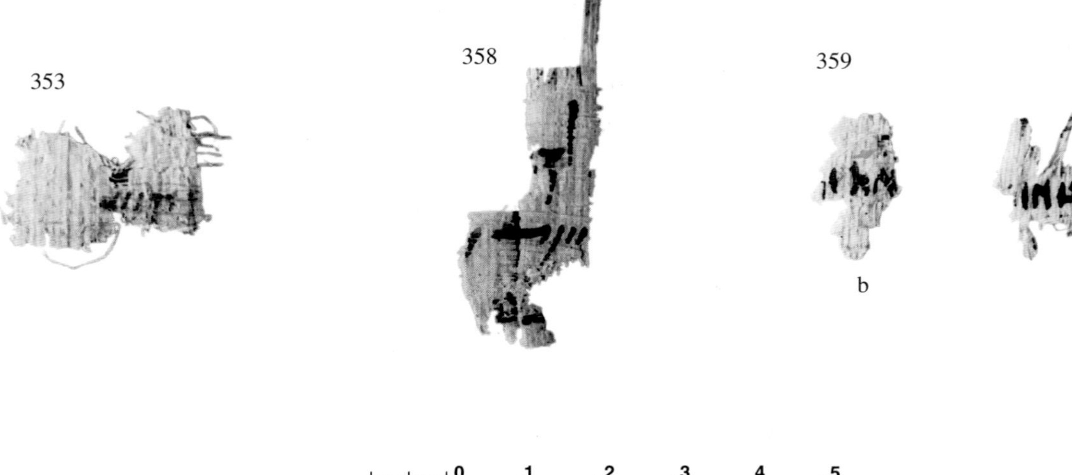

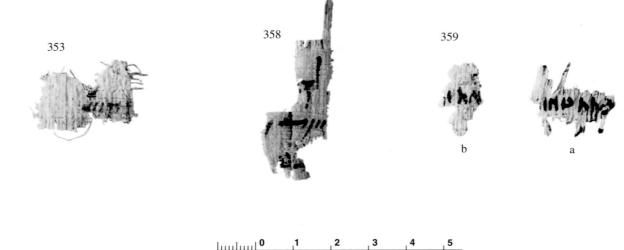

353. 4QpapAccount of Cereal or Liquid ar or heb
358. 4QpapAccount F? ar or heb
359. 4QpapDeed C? ar or heb
PAM 43.406; Mus. Inv. 184

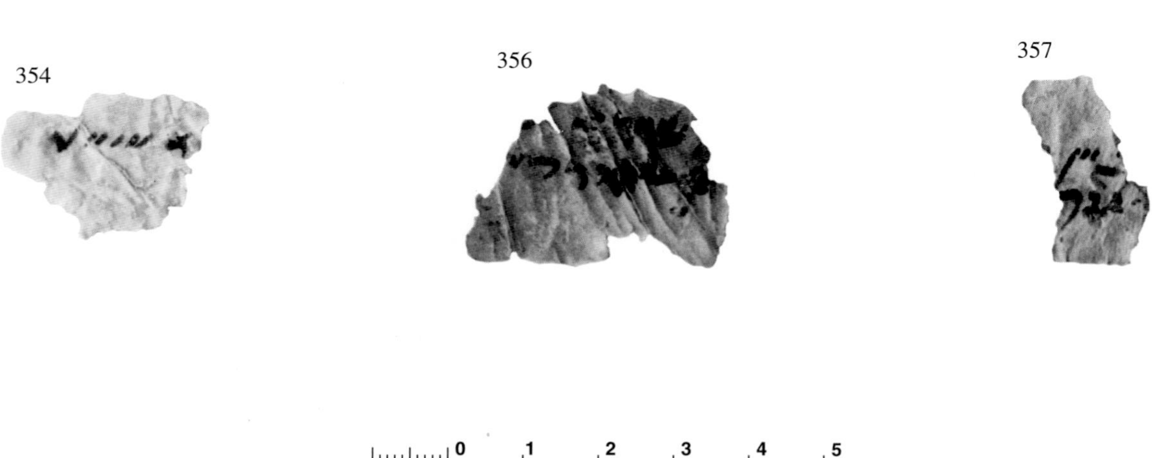

354. 4QAccount B ar or heb
356. 4QAccount D ar or heb
357. 4QAccount E ar or heb
PAM 43.407; Mus. Inv. 603

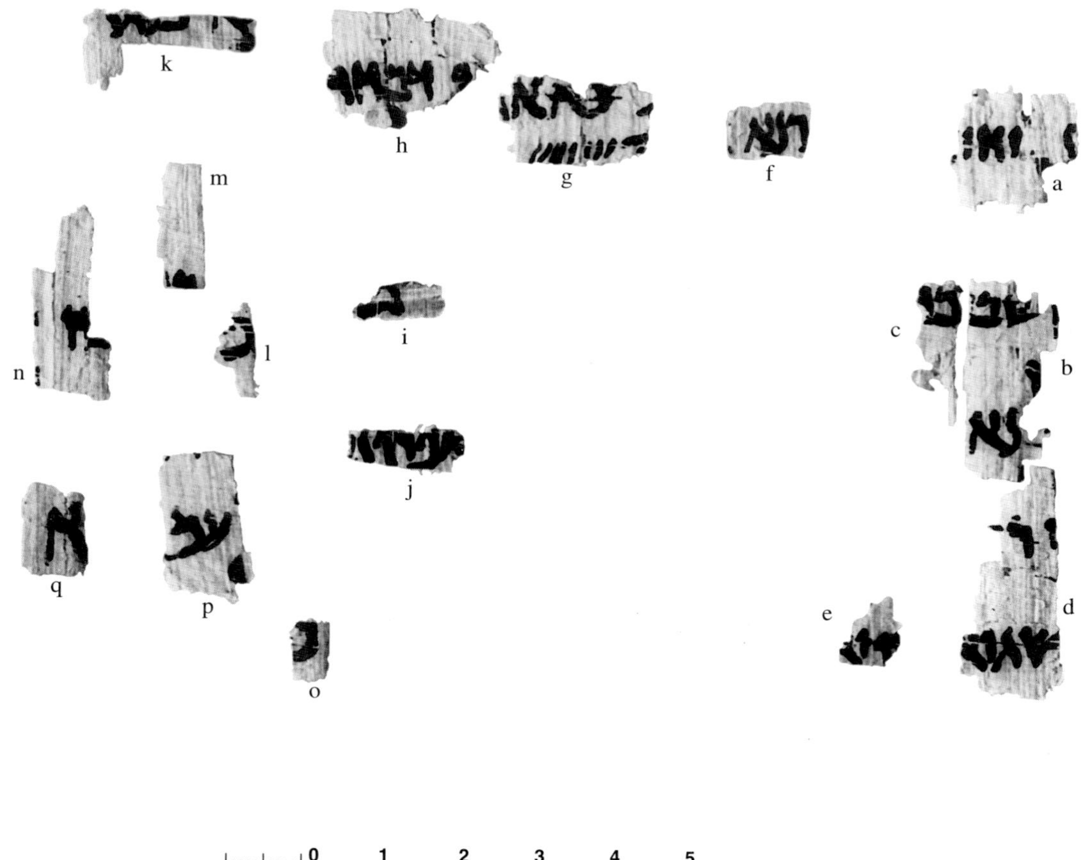

360a. 4QpapUnidentified Fragments B ar
PAM 43.406; Mus. Inv. 184

360b. 4QUnidentified Fragment C
PAM 43.407; Mus. Inv. 603
361. 4QpapUnidentified Fragment gr
PAM 43.406; Mus. Inv. 184